TEXTBOOK

Administrative Law

FOURTH EDITION

MICHAEL T MOLAN
BA, LLM (Lond), Barrister
Head of the Division of Law, South Bank University

OLD BAILEY PRESS

OLD BAILEY PRESS
at Holborn College, Woolwich Road,
Charlton, London SE7 8LN

First published 1997
Fourth edition 2003
Reprinted 2004

© The HLT Group Ltd 2003

ISBN 1 85836 485 X

British Library Cataloguing-in-Publication.
A CIP Catalogue record for this book is
available from the British Library.

Acknowledgement
The publishers and author would
like to thank the Incorporated
Council of Law Reporting for
England and Wales for kind
permission to reproduce extracts
from the Weekly Law Reports, and
Butterworths for their kind
permission to reproduce extracts
from the All England Law Reports.

Printed and bound in Great Britain

Contents

Preface

Old Bailey Press textbooks are written specifically for students. Whatever their course they will find our books clear and concise, providing comprehensive and up-to-date coverage. Written by specialists in their field, our textbooks are reviewed and updated on a regular basis. A companion 150 Leading Cases, Revision WorkBook and Cracknell's Statutes are also published.

Knowledge of recent cases is extremely important for those studying for their examinations. It demonstrates not only an active interest in the law as it develops, but also the dynamic nature of the law which is constantly adapting to changing social and economic trends.

The *Administrative Law* textbook is designed for use by any undergraduates who have Administrative Law within their syllabus. It will be equally useful for all CPE/LLDip students who must study Administrative Law as one of their 'core' subjects.

In addition those studying for certain professional examinations, such as the Institute of Legal Executives, will find this textbook gives them sufficient information for their appropriate examinations in Administrative Law.

The fourth edition of this text reflects recent developments, including the Leggatt Report on the tribunal system and decisions on the openness of inquiry processes, such as *R (On the Application of Persey)* v *Secretary of State for the Environment, Food and Rural Affairs*. The impact of the Human Rights Act 1998 on administrative law is reflected in decisions such as *R (On the Application of Hirst)* v *Secretary of State for the Home Department* and *Lindsay* v *Customs and Excise Commissioners*. The growing importance of the Civil Procedure Rules 1998 as a means of resolving the public/private law dichtonomy is shown in a series of decisions including *R (On the Application of Heather and Another)* v *Leonard Cheshire Foundation* and *R (On the Application of the Oxford Study Centre)* v *The British Council*. Some clarification of the time limits applicable in judicial review is supplied by the House of Lords' decision in *R (On the Application of Burkett)* v *Hammersmith and Fulham London Borough Council* and the operation of estoppel in public law is reviewed in the House of Lords' decision in *R* v *East Sussex County Council, ex parte Reprotech Ltd*.

The law is stated as of 1 January 2003.

Mike Molan
South Bank University

Table of Cases

Table of Statutes and Other Materials

1

Introduction to Administrative Law

1.1 Introduction

1.2 Historical perspective

1.3 Constitutional perspective

1.4 Devices and techniques: who exercises power?

1.5 Judicial review and the ultra vires doctrine

1.6 The limitations of judicial review

1.1 Introduction

To the uninitiated the study of administrative law sounds like a very dull prospect. It perhaps conjures up images of bureaucracy, tedious procedural rules and boring committees, commissions, and tribunals. The reality is very different. It is not overstating the case to claim that in the modern political era administrative law has taken on a pre-eminent role in regulating relations between the machinery of government and the individual citizen. At its core is the control of power – specifically the review by the judiciary of the way in which executive power is used. As a result the subject embraces a huge range of issues, some of them highly politicised. In recent years these have included the legality of a ban on blood sports; whether the courts can order a minister to suspend the operation of a primary Act of Parliament; whether a minister can be in contempt of court for disobeying a court ruling; whether a minister can ban certain types of interview from being broadcast; the powers of local authorities to spend public money, or to refuse to do so; the scope of the discretion vested in chief constables to determine policing policy; the scope of the powers vested in the Home Secretary regarding parole for prisoners convicted of murder; whether the courts could declare invalid an exercise of prerogative power; and the availability of damages in respect of unlawful actions by public bodies.

In the same way that the United Kingdom lacks any formal constitutional arrangement in the form of a single document regarded as providing its constitution, there is no formal basis for the existence of administrative law. As will be seen it is largely the product of judicial activity, although its existence is increasingly recognised in statutory provisions. The growth in administrative law has to a large extent mirrored the increase in the level of state involvement in many aspects of everyday life during the twentieth century, sparking the need for a coherent and effective body of rules to govern relations between individuals and the state. Students of constitutional law will readily recognise that administrative law is in reality an outgrowth of the doctrine of the separation of powers. It is evidence of the judiciary acting as a check on the powers of the executive, and perhaps even the legislature, in some respects. It should not be assumed, however, that any such coherent and effect body of rules actually exists yet. Administrative law is a constantly evolving subject. A brief survey of this textbook will reveal that the topic essentially falls into two sections. First, consideration is given to the various powers exercised by ministers and other administrative agencies, such as local authorities and tribunals. Second, consideration is given to judicial review and the grounds upon which an application for review might be made.

There are many approaches that can be taken to studying administrative law. It is tempting for students to concentrate on the case law as evidence of what administrative law is, and as evidence of how it works, but it should be remembered that there are many administrative law problems that do not come before the courts because of the provision of some statutory remedy, lack of funds for litigation, because access is denied by procedural rules, or because the jurisdiction of the courts has been ousted by statute. In those cases that do reach the courts, the outcome of the decision is not always what was hoped for. Remedies are discretionary and, as will be seen, the courts will often simply quash an unlawful act by the executive, leaving the decision to be taken again.

1.2 Historical perspective

To have a better understanding of the nature of administrative law it helps to be aware of its historical perspective. This can be summarised as falling broadly within three periods.

Pre-1688

Prior to the enactment of the Bill of Rights 1689 most of what we would today recognise as 'administrative functions' for the purposes of administrative law were carried out by Justices of the Peace. They were supervised by judges of assize, who carried out the instructions of the Crown. Real control was centralised in the Privy Council, acting through the Star Chamber. Some features of modern-day administrative law existed, for example the principles of natural justice relating to fair procedures, and the existence of the prerogative remedies of certiorari, prohibition and mandamus. Given the relationship between Parliament and the Crown that obtained during this period however, no direct comparison with present day administrative law is really possible.

1688 to 1900

Fundamental in importance to the development of administrative law was the Civil War and the Revolution of seventeenth century, which resulted in a massive shift in power from the Crown to Parliament, and a change in the supervision of administrative agencies. The Court of King's Bench effectively took over the function of supervising Justices of the Peace and similar bodies. The court developed its role as a provider of remedies in respect of 'inferior' bodies found to have exceeded their jurisdiction. These remedies were in the form of the prerogative orders of mandamus, prohibition and certiorari. During this period, more and more administrative agencies were created by Parliament and provided with statutory powers to perform various tasks. Examples include commissioners of sewers, local boards of works and school boards. In exercising its supervisory jurisdiction over these and Justices of the Peace, the judges of the King's Bench began to gradually develop the doctrine of ultra vires; the theory that if an inferior body (ie not a court of the High Court, therefore a body of limited jurisdiction) purported to act outside the scope of its power, its acts would be quashed.

Until 1888 Justices of the Peace continued to play a significant role in the carrying out of administrative tasks, but from that year many of their functions were transferred to local authorities. Obviously, the supervisory jurisdiction of the High Court extended to these new bodies. With this superficial historical analysis we have now reached the end of the nineteenth century, and one can clearly see the foundations being laid for the system as it exists today. It must not be forgotten, however, that life in England at that time was very different. There was no developed welfare state system. There were a comparatively small number of administrative agencies. Generally, there was much less state involvement in the lives of ordinary citizens and, consequently, less administration and bureaucracy.

> 'Until August 1914 a sensible law-abiding Englishman could pass through life and hardly notice the existence of the State, beyond the post office and the policeman.' (A J P Taylor)

As a result administrative law was barely recognised as a branch of legal study. Writing in *The Law of the Constitution* in 1885, A V Dicey rejected the concept of administrative law, claiming it had no place in the British constitution. His reason for doing so was his adherence to the principle of the rule of law; to his mind everyone should be equal before the law and subject to it. He feared that the development of administrative law would involve the evolution of a special body of rules and principles giving administrative agencies privileges in litigation against the private individual, resulting in a situation whereby they became a law unto themselves. His justification for these views came from comparison with the French droit administratif, and his assumption that the French administrative courts, including the Conseil d'Etat, must be biased in favour of the administration, against the interests of the individual.

The twentieth century

The legal system found itself singularly unprepared to deal with the changes that occurred during the first half of the twentieth century. Administrative law simply did not develop fast enough to deal with the problems created by the enactment of a whole raft of regulatory legislation. For the first time the social and economic policies of central government started to have a significant impact on private property rights, with regulation of areas such as housing, employment, planning, manufacture of goods and pursuit of livelihood. What we would now recognise as welfare rights began to emerge with decisions being taken by administrative bodies in relation to access to housing, education, state pensions and health. It was due to the absence of proper legal controls that many citizens began to become concerned at the powers of the new bureaucracy. The courts during the early part of this century did little to solve the problem: see *Local Government Board* v *Arlidge* [1915] AC 120.

Due to the increasing complexity of the task of governing the country, ministers were increasingly empowered to make delegated legislation in order to introduce significant new measures (see Chapter 2). Ministers were given more significant decision-making powers leading to the development of devices such as the public inquiry in order that the minister's decision should be better informed.

The role played by the judiciary in all of this has changed with circumstances. In the early part of the twentieth century the courts were still finding their feet to some extent, the modern principles of administrative law existing in somewhat embryonic form. During the Second World War the courts deferred almost without question to the wishes of the executive, working on the principle that during a time of national emergency it would be wrong for the courts to intervene and hamper the exercise of executive discretion: see decisions such as *Liversidge* v *Anderson* [1942] AC 206.

Even in the immediate post-war period the judiciary seemed to suffer from the after-effects of this wartime restraint. A number of decisions, dealt with at more length in the appropriate chapters, illustrate the point. In *Racecourse Betting Control Board* v *Secretary for Air* [1944] Ch 114 the Court of Appeal held that there was no power in a supervisory court to quash a decision for error of law on the face of the record; in *Duncan* v *Cammell Laird & Co* [1942] AC 624 the House of Lords allowed the Crown very wide powers to suppress evidence in litigation on the ground that its production was against the national interest; in *Nakkudu Ali* v *Jayaratne* [1951] AC 66 the Privy Council held that the revocation of a licence upon which an individual depended for his livelihood was an administrative act and did not attract the protection of the rules of natural justice.

A parallel development was the increased use of the tribunal, as an alternative to the court, as a means of resolving disputes between individuals and state agencies, and inquiries to resolve disputes over planning matters. There was widespread dissatisfaction with the operation of both these administrative devices, which resulted in the *Report of the Committee on Administrative Tribunals and Inquiries* (the Franks Committee) in 1958. A more detailed account of this is to be found in Chapter 4. It suffices to say here that the very fact a report was thought necessary at all is indicative that all was not well with the system and, further, that much of the Ccommittee's recommendations were subsequently enshrined in the Tribunals and Inquiries Acts 1958, 1971 and, most recently, 1992. This resulted in a tangible improvement in the proceedings of both tribunals and inquiries.

Since the 1960s judges have shown themselves willing to take a more vigorous and dynamic role in the development of the principles of administrative law when it has suited them to do so. Established concepts such as the rules of natural justice have been revitalised, and new heads of review recognised, such as proportionality and 'acting on no evidence'. Through a number of landmark decisions such as *Ridge* v *Baldwin* [1964] AC 40; *Padfield* v *Minister of Agriculture* [1968] AC 997; *Secretary of State for Education and Science* v *Tameside Metropolitan Borough Council* [1976] 3 WLR 641; *Anisminic* v *Foreign Compensation Commission* [1969] 2 AC 147; *O'Reilly* v *Mackman* [1983] 2 AC 237; *Council of Civil Service Unions* v *Minister for the Civil Service* [1984] 3 All ER 935; *R* v *Panel on Take-overs and Mergers, ex parte Datafin* [1987] 2 WLR 699 the position has been reached where, as Lord Denning observed in *Breen* v *AEU* [1971] 2 QB 175 at 189, 'it may truly now be said that we have a developed system of administrative law'.

Whilst the contribution of the judiciary cannot be overstated, it must be remembered that they have developed administrative law very much along their own lines of thought and policy. There are areas where the courts have, in the past, been slow to intervene and exercise their rediscovered power. Cases involving students, trade unionists, the homeless, immigrants and deportees provide evidence that the courts have not always been as steadfast as they might have been in providing a shield against the excesses of executive power. The enactment of the Human Rights Act 1998, and its relevance to courts considering applications for judicial review, is likely to go some way towards remedying these shortcomings: see further Chapter 7.

As indicated in the introduction to this chapter, it should be borne in mind that administrative law is a living subject, and the process of development and refinement goes on. Whatever the predominant political philosophy, danger lies in the fact that all power is capable of misuse or abuse. The problem for the has been and will remain that of trying to cope with the abuse or misuse of public power.

During the 1980s and early 1990s, for example, the political landscape was, to some extent, redrawn with the result that de-regulation and privatisation became key factors in determining the thrust of the legislative programme. In theory this should have meant a reduction in the number of administrative agencies, with a less for the courts to supervise. It could have led to a diminution in the importance of administrative law (assuming of course that one subscribes to the traditional theory that it is concerned with the control of public power). In reality the courts simply adopted the traditional concepts of administrative law and applied them to self-regulatory bodies, regardless of their legal status. Administrative law developed to provide a residual means of control over private bodies: see *R* v *Panel on Take-overs and Mergers, ex parte Datafin* (above), or *R* v *Advertising Standards Authority Ltd, ex parte The Insurance Service plc* (1989) 2 Admin LR 77. The issue remains the exercise of power. If it is public in nature the courts will have the power to control it if they so wish. This issue is of significance in relation to the control of private bodies providing services such as water, prisons and telecommunications.

1.3 Constitutional perspective

A number of basic constitutional principles underpin administrative law.

Parliamentary sovereignty

Since the upheavals of the seventeenth-century Parliament has been seen as the ultimate law-making body in the British constitution. This theory of sovereignty maintains that Parliament can make, amend or repeal any law it sees fit. A corollary of this theory is that the judges cannot question the validity of primary legislation, and can only quash subordinate legislation on limited grounds. That the judiciary gives effect to the legislation passed by Parliament is a political fact as much as a legal one. The issue is really one of judicial loyalty. Even where judges are openly disregarding the wording of primary legislation they can still claim to be acting in furtherance of their duty to give effect to the intention of Parliament: see *Anisminic* v *Foreign Compensation Commission* (above). Consequently, when a primary statute creates an administrative agency and gives it new wide-ranging powers, the courts cannot question the validity of the body itself, or the purposes for which it was created. What the courts can do, however, is review the way in which it exercises power, to ensure that it acts within the scope of the power devolved by Parliament. Parliamentary sovereignty as a doctrine must also be seen in the light of two key developments of the late twentieth century. First, the United Kingdom's membership of the European Community, as effected by the European Communities Act 1972. Certain types of Community law, such as Treaty provisions, regulations and possibly directives are directly applicable in domestic law, and even domestic legislation enacted after 1972 must be read subject to the dictates of EC law. Hence, incompatibility with EC law becomes a ground upon which the courts may be asked to invalidate administrative action.

The second major development is the incorporation of the European Convention on Human Rights in the Human Rights Act 1998. The Act makes it unlawful for any public authority to act in a way which is incompatible with the Convention rights protected thereunder, thus making the Convention something that has to be taken into account when exercising executive discretion and in reviewing the legality of such action. Statutes have to be interpreted so as to ensure compliance with the Convention in so far as this is possible. By the European Communities Act 1972 and the Human Rights Act 1998 Parliament has succeeded in binding its successors in the sense that the courts will bear both statutes in mind in determining the meaning of any domestic legislation. Of course either Act could be repealed, but the political and economic consequences of such decisions ensures that the prospect remains a merely theoretical one for the foreseeable future.

The rule of law

The twentieth century has seen the rapid spread of the philosophy that the state should be primarily responsible for remedying social and economic evils by adopting appropriate policies to be executed by administrative authorities. The state now supervises almost every aspect of a citizen's life from the cradle to the grave, including housing, education, employment, health, pensions, taxation and planning. As early as 1887 Maitland was prompted to observe that:

> 'We are becoming a much-governed nation, governed by all manner of councils and boards and officers ... exercising the powers which have been committed to them by modern statutes.'

In 1922 Lord Sumner in *R* v *Nat Bell Liquors Ltd* [1922] AC 128 summarised the way in which the courts reviewed and controlled this vast new body of administrators:

> '... supervision goes to two points: one is the area of the inferior jurisdiction and the qualifications and conditions of its exercise; the other is the observance of the law in the course of its exercise.'

Thus the rule of law is central to administrative law. It is the basis for judicial review. At its most basic the doctrine means that everyone must act within the confines of the law. When applied to a public body it means that it must act within the confines of its enabling Act and the common law. If it fails to do so its actions will be unlawful or ultra vires. Another way of expressing this concept is to say that a public body, acting with the express or implied authority of the state, must stay within the limits of any power so delegated and cannot be allowed to be 'above the law'. A clear and forceful philosophical justification for the doctrine of the rule of law is to be found in F A Hayek's *The Road to Serfdom* (1944), where he wrote:

> '... stripped of all its technicalities this means that government in all its actions is bound by rules fixed and announced beforehand ... rules which make it possible to foresee with fair certainty how the authority will use its coercive powers in given circumstances, and to plan one's individual affairs on the basis of this knowledge.'

Diagrammatic summary

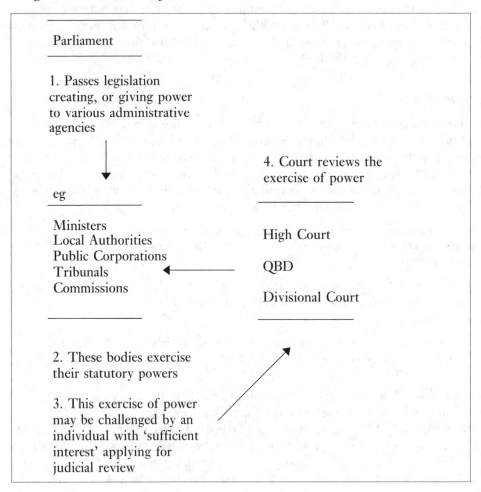

Parliament

1. Passes legislation creating, or giving power to various administrative agencies

eg

Ministers
Local Authorities
Public Corporations
Tribunals
Commissions

4. Court reviews the exercise of power

High Court

QBD

Divisional Court

2. These bodies exercise their statutory powers

3. This exercise of power may be challenged by an individual with 'sufficient interest' applying for judicial review

Responsible government

Although administrative law is by no means limited to judicial control of action taken by ministers of the Crown, it is an aspect of the subject that is of key constitutional significance, not least because ministers tend to exercise the most significant powers. These powers can take the form of a discretion, provided by Parliament in a primary Act, to make decisions affecting the lives of citizens, a discretion to enact delegated legislation, or a ministerial discretion to exercise prerogative power (see further Chapter 2) which can involve making major decisions relating to foreign affairs or legislating by means of Order in Council. The courts will be mindful of the conventions of responsible government in exercising the power to review the exercise of ministerial powers, particularly the fact that a minister may be acting pursuant to a policy agreed at Cabinet level (ie collective responsibility) and the fact that the minister is, in theory, answerable to Parliament for his actions (ministerial responsibility). There may be occasions when the courts conclude that the subject matter of an application for judicial review is so based in policy that it should be left to be determined by the appropriate minister (subject to the decision not being made in bad faith or being an outrageous affront to logic): see for example *R v Home Secretary, ex parte Hosenball* [1977] 1 WLR 766.

The fact that ministerial action has been approved by Parliament may also inhibit judicial intervention: see *Nottinghamshire County Council v Secretary of State for the Environment* [1986] 1 All ER 199 where the House of Lords had to consider a challenge to the action of the Secretary of State, under the Local Government Planning and Land Act 1980, in issuing 'expenditure guidance' which had a directly restraining effect on local authority spending. Before the guidance could take effect it required the approval by resolution of the House of Commons. The authorities challenged the Secretary of State's guidance on the ground, inter alia, that it was unreasonable as it contravened the principles expounded in the judgment of Lord Greene MR in *Associated Provincial Picture Houses Ltd v Wednesbury Corporation* [1948] 1 KB 223 at 229, the leading authority concerning the basis for a challenge to an administrative decision on the ground of unreasonableness. Lord Scarman stated (at p247):

> 'The submission raises an important question as to the limits of judicial review. We are in the field of public financial administration and we are being asked to review the exercise by the Secretary of State of an administrative discretion which inevitably requires a political judgment on his part and which cannot lead to action by him against a local authority unless that action is first approved by the House of Commons ... I cannot accept that it is constitutionally appropriate, save in very exceptional circumstances, for the courts to intervene on the ground of "unreasonableness" to quash guidance framed by the Secretary of State and by necessary implication approved by the House of Commons, the guidance being concerned with the limits of public expenditure by local authorities and the incidence of the tax burden as between taxpayers and ratepayers. Unless and until a statute provides otherwise, or it is established that the Secretary of State has abused his power, these are matters of political judgment for him and for the House of Commons. They are not for the judges or your Lordships' House in its judicial capacity. For myself, I refuse in this case to examine the detail of the guidance or its consequences. My reasons are these. Such an examination by a court would be justified only if a prima facie case were to be shown for holding that the Secretary of State had acted in bad faith, or for an improper motive, or that the consequence of his guidance were so absurd that he must have taken leave of his senses.'

Subsequent decisions, such as *R (On the Application of Javed) v Secretary of State for the Home Department* (2001) The Times 24 May (a Court of Appeal case), indicate that it is the need to leave policy matters to politicians and not the approval of a ministerial order by Parliament that is significant.

1.4 Devices and techniques: who exercises power?

Devices

The use of the word 'devices' refers to the way in which parliament has chosen to put a policy into effect. What sort of administrative agency (inferior body), if any, would be best suited to the task?

Ministers

If the aim is political control of a scheme and consistency, albeit at the expense of impartiality, the implementation of a policy will be entrusted to a Secretary of State as the controlling administrative agency. In constitutional terms there is also the safeguard of ministerial responsibility. The minister will be answerable in the House of Commons, and before select committees, for the way in which he and his officials have discharged their functions. The political advantage lies in the fact that, through exercising his decision-making power, the minister can ensure that government policy is reflected in the choices made. For example, in the sphere of town and country planning, the minister can promote policies regarding the establishment of new towns, or limiting out-of-town shopping developments as the case may be. Similarly, the power to create delegated legislation is normally vested in a minister so that government policy can be reflected in responses to changing circumstances, for example removing welfare benefits from asylum seekers, or banning the sale of beef on the bone (see generally Chapter 2). Subject to any express exceptions the minister's actions will be subject to scrutiny by the Parliamentary Commissioner for Administration (see Chapter 13), and open to judicial review in the courts (see Chapters 5–9 generally).

Tribunals

There may be a number of different reasons for vesting a decision-making power in a tribunal. These issues are considered in more depth in Chapter 4, but suffice to say here that tribunals can provide: a cost-efficient and speedy alternative to the legal process; a means of bringing subject expertise to bear upon a particular type of dispute; and a reasonably independent forum for resolving disputes between the citizen and the state, typically in the sphere of welfare benefits, taxation or licensing. Tribunals normally operate within a statutory framework that provides for appeals, and the referral of points of law to the courts. Where appropriate, the statutory framework may allow for issues to be referred to ministers for consideration. Again the trade off in political terms is between independent and impartial decision-making on the one hand, and loss of political power and influence on the other. Clearly the power to appoint tribunal members can be of key significance.

Public corporations

Public corporations are essentially statutory bodies enjoying a legal identity independent of any government department, empowered to discharge a commercial, regulatory or welfarist function, for example London Transport or the BBC. In the past a variety of procedures have been followed in the creation of public corporations. Where the body has been envisaged as having a welfare or regulatory role the tendency has been to create it by means of the relevant enabling Act; where a corporation has been used to carry out a commercial activity the assets of others engaged in the industry may have been compulsorily acquired and transferred to the new corporation, as was the case with the National Coal Board, subsequently British Coal, under the Coal Industry Nationalisation Act 1946. Alternatively, the government may decide to compulsorily purchase the shares in an industry, thereby gaining control under the normal principles of company law, the shares then being vested in a newly created public corporation. An example of this procedure being followed was provided by the creation of the British Steel Corporation. Finally, functions may be transferred from a government department to a public corporation, a technique used in 1969 when the Post Office was created under the Post Office Act 1969.

The enabling Act will invariably provide for appointments to be made by the relevant minister, thus underlining the political control he can exercise. These appointments are usually for a period of three to five years, the minister retaining the power to remove a board member on grounds of absence, bankruptcy, or physical or mental incapacitation. The minister will seek to appoint a chairman with whom he can establish a good working relationship but, further, one who understands the policy goals that the minister has created for the industry in question. The enabling Act will usually give the minister the power to issue directives to the board of a public corporation, indicating the way in which the industry should proceed. This does not relate to the day-to-day running of the industry, but to more general long-term strategy. Matters covered may range from pricing policy, to buying from British suppliers of goods where possible. Apart from the revenue that their own activities may, where appropriate, generate, public corporations will be largely dependent on central government to make up any shortfall in their accounts. For long-term projects the public corporation may depend on central government for subsidies, or on the minister for the sanctioning of loan agreements. Given this financial dependence, ministers are able to use the granting or withholding of money as a bargaining tool in persuading the board of a corporation to implement government policy.

Given that the boards of public corporations are, by statute, responsible for the day-to-day running of their industry, the minister will not normally be answerable to Parliament for such matters. As mentioned above, the minister is given a statutory power to issue directives to the boards of corporations and, consequently, is answerable to Parliament for these publicly articulated statements of policy.

The problem with accountability concerns the behind-the-scenes activities of ministers and corporation chairmen. They may meet and agree informally on a policy and its implementation yet, when it is carried out, the minister can refuse to answer questions in Parliament about the matter on the ground that it is not his responsibility. Events during the 1984 – 85 miners' strike illustrate this. At various points in the dispute the management of the National Coal Board, led by its chairman, adopted a hard-line attitude to the strike and refused to negotiate with the union members. Allegations were made at the time that the Board was responding to instructions from ministers to adopt this line. When questioned in the House of Commons, however, the Prime Minister and the Energy Secretary both declined to comment on the Coal Board's management of the strike negotiations, claiming that it was not the government's responsibility.

The period since 1979 has seen the implementation of a government policy to return public corporations responsible for commercial undertakings to private ownership, most spectacularly as regards telecommunications, gas, electricity and water. On 1 April 1994 the process of denationalising the railways commenced, with Railtrack taking over some responsibilities from British Rail. The process of 'privatisation' has usually been marked by the vesting of certain controls over pricing in the relevant government minister, and the creation of an independent consumer watchdog group to report on the conduct of the industry concerned. The result is that the functions left to public corporations, other than local authorities, tend now to be welfare-based. As regards regulatory functions, the policy since 1979 has been to leave industries to regulate themselves (eg financial services, advertising, the City), rather than create new regulatory bodies. It is significant that when the system of House of Commons select committees was reorganised in 1979, the Select Committee on Nationalised Industries was abolished and has not since been replaced.

In theory, the ultra vires principle (see Chapters 5–9) applies to public corporations as it does to other public law bodies, but the control may prove more illusory than real. This point is reflected in comments made by Sir John Donaldson MR in *R* v *Independent Broadcasting Authority, ex parte Whitehouse* (1985) The Times 4 April. The applicant alleged that the Director-General of the IBA had acted in breach of s4(1) of the Broadcasting Act 1981 in deciding not to refer his decision to screen the film *Scum*, to other members of the IBA. At first instance declarations were granted that the Director-General of the IBA had committed a grave error in not consulting other members of the institutions, and that the IBA itself had failed to fully inform the Director-General on the procedures relating to referral of controversial films. The Court of Appeal, allowing the appeal, declined to interfere with the Director General's decision. His Lordship observed:

'The relevant duty of the IBA was set out in s4(1), namely, "to satisfy themselves that, so far as possible, the programmes broadcast by the Authority comply with" certain requirements. Those requirements were none of them precise. All required value judgments. The parliamentary intention seemed to have been to create a statutory body, the IBA, consisting of a number of responsible persons as members who would occupy a position analogous to that of the Governors of the BBC. The role of the IBA was to control independent broadcasting and the role of the members to act as policy makers and supervisors. In using the phrase "it shall be the duty of the Authority to satisfy themselves" Parliament was creating what might be described qualitatively as a "best endeavours" obligation and was leaving it to the members to adopt methods of working, or a system, which, in their opinion, was best adapted to securing the requirements set out in s4(1). [T]he IBA's duty was to devise and operate a system designed to ensure that the statutory requirements were met. The court's right and duty to interfere only arose if the system so devised was not operated or if it was such as no reasonable person could have adopted in compliance with the IBA's statutory duty. Their Lordships were quite unpersuaded that the system fell into that category.'

As regards the availability of judicial remedies as a means of controlling public corporations: see further Chapters 11 and 14.

Quangos

The term 'quango' stands for 'quasi-autonomous non-governmental body'. It is a body that has a governmental role, but is not part of the government, operating largely at 'arm's length' from ministerial control. Examples are bodies such as the Health and Safety Commission and Executive, the Environment Agency, the Law Commission, boards of visitors to penal establishments, the Equal Opportunities Commission, the Commission for Racial Equality, the Countryside Commission, Training and Enterprise Councils, the British Council (the largest employing over 6,000 people), the Natural History Museum and the Human Genetics Advisory Commission. The term can also encompass bodies such as NHS local trusts, next steps agencies, which are part of government departments, the Further Education Funding Councils, and the Higher Education Funding Councils for England and Wales.

Essentially quangos are useful because they can be used to discharge functions that need to be carried out at 'arm's length' from ministers, such as regulation or the allocation of funding; they can be used to provide expert advice to ministers on technical or other very specialised issues; they can provide lay persons with an opportunity to contribute to public life; they can be set up quickly in order to respond to a new problem or concern; and they can provide a platform for collaboration between government and industry, or government and the voluntary sector. In summary:

'Quangos can therefore carry out a wide range of important functions best provided by a body which is at arm's length from government, preserving independence in its day-to-day decisions from ministers and their civil servants. Governments of both political persuasions have recognised the value of the voluntary effort of many quango members over many years, the technical expertise they bring to bear, often without pay, and the ability of quangos to work in partnership with other bodies.' (*Opening up Quangos: A Consultation Paper* (1997))

Possibly because of their usefulness, the period between 1980 and 1998 has seen a marked increase in the number of quangos. It has been estimated that there are now over 6,700 such bodies (see *Ego Trip: Extra-governmental Organisations in the UK* by Weir and Hall, Charter 88), many discharging functions that were previously within the jurisdiction of elected bodies, although government figures for 1996 indicate that the total funded by the government is nearer 1,200, compared with over 2,000 in 1979. Government funding for such bodies in 1979 stood at £3 billion. In 1996 the figure was £18.2 billion (6 per cent of government expenditure). Quangos employ more than 100,000 staff, 40 per cent of whom are unpaid. The rationale for transferring powers from elected bodies to quangos is that the latter are more accountable to citizens as the consumers of services than former were to consumers as voters, although this is a view that was hotly contested by the Labour Party in opposition. What is beyond doubt is that quangos are an effective method of executing government policy, via powers of appointment, without the actions of their members having to be held up to periodic democratic scrutiny. Hence the criticisms that quangos are unelected, unaccountable, secretive and unresponsive. Application of the 'Nolan' principles, and possibly a widening of the jurisdiction of the Parliamentary Commissioner for Administration to include more quangos, will have a salutary effect and address some of these criticisms.

Self-regulation
A further option is, of course, not to regulate an activity at all. Where a non-interventionist approach is adopted by a government citizens will have to rely on an industry regulating itself: see for example the Advertising Standards Agency, the Press Complaints Commission, and bodies such as the Banking Ombudsman and Pensions Ombudsman. The courts may still be willing to intervene, however, if they take the view that the function of the body concerned is sufficiently 'governmental': see further Chapter 10.

Whenever considering the actions of an administrative agency consider the question: why was this type of body chosen to perform the function in question?

Techniques

By 'techniques' is meant the way in which the administrative body is empowered to carry out its functions and achieve the policy goals intended. The wording of the enabling Act will often give the court guidance as to the amount of independence that has been vested in an administrative agency, and hence influence its view of any legal challenge.

Duties
Parliament may place duties on administrative agencies, typically by providing that certain action shall be taken etc. It should not be assumed that all such duties are enforceable, however. The courts will again advert to the intention of Parliament in determining whether a given duty is enforceable at the behest of an individual citizen in the courts, or whether an administrative remedy, such as ministerial intervention is more appropriate: see further Chapter 11.

Express limits on powers

The enabling Act may expressly require a particular procedure to be followed before a decision-making power can be exercised, for example prior consultation or notification. Alternatively, a power may be limited in terms of the time during which it can be exercised, the area over which it can be exercised, or in terms of the amount of money that can be spent.

Regulatory powers

Where appropriate an administrative body will be given specific powers, such as: the power to inspect establishments selling food; the power to inspect buildings under construction; or the power to grant licences to those seeking to ply a particular trade, such as taxi drivers. The rationale is that the exercise of power may be best discharged at a local level, where local needs can be taken into account, or by those with particular expert knowledge.

Subjectively worded powers

The enabling Act may provide that a minister or local authority is to have the discretion to decide a matter as it thinks fit. This is known as a subjectively worded power in the sense that the administrative agency appears to be able to decide for itself what it thinks it should do. Whilst the courts will pay due regard to the intention of Parliament where such powers are provided, it should not be assumed that they entitle the administrative body to do literally as it pleases. The courts will still assume that the power is meant to used reasonably and fairly: see further Chapters 5–9.

Exclusion of legal challenge

Parliament may provide that the decisions of a minister, tribunal or local authority are not to be questioned in the courts. Whilst this may, at first, appear to create the danger that wrongdoing could go unchallenged, and injustice unremedied, there will usually be a strong countervailing public policy for such a provision, and possibly some administrative scheme for challenging such decisions: see further Chapter 12.

Again, when considering administrative agencies, consider why they have been empowered to act in a particular way. How is this related to the perceived policy objectives?

1.5 Judicial review and the ultra vires doctrine

In its purest form the ultra vires doctrine holds that an inferior body must act within the scope of its powers, and that if it exceeds its powers its determination will be a nullity. The primary purpose of judicial review is to provide a mechanism whereby the courts examine what a public body has done, or failed to do, with reference to the relevant legislation, and come to a determination as to the legality of the public body's actions. If necessary a reviewing court can quash a decision and order that it be taken again, with due regard being had to the relevant law. How then might an inferior body exceed the scope of its powers? Certain aspects of the answer to this question will be considered at much greater length in the appropriate chapters of this book, for example breach of natural justice (Chapters 5 and 6) and irrationality (Chapter 7). For the purposes of providing an overview, however, the following grounds can be identified.

Error as to jurisdiction

In administrative law the term jurisdiction can most readily be equated with power. Inferior bodies, created by statute, are bodies of 'limited jurisdiction' because they can only do what they are empowered to do by the terms of their enabling Acts. In dealing with most problems involving consideration of the doctrine, therefore, the first matter to be considered is the actual wording of the relevant Act. The jurisdiction of an inferior body will often be expressly stated in the relevant Act, such as where a tribunal has power to determine the rent payable in respect of 'furnished accommodation'. Whether or not the accommodation is furnished is a question of fact that has to answered correctly before the tribunal can proceed to determine what rent should be paid. If it were to conclude that Hyde Park was 'furnished accommodation' and set a rent it would clearly be acting ultra vires. It would be exercising its power in respect of a matter outside its jurisdiction. The term given to such questions is to describe them as disputes on points of 'jurisdictional fact' – facts which must objectively be proved to exist before a body has jurisdiction.

The courts will not normally exercise the power of judicial review regarding findings of fact by inferior bodies, but will intervene if the fact is one that has a bearing on jurisdiction. In *R* v *Fulham, Hammersmith and Kensington Rent Tribunal, ex parte Zerek* [1951] 2 KB 1 a rent tribunal was empowered to assess the correct level of rent payable for unfurnished lettings, and proceeded to reduce the rent payable to a landlord, who contested its decision on the basis that it had no jurisdiction to set a rent because the letting was in fact furnished. The Divisional Court refused his application for certiorari to quash the tribunal's determination, but in the course of so doing Lord Goddard C J stated:

> '... if a certain state of facts has to exist before an inferior tribunal have jurisdiction, they can inquire into the facts in order to decide whether or not they have jurisdiction, but cannot give themselves jurisdiction by a wrong decision upon them; and this court may, by means of proceedings for certiorari, inquire into the correctness of the decision.'

Again, in *White and Collins* v *Minister of Health* [1939] 2 KB 838, the Court of Appeal considered the power of a local authority to exercise compulsory purchase powers over land not forming 'part of any park, garden, or pleasure ground'. The

Court concluded that the question of whether an area of land did, or did not, compromise part of a park or pleasure ground was one of jurisdictional fact. The local authority's decision on such a matter had to be open to challenge in the courts, otherwise it would have been able to exercise its powers of compulsory purchase over any land it chose to, simply by determining that the land did not, in its view, comprise any part of a park etc.

Whilst proof of a jurisdictional fact is normally seen as a precondition to the exercise of power, it can equally be the determinant of whether or not a duty has arisen. In *R* v *South Hams District Council, ex parte Gibbs* (1994) The Times 8 June the Court of Appeal held that before a duty to provide sites for gypsies under the Caravan Sites Act 1968 could arise the question of status (ie was the individual seeking to be provided with a site a gypsy or not) had to be resolved. Provided a local authority applied the correct test in law, the court would not interfere with the authority's conclusions unless the decision could be shown to be vitiated by irrationality, as Parliament must have intended that the detailed inquires necessitated by having to determine whether an individual was or was not a gypsy were to be undertaken by the relevant local authority.

Breach of express limits on power

An enabling Act will often lay down express limitations upon power to be observed once an inferior body enters in upon the task of exercising its jurisdiction. Suppose a tribunal were created to award research funds to publicly funded universities up to a limit of £10 million per university. Whether or not the applicant institution was a publicly funded university would be a jurisdictional fact, as considered above. Once that matter was satisfied the tribunal would have a discretion, but one that could only be exercised subject to the express financial limitation provided for. Hence an award of £11 million to an institution would be ultra vires. Express limitations are frequently encountered in respect of the procedure to be followed by an administrative body when exercising its powers: see further Chapter 6, section 6.2.

Breach of implied limits on power

As indicated above the courts will 'read in' or imply limitations on the exercise of discretion. The courts will assume, for example, that Parliament did not invest a public authority with a discretion on the basis that it might be exercised irrationally or unreasonably. Similarly, a public authority could act ultra vires by acting on irrelevant considerations, failing to take into account relevant considerations, acting on no evidence, acting to achieve an ulterior purpose, acting on bad faith, acting unfairly or taking action disproportionate to that required. Parliament will not state expressly that power must not be exercised in this way – it assumes that it will not be. The reviewing court will simply be giving effect to that assumption. Following the enactment of the Human Rights Act 1998 a public authority will now be acting unlawfully if it contravenes one of the European Convention rights protected by the Act: see further Chapters 7 and 8. Conversely, if a body acts intra vires, that is, within the limits of the power it has been given in its enabling statute, its actions will be immune from review by the courts. Failings such as rudeness, stupidity, loss of documents or inefficiency may be irksome to the citizen but they may not of themselves amount to the type of illegality that triggers an application for judicial review (although a complaint to the Ombudsman might be appropriate (see Chapter 13)).

Obtaining a remedy

Any individual with 'sufficient interest' can apply to the Divisional Court of the High Court for judicial review of an administrative (or inferior) body: see Chapter 10. The remedies available include the private law remedies of injunction, damages and declaration, and the public law remedies, in the form of prerogative orders: certiorari (which quashes an ultra vires action); mandamus (an order to perform a duty); and prohibition (an order to refrain from certain action). From October 2000 these remedies will be known as 'quashing orders', 'mandatory orders' and 'prohibiting orders' respectively. The prerogative orders are those granted by the Crown against an administrative body, hence the citation of many administrative law cases: *R (On the Application of Smith)* v *Fictitious Local Authority*.

The purpose of judicial review

Judicial review looks at the legality of a decision, not its merits. The extent to which this may change with the enactment of the Human Rights Act 1998 remains to be seen (see further Chapter 7), but the likelihood is that the judicial role will be slightly different in cases involving Convention rights because of the issues which the Convention requires a judge to consider (eg whether certain restrictions are 'necessary in a democratic society'). It will remain the case, however, that a court exercising its power of judicial review will not be seeking to substitute its own value judgments for those of an inferior body. The point is illustrated by the Court of Appeal's decision in *R* v *Secretary of State for the Home Department, ex parte Turgut* [2001] 1 All ER 719. The applicant, a Turkish Kurd, evaded military service in Turkey and entered the United Kingdom illegally. His claim for political asylum was rejected, as was his request for exceptional permission to remain in the United Kingdom. The Secretary of State expressed the view that he was not convinced that if the applicant was returned to Turkey he would be subjected to treatment that violated art 3 of the European Convention on Human Rights. The applicant sought review of this decision on the ground that it was irrational. The initial application was refused and the applicant appealed to the Court of Appeal, which reserved to itself the hearing of the substantive application. Simon Brown LJ indicated that a crucial question was as to the proper role of the court in such cases. Should it assume the primary fact-finding role and decide whether the applicant was subject to the risk in question, or should its role be supervisory, bearing in mind that fundamental human rights were at stake? *R* v *Ministry of Defence, ex parte Smith* [1996] QB 517, 554, indicated that the role should be supervisory, although the applicant had contended that if such an approach was taken the United Kingdom would not be satisfying its obligation under art 13 of the Convention to provide an effective remedy for those whose rights were violated. It was further argued that the European Court of Human Rights faced with such a case would come to its own assessment of the risk to the applicant: see *Vilvarajah* v *United Kingdom* (1991) 14 EHRR 248 and *Chahal* v *United Kingdom* (1997) 23 EHRR 413. Dismissing the appeal, Simon Brown LJ concluded that the Court would only quash the decision of the Secretary of State if it was established that there was, on any reasonable view of the facts, a serious risk of inhuman or degrading treatment. And it was further established that no rational Home Secretary could have reached a different conclusion on the material in the case, although he added that, given that fundamental human rights were involved, the area of judgment on issues of fact in relation to which the Court would defer to the Home Secretary as the person primarily entrusted with the decision on the applicant's removal was a decidedly narrow one. It will be noted that there is, inevitably, a very fine dividing line between ascertaining whether the decision was lawful, bearing in mind the quantity and quality of the evidence substantiating the exercise of discretion (the supervisory jurisdiction), and determining whether the decision reached on the basis of that evidence was correct (usurping the role of the primary decision-maker). Judicial review is to be contrasted with a statutory right of appeal where a decision can be overruled and a new decision taken on the merits of the case; with judicial review a decision can be quashed and remitted to the inferior body to take again. By quashing decisions on the grounds that they are ultra vires the courts hope to indicate to public bodies the way in which they should act in future, and through this the courts can promote fairer, and more efficient, administrative practices. The extent to which they succeed in this is a matter for debate.

Damages are not available for loss resulting from acts that are ultra vires per se: see *Dunlop* v *Woollahra Municipal Council* [1982] AC 158. A claim for damages can be added to an application for judicial review, but will only be awarded if they would have been available in an action started by way of writ.

The High Court should only be required to exercise its supervisory jurisdiction in relation to a decision that affects the legal rights and duties of an individual or organisation. A purely administrative decision that does not have either of these consequences is an inappropriate target for judicial review because, if it has no legal effect, there is nothing for judicial review to deal with. Thus, in *R* v *Secretary of State for Employment, ex parte Equal Opportunities Commission and Another* [1992] 1 All ER 545, the House of Lords held (inter alia) that the case was not one where the court would have been empowered to grant a prerogative order, as there was no 'decision' of the Secretary of State to quash, although it should be noted that this does not mean that declaratory relief will necessarily be denied. Similarly, in *R* v *Immigration Appeal Tribunal, ex parte Anderson* (2000) The Times 22 March, the decision by an immigration adjudicator to make or refuse to make a recommendation to the Home Secretary when refusing an appeal under the Immigration Act 1971 was held not to be open to judicial review as such recommendations had no statutory basis and no legal effect: see further the comments of Lord Bridge in *Gillick* v *West Norfolk and Wisbech Area Health Authority* [1985] 3 All ER 402, detailed at Chapter 2, section 2.6.

1.6 The limitations of judicial review

The traditional view of judicial review is that it is the cornerstone of administrative law, representing the importance of independent judicial control over the executive, and providing an important safeguard for the rights of the individual dealing with the state. An examination of the realities of judicial review might suggest a number of factors that operate to limit the extent to which this traditional function can be achieved.

Sporadic nature of review

As with the development of the common law in general, the development of administrative law principles by means of court decisions on applications for judicial review will necessarily be sporadic. The courts can only deal with those cases that come before them. A new concept or new approach must wait for the right conflict to come before the courts before it can be introduced into the law. Further, there may be many 'illegal' administrative practices that are not challenged by way of judicial review because those affected are ignorant, impecunious, cannot be bothered, or simply accept the actions of administrators unquestioningly.

Limits of the ultra vires doctrine

With the now largely academic exception of error of law, review is only possible where an allegation of ultra vires action is made out. The problem here is that there are many forms of intra vires action that are objectionable or questionable, and that cannot be corrected by means of judicial review, such as delay, rudeness, stupidity, or loss of documents. In such cases recourse might instead be had to one of the various 'Ombudsmen' providing the matter falls within his jurisdiction: see further Chapter 13. The joint venture by Justice and All Souls (*Administrative Justice – Some Necessary Reforms* (Clarendon Press, 1988)) examined possible reforms in the law and procedure whereby a person might secure effective redress of grievances suffered as a consequence of acts or omissions of the various agencies of government, including ministers of the Crown, public corporations and local authorities throughout the United Kingdom. The committee's most significant recommendation was that an Administrative Review Commission, along the lines of the Australian Administrative Review Council, should be created. The Commission would be charged with the task of keeping under constant review all the procedures and institutions relating to the citizen's need to challenge the administration. Clearly such a body would have to complement the tasks already discharged by institutions such as the Council on Tribunals and the Parliamentary Commissioner for Administration. The success or failure of such a Commission would depend to a large extent on the duties placed on administrators to consult it for advice, and on the powers it might be given to enforce its findings.

Futility of review

Even when a court has declared a particular decision to have been unlawful, the results may prove the whole process to have been futile. The decision may simply be ignored by the administrative body in question on the assumption that no one will bother to challenge its action in future, thus emphasising the point that a reviewing court is merely deciding one case, and ruling the decision, or procedure adopted in that case, to have been ultra vires. There is no guarantee that the administrative body will not continue to make such decisions, or follow such procedures. The decision declared to have been ultra vires may be retaken by the administrative body and the same conclusion reached, for example, that the individual concerned should not be granted a licence. As the decision has now been taken properly it is immune from review, yet the individual has still not achieved what he really wanted, the grant of a licence.

A court decision on a matter such as entitlement to benefit, or the scope of a minister's powers, may prove so inconvenient to the administrative process that the government of the day responds with amending legislation to nullify the effect of the court's decision. For example, consider *Secretary of State for Education and Science* v *Tameside Metropolitan Borough Council* [1977] AC 1014 and the consequent Education Act 1976.

What the courts see as their proper role in judicial review proceedings

Judicial review is discretionary, consequently immense trust is placed in the judiciary to ensure its proper functioning. Judges have the option of developing judicial review in ways that are dynamic and challenging to the executive, or they can impart the stamp of legality to contentious executive action. Much depends on what the judiciary sees as the 'proper' role of judicial review in this regard. Particular problems arise where review is sought on grounds of unreasonableness, or unfairness, because here, although in theory the courts are only concerned with legality, they will be involved in making value judgments as to what is 'reasonable' and what is 'fair'. Often these value judgments will not accord with the views of the litigant or wider public.

When faced with a challenge to what is effectively a 'rationing' decision by an executive agency, there is an understandable reluctance on the part of the courts to intervene in the absence of manifestly absurd decision-making. This point is well illustrated by the Court of Appeal's ruling in *R* v *Cambridge District Health Authority, ex parte B* [1995] 1 WLR 898. The applicant's daughter was a ten-year-old girl suffering from acute myeloid leukaemia. Doctors treating her determined that a further course of chemotherapy and possible bone marrow transplant could not be justified as the course of treatment would cost in excess of £75,000 and carried with it only a 10–20 per cent chance of success. Without further treatment the girl was assessed as having a life expectancy of between eight and ten weeks. The applicant, suing as the girl's next friend, applied for judicial review of the respondent health authority's refusal to fund further treatment, seeking an order of certiorari to quash the decision and an order of mandamus to compel the authority to fund the treatment. At first instance Laws J rejected the contention that the exercise of discretion by a public body could be assessed purely by reference to the *Wednesbury* test for reasonableness. In his view, given that fundamental issues, such as the right to life, were involved, the public body had to discharge the onus of showing a substantial public interest justification for its decision, and on the facts he was satisfied that the health authority had failed in this regard. He declined to grant an order of mandamus, but did quash the decision not to fund treatment. Allowing the authority's appeal, and rejecting the grounds upon which the decision of the health authority had been criticised in the courts below, Sir Thomas Bingham MR observed that:

> 'Difficult and agonising judgments have to be made as to how a limited budget is best allocated to maximum advantage of the maximum number of patients. That is not a judgment that the court can make. In my judgment, it is not something that a health authority ... can be fairly criticised for not advancing before the court.'

His Lordship went on to observe that it was wholly unrealistic to ask a health authority to appear before the court with evidence of its accounts in order to prove that by treating one patient it would be denying treatment to another: see further *Re Walker's Application* (1987) The Times 26 November considered at Chapter 7, section 7.2 and *R* v *Brent and Harrow Health Authority, ex parte Harrow London Borough Council* (1996) The Times 15 October.

Where the courts decline to intervene the individual may be left without an effective remedy, witness options open to the homeless in the wake of the House of Lords' decision in *R* v *Hillingdon London Borough Council, ex parte Puhlhofer* [1986] 1 All ER 467 not to interfere with the determination of the housing authority concerning the suitability of accommodation provided. In cases such as *Puhlhofer* the courts are influenced, to some extent, by the prospect of increased use of judicial review, which (somewhat curiously) is seen as undesirable.

Occasionally, the reluctance to exercise a reviewing jurisdiction may arise from the courts not wanting to be drawn into what are perceived to be primarily domestic disputes. Some indication as to how the court should approach the question of reviewability was provided by Simon Brown J in *R* v *Chief Rabbi, ex parte Wachman* [1992] 1 WLR 1036, where, in a case involving a challenge to disciplinary proceedings, he expressed the view that, whilst the review jurisdiction of the High Court clearly had been extended to non-statutory bodies, this had only occurred where such bodies performed a governmental or at least quasi-governmental function. The key was to ask if the body performed a regulatory function which, in the absence of such a body, would have been performed by an executive authority. In the light of this he held that there was no question of the state ever regulating religious activities, hence the Chief Rabbi did not come within the scope of 'public law body' as that term was now understood in administrative law. In any event there would be the further problem of the courts ruling upon the fairness of the procedures followed by the rabbinical authorities. Where these were in accordance with Jewish law, but possibly in breach of the principles of natural justice, as those principles were now understood, the court would be placed in the invidious position of having to rule upon the validity of the Jewish laws. He felt such a situation should be avoided if at all possible. See further *R* v *Imam of Bury Park Jame Masjid, Luton, ex parte Sulaiman Ali* (1991) The Independent 13 September.

Deference to national security claims

Even though the court may possess a supervisory jurisdiction over the exercise of ministerial power, there are situations where judicial intervention is unlikely given the non-justiciable nature of the issue involved, typically where the correctness of a decision is more a question of political judgment than of legality. The speeches in *Council of Civil Service Unions* v *Minister for the Civil Service* [1984] 3 All ER 935 identify those matters traditionally considered to fall outside the scope of justiciability, including the conduct of foreign affairs, disposition of troops, appointment of ministers and so forth. Courts are particularly reluctant to intervene where a minister claims to have acted to protect national security, which was itself a key basis for the decision in the *Council of Civil Service Unions* case. In *R* v *Secretary of State for the Home Department, ex parte Cheblak* [1991] 1 WLR 890 the applicant had been made the subject of a deportation order, the minister indicating that he had evidence to suggest that the applicant might engage in terrorist activities if he was allowed to remain in the United Kingdom during the Gulf war. Refusing to grant judicial review of the decision, the Court of Appeal held that it was satisfied that the statutory requirement that reasons be given for detention under the relevant regulations had been met by the statement that the applicant had been detained in the interests of national security. Lord Donaldson MR went out of his way to strenuously deny suggestions that since (at that time) hostilities in the Gulf were imminent the courts would start to become 'executive' minded. He added, however, that the courts would be unlikely to intervene where a decision was being made in the interests of national security, as this was, in his view, a par excellence example of a non-justiciable issue. He regarded the constitutional safeguard in such cases as being supplied by ministerial responsibility to Parliament: see further *R* v *Secretary of State for the Home Department, ex parte Chahal* [1995] 1 WLR 526.

As Sedley J observed in *R* v *Secretary of State for the Home Department, ex parte McQuillan* [1995] 4 All ER 400, under domestic law, once the Secretary of State asserted that his failure to give reasons for the applicant being made the subject of an exclusion order (beyond the bald assertion that he had been involved in terrorist activities) was based on the threat to national security posed by revealing sources of information, the making of the order was rendered non-justiciable issue. Note, however, that the court accepted that, under European Union law, a member state of the European Union had to comply with the principles of proportionality in seeking to limit an individual's right to freedom of movement on the grounds of national security. Hence the question of compliance with European Union law would be referred to the European Court of Justice.

2

Ministers and Their Powers: Delegated Legislation and Prerogative Power

2.1   Introduction

2.2   Delegated legislation in general

2.3   Statutory instruments

2.4   Parliamentary scrutiny

2.5   Scrutiny by the courts

2.6   Other forms of delegated legislation

2.7   Prerogative power

2.8   The exercise of prerogative power on the sovereign's behalf by ministers

2.9   Prerogative and statutory powers

2.10 Judicial review of prerogative power

2.1 Introduction

This chapter is concerned with certain aspects of the exercise of power by central government, ie ministers and their departments. Executive power can be exercised by a number of agencies, such as local authorities, tribunals, chief constables or non-statutory agencies. In constitutional terms, however, the most important executive powers and duties will be those exercised and discharged by ministers heading up the key departments of state. As will be seen most of the powers exercised by ministers are those delegated to them by Parliament in statutes, and as such ministers are subject to the ultra vires doctrine in the exercise of those powers. This means that a minister must not exceed the scope of the power, or exercise it in a manner that is unfair or irrational. Some of these powers are 'legislative' in nature, in the sense that they provide a minister with the discretion to enact delegated legislation if necessary. Some powers are not based on statute at all, notably prerogative powers, dealing with matters such as the conduct of foreign affairs and the defence of the realm.

The exercise of ministerial power is subject to a number of constitutional conventions, primarily the doctrines of collective and ministerial responsibility: see generally Michael T Molan's *Constitutional Law: The Machinery of Government* (4th edn, 2003). In practice this means that a minister is accountable to Parliament for the way in which he exercises his discretion, or the way in which it is exercised on his behalf by his civil servants, and he must have the backing of his colleagues for his actions. In theory a minister who abuses the powers vested in him by Parliament could be called upon to resign if he refuses to account to Parliament for what he has done, or the explanation is deemed to be inadequate. Similarly, a minister who no longer has the confidence and support of his Cabinet colleagues would be forced to resign, or indeed be sacked, by the Prime Minister because of the constraints imposed by the doctrine of collective responsibility. These are, of course, essentially political controls over the exercise of ministerial power, not legal ones. The extent to which they are effective depends upon the extent to which they are observed. The latter part of the twentieth century reveals precious little evidence to support the contention that it is a convention that a minister should resign in the event that there are serious failures within the department that he or she heads. Increasingly there is a tendency to blame failings on officials, blaming the 'execution' of what was in other respects a sound policy.

It is the weakness of the conventions relating to responsible government that make the existence of judicial controls over the exercise of discretion by ministers all the more important. The exercise of statutory discretion and the enforcement of statutory duties in so far as those issues concern ministers are considered generally in the examination of the ultra vires doctrine in Chapters 5 to 9. What follows is an examination of two specific aspects of ministerial discretion: the power to enact delegated legislation and the exercise of prerogative power.

2.2 Delegated legislation in general

The constitutional principle of parliamentary sovereignty means that Parliament can enact or repeal legislation as it sees fit. With a constitutional monarchy the theory is that, following convention, the monarch will always give her assent to any legislation that has successfully passed through both Houses of Parliament. A consequence of this is that the courts cannot question the validity of primary legislation, either on its merits, or on the grounds of procedural impropriety – even when the allegation is one of fraud: see *British Railways Board* v *Pickin* [1974] AC 765. It should be noted that improper action by a government department in a legislative capacity is also beyond the investigative powers of the Parliamentary Commissioner for Administration (the 'Ombudsman'): see Chapter 13. Despite the ever increasing volume of primary legislation (sometimes referred to as the 'parent Act' or the 'enabling Act'), the complexities of governing a sophisticated society necessitate the delegation of legislative functions to inferior bodies, such as ministers and local authorities. Clearly, Parliament does not have the time nor resources to enact every single piece of legislation that is needed in the form of primary legislation which can be fully debated and scrutinised by both houses. As a result various administrative agencies are empowered to enact delegated legislation, under the auspices of the parent Act, that has the force of law.

The most common format for delegated legislation is the statutory instrument (as to which see section 2.3 below) but it must be remembered that it is a generic term, and encompasses bye-laws (enacted by local authorities), ministerial orders, departmental circulars, guidelines and codes of conduct. Caution should be exercised with these last three matters, however, because it is questionable to what extent, if at all, they have any legal effect. Although they are the result of a minister exercising a power that has been delegated to him, if they lack the status of law it would, strictly speaking, be a misnomer to include them under the heading legislation.

As indicated above, the demands placed upon a modern government are such that parliamentary time is at a premium, and consequently a better use of time can be achieved by drafting primary legislation in general terms, providing the relevant minister with wide powers to introduce such measures as he considers necessary in order to implement the policy goals of the enabling Act. This has further advantages in that it allows flexibility, measures can be introduced quickly where this is seen as desirable, and the minister concerned can introduce new measures to deal with unforeseen situations. Clearly this is more efficient than having to introduce a new piece of primary legislation to deal with each emergent problem in a given area. For example, an enabling Act may give a minister general powers to prohibit membership of proscribed organisations or ban the movement of livestock. Similarly, an enabling Act may provide a minister with the powers necessary for providing a public service, such as the running of the prison service. Under the parent Act the minister can be empowered to make rules for the conduct of the service, as may be necessary from time to time: see further the Prison Act 1952 and subsequent Prison Rules 1964 (SI 1964/388).

Not surprisingly, the advantages of delegated legislation outlined above are not without their costs. In the 1920s fears developed about the volume and nature of delegated legislation being produced which was not receiving the parliamentary scrutiny many thought necessary or desirable. In 1929 Lord Chief Justice Hewart published *The New Despotism* in which he railed against what he saw as a dangerous and uncontrolled growth of bureaucratic power. In 1932 the report of the Donoughmore-Scott Committee on Ministers' Powers was issued. The report, amongst other things, explained the inevitability of delegated legislation, but also suggested some safeguards. The report also recommended better scrutiny of the vesting in ministers of 'oppressive' powers. Particular disquiet was engendered by the use of so-called 'Henry VIII' clauses which empower a minister to alter the provisions of the enabling Act itself, so far as may appear to him to be necessary for the purpose of bringing the Act into operation. The conventional wisdom is now that such powers should not be granted except for the purpose of bringing an Act into operation, and should be subject to strict time limitations, usually one year from the passing of the Act.

In the modern constitution the use of delegated legislation is largely taken for granted, albeit it might be seen by some as a 'necessary evil'. Questions nevertheless remain regarding the effectiveness of the scrutiny of delegated legislation in Parliament, and the willingness of the courts to allow judicial review as a means of challenge.

2.3 Statutory instruments

An initial problem is one of definition. Perhaps one way to solve the problem would be to remember that statutory instruments are always delegated legislation, but that not all delegated legislation takes the form of a statutory instrument. The correct approach would be to follow the provisions of s1(1) Statutory Instruments Act 1946 which provides:

> 'Where by this Act or any Act passed after the commencement of this Act power to make, confirm or approve orders, rules, regulations or other subordinate legislation is conferred on His Majesty in Council or on any Minister of the Crown then, if the power is expressed –
> (a) in the case of a power conferred on His Majesty, to be exercisable by Order in Council;
> (b) in the case of a power conferred in a Minister of the Crown, to be exercisable by statutory instrument,
> any document by which that power is exercised shall be known as a "statutory instrument" and the provision of this Act shall apply thereto accordingly ...'

The effect of this provision is that if, under an enabling Act, rules, regulations, orders, and so on, are not stated as being exercisable by statutory instrument, then the provisions of the 1946 Act as to publication and laying do not apply. Note also that even where the 1946 Act does apply, the precise laying procedure to be followed will still be determined by the enabling Act.

Prior consultation

As the creation of delegated legislation is a legislative function, the rules of natural justice do not apply, and failure to consult parties likely to be affected does not amount to a breach of natural justice. In *Bates* v *Lord Hailsham* [1972] 1 WLR 1373 a committee, of which the Lord Chancellor was a member, was empowered by s56 of the Solicitors Act 1957 to make orders prescribing solicitors' remuneration in respect of non–contentious business. Section 56(3) of the Act stated:

> 'Before any such order is made, the Lord Chancellor shall cause a draft to be sent to the council (of the Law Society), and the Committee shall, before making the order, consider any observations in writing submitted to them by the council within one month of the sending to them of the draft, and may then make the order ...'

A draft copy of proposals was sent to the Law Society, but not the British Legal Association of which the plaintiff was one of 2,900 members. He unsuccessfully sought a declaration that it would be ultra vires for the committee to confirm the making of the Order without first giving the British Legal Association an opportunity to give its views. Megarry J observed:

> 'Let me accept that in the sphere of the so-called quasi-judicial the rules of natural justice run, and that in the administrative or executive field there is a general duty of fairness. Nevertheless, these considerations do not seem to me to affect the process of legislation, whether primary or delegated. Many of those affected by delegated legislation, and affected very substantially, are never consulted in the process of enacting that legislation: and yet they have no remedy. Of course, the informal consultation of representative bodies by the legislative authority is a commonplace; but although a few statutes have specifically provided for a general process of publishing draft delegated legislation and considering objections ... I do not know of any implied right to be consulted or make objections, or any principle upon which the courts may enjoin the legislative process at the suit of those who contend that insufficient time for consultation and consideration has been given.'

Where, however, consultation with certain parties is required by the enabling Act, the courts are likely to interpret this as being a mandatory requirement; failure to comply could invalidate any resulting order: see *Agricultural, Horticultural and Forestry Industry Training Board* v *Aylesbury Mushrooms Ltd* [1972] 1 WLR 190.

The nature of the consultation required will depend largely on the circumstances of the case. In *R* v *Secretary of State for Health, ex parte United States Tobacco International Inc* [1991] 3 WLR 529 the Secretary of State was under a statutory duty to consult the applicants prior to issuing a prohibition on the sale of their main product, oral snuff. The applicants were not provided with all the information upon which the Secretary of State proposed to act, and the Divisional Court held that this unfairness justified the invalidation of the delegated legislation. Particular factors leading the court to this conclusion were: the fact that the government had encouraged the applicants to set up a business in Scotland for the manufacturing of oral snuff; the fact that the applicants were the country's sole producers of the product; and the fact that the ban would have a devastating effect on the livelihood of the applicants. In short, with so much at stake, the applicants had been entitled to more by way of consultation.

The 'making' of a statutory instrument

A difficult question arises of when a statutory instrument is actually 'made'. There are a number of ways of approaching the problem. First, that the statutory instrument is made as soon as it is signed by the appropriate minister and it becomes effective from that point onwards, notwithstanding that any publication or laying requirements have not been complied with. Second, that the statutory instrument is made when signed but only comes into effect on a certain date, specified on the order itself. Third, and more commonly, the statutory instrument is signed by the minister and is due to come into effect on some specified date in the future, after one of the various laying procedures have been complied with.

Laying procedures

It is possible for an enabling Act to require ministerial orders to be enacted by way of statutory instrument, but not require any laying procedure at all. This is not uncommon, but obviously raises questions about opportunity of scrutiny in Parliament. Such a possibility should be raised when the enabling Act is progressing through Parliament.

Bare laying procedures

Where an enabling Act simply requires a statutory instrument to be laid before Parliament, s4 of the 1946 Act applies. It states:

> 'Where by this Act or any Act passed after the commencement of this Act any statutory instrument is required to be laid before Parliament after being made, a copy of the instrument shall be laid before each House of Parliament and, subject as hereinafter provided, shall be so laid before the instrument comes into operation.
>
>   Provided that if it is essential that any such instrument should come into operation before copies thereof can be so laid as aforesaid, the instrument may be made so as to come into operation before it has been so laid; and where any statutory instrument comes into operation before it is laid before parliament, notification shall forthwith be sent to the Lord Chancellor and to the Speaker of the House of Commons drawing attention to the fact that copies of the instrument have yet to be laid before Parliament and explaining why such copies were not so laid before the instrument came into operation.'

No further procedure is necessary for the provision to become effective. The statutory instrument is simply drawn to the attention of members, and can come into operation once laid.

Negative resolution procedure

Where the enabling Act requires this procedure to be followed, s5 of the 1946 Act applies. This states:

> 'Where by this Act or any Act passed after the commencement of this Act, it is provided that any statutory instrument shall be subject to annulment in pursuance of resolution of either House of Parliament, the instrument shall be laid before Parliament after being made and the provisions of the last foregoing section shall apply thereto accordingly, and if either House, within the period laid before it, resolves that an Address be presented to His Majesty praying that the instrument be annulled, no further proceedings shall be taken thereunder after the date of the resolution, and His Majesty may by Order in Council revoke the instrument, so, however, that any such resolution and revocation shall be without prejudice to the validity of anything previously done under the instrument or to the making of a new statutory instrument …'

Two points to note regarding this procedure. First, a prayer can only seek the annulment of a statutory instrument, not its amendment. Second, the wording of s5(1) ensures that the annulment of an instrument does not invalidate retrospectively action taken under it by the relevant minister.

Positive resolution procedure

Here the enabling Act requires the instrument to be laid before Parliament, and it can only become law if it receives the affirmative approval of Parliament.

Laying of a draft statutory instrument

A draft instrument is laid before Parliament, and the instrument itself cannot be made until 40 days have passed from the date of the laying of the draft instrument. During this period, the draft instrument may be subject to the negative resolution procedure as outlined above. The procedure is governed by s6 of the 1946 Act, which states:

> 'Where by this Act or any Act passed after the commencement of this Act it is provided that a draft of any statutory instrument shall be laid before Parliament, but the Act does not prohibit the making of the instrument without the approval of Parliament, then, in the case of an Order in Council the draft shall not be submitted to His Majesty in Council, and in any other case the statutory instrument shall not be made, until after the expiration of a period of forty days beginning with the day on which a copy of the draft is laid before each House of Parliament, or, if such copies are laid on different days, with the later of the two days, and if within that period either House resolves that the draft be not submitted to His Majesty or that the statutory instrument be not made, as the case may be, no further proceedings shall be taken thereon, but without prejudice to the laying before Parliament of a new draft ...'

Remedial orders under the Human Rights Act 1998

Under the Human Rights Act 1998 ministers are given the discretion introduce measures by way of statutory instrument or Order in Council in order to remedy defects in either primary or subordinate legislation so as to ensure compliance with the Convention rights protected by the 1998 Act. A minister can take such action either because a United Kingdom court has granted a declaration of incompatibility and rights of appeal have been exhausted, abandoned or become time-barred, or because it appears to a minister that (in the light of a finding of the European Court of Human Rights) a provision of legislation is incompatible with obligations under the Convention. The minister concerned must satisfy himself that there are compelling reasons for making the remedial orders: see s10(1) and (2) of the 1998 Act.

The powers are potentially far-reaching. A minister will be able to amend primary legislation by means of a statutory instrument (s20(1)), and such amendments can be retrospective in effect (but not so as to create criminal liability): see Sch 2 paras 1(1)(b) and 1(4). Schedule 2 provides for two types of procedure for the making of remedial orders, depending upon the urgency of the situation. In most cases a minister will prepare a 'document' comprising the draft order and other details required by Sch 2 para 5 (ie details of the incompatibility to be removed and the reasons for proceeding under s10). There then follows a 60-day consultation period during which representations can be made both inside and outside Parliament. Following this period of consultation the minister lays before Parliament the draft remedial order, together with a summary of the representations made and details of any revisions made to the order in the light of those representations. To come into effect the draft order must have been laid before Parliament for 60 days and must then be approved by Parliament. In urgent cases a minister will be able to bring an order into effect without prior parliamentary approval. The safeguards take the form of requirements that the minister should then lay the 'made' order before Parliament with the details required by Sch 2 para 5. Once 60 days have passed the minister must lay before Parliament a summary of the representations made and details (if any) of revisions made to the order in the light of those representations. At the end of a period of 120 days from the date when the order was first laid before Parliament it will cease to have effect unless approved by both Houses of Parliament. The failure by Parliament to affirm such an order does not affect the validity of actions taken pursuant to that order within the 120-day period. Note that the making of remedial orders lies within the discretion of the minister. No action will lie against him for not laying a proposal for legislation before Parliament or for not making any primary legislation or remedial order: see s6(6)(a) and (b).

Publication

It is widely accepted that ignorance of the law is no excuse. Given the great volume of delegated legislation, however, that doctrine can operate so as to cause severe hardship. As noted above it has been argued that a statutory instrument could come into effect as soon as it was signed by the minister; if this was an instrument creating criminal liability, it could have serious consequences for those concerned. To what extent does the enforceability of a statutory instrument depend upon its having been published? The question arose in *Johnson* v *Sargant & Sons Ltd* [1918] 1 KB 101, where an order was made on one day but its effect made known on the next. Bailache J refused to hold that, at common law, an instrument would come into effect before those affected by it had been notified. The matter remains the subject of debate, however: see Lanham (1974) 37 MLR 510.

Under the 1946 Act two alternative approaches may be taken. Either the enabling Act may itself lay down the procedure that must be followed for publicising any instruments made thereunder, or the enabling Act may provide that the procedures of the 1946 Act are to be followed. Sections 2 and 3 (as amended by the Statutory Instruments (Production and Sale) Act 1996) provide as follows:

'2(1) Immediately after the making of any statutory instrument, it shall be sent to the King's printer of Acts of Parliament and numbered in accordance with regulations made under this Act, and except in such cases as may be provided by any Act passed after the commencement of this Act or prescribed by regulations made under this Act, copies thereof shall as soon as possible be printed and sold by [or under the authority of] the King's printer of Acts of Parliament ...

3(1) Regulations made for the purpose of this Act shall make provision for the publication by His Majesty's Stationery Office of lists showing the date upon which every statutory instrument printed and sold by [or under the authority of] the King's printer of Acts of Parliament was first issued by [or under the authority of] that office; and in any legal proceedings a copy of any list ... shall be received in evidence as a true copy, and an entry therein shall be conclusive evidence of the date on which any statutory instrument was first issued by [or under the authority of] His Majesty's Stationery Office.'

Certain instruments may be exempt in whole or part from the publication requirements of the Act. Section 8 of the 1946 Act as amended, states:

'(1) The Treasury may, with the concurrence of the Lord Chancellor and the Speaker of the House of Commons, by statutory instrument make regulations for the purposes of this Act, and such regulations may, in particular ...

(c) provide with respect to any classes or descriptions of statutory instrument that they shall be exempt, either altogether or to such extent as may be determined by or under the regulations from the requirements of being printed and of being sold by [or under the authority of] the King's printer of Acts of Parliament, or from either of those requirements ...'

The Statutory Instruments Regulations 1947 (SI 1948/1) exempts the following from publication: local acts; temporary instruments; schedules to rules that are too bulky, provided other steps have been taken to bring their contents to the attention of the public; and instruments, the publication of which needs to be suppressed, in the public interest, prior to their coming into operation. In the last three cases the minister concerned must certify that the necessary conditions for the operation of the execution rules have been fulfilled.

Section 3 of the 1946 Act, as amended, does provide a so-called defence of non-publication. It provides as follows:

'(2) In any proceedings against any person for an offence consisting of a contravention of any such statutory instrument, it shall be a defence to prove that the instrument had not been issued by [or under the authority of] His Majesty's Stationery Office at the date of the alleged contravention unless it is proved that at that date reasonable steps had been taken for the purpose of bringing the purport of the instrument to the notice of the public, or of persons likely to be affected by it, or of the person charged.

(3) Save as therein otherwise expressly provided, nothing in this section shall affect any enactment or rule of law relating to the time at which any statutory instrument comes into operation.'

There have been two notable decisions concerning the ambit of this provision. In the first, *Simmonds* v *Newell* [1953] 2 All ER 38, the defendant appealed against a conviction for selling steel at prices higher than those permitted by provisions contained in schedules to a ministerial order. The schedules had not been published on the grounds of bulk. No certificate was produced in evidence exempting them from publication, and the Divisional Court was not satisfied that the Crown had discharged the burden of proving that it had taken reasonable steps to bring the provision to the notice of persons likely to be affected by it.

Compare this with the later decision in *R* v *Sheer Metalcraft Ltd* [1954] 1 QB 586 where a similar defence of non-certification was raised to a prosecution for breaching a price fixing order. The court approached the matter by holding that an instrument could be validly made, and then issued. The very fact that s3(2) created a defence to non-publication meant that an order could be valid without being published. As in the above case, the absence of any exempting certificate placed the burden of proving that reasonable steps to notify those concerned had been taken, on the Crown. In this instance the court was satisfied, on the evidence, that these steps had been taken.

Note in this regard s50 of the draft Criminal Code Bill prepared for the Law Commission (Law Com No 143) which proposes:

'(1) A person would not be guilty of an offence consisting of a contravention of a statutory instrument if –
(a) at the time of his act the instrument has not been issued by Her Majesty's Stationery Office; and
(b) by that time reasonable steps had not been taken to bring the purport of the instrument to the notice of the public, or of persons likely to be affected by it, or of that person.'

Under this proposal the burden of proving the instrument has not been issued by Her Majesty's Stationery Office would be on the defendant.

Publication of other measures

There appears to be no statutory requirement concerning the publication of other measures such as circulars. In *Blackpool Corporation* v *Locker* [1948] 1 KB 349, however, Scott LJ stated, obiter, that given the nature of the circular in question, which delegated powers of compulsory purchase from the minister to local authorities, it was of vital importance that those likely to be affected should be able to ascertain the provisions of the circular.

2.4 Parliamentary scrutiny

Widespread reliance upon delegated legislation to 'flesh out' the basic statutory framework provided in the parent Act inevitably throws into sharp focus the issue of parliamentary controls.

The enabling Act

The first real opportunity for Parliament to exercise some control over the creation of delegated legislation arises when the enabling Act is being debated by the House of Commons, or the House of Lords. Members can consider whether a minister needs to be given powers to issue delegated legislation; if so, the form that the delegated legislation will take, ie whether by statutory instrument or circular; if by statutory instrument, should one of the laying procedures be followed; and generally, whether a minister is being given any wide or unusual powers.

The laying procedures

Provided that the enabling Act requires the use of one of the laying procedures, they do provide a valuable opportunity for scrutiny by members. However, several problems and weaknesses exist with this method. The sheer volume of instruments makes it impossible for any one Member of Parliament to check them all. The laying procedure can be circumvented simply by the enabling Act not requiring any instrument made thereunder to be laid. The affirmative resolution procedure (see section 2.3 above, under 'Positive resolution procedure') clearly provides a much better safeguard against abuse of power than the negative resolution procedure, but does not appear to be employed so frequently. Under the negative resolution procedure, parliamentary time may not be available for the prayers necessary to bring about the annulment of the instrument.

The Joint Committee on Statutory Instruments

Since 1973 it has been the function of the Joint Committee to scrutinise all statutory instruments, draft instruments, schemes requiring approval by way of statutory instrument, and so on. There are particular matters regarding which the attention of the House of Commons will be drawn by the Committee, as follows.

1. Where an instrument imposes a charge on public revenues or contains provisions requiring payments to be made to any public authority in consideration of any licence, or any consent, or of any services rendered.
2. Where an instrument purports to exclude the jurisdiction of the courts.
3. Where an instrument purports to have retrospective effect.
4. Where there appears to have been an unjustifiable delay in laying or publicising the instrument.
5. Where there is doubt as to whether the instrument is intra vires its enabling Act.
6. Where the terms of the instrument require elucidation.
7. Where for any other reason the drafting of the instrument appears to be defective.

It is important to bear in mind that the Committee is concerned neither with the merits of any given instrument nor the soundness of the policy which it seeks to implement. If the Committee does report to the House of Commons on a statutory instrument for any of the reasons outlined above, reliance is placed on the principle of ministerial responsibility to actually achieve some explanation of justification for, or amendment of the instrument.

As David Foulkes has observed:

> 'Within (its) limitations the Committee does useful, thankless and unobtrusive work as a guardian of the constitutional proprieties. It keeps an eye not only on individual instruments but on general developments in delegated legislation. It has shown itself anxious to make full use of its powers and has suggested extensions to its jurisdiction.' (*Administrative Law*, 8th ed, p97)

Where there is agreement between the parliamentary parties, a minister may move that a statutory instrument be referred to one of the Standing (Merits) Committees on Statutory Instruments. The procedure can be adopted provided the instrument is one in relation to which the affirmative resolution procedure applies, or a member has given notice of a motion that it be annulled. Although the committee is able to debate the merits of an instrument, it cannot vote on the matter. The intention is that the House of Commons will take note of the points made in committee, although when the instrument returns to the House there will be no debate on it, simply a vote.

Other measures

No formal parliamentary procedure exists for the scrutiny of other forms of delegated legislation, such as circulars, guidelines and codes of conduct. It should be remembered, however, that the traditional methods of control, such as questions to ministers etc, may be used to highlight apparent irregularities or excesses.

Parliamentary Commissioner for Administration

Although the work of the Ombudsman is dealt with at more length in Chapter 13, it should be noted here that, under s5 of the Parliamentary Commissioner Act 1967, his jurisdiction is limited to administrative functions. This would seem to exclude the Ombudsman from considering complaints concerning delegated legislation. Two points should, however, be borne in mind. First, he can investigate complaints concerning the application of, and effects of, delegated legislation. Second, some measures are not strictly speaking 'legislative', such as guidelines and codes of conduct. It could be argued that ministers act administratively when issuing such documents, and that they are therefore within the scope of the Ombudsman's investigations.

2.5 Scrutiny by the courts

Unlike primary legislation, delegated legislation is reviewable by the courts and can in some cases be completely invalidated. The more detailed heads of review are set out in Chapters 5 to 9. For present purposes it is sufficient to distinguish between cases of procedural ultra vires and substantive ultra vires.

Procedural ultra vires

One of the grounds on which an individual may seek to question the validity of delegated legislation is that the procedure laid down in its enabling Act and/or the Statutory Instruments Act 1946 for making, laying and publishing the measure in question has not been followed. A strict approach would be to say that if the provisions of the enabling legislation have not been observed, then the measure is void. Usually a more subtle technique is employed. The courts will distinguish between procedural requirements that are mandatory – failure to meet these results in invalidity – and directory requirements – failure to meet these does not usually affect validity. The difficulty is in assessing which procedural requirements are likely to be regarded by the courts as mandatory and which as directory.

In *Agricultural, Horticultural and Forestry Industry Training Board* v *Aylesbury Mushrooms Ltd* [1972] 1 WLR 190 failure to comply with a statutory requirement to consult various bodies prior to the making of delegated legislation resulted in the subsequent order affecting them being declared invalid. By contrast, in *Bailey* v *Williamson* (1873) LR 8 QB 118, a conviction under the Rules made pursuant to the Parks Regulation Act 1872 was upheld, even though at the time the Rules had not been laid before Parliament because of the Summer recess. The implication of the conviction was that the Rules did not depend upon the laying procedures for their validity, and that consequently such procedural requirements were merely directory.

In two later cases the courts seem to have adopted a liberal approach to the procedural requirements for the enactment of delegated legislation. First, in *R* v *Secretary of State for the Environment, ex parte Leicester City Council* (1985) The Times 1 February, the applicant local authority applied for judicial review of a draft order under s4(5) of the Rates Act 1984, laid before the House of Commons, specifying the maximum rate to be prescribed to the council. Under s4(1) of the Act this could only be done if the Rate Support Grant Report had been laid before Parliament. In fact the Report had only been laid before the House of Commons. The applicant contended that the subsequent order was, therefore, ultra vires. Dismissing the application, Woolf J was satisfied that in using the word Parliament, the draftsmen meant the House of Commons. He stated, in deciding the effect of s4(1), that it was important to bear in mind that it was dealing with something that was procedural. It was intended that a local authority, prior to being 'rate-capped', should have notice of the maximum proposed so that it could have an opportunity to accept the maximum or reject the maximum or agree a different maximum. The purpose of s4(1) was achieved as long as the authority had a reasonable period to consider the notice. It was unlikely that Parliament had intended that s4(1) should be mandatory. As long as s4(1) was substantially complied with the notice served was not defective. Applying that interpretation, the notice was not invalidated. The report did not have to be re-laid because of technical errors and the notice was not subsequently re-served on the authority.

Consider also *R* v *Secretary of State for Social Services, ex parte Camden London Borough Council* [1987] 2 All ER 560. The minister was empowered to set levels of social security payments by way of statutory instrument. Any such statutory instrument was required to be laid before Parliament and approved by the Treasury. The minister laid the statutory instrument in question before Parliament, and obtained the necessary consents, but details of the maximum amount of benefit payable were set out, not in the statutory instrument, but in a directory published by HMSO which was not laid before Parliament. The applicant, who was a person claiming supplementary benefit, and the local authority in whose area she resided, applied for declarations that the regulations were void for failure to comply with the laying procedures. At first instance and on appeal the application for review was dismissed. The Court of Appeal found that the directory was not part of the statutory instrument and therefore did not have to be laid before Parliament. Further, it was not a document by which the Secretary of State exercised his power to set levels of social security payments. It was quite permissible for him to refer in the statutory instrument to a formula by which levels of benefit would be set, provided he identified the source of the formula with sufficient certainty. This he had done.

Substantive ultra vires

This is a much broader ground of challenge. The applicant may be contending that there is no express or implied power in the enabling Act to justify the impugned subordinate legislation. Alternatively, the applicant may be contending that the power does exist, but has been exercised in a manner that is ultra vires, ie the measure in question: goes beyond what was envisaged by Parliament in the enabling Act; is in conflict with the aims and objects of the enabling Act; is unreasonable, vague, oppressive and incompatible with rights protected under the Human Rights Act 1998; breaches the principle of 'legality; or is contrary to directly applicable EC law having direct effect.

These categories are not, of course, mutually exclusive. In all cases the courts will simply be looking at the enabling Act to determine the intention of Parliament. One of the key issues here, and one that has been given greater significance with the incorporation of the European Convention on Human Rights, is the issue of legality, ie the presumption that, in enacting primary or secondary legislation, Parliament does not seek to undermine or erode long-standing principles of constitutional law relating to civil liberties unless there are clear indications that such was Parliament's intent. As a ground of challenge to delegated legislation this was expressly recognised by the House of Lords in *R* v *Secretary of State for the Home Department, ex parte Simms; Same, ex parte O'Brien* [1999] 3 All ER 400, although there are a number of earlier decisions where concerns as to the effect of delegated legislation on 'fundamental rights' can be seen as a factor.

The refusal of the courts to accept that a minister had been empowered in such a way as to adversely affect certain basic human rights was clearly the basis for the decision of the court in *R* v *Secretary of State for Social Security, ex parte Joint Council for the Welfare of Immigrants* [1996] 4 All ER 385, where the court quashed the Social Security (Persons from Abroad) Miscellaneous Amendments Regulations 1996 (SI 1996/30) issued pursuant to the Social Security (Contributions and Benefits) Act 1992. The regulations had the effect of removing from asylum seekers any entitlement to income benefit where: (1) asylum was sought otherwise than on arrival in the United Kingdom; or (2) an asylum seeker had been refused leave to remain and was awaiting the outcome of an appeal against that decision. Confirming that the 1996 Regulations were ultra vires the 1992 Act, Simon Brown LJ adverted to the fact that Parliament, in enacting the Asylum and Immigration Appeals Act 1993, had given asylum seekers certain rights not to be removed pending determination of their claims to refugee status. The 1996 Regulations, if effective, would have rendered the rights granted by the 1993 Act nugatory, as asylum seekers without private means would either have had to return to countries from which they had fled, or attempted to conduct their claims for asylum whilst living destitute and homeless. The court was of the view that Parliament could not have intended the Secretary of State to be vested with powers, exercisable by way of regulation, that would result in so serious an interference with the rights of asylum seekers. As Simon Brown LJ observed (at p399a–b):

> 'Specific statutory rights are not to be cut down by subordinate legislation passed under the vires of a different Act.'

The court felt it unnecessary to rely on the European Convention on Human Rights (as to which see below) on the basis that the common law existed to ensure that very basic rights were protected. Simon Brown LJ, describing the regulations as 'uncompromisingly draconian' and likely to result in a life for asylum seekers that was 'so destitute that no civilised nation could contemplate it' cited with approval the dictum of Lord Ellenborough CJ in *R* v *Inhabitants of Eastbourne* (1803) 4 East 103 were he observed:

> 'As to there being no obligation for maintaining poor foreigners before the statutes ascertaining the different methods of acquiring settlements, the law of humanity which is anterior to all positive laws, obliges us to afford them relief, to save them from starving ...'

Given that the Social Security (Contributions and Benefits) Act was enacted in 1992, Parliament can be assumed to have had in mind the United Kingdom's obligations under the Conventions on the Status of Refugees of 1951 and 1967, and thus any power to make regulations under the 1992 Act cannot have been intended to empower a minister to derogate from those obligations, either directly or indirectly. On the other hand, the decision can be seen as a clear challenge by the judiciary to the omnipotence of the legislature, given that the regulations were approved by Parliament, and it is significant that the government responded to this ruling by enacting primary legislation, the Asylum and Immigration Act 1996, which had the effect of reversing it.

In *R* v *Lord Chancellor, ex parte Witham* [1997] 2 All ER 779 the applicant, who was unemployed, had no disposable income or savings, and who was in receipt of income support, sought to pursue an action for defamation, in respect of which legal aid was not available. Prior to the enactment of the Supreme Court Fees (Amendment) Order 1996 (SI 1996/3191), amending Supreme Court Fees Order 1980 (SI 1980/821), litigants in person who were on income support were relieved of the obligation to pay certain court fees, and the Lord Chancellor had the discretion to reduce or remit the fee in any particular case on the grounds of financial hardship. The effect of the 1996 Order was to increase the fees for issuing writs, and (by virtue of art 3) to remove the Lord Chancellor's discretion in relation to the remission of fees, with the effect that the applicant was thus unable to pursue his action because of lack of funds. The applicant applied for judicial review of the 1996 Order seeking a declaration that art 3 of that Order was ultra vires the enabling legislation, s130 of the Supreme Court Act 1981. Granting the application, on the ground that access to the courts was a 'constitutional right' that could only be removed by the executive if the power to do so was expressly stated in the parent Act, the court noted that s130 of the 1981 Act contained nothing to indicate that fees might be imposed in circumstances that would amount to citizens being effectively denied access to the courts. Thus, no power existed to introduce such a measure, and the question of whether or not it was reasonable in the circumstances did not arise. In arriving at this conclusion the court noted the distinction between the power of the executive to reduce eligibility for legal aid (effectively a state subsidy for legal representation), something it clearly had the power to do subject to satisfying any applicable test of reasonableness, and the power of the executive to increase court fees that had to be paid regardless of whether or not a litigant was being represented. Regarding the assertion that art 3 was 'unconstitutional' in its effect, Laws J observed:

> 'The common law does not generally speak in the language of constitutional rights, for the good reason that in the absence of any sovereign text, a written constitution which is logically and legal prior to the power of the legislature, executive and judiciary alike, there is on the face of it no hierarchy of rights such that anyone of them is more entrenched by the law than any other. And if the concept of a constitutional right is to have any meaning, it must surely sound in the protection which the law affords to it ... In the unwritten legal order of the British State, at a time when the common law continues to accord a legislative supremacy to Parliament, the notion of a constitutional right can in my

judgment inhere only in this proposition that the right in question cannot be abrogated by the State save by specific provision in an Act of Parliament, or by regulations whose vires in main legislation specifically confers the power to abrogate. General words will not suffice. And any such rights will be creatures of the common law, since their existence would not be the consequence of the democratic political process but would be logically prior to it ...'

Had the challenge been to the level of increase in court fees themselves the court would have accepted that a power to make such increases, in which case the issue would then have been one of reasonableness: see further *R* v *Secretary of State for the Home Department, ex parte Saleem* [2000] 4 All ER 814, where a rule effectively robbing an asylum seeker of the right to appeal against the ruling of a special adjudicator was declared ultra vires on the basis that the right of appeal was to be regarded as a fundamental right – akin to the right of access to the courts – and it could only be cut down where statute clearly indicated that this was to be the case.

The difficulty in all such cases lies in determining the intention of Parliament in enacting the enabling Act. Judges can either bow to what they see as the will of Parliament being exercised by the ministers or take exception at what might be described as the usurpation of the legislative function by the executive. In *R* v *Secretary of State for Social Services, ex parte Stitt* (1990) The Times 5 July the court examined the extent of the powers vested in the Secretary of State by the Social Security Act 1986 (as amended by the Social Security Act 1988). The legislation creating the Social Fund, under which claimants could apply for loans to help meet exceptional needs, indicated specific matters in relation to which funds would be available, such as maternity expenses, cold weather payments and funeral expenses, but as regards 'other needs' the legislation provided the Security Fund officer with a discretion as to whether or not loans should be made. The Secretary of State, who was empowered under ss32 and 33 of the 1986 Act to issue directions to Security Fund officers concerning the exercise of their discretion, instructed Fund officers not to award any loans in respect of the cost of domestic assistance and respite care. Dismissing an appeal against the refusal of the Divisional Court to grant judicial review of the ministerial directions, the Court of Appeal noted that its function was to deal with an ambiguity in the parent Act. Where such ambiguity was found the Court would lean in favour of an interpretation which prevented the executive from acquiring unbridled powers. The legislation in this case had left it to the discretion of the minister to determine how and when loans for 'other needs' should be granted. Whilst the Court found it surprising that Parliament had left such a wide power to a minister to exercise by way of delegated legislation, there was no ground for doubting that this had been what Parliament had intended. The directions in question were subject to annulment by resolution of either House and it was contended on behalf of the applicant that this resulted in very little parliamentary scrutiny of such measures, unlike the positive laying procedure, and that if Parliament had intended the minister to have such wide powers it would have made the exercise of those powers subject to the more exacting positive procedure.

Against this it should be noted that the minister was required to report annually to Parliament on the operation of the Fund. It is of further interest to note that in the course of his submissions, counsel for the minister was unable to point to any previous Act of Parliament granting a minister such wholesale, unregulated and unsupervised powers to enact delegated legislation having such a profound effect on the operation of a primary Act.

In interpreting the scope of a power to make subordinate legislation a court can, in cases of ambiguity, have reference to relevant parliamentary proceedings – see generally *Pepper* v *Hart* [1993] AC 593. In *R* v *Secretary of State for the Environment, Transport and the Regions, ex parte Spath Holme Ltd* [2001] 2 WLR 15, the House of Lords considered the extent to which comments made by a minister during the passage of a Bill could be relied upon in legal proceedings as evidence of the purpose for which a power given in a statute should be exercised.

Lord Bingham observed:

'*Pepper* v *Hart* ... turned on a narrow point, the meaning of "the cost of a benefit" in s63(2) of the Finance Act 1976. The minister gave what was no doubt taken to be a reliable statement on the meaning of that expression. [In the present case] the issue turns not on the meaning of a statutory expression but on the scope of a statutory power. In this context a minister might describe the circumstances in which the government contemplated use of a power, and might be pressed about exercise of the power in other situations which might arise. No doubt the minister would seek to give helpful answers. But it is most unlikely that he would seek to define the legal effect of the draftsman's language, or to predict all the circumstances in which the power might be used, or to bind any successor administration. Only if a minister were, improbably, to give a categorical assurance to Parliament that a power would not be used in a given situation, such that Parliament could be taken to have legislated on that basis, does it seem to me that a parliamentary statement on the scope of a power would be properly admissible.'

Lord Hope agreed with this view, adding:

'The limited exception to the general rule that resort to Hansard is inadmissible which was recognised in *Pepper* v *Hart* is available to prevent the executive seeking to place a meaning on words used in legislation which is different from that which ministers attributed to those words when promoting the legislation in Parliament. That was the situation which appears to have arisen in that case where, as Lord Bridge ... observed ... the argument which was before the House on the first hearing of the appeal raised an acute question as to whether it could be right to give effect to taxing legislation which was capable of two possible interpretations in such a way as to impose a tax which the Financial Secretary to the Treasury had assured the House of Commons it was not intended to impose.

No such issue has been raised in this case. As I have already sought to explain, the passages in Hansard to which your Lordships have been referred deal not with the meaning of words or possible interpretations of expressions that were or might be ambiguous but with statements made by ministers as to matters of policy. I consider that to permit resort to Hansard as a source for material of that kind to define the scope of a discretionary power conferred by Parliament would be to extend the decision in *Pepper* v *Hart* well beyond its proper limits ... it is important that the conditions laid down by the

House in that case should be strictly insisted upon ... if a minister were to give a categorical assurance to Parliament that a discretionary power would not ever be used in a given set of circumstances, that statement would be admissible against the executive in order to control its exercise. But I also think that it is important to stress that as matter of principle the decision in *Pepper* v *Hart* should be confined to cases where the court is concerned with the meaning that is to be given to the words used in legislation by Parliament. It would be contrary to fundamental considerations of constitutional principle to allow it to be used to enable reliance to be placed on statements made in debate by ministers about matters of policy which have not been reproduced in the enactment. It is the words used by Parliament, not the words used by ministers, that define the scope within which the powers conferred by the legislature may be exercised.'

These observations raise a number of interesting problems. Would categorical assurances given by one minister be binding upon his successors in that office? Would the courts be willing to bring issues of estoppel and legitimate expectation to bear on the basis of such assurances?

Although, as can be seen from the foregoing, the judges in United Kingdom courts have professed to have human rights considerations in mind when reviewing the validity of subordinate legislation, such issues become explicit following the enactment of the Human Rights Act 1998. The Act is significant in two respects. First because, under s6, it is unlawful for a public authority to act in a way that is incompatible with the Convention rights protected by the 1998 Act. This should include a minister making rules and regulations by way of subordinate legislation (unless the courts choose to regard him as a person who is exercising functions in connection with proceedings in Parliament – and thus exempt by virtue of s6(3)). Second, by virtue of s3(2)(a) of the 1998 Act, courts and tribunals are to give effect to subordinate legislation 'whenever enacted' in a way which is compatible with Convention rights (ie it applies equally to subordinate legislation that predates the 1998 Act and that which is introduced after the Act takes effect). On an application for judicial review this should enable a court to declare subordinate legislation ultra vires on the ground that it conflicts with Convention rights protected under the 1998 Act. A reviewing court will be required to take account of the jurisprudence of the European Court of Human Rights, resulting in the importation of doctrines such as proportionality as a basis for review of subordinate legislation: see further *R* v *Secretary of State for Health, ex parte Eastside Cheese Company* (1998) The Times 1 December. In the event that a provision in primary legislation prevents the reviewing court from removing the incompatibility, the court will have the power to grant a declaration of incompatibility under s4(4). Although this will not alter the rights of the parties per se, it should prompt the relevant minister to exercise his power to make a remedial order removing the incompatibility. This could enure to the benefit of the applicant seeking to impugn subordinate legislation if the remedial order is made retrospective in effect.

Subordinate legislation that contravenes EC law can be declared to be invalid by domestic courts: see s2(1) European Communities Act 1972. Again, review on the grounds of incompatibility with EC law brings with it the consideration of issues of proportionality.

The courts will strike down subordinate legislation if there is no express or implied authority for it in the relevant enabling Act. Taxation is an area where, traditionally, the courts will closely scrutinise primary legislation for evidence of the authority to raise revenue or impose levies. A leading authority is *Attorney-General* v *Wilts United Dairies* (1922) 91 LJKB 897, where regulations under a milk price fixing scheme, requiring producers to pay a levy to the Food Controller, were invalidated by the House of Lords as amounting to unlawful taxation, since there was no clear statutory authority for such measures. Similarly, in *Customs and Excise Commissioners* v *Cure and Deely Ltd* [1962] 1 QB 340, the Commissioners had made a regulation under which they could determine the amount of tax due from the tax-payer in the event of a tax return being submitted late. The High Court invalidated the regulations on a number of grounds, inter alia, that the Commissioners were only empowered to collect the amount of tax due at law, not the amount they thought fit. They had, therefore, purported to give themselves power by way of delegated legislation going way beyond what was envisaged by Parliament in passing the enabling Act: see further *R* v *Inland Revenue Commissioners, ex parte Woolwich Equitable Building Society* [1990] 1 WLR 1400 and *Hotel and Catering Industry Training Board* v *Automobile Proprietary Ltd* [1969] 1 WLR 677.

Assuming that a power to create the delegated legislation in question can be identified, how will the courts approach the task of examining the way in which that power has been exercised? Essentially the usual principles of the ultra vires doctrine will apply, as to which, see generally Chapters 5 to 9. Hence, a measure can be struck down on the basis that it is unreasonable, or in terms of what might be seen as sub-categories of unreasonableness, if the maker of the delegated legislation has taken into account irrelevant considerations, failed to take into account relevant considerations, has acted without any justifying evidence, or has been motivated by bad faith. Hence, in *Kruse* v *Johnson* [1898] 2 QB 91, the Lord Chief Justice suggested that a bye-law could be invalidated if it was found to be partial and unequal in operation, manifestly unjust, disclosed bad faith, or involved an oppressive, gratuitous interference with the rights of individuals. Similarly, in *R* v *British Airports Authority, ex parte Wheatley* (1983) 81 LGR 794, the Divisional Court held that a bye-law passed by the respondent authority prohibiting licensed hackney carriages was invalid on the grounds that it was unreasonable and oppressive.

A statutory instrument may be quashed on the ground that it simply goes further than is necessary to deal with a particular mischief. In *McEldowney* v *Forde* [1971] AC 632 the House of Lords, by a majority, upheld the validity of a regulation made under emergency powers legislation prohibiting membership of republican clubs but, in the course of their speeches, their Lordships made plain their view that such a measure was at the very limits of what was acceptable.

Rights provided by way of primary legislation may be altered or repealed by way of delegated legislation, for example where regulations are introduced to give effect to Community law, pursuant to s2(2) of the European Communities Act 1972, but it is incumbent on the executive to state in clear terms the substantive rights being affected. Failure to do so can lead to the regulations being struck down by the courts: see further *R* v *Secretary of State for Trade and Industry, ex parte Orange Personal Communications Services Ltd* (2000) The Times 15 November.

Statutory instruments creating criminal offences and bye-laws will be declared void and unenforceable if they are insufficiently certain in their application, or if the drafting is so defective that it is not capable of sensible construction: see *Nash* v *Finlay* (1901) 85 LT 682. In *Staden* v *Tarjanyi* (1980) 78 LGR 614 the court held that a bye-law prohibiting individuals from hang gliding over certain land was void for uncertainty as it did not provide any indication of the height that an individual would have to fly at to escape liability. The test applied by the court to determine whether or not the measure was invalid on the ground of uncertainty was that adopted by Lord Denning in *Fawcett Properties Ltd* v *Buckingham County Council* [1960] 3 All ER 503, to the effect that a planning condition (which, for the purposes of the instant case was equated with a bye-law) should not be regarded as void for uncertainty unless it was impossible to give it any sensible meaning, mere ambiguity not being sufficient. Hence, in *Percy and Another* v *Hall and Others* [1996] 4 All ER 523, the Court of Appeal upheld the validity of the HMS Forest Moor and Menwith Hill Bye-laws 1986, which prohibited entry onto certain restricted tracts of Ministry of Defence land, despite the fact that the prohibited areas were not delineated with the desired degree of clarity. As Simon Brown LJ observed, a degree of uncertainty as to the precise limits of the prohibited area could not make the bye-laws unenforceable against those who deliberately and flagrantly trespassed within the very centre of the prohibited areas.

Whilst the principles upon which the courts will intervene can be broadly stated, the reality is that any party seeking to impugn the validity of delegated legislation may face difficulties peculiar to this area. The fact that subordinate legislation has been approved by a resolution in the House of Commons should not make it immune from judicial review, as Lord Phillips MR observed in *R (On the Application of Javed)* v *Secretary of State for the Home Department* (2001) The Times 24 May, although such action would not be 'unconstitutional', the courts may be less likely to intervene where the measure primarily gives effect to matters of policy falling within the political responsibility of the executive; see *Nottinghamshire County Council* v *Secretary of State for the Environment* [1986] 1 All ER 199, considered below at section 2.6 and in Chapter 1. Where delegated legislation involves issues that are primarily viewed as falling within the sphere of political judgment, judicial intervention will only arise in extreme cases of bad faith or where the decision-maker has apparently taken leave of his senses. An applicant for review of subordinate legislation may also face a not inconsiderable evidential burden, especially where the court is satisfied that Parliament intended the rule-maker to enjoy a wide discretion. For example, in *R* v *The Lord Chancellor, ex parte The Law*

Society (1993) The Times 5 May, the applicants unsuccessfully applied for judicial review of the decision of the Lord Chancellor to introduce a scheme of standard fees for lawyers appearing in magistrates' court cases. The Society had contended that the regulations formulated under the Legal Aid Act 1988 were ultra vires on the grounds (inter alia) that they failed to address the requirement that a solicitor's remuneration had to be reasonable in each individual case. The court, rejecting this contention, found that Parliament had given the Lord Chancellor a wide discretion and was not persuaded that Parliament had intended him to devise a scheme that addressed the level of remuneration to be paid in each case. Significantly, the Lord Chancellor's desire to achieve cost neutrality in devising the revised scheme was not regarded as an irrelevant consideration.

The courts have also accepted the argument that the creation of delegated legislation is a governmental function to which certain legal requirements might not apply. In *R* v *Secretary of State for Social Services, ex parte Nessa* (1994) The Times 15 November, the applicant claimed that the operation of reg 7(1)(c) of the Social Fund Maternity and Funeral Expenses (General) Regulations 1987 (SI 1987/481) contravened s20 of the Race Relations Act 1976, in that it permitted a payment from the Social Fund for funeral expenses provided the funeral took place within the United Kingdom, and thus discriminated against claimants who, for religious reasons, wished to conduct a funeral overseas. Auld J held that s75 of the 1976 Act provided that the Act applied to an act done by or for the purposes of a minister of the Crown as it applied to an act done by a private person. Applying *R* v *Entry Clearance Officer, ex parte Amin* [1983] 2 AC 818, the 1976 Act, like the Sex Discrimination Act 1975, did not, therefore, apply to acts of a minister or officer of the Crown that were of a governmental nature, such as the making of regulations, on the ground that that was a function that would not be performed by a private person.

Whilst it is clear that a reviewing court faced with a challenge to the validity of a statutory instrument may declare it to be ultra vires and thus of no effect, can a tribunal dealing with the same issue act similarly?

The matter was considered by the House of Lords in *Chief Adjudication Officer* v *Foster* [1993] 2 WLR 292. The claimant had been in receipt of income support payments as prescribed by s22 of the Social Security Act 1986. The sum payable included a severe disability premium. The Income Support (General) Regulations 1987, which governed entitlement to the premium, were amended by the Secretary of State, with the effect that the premium would no longer be payable if a claimant was residing with other non-dependent adults. An adjudicator ruled that the claimant should no longer receive the severe disability premium as she was living with her parents. The Social Security Appeal Tribunal confirmed this ruling. The claimant then appealed to the commissioner who ruled that, in its amended form, Sch 2 para 13(2)(a)(ii) and (iii) of the Income Support (General) Regulations 1987 was ultra vires the 1986 Act, and that the claimant was entitled to continue in receipt of the severe disability premium. The Court of Appeal allowed an appeal by the Secretary of State and the Chief Adjudication Officer on the grounds that the commissioner had not had jurisdiction to declare the amendment to the regulations to be ultra vires and, by a majority, that the amendment was not ultra vires the 1986 Act. The House of Lords, dismissing the appeal, held (having referred to Hansard for guidance on what Parliament had intended when creating this statutory framework) that whilst the amendment under consideration in the instant case was within the scope of the amending power vested in the Secretary of State by Parliament, a commissioner did have jurisdiction to question the validity of regulations when an arguable case was raised by a claimant. The significance of the decision lies in the House of Lords' confirmation that welfare claimants need not resort to judicial review to test the validity of delegated legislation relied upon by adjudicators to deny benefit. Adjudication officers and Social Security Appeal Tribunals could simply refuse to apply a regulation on the ground of ultra vires, or apply a regulation and pass the issue on to the next level of appeal, typically a commissioner. Lord Bridge observed that there was a positive benefit in the courts having access to the rulings of social security commissioners as to the validity or otherwise of delegated legislation, since commissioners would be experts in what was acknowledged to be a difficult and complex area of law.

Regarding the role of criminal courts in determining the validity of administrative orders: see *Boddington* v *British Transport Police* [1998] 2 All ER 203, considered in Chapter 10.

Partial invalidity

In some cases the courts may be willing to uphold part of a statutory instrument, or limit the scope of its application so as to render it intra vires. The *Aylesbury Mushrooms* case (above) is one example. Another is the decision of the Divisional Court in *Dunkley* v *Evans* [1981] 1 WLR 1522 where it was held that the Order in question could be restricted so as not to apply to Northern Irish waters, without affecting the validity of the rest of the Order. The basis on which the courts will normally proceed was explained by Cussen J sitting in the Supreme Court of Victoria in *Olsen* v *City of Camberwell* [1926] VLR 58 at 68 where he stated:

'If the enactment, with the invalid portion omitted, is so radically or substantially different a law as to the subject-matter dealt with by what remains from what it would be with the omitted portions forming part of it as to warrant a belief that the legislative body intended it as a whole only, or, in other words, to warrant a belief that if all could not be carried into effect the legislative body would not have enacted the remainder independently, then the whole must fail.'

Perhaps the high water mark of judicial creativity is represented by the decision of the House of Lords in *DPP* v *Hutchinson and Others* [1990] 3 WLR 196. A number of separate cases raised a common point of law for consideration by the court. Under s14(1) of the Military Lands Act 1892 the Secretary of State was empowered to make bye-laws regulating the use of such land. The minister was specifically empowered to prohibit all intrusions on the land, provided that no bye-law took away or prejudicially affected any right of common. The minister, acting pursuant to the 1892 Act, made the RAF Greenham Common Bye-laws 1985. Bye-law 2(b) provided that no person was to remain in the designated area without the permission of an authorised person. The defendants, who were not commoners, were charged with entering the land without permission, and were duly convicted by justices. They appealed successfully to the Crown Court on the basis that the bye-laws were invalid since they prejudicially affected rights of common. The prosecutor appealed successfully to the Divisional Court by way of case stated. The House of Lords allowed the defendants' appeal, holding that bye-law 2(b) was ultra vires the 1892 Act because it prejudicially affected rights in common, and thus offended against the proviso to s1(1) of the 1892 Act. As to whether those aspects of the bye-law that had been successfully impugned could be severed from those that were intra vires, thus leaving the latter to remain in effect as a valid legislative measure, a majority of their Lordships held that for severance to be possible it had to be shown that the part of the bye-law sought to be upheld could stand on its own as something intelligible which still reflected the original legislative purpose of its author. In the present case it was felt that this was clearly not possible, as a bye-law permitting free access by commoners would be fundamentally different in its nature from that which had been enacted. See further *R* v *Inland Revenue Commissioners, ex parte Woolwich Equitable Building Society* (above).

The effect of invalidity

What is the consequence of a court finding that a statutory instrument or bye-law is ultra vires, and therefore invalid? One view is that such a ruling operates retrospectively (ex tunc) on the basis that the measure was never valid, ie it was void ab initio. Against this is the view that such rulings operate from the time of the court's ruling (ex nunc). Whilst the former view is theoretically sound, and appeals on the round of strict logic, it may be extremely difficult to apply in practice. The impugned measure will have operated between parties and have had legal effect until such time as it was struck down. It will often be impossible to go back and unravel all the arrangements entered into on the assumption that the measure was valid. In some cases time limits for challenging decisions will have expired. Schiemann LJ in *Percy* v *Hall* (above) expressed the view that such cases ought not to be approached by applying any rigid doctrine, the 'right' answer depending upon what public policy requires. In *Boddington* v *British Transport Police* [1998] 2 All ER 203 Lord Irvine expressed the view that there was no longer scope for arguing that invalid orders could still have some effect on the basis that they were merely 'voidable' for error of law. He added (at p210e–h):

> 'It is clear, in the light of the *Anismic* case and the later authorities, that [an impugned administrative order] would now certainly be regarded as a nullity (ie as void ab initio),

even if it were to be analysed as an error of law on the face of the record. Equally, the order would be regarded as void ab initio if it had been made in bad faith, or as a result of the [maker] taking into account an irrelevant, or ignoring a relevant, consideration – that is matters not appearing on the face of the record, but having to be established by evidence. Subordinate legislation, or an administrative act, is sometimes said to be presumed lawful until it has been pronounced to be unlawful. This does not, however, entail that such legislation or act is valid until quashed prospectively. ... In my judgment, the true effect of the presumption is that the legislation or act which is impugned is presumed to be good until pronounced to be unlawful, but is then recognised as never having had any legal effect at all. The burden in such a case is on the defendant to establish on a balance of probabilities that the subordinate legislation or the administrative act is invalid.'

Lords Browne-Wilkinson and Slynn preferred to leave the point open. Lord Steyn offered the following (at p225j–26c):

'I see no reason to depart from the orthodox view that ultra vires is "the central principle of administrative law" as Wade and Forsyth ... described it. ... This is the essential constitutional underpinning of the statute based part of our administrative law. Nevertheless, I accept the reality that an unlawful bye-law is a fact and that it may in certain circumstances have legal consequences. The best explanation that I have seen is by Dr Forsyth, who summarised the position as follows in *The metaphysic of nullity invalidity, conceptual reasoning and the rule of law* p159:

"... it has been argued that unlawful administrative acts are void in law. But they clearly exist in fact and they often appear to be valid; and those unaware of their invalidity may take decisions and act on the assumption that these acts are valid. When this happens the validity of these later acts depends upon the legal powers of the second actor. *The crucial issue to be determined is whether that second actor has legal power to act validly notwithstanding the invalidity of the first act.* And it is determined by a analysis of the law against the background of the familiar proposition that an unlawful act is void." (My emphasis.)

That seems to me a more accurate summary of the law as it has developed than the sweeping proposition in *Bugg*'s case. And Dr Forsyth's explanation is entirely in keeping with the analysis of the formal validity of the enforcement notice in *R* v *Wicks* which was sufficient to determine the guilt of the defendant.'

See further Chapter 5, section 5.5 on the status of decisions found to be ultra vires on the ground of breach of natural justice.

Ouster clauses

See Chapter 12 for a discussion of the extent to which the courts will comply with provisions that purport to exclude their jurisdiction.

2.6 Other forms of delegated legislation

Acting pursuant to their statutory powers ministers may also issue measures described as rules, regulations, orders, directions and schemes. As noted above, the extent to which they are legislative in effect will vary from case to case. No set procedure exists for parliamentary scrutiny or publication beyond that required by the relevant enabling Act. Circulars and guidance are issued by ministers and addressed to various interested bodies to indicate the way in which the government department would like to see various rules implemented. For example, the Department of the Environment, Transport and the Regions will issue circulars to local planning authorities as to when they should issue enforcement notices for breach of planning controls.

The codes of practice is a useful administrative device, whereby a government department can make public its aim and policy as regards a particular scheme, but maintain flexibility by being able to alter the contents of the code. The longest standing and best known examples would be the Highway Code and the Codes of Practice issued under s66 of the Police and Criminal Evidence Act 1984. There seems to be little doubt that codes have no legal status as such, but can be called as evidence to support a legal argument. This approach was adopted in *De Falco* v *Crawley Borough Council* [1980] QB 460 where it was held that the defendant authority had to have regard to the Secretary of State's code regarding intentionally homeless persons, but did not have to regard themselves as bound by it. A police officer acting in breach of the Codes of Practice issued under the 1984 Act may, by virtue of s67(8), be liable to disciplinary proceedings, although by virtue of s67(10) a failure on the part of an officer to comply with any provision of such a code will not of itself render him liable to any criminal or civil proceedings. The Codes of Practice are admissible in evidence in civil and criminal proceedings.

A government department may make a public announcement as to the way it is intending to act with respect to a particular matter, such as the collection of outstanding tax, or the enforcement of a new regulation. Such statements have no force in law per se, but may be relevant if the public body concerned then proposes to act contrary to the terms of the statement. The statement may be used as evidence to support an argument that the authority is acting in breach of natural justice (see *Attorney-General of Hong Kong* v *Ng Yuen Shiu* [1983] 2 AC 629); or it might be argued that a quasi-contractual obligation to comply with the public undertaking has arisen: see *R* v *Liverpool Corporation, ex parte LTFOA* [1972] 2 QB 299.

Legal challenge to circulars etc

As will have been noted above, the validity of statutory instruments can be challenged in the courts. Is the same true of matters such as circulars, codes and guidance? The essence of the problem is that if a code or circular has no legal effect as such, there is no purpose in instituting proceedings to assess its validity since, in theory, it can be ignored with impunity. In reality the task of assessing whether or not circulars, codes, memoranda, guidance etc have any legal effect can be rather complex. In *Coleshill and District Investment Co Ltd* v *MHLG* [1969] 2 All ER 525 Lord Wilberforce explained that although circulars had no legal status, they could, through continued reference, acquire weight as persuasive material in the process of statutory interpretation: see further *Bristol District Council* v *Clark* [1975] 3 All ER 976. The courts will certainly not be deterred from assessing the validity of a ministerial pronouncement merely because it is labelled as a circular. They will look at the content not form. In *Jackson Stansfield and Sons* v *Butterworth Ltd* [1948] 2 All ER 558 Scott LJ held that circulars issued by the Minister of Works concerning the delegation of his licensing functions to local authorities were legislative in nature because they were intended to bind the public. A similar view was taken of a ministerial circular which sub-delegated powers of compulsory purchase to a local authority in *Blackpool Corporation* v *Locker* [1948] 1 KB 349.

The courts have acknowledged that there is a distinction to be drawn between ministerial directives and ministerial guidance: see further the judgment of Roskill LJ in *Laker Airways Ltd* v *Department of Trade* [1977] QB 643. Directives are usually mandatory in tone, placing the person to whom they are issued under a legal obligation to comply with their provisions. Guidance, on the other hand, will have little or no legal effect, being merely an indication of the minister's views as to what an administrator ought to bear in mind, although the ultimate decision as to the exercise of discretion rests with the administrator. If ministerial guidance is drafted in terms that appear mandatory, the courts will normally declare it ultra vires on the basis that it purports to limit an administrator's discretion where there is no express ministerial power to do so: see further *R* v *Secretary of State for Social Services, ex parte Stitt* (above). In this respect ministerial directives are much closer to the narrow concept of delegated legislation and are likely to be more closely scrutinised by the courts, especially where the enabling Act makes no further provision for parliamentary approval of any directions so issued: see again *R* v *Secretary of State for Social Services, ex parte Stitt* (above).

If the content of a circular, guidance, or memorandum falls outside the scope of judicial review because it lacks any legal status, the focus of any legal challenge may have to be altered, perhaps to an examination of the minister's decision to issue the circular, code or guidance in the first place. The question arose in *Gillick* v *West Norfolk and Wisbech Area Health Authority* [1985] 3 All ER 402 where the House of Lords was asked to consider the validity of a memorandum issued by the Department of Health and Social Security, which contained advice to the effect that doctors could prescribe contraceptives for girls below the age of 16, without first obtaining the consent of a parent. Lords Fraser and Scarman made obiter comments to the effect that such guidance was amenable to judicial review. Lord Scarman summarised the issue in the following terms (at p415):

'... the case against the department was ... that ... by issuing [the memorandum] it was exercising a statutory discretion in a wholly unreasonable way ...'

Lord Bridge, however, adopted a rather different analysis, questioning whether the actions of the department fell within the scope of the court's supervisory jurisdiction at all. He stated (at p426):

'I ask myself what is the nature of the action or decision taken by the DHSS in the exercise of a power conferred upon it which entitles a court of law to intervene and declare that it has stepped beyond the proper limits of its power. I frame the question in that way because I believe that hitherto, certainly in general terms, the court's supervisory jurisdiction over the conduct of administrative authorities has been confined to ensuring that their actions or decisions were taken within the scope of the power which they purported to exercise or conversely to providing a remedy for an authority's failure to act or decide in circumstances where some appropriate statutory action or decision was called for. ... Now it is true that the [minister] has a general responsibility for the provision of family planning services. But only in a very loose sense could the issue of the memorandum be considered as part of the discharge of that responsibility. The memorandum itself has no statutory force whatsoever. It is not and does not purport to be issued in the exercise of any statutory power or in the performance of any statutory function. It is purely advisory in character and practitioners in the National Health Service are, as a matter of law, in no way bound by it ...'

His Lordship further contended that the decision to issue the memorandum could only be challenged on the grounds of *Wednesbury* unreasonableness where there was a context of specific and detailed statutory provisions in which to consider it, which was not the case here. As a general rule, he felt that the question of whether the advice tendered to administrative bodies in non-statutory guidance was good, bad or unreasonable would not normally be subject to scrutiny in the courts. Lord Bridge was willing to recognise one possible exception to the above proposition, where it was in the public interest for the validity of advice given in a departmental circular or memorandum to be tested in the courts. He accepted that such a situation had arisen in *Royal College of Nursing of the UK* v *DHSS* [1981] 1 All ER 545, wherein the courts had been willing to rule upon the contents of a DHSS circular which had stated that it would be lawful for nurses to perform a particular type of abortion. In the light of this decision, his Lordship (at p427) concluded that:

'... if a government department promulgates in a public document, albeit non-statutory in form, advice which is erroneous in law, then the court has jurisdiction to correct the error of law by an appropriate declaration. But the occasions of a departmental non-statutory publication raising a clearly defined issue of law, unclouded by political moral or social overtones, will be rare. In cases where any proposition of law implicit in a departmental advisory document is interwoven with questions of social and ethical controversy, the court should, in my opinion, exercise its jurisdiction with the utmost restraint, [and] confine itself to deciding whether the proposition of law is erroneous ...'

This restrictive approach to exercising the supervisory jurisdiction of the courts was subsequently illustrated in *R* v *Secretary of State for the Environment, ex parte Greenwich London Borough Council* (1989) The Times 17 May. The Secretary of State had authorised the distribution of a leaflet explaining the operation of the (then) proposed Community Charge to all households in England and Wales. The applicant local authority sought an order of prohibition to prevent the distribution on the ground that the leaflet was inaccurate as it made no reference to the joint liability of spouses or persons living together, and a declaration that the distribution of the leaflet in its present form was ultra vires. The Divisional Court (Woolf LJ and Ian Kennedy J) held, dismissing the application, that the court could only intervene where it was shown that such a leaflet contained errors of law, or was manifestly inaccurate or misleading. Alternatively, the court could intervene on the ground enunciated in the *Wednesbury* case, but this would require proof that no reasonable minister would have taken the decision to publish the leaflet in its present form, or that the leaflet was being issued in its current form to secure some ulterior objective. No such evidence was before the court. The court found that it was inevitable that the leaflets would have to contain a selection of details concerning the Community Charge. The omissions complained of did not render it inaccurate. It is interesting to note further that the applicants had complained that the distribution of the leaflet contravened constitutional conventions concerning the use of public money for the dissemination of information on matters of government policy. Woolf LJ commented that such conventions were observed, not because they had any force in law, but because of the political difficulties that might arise if they were ignored.

It should not be assumed that the existence of a specific statutory power to issue guidance will necessarily be enough of itself to persuade the courts to review the validity of any guidance issued thereunder. In *Nottinghamshire County Council* v *Secretary of State for the Environment* [1986] 1 All ER 199 the House of Lords considered a challenge to the validity of guidance on limits to expenditure issued by the minister to local authorities. Lord Scarman indicated that in the absence of evidence indicating bad faith on the part of the minister, or evidence that the guidance was so absurd that he must have taken leave of his senses, he would not intervene to quash it. It was felt that the issuing of such guidance inevitably involved the exercise of political judgment, and that such matters were for the minister and Parliament. Although Lord Scarman attached great weight in this case to the fact that the order had received express parliamentary approval, even going so far as to assert that '... it is not open to the courts to intervene unless the minister and the House must have misconstrued the statute or the minister has, to put it bluntly, deceived the House', the courts have since distanced themselves from the notion that such approval provides protection from review; see further *R (On the Application of Javed)* v *Secretary of State for the Home Department* (above) – the real issue is justiciability.

2.7 Prerogative power

The conventional wisdom is that, historically at least, the Crown is the ultimate source of power within the constitution. The history of English constitutional law is, however, littered with examples of the skirmishes between the monarchy and the courts and Parliament surrounding the exact scope of prerogative power. The word 'prerogative' comes from the Latin prae (before) and rogo (I demand). The royal prerogative, accordingly, is what the monarch demands and is entitled to in preference to all others. Blackstone defined it as follows:

> 'By the word prerogative we usually understand that special pre-eminence, which the King hath, over and above all other persons, and out of the ordinary course of the common law, in right of his regal dignity ... [I]t must be in its nature singular and eccentrical ... it can only be applied to those rights and capacities which the King enjoys alone, in contradistinction to others, and not those which he enjoys in common with any of his subjects ...'

According to Dicey, the prerogative appeared to be both historically and as a matter nothing else than the residue of discretionary and arbitrary authority, which at any given time was legally left in the hands of the Crown.

Historically the term prerogative has been applied to those special rights and privileges which the King had as a feudal lord, such as, for example, the privilege that he could not be sued in his own courts and, in a more general way, to all the powers and the authority of the King, whether exercised directly by him or through some other agency. The struggle between the Stuart monarchy and Parliament in the seventeenth century culminated in the removal of James II from the throne and his replacement by the Protestant William and Mary, who accepted the new constitutional arrangements set out by Parliament in the Bill of Rights. Some of the complaints listed in the preamble, and some of the articles of the Bill, specifically refer to the issue of prerogative power. The most important legal change brought about by the events of 1689 was the emergence of the general principle that prerogative powers could be limited or even abolished by statute. Since 1689 much prerogative power has been transferred to Parliament and manifests itself in the form of primary and delegated legislation. Primary legislation still requires the assent of the monarch in order to come into effect, thus showing that, again in theory, the Crown is a party to the passing of all Acts of Parliament. Some powers still exist, however, that can be exercised either by the monarch in person, or on behalf of the Crown by ministers; these are what are now generically termed prerogative powers.

The exercise of prerogative power involving the sovereign personally include: the appointment of a Prime Minister; the dissolution of Parliament; the granting of certain honours; and, exceptionally, the dismissal of ministers.

2.8 The exercise of prerogative power on the sovereign's behalf by ministers

Disposition of the armed forces

Under the prerogative and statute the sovereign is the commander-in-chief of the armed forces of the Crown. While many matters regarding the armed forces are now regulated by statute, their control, organisation and disposition is governed by the prerogative. In *China Navigation Co* v *Attorney-General* [1932] 2 KB 197, a case in which the court confirmed the right of the sovereign to determine the military protection to be provided to British subjects overseas, Scrutton LJ observed that:

> 'The administration of the army is in the hands of the King, who unless expressly controlled by an Act of Parliament cannot be controlled by the Court.'

Similarly, in *Chandler* v *DPP* [1964] AC 763, Lord Reid observed:

> 'It is in my opinion clear that the disposition and armament of the armed forces are, and for centuries have been, within the exclusive discretion of the Crown and that no one can seek a legal remedy on the ground that such discretion has been wrongly exercised.'

Today a distinction would be drawn between a legal challenge to a policy decision touching upon the conduct of warfare and foreign affairs on the one hand, and policies adopted by the military relating to the terms and conditions under which members of the armed forces serve on the other. Lord Usher's view expressed in *R* v *Secretary of State for War* [1896] 1 QB 121, to the effect that 'An officer ... cannot as between him and the Crown take proceedings in the courts of law in respect of anything which has happened between him and the Crown in consequence of his being a soldier', is no longer sustainable. Following the decision in the GCHQ case (see section 2.10 below), if the matter is justiciable, the courts will examine the decision to determine its legality. In *R* v *Ministry of Defence, ex parte Smith* [1996] 2 WLR 305 the applicants, one female and three male homosexuals, were administratively discharged from the armed forces pursuant to the Ministry of Defence policy (made under prerogative powers preserved by s138(1) of the Naval Discipline Act 1957 and s11(3) of the Army Act 1957 and of the Air Force Act 1955) prohibiting individuals with homosexual proclivities from serving. The applicants unsuccessfully sought judicial review of the policy, promulgated under the prerogative, on the basis that it was irrational and violated the provisions of the European Convention on Human Rights. The Court of Appeal held that the policy, whilst justiciable and thus reviewable, could not be impugned on the basis of irrationality, having been approved by, amongst others, both Houses of Parliament. Whilst the courts did have an important role to play in ensuring that the rights of citizens were not abused by the unlawful exercise of executive power, the courts could not usurp the position of the primary decision maker in order to regulate the conditions of service of the armed forces of the Crown. The court declined to adjudicate on the point raised concerning the incompatibility of the ban with the provisions of the European Convention on Human Rights, but the Master of the Rolls did observe that the failure of a decision-maker to advert to the Convention when exercising his discretion was not, of itself, a ground upon which the decision could be challenged by way of judicial review.

Prerogative of mercy

The courts are Her Majesty's courts and certain prerogative powers remain in relation to their work. For example, the Attorney-General in England may exercise the prerogative power to enter a nolle prosequi to stop a trial on indictment. On the advice of the Home Secretary, or the Secretary of State for Scotland, the Crown may exercise the prerogative power to pardon convicted offenders or remit or reduce a sentence. The Crown may, under the prerogative, grant leave for appeal from colonial courts to the Judicial Committee of the Privy Council, where the right still exists.

Legislative powers

In addition to the power to summon, prorogue and dissolve Parliament and to assent to Bills considered above, the Crown also has powers to legislate under the prerogative by Order in Council or by letter patent.

Powers relating to external affairs

Under the prerogative the Crown may declare war or make peace. In *R v Bottrill, ex parte Kuechenmeister* [1947] KB 41 a certificate from the Secretary of State denying that a state of war with Germany had ended was accepted as conclusive by the court in habeas corpus proceedings brought by a German national who had been detained as an enemy alien. The making of treaties is also governed by the prerogative. The general rule is that it is a matter exclusively for the Crown whether or not to enter into a treaty, though the treaty cannot give rise to new rights and duties in United Kingdom law unless they are given effect by legislation. The prerogative also includes the power of the Crown to recognise foreign governments, acquire territory, prevent aliens from entering the United Kingdom and to intern enemy aliens.

Emergency powers

In time of war the government (in modern times) acts under statutory powers, but the older prerogative powers remain. In the early seventeenth century it was recognised that in an emergency which threatened the realm, every man might disregard property rights in, for example, creating fortifications and digging trenches to repel the enemy. These powers were apparently not thought of as prerogatives since they were shared by the King with all his subjects. In *The Case of the King's*

Prerogative in Saltpetre (1607) 12 Co Rep 12 it was held that the King had the prerogative right to mine for saltpetre on private property and to carry it away, because it was necessary for the defence of the realm. The scope of the prerogative in time of war was extensively discussed by the House of Lords in *Burmah Oil Company* v *Lord Advocate* [1965] AC 75. In 1942 the British force in Rangoon destroyed the appellant's oil installations to prevent them falling into the hands of the advancing Japanese. The preliminary question for the House was whether the appellants were entitled to compensation. The House accepted that the destruction had been carried out lawfully under the prerogative. Lord Reid said:

> 'The prerogative certainly covers doing all those things in an emergency which are necessary for the conduct of war.'

He linked this to the prerogative right to control the armed forces; the reason for leaving the waging of war to the Executive, he said, was obvious. What was necessary would depend on the circumstances. Their Lordships went on to hold that although the installation had been lawfully destroyed under the prerogative, compensation was payable. The only common law exception to the rule that damage done under the prerogative in time of war gave rise to an entitlement to compensation was that of battle damage – damage actually caused by the use of weapons during conflict. The case was reversed by the War Damage Act 1965 which retrospectively provided that no person is entitled at common law to receive compensation in respect of damage caused by lawful acts of the Crown during, or in contemplation of the outbreak of, a war in which the sovereign is or was engaged. The Act only applies where there is a war and the principle of *Burmah Oil* presumably remains intact in the case of emergencies not amounting to war. As regards the maintenance of domestic law and order, *R* v *Secretary of State for the Home Department, ex parte Northumbria Police Authority* [1988] 1 WLR 356 confirms the existence of a residual prerogative power, vested in the Home Secretary, to provide such assistance as is required to police forces in order to enforce the law.

2.9 Prerogative and statutory powers

The common law rule is that if a prerogative power has been replaced by statute, the courts will proceed on the basis that it is the statutory power that is, and should be, exercised. Such an approach will be of more than merely constitutional significance when there is some distinction between the prerogative and statutory powers in terms of the rights and duties of citizens.

The point is well illustrated by the House of Lords' decision in *Attorney-General* v *De Keyser's Royal Hotel* [1920] AC 508. Troops had been accommodated at the plaintiff's hotel that had been requisitioned by the Crown for this purpose. There appeared to be two different powers under which this could be carried out: the royal prerogative, which was unclear as to the property owner's right to compensation in such circumstances; and the Defence Regulations of 1803 and 1842 which provided a code for the making of compensation payments in the event of property being requisitioned.

In the statute under which the regulations were made there was no mention of the co-extensive prerogative power, and the Crown was not expressly bound by the statute. It was held that if an area of prerogative power is subsequently covered, or 'overlapped' by a statutory provision, the statutory provision should prevail. In this case compensation was, therefore, payable under the Defence Regulations.
As Lord Dunedin observed:

> 'Inasmuch as the Crown is a party to every Act of Parliament it is logical enough to consider that when the Act deals with something which before the Act could be effected by the prerogative, and specially empowers the Crown to do the same thing, but subject to conditions, the Crown assents to that, and by that Act, to the prerogative being curtailed.'

Lord Atkinson added:

> '... after the statute has been passed, and while it is in force, the thing it empowers the Crown to do can thenceforth only be done by and under the statute, and subject to all the limitations, restrictions and conditions by it imposed, however unrestricted the Royal Prerogative may theretofore have been.'

These principles were subsequently followed in *Laker Airways Ltd* v *Department of Trade* [1977] QB 643, where it was held that the Secretary of State could not use his prerogative power to withdraw the designation of the respondent airline as a recognised carrier on the transatlantic route, under the Bermuda Agreement of 1946, since the matter was, by then, regulated by the Civil Aviation Act 1971.

A distinction will be drawn by the courts where the prerogative power is not entirely replaced by a statutory provision. In *R* v *Secretary of State for the Home Department, ex parte Northumbria Police Authority* [1988] 1 All ER 556 the Secretary of State, claiming to act either under s41 of the Police Act 1964, or under his prerogative powers, issued a circular to chief constables indicating that central government would supply them with riot equipment such as CS gas, in the event of a local police authority refusing to sanction the purchase of such equipment. The applicant authority contended that s4(4) of the 1964 Act gave police authorities the exclusive power to equip local police forces, and that this statutory power usurped any remaining prerogative power in the Secretary of State to supply such equipment. The Court of Appeal held that, notwithstanding the power granted to the Secretary of State under s41 of the 1964 Act, s4(4) of the Act had not replaced the prerogative power of the Secretary of State to maintain law and order. Crucial to this reasoning was the finding that s4(4) did not give local police authorities a monopoly over the supply of such equipment.

The correct approach to be adopted where the prerogative power is replaced with one under statute, but the statute has not yet been brought in to force, was considered by the House of Lords in *R* v *Secretary of State for the Home Department, ex parte Fire Brigades Union and Others* [1995] 2 WLR 464. A scheme existed for allocating public funds by way of compensation for the victims of crime, administered by the Criminal Injuries Compensation Board, under the prerogative. Sections 108–117 of the Criminal Justice Act 1988 sought to codify this scheme and place it on a statutory basis, leaving the quantum of any funds awarded to be determined by application of the common law principles. Section 171(1) empowered the Secretary of State to bring the scheme into effect on a day to be announced. In November 1993, in the exercise of his prerogative powers, the Secretary of State announced a new tariff scheme under which set amounts would be payable to the victims of crime, depending upon how their claims were categorised. The effect of this new tariff scheme was that much lower awards would be made in the future, resulting in a halving of the cost of the criminal injuries compensation scheme by the year 2000. The application for judicial review of the Secretary of State's failure to implement the statutory scheme under the 1988 Act and his exercise of prerogative power in introducing the revised tariff for awards was dismissed at first instance. On appeal the Court of Appeal held that, whilst the Secretary of State was under no duty to introduce the statutory scheme, it was an abuse of his common law prerogative powers to introduce a compensation scheme other than that contained in the 1988 Act. The Secretary of State appealed to the House of Lords and the applicants cross-appealed where it was held (by a majority), dismissing both the appeal and cross-appeals, that, as the Secretary of State had a discretion under s171(1) of the 1988 Act to bring the scheme into effect at some future date, the applicant's contention, to the effect that the Secretary of State had to bring the scheme into effect at some time, if correct, would mean the courts being able to grant an order of mandamus to this effect. Lord Browne-Wilkinson observed that it would be undesirable for the courts to be seen to be intervening in the legislative process to this extent, as it would involve the courts in treading 'dangerously close to the area over which Parliament enjoys exclusive jurisdiction, namely the making of legislation'. The section was to be read as conferring a discretion upon the Secretary of State that had to be exercised (or not) according to law. In this case the House of Lords felt that the Secretary of State had acted unlawfully in determining that he would never exercise his powers under s171(1). Regarding the exercise of prerogative power, the fact that the statutory scheme had not come into effect meant that, unlike the position in the *De Keyser* case, the prerogative power continued to exist and could be invoked by the Executive. The existence of the embryonic statutory scheme was, however, a factor that had to be borne in mind by a minister exercising the prerogative power, and limited the way in which that power could lawfully be used. In the present case the Secretary of State could not rely on his own act of introducing a revised scheme for compensation under the prerogative as a ground for not exercising his discretion under s171(1). Hence the introduction of the revised scheme under the prerogative, given the pre-existing statutory scheme, constituted an abuse of power and was thus ultra vires.

The constitutional significance of the case lies in the extent to which the majority was willing to provide a brake on the actions of the Executive, and risk accusations of judicial supremacisim. Mindful of such criticisms, Lord Keith (dissenting) viewed the decision as to whether or not to implement the legislation as one that was essentially administrative or political, in respect of which the Secretary of State owed a duty to Parliament, not the public at large. Hence, in his view, it would have been inappropriate for the courts to intervene.

2.10 Judicial review of prerogative power

The traditional judicial approach to prerogative power, as evidenced by some of the older cases cited above, was that once a power was identified as falling within the scope of the prerogative, the manner in which it was exercised was a matter for the minister, who was accountable to Parliament and the wider electorate, not the courts. Lord Denning's judgment in *Laker* (above) was indicative of a growing unwillingness to accept the ritualistic reliance on prerogative power as a bar to the supervisory jurisdiction of the courts by way of judicial review. Indeed, a rejection of the 'traditional' approach had arguably already occurred in *R* v *Criminal Injuries Compensation Board, ex parte Lain* [1967] 2 QB 864.

The question before the Divisional Court in that case was whether or not certiorari would lie to quash a decision of the Board for error of law on the face of the record. The Board (at that time) was not a statutory body but had been created pursuant to an act of the Executive under prerogative powers, and it was contended, as a consequence, that its decisions were not amenable to review by the High Court. The court, held that the Board's decisions were reviewable because it was a public body – ie making decisions affecting the rights of subjects, under a duty to act judicially, and making awards to claimants from the public purse. In so holding the court clearly abandoned the traditional approach of looking at the source of the power in question as the determinant of reviewability, in favour of looking at the nature of the power and the effect of its use. In some senses *ex parte Lain* could have been regarded as something of an exception to the rule, possibly because it dealt with delegated prerogative power, and it was not until 1984 that the House of Lords was presented with the opportunity to assess in depth the question of the reviewability of prerogative power.

The litigation giving rise to *Council of Civil Service Unions* v *Minister for the Civil Service* [1984] 3 All ER 935 arose as a consequence of actual and threatened industrial action at the government's communications headquarters (GCHQ). The Minister for the Civil Service issued an oral instruction to the effect that civil servants employed there would be prohibited from membership of any trade union. The staff of GCHQ were not consulted prior to the taking of this decision, which was made pursuant to the Minister's powers, under art 4 of the Civil Service Order in Council 1982, to give instructions 'for controlling the conduct of the Service, and providing for ... the conditions of service', the Order itself being made under the royal prerogative.

The House of Lords held that simply because a decision-making power was derived from a common law and not a statutory source it should not, for that reason only, be immune from judicial review. According to Lord Diplock, judicial review had developed to a stage where one could classify under three heads the grounds on which administrative action was subject to control by the courts: 'illegality', 'irrationality' and 'procedural impropriety'. As regards 'procedural impropriety', his Lordship saw no reason why it should not be a ground for judicial review of a decision made under powers of which the ultimate source was the prerogative.

Lord Roskill thought that the right of challenge could not, however, be unqualified. It must depend on the subject matter of the prerogative power that was exercised. Prerogative powers such as those relating to the making of treaties, the defence of the realm, the prerogative of mercy, the grant of honours, the dissolution of Parliament and the appointment of ministers were not, he thought, susceptible to judicial review because their nature and subject matter was such to render them not amenable to the judicial process. It was also pointed out that prerogative decisions would usually involve the application of government policy of which the courts were not the appropriate arbiters. According to Lord Diplock:

'... the kind of evidence that is admissible under judicial procedures and the way in which it has to be addressed tend to exclude from the attention of the court competing policy considerations which, if the executive discretion is to be wisely exercised, need to be weighed against one another – a balancing exercise which judges by their upbringing and experience are ill-qualified to perform.'

Their Lordships agreed therefore that Executive action based on common law or the use of a prerogative power was not necessarily immune from review. This was especially so in the present case where the prerogative derived from an Order in Council, which was virtually indistinguishable from an order deriving from statute. In such cases the decision might be reviewed by the courts just as it would have been if it had rested on statutory powers. In the instant case, the decision rested upon the minister's consideration of national security, a matter the House of Lords thought it was for the Executive to weigh and decide. Their Lordships accepted that the overriding element of national security, in maintaining services at GCHQ, displaced any right the unions may have had to judicial review of the order.

Application of the GCHQ decision

Despite the extent to which the House of Lords' decision in *Council of Civil Service Unions* v *Minister for the Civil Service* represented a breakthrough in the extension of the ambit of judicial review, it should be borne in mind that an old limitation was largely being replaced with a modern one. Whereas previously the constitutional history of the prerogative may have made the judiciary reluctant to question the way in which it was exercised, the modern determinant of judicial intervention is the concept of justiciability. Is the exercise of the prerogative being challenged one in relation to which the judges are qualified to express a view? As a broad guide it is probably accurate to suggest that the greater the element of policy involved in the exercise of the prerogative, the less likely it is that the courts will interfere with the minister's decision. There has been no evidence that the courts would be prepared to adjudicate upon the exercise of prerogative power involved in decisions such as those to commit troops to the Gulf war, or to permit the use of British air bases for the launch of bombing raids on Libya.

Where the exercise of prerogative power involves the exercise of ministerial discretion in relation to the rights of individual citizens, and in the absence of considerations of foreign policy and national security, the courts have shown themselves willing to exercise this new found jurisdiction, not least because they may be concerned with cases where, but for judicial review, the citizen would have no other means of challenging the decision in question. In *R v Secretary of State for Foreign and Commonwealth Affairs, ex parte Everett* [1989] 1 All ER 655 the Court of Appeal confirmed that the issuing of passports, although falling within the scope of prerogative power, was, following the GCHQ decision, a matter that could be the subject of review. In reversing the decision of the Divisional Court, it was held that the Foreign Office policy, of not renewing the passports of individuals in respect of whom an arrest warrant had been issued, was clearly sound, but that the applicant should have been informed of the grounds for the refusal, and notified that the policy might be departed from in exceptional circumstances. On the facts, however, it was felt that the applicant had sustained no injustice since by the time the matter had reached the Divisional Court he had discovered the grounds for the refusal to renew his passport and, as there were no exceptional circumstances before that court, there were no grounds for granting the order of certiorari. Similarly the prerogative powers exercised by the Home Secretary in respect of immigration and deportation decisions will be subject to review, but not on the grounds that, in exercising those powers, he has failed to take into account the terms of an international treaty not yet incorporated into domestic law: see *R v Secretary of State for the Home Department, ex parte Ahmed and Others* (1998) The Times 15 October.

The courts have also shown themselves willing to intervene in issues related to the administration of justice. In *R v Criminal Injuries Compensation Board and Another, ex parte P; Same, ex parte G* [1995] 1 WLR 845, a decision which effectively vindicates the approach taken some 30 years previously in *ex parte Lain* (above), the Court of Appeal confirmed that it had jurisdiction to review the operation of the Criminal injuries Compensation Scheme, despite the fact that it had been established, and was administered, pursuant to the exercise of prerogative power. Evans and Peter Gibson LJJ were also of the view that the court had jurisdiction to consider the exercise of executive discretion in this matter, as the grant of moneys by Parliament for distribution by the Board implied that the making of awards had to be both fair and rational. Interestingly, Neill LJ, dissenting, took the view that whilst the Board's decisions were reviewable per se, the distribution of funds by the Board was not a justiciable issue. Would Neill LJ have been content to rule that the distribution of funds was not justiciable if the decision impugned had nevertheless been prima facie irrational? On this point, note the comments made by Peter Gibson LJ:

> 'To take the fanciful but archetypal example of perversity, if the schemes had been revised in 1979 to exclude only redheaded victims of crimes committed by persons under the same roof, I would have thought that the court could intervene on the application of a redheaded victim, notwithstanding that (a) the decision to introduce such a revised scheme was an exercise of the executive's discretion on how public moneys were to be distributed and (b) the decision affected no right nor any legitimate expectation, in the sense of an expectation arising from a previously prevailing benefit or from an assurance of the applicant.'

The reviewability of the exercise of the prerogative of mercy was confirmed in *R v Secretary of State for the Home Department, ex parte Bentley* [1994] 2 WLR 101. The applicant's brother, Derek Bentley, was convicted of the murder of a police officer in 1952 and, despite the jury's recommendation, and the advice of Home Office officials to the effect that the death penalty should not be enforced, was subsequently executed in 1953. In 1992 the Home Secretary, whilst indicating that he had some sympathy for the view that Bentley should not have been hanged, refused to grant him a posthumous pardon, on the ground that it was not Home Office policy to do so unless the defendant concerned had been proved to be both technically and morally innocent of any crime, and that, following a review of his case, he was satisfied that Bentley's innocence had not been established. The Divisional Court declined to make any order, but invited the Home Secretary to look again at the range of options that might permit some formal recognition to be given to the generally accepted view that Bentley should not have been hanged. Watkins LJ saw no reason why, in the light of the House of Lords' decision in the GCHQ case, the exercise of the prerogative of mercy should not be susceptible to review. Whilst the formulation of policy relating to the granting of pardons might not be justiciable, the failure by a Home Secretary to consider the variety of ways in which that prerogative might be exercised could be reviewed. In the instant case the Home Secretary should have considered whether or not the grant of a conditional posthumous pardon was appropriate as recognition that the state had made a mistake, and that Bentley should have had his sentence commuted: see further *R v Secretary of State for the Home Department, ex parte Harrison* [1988] 3 All ER 86 and *R v Solicitor-General, ex parte Taylor* (1995) The Times 14 August (no judicial review of decision not to institute contempt proceedings).

As indicated above the availability of some other form of redress is a factor that can weigh heavily with the court in its decision as to whether or not it should intervene. As May LJ observed, in *R v Civil Service Appeal Board, ex parte Bruce* [1989] 2 All ER 907, the mere fact that a body, such as the Board, derived its powers from the prerogative did not automatically mean that its decisions would be amenable to judicial review as a matter of course. The availability of other means of legal challenge such as, in that case, the possibility of an action for breach of contract, might persuade the courts not to exercise its jurisdiction. On the facts the court declined to determine the question of whether a civil servant had a contract of employment, but was satisfied that, even if the decisions of the Board were amenable to review, the application would be dismissed since the applicant could pursue any allegations of unfairness in proceedings before an industrial tribunal.

The Human Rights Act 1998 raises the prospect of an exercise of prerogative power being challenged on the basis that it conflicts with Convention rights protected by the Act. Section 6(1) provides that it is unlawful for a public authority to act in a way which is incompatible with a Convention right and this would certainly encompass a minister exercising prerogative power. For breach of Convention rights as a basis for judicial review: see further Chapters 7 and 8.

3

Local Government

3.1 Introduction

By means of primary legislation Parliament has created a range of executive bodies designed to carry out various aspects of central government policy. Examples include the Post Office, the Independent Television Commission, the Radio Authority, the Health and Safety at Work Executive, the Civil Aviation Authority, the Commission for Racial Equality and the Equal Opportunities Commission. In addition, public corporations have been created in the past to provide public welfare services, such as area health authorities. Historically, the rationale for creating public corporations to undertake commercial activities has been based on arguments that the products and services involved could not be made at a profit by private enterprise, but were seen as essential to the economy, such as steel, coal, or railway services; that it may be more practical for one large undertaker to supply a service, such as gas, or electricity; or, on a more ideological level, that there may be a view that certain goods and services are so important their supply should not be left in private hands and that further, any profit made should be returned to the nation, or the business not run at a profit at all, thus reducing costs to the consumer. The move to privatisation since 1979 has seen a shift back to reliance on the private sector.

Local authorities, as public corporations, are statutory bodies with responsibilities for the delivery of social, environmental and commercial services at local level. All owe their existence to statute, with the exception of the Corporation of the City of London. The rationale for the existence of local authorities is clear – central government cannot be responsible for the level of detail involved in the provision of services locally, and local government is likely to have a much better idea of what is in the interests of local people. The issue that has proved problematic for many years, however, is that of control. How can central government ensure a uniform level of provision if local authorities are to enjoy a high degree of autonomy in they way they provide services? Should local authorities be allowed to spend money as they wish and merely be answerable to the local electorate, or should central government exercise close control? How should disputes over policy be resolved where central government and local government are ideologically opposed to each other?

3.2 Organisation of local government

England and Wales

The current structure of local government in England and Wales (excluding London, as to which see below) is still largely based upon the changes introduced by the Local Government Acts 1972 and 1985. Under the 1972 Act England was divided into 39 county councils and six metropolitan counties. The 39 county councils were further sub-divided into 296 district councils, these district councils being further sub-divided into local parish councils (in Wales, community councils). The metropolitan counties were sub-divided into 36 metropolitan districts. In 1986 the six metropolitan county councils were abolished, and their functions transferred to either residuary bodies or joint authorities made up of members from district councils. The Conservative government of the late 1980s was of the view that there could be significant savings in costs if the 'two-tier' system of county and district councils was replaced by a system based on unitary authorities. A Commission chaired by John Banham investigated the issue and recommended a series of changes that represented something of a compromise position. Unitary authorities have been introduced in some areas, where this appears to be the most efficient basis for local government, and the 'two-tier' structure has been retained elsewhere. As a result of the Scotland (Local Government) Act 1994 and the Local Government (Wales) Act 1994 there are now 32 unitary authorities in Scotland and 22 in Wales. In England there are 46 unitary authorities, and 34 'old-style' county councils sub-divided into 238 district councils.

Allocation of functions

A local authority is an example of an administrative device by which means executive functions can be discharged. In allocating functions to local authorities, central government may be motivated by the belief that certain matters should be under the control of locally elected representatives, as this ensures that the views of local people are reflected in decision-making. Alternatively, and more cynically, it may be that central government does not want to have responsibility for certain functions. The main provision governing the distribution of functions between the different tiers of local government is the Local Government Act 1972.

County councils have responsibility for education, town and country planning (some functions shared with district and borough councils), social services, major highways, libraries and recreation facilities, fire and police services and public transport. District or borough councils are responsible for housing, including slum clearance, public health and sanitary services, refuse collection, minor roads and local licensing matters. Parish councils (community councils in Wales) deal with footway lighting, allotments, bus shelters, burial grounds, village greens and parking places for motor cycles and bicycles.

London

Originally, under the London Government Act 1963, Greater London was given two tiers of local government. The 'upper' tier authority was known as the Greater London Council (GLC) (replacing the old London County Council) and the 'lower' tier authorities were the 32 London borough councils. The Corporation of the City of London remained unaffected by these changes and Inner and Middle Temple also retained their ancient status as local authorities. The GLC was abolished by the Local Government Act 1985, leaving London without any overall local government body. The Labour Party included a commitment to re-introduce an elected Assembly for London in the manifesto on which it fought and won the 1997 general election. Following a referendum held in spring 1998 indicating popular support for such a move the Greater London Authority Act 1999 was enacted leading to the establishment of a London-wide Assembly headed by a directly elected Mayor. The Assembly comprises 25 members, 14 elected by constituencies in London and 11 members elected on a London-wide basis. The Assembly does not have any tax-raising powers but can oversee the transport and economic policies developed by the Mayor. The Assembly can question the Mayor about the discharge of these functions. A new police authority has also been established to oversee the Metropolitan Police, along with a new fire and emergency planning authority.

3.3 Constitution of local government – arrangements under the Local Government Act 1972

Under the Local Government Act 1972 the typical constitutional arrangement for a local authority is for it to meet in plenary session to make policy and agree a budget. Councillors are normally grouped on a party political basis with the leader of the council being the leader of the largest or majority grouping. Council committees meet to give effect to policy, with decisions being ratified by full council meetings where appropriate.

Council meetings

Council meetings are held according to the requirements of the standing orders that each authority produces for this purpose. Council meetings must be held at least once a year, and a quorum is 25 per cent of all members. Prior notice of a meeting must be given, and the agenda and any reports to be considered must be available for inspection at least three days before the meeting. Decisions are normally made on the basis of a majority vote at council meetings. The duties of councillors exercising their voting powers was considered by the Court of Appeal in *R* v *Waltham Forest London Borough Council, ex parte Waltham Forest Ratepayers' Action Group* (1987) The Times 2 October, where the local authority, which was controlled by the Labour Party, had voted to increase rates by over 60 per cent. A number of Labour councillors had privately expressed their disquiet at the proposed increase, but had voted in favour of the resolution, rather than resign the party whip. The challenge to the validity of the council's resolution, which had been brought on the basis that the councillors who had voted in favour had either taken into account an irrelevant consideration, the party whip system, or else the party whip system had had the effect of causing them to abdicate the exercise of their discretion, failed on the ground that there was insufficient evidence that those councillors who had supported the rates increase had blindly followed party policy in the way in which they had cast their votes. Lord Donaldson MR observed that the voting by the councillors could not be impugned simply because there was a party whip system in operation. The whip might have been a relevant factor in determining how votes might be cast, but it was only one of several. To impugn the whip system would be to call into question the way in which Parliament itself operated. His Lordship felt that such a system would only become objectionable if a councillor were to be forced to resign not only from his party, but also the council itself, if he decided to defy the relevant party whip.

Where the votes cast at a council meeting produce a tied result the chair or mayor can use his or her casting vote to resolve the matter. The question of whether such a power should or should not be exercised with reference to party political loyalties was considered in *R* v *Bradford City Council, ex parte Wilson* [1989] 3 All ER 140, the Divisional Court holding that it was clearly the mayor's (or the chairman's) duty to act impartially to ensure that council meetings proceeded efficiently and effectively, with a full and fair debate involving various viewpoints. It did not necessarily follow, however, that when such a person came to consider the exercise of his own vote he had to remain above party politics. In particular there was no authority for the proposition that a casting vote should be used in a manner that would ensure that debate on a particular topic could be continued. Bingham LJ expressly rejected any analogy between the role of a lord mayor in chairing council meetings, and the role of the Speaker in the House of Commons. This decision was followed in *R* v *Bradford Metropolitan County Council, ex parte Corris* [1989] 3 All ER 156. Note that the Local Government Finance Act 1992 provides that councillors who fail to pay the council tax can be disqualified from voting at council meetings as a consequence.

Council committees

Under the Local Government Act 1972 much decision-making is actually delegated to committees. Section 101 of the 1972 Act allows local authorities to arrange for the discharge of their functions by committees, sub-committees, officers, or other local authorities, although this does not prevent the full council from exercising this function as well. Certain committees have to be established in order to ensure compliance with statutory requirements. Thus education committees, social services committees and (in non-metropolitan county councils) police committees must be established. A local authority is empowered, under s111 Local Government Act 1972, to discharge its functions by establishing a working party where this is appropriate, and there is no common law requirement that a councillor should be allowed to attend: see *R* v *Eden District Council, ex parte Moffat* (1988) The Times 24 November.

Prior to the introduction of the Local Government and Housing Act 1989 it appeared that the courts would not necessarily intervene where the majority group on a local authority voted to exclude opposition members from committees: see *R* v *Rushmore Borough Council, ex parte Crawford* (1981) 27 November (unreported). Under the 1989 Act appointments to relevant committees and sub-committees are required to achieve a political balance. The appointment committee of a local authority is required to review the political balance of the authority and to ensure that this is reflected in the composition of its committees. In particular an authority should ensure that not all seats on a committee are allocated to one political group, and that the committee reflects the fact that there is a controlling group on the council as a whole if this is the case.

Subject to the requirements of the 1989 Act, however, it remains open to an authority to prevent a councillor from sitting on a particular committee. The question of a councillor's right to sit on a committee and to see documents before it was considered in *R* v *Hackney London Borough Council, ex parte Gamper* [1985] 3 All ER 275, wherein a Liberal councillor, who was a member of the respondent authority, applied successfully for judicial review of its decision to deny him access to meetings and the documents of the direct labour organisation sub-committees. Lloyd J held that the authority should have asked itself whether the applicant had a need to know such information in order to properly perform his duties as a councillor, even though he was not a member of the sub-committee in question. His Lordship was satisfied that on the facts the decision to exclude the respondent was one that no reasonable authority could have made. Similarly, in *R* v *Sheffield City Council, ex parte Chadwick* (1985) The Times 17 December, a Liberal councillor successfully applied for judicial review of a decision of the Council to deny him admission to meetings of its budget sub-committee and to refuse him copies of its reports. The applicant was a member of the council's policy committee, but not of the budget sub-committee, which consisted entirely of Labour councillors, the Labour Party having control of the council as a whole. The applicant's exclusion was held to be unlawful since he would not be properly informed when, as a member of the policy committee, he was called upon to endorse or reject the recommendations of the budget sub-committee. Following *R* v *Hackney London Borough Council, ex parte Gamper* (above), the applicant had a need to know what the deliberations of the budget sub-committee had been in order to perform his duties properly. Further, in coming to its conclusion to exclude the applicant, the committee had taken into account considerations that were irrelevant, eg the desire to maintain the secrecy of what were in reality party policy discussions taking place in sub-committee meetings.

Neither would the 1989 Act prevent an authority from resolving to remove a councillor from one of its committees, although regard would have to be had to any standing orders applying to such procedures. The courts will not intervene to assist council members excluded from committees unless such exclusion is unreasonable. In *R* v *Greenwich London Borough Council, ex parte Lovelace* [1990] 1 All ER 353 the respondent Labour controlled local authority was pursuing a policy of increasing council house rents, the policy being implemented by the authority's housing committee, of which the applicants, who were both Labour Party councillors, were members. The applicants were opposed to the policy and voted against it at meetings of the committee, action that prompted the controlling Labour group, exercising its discretion under the authority's standing orders, to remove the applicants from the housing committee. The Court of Appeal, dismissing the applicants' appeals against the Divisional Court's refusal to allow an application for judicial review of the authority's actions, held that since the local authority clearly had the power under its standing orders to dissolve any committee or alter its membership at any time, the crucial questions became: what was the reason for removing the applicants from the housing committee, and was the reason legitimate? The court accepted that local authorities invariably operated on party political lines, and recognised that the modern reality was that a political party would seek cohesion amongst its members so as to promote party policy. The applicants had been removed because their membership of the committee prevented it from giving effect to party policy which was to present a balanced budget. The reason for the removal of the applicants was, therefore, legitimate. The line that had to be drawn was between steps taken to impose party discipline, which were prima facie lawful, and steps taken primarily to punish an individual councillor that would be unlawful. Deciding on which side of that line a particular action fell could be problematic, but it was a function that the courts were well equipped to perform: see further *R* v

Waltham Forest London Borough Council, ex parte Waltham Forest Ratepayers' Action Group (above).

A realistic approach by the courts to the role played by party politics in the decision-making processes of council committees is also evidenced by *R v Amber Valley District Council, ex parte Jackson* [1984] 3 All ER 501 and *R v Local Commissioner for Administration in North and North East England, ex parte Liverpool City Council* (2000) The Times 3 March. Note, however, that in the latter case the Court of Appeal found that the use of 'agreed voting' procedures (ie based on party allegiance) in respect of the consideration of planning applications, could amount to maladministration, as it rendered subsequent debate in committees and the council chamber meaningless. The provisions of para 4 of the National Code of Local Government Conduct (relevant at the time of the application) imposed a more stringent regime than the common law by providing the following advice to councillors:

> 'Whilst you may be strongly influenced by the views of others, and of your party in particular, it is your responsibility alone to decide what view to take on any particular question which councillors have to decide.'

The Court expressed the view that if the Code was less permissive than the common law it was the Code that had to be followed. Given the multiplicity of committees and sub-committees through which a local authority discharges its functions, a degree of overlap in committee membership is inevitable. In *R v Hereford and Worcester County Council, ex parte Wellington Parish Council* (1996) 160 LGR 161 the fact that three members of a planning sub-committee, who had voted in favour of granting permission for a gypsy site, were also members of the gypsy sub-committee was held not to be in breach of the rules of natural justice on the grounds of bias. Given that the relevant legislation does not forbid such intermingling of functions, it could be contended that it is impliedly endorsed by Parliament.

Council officers

The appointment of staff is within the discretion of the authority: see s112 of the 1972 Act. Certain officers, such as chief education officers, and inspectors of weights and measures, must be appointed. The terms and conditions under which council officers are employed is essentially a matter for each local authority as employer to determine, subject to a general requirement that contractual terms should be reasonable: see s112(2). In most large local authorities today the senior council officer will be designated as the chief executive officer and will discharge the functions of general manger of the authority. Although servants of the authority, and notwithstanding that they will not be permitted to participate in any votes, senior council officers will often have considerable influence on the formulation and execution of policy, given their experience and areas of expertise.

The Widdicombe Committee report into local government in 1985 led to the enactment of the Local Government and Housing Act 1989, and the Local Government Officers (Political Restrictions) Regulations 1990 (SI 1990/851) issued thereunder, which resulted in certain restrictions being imposed upon the political activities of council officers occupying more senior salaried posts. The holder of a post designated under the Act and Regulations as 'politically restricted' may not be a member of another local authority, canvass on behalf of a political party or serve as an MP. Teachers and lecturers employed by local authorities are exempt from these provisions.

The validity of these restrictions was tested before the European Court of Human Rights in *Ahmed and Others* v *United Kingdom* Case No 65/1997/849/1056 (1998) The Times 2 October, the applicants contending that the restrictions amounted to a violations of their rights to freedom of expression and assembly, contrary to arts 10 and 11 of the European Convention on Human Rights (ECHR) and their rights to participate fully in the electoral process, contrary to art 3 of Protocol 1 to the ECHR. By six votes to three the Court held that, whilst the Regulations did interfere with the applicants' rights under art 10, they were not in conflict with the Convention as claimed. The Court found that, contrary to the applicants' submissions, the restrictions imposed by the Regulations were sufficiently precise to meet the requirement that they should be 'prescribed by law'. The Court noted that the Regulations could not be expected to define political activity with absolute precision, bearing in mind also that they applied to a substantial number of officers. Second, the Court concluded that the restrictions imposed by the Regulations were in pursuit of a legitimate aim, namely ensuring the effectiveness of local political democracy and preventing the diminution of the neutrality of certain categories of officers. The Regulations were also seen as protecting the rights of council members and the electorate to effective political democracy at the local level. In particular the Court attached great importance to what it saw as the long tradition of political neutrality which local government officers owed to elected council members. Third, the Court held that the Regulations were 'necessary in a democratic society'. In reaching this conclusion the Court took notice of the work done by the Widdicombe Committee and the evidence of abuse that it had uncovered. The response, in the form of the Regulations, was within the respondent state's margin of appreciation. By restricting the operation of the Regulations to certain specified categories of officer, and restricting only partisan comment, the government had tried to ensure that the interference with rights under the ECHR had been minimised in so far as this was possible given the purpose of the Regulations. Rights such as freedom to join political parties remained unaffected by the Regulations. The factors justifying the interference with the applicants' rights under art 10 applied equally to the alleged violation of the rights to freedom of association guaranteed under art 11. The Court also regarded it as significant that the Labour government elected in May 1997 had reviewed the operation of the Regulations and determined that they should remain in effect.

A local authority will normally be vicariously liable for any torts committed by a council officer in the course of his employment. Where, however, a council officer acts outside the scope of his delegated authority he may incur personal liability. In *Burgoine and Another* v *Waltham Forest London Borough Council* (1996) The Times 7 November the council resolved to indemnify certain council officers in respect of any liabilities incurred in the course of their acting within the scope of the authority delegated by the council. An indemnification clause to this effect was included in the contracts of employment of Burgoine, the council's Chief Executive, and Cooke, the council's Assistant Director of Finance. Later that year, the council, purporting to exercise its powers under s19 of the Local Government (Miscellaneous Provisions) Act 1976, created a company, Waltham Forest Water Park Ltd (the company), in order to provide a public water park. Burgoine and Cooke were appointed as directors of the company. The venture ran into financial difficulties, resulting in the company being put into liquidation. The company's creditors subsequently sought to recover substantial sums from the directors. Burgoine and Cooke, in turn, sought to invoke the indemnification clauses in their contracts of employment so as to shift their personal liability onto their employers. The court held that the indemnification clauses were not binding on the council where the activities of those employees it sought to indemnify were in fact ultra vires the council. Following *Credit Suisse* v *Waltham Forest London Borough Council* [1996] 4 All ER 176 and *Credit Suisse* v *Allerdale Borough Council* [1996] 4 All ER 129, it was agreed on all sides that the setting up of the water park company had been ultra vires the council, hence the appointment of Burgoine and Cooke as directors had been ultra vires, and hence they could not have been pursuing duties on behalf of the council when acting as directors. An indemnity contract that was ultra vires as a matter of public law could not be invoked in private law proceedings. Section 101 of the Local Government Act 2000 now provides that the Secretary of State may by order make provision for conferring power on local authorities to provide indemnities to some or all of their members and officers.

3.4 Constitution of local government – the Local Government Act 2000

Part II of the Local Government Act 2000 introduced new constitutional arrangements for local authorities as regards their executives. Section 11 provides for three models and local authorities are required to adopt that which is most suitable for them. Model One, the 'mayor and cabinet executive' system, is based on an elected mayor of the authority and two or more councillors of the authority appointed to the executive by the elected mayor. Model Two is the 'leader and cabinet executive' system, comprising a councillor of the authority elected as leader of the executive by the authority and two or more councillors of the authority appointed to the executive by the executive leader or the authority. Model Three is the 'mayor and council manager' system, which may comprise an elected mayor of the authority and an officer of the authority (council manager) appointed to the executive by the authority. Under s24 executive committees are not required to reflect the political balance of the full council in their composition.

Section 13 provides for the functions to be carried out by an executive, much of the detail being provided for in ministerial regulations. Regardless of the model adopted, the broad division of functions between executive, council and members in committee is as follows. The executive proposes the broad policy framework for the authority and the draft budget. The full council meeting debates and approves the policy framework and the budget. The executive then has the task of implementing the policy framework and giving effect to budgetary decisions. Overview and scrutiny committees of the authority hold the executive to account in respect of the implementation of the policy framework and budget, especially as regards the securing of 'best value' under the Local Government Act 1999 (see below). These committees in some ways resemble parliamentary select committees in that they are empowered to call members of the executive and officers of the authority to appear before them, and have the power to ask for decisions to be reconsidered by the executive.

Prior to adopting one of the three models for executive arrangements, a local authority must propose a scheme and consult its electorate. Where a 'mayor and cabinet executive' model or a 'mayor and council manager' model is proposed a local authority is required to conduct a referendum of local electors. Once a model of executive is adopted it has to be ratified by a full council meeting of the authority. The Secretary of State is empowered by s34 to introduce regulations whereby a local authority is required to hold a referendum on an executive arrangement involving a directly elected mayor if 5 per cent of electors petition in favour. Elected mayors are normally elected using the supplementary vote system of proportional representation. However, if there are only two candidates a simple majority system is used; see further the Local Authorities (Referendums) (Petitions and Directions) (England) Regulations 2000 (SI 2000/2852).

The aim of these changes was to enable local authority decision-making to be more effective, responsive and accountable. Section 13 provides that s101 of the 1972 Act can be disapplied in respect of any functions which are not (on the basis of ministerial orders) to be functions of the executive; see further the Local Authorities (Functions and Responsibilities) (England) Regulations 2000 (SI 2000/2853).

3.5 Ensuring proper standards

Public access

The public has a general right to attend meetings of local authorities, under the Public Bodies (Admission to Meetings) Act 1960. Section 100 of the Local Government Act 1972 extends the scope of this right of attendance to meetings of committees and sub-committees. Section 100 has in turn been amended by the Local Government (Access to Information) Act 1985, which increases public access to local authority meetings, reports and documents. Members of the public and press have the right to attend meetings of principal councils (previously local authorities had a discretion to exclude the public and the press from access to such meetings and materials), but this can be displaced by the authorities' duty to exclude the public where evidence, the disclosure of which would constitute a breach of confidence, is to be considered. Confidential information comprises information which government departments provide on terms forbidding disclosure, and information, disclosure of which is otherwise forbidden by law. Where 'exempt information' may be disclosed at a meeting the local authority may pass a resolution excluding the public. Exempt information is defined in Sch 1 of the Act and includes: any information relating to particular individuals; any information relating to prevention, investigation or prosecution of crime; any information connected with legal proceedings; and the identity of a protected informant. Local authorities whose meetings are governed by s100A of the 1972 Act retain a residual power to exclude members of the public who have been admitted to a meeting, if such action is considered necessary in order to maintain order.

Bodies such as parish or community councils, and meetings of regional or district health authorities, continue to be governed by the Public Bodies (Admission to Meetings) Act 1960. The Act provides a power to exclude the public where confidential information is to be considered, and where there are 'special reasons' for exclusion, for example where the meeting is considering a report from one of its officers. Thus, in *R* v *Liverpool City Council, ex parte LTFOA* [1975] 1 All ER 379, a local authority committee, meeting to consider the issuing of taxi cab licences, passed a resolution under the 1960 Act excluding the public from the meeting because of the small number of seats available (most were occupied by members and officers of the local authority), and the belief that its business could not be properly conducted in the presence of those competing to be granted licences. The Divisional Court upheld the validity of the resolution on the basis that the two reasons relied upon were entirely justified, and the failure to state these reasons in the resolution was a breach of a directory not mandatory provision. Further, the applicants were unable to show any significant injury in consequences of the irregularity. Similarly, in *R* v *Brent Health Authority, ex parte Francis* [1985] 1 All ER 74, where the applicant, a member of the public, applied unsuccessfully for an order of certiorari, to quash the respondent authority's decision to exclude the public from its meetings where spending cuts were being considered, three previous meetings on the same topic having resulted in disorderly conduct on the part of members of the public attending. Forbes J held that a public body had a common law right to exclude the public from its meetings, notwithstanding the Public Bodies (Admissions to Meetings) Act 1960, where it feared on reasonable grounds that members of the public planned to disrupt the meeting. On the facts the court was satisfied that the power had been exercised bona fide.

Under s22 of the Local Government Act 2000 meetings of a local authority executive, or a committee of such an executive, may be held in private at the discretion of the executive, although a written record must be kept of any such private meetings; see further the Local Authorities (Executive Arrangements) (Access to Information) (England) Regulations 2000 (SI 2000/3272).

A code of conduct for local authority members and employees

Part III of the Local Government Act 2000 deals with the conduct of local government members and employees. Following on from recommendations made in the Nolan Committee's *Third Report on Standards in Public Life* in July 1997, every local authority is now required to adopt a code of conduct covering the behaviour of officers and elected members, and to establish a standards compliance committee and appoint a monitoring officer: see s53 and s54. The monitoring officer is also required to establish and maintain a register of the interests of members of the relevant authority: see s81. The Secretary of State has responsibility for publishing a model code of conduct (s49) that authorities can adapt and adopt: see ss51 and 52.

A new non-departmental public body known as the Standards Board for England has been established to investigate allegations of unethical conduct by relevant authority members. In Wales this function is discharged by the Commissioner for Local Administration in Wales.

Allegations are investigated by an ethical standards officer: ss60–62. Upon completing his investigations on behalf of the Board the ethical standards officer may determine: that the allegation is unfounded; that no action is required; that the matter should be referred to the relevant local authority's compliance committee; or that the matter should be referred to the Adjudication Panel: s76. The panel can have the matter remitted to a case tribunal to adjudicate on the findings. The case tribunal can make suitable recommendations regarding sanctions.

Criminal sanctions

There are various ways in which both the members and officers of a local authority can fall foul of the civil and criminal law by failing to declare vested interests, accepting corrupt payments or wilfully causing financial loss to the authority and its inhabitants.

Sections 94–98 Local Government Act 1972 provide that any member of a local authority who has any pecuniary interest, direct or indirect, in any contract, proposed contract or other matter, and is present at a meeting of the local authority at which the contract or other matter is the subject of consideration, must disclose his interest and not take any further part in any discussion of, or vote on, the issue. The prohibition is against participation of any kind, including voting against the matter and thereby against the member's own interest: see *Brown* v *DPP* [1956] 2 QB 369. A pecuniary interest, for these purposes, includes an interest of a spouse, or a partner, or being a member of a company which has an interest. The words 'contract or other matter' have been given a wide interpretation by the courts. In *Rands* v *Oldroyd* [1959] 1 QB 204 it was held that a councillor had an interest by virtue of being a local building contractor participating in a vote on the council's direct labour workforce. Prosecutions for these offences can only be instituted on behalf of the DPP. By analogy with the position of private companies entering into ultra vires contracts, any contract entered into by a local authority following the illegal involvement of a councillor is likely to be voidable at the instance of the authority: see *Hely-Hutchinson Ltd* v *Brayhead Ltd* [1967] 1 QB 549.

These criminal sanctions have now been augmented by regulations made under s19 of the Local Government and Housing Act 1989 requiring each member to give a general notice to the appropriate officer of the authority setting out his direct and indirect pecuniary interests as required: see Local Authorities (Members Interests) Regulations 1992 (SI 1992/618). Section 117 of the 1972 Act provides similar restrictions on officers of an authority having direct or indirect pecuniary interests in any matter before the council.

Local authorities, as contractors, have considerable powers of patronage, and the scope for corruption in the form of bribery of council members, or the solicitation of bribes by council members, is, in theory, considerable.

To deter such activities the Public Bodies Corrupt Practices Act 1889 provides that it is an offence to solicit bribes in return for taking certain action, or refraining from a certain course of action (s1(1)); and similarly that it is an offence to offer bribes: s1(2). The offences encompass both members and officers of local authorities. The Prevention of Corruption Act 1906 extends similar offences to Crown servants.

R v *Bowden* [1995] 4 All ER 505 confirms that, notwithstanding the statutory offences referred to above, a council officer may be prosecuted under the common law offence of misconduct in public office. The appellant, a maintenance manager employed by a local authority, had authorised the carrying out of repair work by employees of the local authority at premises occupied by a friend. The appellant's contention that the common law offence only applied to officers of the Crown, or alternatively that it could only apply to more senior local government officers, was rejected by the court, which held that the common law offence applied to every person who was compensated from public funds for discharging a public duty.

In March 1998 the Law Commission published its proposals for reforming the law relating to corruption: see Law Commission Consultation Paper No 145. If brought into effect the law relating to both the private and public sectors would be affected. The proposals include four new offences: corruptly conferring or offering or agreeing to confer an advantage; corruptly obtaining, soliciting or agreeing to obtain an advantage; corrupt performance by an agent of his or her functions as an agent; and receipt by an agent of a benefit which consists of, or is derived from, an advantage which the agent knows or believes to have been corruptly obtained. An agent would be a person agreeing to perform functions for another person or for the public (other than an MP). Local councillors are specifically included within the definition of agent for these purposes. Corruption would be defined in terms of the state of mind of the provider of the advantage or the recipient. To this end a person would be regarded as corruptly conferring an advantage if it was his intention that the recipient agent should do something, and that if the agent so acts it would probably be in return for the advantage as opposed to some other legitimate factor. A criminal offence would be committed, for example, if it could be shown that a contract was awarded because of the 'corporate hospitality' that had been provided, and that the hospitality was out of all proportion to that which would be normal.

Surcharge and advisory notice

As part of the financial controls exercised over local authorities the District Auditor could, acting pursuant to s20 of the Local Government Finance Act 1982, apply to the High Court for an order that any person responsible for incurring illegal expenditure on the part of the local authority should be required to repay the sum involved. If the sum exceeded £2,000 the court could order the disqualification of a council member. No order could be made if the member acted on the basis of a reasonable belief that that the expenditure was authorised by law. Similarly, a councillor could be surcharged in respect of any failure to bring into account sums due to a local authority, or where a loss had been incurred because of the wilful misconduct of a councillor. Earlier incarnations of the provision were used to notable effect during the 1970s and 1980s in respect of councillors in Clay Cross, Derbyshire, who refused to increase council house rents in accordance with the government's 'Fair Rents' policy (1973); councillors in Lambeth, South London who refused to set a legal rate (1985); and against Labour councillors in Liverpool in 1986: see further *Lloyd* v *McMahon* [1987] AC 625.

The nature of 'wilful misconduct' for these purposes was considered by the House of Lords in *Magill* v *Porter; Weeks* v *Magill; Hartley* v *Magill; England* v *Magill; Phillips* v *Magill* [2002] 2 WLR 37. In May 1986 the Conservative grouping on the City of Westminster council took control. Porter and Weeks were, respectively, the Conservative leader and Conservative deputy leader of the council at the time. The council adopted a policy of 'building stable communities' that involved selling off council-owned properties in addition to sales of properties under the 'right to buy' scheme. Legal advice was obtained indicating that the scheme was lawful and the policy was duly approved by the council's Housing Committee of which Porter and Weeks were not members. The policy of sales was fiercely opposed by Labour councillors who claimed that Porter and Weeks had been seeking to achieve an ulterior motive, ie an increase in the numbers of those moving into marginal wards who would be more likely to vote Conservative. The district auditor investigated claims of abuse of power and concluded, pursuant to s20 of the Local Government Finance Act 1982, to the effect that Porter and Weeks, and other councillors, had been guilty of wilful misconduct in pursuing the policy. Lord Bingham, concurring with this finding, observed that what had to be established was that a councillor had deliberately done something which was wrong, knowing it to be wrong or with reckless indifference as to whether or not it was wrong. He accepted that elected politicians could pursue policies that they hoped or expected would be popular with the electorate, and thus boost their chances of re-election at the next opportunity, but could not (as had been the case with Porter and Weeks) exercise a public power in order to promote the electoral advantage of their political party. Significantly the House of Lords rejected the argument that a councillor could hide behind the protection of legal advice when faced with an allegation of wilful misconduct. This perhaps seems a little harsh, but should be seen in the context of the facts of this particular case. The loss to the local authority exceeded £26 million, and the behaviour of the council leader and her deputy was described by Lord Bingham as a deliberate, corrupt, blatant and dishonest misuse of public power that the auditor had been right to stigmatise as disgraceful.

In its third report (see above) the Nolan Committee investigated misconduct in local government and recommended a number of changes. Essentially, the committee contended that criminal sanctions should be retained to deal with instances of corruption, but that surcharging should be abolished, to be replaced with more appropriate disciplinary measures. The surcharging system was seen as being inappropriate, not only because of the disproportionate size of the amounts surcharged, but also because of the district auditor's role as prosecutor, judge and jury in the process. The Committee also suggested that there ought to be constraints over council officers taking up positions with private companies providing council services that have been put out to tender. Section 91 of Part V of the Local Government Act 2000 gives effect to these recommendations by abolishing the system of surcharging errant councillors and replacing it with an 'advisory notice' scheme whereby auditors will be able to seek judicial guidance as to the legality of proposed action. The auditor may issue an advisory notice if he has reason to believe that the local authority or an officer of the authority: is about to make or has made a decision which involves or would involve the body incurring expenditure which is unlawful; is about to take or has begun to take a course of action which, if pursued to its conclusion, would be unlawful and likely to cause a loss or deficiency; or is about to enter an item of account, the entry of which is unlawful. The auditor must give reasons for serving the notice. Once a notice has been served it becomes unlawful for the local authority or one of its officers to make or implement the decision, course of action, or enter the item of account to which the notice relates.

3.6 Local government elections

Elections

Prior to 1992 local government constituency boundaries were established by the Local Government Boundary Commissions for England and Wales. Under the Local

Government Act 1992, the Local Government Commission replaces the Local Government Boundary Commission. The Local Government Commission makes recommendations to the Secretary of State as to structural, electoral or boundary changes. Following the recommendations of the Commission the Secretary of State may make orders concerning the areas of authorities, the establishment of new authorities and the abolition of existing authorities.

County council elections normally take place every four years and all the councillors retire together. Metropolitan district council elections normally take place in each year in which there is no county council election and councillors retire one-third at a time.

In other district councils there is normally an option between all the councillors retiring simultaneously for an election every four years, or the system of one-third retiring at a time in years where there is no county council election. Parish and community council elections take place every four years and all the councillors retire together. London borough council elections take place every four years and all the councillors retire together.

Part IV of the Local Government Act 2000 makes provision for altering the frequency of local government elections and the number of authority members being re-elected at any one time. Section 85 provides for three different schemes: (1) all-out elections, with the whole council being elected once every four years; (2) elections by halves, with half the councillors being elected every other year; and (3) elections by thirds, with one-third of the councillors being elected each year for three years out of four. It is envisaged that this latter model should become the norm as it imposes some form of annual accountability towards the electorate. The Secretary of State is empowered to impose a particular scheme on a local authority.

A register of electors must be prepared each year and is effective for elections occurring in the 12 months commencing 16 February. The register serves both parliamentary and local government elections. The Representation of the People Act 1983, as amended by the Representation of the People Act 2000, provides that a person is eligible to vote at a local government election if: at the qualifying date he has a qualification based on residence or alternatively has a service qualification or a qualification as a merchant seaman or a qualification as a voluntary mental patient; and on the qualifying date and the date of the poll is a Commonwealth citizen or a citizen of the Republic of Ireland, and not suffering from any legal incapacity to vote; and on the date of the poll is of voting age, ie 18 years or over, provided that he is registered as an elector. Unless disqualified, a person is qualified to be elected and to be a member of a local authority if he is a British subject or a citizen of the Republic of Ireland and on the 'relevant day' he is 21 years of age; he is and thereafter continues to be a local government elector for the area of the authority; or he has during the whole of the 12 months preceding that day occupied as owner or tenant any land or other premises in that area; or his principal or only place of work during that 12 months has been in that area; or he has during the whole of those 12 months resided in that area; or in the case of a member of a parish or community council he has during the whole of those 12 months resided either in the parish or community or within three miles of it. The 'relevant day' is the day of nomination and the day of the poll if there is one.

A person is disqualified from being elected or being a member of a local authority if: he holds any paid office or employment (other than that of chairman, vice-chairman or deputy chairman) appointments to which are made or confirmed by the local authority or a committee or sub-committee of the authority, or by a joint board, joint authority or joint committee on which the authority is represented, or by any person who is himself in the employment of the authority; or is a person who has been adjudged bankrupt, or made a composition or arrangement with his creditors; or has within five years before the day of election or since his election been convicted of any offence and has had passed on him any sentence of imprisonment (whether suspended or not) for a period of not less than three months without the option of a fine; or is disqualified from being elected or being a member of that authority under Part III of the Representation of the People Act 1983 (which relates to corrupt or illegal practices); or is disqualified from membership for a specified period by order of the court because of his involvement in expenditure contrary to law; or is disqualified from membership for five years following an auditor's certificate that a loss or deficiency has been caused by his wilful misconduct while a member of a local authority; or holds a politically restricted post under the local authority or any other local authority in Great Britain. The Representation of the People Act 1989 increased fourfold the permitted level of expenses for candidates for local government elections, without altering the limits for parliamentary elections.

Prompted by concerns about very low participation rates in local government elections, s10 of the Representation of the People Act 2000 provides that a local authority may apply for ministerial approval to hold local elections in a manner that differs from the pattern laid down by the 1983 Act in respect of: when, where and how voting at the elections is to take place; how the votes cast at the elections are to be counted; and the sending by candidates of election communications free of charge for postage. The local authority concerned will be required to report to the Secretary of State on the success of the scheme in terms how it has facilitated voting, encouraged an increased turnout and enabled electors to make a more informed choice.

3.7 Control by central government

The whole purpose of local government is that there should be some control over local matters, by locally elected local persons, independent of central government. The extent to which the foregoing is met by reality is open to question. The following examples of central government control indicate all too clearly where real power lies. Many problems seem to arise from the fact that central government is organised along party political lines, as is local government; when the two are of different political beliefs, conflict is inevitable. As local authorities are creatures of statute, the ultimate sanction rests with Parliament in the form of repealing an enabling Act and destroying a local authority by removing its legal personality. As mentioned above, this was the fate that overtook the GLC and the six metropolitan counties in 1986.

Directives, orders, guidance, codes and ministerial approval

Ministers can exercise control and influence over the actions of local authorities by statutory and non-statutory means. For example, wide powers exist under the Local Government Acts 1972, 1999 and 2000 by which ministers can issue statutory orders concerning local authority functions. Many other statutes have within them provisions empowering the relevant minister to take such action as he deems necessary, for example, by issuing a directive to make a local authority conform with a particular policy: see *Secretary of State for Education* v *Tameside Metropolitan Borough Council* [1977] AC 1014 and its aftermath, the Education Act 1976. In *De Falco* v *Crawley Borough Council* [1980] QB 460, where the Secretary of State had issued a code to local authorities on how the Housing (Homeless Persons) Act 1977 Act should be implemented, the Court of Appeal held that, although the code did not have the force of statute, the local authority had to have regard to it in deciding whether a person was 'intentionally homeless'.

In *R* v *Secretary of State for the Environment, ex parte Hackney London Borough Council* (1984) The Times 21 March the local authority applied for a judicial review of the expenditure guidance for 1984–85 issued to it by the Secretary of State, on the ground that such guidance was ultra vires s59 of the Local Government Planning and Land Act 1980. The local authority contended that such guidance was only lawful if it was possible for the recipient authority to comply with it without precluding the reasonable discharge of its statutory duties. It was further argued that it could not, in fact, comply with the guidance and fulfil all its statutory duties. Dismissing the application, the court held that it was open to the Secretary of State to issue spending guidelines which he knew could not be achieved by the local authority, and thus force an increase in rates if he believed that was necessary in order to reduce the level of local authority expenditure. The court felt that the guidance was certainly not unreasonable in the *Wednesbury* sense, as it was clearly the Secretary of State's view that pressure from the ratepayers to reduce council spending was likely to be more effective than pressure from central government. The court felt that it was not equipped to adjudicate on the merits of policies on local government spending.

In other fields, such as town and country planning, it is common practice for the minister to issue circulars to local authorities indicating the view of central government as to how a scheme should be administered, or certain cases dealt with.

Local authorities are empowered to promulgate bye-laws. These will be rules that are local in operation, deemed necessary by the authority in question for the regulation and management of their areas or enterprises. Local authority bye-laws must be made under the seal of the council and submitted to the Secretary of State for approval. Steps must be taken to ensure publicity in the local press and a copy must be available for local inspection.

Default powers

Although the 1972 Act itself contains no overall default power allowing for the Secretary of State to take over the functions of a local authority, many of the statutes imposing duties on the authorities provide for default powers which allow the minister to take over specific functions if this appears necessary. Instances of such default powers being exercised are rare, but see for example the litigation resulting in *Asher* v *Lacey* [1973] 3 All ER 1008 and *Asher* v *Secretary of State for the Environment* [1974] Ch 208, arising out of the refusal of Clay Cross Urban District Council to implement the Housing Finance Act 1972 and increase council house rents. The Secretary of State under ss95–99 of the Act appointed a 'housing commissioner' to take over the authority's functions, and issued a 'default' order against them.

Other forms of control

The Local Commissioners Act 1974 provides for local government 'ombudsmen' in England and Wales, who are empowered to investigate complaints of maladministration by local authorities and can produce a report on their findings. In England and Wales such reports carry no compulsory effect and are often ignored by local authorities: see further Chapter 13.

The Local Government Finance Act 1982 created the Audit Commission, absorbing much of the District Audit Service, which has as its main aims the scrutiny of local government spending to ensure that instances of unlawful, or wasteful, expenditure are brought to light, and the introduction of commercial accounting methods into local government finance to encourage greater cost-effectiveness. In practice the auditing function can be carried out by a district auditor or an approved private accountant auditor. If an auditor discovers what he believes to be evidence that there has been unlawful expenditure he may issue and advisory notice under the Local Government Act 2000: see above.

Finance – raising revenue

Local authorities cannot act without resources. Central government clearly has the power to determine how those resources are to be provided, and in particular what method of local taxation is to be employed in order to raise revenue for local authority functions. The current system is governed by the Local Government

Finance Act 1992 which introduced the council tax as the replacement for the community charge. The council tax represents a move back towards a property-based tax, like the old rating system, with relief available to those who are sole occupants. Each year, in the budget, the government announces the amount that it expects local government to spend in the forthcoming financial year. This figure is known as the Total Standard Spending (TSS). The money received by local authorities from central government is known as Aggregate External Finance (AEF) and comprises three elements: income from uniform business rates (28 per cent of total income), specific grants (11 per cent of total income) and revenue support grant (41 per cent of total income). The remaining 20 per cent of income comes from the council tax levied on householders. The shortfall between the AEF and the TSS has to be funded by local authorities themselves, usually by increasing levels of council tax, or eating into cash reserves. The extent to which local authorities can increase their budgets is limited to levels imposed by the Department of the Environment known as Standard Spending Assessments (SSAs). In political terms these procedures can be useful to central government in that it passes the blame for increased council tax bills to local authorities, unless they are prepared to cut local services. The raising of loans by local authorities has to be sanctioned by the Secretary of State, whose decision may rest upon the government's view as to the desirability of the proposals for which finance is sought.

Finance – achieving best value

The Local Government Act 1999, which came into effect in July 2000, seeks to address the problem of providing local authorities with a degree of financial autonomy whilst maintaining some central government control by introducing the concept of 'best value'. Under s1 of the 1999 Act most major local authorities are designated as 'best value' authorities. Section 3 places local authorities under a duty to make arrangements 'to secure continuous improvement in the way in which its functions are exercised, having regard to a combination of economy, efficiency and effectiveness'.

Whilst local authorities can decide for themselves how to achieve these goals, s4 empowers the Secretary of State to establish performance indicators by which the relative success or failure of each authority in achieving these goals can be assessed. Under s5 each 'best value' authority is under a duty to review its functions to ensure that the goals are being achieved. Each 'best value' authority is required under s6 to adopt a plan for achieving best value for the coming financial year. Each 'best value' authority is subject to a best value audit (s7) and must respond to issues requiring action as identified in any best value audit: s9. As directed by the Secretary of State the Audit Commission may conduct investigations into the running of a 'best value' authority in order to check on compliance. Section 14 of the 1999 Act makes specific provision for inspection of the way in which an authority is administering the payment of housing benefit and council tax, and s15 empowers the Secretary of State to take remedial action where failings are uncovered.

As a corollary of the introduction of 'best value', previous legislation requiring local authorities to put certain types of contract out to competitive tendering have been repealed. Part II of the 1999 Act abolishes the rate-capping powers used by ministers to deal with overspending councils and replaces them with a complex system of budgetary overview whereby the Secretary of State will examine a local authority's budget over a period of time, the degree of local support for high levels of spending and an authority's performance in terms of achieving 'best value'. Where the Secretary of Sate does intervene to deal with overspending or the setting of a high rate of council tax a local authority can given a target budget that must be achieved over a number of years. In Wales the National Assembly for Wales will exercise the powers of the Secretary of State in this regard.

3.8 Powers and duties of local authorities

Local authorities, as public bodies, are subject to the constraints imposed by the ultra vires principle. This means that a local authority cannot act unless it can point to a legal power, express or implied, that justifies the action. Many of the most significant and historic cases in administrative law have concerned the legality of the exercise of discretion by local authorities, whether in respect of the exercise of licensing functions, raising revenue or expenditure. Decisions such as *Associated Provincial Picture Houses* v *Wednesbury Corporation* [1948] 1 KB 223, *Roberts* v *Hopwood* [1925] AC 578, *Prescott* v *Birmingham Corporation* [1955] Ch 210 and *Bromley London Borough Council* v *GLC* [1983] 1 AC 768 provide key examples. For consideration of the ultra vires principle: see further Chapters 5 to 9.

'General powers' under ss111 and 137 of the Local Government Act 1972

Mindful of the fact that rigid adherence to the ultra vires principle could well hinder the perfectly proper exercise of discretion by local authorities, not least in respect of action required to deal with situations not envisaged by Parliament at the time any given power was provided, s111 of the Local Government Act 1972 empowers a local authority to do anything that is calculated to facilitate or is conducive to or incidental to the discharge of any of its functions.

The latitude that such a provision provides was illustrated in *Attorney-General* v *Crayford Urban District Council* [1962] Ch 575. The local authority acted as agents for an insurance company, encouraging its tenants to take out policies covering their household contents. The premiums were collected along with the rent and rates and, after deducting commission, the local authority paid the balance over to the Municipal Mutual Insurance Ltd. The Attorney-General, at the relation of the Prudential Insurance Staff Union, sought a declaration that the authority was acting outside the scope of s111 of the Housing Act 1957 (which was in terms similar to s111 of the 1972 Act) in carrying on this activity. Holding that the conduct of the insurance business was within the powers of the local authority, Lord Evershed MR observed:

> 'It must be the concern, if not the duty, of a local authority to maintain the general quality and standard of its housing estate which it is its duty to provide and to take such steps as may fairly be regarded as prudent to that end, and also so as to ensure, so far as may be, that the rents due to it will be paid and that the council will not be unduly involved in the consequences that would follow from a tenant's failure to pay his rent and observe the ordinary obligations of his tenancy.'

Whilst the usefulness of provisions such as s111 is obvious, the courts will be alive to the possibility that local authorities might invoke its terms to engage in activities that cannot properly be said to be merely ancillary to other legitimate activities. In *McCarthy & Stone Developments Ltd* v *Richmond London Borough Council* [1991] 3 WLR 941 the council had adopted a policy of charging property developers in respect of the cost of handling inquiries relating to speculative development or redevelopment proposals, relying on s111 as authority. The House of Lords held that, in the absence of an express statutory provision, there was no power to levy the charges in question. The requirement of express statutory authority for the raising of revenue is well established (see *Attorney-General* v *Wilts United Dairies* (1921) 37 TLR 884) but, as Lord Lowry observed, s111 could not provide such authority. The House of Lords expressed the view that the mainstream function of the council, as a planning authority, was the consideration and determining of planning applications. The provision of a planning inquiry and consultation service could be authorised by s111 as ancillary to that function, but to suggest that it provided a power to charge for such a service was to claim that it provided the power to engage in activities which were ancillary to an activity which was in itself ancillary to its statutory planning functions. Similarly, in *Hazell* v *Hammersmith and Fulham London Borough Council* [1991] 2 WLR 372, the House of Lords held that, whilst borrowing was a function of the local authority that could be facilitated by reliance upon s111, so-called interest rate swap agreements, being largely speculative in nature, were ultra vires the authority's borrowing powers and could not, therefore, be legitimised by reliance upon s111.

A number of local authorities sought to rely on the terms of s111 in order to circumvent the centrally imposed controls on local authority borrowing and expenditure, particularly in the sphere of public housing. In *Credit Suisse* v *Allerdale Borough Council* [1996] 4 All ER 129 the council had sought to develop a leisure pool complex, for the use of local people and tourists, without imposing any burden on the local taxpayers. Having taken counsel's opinion as to how it might circumvent the tight statutory controls on local government expenditure, the council resolved to created a company (A Ltd), which would borrow money in the commercial market to fund the proposed development. The scheme included plans to build and sell time-share apartments, it being envisaged that the profit from this aspect of the project would offset the cost of building the leisure complex. The plaintiff bank lent A Ltd £6 million in order to finance the project, the loan being underwritten by guarantees provided by the council. In due course sales of the time-share units were considerably lower than anticipated and A Ltd did not have the income to service the loan advanced by the plaintiff bank. In 1990 the council passed a resolution that A Ltd be put into voluntary liquidation. The plaintiff bank's claim to have the loan repaid under the terms of the guarantee was resisted by the council. The Court of Appeal held that, although the Local Government (Miscellaneous Provisions) Act 1976 Act did empower local authorities to provide recreational facilities, it did not expressly empower them to create companies in order to raise capital outside the normal statutory constraints in order to achieve this goal. Nor could any such power be implied under s111 of the Local Government Act 1972. The only borrowing powers implied by s111 had to be borrowing by the local authority itself. As Neill LJ observed:

'The implied powers in s111 do not provide an escape route from the statutory controls. In my view that is clear not only as a matter of principle but also on the construction of s111 itself … [T]he establishment of the company and the giving of the guarantee were part of an ingenious scheme designed to circumvent the no-doubt irksome controls imposed by central government. The council, however, could only do what it was empowered to do by statute. Neither the establishment of the company nor the giving of the guarantee fell within the express or implied powers of the council.'

Regarding the contention that, in declaring the guarantee to be ultra vires, the court would be permitting the council to profit from its own illegality he added:

'I do not consider the present law to be satisfactory. I say nothing about the merits of this case which have not been investigated. But there may be cases where it is beyond argument that a third party has entered into a contract with a public body in ignorance of any procedural defect which may later entitle the public body to claim that the contract was made ultra vires and so reject liability under it. But if, as I believe there to be, there is only one category of ultra vires decisions where a local authority is concerned, I see no room for a judicial discretion.'

Similarly, in *Credit Suisse* v *Waltham Forest London Borough Council* [1996] 4 All ER 176, where the council had taken a 50 per cent interest in a company that would buy and sell houses in order to alleviate the problem of homelessness in the council's area, the Court of Appeal refused to enforce a guarantee given by a local authority in respect of borrowings by the company. The court held that the statutory function under s65 of the Housing Act 1985 was to be discharged within the terms of s69 of that Act. The power to engage in activities that were incidental to, conducive to, or facilitated the discharge of other functions did not implicitly empower the council to enter into contracts of indemnification on behalf of a limited company. See further *Morgan Grenfell & Co Ltd* v *Sutton London Borough Council* (1996) The Times 7 November, where the court refused to enforce a guarantee provided by the local authority in the event of a housing association failing to repay a loan advanced by the plaintiff bank. Again the court reaffirmed the principle that where Parliament had made detailed statutory provision as to how certain local authority functions were to be discharged there was no scope for implying additional powers outwith that statutory scheme.

The promotion of economic, social or environmental well-being under the Local Government Act 2000

Under s137 of the Local Government Act 1972 local authorities were given a margin of discretion to spend up to the product of a 2p rate on purposes for which they had no other express statutory power and which they considered to be in the interests of their area. The provision was narrowly construed and proved to be ineffective in many cases. Part I of the Local Government Act 2000 aims to return the initiative to local authorities in deciding what is best for their areas. Under s2 a local authority is empowered to do anything which it considers will achieve any one or more of the following objects in respect of its area: improvement of economic well-being; the promotion or improvement of social well-being; or the promotion or improvement of environmental well-being.

A local authority is empowered to incur expenditure for this purpose and can enter into the necessary agreements to give effect to its plans. A local authority must also have a strategy for promoting these goals: see s4. At first blush the power seems very wide-ranging and a far cry from the narrowly interpreted s137 of the 1972 Act. Buried within the details, however, are a number of significant limitations, notably s3(1) which provides that s2 does not enable a local authority to do anything which it is unable to do by virtue of any prohibition, restriction or limitation on its powers in any enactment. Nor does the power under s2 enable a local authority to raise money. The Secretary of State may also, by order, make provision preventing local authorities from doing, by virtue of s2(1), anything that is specified in any such order. To assist local authorities the Secretary of State is empowered under s5 to amend, repeal, revoke or disapply any enactment if he is of the opinion that it has the effect of preventing local authorities from properly exercising their powers under s2. In effect s137 of the 1972 Act is now only of relevance to parish or community councils: see further s8.

4

Tribunals and Inquiries

4.1   Introduction to tribunals

4.2   Tribunal functions

4.3   Tribunal constitution and membership

4.4   Tribunal procedure

4.5   Challenging tribunal decisions in the courts

4.6   The Council on Tribunals

4.7   Future reform of the tribunal system: the Leggatt Report

4.8   Introduction to inquiries

4.9   Inquiry procedures

4.10 The role of the minister

4.11 Problems arising from the use of inquiries

4.1 Introduction to tribunals

Tribunals were conceived principally as an alternative form of dispute resolution. Parliament enacts legislation giving effect to a particular policy aim, perhaps the setting up of a welfare scheme, licensing or rent regulation. The legislation provides for the setting up of tribunals for the resolution of disputes arising from the operation of the scheme. Such disputes could obviously be left to be resolved by the courts, but in many cases Parliament views it as inappropriate for such problems to be dealt with by means of full-scale litigation, with all its attendant drawbacks. Since 1945 there has been a proliferation of administrative tribunals dealing with many aspects of public life, this proliferation largely mirroring the changing role of the state in modern society.

Since the early part of the twentieth century concern had been growing about the scope and power of the administration; the report on Ministers Powers (1932) (see Chapter 2, section 2.2) evidenced this. Little came of that report, however, and it was not until the post-war period that any thoroughgoing review of administrative processes was initiated. Particular concern existed regarding the independence of many tribunals, and also the extent to which their decisions were beyond the control of the courts. Similarly, with inquiries, there was widespread dissatisfaction with procedures adopted and ministerial responses to inspectors' reports. The response of the government was the setting up of a committee under Sir Oliver Franks to review the operation of such bodies (hereinafter referred to as the Franks Committee). Its report was published in 1957 (Cmnd 218, hereinafter referred to as the Franks Report). The Franks Committee explained its own scope of reference as follows:

'Our terms of reference involve the consideration of an important part of the relationship between the individual and authority. At different times in the history of this country it has been necessary to adjust this relationship and to seek a new balance between private rights and public advantage between fair play for the individual and efficiency of administration. The balance found has varied with different governmental systems and different social patterns. Since the war the British electorate has chosen governments that have accepted general responsibilities for the provision of extended social services and for the broad management of the economy. It has consequently become desirable to consider afresh the procedures by which the rights of individual citizens can be harmonised with wider public interests.' (Part 1: Chapter 2, para 5.)

The Franks Committee was subsequently criticised for confining its investigation to procedures that were basically sound anyway. As the Committee stated in its own report (Chapter 2, para 9), it was concerned only with decisions subject to some statutory procedure – not decisions where no formal procedure was prescribed. Such an approach is criticised because many of the most important administrative decisions affecting the individual's rights and liberties were taken without any formal statutory procedure having to be followed; by adopting these narrow terms of reference the Franks Committee inevitably shut its eyes to those aspects of administrative decision-making most in need of scrutiny.

As the Committee itself observed:

'It follows therefore that the celebrated case of Crichel Down, which is widely regarded as a principal reason for our appointment, itself in fact falls outside the subjects with which we have been asked to deal. It is true that an enquiry was held in this case, but it was an ad hoc enquiry for which there was no statutory requirement. It resulted from the exercise of those informal methods of raising objection to which we have referred, and was therefore unlike the enquiries with which we are concerned.'

The Committee affirmed its view that in laying down procedures for tribunals, Parliament was assumed to be seeking to promote good administration and public confidence in the decisions of tribunals. The Committee's Report states:

'Administration must not only be efficient in the sense that the objectives of policy are securely attained without delay. It must also satisfy the general body of citizens that it is proceeding with reasonable regard to the balance between the public interest which it promotes and the private interest which it disturbs ... adjudications must be acceptable as having been properly made. It is natural that Parliament should have taken this view of what constitutes good administration. In this country government rests fundamentally upon the consent of the governed. The general acceptability of these adjudications is one of the vital elements in sustaining that consent.'

Openness, fairness and impartiality were identified by the Committee as essential characteristics of tribunal procedures. As the Report states:

'Take openness. If these procedures were wholly secret, the basis of confidence and acceptability would be lacking. Next take fairness. If the objector were not allowed to state his case, there would be nothing to stop oppression. Thirdly, there is impartiality. How can the citizen be satisfied unless he feels that those who decide his case come to their decision with open minds?

Difference in the nature of the issue for adjudication may give good reason for difference in the degree to which the three general characteristics should be developed and applied. Again, the method by which a Minister arrives at a decision after a hearing or enquiry cannot be the same as that by which a tribunal arrives at a decision. This difference is brought out later in the Report. For the moment it is sufficient to point out that when Parliament sets up a tribunal to decide cases, the adjudication is placed outside the Department concerned. The members of the tribunal are neutral and impartial in relation to the policy of the Minister, except insofar as that policy is contained in the rules which the tribunal has been set up to apply. But the Minister, deciding in the cases under the second part of our terms of reference, is committed to a policy which he has been charged by Parliament to carry out. In this sense he is not, and cannot be, impartial.'

The Committee concluded that tribunals were not to be viewed as courts of law, but neither were they to be regarded as appendages of government departments. It seems clear from the tenor of its Report, however, that the Committee saw tribunals as being closer to courts than to the machinery of administration. There was no evidence found of partiality among tribunal members, and the Committee was satisfied with the degree of independence from central government, but it did recommend the appointment of chairman to be the responsibility of the Lord Chancellor, and that chairmen should ordinarily be legally qualified. On this issue the Report provides:

'We appreciate the force of the contention that all appointments to tribunals should be made by the Lord Chancellor so as to demonstrate clearly the intention that tribunals should be wholly independent of departmental influence. But we feel that the best practical course would be for the responsibility of the Lord Chancellor for such appointments not to be extended beyond the chairman, though we consider that he should retain his present responsibility for appointing members of certain tribunals and that there may be scope for extending this responsibility to a few other tribunals.

Although we are unable to recommend that all members of tribunals should be appointed by the Lord Chancellor we are satisfied that their appointment should not rest with the Ministers concerned with the subject matter of the adjudications. In order to enhance the independence of tribunals, both in appearance and in fact, we consider that the Council on Tribunals should make these appointments. We see no need for the Council to review any existing appointments.'

The Committee rejected the proposal that clerks to tribunals should be drawn from a newly created corps of clerks under the Lord Chancellor's Department, the reasoning being that a career structure might be difficult to create for such persons. Given that the role of the clerk can be very influential, and that they are frequently seconded from relevant government departments, thus giving rise to doubts as to their impartiality, this reasoning of the Committee has always seemed difficult to support. The Report provides:

'The practice whereby the majority of clerks of tribunals are provided by the Government Departments concerned from their local and regional staffs seems partly to be responsible for the feeling in the minds of some people that tribunals are dependent upon and influenced by those Departments. Not only for this reason but also because there would appear to be advantages in improving the general quality of tribunal clerks we have considered the possibility of establishing under the Lord Chancellor's Department a central corps of clerks from which a service could be provided for all tribunals.

Though this idea has many attractions we have, after careful consideration, rejected it. It would have the advantage of further enhancing the independence of tribunals, and it would be more appropriate for independent clerks to advise and help applicants than for departmental clerks to do so. The main objection is that it is difficult to see how any reasonable prospect of a career could be held out to the members of such a general service. It would also be difficult to arrange sittings for the various tribunals in one area in such a way that the clerks were fully occupied and the tribunals could meet when most convenient to the members. Finally, it would no longer be possible for the social service Departments to give some members of their staff a period of service as clerks of tribunals which is doubtless valuable in developing the outlook appropriate to the administration of a social service.

We therefore consider that the present arrangements for providing clerks of tribunals should continue. In order, however, to ensure that departmental clerks cannot exercise a departmental influence upon tribunals, we regard it as essential that their duties and conduct should be regulated on the advice of the Council on Tribunals. The general principles to be followed are that the duties of a clerk should be confined to secretarial work, the taking of such notes of evidence as may be required and the tendering of advice, when requested, on points connected with the tribunal's functions. Like a magistrates' clerk he should be debarred from retiring with the tribunal when they consider their decision, unless he is sent for to advise on a specific point.'

The Report made no effective recommendations as to standardisation of procedures at tribunals, which is possibly one of its major failings. On the need for a more informal atmosphere at tribunal hearings, the Report stated:

'Informality without rules of procedure may be positively inimical to right adjudication, since the proceedings may well assume an unordered character which makes it difficult, if not impossible, for the tribunal properly to sift the facts and weigh the evidence. It should here be remembered that by their very nature tribunals may well be less skilled in adjudication than courts of law. None of our witnesses would seek to make tribunals in all respects like courts of law, but there is a wide measure of agreement that in many instances their procedure could be made more orderly without impairing the desired informality of atmosphere. The object to be aimed at in most tribunals is the combination of a formal procedure with an informal atmosphere. We see no reason why this cannot be achieved. On the one hand it means a manifestly sympathetic attitude on the part of the tribunal and the absence of the trappings of a court, but on the other hand such prescription of procedure as makes the proceedings clear and orderly.'

The Committee was of the view that proceedings should be in public wherever possible, in camera sessions only being necessary in cases involving national security, financial details personal to the individual involved, or the professional reputation of the individual. Where possible the Committee felt that reasons should be given for a tribunal's decision, preferably in writing. The Committee generally favoured the proposition that each tribunal should have an appellate body to deal with appeals on fact, law or merits, save where the tribunal of first instance was exceptionally well qualified, and was firmly of the opinion that appeal on a point of law should lie from all tribunal decisions to the High Court.

Reaction to the Franks Report

The achievements of the Franks Committee should not be underestimated. Most, if not all, of its recommendations were implemented, albeit in a substantially modified form in some cases, and the details of these reforms are given, where appropriate, in the sections that follow. In addition to addressing the constitutional and procedural aspects of the work of tribunals and inquiries, however, the Franks Committee is largely responsible for the creation of the Council on Tribunals, a body having a potentially important supervisory role.

4.2 Tribunal functions

The tasks performed by tribunals can, to a large extent, be divided into two categories. The resolution of disputes between the individual and the state, and the resolution of disputes between private individuals. Examples of the former include Mental Health Review Tribunals, entrusted with the task of reviewing the continued detention of persons suffering from mental disorders, where they have been made the subject of a compulsory hospital attendance order; various National Health Service Tribunals dealing with such diverse matters as complaints against general practitioners, and other matters relating to services provided by National Health Service personnel; and Income Tax Commissioners dealing with disputed assessments of liability to pay taxation. A par excellence example of the latter is the Employment Tribunal, the jurisdiction of which extends to matters such as unfair dismissal, sex discrimination in employment, redundancy payments, and health and safety at work issues.

In entrusting decision-making to a tribunal, Parliament will have made a conscious choice between various other methods of dispute resolution. Where the problem is one of resolving disputes between individuals and government departments, the task could be carried out by a minister (or more realistically a civil servant acting on his behalf) exercising his discretion, but only by sacrificing impartiality. The individual concerned would, quite legitimately, feel that the minister was bound to suffer from 'pro-departmental bias'. As an alternative, such disputes could be left to be resolved by the courts, but for a number of reasons tribunals are likely to be more suitable. Many disputes before tribunals require swift resolution. The delays attendant upon litigation are well known. A claimant seeking a welfare benefit clearly cannot wait months to have the validity of his claim determined. The tribunal procedure should involve far less expense than going to court. Savings result partly from the speed and brevity of proceedings, partly from the reduced role played by lawyers, and partly from the fact that the schemes will be financed by central government. By promoting an atmosphere less formal than that to be found in courts of law, tribunals hope to encourage individuals to represent themselves. The extent to which this has been achieved, or is indeed desirable, is debatable. In normal court proceedings, a considerable amount of time is taken up presenting expert evidence, simply to explain to the trial judge the complex issues involved. Tribunals have an advantage in that members can be appointed who have an expert knowledge of the subject matter raised in disputes brought before them. For example, persons with knowledge of the social services, local property values or industrial relations. Although not courts of law, tribunals are, in theory, independent of government departments who may be party to disputes before them. Regardless of the reality of the situation, an important factor is the impression made upon the individual bringing his case before the tribunal; it must at least appear to be separate from government.

Workload

The following statistics, derived from the annual report of the Council on Tribunals for 2000/2001, provide a 'snapshot' of the workload of certain key tribunals under the direct supervision of the Council on Tribunals.

Tribunal	Cases received 2001	Cases decided 2001	Cases received 2000	Cases decided 2000
Parking Adjudicators	40,441	30,472	42,279	31,933
Employment Tribunals	107,357	28,808	114,983	31,016
Valuation Tribunals	760,483	34,482	798,973	36,199
Appeals Service	236,251	151,290	274,472	178,521
Schools Admissions Appeals Panels	66,555	43,978	89,182	62,655
Rent Assessment Panels	10,020	8,185	10,476	8,542
General Commissioners of Income Tax	72,787	12,739	78,746	13,905
Mental Health Review Tribunal	20,421	11,266	21,461	11,833
Traffic Commissioners	8,531	7,899	9,971	9,308

4.3 Tribunal constitution and membership

As regards those tribunals listed in Sch 1 to the Tribunal and Inquiries Act 1992, the procedure for the appointment of tribunal chairman is set out in the 1992 Act itself. Section 5(1) provides that the Council on Tribunals may make to the appropriate minister general recommendations as to the making of appointments to membership of any tribunals. The minister is required to have regard to the recommendations. By virtue of s6(1), the chairman will be selected from a panel of persons appointed by the Lord Chancellor.

Under s7(1), the power of a minister, other than the Lord Chancellor, to terminate a person's membership of any tribunal can only be exercised with the consent of the Lord Chancellor. Terms and conditions of service vary with the enabling Act.

Note in this regard the recommendations of the Franks Committee:

'There has been substantial agreement among witnesses that at any rate the majority of chairmen of tribunals should have legal qualifications. We attach great importance to the quality of chairmanship. Objectivity in the treatment of cases and the proper sifting of facts are most often best secured by having a legally qualified chairman, though we recognise that suitable chairmen can be drawn from fields other than the law. We therefore recommend that chairmen of tribunals should ordinarily have legal qualifications but that the appointment of persons without legal qualifications should not be ruled out when they are particularly suitable.

It is impossible, we think, to lay down any such general desideratum in the case of members because of the wide variety of experience that has to be drawn on for the different tribunals. Such evidence as we have received indicates that the quality of members is on the whole satisfactory, and we have ourselves no general proposals to make with regard to their qualifications. The new arrangements which we have recommended for the appointment of members will maintain and may well improve their quality.'

The coming into effect of the Human Rights Act 1998 may call for a reassessment of the extent to which current arrangements for the appointment of tribunal members are consistent with the European Convention on Human Rights. Under art 6 an individual has the right to have a determination as to his civil rights and obligations determined by an independent and impartial tribunal. In *Smith* v *Secretary of State for Trade and Industry* (1999) The Times 15 October the Employment Appeal Tribunal highlighted a number of factors that might support a claim under art 6 where the respondent in the employment tribunal hearing was the Secretary of State. These were the fact that: the lay members of the tribunal were appointed and paid by the Secretary of State; the terms of appointment were laid down by and could be varied by the Secretary of State; and the remuneration of the tribunal chairman was determined by the Secretary of State who also determined the rules of procedure.

Constitution of tribunals

A tribunal will normally comprise a legally qualified chairman and two members able to represent a range of relevant interests. For example, as is the case with employment tribunals, the interests of trade unions on the one hand and employers on the other. Unless statute provides otherwise, a tribunal may determine a question by a majority decision. A decision will normally be arrived at by all members meeting together. Indeed a failure to do so can render a decision a nullity; see *R v Department of Health, ex parte Bhaugeerutty* (1998) The Times 1 May. The courts might, however, be willing to overlook apparent procedural irregularities where the evidence indicates that all three tribunal members agree, and there is no statutory requirement that they physically meet together to consider their decision: see *R v Greater Manchester Valuation Panel, ex parte Shell Chemicals UK Ltd* [1982] 1 QB 255. Frequently a panel of potential members is drawn up and they serve in rotation. Depending on the nature of the tribunal, sittings may be local, regional or national.

The clerks to tribunals and other administrative staff connected with a tribunal will usually be civil servants, frequently members of the government department that is a party to the disputes before the tribunal, a matter that has raised questions as to apparent impartiality.

4.4 Tribunal procedure

Great progress has been made towards a standardisation of tribunal procedure. Although, in theory, an Act providing for a tribunal can specify a particular procedure to be followed (usually as designated in delegated legislation made by the relevant minister or authority), the trend is towards following a model procedure. Section 8 of the Tribunals and Inquiries Act 1992 provides that the Council on Tribunals should be consulted when procedural rules are being devised. The Council on Tribunals has also published its *Model Rules of Procedure for Tribunals* (Cmnd 1434) (1991). The Human Rights Act 1998, at s7(11), further provides that:

> 'The Minister who has power to make rules in relation to a particular tribunal may, to the extent he considers it necessary to ensure that the tribunal can provide an appropriate remedy in relation to an act (or proposed act) of a public authority which is (or would be) unlawful as a result of s6(1), by order add to –
> (a) the relief or remedies which the tribunal may grant; or
> (b) the grounds on which it may grant any of them.'

Public hearings

The Franks Committee regarded openness as one of the three essential features of the satisfactory working of tribunals. It was therefore of the view that tribunal proceedings should normally be held in public. The Report stated:

> 'We are in no doubt that if adjudicating bodies, whether courts or tribunals, are to inspire that confidence in the administration of justice which is a condition of civil liberty they should, in general, sit in public. But just as on occasion the courts are prepared to try certain types of case wholly or partly in camera so, in the wide field covered by tribunals, there are occasions on which we think that justice may be better done, and the interests of the citizen better served, by privacy.
>
> The first type of case is where considerations of public security are involved. Such cases are not often likely to arise before tribunals, but provision should be included in the codes of procedure for enabling a tribunal to sit in private on this type of case.
>
> The more frequent type of case in which privacy is desirable is that in which intimate personal or financial circumstances have to be disclosed. Few people would doubt the wisdom of the practice whereby hearings before the General and Special Commissioners of Income Tax are held in private in order that details of taxpayer's affairs shall not become public knowledge ... Another case in which the privacy of proceedings is justified is the hearing at which a medical examination of the applicant may take place.
>
> A third type of case in which privacy is on balance desirable is that involving professional capacity and reputation where the machinery includes provision for a preliminary and largely informal hearing before any decision is made to institute formal proceedings which may involve penalties ... Accordingly we recommend that where a tribunal is of a class which has to deal almost exclusively with any of these three types of case the hearing should continue to be in private. In the case of all other classes of tribunal, however, the hearing should be in public, subject to a discretionary power in the chairman to exclude the public should he think that a particular case involves any of these considerations.'

The power to sit in camera is addressed in the procedural rules as devised for each tribunal. Prior to September 1994 hearings of the Special Commissioners of Income Tax were held in private, because of the desire to maintain confidentiality concerning taxpayers' wealth. Revised procedural rules now ensure that the hearings are open to the public. The fundamental importance of public access to tribunals is reflected in the Court of Appeal's ruling in *Storer* v *British Gas plc* [2000] 2 All ER 440. The appellant, S, brought proceedings against his former employer for constructive dismissal. Because he brought the claim outside the three-month time limit it was necessary for him to show that it had not been reasonably practicable for him to have brought his claim within that time limit. The employment tribunal chairman, sitting alone, had ruled that there should be no extension of time in the appellant's favour. Because of the shortage of courtroom accommodation this hearing took place in the office of the regional chairman, a secure area protected by a push-button, coded lock on the door. On appeal the appellant raised the point that the first instance hearing had not been held in public – as required by reg 8(2) of Sch 1 to the Industrial Tribunal (Constitution and Rules of Procedure) Regulations 1993. The Employment Appeal Tribunal accepted that the hearing had been held in a secure part of the building but also accepted that no member of the public had been prevented from entering, but the Court of Appeal rejected this contention. Citing with approval Bentham's view that 'publicity was the soul of justice', the Court noted that not only had Parliament expressly required a public procedure, it had not legislated for any alternative. The requirement to proceed in public was, therefore, mandatory. The Court rejected the contention that members of the public would have been admitted to the first instance hearing had they so requested. Given its location there was little chance of any member of the public being aware that the hearing was taking place, let alone that they were permitted to enter. As the tribunal had no right to sit in private it had acted without jurisdiction. Note further in this regard the requirement in art 6 of the European Convention on Human Rights, to the effect that hearings regarding the determination of an individual's civil rights should be held in public, subject to certain restrictions.

Natural justice

The common law rules of natural justice apply to tribunals, just as they do to any other administrative body exercising 'quasi-judicial' powers. The extent and content of these rules is detailed in Chapters 5 and 6. Broadly, the common law would require adherence to a number of the following basic principles, to a lesser or greater extent depending on the context of the case. To the extent that these matters are dealt with in the procedural rules laid down for any particular tribunal they can be assumed to have displaced the common law.

A person appearing before a tribunal should be given proper notice of the scheduling of the hearing, and where appropriate adequate notice of the case against him. As the Franks Report notes:

> 'The second most important requirement before the hearing is that citizens should know in good time the case which they will have to meet, whether the issue to be heard by the tribunal is one between citizen and administration or between citizen and citizen. This constituent of fairness is one to which much of the evidence we have received has rightly drawn attention ... We do not suggest that the procedure should be formalised to the extent of requiring documents in the nature of legal pleadings. What is needed is that the citizen should receive in good time beforehand a document setting out the main points of the opposing case. It should not be necessary, and indeed in view of the type of persons frequently appearing before tribunals it would in many cases be positively undesirable, to require the parties to adhere rigidly to the case previously set out, provided always that the interests of another party are not prejudiced by such flexibility.'

A tribunal should permit legal representation when requested, unless there are compelling policy reasons for excluding it. In reality legal representation is permitted at all tribunals except those hearing complaints against NHS practitioners, largely because doctors will almost always be able to afford representation, whilst those appearing against them will not. Frequently individuals are represented by friends, family, trade union officials and so on. Publicly funded assistance for legal representation before tribunals is normally only available in the case of the Lands

Tribunal, Employment Appeal Tribunal or Commons Commissioners, although some limited assistance is available in respect of proceedings before Mental Health Review Tribunals. Legal advice may be available to help an individual prepare his case for presentation before a tribunal.

Each party should be permitted to put its case, calling and cross-examining witnesses as appropriate. Tribunals are generally not bound by the strict rules of evidence. In *R* v *Deputy Industrial Injuries Commissioner, ex parte Moore* [1965] 1 QB 456 Diplock LJ observed:

> '... "evidence" is not restricted to evidence which would be admissible in a court of law. For historical reasons, based on the fear that juries who might be illiterate would be incapable of differentiating between the probative values of different methods of proof, the practice of the common law courts has been to admit only what the judges then regarded as the best evidence of any disputed fact, and thereby to exclude much material which, as a matter of common sense, would assist a fact-finding tribunal to reach a correct conclusion ... These technical rules of evidence, however, form no part of the rules of natural justice. The requirement that a person exercising quasi-judicial functions must base his decision on evidence means no more than it must be based upon material which tends logically to show the existence or non-existence of facts relevant to the issue to be determined, or to show the likelihood or unlikelihood of the occurrence of some future event the occurrence of which would be relevant. It means that he must not spin a coin or consult an astrologer, but he may take into account any material which, as a matter of reason, has some probative value in the sense mentioned above. If it is capable of having any probative value, the weight to be attached to it is a matter for the person to whom Parliament has entrusted the responsibility of deciding the issue. The supervisory jurisdiction of the High Court does not entitle it to usurp this responsibility and to substitute its own view for his.'

See further *Mahon* v *Air New Zealand Ltd* [1984] 3 All ER 201 (PC). Tribunal members are, of course, frequently appointed on the basis of their expertise, and they can rely on their own knowledge to determine an issue, even though the parties themselves have not referred to this information. The vital point is that if a tribunal chairman wishes to rely on evidence not adduced by the parties, he must inform them of this, and invite their representations upon it. In *Kavanagh* v *Chief Constable of Devon and Cornwall* [1974] 1 QB 624 the Court of Appeal held that when a Crown Court was considering K's appeal against the chief constable's refusal of a firearms certificate under the Firearms Act 1968, it was acting in an administrative capacity, and as such the normally strict rules of evidence could be relaxed, permitting the chief constable to put forward hearsay evidence to support his decision. As Lord Denning MR observed:

> 'It seems to me that the Crown Court is in the same position as the court of quarter sessions ... justices never held themselves bound by the strict rules of evidence. They acted on any material that appeared to be useful in coming to a decision, including their own knowledge. No doubt they admitted hearsay, though there is nothing to be found in the books about it. To bring the procedure up to modern requirements, I think they should act on the same lines as any administrative body which is charged with an inquiry.

They may receive any material which is logically probative even though it is not evidence in a court of law. Hearsay can be permitted where it can fairly be regarded as reliable.'

See further *T A Miller Ltd* v *Minister of Housing and Local Government* [1968] 1 WLR 992 and *Dugdale* v *Kraft Foods Ltd* [1977] ICR 48. At present only a limited number of tribunals have the power to administer the oath and receive sworn evidence. The Law Commission has recommended that all tribunals should have a discretion to accept sworn evidence where appropriate. It should be noted that this may be at the expense of informality.

Precedent

A system of precedent can only operate if decisions are reported. At present there is only a limited system of reporting tribunal decisions at first instance. Various appeal tribunals have their decisions more widely published in specialist reports. Selected decisions of the Social Security Commissioner, and of the Lands Tribunal, are available, but even then are only persuasive, not binding, on future cases. Tribunals clearly have to follow previous decisions of courts of law. The Council on Tribunals has shown itself to be in favour of the more important tribunal decisions being reported, as this would be a major aid in promoting consistency in decision-making.

Human Rights Act 1998

By virtue of s7 of the Human Rights Act 1998:

'... a person who claims that a public authority has acted (or proposes to act) in a way which is made unlawful by s6(1) may ... bring proceedings against the authority under this Act in the appropriate court or tribunal, or rely on the Convention right or rights concerned in any legal proceedings ...'

Hence, since October 2000, the protection of Convention rights (ie rights protected by arts 2–12 and 14 of the Convention, arts 1–3 of the First Protocol and arts 1 and 2 of the Sixth Protocol) has become an issue that can be asserted in proceedings before a tribunal. This means that in arriving at its determination a tribunal has to have regard to the jurisprudence of the European Court of Human Rights, in particular any '(a) judgment, decision, declaration or advisory opinion of the European Court of Human Rights, (b) opinion of the Commission given in a report adopted under art 31 of the Convention, (c) decision of the Commission in connection with arts 26 or 27(2) of the Convention, or (d) decision of the Committee of Ministers taken under art 46 of the Convention' (see s2(1), to the extent that the tribunal considers it relevant to the proceedings in which that question has arisen).

The tribunal's duty is to read and give effect to primary legislation and subordinate legislation in such a way as is compatible with the Convention rights (insofar as this is possible). This duty applies regardless of whether the primary legislation and subordinate legislation was enacted before or after the introduction of the Human Rights Act 1998: see s3 of the 1998 Act.

If a tribunal finds that a public authority has acted unlawfully, as that term is understood in the context of the 1998 Act, 'it may grant such relief or remedy, or make such order, within its powers as it considers just and appropriate': see s8(1).

Privilege

Proceedings in courts of law are normally protected by absolute privilege, so that no action can be brought for defamation in respect of anything said during a trial. Whether proceedings before tribunals are similarly protected depends, to some extent, on the nature of the hearing. *Trapp* v *Mackie* [1979] 1 All ER 489 establishes that absolute privilege can apply, although there is no one factor that is conclusive in this regard. Lord Diplock identified the factors that would be persuasive as being whether:

1. the tribunal was authorised by law, ie constituted pursuant to an Act of Parliament;
2. the tribunal was inquiring into an issue in dispute between adverse parties of a kind similar to issues that commonly fall to be decided by courts of justice;
3. the hearing was held in public;
4. decisions as to what oral evidence should be led, and what documents should be tendered or their production called for by the adverse party were left to the contending parties;
5. witnesses whom either of the adverse parties wished to call were compellable, under penal sanctions, to give oral evidence or to produce documents, and were entitled to the same privilege to refuse to answer a question or to produce a document as would apply if the inquiry were a proceeding in a court of law;
6. the oral evidence was give upon oath;
7. witnesses who gave oral testimony were subject to examination-in-chief and re-examination by the party calling them and to cross-examination by the adverse party, in accordance with the normal procedure of courts of law;
8. the adverse parties were entitled to be, and were in fact, represented by legally qualified advocates or solicitors and these were given the opportunity of addressing the tribunal on the evidence that had been led;
9. the decision of the tribunal was conclusive, as opposed to advisory;
10. expenses were recoverable in the same manner as expenses incurred in a civil action in a court of law.

In *Daniels* v *Griffiths* (1997) The Times 2 December the Court of Appeal held that, whilst communications between the victim of a crime and the Parole Board would attract qualified privilege, it would be inappropriate, given the history and status of the Parole Board, to extend the protection of absolute privilege to such communications.

Contempt

As with the issue of absolute privilege, the extent to which proceedings before a tribunal will be protected by the law of contempt will also vary depending upon the nature and constitution of the tribunal. The fact that a body may have the word 'court' as part of its nomenclature will not to be regarded as decisive of the matter; the courts will take into account the history and pedigree of the body in question: see *Attorney-General* v *BBC* [1981] AC 303, where the House of Lords held that a Valuation Court was not a 'court of law' within the terms of the Contempt of Court Act 1981.

In *Pickering* v *Liverpool Daily Post and Echo Newspapers plc and Others* [1991] 2 WLR 513 the House of Lords accepted that a Mental Health Review Tribunal was a court of law for the purposes of s19 of the Contempt of Court Act 1981, on the basis that it had the power to subpoena witnesses and make decisions affecting the liberty of individuals. Note that Lord Donaldson MR, in the Court of Appeal, had thought it significant that the European Convention on Human Rights required the lawfulness of an individual's detention to be determined by a court, and that if the tribunal was not to be regarded as a court, art 5(4) of the European Convention was not being complied with, a view endorsed by the House of Lords.

Perhaps the most useful checklist of factors that will determine whether or not the 1981 Act will apply to a tribunal's proceedings was provided in *Peach Grey & Co (A Firm)* v *Sommers* [1995] 2 All ER 513, a case involving alleged interference with witnesses due to appear before an Employment Tribunal. In confirming that the tribunal's proceedings were protected by contempt, the court indicated that it was persuaded by the fact that it was presided over by a legally qualified person; sat in public; decided cases affecting the rights of parties; could compel the attendance of witnesses; could administer the oath; heard from parties permitted legal representation; had to give reasons for its decisions; and made decisions which could be taken on appeal, on a point of law, to the Employment Appeal Tribunal. Note the extent to which these are the same factors that relate to whether or not proceedings attract absolute privilege.

The giving of reasons

Unless special reasons exist, one is entitled to cast doubt on the merits of a decision for which reasons will not be provided. At common law, failure to give reasons may amount to a breach of natural justice, and be remediable by way of judicial review. The view of the Franks Committee as evidenced in its Report was expressed thus:

> 'We are convinced that if tribunal proceedings are to be fair to the citizen reasons should be given to the fullest practicable extent. A decision is apt to be better if the reasons for it have to be set out in writing because the reasons are then more likely to have been properly thought out. Further, a reasoned decision is essential in order that where there is a right of appeal, the applicant can assess whether he has good grounds of appeal and know the case he will have to meet if he decides to appeal.'

If a tribunal is listed in Sch 1 to the Tribunals and Inquiries Act 1992 it is, by virtue of s10 of that Act, under a duty to give reasons for its decisions if requested to do so. Reasons may by refused, or the specification of the reasons restricted, on grounds of national security, and a tribunal may refuse to furnish reasons to a person not primarily concerned with the decision, or if of the opinion that to furnish it would be contrary to the interests of any person primarily concerned. Any reasons that are provided become, by virtue of s10(6), part of the decision and accordingly are regarded as having been incorporated in the record.

The reasons given must be sufficient and adequate in the context of the decision; see *Mountview Court Properties Ltd* v *Devlin* (1970) 21 P & Cr 689. In *Elliot* v *Southwark LBC* [1976] 2 All ER 781, James L J stated obiter that:

> 'The duty to give reasons pursuant to statute (was) a responsible one and (could not) be discharged by the use of vague general words ...'

Generally, the reasons given should indicate the important points in the decision; demonstrate that the mind of the decision-maker has been directed to these points; show what view he has taken on these points; and be clear and intelligible. If the duty to give reasons is not complied with, the courts may order the tribunal to produce them by way of a mandatory order.

4.5 Challenging tribunal decisions in the courts

In many cases where a tribunal has been created by statute, provision will also have been made for an appellate tribunal to consider appeals. Appeals can deal either with a mixture of fact and law, or appeal may only be available on a point of law. Where appeal is available against findings of fact and law there is in effect a complete rehearing of the case, and the appellate tribunal can uphold the decision at first instance, or quash it and substitute its own. Clearly appeal on a point of law is more limited. A problem arises where no provision is made for appeals to be heard, as there is no common law right to appeal against a tribunal's decision; it is only possible where statute so provides. A situation may arise, therefore, where an individual is dissatisfied with a tribunal's determination on a point of fact, and in the absence of any right to appeal, or perhaps only being able to appeal on a point of law, the tribunal's decision is unchallengeable – subject to what is said about judicial review, below. The Franks Report recommended that there should always be a right of appeal, but this has not been implemented. Where an enabling Act does provide for an appeal, however, this should be an individual's first resort.

Appeal on a point of law to the High Court

If a tribunal is listed in Sch 1 to the Tribunals and Inquiries Act 1992, s11 provides that an appeal will lie to the High Court on a point of law. A Sch 1 listing is therefore obviously a useful safeguard where no appellate body is provided. Section 11 provides (inter alia):

'... if any party to proceedings before any tribunal specified [in] Sch 1 is dissatisfied in point of law with a decision of the tribunal he may, according as rules of court may provide, either appeal from the tribunal to the High Court or require the tribunal to state and sign a case for the opinion of the High Court.'

While providing an important avenue of challenge to a tribunal decision, there remains a problem of identifying a 'point of law'. It is not possible to provide a categorical definition, but it would appear that the courts are willing to take a liberal view, where there is a desire to intervene. As H W R Wade has commented:

'The courts ought ... to guard against any artificial narrowing of the right of appeal on a point of law, which is clearly intended to be a wide and beneficial remedy. Very difficult questions of law have to be determined by many tribunals and for the sake of consistency and fairness it is important that the guidance of the courts should be available.' (*Administrative Law*, 6th ed, p943.)

Examples include *Woodhouse* v *Peter Brotherhood Ltd* [1972] 2 QB 520 (whether there had been a transfer of business for the purposes of the Redundancy Payments Act); *O'Brien* v *Associated Fire Alarms Ltd* [1969] 1 All ER 93 (the construction of a contract of employment held to constitute a point of law); *Lord Advocate* v *Reliant Tool Co Ltd* [1968] 1 All ER 162 (statutory interpretation held to involve a point of law); and *Tandon* v *Trustees of Spurgeon's Homes* [1982] 2 WLR 735 (the question of whether a building constituted a house for the purposes of the Housing Acts was one of law): see further the discussion of this problem in *Edwards* v *Bairstow* [1956] AC 14.

Judicial review

Judicial review is available as a largely residual way of supervising tribunal decision-making where a decision is believed to be ultra vires, for example on the grounds of unreasonableness, or breach of natural justice. Review must be contrasted with appeal. Review is a common law remedy, appeal is only available where statute so provides. An appeal can look into the merits of a decision to determine whether it was 'good' or 'bad'; review is concerned solely with legality – was the decision ultra vires? Finally, as noted earlier, an appeal can result in a first instance decision being quashed, and the appellate body substituting its own decision; review can only quash or remit the decision to be taken again where appropriate. Judicial review is discretionary, as are the remedies thereunder. Review may be refused where Parliament has provided a more suitable channel of challenge to a tribunal's decision, for example a right of appeal to an appellate tribunal or minister, or appeal on a point of law under s11 of the 1992 Act. Parliament may expressly wish to exclude any recourse to the courts by including an 'ouster' clause in the enabling Act: for example, see *Anisminic* v *Foreign Compensation Commission* [1969] 2 AC 147. Such clauses have proved largely unsuccessful in preventing intervention by the courts; the only type to have been in any way effective are the 'partial' ouster clauses that allow a decision to be challenged within a short period of time. In this respect note s12 of the 1992 Act, which provides (as regards England and Wales):

'(a) any provision in an Act passed before 1 August 1958 that any order or determination shall not be called into question in any court, or
(b) any provision in such an Act which by similar words excludes any of the powers of the High Court,
shall not have effect so as to prevent the removal of the proceedings into the High Court by order of certiorari or to prejudice the powers of the High Court to make orders of mandamus.'

Subsection 12(3) states that the section does not apply to any order or determination of a court of law, or where an Act makes special provision for application to the High Court or the Court of Session within a time limited by the Act.

4.6 The Council on Tribunals

In para 43 of the Franks Report, the Committee recommended the setting up of standing councils in England and Scotland 'to keep the constitution and working of tribunals under continuous review'. It further recommended that the councils should be consulted whenever it was proposed to establish a new type of tribunal and should have the power to appoint tribunal members, formulate procedural rules for tribunals and advise on associated matters. The Council on Tribunals was eventually brought to life by the Tribunals and Inquiries Act 1958 (now the 1992 Act). As will be seen, the Council was not blessed with quite the range of powers envisaged by the Franks Committee.

The tribunals and decision-makers under the direct supervision of the Council on Tribunals (as of May 2001) are listed below.

Agriculture/fishing/forestry/food

1. Agricultural Arbitrators appointed (otherwise than by agreement) under Sch 11 to the Agricultural Holdings Act 1986.
2. Agricultural Land Tribunals established under s73 of the Agriculture Act 1947.
3. The Controller of Plant Variety Rights and any officer authorised to exercise the functions of the Controller under Sch 1 to the Plant Varieties Act 1997.
4. The Dairy Produce Quota Tribunal for England and Wales constituted under reg 35(1) of the Dairy Produce Quotas Regulations 1991.
5. Forestry Committees appointed in England and Wales under ss16, 17B, 20, 21 or 25 of the Forestry Act 1967.
6. The Meat Hygiene Appeals Tribunal constituted in accordance with regulations under Pt II of the Food Safety Act 1990.

7. The Plant Varieties and Seeds Tribunal referred to in s42 of the Plant Varieties Act 1997.
8. The Sea Fish Licence Tribunal established under s4AA of the Sea Fish (Conservation) Act 1967.

Competition/fair trading

1. Competition Commission Appeal Tribunals established under s48 of the Competition Act 1998.
2. The Director General of Fair Trading in respect of his functions under the Consumer Credit Act 1974 and the Estate Agents Act 1979, and any member of his staff authorised to exercise those functions under Sch 1 to the Fair Trading Act 1973.

Criminal injuries compensation

1. Criminal Injuries Compensation Appeal Panel adjudicators appointed under s5 of the Criminal Injuries Compensation Act 1995.

Education

1. Admission Appeal Panels constituted in accordance with Sch 24 or para 3 of Sch 25 to the Schools Standards and Framework Act 1998.
2. Exclusion Appeal Panels constituted in accordance with Sch 18 to the Schools Standards and Framework Act 1998.
3. The Independent Schools Tribunal constituted under s476 of, and Sch 34 to, the Education Act 1996.
4. The Registered Inspectors of Schools Tribunal constituted under Sch 2 to the Schools Inspections Act 1996.
5. Schools Adjudicators appointed under Sch 5 of the Schools Standards and Framework Act 1998.
6. The Special Educational Needs Tribunal constituted under s333 of the Education Act 1996.

Employment/industry

1. Employment Tribunals for England, Scotland and Wales established under s1(1) of the Industrial Tribunals Act 1996.
2. The Industrial Arbitration Tribunal established under Sch 3 to the Industry Act 1975.
3. Industrial Training Levy Exemption Referees established by the Industrial Training (Levy Exemption References) Regulations 1974.

4. The Police Appeals Tribunal constituted under the Police Act 1996 and the Police Act 1997.
5. Reserve Forces Appeal Tribunals constituted under Pt IX of the Reserve Forces Act 1986.
6. Reserve Forces Reinstatement Committees and Umpires appointed under Sch 2 to the Reserve Forces (Safeguard of Employment) Act 1985.

Finance/revenue

1. The Banking Appeal Tribunal constituted under s28 of the Banking Act 1987.
2. The Building Societies Appeal Tribunal constituted under s47 of the Building Societies Act 1986.
3. The Financial Services Tribunal established by s96 of the Financial Services Act 1986.
4. The Friendly Societies Appeal Tribunal constituted under s59 of the Friendly Societies Act 1992.
5. General Commissioners of Income Tax (for England, Wales, Scotland and Northern Ireland) acting under s2 of the Taxes Management Act 1970.
6. The Insolvency Practitioners Tribunal referred to in s396 of the Insolvency Act 1986.
7. The National Lottery Commission in respect of its functions under ss10 and 10A of, and Sch 3 to, the National Lottery Act 1993, and any member, employee or committee of that Commission authorised under Sch 2A to that Act to exercise any of those functions.
8. The National Savings Bank and National Savings Stock Register Adjudicator appointed under s84 of the Friendly Societies Act 1992.
9. The s703 Tribunal for the purposes of the Income and Corporation Taxes Act 1988.
10. Special Commissioners of Income Tax appointed under s4 of the Taxes Management Act 1970.
11. VAT and Duties Tribunals for England and Wales established under Sch 12 to the Value Added Tax Act 1994.

Health and social services

1. Health Authority Discipline Committees established under reg 3 of the National Health Service (Service Committee and Tribunal) Regulations 1992 (as amended).
2. Mental Health Review Tribunals constituted or having effect as if constituted under s65 of the Mental Health Act 1983.
3. The National Health Service Tribunal constituted under s46 of the National Health Service Act 1977.
4. Registered Homes Tribunals constituted under Pt III of the Registered Homes Act 1984.

Immigration/asylum

1. Asylum Support Adjudicators established under s102 of the Immigration and Asylum Act 1999.
2. Immigration Adjudicators established under s57 of the Immigration and Asylum Act 1999.
3. The Immigration Appeal Tribunal established under s56 of the Immigration and Asylum Act 1999.
4. The Immigration Services Tribunal established under s87 of the Immigration and Asylum Act 1999.

Information

1. The Information Commissioner appointed under s6 of the Data Protection Act 1998.
2. The Information Tribunal constituted under s6 of the Data Protection Act 1998, and in respect of its jurisdiction under s48 of that Act.

Land/housing

1. Commons Commissioners and Assessors appointed under s17(2) and (3) of the Commons Registration Act 1965.
2. The Lands Tribunal constituted under s1(1)(b) of the Lands Tribunal Act 1949.
3. London Building Acts Tribunals constituted in accordance with s109 of the London Building Acts (Amendment) Act 1939.
4. Leasehold Valuation Tribunals under s142 of the Housing Act 1988, Rent Tribunals under s72, and hearings under ss14 or 22 of the Housing Act 1988; Rent Assessment Committees constituted in accordance with s10 of the Rent Act 1977.
5. Valuation Tribunals established by regulations under Sch 11 to the Local Government Finance Act 1988.

Patents/designs/trademarks/copyrights

1. The Comptroller General of Patents, Designs and Trade Marks and any other officer authorised to exercise the functions of the Comptroller under s62(3) of the Patents and Designs Act 1907 (includes design rights, licence of right, matters under the Copyright, Designs and Patents Act 1988).
2. The Copyright Tribunal constituted under s145 of the Copyright, Designs and Patents Act 1988.

Pensions

1. Fire Service Pensions Appeal Tribunals constituted under s26 of the Fire Services Act 1947.
2. The Occupational Pensions Regulatory Authority established by s1 of the Pensions Act 1995.
3. The Pensions Compensation Board established by s78 of the Pensions Act 1995.
4. The Pensions Ombudsman established under Pt X of the Pensions Schemes Act 1993 in respect of his functions under or by virtue of s146(1)(c) and (d) of that Act.
5. Police Pensions Appeal Tribunals appointed under s1 of the Police Pensions Act 1976.

Road traffic/transport/aviation

1. The Aircraft and Shipbuilding Industries Arbitration Tribunal established under s42 of the Aircraft and Shipbuilding Industries Act 1977.
2. The Civil Aviation Authority established under s2 of the Civil Aviation Act 1982.
3. Parking Adjudicators (of the National Parking Adjudication Service and the Parking and Traffic Appeals Service) appointed under s73(3)(a) of the Road Traffic Act 1991.
4. Traffic Commissioners for any area constituted for the purposes of the Public Passenger Vehicles Act 1981.
5. The Transport Tribunal constituted under Sch 4 to the Transport Act 1985.

Social security

1. Appeals Service Tribunals constituted under Chapter I of Pt I of the Social Security Act 1998.
2. Pensions Appeal Tribunals for England and Wales constituted under s8 of the War Pensions (Administrative Provisions) Act 1919 or the Pensions Act 1943.
3. Social Security and Child Support Commissioners appointed under Sch 4 to the Social Security Act 1998 and s22 of the Child Support Act 1991, and any tribunal presided over by such a Commissioner.

Other

1. The Antarctic Act Tribunal established under reg 11 of the Antarctic Regulations 1995.
2. The Foreign Compensation Commission established under s1 of the Foreign Compensation Act 1950.
3. The Horse Race Betting Levy Appeal Tribunal for England and Wales established under s29 of the Betting, Gaming and Lotteries Act 1963.

4. Mines and Quarries Tribunals for the purposes of s150 of the Mines and Quarries Act 1954.
5. The Misuse of Drugs Tribunal in England and Wales constituted under Pt I of Sch 3 to the Misuse of Drugs Act 1971.
6. The Wireless Telegraphy Appeal Tribunal established under s9 of the Wireless Telegraphy Act 1949.

Powers and functions of the Council on Tribunals

The primary function of the Council is to keep under review the constitution and working of the tribunals specified in Sch 1 to the Tribunals and Inquiries Act 1992. It is also required to consider and report on particular matters referred to the Council by the Lord Chancellor and the Lord Advocate with respect to any tribunal other than an ordinary court of law, whether or not specified in Sch 1 to the 1992 Act; and to consider and report on such matters as may be so referred, or as the Council may consider to be of special importance, with respect to administrative procedures which may involve the holding by or on behalf of a minister of a statutory inquiry. The Council has to be consulted by the appropriate rule-making authority before the procedural rules are made for any tribunal specified in Sch 1 to the 1992 Act; similarly with procedural rules made by the Lord Chancellor in connection with statutory inquiries. It must also be consulted before any tribunal is exempted from the requirement of giving reasons for its decision under s12 of the Tribunals and Inquiries Act 1992. The Council can make recommendations to relevant ministers on tribunal membership, and is required to make an annual report to the Lord Chancellor on the workings of the tribunal and inquiry system.

Staffing and operation of the Council on Tribunals

There are between ten and 15 part-time members, generally appointed for terms of three years. Some of the members are lawyers. The Parliamentary Commissioner for Administration is an ex-officio member. The Council meets 11 times a year. Some members visit tribunals and inquiries to see them in operation, and members have frequent meetings with representatives of government departments. The Council possesses a small secretariat and has to deal with a considerable volume of communications from the general public.

The contribution of the Council on Tribunals

In 1980 the report entitled *The Functions of the Council on Tribunals* (Cmnd 7805) stated:

'Our most important contribution over the years has, we believe, been our constant effort to translate the general ideals of the Franks Committee into workable codes of principles and practice, accepted and followed by all those who are responsible for setting up administrative tribunals, devising their manner of operation and, indeed, serving upon them as chairmen and members.'

The Council has succeeded in promoting the standardisation of procedures at statutory inquiries, ensuring an effective implementation of the Franks Committee goals of fairness, openness and impartiality. It has been influential as regards the content of draft legislation, and in developing a convention of prior consultation by government departments. Further, the Council has promoted the 'presidential' system of organising tribunals, whereby a particular class of tribunal has a national president or chairman – thus providing for better communications between tribunals of the same class. In addition, the Council has published guidelines for tribunal members, and helped organise training conferences and meetings of chairmen.

On the debit side, the Council, whilst under a duty to review the workings of specified tribunals, has no corresponding duty as regards statutory inquiries. Its power to consider and report on the workings of certain tribunals is limited, whilst no such limit exists on its power to report on the workings of inquiries. By its own admission the Council is understaffed and underfinanced. To be more effective it requires full-time members meeting on a more regular basis. Its powers are consultative and advisory, not executive. In short the Council can achieve nothing of its own volition. It cannot appoint tribunal members, nor make binding procedural rules independently of the Lord Chancellor. There is no requirement that the Council be consulted during the drafting of primary legislation, and it lacks any statutory jurisdiction to deal with complaints from members of the public. In the report on *The Functions of the Council on Tribunals*, the Council itself proposed:

'... that we should be given specific responsibility for complaints in relation to our field of works, it is important that the extent of our jurisdiction be clearly defined. The power could be on the following lines:

A member of the public alleging a procedural irregularity in a hearing before a tribunal or statutory inquiry would be entitled to make a formal complaint to us ... We would then have to consider whether the complaint prima facie raised a substantial point of principle relating to procedure ... If we came to that conclusion, we would be empowered to obtain papers and other information from the relevant tribunal or inquiry and from the Government department concerned, to question the complainant and any other person involved, and to submit a report to the complainant, the department and, at our discretion, to anyone else ...

If we decided that the complaint did not prima facie raise a substantial point of principle we would refer the matter without comment to the department concerned, who would be required to report to us the outcome of their own enquiries. In addition to this action on complaints from members of the public, we would be empowered at our discretion to conduct an investigation into an alleged procedural irregularity referred to us by the department concerned. We would not, however, at any time investigate a complaint relating to the merits of a decision or recommendation; or concerning the conduct of chairmen or members; or which fell within the competence of the Parliamentary Commissioners; or which could reasonably form the basis for an appeal or some other proceeding in a court of law ... This solution would not remove the slight overlap of functions between the Parliamentary Commissioner and ourselves, which already exists. The Parliamentary Commissioner would retain his jurisdiction to investigate complaints of maladministration against Government departments in relation to procedures which included public inquiries, and in relation to the pre-hearing and post-decision administrative handling by departments of matters referred to tribunals. Our jurisdiction would be limited to the form and operation of procedures, but within that limitation it would extend to events which took place within the doors of the tribunal or inquiry.'

At present the Council lacks the resources for carrying out any detailed research into the workings of the tribunal and inquiry system. There are no formal channels through which it can carry out such monitoring. Finally, it is generally accepted that the Council has failed to stop the proliferation in the number of tribunals, and has further failed to introduce anything approaching a standardised procedure for such bodies.

It should be evident from the above that the hopes of the Franks Committee as regards the Council on Tribunals were only partly realised. The Council itself is strongly of the view that it needs much wider powers, and a much expanded administrative support if it is to function properly. It has been entrusted with an increasingly important yet complex task, and in failing to discharge its duties properly it can fairly point the finger of blame at successive governments who have failed to take the action necessary to rectify the situation. For the present it seems as though the Council will continue its good work as best it can, providing administrative lawyers with an invaluable insight into how the administrative machine operates, by means of its annual reports. As the 1980 report *The Functions of the Council on Tribunals* concludes:

'The case for a statutory advisory body with ... (a) ... general oversight appears to us to be even stronger now than at the time of the Franks Committee. Since then the tendency for issues arising out of legislative schemes to be referred to tribunals has continued unabated, in a largely piecemeal manner. Not only has there been considerable growth in the number of tribunals, they are operating increasingly in difficult and sensitive areas – for example, immigration, compulsory detention under mental health legislation, misuse of drugs, equal pay, redundancy, unfair dismissal from employment, and supplementary benefits.

Moreover, the changed situation since 1957 is not confined to tribunals. Statutory inquiries have assumed an increasingly controversial role. Planning, redevelopment, land usage, highway policy, siting of major airports, development of natural resources and exploitation of new sources of energy are raising issues of a greater order of magnitude than those current at the time of the Franks Committee. Our position as an independent statutory advisory body with the broadest range of knowledge in this field is being recognised by Ministers, Government departments and other organisations.

Since we were set up, significant changes have also taken place in the general constitutional and administrative climate. There is, for example, a movement towards greater formalism in procedures for settling disputes. The process started with reforms following the Franks Report which, in general, made tribunals more like courts. It had to be demonstrated that tribunals were not adjuncts of Government departments and that in their decision-making they followed a judicial process. Since then the trend towards judicialisation has gathered momentum with the result that tribunals are becoming more formal, expensive and procedurally complex. Consequently they tend to become more difficult for an ordinary citizen to comprehend and cope with on his own. There is, we believe, an urgent need to keep the whole of this movement under the closest scrutiny. We believe that we are in a position to play a key role in the achievement of a right balance.

There is also a constant need, as was emphasised in discussion with our Committee, for an independent body able to offer advice to Government on what kinds of dispute are appropriate or inappropriate for adjudication by tribunals. We believe that we can exercise this function, and can develop criteria indicating the kinds of decision which, if disputed, should be subject to review by processes external to the departments concerned; the most appropriate form of review; the degree of formality required, according to the type of decision; and whether a proposed tribunal should come under our supervision.

Finally, we draw attention to particular problems running across the whole field which need co-ordinated rather than piecemeal approach: for example, a much wider system for recruitment of tribunal members, including more women; arrangements for training of both chairmen and members; the presidential system; conferences and seminars; the publication of explanatory leaflets; and the clarification and simplification of official forms.

... At present, we are perhaps in a better position than any other official body to appreciate the wider implications of the particular matters referred to us, and to consider the important issues relating to the system as a statutory power of the Council to act as a general advisory body in the field of administrative adjudication be placed beyond doubt.'

Summary

A number of significant criticisms can still be aimed at the tribunal system. There is no standardised procedure before tribunals despite the efforts of the Council on Tribunals. Not all tribunals have an appellate body that can provide for a rehearing. The non-availability of public funding must undoubtedly prejudice the less able litigant. Training for, and co-ordination of, tribunal members could undoubtedly be improved. In the case of some tribunals there have been criticisms of creeping 'judicialisation' – partly due to the presence of lawyers, resulting in an intimidating atmosphere in which some individuals find it difficult to express their views. Such research that has been conducted indicates that some chairmen fail to prevent purely prejudicial evidence being submitted, and in some tribunals there is an inability amongst tribunal members to differentiate properly between government policy, for example non-statutory guidance, and the law that has to be applied. Finally, concern inevitably persists over the extent to which some tribunals can truly be said to be independent of government departments, when they sometimes hold their sittings in the same building as that occupied by the department, and are staffed by civil servants. Ministers still exercise considerable control over tribunals by appointing members, and deciding not to re-appoint members when their period of service expires.

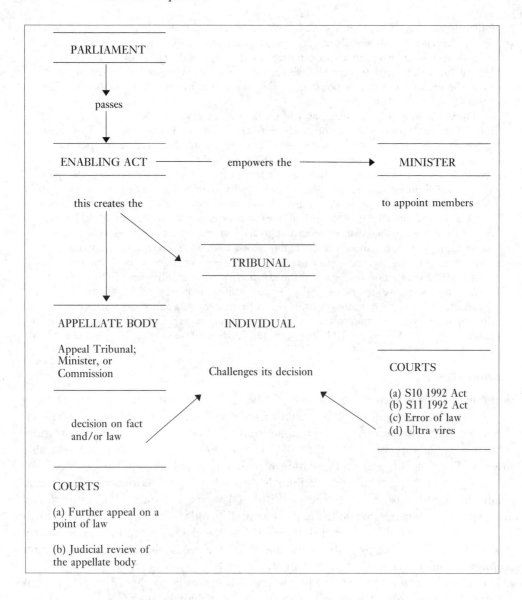

4.7 Future reform of the tribunal system: the Leggatt Report

In June 2000 the Lord Chancellor invited Sir Andrew Leggatt to undertake a wide-ranging review of tribunals – the first time a systematic investigation into the working of tribunals has been put in train since the Franks Report in the late 1950s. The context in which the review took place was the massive growth in the use of tribunals to provide administrative justice – from 30 in 1957 to over 100 today.

There has also been an increase in the use of other regulatory bodies with judicial functions. The main concerns to occupy the review team were the lack of coherence in the tribunal system and the variations in tribunal procedure and practice. The review team's terms of reference were as follows:

> 'To review the delivery of justice through tribunals other than ordinary courts of law, constituted under an Act of Parliament by a Minister of the Crown or for purposes of a Minister's functions; in resolving disputes, whether between citizens and the state, or between other parties, so as to ensure that:
> – There are fair, timely, proportionate and effective arrangements for handling those disputes, within an effective framework for decision-making which encourages the systematic development of the area of law concerned, and which forms a coherent structure, together with the superior courts, for the delivery of administrative justice;
> – The administrative and practical arrangements for supporting those decision-making procedures meet the requirements of the European Convention on Human Rights for independence and impartiality;
> – There are adequate arrangements for improving people's knowledge and understanding of their rights and responsibilities in relation to such disputes, and that tribunals and other bodies function in a way which makes those rights and responsibilities a reality;
> – The arrangements for the funding and management of tribunals and other bodies by government departments are efficient, effective and economical; and pay due regard both to judicial independence, and to ministerial responsibility for the administration of public funds;
> – Performance standards for tribunals are coherent, consistent, and public; and effective measures for monitoring and enforcing those standards are established; and
> – Tribunals overall constitute a coherent structure for the delivery of administrative justice.'

The Consultation Paper, *Review of Tribunals*, stated that the 'overarching requirement of the tribunal system ... is that it should be seen to be fair' and to this end the concept of fairness was seen as encompassing the Franks Report notions of openness and impartiality. The paper proposed a number of benchmarks against which the achievement of fairness should be measured. These included matters such as: independence, accessibility, simple procedures, proportionate remedies, speed of decision-making and cost-effectiveness.

In March 2001 the 'Report of the Review of Tribunals' chaired by Sir Andrew Leggatt, was published under the title *Tribunals for Users: One System, One Service*. Its main recommendations were as follows.

1. The tribunal system should be more independent of central government. This aim would be achieved by:

   a) ensuring separation between the ministers and other authorities whose policies and decisions are tested by tribunals, and the minister who appoints and supports tribunal members;

   b) making the administration of tribunals the responsibility of the Lord Chancellor;

c) making the Lord Chancellor responsible for all appointments to tribunals (in consultation, as necessary) – all appointments should be for a period of five or seven years. Subject to age, renewal for further such periods should be automatic, except for cause. Grounds for removal should be prescribed by the Lord Chancellor, with the concurrence of the appropriate minister in the devolved administrations and the relevant head of the judiciary. A Judicial Appointments Commissioner should be responsible for supervising tribunal appointments, and in particular for the appointment of lawyers. Another Commissioner should be responsible for the appointment of non-lawyers. The Judicial Appointments Commission should establish a separate committee to oversee its work on tribunals.

2. The Tribunal system should be made more coherent. This aim would be achieved with the following actions.

   a) Present the citizen with a single, overarching structure, giving access to all tribunals.
   b) Include local government tribunals, citizen and state tribunals and party tribunals in the tribunals system.
   c) Give tribunals the separate rules and procedures they need – the Lord Chancellor's Department being required to adapt the civil justice reforms to the different circumstances of litigation before tribunals as quickly as possible, to ensure that procedures are as speedy, proportionate and cheap as the nature of each case allows.
   d) Establish a Tribunals Service (as an executive agency of the Lord Chancellor's Department, separate from the Court Service) committed to producing a service and approach of the highest quality, and responsive to the user. In addition to measures to test the efficiency and effectiveness of the tribunals system, the Tribunals Service should set out for users the standards of service which they can expect, and what to do if they do not think those standards have been met.
   e) Establish a tribunals system divided by subject matter into divisions in a structure which is at once apparent to the user – the divisions composed by creating sensibly coherent areas of work, and by bringing together, as far as possible, the tribunals for which each government department currently has overall responsibility. First-tier tribunals should be grouped into eight divisions to deal with disputes between the citizen and the state, and one to deal with disputes between citizens.
   f) Establish a single route of appeal for all tribunals, to a single appellate division – this would involve creating appellate tribunal jurisdictions covering the areas of education, health and regulatory matters. Generally, there should be a right of appeal on a point of law, by permission, on the generic ground that the decision of the tribunal was unlawful, from first-tier tribunals to second-tier tribunals, and from second-tier tribunals to the Court of Appeal.

The appellate body should have power in its discretion, if it upholds an appeal, to quash the decision, to remit it for reconsideration, to grant declaratory relief or (if there was no substantial prejudice) to give no relief.

g) Introduce a common time limit for appealing a tribunal's decision of six weeks from the date of issue of the tribunal's reasoned decision, or for particular tribunals such other period as may exceptionally be prescribed by Statutory Instrument.

h) Clarify the rules on precedent so that first-tier tribunals should continue to consider each case on its merits and decide it as the public interest may require – their decisions should not set binding precedents. The system of designating binding cases (or limiting the cases which are permitted to be cited in argument) as used by the Social Security Commissioners and the IAT should be adopted throughout the appellate Division. Decisions about binding precedents should be taken by the President of each appellate tribunal, with the approval of the Tribunals Board.

i) Enact a statutory provision to exclude the decisions of second-tier tribunals from the supervisory jurisdiction of the High Court, and enacting a statutory provision excluding judicial review of the decisions of first-tier tribunals if rights of appeal have not been exhausted.

j) Appoint a High Court judge as the Senior President to head the Tribunal System, and a Tribunals Board, to direct the Tribunals System, consisting of the Senior President, the Presidents of the appellate tribunals who are judges of the High Court, and the Presidents of first-tier Divisions, together with the Chairman of the Council on Tribunals, the Chairman of the Tribunals Committee of the Judicial Studies Board, and the Chief Executive of the Tribunals Service. The Board's functions should include advising the LCD on qualifications for chairmen and members, overseeing the appointment of members, co-ordinating their training, investigating complaints against them, and recommending changes to the rules of procedure governing all Divisions.

k) Tribunal practice should be based on the Council on Tribunal's Model Rules, with procedures revised over time to achieve the greatest possible coherence across the system, whilst recognising the needs of different divisions (and perhaps classes of case within divisions) at least for different time limits.

3. The tribunal system should be made more user-friendly. This aim would be achieved with the following actions.

a) Provide users with information about how to start a case, prepare it for submission to the tribunal and present it at a hearing – the aim being that tribunal users should be able to prepare and present their cases.

b) Develop a consistent approach and common standards, on which the Council on Tribunals should be consulted.

c) Explore the feasibility of specifying in regulations, rules of procedure or codes of practice the documents and information that decision-makers in both central and local government should be under a duty to supply to appellants.

d) Provide customer service points in all tribunal offices.

e) Provide appellants with timely advice and ensure procedures are in place for examining financial eligibility for public funding – the Community Legal Service contract scheme being extended to key advice organisations, and used to assure the quality of advice and assistance users receive. State assistance should be directed to helping users to: understand their case and its merits; take a view about whether to proceed with an appeal; and if so, to find out how to prepare for a hearing.

f) Exploit information technology to provide: common administrative systems across the tribunals system; case administration systems and electronic filing systems integrated as one system; document production systems that ensure the standard production of letters, directions, rulings, forms, decisions and publications; online publication of tribunal decisions; web-based interactive systems to help parties prepare their cases, and web-based tracking to help them follow the progress of their actions; and a website to help citizens and organisations to identify the most appropriate forums for the resolution of their disputes.

4. The management and supervision of tribunals should be improved. This aim would be achieved with the following actions.

a) Emphasise in the advertisements for tribunal members the distinctive nature of tribunal proceedings and the need for interpersonal skills, as well as other professional skills and knowledge.

b) Require the Presidents to: promote by leadership and co-ordination both consistency of decision-making and uniformity of practice and procedure; hear personally those cases which raise the most difficult, novel and complex issues, and those which raise general issues of practice and procedure for the system or its divisions; be responsible for training and the co-ordination of the programmes developed by the Judicial Studies Board (JSB) and the implementation of training in their respective divisions.

c) Ensure that: non-lawyers appointed as tribunal members are appointed on the basis of the specific contribution which each has to make to the tribunal's work, the relevant criteria for appointment being stipulated by Parliament; non-lawyers receive careful training and, where appropriate, guidance from the chairman in the process of finding facts and in the weighing of evidence.

d) Provide improved training for chairmen and members in the interpersonal skills peculiar to the distinctive approach of tribunals – the skills required for the efficient conduct of a tribunal being imparted by means of introductory training in core competencies, sustained by continued training. Instruction should be provided in the additional competencies needed by chairmen, especially those needed to help them overcome the communication, language and literacy difficulties experienced by some users.

e) Give the JSB responsibility for the organisation and delivery of training for tribunal chairmen and members, for recommending training policy, for establishing national training standards and for monitoring the structure and content of training across all tribunals in England and Wales.

f) Encourage the Council on Tribunals, through its programme of visits, to identify training needs: the JSB should consult the Council on training requirements.

g) Extend the role of the Council on Tribunals to: encompass the monitoring of the development of the new tribunals system during the first few years of its existence, and check that the practices and procedures of government departments are compliant with the European Convention on Human Rights; champion users' causes; take evidence from user groups, the Tribunals Service, departments and the JSB about how well the system is working; monitor the training of chairmen and members, proposals for procedural change, the development of information technology, the usefulness of the information provided for users by the Tribunals Service and the adequacy of independent sources of assistance and advice for users; continue its own programme of visits, albeit scaled down, and after each visit report its findings at once to the Senior President and to the President of the division concerned; ensure that the various mechanisms for redressing the grievances of users work together coherently and efficiently; commission research into the operation of administrative justice both in the UK and abroad; and promote conferences, more detailed tribunal information, specialised reports, and more guidance on standards and best practice. In the longer term, the Council should be made responsible for upholding the system of administrative justice and keeping it under review, for monitoring developments in administrative law, and for making recommendations to the Lord Chancellor about improvements that might be made to that system.

5. Tribunals should move towards a system of active case management. This aim would be achieved with the following actions.

a) Improve arrangements for scheduling hearings, inter alia, by measuring the time taken for an appeal from the date of the initial decision, setting down time limits to show when cases are expected to be heard, giving tribunals any sanctions needed to ensure adequate case progression and making effective use of information technology to monitor work flow.

b) Make Chairmen responsible for ensuring that cases adhere to time limits, for supervising the listing and allocation of cases, for conducting hearings and for promulgating clear decisions promptly.

c) Ensure difficulties are identified in advance by: making more use of pre-hearing procedures and review; giving directions about how to prepare for the hearing; appoint a legally qualified registrar to each division empowered to order the production and exchange of documents, to order parties and witnesses to attend oral hearings, to issue directions and to refer parties who abuse tribunal procedures to court for contempt action; empower registrars to carry out pre-hearing work for each tribunal, under its direction, and give legal or procedural advice to tribunal members and administrators, if required; encourage registrars to consider the suitability of alternative dispute resolution during pre-hearing procedures.

d) Publish rules and Practice Directions outlining the arrangements for case management, using that term in its widest sense to denote minding cases during their progress through the tribunal.

e) Ensure that case management procedures approximate to modern court procedure.

4.8 Introduction to inquiries

Inquiries take a number of forms, but their chief purpose is usually the conduct of an investigation of some sort, whether into planning proposals, natural disasters or political scandals. Unlike tribunals, where the body concerned will be a decision-making one, inquiries usually produce reports, written by an inquiry inspector, with the subsequent decision being taken by a different administrative body, such as a minister, although provisions exist for decisions to be taken by the inquiry inspector himself.

Whereas tribunals will normally be called upon to resolve a dispute between two parties by arriving at a determination, the public inquiry has, traditionally, been seen as an administrative device through which evidence can be gathered and views canvassed, prior to a decision being made, typically by a minister. It is in the sphere of planning control that public inquiries play their most significant role. Under s320 of the Town and Country Planning Act 1990 (consolidating the previous Act of 1971) the Secretary of State may cause a local inquiry to be held for the purposes of exercising any of his functions under any of the provisions of the Act. In effect this means that an inquiry might be held into a matter such as the compulsory purchase of property, the refusal of planning permission, alterations to listed buildings, the placing of advertising hoardings etc. Some inquiries deal with issues of very localised concern, for example a road-widening scheme; others will raise issues of national significance, ie inquiries into major developments such as airports or power stations. Inevitably questions are raised as to the extent to which the public inquiry is an appropriate means of dealing with such a wide range of problems. Under s101 of the 1990 Act the Secretary of State can appoint a Planning Inquiry Commission, to consider planning appeals that have wide implications beyond the locality of the site in question, or involve very complex technicalities. The Commission, if appointed, should consist of a chair and not less than two or more than four other members appointed by the Secretary of State. The rationale for these provisions is that issues of this nature are not suitable for consideration by a local public inquiry. Planning Inquiry Commissions are allowed to consider the broader implications of the planning appeal, such as possible alternative sites for the development. To date no use has been made of this special inquiry procedure, despite the recommendation of the House of Common's Select Committee in 1986 that the possibilities offered by the Commission should be exploited, and despite the suitability of some planning applications such as those relating to the building of a nuclear fuel reprocessing plant at Windscale, in Cumbria; or the National Coal Board's application to mine coal in the Vale of Belvoir.

Under the Tribunals of Inquiry (Evidence) Act 1921 a tribunal can be appointed to inquire into 'a definite matter of urgent public importance'. Despite the misleading title the procedure more closely resembles that of an inquiry than a tribunal. The tribunal, chaired by a lawyer who sits with two other persons, conducts its business in an inquisitorial fashion. It can compel the attendance of witnesses and production of documents; witnesses are privileged in giving their evidence, and can be legally represented. The tribunal does not make any decisions or hand down punishments, but produces a report on its findings, which is forwarded to the appropriate minister. Examples of the sort of matters referred to the tribunal in the past include: disclosure of budget secrets; the causes of the 1966 Aberfan disaster; the events in Londonderry in January 1972; and the failure of the Vehicle and General Insurance Company. Many of the matters investigated also fall within the ambit of the Parliamentary Commissioner for Administration, but are dealt with under the 1921 Act because of the scale of the maladministration involved, and the need for a public investigation.

In addition to the above cases, many 'ad hoc' inquiries are established, under the prerogative, on a 'one off' basis to enquire into a specific event or issue. Examples include: the inquiry under Lord Scarman into the Brixton riots of April 1981; the inquiry into events leading up to the Falklands War; and the inquiry into the fire at Bradford City Football Club in May 1985. The most significant, most recent, example is the Scott inquiry into the so-called 'Iraqi Supergun' affair, and it is interesting to note that Scott LJ was promised that he would be given powers similar to those enjoyed by Tribunals of Inquiry under the 1921 Act if he requested them.

The Franks Committee's findings regarding inquiries

Most of the evidence before the Franks Committee concerned the workings of inquiries dealing with land use. The Committee saw inquiries as having a two-fold purpose: to provide an opportunity for public participation in decision-making and to enable a minister to arrive at a better informed decision. As to the question of whether inquiries were administrative or judicial in nature, the Committee commented:

'Our general conclusion is that these procedures cannot be classified as purely administrative or purely judicial. They are not purely administrative because of the provision for a special procedure preliminary to the decision – a feature not to be found in the ordinary course of administration – and because this procedure, as we have shown, involves the testing of an issue, often partly in public. They are not on the other hand purely judicial, because the final decision cannot be reached by the application of rules and must allow the exercise of a wide discretion in the balancing of public and private interest. Neither view at its extreme is tenable, nor should either be emphasised at the expense of the other.

If the administrative view is dominant the public enquiry cannot play its full part in the total process, and there is a danger that the rights and interests of the individual citizens affected will not be sufficiently protected. In these cases it is idle to argue that Parliament can be relied upon to protect the citizen, save exceptionally. We agree with the following views expressed in the pamphlet entitled Rule of Law: Whatever the theoretical validity of this argument, those of us who are Members of Parliament have no hesitation in saying that it bears little relation to reality. Parliament has neither the time nor the knowledge to supervise the Minister and call him to account for his administrative decisions.

If the judicial view is dominant there is a danger that people will regard the person before whom they state their case as a kind of judge provisionally deciding the matter, subject to an appeal to the Minister. This view overlooks the true nature of the proceeding, the form of which is necessitated by the fact that the Minister himself, who is responsible to Parliament for the ultimate decision, cannot conduct the enquiry in person.

Most of the evidence which we have received, other than the evidence from Government Departments, has placed greater emphasis on judicial aspects of the procedure. The view is that present procedure, either in regard to actual law or to practice, do not sufficiently reflect the essentially adjudicative nature of the process. From the point of view of the citizen what begins in many ways like an action at law, with two or more parties appearing before a judge-like inspector and stating their case to him, usually in public, is thereafter suddenly removed from public gaze until the ministerial decision is made. Often the main factors at the enquiry seem to have counted for little in the final decision. New factors – they may have been considerations of broad policy – have come in so that the final decision does not seem to flow from the proceedings at the enquiry.

... we shall ... address ourselves to the task of finding a reasonable balance between the conflicting interests. On the one hand there are Ministers and other administrative authorities enjoined by legislation to carry out certain duties. On the other hand there are the rights and feelings of individual citizens who find their possessions or plans interfered with by the administration. There is also the public interest, which requires both that Ministers and other administrative authorities should not be frustrated in carrying out their duties and also that their decisions should be subject to effective checks or controls, and these, as we have pointed out, can no longer be applied by Parliament in the general run of cases.'

The Committee further recommended that the case against which objections were being raised at an inquiry should be clearly made out, and the objections themselves developed with sufficient detail to permit proper consideration. As regards the position of inquiry inspectors, and the respective merits and demerits of both departmental and independent inspectors, the Committee recommended that inspectors be brought under the control of the Lord Chancellor's Department, thereby stressing their unquestioned independence and impartiality. It was nevertheless accepted that inspectors would have to be kept informed of central government policy, where appropriate. Many of these recommendations now form part of the Town and Country Planning (Inquiries Procedure) Rules 1992 (SI 1992/2038).

4.9 Inquiry procedures

As with tribunals there is no universal procedure adopted by all inquiries. The Council on Tribunals has, however, been successful in introducing a measure of consistency as regards the procedure adopted by inquiries dealing with land use. Section 9 of the Tribunals and Inquiries Act 1992 provides:

'(1) The Lord Chancellor, after consultation with the Council, may make rules regulating the procedure to be followed in connection with statutory inquiries held by or on behalf of Ministers; and different provision may be made by any such rules in relation to different classes of such inquiries.

(2) Any rules made by the Lord Chancellor under this section shall have effect, in relation to any statutory inquiry, subject to the provisions of the enactment under which the inquiry is held, and of any rules or regulations made under that enactment.

(3) Subject to subs(2), rules made under this section may regulate procedure in connection with matters preparatory to such statutory inquiries as are mentioned in subs(1), and in connection with matters subsequent to such inquiries, as well as in connection with the conduct of proceedings at such inquiries.'

For these purposes, s16(1) defines a statutory inquiry as:

'(a) an inquiry or hearing held or to be held in pursuance of a duty imposed by any statutory provision, or

(b) an inquiry or hearing, or an inquiry or hearing of a class, designated for the purposes of this section by an order under subs(2).'

Section 16(2) further provides:

'The Lord Chancellor and the Lord Advocate may by order designate for the purposes of this section any inquiry or hearing held or to be held in pursuance of a power conferred by any statutory provision specified or described in the order, or any class of such inquiries or hearings.'

To date over 100 inquiries have been so designated.

The standard procedural rules for land use inquiries are now to be found in the Town and Country Planning (Inquiries Procedure) Rules 1992 (SI 1992/2038) (replacing the 1988 rules). The revised inquiry procedure rules, which came into effect on 30 September 1992, apply to: any local inquiry caused by the Secretary of State to be held in England or Wales before he determines; an application in relation to planning permission referred to him under s78 of the Town and Country Planning Act 1990; an application for consent referred to him under a tree preservation order or an appeal to him under such an order; an application in relation to listed building consent, or an appeal to him under s20 of the Planning (Listed Buildings and Conservation Areas) Act 1990.

Subject to certain exceptions, s321 of the 1990 Act provides that all oral evidence at local inquiries must be given in public and the documentary evidence must be available to the public for inspection. The aim of the rules is to ensure fairness and openness, so far as is compatible with the purpose of the inquiry.

Rule 4 details the preliminary information to be supplied by the local planning authority; r5 provides for the procedure to be followed where the Secretary of State causes a pre-inquiry meeting to be held in order to address those matters that need to be resolved in order to ensure that the inquiry itself is conducted effectively and efficiently; and r6 deals with the statements that have to be served by the various interested parties prior to the inquiry. Rule 11 details those entitled to appear at the inquiry, the list includes the applicant (ie the appellant), the local planning authority, other statutory bodies such as local authorities, National Parks Committees, and any other person permitted to appear at the discretion of the inquiry inspector.

A representative of the relevant government department may attend if the applicant so requests, but note that under r12(4) the representative is not required to answer any question which in the opinion of the inspector is directed to the merits of government policy. Under r11(3), any person entitled or permitted to appear may be represented by counsel, solicitor, or some other person. Under r14 the inspector will invite the applicant to commence the proceedings and will permit him the right of final reply. Others entitled or permitted to appear are heard in such order as the inspector may determine. A person entitled to appear at an inquiry is entitled to call evidence and the applicant, the local planning authority, and a statutory party will be entitled to cross-examine any person giving evidence. In all other cases the calling of evidence and the cross-examination of persons giving evidence is at the inspector's discretion. The inspector may refuse to permit the giving or production of evidence, the cross-examination of persons giving evidence, or the presentation of any other matter, which he considers to be irrelevant or repetitious. Any person refused permission to present oral evidence may put evidence in writing before the close of the inquiry. The inspector has powers to maintain order at the inquiry. Under r14(7) he may require any person appearing or present at an inquiry who, in his opinion, is behaving in a disruptive manner to leave and may refuse to permit that person to return, or may permit him to return only on such conditions as he may specify. The rules place on a legislative basis decisions such as *Lovelock* v *Secretary of State for Transport* (1979) P & CR 468 in which it was held that an inspector ordering the exclusion of a disruptive member of the public or participant would not be acting in breach of natural justice.

Where he considers it necessary to do so, the inspector may visit the site relevant to the inquiry. Under r15 he may make an unaccompanied inspection of the land before or during an inquiry without giving notice of his intention to the persons entitled to appear at the inquiry, or may, during an inquiry or after its close, inspect the land in the company of the applicant, the local planning authority and any statutory party. In addition, he is required to make such an inspection if requested to do so by the applicant or the local planning authority before or during an inquiry.

Natural justice

Whilst it is trite law to state that the rules of natural justice apply to the public inquiry process, as Kerr J stated in *Lake District Special Planning Board* v *Secretary of State for the Environment* (1975) JPL 220:

> '... [the litigant] faces a heavy burden in seeking to establish a breach of the rules of natural justice when the allegation in question relates to something which is comprised within the scope of a statutory procedure ... which is itself designed to lay down the requirements which must be complied with to ensure that justice is done, but when no breach of this procedure has been established.'

There are, however, some notable instances of the rules of natural justice being applied to the actual inquiry procedure. In *Fairmount Investments Ltd* v *Secretary of State for the Environment* [1976] 2 All ER 865 a compulsory purchase order was quashed when an inspector attached great weight in his report to a matter not directly raised during the inquiry; on this point see also *H Sabey and Co* v *Secretary of State for the Environment* [1978] 1 All ER 586. In *R* v *Secretary of State for the Environment, ex parte Fiedler Estates (Canvey) Ltd and Another* (1988) The Times 10 June the applicants for review had applied unsuccessfully for planning permission to build houses in the vicinity of Canvey Island, and appealed to the Secretary of State who had instituted a public inquiry which was expected to last for three days. One interested group, the Canvey Ratepayers' Association, sought to give evidence, through its chairman, on the second day of the inquiry. By the end of the first day of the inquiry all those present who had wanted to give evidence had done so, and the inspector declared the inquiry closed. The Association's chairman arrived to give evidence the following day only to find the inquiry had closed. On receiving a complaint from the Association, the Secretary of State decided to hold a new inquiry at which the Association gave evidence, but he failed to notify any of the other interested parties of this decision. The Divisional Court held that the conduct of the Secretary of State, in failing to notify the other parties of his decision to hold a fresh inquiry, was so unreasonable that it verged on the absurd and amounted to a failure to comply with procedural fairness. He had acted ultra vires in hearing one side in the absence of the other. Roche J expressed the view that the minister could quite properly have dealt with the matter by receiving written evidence from the Association after the inquiry and asking the applicants to comment upon it.

The decision of the House of Lords in *Bushell* v *Secretary of State for the Environment* [1981] AC 75 involved a valuable discussion by their Lordships of the extent to which natural justice applied to inquiry proceedings where no statutory rules were in force. Lord Diplock was at pains to point out that it was wrong to equate a public inquiry with a court of law. In the absence of any particular procedural rules which may require certain steps to be taken, his Lordship felt that all that natural justice required of public inquiries was fairness to 'all those who have an interest in the decision that will follow'. He held that natural justice was satisfied by objectors to a proposed motorway scheme being allowed to put their objections before the inspector; it did not necessitate their being allowed to cross-examine departmental representatives on the veracity of their evidence. In *R* v *Secretary of State for Transport, ex parte Gwent County Council* [1987] 2 WLR 961 the Court of Appeal endorsed the views of Lord Diplock expounded in *Bushell* (above), where the Court stressed that the inquiry process should be looked at as a whole. Some degree of procedural impropriety by the inspector could be remedied by the minister when considering the inspector's report.

Openness

Save where statute provides expressly that a particular type of inquiry should proceed in public, the question as to whether or not fairness and confidence in public procedures necessarily requires that inquiries should be held in public is one that very much depends on the context in which the inquiry is held. In *R* v *Secretary of State for Health, ex parte Wagstaff and Others* [2001] 1 WLR 292 the Secretary of State, acting under s2 of the National Health Service Act 1977, ordered an inquiry into the events surrounding the murder by Doctor Harold Shipman of over 15 of his patients. The Secretary of State had determined that the inquiry should receive evidence in private. The families of those killed and the press wanted the inquiry to be conducted in public. The Secretary of State refused to accede to these requests, pointing out that although the procedure would be private the resultant report would be made public. The applicants successfully sought judicial review of the decision to proceed with a private hearing, contending that either there was, in the light of art 10 of the European Convention on Human Rights, a legitimate expectation that the proceedings would be in public or, alternatively, that the decision to proceed with a private hearing was irrational. The Divisional Court attached great importance to the fact that the inquiry was dealing with a matter of very serious and genuine public concern – public confidence in the National Health Service was at stake. A public hearing, it was felt, helped guard against exaggeration of evidence and the passing on of blame. The wishes of the victims' families was also a significant factor. No sound operational reasons had been put forward for not proceeding in public. There was no indication that a private procedure would be speedier, would yield more evidence, or that it would be more rigorous and exacting than a public hearing. If anything there was a presumption in favour of a public hearing where a truly public inquiry was concerned, as opposed to where the inquiry was a purely internal or domestic affair. As to art 10, the court was of the view that it simply restated the common law position concerning the right to receive and impart information and was, as such, not decisive of the matter. The decision to proceed with a private hearing was, therefore, irrational.

Against this, in *R (On the Application of Persey)* v *Secretary of State for the Environment, Food and Rural Affairs* (2002) The Times 28 March, the Divisional Court held that the decision of the Secretary of State for the Environment, Food and Rural Affairs to hold the 'Lessons Learned' inquiry into the foot and mouth outbreak in private was lawful. The court stressed that there was no legal presumption that an inquiry would be held in public. Contrasting the application with that in *Wagstaff*, Simon Brown LJ observed:

> 'The principal differences are surely these. The terms of reference of the [present] … inquiry are … "markedly narrower" … than those under consideration in *Wagstaff* … Secondly, no-one suggests that an open public inquiry into [foot and mouth] would take no longer than Dr Anderson's proposed six-month inquiry (scheduled to report in June 2002). On the contrary, however inquisitorial the procedure and however firm the chairmanship, all experience dictates that an open inquiry would take very appreciably longer, even putting aside the need to set it up entirely afresh. One does not need to reflect on the Saville Inquiry to recognise the risk of timetables slipping. Thirdly, the case on candour which the defendant advances here seems to me both stronger than, and in an important respect different from, that advanced in *Wagstaff*. The court there … quoted a statement made by Sir Louis Blom-Cooper QC in support of public inquiries being conducted openly, remarking that "there was no evidence put before us to the opposite effect" (albeit reference was made to Sir Cecil Clothier's report on the Allitt Inquiry providing some support for the contrary view). In the present case not only is there a statement from a witness, Mr Richard Lingham, with great personal experience of health service inquiries, who expresses himself as "… firmly in favour of … an inquiry that hears evidence in private" … but Sir Louis himself takes a perhaps more ambivalent view than *Wagstaff* suggested. In his statement before us, he says this:
>
>> "It is frequently asserted that witnesses before an inquiry held in private are thereby more inclined to be candid about their testimony. My experience on the whole accords with that view, but there is a distinct downside to that benefit."
>
> Having then explained that downside, essentially that witnesses in private tend to be careless about accusations against others, Sir Louis concludes:
>
>> "On balance I prefer the even-handed approach which gives equal weighting to the evidence."
>
> A view arrived "on balance" hardly suggests that the evidence is all one way. In *Wagstaff*, moreover, the court did not have the benefit of [the] … evidence that, because the BSE Inquiry was held in public, "those with experience and knowledge [did not] make constructive suggestions about the management of the disease and its handling which could have contributed to the Inquiry's thinking". In other words, in an inquiry into a broadly comparable area of concern, witnesses tended to be defensive rather than constructive in their evidence.'

Simon Brown LJ concluded that the decision to proceed with the inquiry in private was one that was 'pre-eminently a judgment for government'.

Simon Brown LJ also rejected the contention that art 10 of the European Convention on Human Rights carried with it a right of access to information. As a result the Secretary of State was not under a legal duty to hold an inquiry in public by virtue of art 10. As Simon Brown LJ explained:

'... we have had the advantage of substantially fuller argument on the point than the court enjoyed in *Wagstaff* and have been referred to a number of additional cases. In the result I for my part have come to the clear conclusion that art 10 is simply not engaged by a decision, as here, to hold a closed public inquiry. Let me as briefly as possible explain why ... the court in *Wagstaff* cited part only of para 74 of *Leander* v *Sweden* (1987) 9 EHRR 433, the first of the three Strasbourg cases referred to, and observed that it could not assist the government's case. It seems to me, however, necessary to cite the paragraph rather more fully:

"... the right to freedom to receive information basically prohibits a government from restricting a person from receiving information that others wish or may be willing to impart to him. Article 10 does not in circumstances such as those of the present case, confer on the individual a right of access to a register containing information on his personal position, nor does it embody an obligation on the government to impart such information to the individual."

... The crucial point made by *Leander* is that freedom of expression – whether the right to receive, or the right to impart, information – is one thing, access to information quite another, and that art 10, whilst naturally conferring the former, does not accord the latter. That distinction appears to me central to this case. The true analysis of the complaint made here is that the form of inquiry decided upon by government and now being undertaken by Dr Anderson denies public access to the information being imparted at the closed sessions. That, to my mind, is not a legitimate complaint. The fact that a particular participant may be willing, even anxious, to have his contribution broadcast is nothing to the point. He is, of course, entirely at liberty to say what he likes to whomsoever he wishes. The conduct of the inquiry is not, however, in his hands and it is the willingness or unwillingness of whoever controls the inquiry's proceedings which must determine whether the public shall have direct access to the information being imparted. Someone attending a closed session of the Lessons Learned Inquiry is no more entitled to be accompanied by the press and television cameras than if he were invited to participate in a departmental meeting or, indeed, advise the Minister in his private office. In truth, under the guise of seeking merely to remove supposedly impermissible restrictions on the ability of willing participants to communicate their contributions more widely and more accurately than is possible without media intervention, the claimants and interveners are in reality seeking to enforce the setting up of a quite different form of inquiry, namely an open public inquiry such as Lord Phillips held into BSE. Article 10 contains no warrant for such an exercise. It is not a corollary of the right to freedom of expression that public authorities can be required to put in place additional opportunities for its exercise. Article 10 imposes no positive obligation on government to provide, in addition to existing means of communication, an open forum to achieve the yet wider dissemination of views. Article 10 prohibits interference with freedom of expression: it does not require its facilitation. In reality, as it seems to me, the claimants' argument here seeks to pull itself up by its own bootstraps. Had no inquiry been set up, art 10 would manifestly not be engaged. A closed form of inquiry having been determined upon, art 10 cannot then be invoked to transform it into some quite different process ... There seems to me to be some force too in the Attorney-General's argument that were art 10 to have the effect here contended for, it would not be necessary for art 6(1) to specify the entitlement of litigants to a "public hearing" of their disputes. The very fact that art 6 makes express provision for this suggests that no such right exists in relation to other forms of state inquiry.'

The decision suggests that the ruling in *Wagstaff* should be seen as the exception rather than the rule. It should also be borne in mind that in *Wagstaff* the terms of reference for the inquiry were very wide, and many people had received the clear impression that the inquiry would sit in public. Also see *R (On the Application of Howard)* v *Secretary of State for Health* (2002) The Times 28 March where the court applied the ruling in *Persey* to conclude that the Secretary of State for Health had not acted unlawfully in refusing to hold an inquiry into professional misconduct by a doctor in public.

Inquiry inspectors

Although the format of inquiries can vary widely, the majority of those concerned with issues of land use will be held by inquiry inspectors. The Franks Committee recommended that inspectors should be appointed by the Lord Chancellor. In practice, where the inquiry inspector is adjudicating between a local authority and a citizen, he will be from the Department of the Environment Inspectorate. Where a government department is promoting a scheme, an independent inspector will be appointed, eg a QC (Sizewell), or High Court judge (Windscale). There are approximately 400 inspectors, a quarter of whom are freelance the rest civil servants. Under the Town and Country Planning Appeals (Determination by Inspectors) (Inquiries Procedure) Rules 1992 (SI 1992/2039) (replacing the 1988 Rules), the minister may appoint an inspector to act on his behalf and decide upon the outcome of the inquiry process. Recent statistics indicate that a great many inquiries are now determined by inspectors. When determining the outcome of an inquiry on behalf of the minister, inspectors are subject to supervision by the courts to ensure that they act lawfully. For example, in *Surrey Heath Borough Council* v *Secretary of State for the Environment* (1986) The Times 3 November, an inquiry inspector's decision was quashed on the basis that he had paid too much regard to the minister's circular suggesting that development that would bring employment should be encouraged, whilst failing to pay sufficient regard to the local structure plan which discouraged speculative development.

4.10 The role of the minister

As far as planning inquiries are concerned, unless the inquiry is one in respect of which the inspector has been empowered to determine the matter on behalf of the minister, he will normally make a report in writing, following the close of the inquiry, setting out his recommendations for consideration by the minister. The minister's discretion to disagree with the inspector's findings is rather narrow. Under r16(4), if, after receiving the inspector's report, the minister is minded to differ on any material factual point, or take into consideration new evidence on any matter of fact, with the result that he is disposed to disagree with the inspector's recommendations, he must first notify those who were entitled to appear at the inquiry and inform them of his reasons for so doing. He must further allow at least 21 days for those who were entitled to attend the inquiry to make representations, or re-open the inquiry.

The result is that the minister is not bound by the inspector's findings, but cannot disagree with him on a question of fact without reopening the issue. Note that he is clearly free to reject the inspector's findings on policy grounds: see *Lord Luke of Pavenham* v *MHLG* [1967] 1 QB 172 and *Nelsovil Ltd* v *MHLG* [1963] 1 All ER 423.

By virtue of r17(1), the minister is obliged to give reasons for his decision. Where reasons are required by statute, the basic principles, established in *Re Poyser and Mills Arbitration* [1964] 2 QB 467, are that the reasons given should be proper, intelligible and adequate. The first two criteria are unlikely to give rise to difficulties in the context of r17, but the latter issue of adequacy has been considered by the House of Lords in *Save Britain's Heritage* v *Number 1 Poultry Ltd* [1991] 1 WLR 153. Lord Bridge, whilst accepting that on the facts of the case before him the Secretary of State's reasons lacked clarity and precision, rejected the notion that courts were required to set a standard of draftsmanship that decision letters had to achieve. In his view the essential issue was that the reasons given for a decision should enable a person entitled to contest it to make a proper assessment as to the validity of the decision. He stated (at p167):

> 'Whatever may be the position in any other legislative context, under the planning legislation, when it comes to deciding in any particular case whether the reasons given are deficient, the question is not to be answered in vacuo. The alleged deficiency will only afford a ground for quashing the decision if the court is satisfied that the interests of the applicant have been substantially prejudiced by it. This reinforces the view I have already expressed that the adequacy of reasons is not to be judged by reference to some abstract standard. There are in truth not two separate questions: (1) were the reasons adequate? (2) if not, were the interests of the applicant substantially prejudiced thereby? The single indivisible question, in my opinion, which the court must ask itself whenever a planning decision is challenged on the ground of a failure to give reasons is whether the interests of the applicant have been substantially prejudiced by the deficiency of the reasons given.'

With the coming into effect of the Human Rights Act 1998 there were concerns regarding aspects of the ministerial role in determining the outcome of planning inquiries. For example, in *County Properties Ltd* v *The Scottish Ministers* (2000) The Times 19 September the Outer House of the Court of Session allowed a petition for judicial review by the applicant company after the relevant minister had 'called in' a planning application. The company had sought listed building consent in respect of a property and a government agency, Historic Scotland, had objected. The minister had then appointed a reporter to establish a tribunal to look into the application and report back to the minister. Had the application not been called in it would have been determined in the normal way by the local planning authority. The court held that the procedure adopted by the minister could amount to a violation of the right to a fair determination guaranteed by art 6 of the European Convention on Human Rights because neither the reporter nor Historic Scotland could be regarded as being sufficiently independent of the minister, and the minister would, ultimately, be presiding over a dispute between the petitioners and his own executive agency. It was felt that the existence of a right to appeal to the courts on a point of law did not cure this irregularity as much of the case would turn on issues of aesthetic judgment rather than points of law.

The matter seems, for time being, to have been settled firmly in the minister's favour by the later House of Lords' decision in *R (On the Application of Holding and Barnes plc) v Secretary of State for the Environment, Transport and the Regions; R (On the Application of Alconbury Developments Ltd) v Secretary of State for the Environment, Transport and the Regions; Secretary of State for the Environment, Transport and the Regions v Legal and General Assurance Society Ltd* [2001] 2 WLR 1389. The case involved conjoined applications for judicial review in respect of the decisions of the Secretary of State in regard of 'called in' applications for planning permission, and recovered appeals against the refusal of planning permission under the Town and Country Planning Act 1990 and orders under the Transport and Works Act 1992, the Highways Act 1980 and the Acquisition of Land Act 1981. The applicants contended that as the Secretary of State was responsible for determining national planning policy, he could not be an impartial tribunal as regards the determination of the applicant's civil rights where he decided to intervene in the determination of planning applications and appeals. The House of Lords held that it was wrong to think of the minister as an impartial figure in the planning process. His involvement was a deliberate feature of the process, as he was responsible for the development and execution of a national planning policy for which he was answerable to Parliament. The European Court of Human Rights had recognised that the determination of some civil rights would be in the hands of elected representatives. This was permissible provided adequate judicial safeguards were provided to challenge such decisions. Those judicial safeguards did not have to be procedures that provided for a complete rehearing of the case or a comprehensive challenge to the merits of a decision, as this would undermine the whole basis of giving the decision-making power to an elected representative. The application for judicial review procedure and the statutory rights of appeal provided in the relevant planning legislation did provide for adequate safeguards, as they allowed for challenges if the decision-maker erred in law, exceeded his powers or adopted an unfair procedure.

4.11 Problems arising from the use of inquiries

There are conflicting views of the purpose that local planning inquiries are supposed to serve. On the one hand they are seen as providing a forum for public participation in decision-making. On the other they provide a means by which the person entrusted with decision-making powers (inspector or minister) can arrive at a better informed decision.

The House of Lords in *Bushell* v *Secretary of State for the Environment* (above) adhered very much to the latter approach, holding that inquiries were not like courts of law because there was 'nothing at stake'. Nobody was going to 'win' anything. As a consequence natural justice did not require the procedure adopted at an inquiry to mirror that found in a court of law, reflecting an 'administrative' as compared to 'judicial' approach to inquiries. As Lord Diplock stated:

> 'The purpose of the inquiry is to provide the minister with as much information about those objections as will ensure that in reaching his decision he will have weighed the harm to local interests and private persons who may be adversely affected by the scheme against the public benefit which the scheme is likely to achieve and will not have failed to take into consideration any matters which he ought to have taken into consideration.'

Cynics might argue that inquiries, those into large-scale projects at least, are really an exercise in public relations by the promoting authority or department, with the aim of making the public feel as though they have participated in some way in the decision-making process, or at least allowing them to 'let off steam'.

Where the inquiry is a relatively small-scale one, into development being proposed by a private individual, then the views of individual members of the public might actually influence the outcome. Where the development is of regional or national significance, it is likely to be departmental policy that the development is going to go ahead, therefore individual objections are going to count for very little. The problems arise when members of the public become frustrated through their inability to effectively challenge the latter style of proposal. The problem manifests itself either as a long-lingering suspicion of the processes of government, or in scenes of public disorder at the inquiry itself. Perhaps the fact that central government policy cannot be questioned or changed at inquiries should be made clearer. Those objecting to proposed development are often handicapped at inquiries, either by their lack of resources which prevents them from presenting a better researched case, or because, as sometimes is the case with highway inquiries, the inquiry into the development is split into sections, concerned only with a small stretch of the proposed route, and the overall plan for the motorway cannot be challenged.

As the holding of an inquiry is frequently a procedural prerequisite before development can take place, the easiest way to prevent development is to disrupt the inquiry.

The inquiry process, in its current form, causes delays and is very expensive due in part to the adversarial approach adopted by some parties but also due to the time taken in preparing and deciding upon the inspector's report. It is not surprising that there has been a tendency in recent years for the government to seek specific statutory approval for large-scale development projects, thus side-stepping the framework of the planning legislation.

5

The Nature and Scope of Natural Justice

5.1 Introduction

5.2 Development of natural justice

5.3 Where natural justice may not apply

5.4 Invoking natural justice – the concept of legitimate expectation

5.5 Consequences of a breach of natural justice

5.1 Introduction

Many have observed that the term 'natural justice' is misleading in that there is nothing necessarily natural about justice, and often very little justice in nature. For administrative lawyers, however, it is one of the key grounds upon which executive action can be challenged in the courts. Reference is often made to the 'rules of natural justice', a phrase suggestive of clear and immutable principles governing administrative procedures. As will be seen in both this and the following chapter, however, determining when and how these rules apply can pose very difficult questions for the litigant, advocate and judge.

The traditional analysis is that the rules of natural justice encompass two propositions: audi alteram partem – no man is to be condemned without a hearing; and nemo judex in causa sua – no man should sit as a judge in his own case.

Both rules, as will be seen, are actually concerned with procedure. If an applicant applies for judicial review on the ground that there has been a breach of natural justice he will be alleging that an unfair procedure has been adopted. Strictly applied, this approach means that the courts are not interested in the merits of the decision that has actually been arrived at, but the legality of that decision. The courts will often take the view that an administrative body does not have the jurisdiction to act unless it has followed a fair procedure in arriving at its conclusion as to how it should exercise its discretion. In other words, a decision that has been arrived at following the adoption of an unfair process will, in theory, be ultra vires.

Difficulty arises because the courts have considerable discretion in the application of the rules of natural justice. Precisely what is required to ensure compliance will vary with the circumstances of each case, such as the nature of the decisions being taken, the status of the applicant, and the interest at stake. Where Parliament delegates a decision-making power to an administrative agency it is unlikely to ever add the injunction that the power must be exercised fairly. The courts derive their jurisdiction in relation to natural justice by treating it as an implied precondition to the exercise of statutory power, on the basis that Parliament cannot have intended that the power be exercised unfairly.

5.2 Development of natural justice

Breach of natural justice has been recognised by the courts as a valid ground of challenge for centuries. Some of the earliest reported cases show the courts applying principles that are still readily recognisable today, eg *Bagg's* Case (1615) 11 Co Rep 936, where the disfranchisement of a freeman of Plymouth was declared void because he was not given a hearing prior to this privilege being revoked. Almost subconsciously the courts began to apply these principles to cases involving disputes between the citizen and the administration to ensure that those with executive power exercised it with a modicum of fairness. Hence, in *Cooper* v *Wandsworth Board of Works* (1863) 14 CBNS 180, where the house that the plaintiff had built without obtaining a licence was pulled down by the Board's employees without his being given any prior notice, the court held that the plaintiff could succeed in an action for trespass. Although the statute in question did not provide for property owners to be heard before their buildings were demolished, Byles J stated that there was a long line of authority to the effect that a man was not to be deprived of his property without first being heard, and in any event the common law would supply the omission of the legislature and provide that a hearing should be granted.

At the beginning of the twentieth century, as the scale and power of executive agencies began to increase, the courts started to develop a more generalised concept of natural justice, reflecting a requirement of fairness on the part of those wielding public power. In *Board of Education* v *Rice* [1911] AC 179 Lord Loreburn LC observed that administrative agencies, such as the Board, were required to ascertain the law and the facts in good faith and listen fairly to both sides as, in his view, that was a 'duty laying upon every one who decides anything'.

From these promising beginnings, the courts somewhat lost their way during the ensuing 50 years, effectively abdicating their role of ensuring that the administration conformed with the common law concepts of fairness. The courts seemed unable, or unwilling, to apply the principles to the actions of inferior bodies, remaining firmly committed to the view that compliance with the requirements of natural justice was required only by those discharging judicial functions. As most inferior bodies such as commissioners, tribunals and ministers exercised what were perceived to be administrative functions, their actions were effectively immune from attack on grounds of failing to apply the rules of natural justice.

This retreat from natural justice was reflected in a number of key decisions. In *Local Government Board* v *Arlidge* [1915] AC 120 the House of Lords held that the standards of fairness required of a court of law could not be demanded of a government department, with the result that it was not a violation of natural justice for the Board to refuse to disclose the contents of a report to Arlidge which contained the evidence upon which it had upheld a decision to demolish his property. Similarly, in *Franklin* v *Minister of Town and Country Planning* [1948] AC 87 where the House of Lords held that the minister's statutory duties, including the making of a draft order designating Stevenage as a 'new town', were 'purely administrative' with the result that allegations that he had acted in breach of natural justice were irrelevant, even where the challenge was on the ground of bias.

It was not just in respect of the actions of government departments that the courts were unwilling to intervene on the grounds of fairness. *R* v *Metropolitan Police Commissioner, ex parte Parker* [1953] 2 All ER 353 and *Nakkuda Ali* v *Jayaratne* [1951] AC 66 provide evidence of the courts' refusal to apply the principles of natural justice to the exercise of regulatory jurisdictions. In the former case the Divisional Court refused to quash the revocation of the applicant's licence to operate as a cab driver despite the fact that he had not been granted a hearing before this was done. The court held that the Commissioner's powers of revocation were 'administrative' and therefore certiorari was not available to quash the decision. In the latter, the Privy Council had to consider the validity of the action of the Controller of Textiles of Ceylon who had cancelled the appellant's textile licence, because he had reasonable grounds to believe that the appellant was unfit to continue in business. The appellant argued that the hearing he had been given before revocation of his licence had been inadequate, and therefore the revocation had been in breach of natural justice. The Privy Council held that the Controller, in cancelling licences, was exercising powers that were administrative in nature, consequently there was no obligation upon him to grant the appellant any hearing, let alone an adequate one.

Natural justice restored

Taken to its natural conclusion, the trend established in the four cases considered above would have severely restricted the scope of judicial review of administrative action. Given the extent to which the state, via its executive agencies, was coming increasingly to make decisions affecting the existing and prospective rights of citizens, it was clear that a fresh approach was required. The turning point, and the decision that effectively reinstated breach of natural justice as a ground for challenging executive power, was the House of Lords' decision in *Ridge* v *Baldwin* [1964] AC 40. Charles Ridge had been dismissed from his position as Chief Constable of the County Borough of Brighton by the local watch committee. He contended before the House of Lords that the principles of natural justice applied to the exercise of powers to dismiss him, and that these principles had been breached by not allowing him to know the full case against him, and by not allowing him to put his case properly. The House of Lords allowed his appeal, holding that natural justice did apply and had not been observed. Lord Reid identified three types of case involving dismissal from a position, and explained the way in which the rules of natural justice might, or might not, apply in each case.

First, there were what he described as 'master and servant' cases where natural justice did not really have any relevance. A master was free to dispense with a servant's services as he wished, without granting the latter any hearing. The servant's remedy lay in an action for breach of contract (hence the creation of Industrial Tribunals). Second, there were cases where individuals held office 'at pleasure', such as Crown servants. Such persons had no right to be heard before being dismissed (but note internal Civil Service safeguards). Third, there were cases, like that of Charles Ridge, where an individual was being stripped of some office or status. Lord Reid stated that there was, in his view, an unbroken line of authority to the effect that a man could not be denied an office, without first being told what it was that was being alleged against him, and being given an opportunity of putting his defence or providing an explanation.

Of the judicial/administrative dichotomy, Lord Reid explained that previous cases may have been wrongly decided by courts assuming that certiorari was only available to quash a decision, arrived at following a procedure that had breached natural justice, where the decision-making body was acting ' judicially'. In his view Atkin LJ's dictum in *R* v *Electricity Commissioners, ex parte London Electricity Joint Committee Co (1922) Ltd* [1924] 1 KB 171, to the effect that certiorari was only available in respect of bodies having a duty to act judicially, had been taken too literally in subsequent cases, with the result that the remedy had not been extended to administrative bodies making decisions affecting the rights of individuals. Lord Reid suggested that the 'judicial' element should be deduced from the nature of the power being exercised. In short, the applicability of the rules of natural justice should not depend so much on a sterile academic classification of powers as administrative or judicial, but on the importance of what was at stake for the individual whose rights were affected by the decision.

The interests protected

In many of the early cases concerning natural justice it is possible to identify some property interest that the plaintiff or applicant was seeking to protect. Indeed, in *Ridge* v *Baldwin*, it seems likely that Ridge was principally concerned with protecting his pension rights. In most cases where a property right is affected there is likely to be a private law right of action that the injured party can pursue, in respect of breach of contract or tort.

In light of the role of the modern state, however, particularly the extent to which citizens' activities are regulated by powers of licensing and inspection, and the extent to which rights are created which have no parallel in private law (eg welfare benefits etc), it has been incumbent upon the courts to extend the scope of natural justice to apply to these areas.

Given that judicial review has developed a residual function of providing a means of challenging public law decisions where no other procedure for challenge exists, it is not entirely surprising to find the principles of natural justice being invoked in circumstances that would have been unthinkable 50 years previously. In *R* v *Deputy Governor of Parkhurst Prison, ex parte Leech* [1988] 1 All ER 485 the applicants sought judicial review of the decisions of a prison governor in relation to his imposition of punishments for breach of prison rules, alleging that he had acted in breach of natural justice. The House of Lords held that, in exercising his statutory powers to discipline prisoners, a prison governor was amenable to judicial review because he was exercising a power which affected the legitimate expectations or rights of citizens, and such a power had to be exercised in accordance with the rules of natural justice. In the course of his speech, Lord Bridge stressed the significance of the rights affected as the key to the application of natural justice:

> 'Can it then be right for the court to refuse jurisdiction to afford what seems prima facie to be both the appropriate and the necessary remedy on the ground of "public policy"? My Lords ... It may be a virtual certainty that a number of trouble makers will take every opportunity to exploit and abuse the jurisdiction. But that is only one side of the coin. On the other side it can hardly be doubted that governors and deputy governors dealing with the offences against discipline may occasionally fall short of the standards of fairness which are called for in the performance of any judicial function. Nothing, I believe, is so likely to generate unrest among ordinary prisoners as a sense that they have been treated unfairly and have no effective means of redress. If a prisoner has a genuine grievance arising from disciplinary proceedings unfairly conducted, his right to petition a faceless authority in Whitehall for a remedy will not be of much comfort to him. Thus, I believe, it is at least possible that any damage to prison discipline that may result from frivolous and vexatious applications for judicial review may be substantially offset by the advantages which access to the court will provide for the proper ventilation of genuine grievances and perhaps also that the availability of the court's supervisory role may have the effect on the conduct of judicial proceedings by governors which it appears to have had in the case of boards of visitors of enhancing the standards of fairness observed ... I am firmly of the opinion that, if the social consequences of the availability of judicial review to supervise governors' disciplinary awards are ... detrimental to the proper functioning of the prison system ... it lies in the province of the legislature, not of the judiciary, to exclude the court's jurisdiction.'

Similarly, in *R* v *Board of Governors of London Oratory School, ex parte R* (1988) The Times 17 February, McCullough J observed that there was no reason why the rules of natural justice should not apply to the decision of school governors to expel a pupil. The court was mindful of the consequences of expulsion for the pupil, regarding them as at least as serious as those resulting from an undergraduate being 'sent down'. In terms of procedure, the court was of the view that a pupil threatened with expulsion was entitled to know the case against him, and should be granted a hearing before an unbiased tribunal.

Natural justice and reasonableness

Although considered separately for the purposes of exposition, it would be erroneous to assume that breach of natural justice and unreasonableness (see Chapters 7–9) were mutually exclusive as grounds of challenge. A decision based on a defective procedure could be attacked as one that has been arrived at without relevant considerations being taken into account or, conversely, as one in relation to which irrelevant considerations were taken into account. This failure to observe natural justice could form the basis of a challenge to the substance of the decision itself.

Administrative bodies will frequently have discretion as to the procedure to be adopted in arriving at a decision. This exercise of discretion can be challenged on the ground of unreasonableness, if it is so unreasonable that it is a decision that no reasonable decision-maker would have arrived at. A number of cases illustrate this type of challenge. In *R* v *Secretary of State for the Home Department, ex parte Tarrant* [1984] 1 All ER 799 the decision of the Board of Visitors not to allow a prisoner legal representation was regarded as both unfair and unreasonable by the court on the ground that no reasonable tribunal would have refused the prisoner representation given the gravity of the charges and the possible loss of remission. In *R* v *Norfolk County Council, ex parte M* [1989] 2 All ER 359 the court considered the case of an applicant who was alleged to have behaved indecently towards a 13-year-old girl whilst working at her parent's house as a plumber, allegations that he had strenuously denied. Without giving any notice to the applicant, the social services department of the local authority convened a case conference at which the decision was taken to place his name on the authority's register of child abusers. Once aware of the decision the applicant was given an opportunity to appear with a solicitor before a re-convened case conference in order to make representations, but declined this invitation in the light of the course that the proceedings had already taken. The Divisional Court, granting his application for an order of certiorari to quash the registration, held that the consequences of registering a person as a child abuser were sufficiently serious to require the local authority to act fairly towards that person. Natural justice had not been observed, in that the applicant had not been given advance warning of the decision, had not been consulted, and had not been made aware of all the circumstances surrounding the decision. The court felt that the actions of the authority were so much at odds with the requirements of fairness that they could properly be described as unreasonable in the *Wednesbury* sense (see Chapter 7). See further *R* v *Secretary of State for Health, ex parte C* (2000) The Times 1 March.

5.3 Where natural justice may not apply

The courts have recognised that, whilst the traditional rules of natural justice, in terms of the right to a hearing and the rule against bias, may not apply in full to every decision-making process, fairness is a concept that ought to pervade all aspects of the administration. As Lord Parker CJ observed in *Re HK (An Infant)* [1967] 2 QB 617:

> '... even if an immigration officer [determining whether a person arriving in the United Kingdom has the right to remain in the country] is not acting in a judicial or quasi-judicial capacity, he must at any rate give the immigrant an opportunity of satisfying him of the matters in the subsection, and for that purpose let the immigrant know what his immediate impression is so that the immigrant can disabuse him. That is not, as I see it, a question of acting or being required to act judicially, but of being required to act fairly.'

The difficulty with the 'duty to act fairly' is that what it requires in any given situation may be fairly minimal, to the point where a successful challenge before the courts becomes a distant possibility. It would appear that there is, to some extent, a link between the rights that the applicant seeks to have protected, and the rigour with which the duty to act fairly is enforced.

Where the litigant is seeking to challenge the denial of some privilege to which he had no pre-existing right the courts have tended to take the view that few procedural safeguards need be observed. Hence, in *R* v *Gaming Board for Great Britain, ex parte Benaim and Khaida* [1970] 2 QB 417, the decision of the Board refusing the applicants a gaming licence was upheld even though they had not been given reasons for the refusal or notified of the case they had to answer. As Lord Denning subsequently explained in *Breen* v *AEU* [1971] 1 All ER 1148:

> 'If a man seeks a privilege to which he has no particular claim ... then he can be turned away without a word. He need not be heard. No explanation need be given ...'

In *McInnes* v *Onslow-Fane* [1978] 1 WLR 1520 Megarry V-C expressed the view that the Board dealing with an application for a boxing manager's licence was under a duty to act fairly, but that did not necessitate granting an oral hearing, or informing the applicant of the case against him. It merely required the body making the decision to do so honestly, without bias and caprice. See further *Central Council for Education and Training in Social Work* v *Edwards* (1978) The Times 5 May (an applicant for a place on a polytechnic course held to have no right to a hearing, or to be given the reasons for being denied a place).

Legislative process

The rules of natural justice cannot normally be invoked to challenge the validity of legislation or of the legislative process. In *Bates* v *Lord Hailsham* [1972] 1 WLR 1373 the court held that a failure to consult prior to exercising powers to create delegated legislation, in the absence of any statutory requirements to do so, could not invalidate the process. The rules of natural justice simply did not apply.

Domestic procedures

The courts may decline jurisdiction over what they perceive to be decisions of internal/domestic bodies, such as the disciplinary panels of clubs and federations, on the basis that it is not appropriate to over-judicialise such proceedings. Much depends on what is at stake for the applicant/plaintiff. In *Currie* v *Barton* (1988) The Times 12 February O'Conner LJ expressed the view that the courts should not intervene in the affairs of domestic bodies unless such bodies were in a contractual relationship with those affected by their decisions, or their decisions affected the ability of an individual to pursue his/her livelihood.

Preliminary procedures

There are a number of authorities suggesting that natural justice will not apply where action is merely preparatory to the making of a decision, or 'purely administrative' as it is sometimes described. In both *Furnell* v *Whangarei High Schools Board* [1973] AC 660 and *Herring* v *Templeman* [1973] AC 660 it was held that an individual had no right to be heard by a subordinate body instructed to prepare a report for a disciplinary body. Only when the charges were put to the individual concerned did the right to be heard apply. Similar reasoning was adopted in *Norwest Holst Ltd* v *Secretary of State for Trade* [1978] Ch 201, where it was held that the company had no right to be heard prior to the appointment of inspectors to investigate the company's affairs. Such appointments were 'purely administrative' decisions: see also *Lewis* v *Heffer* [1978] 3 All ER 354. Note that in *R* v *Norfolk County Council, ex parte M* (above) the court rejected the submission by counsel for the authority that the decision to register the applicant as an abuser was not one amenable to judicial review because it was clerical or administrative in nature, the court being guided to its conclusion by the effect that such a decision could have upon an individual.

5.4 Invoking natural justice – the concept of legitimate expectation

As has been noted above, the search for the touchstone that will bring into play the rules of natural justice has progressed from identifying a process as 'judicial' to looking at the rights affected, and the concept of 'rights affected' has itself developed to encompass what would now be called 'public law' rights, as opposed to property-related rights. As a basis for the court's jurisdiction, however, this still represents a rather vague test. In the search for something more concrete the courts have, over the last 25 years, through decisions such as *Schmidt* v *Secretary of State for Home*

Affairs [1969] 2 Ch 149, *McInnes* v *Onslow-Fane* (above) and *Cinnamond* v *British Airports Authority* [1980] 1 WLR 582, gradually developed the concept of 'legitimate expectation' as a basis for determining whether or not they should intervene on the grounds of breach of natural justice.

The matter was reviewed at length in *R* v *Devon County Council, ex parte Baker and Another; R* v *Durham County Council, ex parte Curtis and Another* [1995] 1 All ER 73, a case involving challenges to decisions by local authorities to close homes for the elderly. Although careful to point out that his was not to be taken as an exhaustive analysis of the issue, Simon Brown LJ went on to identify four broad categories of case in which the concept might be relevant, and it is submitted that this provides a useful starting point for examination of a notoriously fluid and conceptual topic.

The first category involves those cases where the litigant asserts a substantive right, in the form of an entitlement that should not be denied him. In *R* v *Secretary of State for the Home Department, ex parte Khan* [1985] 1 All ER 40 the Home Office published a circular indicating the criteria that would be applied when persons in the United Kingdom wished to adopt a child from abroad. The applicant, who sought to adopt the child of a relative who lived in Pakistan, applied for an entry clearance certificate for the child, but his request was refused by the Secretary of State who applied criteria other than those set out in the circular. The applicant applied for judicial review of the Secretary of State's refusal, contending that he had a 'legitimate expectation', arising out of the circular, that the procedure set out therein would be followed. The Secretary of State claimed that his discretion in such matters was unfettered. The court held that, provided the circular did not conflict with the minister's statutory duty, he was under a duty to apply the criteria and could only resile from the provisions of the circular if there was: an overriding public interest that he should do so; and interested persons were first afforded a hearing. In the circumstances the court felt that the Secretary of State had acted unfairly and unreasonably in deciding the applicant's case after applying criteria different from those set out in the circular.

In *R* v *North and East Devon Health Authority, ex parte Coughlan* [2000] 2 WLR 622 the Court of Appeal held that the respondent authority should be held to its undertaking to the applicant that she would have a 'home for life' at a particular specialist nursing home. Lord Woolf MR expressed the view that the undertaking gave rise to a legitimate expectation on the part of the applicant that she would not be moved to another location against her wishes. Although the authority was not irrevocably bound by the undertaking, the key to the recognition of the legitimate expectation here was the Court's view that there was no overriding public interest that justified allowing the authority to resile from the promise. Compare with the approach taken by the House of Lords to the argument put forward by Myra Hindley to the effect that she had a legitimate expectation of not having to serve the remainder of her life in prison to satisfy the retribution and deterrence elements of the life sentence imposed on her for murder: *R* v *Secretary of State for the Home Department, ex parte Hindley* [2000] 2 All ER 385.

Similarly, in *R* v *Secretary of State for the Home Department, ex parte Ruddock* [1987] 2 All ER 518 the court held that, since the Secretary of State had repeatedly confirmed, between 1952 and 1982, that the criteria for authorising phone-tapping would be complied with, there arose a legitimate expectation that he would in fact comply with such criteria. Taylor J observed that the doctrine of legitimate expectation was not limited to those cases involving a legitimate expectation of a hearing before some right was affected, but also extended to situations where, although no right to be heard existed, fairness required a public body to act in compliance with its public undertakings and assurances: see also *R* v *Brent London Borough Council, ex parte MacDonagh* (1989) The Times 22 March.

This first category, therefore, would appear to involve cases where the litigant can say that because of an existing published policy he has an identifiable substantive right – not just as to the procedure to be followed, but as to a decision being made in his favour provided established criteria are met, ie that a child will be allowed to enter the country, or that phone-tapping will not be authorised.

As Simon Brown LJ observed:

'[The authorities] show that the claimant's right will only be found established when there is a clear and unambiguous representation upon which it was reasonable for him to rely. Then the administrator or other public body will be held bound in fairness by the representation made unless only its promise or undertaking as to how its power would be exercised is inconsistent with the statutory duties imposed upon it. The doctrine employed in this sense is akin to estoppel. In so far as the public body's representation is communicated by way of a stated policy, this type of legitimate expectation falls into two distinct sub-categories: cases in which the authority are held entitled to change their policy even so as to affect the claimant, and those in which they are not. An illustration of the former is *R* v *Torbay BC, ex parte Cleasby* [1991] COD 142; of the latter *ex parte Khan*.'

In a subsequent decision, *R* v *Commissioners of Inland Revenue, ex parte Unilever plc* [1996] STC 681, Simon Brown LJ appears to have relaxed these preconditions somewhat by holding that, even where the representations made by the public body are someway short of unqualified and unambiguous, the public body will be bound by them if it would be unfair and an abuse of power for it to act otherwise. Given that public bodies must be granted the freedom to exercise discretion in the public interest, it has to be accepted that policies can be changed in a way that might adversely affect the existing interests and rights of individuals. The real issues in such cases, it is submitted, relate to how the policy is changed and the reasons for so doing. The legality of any such change, being a substantive issue, is to be judged according to the *Wednesbury* criteria, as the Court of Appeal has reaffirmed in *R* v *Secretary of State for the Home Department and Another, ex parte Hargreaves and Others* [1997] 1 WLR 906.

In *R* v *Ministry of Agriculture, Fisheries and Food, ex parte Hamble (Offshore)*

Fisheries Ltd [1995] 2 All ER 714, a case concerning an unsuccessful challenge to a change of policy in the granting of fishing licences for North Sea trawlers, Sedley J noted that the reasons given by the MAFF for changing its policy and refusing to make an exception that would have permitted the applicants to continue fishing were legitimate in the circumstances (desire to conserve fishing stocks), and the very existence of other exceptions showed that the MAFF had addressed the issue of rigidity. Regarding legitimate expectation, he rejected the view expressed by Laws J in *ex parte Richmond-upon-Thames LBC* [1994] 1 WLR 74, to the effect that the concept of legitimate expectation only extended to procedural expectations, citing *ex parte Ruddock* (above), *Findlay* v *Secretary of State for the Home Department* [1985] AC 318 and a number of European Court decisions as authorities to the contrary. He further rejected any notion that the degree of reliance, on the part of the applicant, had any bearing on the legitimacy of the expectation, as this could indirectly amount to an estoppel (on this point, see also *R (On the Application of Bibi)* v *Newham LBC* (2001) The Times 10 May). Citing the jurisprudence of the European Union in relation to the need for legal certainty and non-retrospectivity, he observed that what was important was whether or not the applicant could demonstrate an 'expectation' that was worthy of protection, ie that it was legitimate. Where an expectation arose from custom and practice, based on a particular policy, the court had to be alive to the possibility that the policy might have to be revised from time to time, as the public interest required. His Lordship endorsed the view that, whilst an individual might have an expectation regarding the procedure to be adopted by a public body, or an expectation that he might be permitted to continue to enjoy some right or privilege, for that expectation to be protected in public law it was not sufficient that it should merely be a reasonable expectation. As he observed:

> '... legitimate expectation is now in effect a term of art, reserved for expectations that are not only reasonable but which will be sustained by the court in the face of changes of policy ... whether this point has been reached is determined by the court, whether on grounds of rationality, of legality or of fairness, of all of which the court, not the decision-maker, is the arbiter.'

A second category identified in *ex parte Baker* arises where the applicant's interest lies in some ultimate benefit which he hopes to attain or, possibly, retain. This classification can be traced back to decisions such as *Schmidt* v *Secretary of State for Home Affairs* (above), where two Scientology students, who were refused an extension of their permission to remain in the United Kingdom when their right to remain had expired, complained that they had not been granted a hearing. The Court of Appeal held that there had been no breach of natural justice, Lord Denning stating that as they had no right to remain in the country, they had no legitimate expectation of being granted a hearing. Significantly, however, he was willing to accept that the situation might have been different if their right to stay had been revoked before its expiry, ie they had had an expectation that their right to remain would not be revoked prior to its expiry.

As Simon Brown LJ explained in *ex parte Baker*:

'... it is the interest itself rather than the benefit that is the substance of the expectation. In other words the expectation arises not because the claimant asserts any specific right to a benefit but rather because his interest in it is one that the law holds protected by the requirements of procedural fairness; the law recognises that the interest cannot properly be withdrawn (or denied) without the claimant being given an opportunity to comment and without the authority communicating rational grounds for any adverse decision. ... Whether or not [the claimant] can ... legitimately expect procedural fairness ... will depend upon the court's view of what fairness demands in all the circumstances of the case ... in the category 2 sense [legitimate expectation] seems to me no more than a recognition and embodiment of the unsurprising principle that the demands of fairness are likely to be somewhat higher when an authority contemplates depriving someone of an existing benefit or advantage than where the claimant is a bare applicant for a future benefit.'

Relying on a passage from the speech of Lord Diplock in *Council of Civil Service Unions* v *Minister for the Civil Service* [1985] AC 374 at 408, he further expressed the view that the only touchstone for a 'category 2' interest was that the claimant had in the past been entitled to enjoy some benefit or advantage. In *R* v *Rochdale Metropolitan BC, ex parte Schemet* (1992) 91 LGR 425 the applicants successfully established a 'category 2' claim in respect of the local authority's decision to abandon its policy of paying the travelling expenses of children attending schools maintained by a neighbouring authority. Roch J observed that the parents of such children:

'... had a legitimate expectation that that benefit would continue until there had been communicated to them some rational grounds for withdrawing it on which they had been given an opportunity to comment.'

Further evidence of this approach (although the challenged failed on the facts) is provided by the Court of Appeal's decision in *R* v *Secretary of State for Transport, ex parte Richmond-upon-Thames London Borough Council (No 4)* [1996] 1 WLR 1460.

Compare with *R* v *Department of Education and Employment, ex parte Begbie* (1999) The Times 14 September, where the Court of Appeal held that a pre-election promise by an opposition spokesman, to the effect that any child already attending a fee-paying school under the assisted places scheme prior to the election would be allowed to complete her education even though the scheme was to be abolished if Labour were elected, was held not to give rise to a legitimate expectation that, if elected, the statement would be put into effect as policy. Peter Gibson LJ observed that no issue of estoppel could arise as an opposition spokesman did not speak on behalf of a public authority. Moreover, he felt that the consequences of a failure to enact pre-election promises should be political, not legal. In any event, the doctrine of legitimate expectation had to yield to the intention of Parliament as expressed through legislation. The terms of the relevant legislation, the Education (Schools) Act 1997, were incompatible with the legitimate expectation alleged.

The third category referred to by Simon Brown LJ in *ex parte Baker* arises where the concept of legitimate expectation is used to refer to the fair procedure itself, ie the applicant claims to have a legitimate expectation that the public body will act fairly towards him. His Lordship criticised the use of legitimate expectation in this sense as being 'superfluous and unhelpful' because it confuses the interest which is the basis of the requirement of procedural fairness with the requirement itself.

The fourth and final category identified in *ex parte Baker* involves those cases where a particular procedure, not otherwise required by law, has to be followed as a result of a previous promise or course of dealing. Simon Brown LJ cited, as illustrative of this fourth category, the decision of the Privy Council in *Attorney-General of Hong Kong* v *Ng Yuen Shiu* [1983] 2 All ER 346. In that case the Hong Kong government had made public its changed policy towards illegal immigrants, stating that each one, if he or she came forward, would be interviewed and, although no guarantee would be given that they would not subsequently be removed, each case would be treated on its merits. The respondent, who had entered Hong Kong illegally in 1976, was interviewed by an immigration officer and subsequently detained pending the making of a removal order. His appeal to the immigration authorities was dismissed without a hearing, but the Court of Appeal of Hong Kong granted the respondent an order of prohibition preventing his removal, pending a proper hearing of his case, a decision in respect of which the Attorney-General of Hong Kong appealed to the Privy Council. Quashing the order of prohibition, the Privy Council held that, assuming there was no general right in an alien to have a hearing in accordance with the rules of natural justice before the making of a removal order against him, a person was nevertheless entitled to a fair hearing before a decision adversely affecting his interests was made by a public official or body if he had a legitimate or reasonable expectation of being accorded such a hearing. Such an expectation might be based on some statement or undertaking by, or on behalf of, the public authority which had the duty of making the decision if the authority had through its officers, acted in a way which would make it unfair or inconsistent with good administration to deny the person affected an inquiry into his case. That principle was as much applicable where the person affected was an alien as where he was a British subject, because a public authority was bound by its undertaking as to the procedure it would follow, provided those undertakings did not conflict with its statutory duty. It followed that the government undertaking that each case would be treated on its merits had not been implemented since the respondent had been given no opportunity to explain the humanitarian grounds on which he might have been allowed to remain in Hong Kong, in particular that he was a partner in a business which employed a large number of workers.

Similar reasoning can be identified in *Council of Civil Service Unions* v *Minister for the Civil Service* (above), to the extent that the House of Lords accepted that, because there had been a previous regular practice of consultation between the minister and the unions on matters relating to conditions of service, the unions had a legitimate expectation of being consulted as to future changes.

The distinction between 'category 1' and 'category 4' cases would seem to lie in the fact that the first grouping relate to the litigant's claim to have a decision made in his favour, in accordance with a stated policy; in the latter grouping the litigant has an expectation relating to the way in which decisions will be made. For example, in *Ng Yuen Shui*, it could not be contended that the applicant had a legitimate expectation that he would not be deported, merely that he would be given a hearing prior to any decision being made.

It is submitted that the categories are unlikely to be mutually exclusive, as cases can often involve a mixture of policy statements and undertakings. For example, in *R v Brent London Borough Council, ex parte MacDonagh* (above) the local authority had sent a letter to each of the gypsies occupying a local authority site informing them that they would not be evicted from the site in future, unless the local authority provided suitable alternative accommodation. In 1988, in the light of the extent to which conditions on the site had deteriorated, the local authority took the decision to evict. The Divisional Court, granting an order of certiorari to quash the decision, and an injunction to prevent the local authority from revoking its consent to the occupation of the site without consultation with the gypsies, held that the letters, and the previous conduct of the local authority, gave rise to a legitimate expectation that there would be no evictions without some alternative accommodation being made available. Was this a case of substantive rights arising because of a stated policy that it was lawful for the authority to adopt, or did the legitimate expectation arise from the assurances from the authority as to the procedures it would adopt? The question is not simply of academic interest. Presumably the litigant would prefer to be regarded as falling within 'category 1' as what he wants is the substantive right. If denied the right that he asserts he is unlikely to be mollified by an explanation that points out that a fair procedure was nevertheless followed.

It could be contended that, because the distinction between procedures and substantive entitlements may come down to mere semantics, the courts should abandon notions of categorisation, and simply address the issue of fairness in the substantive sense. In *R v Commssioners of Inland Revenue, ex parte Unilever plc* (above), there was evidence that, for over 20 years, the Revenue had allowed the applicants to submit an annual claim to tax relief after the official deadline. In 1992, without notice, the Revenue decided to alter its past practice and refused to accept the late claim for that year. Notwithstanding that there was no evidence of the Revenue ever having sanctioned the making of claims out of time, the Court of Appeal held that it was an abuse of power for the Revenue to suddenly alter its practices to the detriment of the applicant. In effect, the Revenue's custom and practice had lulled the applicants into a false sense of security regarding adherence to time limits. Simon Brown LJ made it clear that he regarded the matter as falling within *Wednesbury* concept in the sense that it would have been 'illogical or immoral or both for a public authority to act with such conspicuous unfairness'. Again, the case could be seen as being concerned with expectations regarding procedures, the handling of late claims, or as one concerned with an expectation as to how discretion would be exercised. Either way the Revenue's behaviour foundered on the concept of irrationality.

Where the assurance given is based on a mistake by the promisor as to the promisee's legal rights, the courts will not hold that a legitimate expectation has arisen in favour of the promisor, not least because the court might be in danger of extending the promisor's power in a manner not permitted by statute: see generally Chapter 9, section 9.5. In *R* v *Secretary of State for the Home Department, ex Silva and Another* (1994) The Times 1 April the applicants, prisoners originally from Colombia, serving prison sentences for drugs offences, were informed of the Home Secretary's intention to deport them in a letter that erroneously referred to the applicants being permitted a right to appeal against the decision. The mistake was subsequently rectified and the applicants were notified that they were to be deported pursuant to s3(6) of the Immigration Act 1971, which did not provide for any right of appeal. Considering the application for judicial review of the Home Secretary's decision to order deportation, on the ground that his initial letter had given rise to a legitimate expectation that the deportation would be ordered under s3(5)(b) of the 1971 Act, which did permit a right of appeal, the Court of Appeal held that applicants' reliance on *Ng Yuen Shiu* (above) was misguided, as they had not shown that it would be unfair or detrimental to the principles of good administration for the Home Secretary to depart from his initial decision.

5.5 Consequences of a breach of natural justice

What happens once a decision has been taken in breach of natural justice? Is it 'void', or 'voidable'? Can an individual ignore the decision with impunity and rely on its invalidity as justification in any subsequent action taken against him? Can a breach of natural justice at first instance be cured by a valid hearing on appeal? Historically the position has been that an intra vires decision is valid; an intra vires decision vitiated by an error of law is voidable, in the sense that it continues in force as a valid decision unless and until it is quashed by an order of certiorari; and an ultra vires decision is void, of no effect – it is as if no decision was ever taken.

Whilst this approach may have the advantage of simplicity, how is an individual to know if a decision is in breach of natural justice, and therefore ultra vires? It would be rather dangerous, for example, where a market trader's licence has been revoked, for him to assume on his own, or even his legal adviser's, judgment that because there had been a breach of natural justice the revocation was void, and he could therefore continue legally to trade. In *Ridge* v *Baldwin* (above) the House of Lords made it clear that there are no 'degrees of nullity', an ultra vires decision is void. As Lord Reid commented:

'... there was considerable argument whether in the result the watch committee's decision is void or merely voidable. Time and again in the cases I have cited it has been stated that a decision given without regard to the principles of natural justice is void and that was expressly decided in *Wood* v *Wood* (1874) LR 9 Exch 190. I see no reason to doubt these authorities. The body with the power to decide cannot lawfully proceed to make a decision until it has afforded to the person affected a proper opportunity to state his case.'

Professor Wade suggests that decisions should be regarded as voidable, where there is an error of law; 'void', where there appears to be evidence that the body has acted ultra vires, but this is yet to be confirmed by the courts; and void where a decision has been declared to be such by the courts and its effects can safely be ignored. The danger of describing an ultra vires decision as void in any absolute sense until declared to be such by the courts is illustrated by those decisions which, after the expiry of a time limit, become unchallengeable in the courts. It would be odd to say that an absolutely void decision had nevertheless to be observed because of the partial 'ouster' clause that prevents legal challenge. See further *R* v *Bassetlaw District Council, ex parte Oxby* (1997) The Times 18 December.

In *Boddington* v *British Transport Police* [1998] 2 All ER 203 Lord Irvine expressed the view that, following *Anisminic* v *Foreign Compensation Commission* (considered further at Chapter 12, section 12.2), an impugned decision or order would now be regarded as a nullity (ie as void ab initio), even if it were to be analysed as an error of law on the face of the record. Equally, a decision or order would be regarded as void ab initio if it was made in bad faith, or as a result of irrelevant matters being taken into account, relevant considerations not being taken into account etc. Lord Browne-Wilkinson preferred to reserve his position on this point, observing (at p218g–h):

'... my noble and learned friend Lord Irvine of Lairg LC ... attaches importance to the consideration that an invalid bye-law is and always has been a nullity. The bye-law will necessarily have been found to be ultra vires; therefore it is said it is a nullity having no legal effect. I adhere to my view that the juristic basis of judicial review is the doctrine of ultra vires. But I am far from satisfied that an ultra vires act is incapable of having any legal consequence during the period between the doing of that act and the recognition of its invalidity by the court. During that period people will have regulated their lives on the basis that the act is valid ... I prefer to express no view at this stage on those difficult points ...'

Lord Slynn also declined to give an authoritative view on this point, but observed (at p219f–j):

'I consider that the result of allowing a collateral challenge in proceedings before courts of criminal jurisdiction can be reached without it being necessary in this case to say that if an act or bye-law is invalid it must be held to have been invalid from the outset for all purposes and that no lawful consequences can flow from it. This may be the logical result and will no doubt sometimes be the position but courts have had to grapple with the problem of reconciling the logical result with the reality that much may have been done on the basis that an administrative act or a bye-law was valid. The unscrambling may produce more serious difficulties than the invalidity. The European Court of Justice has dealt with the problem by ruling that its declaration of invalidity should only operate for the benefit of the parties to the actual case or of those who had begun proceedings for a declaration of invalidity before the court's judgment. In our jurisdiction the effect of invalidity may not be relied on if limitation periods have expired or if the court in its discretion refuses relief, albeit considering that the act is invalid. These situations are of course different from those where a court has pronounced subordinate legislation or an administrative act to be unlawful or where the presumption in favour of their legality has been overruled by a court of competent jurisdiction. But even in these cases I consider that the question whether the acts or bye-laws are to be treated as having at no time had any effect in law is not one which has been fully explored and is not one on which it is necessary to rule in this appeal and I prefer to express no view upon it.'

Invalidity and appeals

If a hearing at first instance is vitiated by a procedural error that amounts to a breach of natural justice, to what extent, if at all, can such errors be rectified by a properly conducted and constituted appeal hearing? On the one hand there is the logical difficulty created by the fact that a hearing in breach of natural justice is a nullity, and there cannot be an appeal from a nullity; on the other hand an appeal, unlike judicial review, can involve a complete rehearing of a case and is in effect the decision being taken all over again. In *Leary* v *National Union of Vehicle Builders* [1970] 2 All ER 713 the court held that a defective hearing could not be cured by a properly conducted appeal, Megarry J observing that:

> 'If the rules and the law combine to give the member the right to a fair trial and the right of appeal, why should he be told that he ought to be satisfied with an unjust trial and a fair appeal? ... As a general rule ... I hold that a failure of natural justice in the trial body cannot be cured by a sufficiency of natural justice in an appellate body.'

This view was not followed by the Privy Council, however, in *Calvin* v *Carr* [1979] 2 All ER 440, where the claim of a jockey, to the effect that a hearing of his case before the stewards, which resulted in his disqualification, was in breach of natural justice and could not, therefore, be remedied by a properly conducted appeal hearing before an appellate committee of the Australian Jockey Club, was dismissed. Instead the Privy Council suggested that guidance could be derived from classifying cases according to the type of procedure involved. As Lord Wilberforce explained:

> 'First there are cases where the rules provide for a rehearing by the original body, or some fuller or enlarged form of it ... It is not difficult in such cases to reach the conclusion that the first hearing is superseded by the second ... At the other extreme are cases where, after examination of the whole hearing structure, in the context of the particular activity to which it relates (trade union membership, planning, employment etc) the conclusion is reached that a complainant has the right to nothing less than a fair hearing both at the original and at the appeal stage.'

Lord Wilberforce continued by describing a third, intermediate, situation where the possibility of defects at an initial hearing being remedied on appeal would depend on the circumstances. As he observed:

'... it is for the court, in the light of the agreements made, and in addition having regard to the course of proceedings, to decide whether, at the end of the day, there has been a fair result, reached by fair methods, such as the parties should fairly be taken to have accepted when they joined the association. Naturally there may be instances when the defect is so flagrant, the consequences so severe, that the most perfect of appeals or rehearings will not be sufficient to produce a just result.'

A case that is arguably a good example of Lord Wilberforce's 'intermediate' category arose in *R* v *Governors of St Gregory's RC Aided High School, ex parte Roberts* (1995) The Times 27 January, where the applicant, a pupil at the respondent school, was found to have sworn at a master. The headmaster of the school ordered the applicant's exclusion from the school, a decision subsequently upheld following a meeting of the governors at which the applicant was not permitted to give evidence, although his mother had been present, had been permitted to cross-examine the headmaster, and had made representations on her son's behalf. The decision of the governors was subsequently upheld by an appeals committee, at which the previously gathered evidence was reviewed, and the applicant was permitted to speak. Dismissing the application for judicial review, the court held that the defects in the procedure followed by the governors had been cured by the proceedings before the appellate committee, which had investigated the case very thoroughly.

In the light of this decision, therefore, and others such as *R* v *Brent London Borough Council, ex parte Gunning* (1985) 84 LGR 168 and *R* v *Visitors to the Inns of Court, ex parte Calder* [1993] 3 WLR 287, the position would appear to be that the courts are more likely to regard an appeal process as curing defects in procedure at first instance if the appeal process is concerned with the deliberations of a 'domestic' tribunal, as opposed to a statutory one, and the appellate hearing involves a thorough review of the evidence, allows the interested party a hearing, and acts without bias.

6

What Are the Requirements of a Fair Hearing?

6.1 Introduction

6.2 Failure to comply with express statutory procedural requirements

6.3 Procedural fairness at common law

6.4 The common law right to legal representation

6.5 The right to a reasoned decision at common law

6.6 The rule against bias

6.1 Introduction

This chapter is concerned with the procedures to be observed by a public decision-maker to comply with the requirements of natural justice. The preceding chapter sought to deal with the question of when natural justice applies, and it will be recalled that some situations seem to require the full panoply of 'judicial' type procedural safeguards, whilst in others there is only a 'duty to act fairly'. The problem is that the extent to which natural justice applies to a situation, and if it does what procedural requirements must be observed, will necessarily vary from one situation to another, depending upon context, subject matter and the rights of those affected. Where a statute specifies the procedure to be followed the role of the courts is primarily to ensure that the procedure has been followed in so far as it needs to be. Where the procedure to be followed is at the discretion of the decision-making body all that can be said with any certainty is that if the process is one to which natural justice or a duty to act fairly does not apply, such as might be the case with the discharge of purely administrative functions, the procedural requirement considered in the course of this chapter will be largely irrelevant. If, on the other hand, the situation is one that requires some compliance with natural justice or the duty to act fairly, then the procedural requirements detailed here will have to be followed to a degree. With the enactment of the Human Rights Act 1998 one should also bear in mind the residual duty placed upon public authorities to act in compliance with the Convention rights. Of particular relevance here is art 6 which provides for the right to a 'fair and public hearing within a reasonable time by an independent and impartial tribunal' where an individual's civil rights and obligations are being determined.

That art 6 rights may be engaged where an act is of an administrative nature was confirmed by Lord Clyde in *R (On the Application of Holding and Barnes plc)* v *Secretary of State for the Environment, Transport and the Regions; R (On the Application of Alconbury Developments Ltd)* v *Secretary of State for the Environment, Transport and the Regions; Secretary of State for the Environment, Transport and the Regions* v *Legal and General Assurance Society Ltd* [2001] 2 WLR 1389, where he observed that:

> 'It is thus clear that art 6(1) is engaged where the decision which is to be given is of an administrative character, that is to say one given in an exercise of discretionary power, as well as a dispute in a court of law regarding the private rights of the citizen, provided that it directly affects civil rights and obligations and is of a genuine and serious nature.'

See further *R (On the Application of McLellan)* v *Bracknell Forest Borough Council* [2002] 1 All ER 899.

Whether or not a procedure complies with the requirements of fairness as required by art 6 will fall to be determined by looking at the procedure as a whole – including the availability of appeal procedures and judicial review. As Simon Brown LJ observed in *R (On the Application of Adlard)* v *Secretary of State for the Environment, Transport and the Regions* (2002) The Times 31 May:

> 'The question whether or not art 6 is satisfied ... falls to be considered by reference not merely to the initial decision-making process but also in the light of the High Court's review jurisdiction ... For my part, I can find no warrant, whether in domestic or in Strasbourg jurisprudence, for concluding that where ... the administrative decisions taken at first instance are generally likely to turn on questions of judgment and discretion rather than on findings of fact, the statutory scheme must provide for an oral hearing at that initial stage ... The remedy of judicial review in my judgment amply enables the court to correct any injustice it perceives in an individual case. If, in short, the court were satisfied that exceptionally, on the facts of a particular case, [that a decision-maker had] acted unfairly or unreasonably in denying an objector any, or any sufficient, oral hearing, the court would quash the decision and require such a hearing to be given ...'

6.2 Failure to comply with express statutory procedural requirements

Parliament may determine the procedure to be followed by a decision-making body by making express provision in the relevant enabling Act. The nature of the procedure proscribed will depend upon the aims that Parliament is trying to achieve. Time limits for the making of applications to a decision-making body are often laid down to reduce delays. Matters are required to be recorded in writing to aid certainty. Notice of decisions being taken and of rights of appeal are provided to promote fairness. The requirement of prior consultation may, in addition to promoting fairness, result in a better informed decision.

What is the consequence of a decision-making body failing to comply with a procedural requirement laid down in its enabling Act? A logical response might be that if an inferior body fails to act in a way prescribed by statute the result must be that its decision is ultra vires. In reality the answer is not so simple. Procedural requirements have traditionally been allocated to one of two broad categories. Either the requirement is mandatory, where failure to observe the requirement normally renders any subsequent action void, or the requirement is directory, where failure to observe the requirement will not normally be fatal to the validity of the ensuing determination.

Making the distinction

How is the distinction made between a procedural requirement that is mandatory and one that is directory? There is no one simple test. Everything depends on context. In *Howard* v *Boddington* (1877) 2 PD 203, Lord Penzance expressed the problem thus:

> 'You cannot safely go further than that in each case you must look to the subject matter; consider the importance of the provision that has been disregarded and the relation of that provision to the general object intended to be secured by the Act.'

Inevitably the courts will want to avoid an over-rigid approach and retain for themselves a degree of discretion to be exercised on a case by case basis. As Lord Hailsham LC observed in *London and Clydeside Estates Ltd* v *Aberdeen District Council* [1980] 1 WLR 182:

> 'When Parliament lays down a statutory requirement for the exercise of legal authority it expects its authority to be obeyed down to the minutest detail. But what the courts have to decide in a particular case is the legal consequence of non-compliance on the rights of the subject viewed in the light of a concrete state of facts and a continuing chain of events. It may be that what the courts are faced with is not so much a stark choice of alternatives but a spectrum of possibilities in which one compartment or description fades gradually into another. At one end of this spectrum there may be cases in which a fundamental obligation may have been so outrageously and flagrantly ignored or defied that the subject may safely ignore what has been done and treat it as having no legal consequences upon himself. In such a case if the defaulting authority seeks to rely on its action it may be that the subject is entitled to use the defect in procedure simply as a shield or defence without having taken any positive action of his own. At the other end of the spectrum the defect in procedure may be so nugatory or trivial that the authority can safely proceed without remedial action, confident that, if the subject is so misguided as to rely on the fault, the courts will decline to listen to his complaint. But in a very great number of cases, it may be in a majority of them, it may be necessary for a subject, in order to safeguard himself, to go to the court for declaration of his rights, the grant of which may well be discretionary, and by the like token it may be wise for an authority (as it certainly would have been here) to do everything in its power to remedy the fault in its procedure so as not to deprive the subject of his due or themselves of their power to act. In such cases, though language like "mandatory", "directory", "void", "voidable",

"nullity" and so forth may be helpful in argument, it may be misleading in effect if relied on to show that the courts, in deciding the consequences of a defect in the exercise of power, are necessarily bound to fit the facts of a particular case and a developing chain of events into rigid legal categories or to stretch or cramp them on a bed of Procrustes invented by lawyers for the purposes of convenient exposition ... I do not wish to be understood in the field of administrative law and in the domain where the courts apply a supervisory jurisdiction over the acts of subordinate authority purporting to exercise statutory powers, to encourage the use of rigid legal classifications. The jurisdiction is inherently discretionary and the court is frequently in the presence of differences of degree which merge almost imperceptibly into differences of kind.'

Even when the distinction appears to have been made, and one has decided that a requirement must be mandatory because of its significance, one still has to bear in mind the doctrine of substantial compliance. This operates with the effect that, even though a requirement is generally mandatory, an inferior body's actions will not be invalidated because it has failed to comply with it in some minor way: see *Coney* v *Choice* [1975] 1 All ER 979, discussed further below.

A further complication is that the classification of a requirement as mandatory or directory may depend to some extent on the extent to which it has been breached. An example of this problem is provided by the decision in *Cullimore* v *Lyme Regis Corporation* [1962] 1 QB 718. (When considering this decision, bear in mind the point that time limits are generally regarded as being directory.) The local authority was empowered to carry out coastal protection works and levy charges on landowners for the work done. Charges had to be levied within six months of the work being carried out. The local authority delayed for nearly two years before submitting its charges. The court held the charges to be void as a result of being out of time. Note that this means the time limit must have been regarded as mandatory. The court went on to point out that if the charges had been levied only a few days late they would have been valid. This is either an application of the substantial compliance doctrine, or implicit recognition that the time limit would normally have been regarded as directory.

Further warnings against over-zealous adherence to the mandatory/directory distinction are to be found in *R* v *Secretary of State for the Home Department, ex parte Jeyeanthan* [1999] 3 All ER 231.

Lord Woolf MR reviewed the nature of the mandatory/directory dichotomy as it applied to express statutory procedural requirements and observed:

'The position is more complex than [the dichotomy suggests] and this approach distracts attention from the important question of what the legislator should be judged to have intended should be the consequence of the non-compliance. This has to be assessed on a consideration of the language of the legislation against the factual circumstances of the non-compliance. In the majority of cases it provides limited, if any, assistance to inquire whether the requirement is mandatory or directory ... Because of what can be the very undesirable consequences of a procedural requirement which is made so fundamental that any departure from the requirement makes everything that happens thereafter irreversibly a nullity it is to be hoped that provisions intended to have this effect will be few and far between. In the majority of cases, whether the requirement is categorised as directory or mandatory, the tribunal before whom the defect is properly raised has the task of determining what are to be the consequences of failing to comply with the requirement in the context of all the facts and circumstances of the case in which the issue arises. In such a situation that tribunal's task will be to seek to do what is just in all the circumstances … An examination of the relevant authorities, the leading textbooks and the numerous authorities to which they refer confirm the limitations of applying a solely mandatory/directory classification … Frequently the investigation involves doing no more than deciding the sense in which the word "shall" has been used as part of a particular procedural requirement. As the word "shall" is normally inserted to show that something is required to be done, the exercise tends to be an unrewarding one. Much more important is to focus on the consequences of non-compliance. Here the authorities show no constant pattern. This is the result of courts in those cases focusing on the issue of whether or not a requirement is mandatory and ignoring or failing to pay sufficient attention to the issue of the consequences of non-compliance with, in particular, a mandatory requirement.'

Lord Woolf MR referred to the comments of Lord Hailsham of St Marylebone LC in his speech in *London and Clydeside Estates Ltd* v *Aberdeen District Council* (above) and continued:

'Bearing in mind Lord Hailsham LC's helpful guidance I suggest that the right approach is to regard the question of whether a requirement is directory or mandatory as only at most a first step. In the majority of cases there are other questions which have to be asked which are more likely to be of greater assistance than the application of the mandatory/directory test. The questions which are likely to arise are as follows: is the statutory requirement fulfilled if there has been substantial compliance with the requirement and, if so, has there been substantial compliance in the case in issue even though there has not been strict compliance? (The substantial compliance question.) Is the non-compliance capable of being waived, and if so, has it, or can it and should it be waived in this particular case? (The discretionary question.) I treat the grant of an extension of time for compliance as a waiver. If it is not capable of being waived or is not waived then what is the consequence of the non-compliance? (The consequences question.) Which questions arise will depend upon the facts of the case and the nature of the particular requirement. The advantage of focusing on these questions is that they should avoid the unjust and unintended consequences which can flow from an approach solely dependent on dividing requirements into mandatory ones, which oust jurisdiction, or directory, which do not. If the result of non-compliance goes to jurisdiction it will be said jurisdiction cannot be conferred where it does not otherwise exist by consent or waiver.'

The current approach can be summarised thus: (1) first assess the legislative intention – will substantial compliance suffice?; (2) if there is non-compliance can it be waived, has it been waived, should it have been waived?; (3) what was the consequence of non-compliance (assuming it could have been or was waived)?

Statutory requirement to consult

A statutory requirement that a body should consult prior to using its powers is almost invariably regarded as mandatory by the courts. In *Agricultural, Horticultural and Forestry Industry Training Board* v *Aylesbury Mushrooms Ltd* [1972] 1 All ER 280 the minister had failed to consult a small group of workers in the mushroom growers' industry, as he was expressly required to do by the relevant statute, as a precondition of establishing a training board scheme, to which those affected would have to contribute a levy. The court held that the scheme was invalid, as against the mushroom growers, as they had not been consulted. They did not, therefore, have to make a contribution. Note, however, that the court did not invalidate the whole scheme.

Similarly, in *Grunwick Processing Laboratories* v *ACAS* [1978] AC 655, the House of Lords held that a failure by ACAS to consult the whole of the workforce at the appellant's factory rendered the subsequent report produced by ACAS invalid, because the express statutory requirement of consultation had not been satisfied. Lord Diplock refused to imply the words 'so far as is practicable' into the statutory duty to consult: see further *R* v *Tunbridge Wells Health Authority, ex parte Goodridge* (1988) The Times 21 May.

Statutory requirement to give prior notice of decision-making

The requirement that prior notice be given of a decision is generally regarded as mandatory. In *R* v *Swansea City Council, ex parte Quietlynn* (1983) The Times 19 October a local authority proposed to introduce a statutory scheme for licensing 'sex establishments' under which it became a criminal offence to run such an enterprise without first obtaining a licence from the local authority. Twenty-eight days' clear notice had to be given by the authority of the scheme's introduction. The local authority conceded that this time limit had not been observed, and certiorari was granted to quash the refusal of the application. The importance of the notice provision relates not only to the natural justice issue of giving a person affected adequate time to prepare a case, but also the seriousness of the consequences – the possibility of criminal liability being imposed. Where, however, there has been a genuine attempt to comply with the requirement of giving notice, and the failure to secure complete compliance does not cause any quantifiable prejudice, the courts will exercise their discretion to uphold the validity of the consequent administrative action. In *Coney* v *Choice* (above) the Education Act 1944 required a local education authority to place notices outside all schools in its area that were due to be made the subject of a comprehensivisation scheme. Templeman J observed:

'... here is an Act, which is concerned with the administration of education in which ... the ramifications can be considerable as regards different areas and as regards a host of children. It would in my judgment be lamentable if the carrying out of the purposes of the Education Act 1944 (as amended) were hampered by a strict insistence on the letter of the regulations being carried out subject to the dire penalty of the whole thing being invalid. In my judgment, this is a case where the regulations must be treated as directory. Both the object and the terms of the regulations themselves seem to me to support that, and the consequences of the contrary also seem to me to require it. I accept there must be substantial compliance with the regulations, and in my judgment there has been. Asking myself whether any substantial prejudice has been suffered by those for whose benefit the requirements were introduced, I am quite satisfied the answer is "No". The plaintiffs, having lost the battle on the merits, are now fighting a battle purely on the technicalities. I make no criticism. If the Education Act 1944 is so full of technicalities that the proposals can be tripped up, well, the plaintiffs are entitled to do just that. But in my judgment this is not an Act where Parliament intended that the technicalities should rule rather than the spirit of the law.'

Presumably a woeful failure on the part of the local education authority to provide the required notices would have invalidated the scheme, but would this have been because the requirement was mandatory, or because of the failure to comply with what Templeman J described as a directory requirement? Again, it suggests that a normally mandatory requirement becomes directory in cases of substantial compliance so as to justify upholding the validity of the following administrative action. It would perhaps aid certainty to adopt the view that such requirements are in fact mandatory, but where there has been substantial compliance the courts will not intervene to provide relief.

Where notice is required it should be given in the correct form. In *R v Lambeth London Borough Council, ex parte Sharp* (1986) 55 P & CR 232 Lambeth London Borough Council granted itself deemed planning permission in respect of the construction of an athletics track within a conservation area. The relevant regulations required that the authority should publish in a local newspaper, and display on or near the land, notices describing the development, and in each case such notice was required to state that any objection to the proposal should be made to the authority in writing within a specified period. The notice that the council had published in a newspaper had referred to 'representations' rather than 'objections' and had not specified the period within which objections were to be made; and neither notice had indicated that objections should be in writing. The appellant successfully contended that these irregularities invalidated the deemed grant of planning permission, the court holding that the requirements as to the giving of notice were mandatory.

Statutory requirement that matters be put in writing

Where statute requires certain matters to be put in writing, the requirement is generally regarded as being mandatory. In *Epping Forest District Council v Essex Rendering Ltd* [1983] 1 WLR 158 the House of Lords held that the requirement, that the consent of a local authority under s107 of the Public Health Act 1936 to the establishment of an offensive trade was to be in writing in accordance with s283(1) of that Act, was mandatory and not directory, because the object of s107 was to protect the public by making the establishment of an offensive trade without written consent a criminal offence. It was, therefore, important that the grant of consent should not be accidental, vague or informal. Since the appellants had not obtained the written consent of the authority they had been rightly convicted of an offence. Similarly, in *Howard* v *Secretary of State for the Environment* [1975] QB 235 the requirement that an appeal against an enforcement notice be put in writing was regarded as mandatory, in the interests of certainty. The administration had to have a permanent record of whether an appeal had been made or not.

Statutory requirement that notice of the right to appeal be given

This procedural requirement is almost always regarded as mandatory. In *London and Clydeside Estates Ltd* v *Aberdeen District Council* [1979] 3 All ER 876 the House of Lords held a certificate issued in connection with a compulsory purchase order to be invalid for failing to inform the plaintiff of his right of appeal, such a requirement being mandatory. Similarly, in *Agricultural, Horticultural and Forestry Industry Training Board* v *Kent* [1970] 2 QB 19, it was held that not only was the requirement of giving notice of the right to appeal mandatory but also failure to give adequate details of how to appeal could result in invalidity.

Statutory time limits

Generally time limits will be regarded as directory, especially where no substantial hardship can be made out, but note the observations in *Cullimore* v *Lyme Regis Corporation* (above). Further, time limits may be regarded as directory on grounds of administrative convenience. See *Simpson* v *Attorney-General* [1955] NZLR 271 where the court refused to invalidate a general election result on the ground that the writ for it had been issued out of time.

6.3 Procedural fairness at common law

Where there is no procedure proscribed by statute, or a statute is silent as to particular aspects of procedure, the question of what fairness requires will fall to be determined at common law.

Notice of the decision-making process

A basic requirement of a fair administrative process is that those likely to be affected by decisions are given adequate notice that they are going to be made. Adequate notice allows an individual to prepare his case properly and conduct his affairs accordingly. Note that in some situations the administrative process denies an individual any notice that a decision affecting him has been taken. For example, in the sphere of town and country planning, property owners are given no official warning that their properties are about to be listed, a designation bringing with it considerable restrictions on the rights of owners to deal with their properties as they choose. The justification, for what would otherwise be a clear breach of natural justice, is expediency. Many property owners, on being informed that their properties are about to be listed, would simply have them demolished rather than be stuck with a building over which they have restricted rights and this would clearly frustrate the whole purpose of listing. The case law illustrates situations where the courts will intervene. In *Cooper* v *Wandsworth Board of Works* (1863) 14 CBNS 180 the plaintiff succeeded in an action against the Board for trespass on the grounds that they failed to notify him of their decision and consider any representations he might have to make. As Viscount Haldane LC stated in *Local Government Board* v *Arlidge* [1915] AC 120, 132:

> 'My Lords, when the duty of deciding an appeal is imposed, those whose duty it is to decide it must act judicially. They must deal with the question referred to them without bias, and they must give to each of the parties the opportunity of adequately presenting the case made.'

In *Willis* v *Childe* (1851) 13 Beav 117 it was held that a schoolmaster, who was informed, a few hours before a meeting of the trustees was due to take place, that they would be considering representations from him on their decision to dismiss him, had been given inadequate notice of the meeting and its subsequent proceedings were of no effect. In *R* v *Thames Magistrates' Court, ex parte Polemis* [1974] 2 All ER 1219 the applicant, the master of a ship moored on the Thames from which it was alleged that oil had been discharged, received a summons to attend trial at the magistrates' court at 10.30 am on the morning of the day his ship was due to sail. His solicitor applied unsuccessfully for an adjournment. The applicant was eventually convicted and fined £5,000, and successfully sought an order of certiorari to quash the conviction on the ground that he had not had reasonable time to prepare his defence, with a consequent breach of natural justice. In granting relief Lord Widgery CJ rejected the 'futility of giving proper notice' argument, observing:

> 'It is again absolutely basic to our system that justice must not only be done but must manifestly be seen to be done. If justice was so clearly not seen to be done, as on the afternoon in question here, it seems to me that it is no answer to the applicant to say: "Well, even if the case had been properly conducted, the result would have been the same." That is mixing up doing justice with seeing that justice is done, so I reject that argument.'

Similarly, in *Glynn* v *Keele University* [1971] 1 WLR 487, a breach of natural justice was held to have occurred where a student was fined by the University without first being told the reasons why or being granted a hearing, although relief was denied on other grounds. Note, however, that the requirements of giving notice may be relaxed somewhat where the case is straightforward and the issues well known to the parties. In *R* v *Brent London Borough Council, ex parte Assegai* (1987) 151 LG Rev 891 a school governor was dismissed, without being given notice of the decision, and without being given the opportunity to reply in writing to complaints that had been made against him. Although he was unsuccessful in applying for judicial review of the local authority subcommittee decision to dismiss him, the court held that natural justice required him to be given some notice of the proceedings because his appointment was supported by legislation, had a public law element, and was in the nature of a status or office. Woolf LJ observed that the only possible relationships in which all the requirements of natural justice were excluded were ones in which there was no element of public employment or service, nor support by statute, and nothing in the way of an office or status which was capable of protection. See also *R* v *Chief Constable of Thames Valley Police, ex parte Stevenson* (1987) The Times 22 April.

Changes in nature of the hearing

Where natural justice requires some notice to be given of an impending decision, it also requires the decision-making body to provide some information as to the nature of the hearing, what is being determined etc. If this were otherwise, giving notice of the decision being taken would be pointless as the individual would not be able to prepare his case properly. The logical extension of this line of reasoning is that if a decision-making body informs an individual that a hearing is to be held to consider 'X' and once at the hearing the individual finds that the decision-making body has decided to deal with 'Y', there will have been a breach of natural justice because the decision-making body will not have kept to the terms of the notice given. In *Andrews* v *Mitchell* [1905] AC 78 a member of a friendly society appeared before its disciplinary body on a charge of misconduct punishable by way of a fine. At the conclusion of the hearing the disciplinary body decided to expel him on a different charge under a different rule. This was held to be a clear breach of natural justice.

The right to make representations

It is frequently assumed that, if natural justice or a duty to act fairly applies to a procedure, then an individual automatically has a right to be heard. This is not necessarily the case. Where a person's livelihood is at stake, or allegations have been made which amount to an attack on an individual's integrity, then representations will almost certainly have to be allowed. In *R* v *Wear Valley District Council, ex parte Binks* [1985] 2 All ER 699 the respondent authority terminated the applicant's oral contractual licence to sell take-away food from a caravan. The business was her only source of livelihood. She was given no notice of the decision, and four weeks notice to remove her caravan. On an application for judicial review, Taylor J held that the local authority was obliged to comply with the rules of natural justice in terminating the licence, and that this required that the applicant should be given an opportunity to be heard before the decision was taken, and should be given reasons for the decision. The court regarded as significant the fact that the applicant's licence was one that permitted her to trade in a public place, and that it was her sole means of livelihood.

The right to know the evidence available to the decision-maker

If an applicant is to be permitted to make any representations, compliance with a fair procedure should require that he is informed of the case against him, to the extent that there is one, so that he can tailor his submissions accordingly and, where appropriate, refute some of the allegations, correct mistakes, or explain away otherwise damaging evidence. Hence in *Re Pergamon Press Ltd* [1971] Ch 388 it was held that inspectors investigating a company's affairs had to give an outline of the charges against the company and provide it with a fair opportunity of correcting or criticising the evidence, although this did not necessarily extend to providing transcripts of evidence. Similarly, in *Maxwell* v *Department of Trade and Industry* [1974] QB 523, it was held to be sufficient for inspectors to put to the plaintiff any substantially prejudicial points that had been made against him.

The principal argument against disclosure will usually be the need to maintain confidentiality but, as the court held in *R* v *Department of Education and Science, ex parte Kumar* (1982) The Times 18 November, such objections can be overcome to some extent by the applicant being given an opportunity to comment on the gist of the allegations. See further *R* v *Governors of Dunraven School, ex parte B* (2000) The Times 3 February. The refusal of the Home Secretary to allow prisoners, who had applied for their convictions to be referred to the Court of Appeal, to know the outcome of the police findings upon which he based his decisions as to referral, was declared to be unlawful by the Divisional Court in *R* v *Secretary of State for the Home Department, ex parte Hickey and Others* [1995] 1 WLR 734, Simon Brown LJ observing that:

> 'Once it is conceded that [such] determinations are reviewable ... principle dictates that, absent powerful countervailing considerations, advance disclosure is required ... without it an adverse decision may not be right; and even if it is, it will certainly not be fair.'

In his view natural justice required that applicants should be permitted to make representations to the Secretary of State, in the light of the evidence provided by the police, before he made his decision as to whether or not the case ought to be referred to the Court of Appeal. In rejecting the 'confidentiality' argument his Lordship noted that the Secretary of State was seeking to create 'something akin to the very public interest immunity class claim which the House of Lords ... [had] recently abolished in *ex parte Wiley* [1994] 1 AC 274'.

In reviewing the Secretary of State's policy Simon Brown LJ endorsed the view expressed by Lord Mustill in *R* v *Secretary of State for the Home Department, ex parte Doody* (below), to the effect that it was not the task of the court to say how it would operate the scheme if given a free hand, the only issue being whether the way in which the scheme was administered fell below the minimum standard of fairness, thus neatly underlining the point that the court is concerned with the legality of the procedure adopted.

In addressing the issue as to what might constitute the 'gist' of the evidence in any given case, Lightman J observed in *R v Secretary of State for the Home Department, ex parte Harry* [1998] 3 All ER 360 (at p370g):

> '... what is sufficient to constitute the gist for one purpose may not be sufficient for another. When a fundamental right is in issue, a more expansive and informative summary may be called for. The detail required must depend on what ... fairness requires to enable the making of meaningful and focused representations ... Good administrative practice may call for the production of a document where this is necessary to avoid the risk of a legitimate sense of concern or grievance and there is no countervailing consideration of any weight and no legitimate reason for wishing to withhold it.'

In *R v Chief Constable of North Wales Police, ex parte AB* [1998] 3 All ER 310 the Court of Appeal noted that whilst individuals should be given the opportunity to comment on material to be disclosed, exceptions might have to be made depending upon: the time scale involved; whether the person concerned would be likely to add any information of any value; whether the person concerned had already had an opportunity to comment; the sensitive nature of the material. And see further *Elliot v Chief Constable of Wiltshire* (1996) The Times 5 December and *Hellewell v Chief Constable of Derbyshire* [1995] 4 All ER 473.

Clearly the more that is at stake for the applicant, the greater the obligation to give notice of the case to be met. Hence, in *R v Secretary of State for the Home Department, ex parte Mohammed Al Fayed* [1997] 1 All ER 228, the Court of Appeal (Kennedy LJ dissenting) held that the applicants ought to have been given an outline of the concerns harboured by the Home Secretary that caused him to believe that they were not of sufficiently good character to warrant having British citizenship bestowed upon them. Not only did the refusal amount to a slur upon their characters, but also it deprived them of the benefits of British and European Union citizenship. Similarly, a Category A prisoner preparing his case before a categorisation committee meeting is entitled to know the gist of the reports made available to the committee: *R v Secretary of State for the Home Department, ex parte McAvoy* (1997) The Times 12 December whereas a Category C prisoner hoping to be downgraded to Category D has no such common law right, the reclassification having only limited significance: see *R v Governor of Maidstone Prison, ex parte Peries* (1997) The Times 30 July.

Must representations be oral?

It is again sometimes wrongly assumed that if natural justice requires a person to be allowed to make representations, they must take the form of an oral hearing. In fact, an oral hearing is the exception, not the rule. In many cases an individual can put all necessary evidence before a decision-making body in the form of written representations.

Certainly an investigative body can act fairly where it collects written evidence instead of hearing witnesses orally, as in *Selvarajan v Race Relations Board* [1976] 1

All ER 12. Where the facts are well known and accepted by both sides, or the individual concerned admits to some wrongdoing and merely seeks to make a plea in mitigation, written representations may be adequate: see *Brighton Corporation* v *Parry* (1972) 70 LGR 576 and *R* v *Aston University Senate, ex parte Roffey* [1969] 2 QB 538. The gravity of the matters under consideration, as regards the applicant, will clearly be a factor weighing heavily with the court.

A leading authority on this issue is the decision of the House of Lords in *Lloyd and Others* v *McMahon* [1987] 2 WLR 821, a case concerning the surcharging of councillors who refused to set a lawful rate within the required time limit, causing consequent financial loss to the authority of which they were members. The appellants were notified by the district auditor that they could make representations in writing before he reached a final decision, and they responded collectively with documentary evidence explaining that they had delayed setting a rate pending any decision by central government to increase its grant support for the council. During the hearing of their appeal against certification the Divisional Court invited the councillors to give oral evidence in support of their case but they declined to do so. Dismissing their further appeals, the House of Lords held that there was clear evidence of wilful misconduct by the councillors, and that the district auditor had not acted unfairly in refusing to allow them an oral hearing prior to his issuing of the certificate under the 1982 Act. As Lord Keith stated (at p872):

'It is easy to envisage cases where an oral hearing would clearly be essential in the interests of fairness, for example where an objector states that he has personal knowledge of some facts indicative of wilful misconduct on the part of a councillor. In that situation justice would demand that the councillor be given an opportunity to depone to his own version of the facts. In the present case the district auditor had arrived at his provisional view upon the basis of the contents of documents, minutes of meetings and reports submitted to the council from the auditor's department and their own officers. ... No facts contradictory of or supplementary to the contents of the documents were or are relied on by either side. If the appellants had attended an oral hearing they would no doubt have reiterated the sincerity of their motives from the point of view of advancing the interests of the inhabitants of Liverpool. It seems unlikely, having regard to the position adopted by their counsel on this matter before the Divisional Court, that they would have been willing to reveal or answer questions about the proceedings of their political caucus. The sincerity of the appellants' motives is not something capable of justifying or excusing failure to carry out a statutory duty, or of making reasonable what is otherwise an unreasonable delay in carrying out such a duty. In all the circumstances I am of opinion that the district auditor did not act unfairly, and that the procedure which he followed did not involve any prejudice to the appellants.'

As Lord Mustill later observed in *R* v *Secretary of State for the Home Department, ex parte Doody and Others* [1993] 3 WLR 154, in relation to whether or not a prisoner sentenced to mandatory life imprisonment should be given the opportunity to make representations prior to the Home Secretary's determination of the minimum period to be served:

'What does fairness require in the present case? My Lords I think it unnecessary to refer by name or to quote from, any of the oft-cited authorities in which the courts have explained what is essentially an intuitive judgment. They are far too well known. From them, I derive the following. (1) Where an Act of Parliament confers an administrative power there is a presumption that it will be exercised in a manner which is fair in all the circumstances. (2) The standards of fairness are not immutable. They may change with the passage of time, both in the general and in their application to decisions of a particular type. (3) The principles of fairness are not to be applied identically by rote in every situation. What fairness demands depends on the context of the decision, and this is to be taken into account in all its aspects. (4) An essential feature of the context is the statute which creates the discretion, as regards both its language and the shape of the legal and administrative system within which the decision is taken. (5) Fairness will very often require that a person who may be adversely affected by the decision will have an opportunity to make representations on his own behalf either before the decision is taken with a view to producing a favourable result, or after it is taken, with a view to procuring its modification, or both. (6) Since the person affected cannot usually make worthwhile representations without knowing what factors may weigh against his interests fairness will very often require that he is informed of the gist of the case that he has to answer.'

The requirements of a fair hearing are not, of course, fixed, but will vary with the circumstances of the case, as the above extracts indicate. Compare the factors that led Lord Keith to deny the need for an oral hearing in the *Lloyd* case (above) with those persuading the court in *R v Army Board of the Defence Council, ex parte Anderson* [1991] 3 All ER 375 to conclude that the hearing given there had been inadequate. Anderson had complained to the Council that he had been the victim of racial discrimination whilst a serving soldier. The Council, which acted as a forum of last resort in respect of soldiers' complaints, subject only to the possibility of judicial review, wrote to the applicant stating that his request for redress of grievance had been denied. In allowing his application for review of the Council's decision Taylor LJ took the *Lloyd* case as authoritative. His Lordship indicated that relevant factors in the case before him were the statutory framework within which the Council operated, the kind of decision it had to take, and the nature of the decision-making body itself. The fact that the legislation in question provided for a particular procedure did not mean that the courts would not imply further requirements where it was necessary to do so to ensure fairness. A crucial factor in the present case was that the Council was a tribunal of last resort. As such it was required to do more than simply act bona fides, without bias or caprice.

His Lordship, summarising what he regarded as the correct approach to ensure fairness in hearings where the tribunal was exercising a disciplinary function, not merely making an administrative decision, observed that an oral hearing was not essential to fairness but was probably required where there were substantial differences on issues of fact which could not be resolved on the papers. It was clear in that particular case that the respondents were not entitled to adopt, as an inflexible policy, the approach that oral hearings would never be permitted. The question of whether evidence should be tested by cross-examination stood or fell with the question of whether or not an oral hearing should be granted. Further, even if an oral hearing was not granted, a complainant should be given the opportunity to respond to the respondent body's findings of fact following its investigations, subject to public interest immunity.

Even where the rules of natural justice would normally require some form of consultation with the person affected by a decision, the court may disregard them in order to achieve a wider policy goal. For example, in *R* v *Life Assurance Unit Trust Regulatory Organisation Ltd, ex parte Ross* [1991] NLJ 1001, where the applicant had not been consulted by LAUTRO prior to its decision to instruct leading companies not to deal with his company, Mann LJ expressed the view that the most important factor was that LAUTRO should be able to effectively protect investors. He stated:

> 'The achievement of that purpose must on occasion require action which has urgently to be taken, and the entertainment of representations may not be compatible with urgency. ... In my judgment once it is recognised, as inevitably it must be, that a self-regulating organisation may have to act with urgency in order to achieve its purpose, then it would be undesirable to encumber it with the necessity to make a judgment as to whether time admits of an opportunity to make representations.'

See also *R* v *Parole Board, ex parte Mansell* [1996] COD 327, where the court rejected the contention that prisoners serving fixed term sentences were entitled to oral hearings before the Parole Board, not least because of the practical consequences of granting such procedural safeguards.

Hearing denied on grounds of futility

It has been argued, from time to time, that there is no right to be heard where the hearing would make no difference to the outcome, or would be a 'useless formality'.

In *Glynn* v *Keele University* (above) the court refused to invalidate disciplinary action taken in respect of the student concerned, despite the fact that he had been denied a hearing, on the ground that nothing he could have said would have made any difference to the outcome. Similarly, in *Cinnamond* v *British Airports Authority* [1980] 1 WLR 582, Lord Denning MR stated that orders issued by the defendant authority banning the plaintiffs from entering Heathrow Airport, otherwise than as bona fide passengers, were not invalid on the ground that the plaintiff taxi-drivers had not been granted a hearing prior to the orders being made. His Lordship took the view that a hearing was unnecessary and, by implication, that it would have been pointless, especially as the plaintiffs knew exactly why the banning orders had been made. For earlier evidence of Lord Denning MR's robust approach to such cases: see *Ward* v *Bradford Corporation* (1972) 70 LGR 27. Despite the above, it is submitted that the conventional wisdom is that futility will not suffice as a general ground for refusing a hearing. As Lord Reid observed in *Ridge* v *Baldwin* [1964] AC 40:

> 'It may be convenient at this point to deal with an argument that, even if as a general rule a watch committee must hear a constable in his own defence before dismissing him, this

case was so clear that nothing that the appellant could have said could have made any difference. It is at least very doubtful whether that could be accepted as an excuse. But even if it could the watch committee would in my view fail on the facts. It may well be that no reasonable body of men could have reinstated the appellant. But as between the other two courses open to the watch committee the case is not so clear. Certainly on the facts as we know them the watch committee could reasonably have decided to forfeit the appellant's pension rights, but I could not hold that they would have acted wrongly or wholly unreasonably if they had in the exercise of their discretion decided to take a more lenient course.'

Further, in *Malloch* v *Aberdeen Corporation* [1971] 1 WLR 1578, Lord Reid again warned against adopting a too generalised approach to the denial of a hearing on grounds that it would serve no purpose. Under the Education (Scotland) Act 1946, as amended, every teacher employed by an education authority was required to be registered with the General Teaching Council (a statutory body). Malloch declined to register. The Aberdeen Education Authority were advised that they had no option but to dismiss him. Subsequently Malloch was informed that a meeting of the education committee was to be held in order to initiate steps to dismiss him. He was not allowed to make representations to the committee even though he wished to. The committee passed a resolution to dismiss him. Malloch sought to impugn the resolution being passed on the ground that it was contrary to natural justice. The House of Lords allowed Malloch's appeal (by a majority). Per Lord Reid:

'Then it was argued that to have afforded a hearing to the appellant before dismissing him would have been a useless formality because whatever he might have said could have made no difference. If that could be clearly demonstrated it might be a good answer. But I need to decide that because there was here, I think, a substantial possibility that a sufficient number of the committee might have been persuaded not to vote for the appellant's dismissal. The motion for dismissal had to be carried by a two-thirds majority of those present, and at the previous meeting of the committee there was not a sufficient majority to carry a similar motion. Between these meetings the committee had received a strong letter from the Secretary of State urging them to dismiss the teachers who refused to register. And it appears that they had received some advice which might have been taken by them to mean that those who failed to vote for dismissal might incur personal liability. The appellant might have been able to persuade them that they need not have any such fear.'

Note that in the course of the above passage Lord Reid does seem to countenance the possibility of a hearing being denied in very clear cases. See further *R* v *Chief Constable of Thames Valley Police, ex parte Stevenson* (above).

Evidence at the hearing

The strict rules of evidence one would expect to see applied in a court of law are not binding on statutory tribunals, and even less so in the case of domestic bodies. An adjudicator may be allowed to act on his own knowledge, provided he puts those points to the parties before him and invites representations thereon. In *Wetherall* v

Harrison [1976] QB 773 the prosecutor appealed against the justices' ruling that the case against the defendant, who had been charged with failing to supply a specimen for the purposes of a 'drink-driving' offence, should be dismissed on the basis that his failure had arisen from a genuine fit induced by the prospect of a blood sample being taken. The justices had been persuaded to their conclusion in the light of the expert knowledge of one of their number, a doctor. The court held that it was acceptable for a tribunal member to rely on his own personal knowledge when coming to a decision provided he used it as a means of interpreting the evidence given in court and not as a replacement for it. As Lord Widgery CJ observed:

> 'Laymen ... considering a case which has just been heard before them lack the ability to put out of their minds certain features of the case. In particular, if the justice is a specialist, be he a doctor, or an engineer or an accountant, or what you will, it is not possible for him to approach the decision in the case as though he had not got that training, and indeed I think it would be a very bad thing if he had to. In a sense, the bench of justices are like a jury, they are a cross section of people, and one of the advantages, which they have is that they bring a lot of varied experience into the court room and use it.'

Cross-examination at the hearing

As a rule, if an individual is afforded the right to make oral representations he will normally be allowed the right to cross-examine those giving evidence against him. The purpose of cross-examination, it should be remembered, is to test the veracity of evidence. In *University of Ceylon* v *Fernando* [1960] 1 All ER 631 the Privy Council held it was not a breach of natural justice for an inquiry into allegations of misconduct at examinations not to inform the plaintiff of his right to cross-examine a witness, but it may have been if the plaintiff had been denied permission to cross-examine the witness.

Public inquiries present a particular problem here. Participants will seek to destroy the credibility of the opponent's evidence by cross-examination, but it must be borne in mind that inquiries are not courts of law. In *Nicholson* v *Secretary of State for Energy* (1978) 76 LGR 693 the plaintiff was not allowed to cross-examine witnesses from local authorities at a public inquiry into an application to carry out open cast mining. The court had no option but to quash the minister's grant of permission to carry out the works in the light of the breach of natural justice. The relevance of the local authority evidence to the plaintiff's case may have been a deciding factor. Compare this with the House of Lords' decision in *Bushell* v *Secretary of State for the Environment* [1981] AC 75, where it was held not to be a breach of natural justice for an inquiry inspector to refuse objectors the right to cross-examine representatives of a government department on the accuracy of traffic flow predictions, upon which the policy of building motorways was based. Lord Diplock expressed the view that cross-examination on such a topic would achieve no useful result; the purpose of an inquiry was to prepare a report for the information of the minister, it was not like civil litigation where the party that best proved its case and destroyed its opponent's would win.

The safest course for a decision-maker to adopt, perhaps, is to permit cross-examination in those cases where, assuming a hearing has been granted, there is a conflict of evidence relating to a matter of fact, and the issue at stake is of significance to the applicant, eg livelihood: see further *Errington* v *Williams* (1995) The Times 2 June.

Adjournment of the hearing

Refusal of an adjournment may result in a breach of natural justice if, as a result, the applicant is unable to continue with a proper presentation of his case. In *Priddle* v *Fisher & Sons* [1968] 3 All ER 506 an Industrial Tribunal, considering the appellant's claim for redundancy payments against his former employer, proceeded to deal with the case despite the fact that it had been informed that the appellant himself was unable to attend because of severe weather conditions, and that his representative had fallen ill and was therefore unable to conduct the case on his behalf. The Court of Appeal held that the tribunal possessed a discretion as to when to allow an adjournment and had erred in law by not exercising that discretion in the instant case. Lord Parker CJ commented that in his judgment:

'... the exercise of a judicial discretion on wrong principles does amount to a point of law, and accordingly this court has jurisdiction to deal with the matter. ... The matter can be put in many ways, but the way in which it appeals to me is that a tribunal is acting wrongly in law if, knowing that an appellant has all along intended to attend and give evidence in support of his claim, and being satisfied, as they must have been, that he was unable for one reason or another to attend, they refuse to adjourn merely because he had not asked expressly for an adjournment. Before deciding to continue the tribunal should be satisfied that he was inviting them to continue in his absence. The matter is even more clear when one realises here that the burden is on the employers and the appellant has a right to cross-examine them to show, if he can, that the reason given for dismissal was a disguise for a dismissal on the ground of redundancy.'

Similar views were expressed in *R* v *South West London Supplementary Benefit Appeal Tribunal, ex parte Bullen* (1976) 120 SJ 437. The interests of fairness may, in certain circumstances, have to give way to administrative expediency, however. In the context of a public inquiry, the granting of an adjournment may cause great inconvenience to other participants. In *Ostreicher* v *Secretary of State for the Environment* [1978] 3 All ER 82 the applicants unsuccessfully sought an adjournment of an inquiry into objections to a clearance order on the ground that the inquiry would coincide with the Jewish Passover period. Lord Denning MR observed that in any given case the court simply had to consider what was fair to the parties concerned, but sought to draw a distinction between an administrative inquiry and judicial proceedings before a court. He stated:

'An administrative inquiry has to be arranged long beforehand. There are many objectors to consider as well as the proponents of the plan. It is a serious matter to put all the arrangements aside on the application of one objector out of many. The proper way to deal with it, if called upon to do so, is to continue with the inquiry and hear all the representatives present: and then, if one objector is unavoidably absent, to hear his objections on a later day when he can be there. There is ample power in the rules for the inspector to allow adjournments as and when reasonably required.'

Note that under the Town and Country Planning (Inquiries Procedure) Rules 1992 an inspector may proceed with an inquiry in the absence of any person entitled to attend (r14(9)), and may adjourn the inquiry from time to time (r14(11)).

The courts will not look kindly on the ineptitude of those representing the applicant, even if this involves punishing the applicant for the failings of his advisers. In *Al-Mehdawi* v *Secretary of State for the Home Department* [1989] 3 All ER 843 the House of Lords considered an application for certiorari to quash a decision of an immigration adjudicator who had ordered the deportation of the applicant. The applicant had been invited to attend before the hearing of his appeal against the deportation, but due to the ineptitude of his solicitors, notification did not reach him in time, and the appeal proceeded in his absence. The applicant then sought to quash the adjudicator's dismissal of his appeal on the basis that he had been denied a hearing in breach of natural justice. The House of Lords held that certiorari would not lie to quash the decision as the unfairness did not result from the actions of the adjudicator.

Must decision-makers meet as a committee?

Where there are statutory provisions dealing with procedural issues it is not uncommon to find a requirement that a decision-making body must meet as a committee to determine given issues, and there may also be a requirement as regards a quorum for such meetings. What is the position at common law? Much depends upon the nature of the decision-making body and the issue before it, but there is perhaps a presumption that if statute has provided for an issue to be determined by a multi-member body it ought to meet as such to determine the issues referred to it. Hence, in *R* v *Army Board of the Defence Council, ex parte Anderson* (above), it was held that members of the Defence Council had to meet as a committee, rather than consider cases individually, because of the disciplinary function exercised by the Council. In *R* v *Legal Aid Board, ex parte Donn & Co* [1996] 3 All ER 1 a local area legal aid committee rejected a tender submitted by the applicants, unaware that the documentation was incomplete because of a clerical error at the Legal Aid Board. When the error was discovered the chair of the local committee contacted its members individually. Notwithstanding that six out of the seven committee members indicated that they would not have come to a different conclusion even if they had had the full documentation, the court held that natural justice had not been complied with. Ognall J was persuaded by *ex parte Anderson*, to the effect that a proper hearing of the tender application required that the adjudicating body should meet as a whole, and not come to a conclusion as individuals. As he observed:

> 'The whole rationale of a committee is that, like a jury, they meet together to exchange views; to be prepared to submit themselves to the give and take of debate; to accept that no view formed in isolation is immutable, even a view which may, at the first time of assembly, be apparently shared by a majority ... [A]ssuming for this purpose ... that the committee was [not already functus officio] ... their only lawful option ... was to reconvene, revoke their earlier decision and reconsider ... in committee as a whole.'

6.4 The common law right to legal representation

When considering this aspect of natural justice it is important to distinguish between cases where an individual has been refused the right to be legally represented, and cases where the right exists, but the individual has not availed himself of it. That legal representation is an acknowledged aspect of a fair procedure is evidenced by the fact that nearly all tribunals permit applicants to have legal representation if they so wish. That absence of legal representation does not, of itself, invalidate a hearing, is evidenced by the number of unrepresented defendants convicted in the magistrates' courts. The principal concern here is with cases where representation is denied.

Much may depend on what is at stake for the individual concerned as a result of the tribunal's decision. In *Maynard* v *Osmond* [1977] QB 240 the Court of Appeal held that statutory regulations governing police disciplinary proceedings, which provided that a police constable could conduct his own defence or be represented by another officer, did not entitle a constable to representation by a lawyer. The regulations had excluded a right, which might have existed at common law, to legal representation. The fact that legal representation was allowed to more senior officers was held to be evidence that Parliament had not intended it to be available to more junior ranks, who in any event had less to lose than their more senior colleagues.

Rules of private associations excluding the right of legal representation before disciplinary committees have generally been upheld. In *Enderby Town FC* v *FA Ltd* [1971] Ch 591 the Court of Appeal upheld the validity of the Football Association's decision prohibiting legal representation in cases before it. As Lord Denning MR observed:

> 'In many cases it may be a good thing for the proceedings of a domestic tribunal to be conducted informally without legal representation. Justice can often be done in them better by a good layman than by a bad lawyer. This is especially so in activities like football and other sports, where no points of law are likely to arise, and it is all part of the proper regulation of the game. But I would emphasise that the discretion must be properly exercised. The tribunal must not fetter its discretion by rigid bonds. A domestic tribunal is not at liberty to lay down an absolute rule: "We will never allow anyone to have a lawyer to appear for him." The tribunal must be ready, in a proper case, to allow it.'

Where an individual's reputation or livelihood is at stake there may be a much stronger argument in favour of legal representation: see *Pett* v *Greyhound Racing Association* [1969] 1 QB 125. In *Fraser* v *Mudge* [1975] 3 All ER 78 the Court of Appeal held that prisoners subjected to the disciplinary regime of the prison did not have full rights of legal representation. In certain circumstances, however, such hearings can have serious consequences for those concerned, such as loss of significant amounts of remission, and the importance of such hearings has now been recognised by the courts, as evidenced by decisions such as *R* v *Secretary of State for the Home Department, ex parte Tarrant* [1984] 1 All ER 799, where it was held that, although a prisoner appearing before a board of visitors on a disciplinary charge did not have an automatic right to legal representation, the board did have a discretion to permit it. In that case it had been a breach of natural justice to deny the prisoner legal representation, given the grave nature of the charge, and the consequences for the prisoner of his being found guilty.

In *R* v *Board of Visitors of Swansea Prison, ex parte McGrath* (1984) The Times 21 November, however, it was held that apart from exceptional cases the board of visitors was under no duty to consider exercising its discretion to grant legal representation to a prisoner, unless the prisoner so requested. Further, in *R* v *Board of Visitors of the Maze Prison, ex parte Hone* [1988] 1 All ER 321, where the applicants were prisoners charged with serious offences against prison discipline who had not been permitted legal representation at the hearing of their cases by the prison board of visitors, and who contended that there had, therefore, been breaches of natural justice, the House of Lords held that simply because the charge facing a prisoner was one which, if he were a defendant in a criminal court, would automatically entitle him to legal representation, did not mean that he had an automatic right under the rules of natural justice to legal representation when appearing before the prison board of visitors on a corresponding charge against prison discipline. Boards of visitors had a discretion to allow legal representation, and this would depend on the facts of each case.

6.5 The right to a reasoned decision at common law

Citizens will normally expect reasons to be given by a public body for a decision, particularly where the decision is one adverse to their interests. For a significant range of tribunals the giving of reasons, where requested, is not a matter of discretion but a duty imposed by s10 of the Tribunals and Inquiries Act 1992, provided the tribunal in question is one listed in Sch 1 to the Act. Whether or not there exists, as regards other decision-makers, a duty to give reasons at common law, is rather less clear. While an unreasoned decision is the exception rather than the norm, the absence of reasons will not necessarily lead the courts to invalidate a decision on that basis alone. As Lord Keith commented in *Lonrho plc* v *Secretary of State for Trade and Industry* [1989] 1 WLR 525 at 539:

'The only significance of the absence of reasons is that if all other known facts and circumstances appear to point overwhelmingly in favour of a different decision, the decision-maker who has given no reasons cannot complain if the court draws the inference that he had no rational reason for his decision.'

Traditionally the law has taken the view that those coming within the category of 'mere applicants' for a particular privilege, and particularly prisoners seeking to challenge decisions made in respect of 'executive sentencing', have had little or no right to be told of the reasons for decisions. In *R v Gaming Board for Great Britain, ex parte Benaim and Khaida* [1970] 2 QB 417, where the applicants had been refused consent to apply for a gaming licence by the Board, which had refused to give reasons for its decision, the Court of Appeal held that the Board was not obliged to disclose the sources of the information upon which it had acted. Apart from the fact that much of the evidence had been supplied in confidence, the Board was not obliged to state the reasons for the refusal as, in any event, the applicants were being denied a privilege not a right. Lord Denning MR reiterated this view in *Breen v AEU* [1971] 2 QB 175. Megarry V-C in *McInnes v Onslow-Fane* [1978] 1 WLR 1520 suggested that a mere applicant would only be entitled to reasons for a decision where, for example, the refusal of a licence involved a slur on his reputation. In many such cases there was 'no case against' the applicant as such, the decision-making body simply considered him to be unsuitable. Megarry V-C said:

'... in the absence of anything to suggest that the [members of the tribunal] have been affected by dishonesty or bias or caprice, or that there is any other impropriety, I think that [they] are fully entitled to give no reasons for their decision, and to decide the application without any preliminary indication to the plaintiff of those reasons.'

Perhaps the high water mark of the 'executive minded' approach was exemplified by the decision of the Court of Appeal in *Payne v Lord Harris* [1981] 1 WLR 754, where it was held that a prisoner was not entitled to know the reasons for the rejection of his application to be released on licence. Lord Denning MR stated:

'No doubt it is the duty of all those concerned ... to act fairly. That is the simple precept which now governs the administrative procedure of all public bodies. But the duty to act fairly cannot be set down in a series of propositions. Each case depends on its own circumstances. Sometimes fairness may require that the man be told of the outline of the case against him. At other times it may not be necessary to have a hearing or even to tell the man the case against him, because it must be obvious to him.'

In particular he felt that there was a danger that reasons, if given, would tend to become short and stereotyped rather than full and informative. He continued:

'If [the reasons] were full and informative, they would give the prisoner an opening with which he could challenge the refusal. He could lodge an application for judicial review, complaining that the Board took things into account which they should not have done – or that their decision was unreasonable. If he were refused judicial review he would harbour grievance which would become obsessive – just as much as if he is refused parole without reasons being given.'

As will be seen, the courts have since moved away from this conservative approach to executive accountability, but note the significance of this restrictive approach for litigants; without the reasons for a decision it may be impossible to substantiate the grounds for an application for review, such as error of law, or failure to take into account relevant considerations. The approach advocated by Lord Denning MR in respect of the Parole Board would have effectively made judicial review of such determinations impossible.

The trend now is towards greater openness in decision-making, the courts approaching the issue on the basis of requiring reasons unless there are some compelling public policy reasons for their not being provided. In *R v Civil Service Appeal Board, ex parte Cunningham* [1991] 4 All ER 310 the applicant, who had been employed as a prison officer, was accused of assaulting a prisoner and dismissed. On appeal, the Civil Service Appeal Board found his dismissal to have been unfair and recommended his reinstatement, but this was not accepted by the Home Office. The Board thereupon awarded him £6,500 for the loss of his position but declined to give reasons for the level of the award. The applicant regarded the award as being far too low, and applied to the courts for an order that the Board should supply the reasons for its decision. Otton J, for the Divisional Court, held that the Board would be ordered to provide the reasons sought. Although in his Lordship's view there was no general duty at common law requiring administrative bodies to give reasons for their decisions, and despite the fact that he was unwilling to infer (in this particular case) that the absence of reasons necessarily meant that there were no good reasons for the decision, there was no evidence to suggest that the proper working of the Board would be undermined by its having to supply a short statement of reasons, simply to put the applicant's mind at rest. The Court of Appeal upheld this ruling. It is, perhaps, not without significance that the applicant was unable, as a prison officer, to take his case before an industrial tribunal that would have been required to give reasons for its decisions. The aim of the Civil Service Pay and Conditions Code is to ensure that Crown servants are in no less a favourable position than other employees. Where reasons are given they should be adequate in the sense of being intelligible and indicative of the basis for the decision: see *R v Criminal Injuries Compensation Board, ex parte Cummins* (1992) The Times 21 January.

A key development in the trend towards more open decision-making was the House of Lords' decision in *R v Secretary of State for the Home Department, ex parte Doody and Others* (above). The Secretary of State, acting under s61 of the Criminal Justice Act 1967, had the power to determine the first date upon which prisoners who had received mandatory life sentences for murder might be considered for release (ie the point at which the 'penal element' of the sentence would expire). The procedure adopted involved the Secretary of State obtaining the views of the trial judge and the Lord Chief Justice prior to informing a prisoner of the first date for review of his continued detention. The effect was that a prisoner would then be aware of his minimum period of imprisonment. The applicants, each of whom was a prisoner serving a life sentence following conviction for murder, sought to challenge the decision of the Secretary of State in respect of the date set for review as regards their own cases. Inter alia, they each sought a declaration to the effect that the Secretary of State should inform a prisoner of his reasons for departing from the judicial recommendation if this was what he intended to do. The House of Lords held that the Secretary of State was obliged to give reasons for departing from the period recommended by the judiciary as regards the 'penal element' of the sentence.

Lord Mustill, whilst confirming that there was no general legal duty to give reasons for an administrative decision, went on to observe that it was important that there should be 'an effective means of detecting the kind of error which would entitle the court to intervene' should a decision as to sentencing be wrong in law. In his Lordship's view, a requirement that reasons be given for departing from a judicial recommendation as to the minimum term could provide evidence of any such errors. Lord Mustill regarded *Payne* v *Lord Harris of Greenwich* (above) as reflecting an outmoded view of the duty to give reasons. In particular he felt that in the 13 years since that decision the perception of society's obligation towards persons serving prison sentences had changed noticeably, and that the trend in administrative law was now firmly towards openness in decision-making. He observed:

> 'There is no true tariff, or at least no tariff exposed to the public view which might give the prisoner an idea of what to expect. The announcement of his first review date arrives out of thin air, wholly without explanation. The distant oracle has spoken and that is that ... I doubt whether in the modern climate of administrative law such an entirely secret process could be justified.'

This discernible trend towards 'transparent' decision-making where individual liberty is at stake has been promoted further by decisions such as that in *R* v *Secretary of State for the Home Department, ex parte Duggan* [1994] 3 All ER 277, where the Divisional Court held that a prisoner who had been classified as a category 'A' risk, and thus subject to greater restrictions, was entitled to be provided with the gist of the reports compiled for the category A section, so that he could comment upon them, and should be provided, subject to the constraints required by public interest immunity, with the reasons for any subsequent decision. As Rose LJ observed:

> '... to my mind the authorities show an ever-increasing variety of situations where, depending on the nature of the decision and the process by which it is reached, fairness requires that reasons be given.'

His Lordship added that if the principles of natural justice applied to a prison governor adjudicating upon infractions of prison discipline (per Lord Oliver in *R* v *Deputy Governor of Parkhurst Prison, ex parte Leech* [1988] AC 533 at 578) then, a fortiori they applied to a decision that impacted upon the ultimate date on which a prisoner would be released. See further *R* v *Governor of Maidstone Prison, ex parte Peries* (above); *R* v *Ministry of Defence, ex parte Murray* [1998] COD 49 (court martial required to give reasons for sentence – see useful summary of principles provided by Lord Bingham CJ); *R* v *City of London Corporation, ex parte Matson* [1997] 1 WLR 765 (Court of Aldermen required to give reasons for not endorsing the election of an alderman); *R* v *Birmingham City Council, ex parte M* (1998) The Times 13 October (education committee required to give reasons for not allocating a child to his 'first choice' school); *R* v *Criminal Injuries Compensation Authority, ex parte Leatherland* (2000) The Times 12 October (public interest in evidence underpinning decision); and *Stefan* v *General Medical Council* (1999) The Times 11 March (PC) (health committee of General Medical Council required to give reasons for indefinitely suspending a doctor from practice on medical grounds). In this last case note that the Privy Council expressed the view that the provision of a right of appeal indicated that reasons should be given so that the person affected might discern whether or not there were grounds calling for the exercise of the right to appeal.

Sitting as a deputy High Court judge in *R* v *Lambeth London Borough Council, ex parte Walters* (1993) The Times 6 October, Louis Blom-Cooper QC went so far as to assert that there was now at least a general duty to give reasons at common law, it being in his view:

'... hard to envisage any situation, except possibly where the giving of reasons would reveal some aspect of national security, or unintentionally disclose confidential information or invade privacy, where an individual should not know the reasons for the decision which had been made.'

Such claims are, with respect, somewhat premature. More accurate is the summary of the current law provided by Sedley J in *R* v *Higher Education Funding Council, ex parte Institute of Dental Surgery* [1994] 1 All ER 651, where he observed:

'1. There is no general duty to give reasons for a decision, but there are classes of case where there is such a duty.

2. One such class is where the subject matter is an interest so highly regarded by the law – for example personal liberty – that fairness requires that reasons, at least for particular decisions, be given as of right.

3. (a) Another such class is where the decision appears aberrant. Here fairness may require reasons so that the recipient may know whether the aberration is in the legal sense real (and so challengeable) or apparent.

(b) It follows that this class does not include decisions which are in themselves challengeable by reference only to the reasons for them. A pure exercise of academic judgment is such a decision.

(c) Procedurally, the grant of leave in such cases will depend upon prima facie evidence that something has gone wrong. The respondent may then seek to demonstrate that it is not so and that the decision is an unalloyed exercise of an intrinsically unchallengeable judgment. If the respondent succeeds, the application fails. If the respondent fails, relief may take the form of an order of mandamus to give reasons, or (if a justiciable flaw has been established) other appropriate relief.'

On the basis of this ruling there may still be a swathe of administrative decision-making immune from any duty to give reasons, eg the rejection by a university of an application for a place on a degree course; the decision to transfer a prisoner to separate detention under r43(1) of the Prison Rules 1964 (SI 1964/388) (see *R v Deputy Governor of Parkhurst Prison, ex parte Hague* [1992] 1 AC 58, *R v Deputy Governor of Parkhurst Prison, ex parte Leech* [1988] AC 533, *R v Secretary of State for the Home Department, ex parte Gunnell* (1984) The Times 7 November and *R v Secretary of State for the Home Department, ex parte Mehmet* (1999) The Times 18 February); and a local planning authority's decision to allow an appeal against a refusal of planning permission: see *R v Aylesbury Vale District Council and Another, ex parte Chaplin* (1996) The Times 23 July.

6.6 The rule against bias

The rule against bias is a common law doctrine that provides that no man should be a judge in his own cause. It is frequently referred to as one of the two 'rules' of natural justice – the other being the right to a fair hearing. In reality the rule against bias is an aspect of fair procedure. If the applicant has a right to a fair hearing then, by definition, the tribunal should be free from bias.

The common rule is also reflected in the European Convention on Human Rights, art 6 of which provides that in the determination of his civil or criminal liabilities every person is entitled to a hearing before an impartial tribunal. The rule against bias also exists to ensure that confidence is maintained in the integrity of the judicial and administrative process. As Lord Hewart CJ memorably observed in *R v Sussex Justices, ex parte McCarthy* [1924] 1 KB 256, the rule against bias is not only concerned with ensuring that instances of actual bias are rooted out, but also with ensuring that justice is seen to be done, ie it is important that, even where there is no actual bias, those appearing before a tribunal do not have grounds to suspect that there might be bias or impartiality.

Where bias gives rise to automatic disqualification of the decision-maker

Actual bias
If a party to a hearing can establish actual bias on the part of a decision-maker a reviewing court will regard that decision-maker as automatically disqualified on the grounds of bias. Such cases will be rare. A decision-maker may harbour prejudices but keep them to himself. In any event it is most unlikely that a party to a hearing will be given the opportunity to cross-examine the decision-maker as to his or her views, thus making the task of collecting evidence of actual bias a daunting one.

Pecuniary interest
In the majority of cases pecuniary interest by a decision-maker in a matter subject to his influence is sufficient to automatically invalidate any resulting determination. The leading case is *Dimes v Grand Junction Canal Proprietors* (1852) 3 HL Cas 759,

where Lord Cottenham LC had affirmed decrees made by the Vice-Chancellor in litigation between Dimes and the canal proprietors. Dimes discovered that, despite the fact that the Lord Chancellor had for a long period held shares in the canal company in his own right and as trustee, he had continued to hear matters arising out of the litigation relying on the advice of the Master of the Rolls who sat with him. Dimes appealed to the House of Lords against all the decrees made by the Lord Chancellor on the ground that he was disqualified by interest. The House of Lords set aside the decrees issued by the Lord Chancellor on the ground of pecuniary interest. In the course of his speech Lord Campbell stated:

> 'No one can suppose that Lord Cottenham could be, in the remotest degree, influenced by the interest that he had in this concern; but, my Lords, it is of the last importance that the maxim that no man is to be a judge in his own cause should be held sacred. And that is not to be confined to a cause in which he has an interest. Since I have had the honour to be Chief Justice of the Court of Queen's Bench, we have again and again set aside proceedings in inferior tribunals because an individual, who had an interest in a cause, took a part in the decision. And it will have a most salutary influence on these tribunals when it is known that this High Court of last resort, in a case in which the Lord Chancellor of England had an interest, considered that his decree was on that account a decree not according to law, and was set aside. This will be a lesson to all inferior tribunals to take care not only that in their decrees they are not influenced by their personal interest, but to avoid the appearance of labouring under such an influence.'

The rule against pecuniary interest is subject to a number of qualifications. First, it is subject to a remoteness principle, to the effect that where the pecuniary interest is so minimal or indirect as to be of negligible significance it will not be used as justification for invalidating a decision. In *R v Rand* (1866) LR 1 QB 230 the court was asked to quash a certificate issued by justices permitting Bradford Corporation to take water from a certain reservoir. The justices were trustees of institutions that held Bradford Corporation bonds, and it was contended that this interest disqualified them from acting, and invalidated the certificate granted. The court refused to quash the certificate, holding that any pecuniary interest on the part of the justices was more theoretical than real.

Second, the operation of the rule against pecuniary interest may be affected by statute. An Act of Parliament can effectively displace the common law presumption of bias: see for example s193 Licensing Act 1964, as applied in *R v Barnsley County Borough Licensing Justices, ex parte Barnsley and District Licensed Victuallers Association* [1960] 2 QB 167. Alternatively, the rule can be extended by statute, as for example by ss94–98 of the Local Government Act 1972, which provide that it is a criminal offence for a councillor to participate in any discussion or vote on a matter in which he has a direct or indirect pecuniary interest, the prohibition extending to a councillor voting against his own interests: see further *R v Hendon Rural District Council, ex parte Chorley* [1933] 2 KB 696.

Third, the rule may be disregarded where the decision-maker has a pecuniary interest, but the decision is challenged by an individual who is not a party to the proceedings in question: see further *David Eves* v *Hambros Bank (Jersey) Ltd* [1996] 1 WLR 251.

Fourth, where the pecuniary interest is that of a decision-maker's partner or relative, the automatic disqualification rule will not apply unless it can be said that the interest of the partner or relative is indistinguishable from that of the decision maker: see *Locabail (UK) Ltd* v *Bayfield Properties Ltd; Locabail (UK) Ltd* v *Waldorf Investment Corporation; Timmins* v *Gormley; Williams* v *Inspector of Taxes; R* v *Bristol Betting and Gaming Licensing Committee, ex parte O'Callaghan* [2000] 1 All ER 65.

Finally, the rule may be disregarded where the pecuniary interest is so small as to be ignored under the de minimis principle.

Connection with the parties or espousal of the cause in issue

In *R* v *Bow Street Metropolitan Stipendiary Magistrate, ex parte Pinochet Ugarte (No 2)* [1999] 1 All ER 577 the House of Lords confirmed that automatic disqualification of a decision-maker on grounds of bias was not limited to cases of pecuniary interest alone. The rule also applied where the adjudicator was a supporter of, or was connected with, a cause or interest group involved in the case before him. In the *Pinochet* case Lord Hoffmann was held to have been automatically disqualified from sitting on the appeal arising out of the extradition hearings because he was a director of a charity linked to, and sharing the same aims as, Amnesty International, one of the parties to the litigation. Lord Browne Wilkinson explained (p588d–e):

> 'My Lords, in my judgment, although the cases have all dealt with automatic disqualification on the grounds of pecuniary interest, there is no good reason in principle for so limiting automatic disqualification. The rationale of the whole rule is that a man cannot be a judge in his own cause. In civil litigation the matters in issue will normally have an economic impact; therefore a judge is automatically disqualified if he stands to make a financial gain as a consequence of his own decision of the case. But if, as in the present case, the matter at issue does not relate to money or economic advantage but is concerned with the promotion of the cause, the rationale disqualifying a judge applies just as much if the judge's decision will lead to the promotion of a cause in which the judge is involved together with one of the parties. Thus in my opinion if Lord Hoffmann had been a member of Amnesty International he would have been automatically disqualified because of his non-pecuniary interest in establishing that Senator Pinochet was not entitled to immunity.'

In the light of Lord Browne-Wilkinson's comments it is submitted that cases such as *R* v *Sussex Justices, ex parte McCarthy* (above) might now be regarded as 'automatic disqualification' cases. In that case a solicitor who was representing a client against McCarthy in a motoring accident also worked as a clerk to the Sussex justices who were trying McCarthy on a criminal charge arising out of the same motoring incident. When the justices retired to consider their verdict, the clerk retired with them and they convicted the defendant of dangerous driving. The conviction was quashed on the ground that the appearance of bias was fatal. Similarly, in *R* v *Altrincham Justices, ex parte Pennington* [1975] QB 549 the conviction of the defendant for selling underweight quantities of vegetables to various schools was quashed on discovery that the chairman of the court was also a co-opted member of the local authority's education committee.

There is no reason to suppose that the extension of the automatic disqualification concept should not encompass quasi-judicial bodies such as tribunals. In *Metropolitan Properties Co* v *Lannon* [1968] 3 All ER 304 a number of tenants applied to the rent officer to fix a fair rent for their flats. The landlord objected to the rent officer's decision and appealed to the rent assessment committee, the chairman of which was a solicitor who lived with his father, who was himself a tenant of the company which was associated with the landlords in the present case. The chairman's firm had from time to time acted for his father's fellow tenants against the associated company on matters similar to the ones in issue here; the chairman himself had assisted his father in writing to the rent officer. The committee fixed rents for the flats below that assessed by the experts and below that asked for by the tenants themselves. The Court of Appeal held that the committee's decision was vitiated by bias. It seems likely that if such facts were to come before the courts again this would be seen as a case warranting automatic disqualification.

The extension of the automatic disqualification rule to cases of non-pecuniary interest is likely to cause some uncertainty. As indicated above, a pecuniary interest is easily identified, subject only to the de minimis rule and arguments on remoteness. Assessing the effect of allegiances on impartiality involves a more qualitative assessment. For example, in *R* v *Holderness Borough Council, ex parte James Roberts Developments Ltd* [1993] 1 PLR 108, a case where a refusal of planning permission was upheld despite the fact that planning committee had a local builder and developer as one of its members, Simon Brown LJ expressed the view that it was going too far to say that merely because a member of the committee was a local builder he was for that reason alone to be disqualified and any decision made by the committee vitiated. Butler-Sloss LJ added that if a builder were to be disqualified in such a case, it was likely that a solicitor or surveyor involved in local developments would be similarly disqualified, and consequently such a prohibition would be too wide. Dillon LJ, dissenting, felt that in the light of what he saw as the great dangers of bribery and corruption in local government, particularly where planning matters were concerned, it was felt it vital that justice should be seen to be done.

Where the appearance of bias may lead to disqualification

In *Locabail (UK) Ltd* v *Bayfield Properties Ltd etc* (above) the court sought to offer some general guidance on factors that might or might not lead to a finding of bias in those cases where disqualification was not otherwise automatic. It was thought that no sensible objection could ever be based on factors such as religious persuasion, ethnic origin, gender, age, class, means or sexual orientation. The court doubted whether a challenge could ever succeed on the basis that the adjudicator had a particular social or educational background, employment history, political associations, was a member of any social, sporting or charitable bodies, or had Masonic associations. Also regarded as unimportant were previous judicial decisions, extracurricular utterances, membership of the same Inn, circuit, or local Law Society. By contrast it was felt that a real danger of bias might arise where there was a friendship or personal animosity between the judge and a member of the public involved in a case, or if the judge had doubted the credibility of a party in previous proceedings in outspoken terms suggesting that he was unable to approach a party's evidence with an open mind, or if for any other reason there were real grounds for doubting the judge's ability to ignore extraneous considerations and bring an objective judgment to bear on the issues before him.

Politics and preferences

It some cases allegations of bias will arise because an adjudicator makes his committed views on a relevant topic known in such a manner that the resulting appearance of bias disqualifies him from exercising his discretion. In a sense the decision-maker can be regarded as acting unreasonably since by definition he is taking into account irrelevant considerations, ie he is motivated by factors unconnected with the merits of the case. A striking example of this problem is provided by *R* v *Inner West London Coroner, ex parte Dallaglio and Others* [1994] 4 All ER 139. The applicants were relatives of those who had died as a result of the *Marchioness* disaster in August 1989 when a pleasure boat sunk as a result of a collision with another vessel on the Thames. The inquests into the deaths had been opened, but subsequently adjourned following the intervention of the DPP. A newspaper article concerning the conduct of the inquest suggested that there might have been some form of official cover-up, particularly in light of the fact that some relatives had been denied sight of the bodies of those killed. The coroner met with journalists in an attempt to rectify what he saw as misrepresentations by the press. In the course of his discussions he alleged that one of the applicants had been 'unhinged' by grief following her son's death, and that others were 'mentally unwell'. He subsequently resisted the applicants' demands that the inquest be reopened on the basis that the majority of relatives now wanted to treat the event as closed. The applicants, initially unsuccessful in applying for judicial review of the coroner's refusal to remove himself from the inquest on the grounds of apparent bias, and his refusal to reopen the inquest, succeeded before the Court of Appeal, where the coroner's comments were described as injudicious, insensitive and gratuitously insulting and thus fell foul of the test for bias (considered below). See also the quashing of the decision in *Timmins* v *Gormley* (*Locabail et al* above) on the grounds that the judge's publicly expressed trenchant views on the role of insurance companies in personal injury litigation disqualified him from hearing a case involving a claim for damages brought by a road user.

Earlier cases that would presumably also fall foul of the test for apparent bias include: *R* v *Halifax Justices, ex parte Robinson* (1912) 76 JP 233 (licensing justice who declared that he would have been a traitor to the strict temperance sect of which he was a member, if he voted in favour of granting a liquor licence); and *R* v *Bingham Justices, ex parte Jowitt* (1974) The Times 3 July (chairman of the bench had stated that he would always believe the evidence of a police officer in preference to that of a member of the public). An obvious point to be noted about all these examples is that the issue of bias may not have been aired but for the 'confession' by the decision-maker as to his strongly held views: see further *R* v *Nailsworth Licensing Justices, ex parte Bird* [1953] 1 WLR 1046.

It may be the case that a more relaxed view is taken where the decision-making body is exercising a more administrative role, as opposed to the judicial or quasi-judicial functions encountered in the examples considered above. In *R* v *Amber Valley District Council, ex parte Jackson* [1984] 3 All ER 501, a company applied to the council for planning permission to develop an amusement park on a site in its area. The applicant sought an order of prohibition to prevent the council from considering the matter on the basis that the council was Labour controlled, and the Labour group was, as a matter of policy, in favour of the development and could not, therefore, make an unbiased decision on the application. The court held a publicly stated policy preference did not disqualify the councillors from adjudicating on the planning application, provided they observed their duty to act fairly and take into account all material considerations, including objections.

Similarly, in *R* v *Hereford and Worcester County Council, ex parte Wellington Parish Council* (1996) 160 LGR 161, the Divisional Court upheld a grant of planing permission for the development of a gypsy site, notwithstanding that three members of the planning sub-committee were also members of the authority's gypsy sub-committee that had recommended the development. In the view of the court this overlapping of functions did not mean that the committee members concerned were incapable of considering the planning application honestly, fairly and with an open mind. Their being predisposed towards the development could not be equated with bias.

A more stringent line may be taken where councillors agree to be bound by the National Code of Local Government Conduct: see *R* v *Local Commissioner for Administration in North and North East England, ex parte Liverpool City Council* [1999] 3 All ER 85. Under the Code the test adopted is whether a reasonable member of the public would have felt that a councillor might have been significantly influenced by his personal allegiances or party loyalty.

Intermingling of functions: first instance and appeal

Difficulties may arise where, for example, disciplinary action is taken by a subordinate body and has to be approved by an appellate or executive body, and members of the disciplinary body are also members of the appellate or executive body. Such 'intermingling of functions' may result in a decision being invalidated on grounds of bias. Clearly the fear is that those who make a decision at first instance are unlikely to disagree with their own decisions if they sit in judgment on them on an appellate body. In *Hannam* v *Bradford Corporation* [1970] 1 WLR 937 the plaintiff was a teacher who had gone absent without leave from the school at which he taught. The school governors met and decided to sack him. The staff sub-committee of the local authority met to consider this decision (note that this hearing was not an appeal by Hannam). The sub-committee had the power to prohibit the dismissal, but decided not to exercise this power. Three of the ten sub-committee members were also governors of the school at which Hannam had taught, but they had not attended the meeting of governors at which the decision to dismiss him had been taken. The sub-committee's decision was subsequently ratified by the full council. Hannam brought an action for breach of contract, claiming that the question of his dismissal should have been determined by a properly constituted tribunal. The Court of Appeal held that as the staff sub-committee, when considering the plaintiff's dismissal, was exercising a quasi-judicial function, its decision to allow the dismissal to stand was invalid. The three governors on the sub-committee were sitting in judgment on a decision of a body to which they belonged. The fact that they had taken no part in the original decision was irrelevant. As Sachs LJ observed, the governors did not, on donning their sub-committee hats, cease to be an integral part of the body whose action was being impugned. The quorum for the sub-committee was three. What if the only members had been the governors? In his view, no one could seriously suggest that their decision would have been allowed to stand. In the event the plaintiff's action for breach of contract failed on other grounds.

Similarly in *R* v *Kent Police Authority, ex parte Godden* [1971] 2 QB 662, where the applicant, who had been a chief inspector in the Kent Police, was moved to administrative duties in 1969. He complained of malpractices by his superiors, an inquiry was held, but nothing was found to justify his allegations. In 1970 his desk was searched and erotic material discovered. Godden was seen by the force's chief medical officer, declared paranoid, and placed on sick leave. Following examination by his own doctor he was declared to be perfectly normal. In early 1971 the Kent Police appointed the same chief medical officer to determine whether Godden should be permanently retired, whereupon Godden applied for prohibition and mandamus, on the basis that any such examination by the force's own medical officer would be vitiated by bias. The Court of Appeal held that his application should succeed. It was the view of Lord Denning MR that a doctor examining a man to determine whether he should be retired was undoubtedly acting in a judicial capacity. The chief medical officer was disqualified from acting because of his earlier diagnosis of Godden. In effect he would be sitting on appeal from his own earlier decision. It should not always be assumed, however, that procedural irregularity will of itself persuade the court to intervene. In *Ward* v *Bradford Corporation* (1972) 70 LGR 27 a local disciplinary committee decided to expel a student teacher living in college accommodation because she had allowed a man to remain in her hall of residence room overnight, the committee's decision being approved by a governing body, three of whose members were also members of the committee. Despite the obvious potential for the intermingling of function, the Court of Appeal upheld the validity of the expulsion, holding the governing body had acted fairly throughout, and noting that the three members of the committee entitled to sit on the governing body had not done so. Lord Denning MR took the view that the complainant had not 'lost anything' even if there had been bias, as she clearly would never have made a good teacher.

There may be situations where the intermingling of functions is an unavoidable consequence of the scheme approved by Parliament, in which case the courts are most unlikely to overturn any decisions arrived at as a result of complying with the statutory procedure: see *Franklin* v *Minister of Town and Country Planning* [1948] AC 87.

Intermingling of functions: investigator and prosecutor

In *R* v *Barnsley Metropolitan Borough Council, ex parte Hook* [1976] 1 WLR 1052, the applicant, a market trader licensed by the local authority, was seen urinating in the street by two council workmen. The applicant had done this because the council lavatories were shut. Heated words were exchanged, and the incident was reported to the market manager, who wrote to the applicant revoking his licence. The applicant appealed unsuccessfully to two council committees, the market manager having been present whilst these committees had deliberated on the outcome of these appeals. The Divisional Court refused to grant certiorari on the ground that the revocation was merely an administrative act. The Court of Appeal held that the relief sought would be granted, on the basis that in revoking a trader's licence the council was under a duty to act judicially, the duty being inferred from the fact that the decision was one affecting the applicant's livelihood. The decision had been vitiated by the market manager's presence throughout the committees' proceedings, as this amounted to the prosecutor being present, in the absence of the accused, when the adjudicators were making their decisions.

Intermingling of functions: previous knowledge of the issues and inevitable bias

There may be situations were those exercising discretion in respect of an applicant's rights have prior knowledge of the applicant or have otherwise been involved at an earlier stage in the decision-making process. To what extent are they prohibited, by the rule against bias, from any further involvement? What if this involvement at more than one stage in the process is the result of a scheme enacted by Parliament? As will be seen, much depends on the extent to which the courts feel the decision-maker is able to come to the matter with an open mind, the extent to which there is a sound public policy reason for involvement at various stages and the extent to which resort to judicial review can provide a sufficient safeguard.

In *R* v *Board of Visitors of Frankland Prison, ex parte Lewis* [1986] 1 All ER 272 the applicant, a prisoner who had been found guilty of an offence against prison discipline by the prison's board of visitors, subsequently discovered that the chairman of the board had also been involved in a consideration of his application to the parole board and hence had knowledge of his background, in particular his previous convictions. Considering his application for judicial review of the board's finding of guilt on the basis that it was vitiated by bias, the court held that although prison boards of visitors were under a duty to act judicially when considering disciplinary hearings, a member was not disqualified from acting simply because he had acquired information about the prisoner in a different administrative capacity. Woolf J felt that it was inevitable that members of boards of visitors would know more about those appearing before them than, for example, magistrates, because of the administrative duties they frequently performed, such as considering the suitability of prisoners for release on parole. A board of visitors always had a discretion not to proceed with a hearing if it was of the opinion that, as presently constituted, it would be improper for it to proceed. He regarded it as significant that Parliament had constituted these bodies to act on the basis of their special knowledge of the prison system, thus their members should not be too ready to regard a general background knowledge of the prisoner as a ground for not adjudicating. In this case his Lordship felt that a reasonable and fair-minded person would not have regarded the chairman as disqualified. Similarly, in *R v Oxford Regional Mental Health Review Tribunal, ex parte Mackman* (1986) The Times 2 June, where the applicant, a patient at Broadmoor, appeared before the Mental Health Review Tribunal on 16 January 1985, unsuccessfully seeking an order for his discharge. Renewing his application in November 1985, only to find that the President of the tribunal on this occasion was the same person who had presided over, and refused, his earlier application, the applicant unsuccessfully sought an adjournment so that the application might be heard by a differently constituted tribunal. The subsequent request for a discharge was refused. In refusing the application for (inter alia) certiorari to quash the decision, McNeill J pointed out that there was no statutory requirement that a tribunal member should not sit on successive applications.

It would appear that a distinction can be drawn in this matter between courts of law on the one hand, and tribunals on the other, in that, in some areas, it may be inevitable that a tribunal member is going to be involved in dealing with more than one case involving an individual, especially when the tribunal deals with a somewhat specialised subject matter. In magistrates' courts there is arguably greater scope for magistrates declining to sit in a particular case and being replaced by a colleague. This distinction is supported by the decision of the Divisional Court in *R v Downham Market Magistrates' Court, ex parte Nudd* (1988) The Times 14 April, where the applicant appeared before the same chairman of justices in respect of three separate offences in a space of 13 months. The applicant successfully sought judicial review of the latter conviction on the basis of bias, in that the chairman of the bench already knew of the applicant's antecedents, the court holding that the chairman should not have sat in this case, given his prior experience of the applicant's background, and in the light of the fact that the conviction complained of turned on a conflict of evidence between the applicant and a police officer. The court felt that the test for bias may have been made out in that the chairman might have been unduly influenced by his prior knowledge of the applicant, and thus been unable to give him a fair hearing. See further *R* v *Board of Visitors of Walton Prison, ex parte Weldon* (1985) The Times 6 April.

These authorities, self-evidently, pre-date the incorporation of the European Convention on Human Rights by means of the Human Rights Act 1998. How has this altered the approach of the courts, if at all, as regards 'inevitable bias'? The matter was addressed by the European Court of Human Rights in *Kingsley* v *United Kingdom* (2001) The Times 9 January in respect of decision by the Gaming Board to revoke certain licences granted to the applicant that were a precondition to his being permitted involvement in the running of casinos. The applicant applied for judicial review of the revocations on the ground of bias, evidence being produced that members of the Gaming Board who had agreed that the applicant's certificate should be revoked had been involved in earlier meetings of the Gaming Board where the revocation had been proposed and agreed. Whilst the Court noted that the procedures adopted by the Gaming Board lacked the required appearance of impartiality, and thus caused a violation of the applicant's rights under art 6 of the Convention, those failings could have been cured if there had been sufficient judicial safeguards. That begged the question of whether judicial review provided a sufficient judicial safeguard in the circumstances. The Court observed that, although the Gaming Board had conceded the appearance of bias at the judicial review hearings, Jowitt J had taken the view at first instance that the test for bias was not satisfied and that, in any event, Parliament had not provided for any other body to make the initial decision – thus it was a case of inevitable bias. The Court of Appeal also recognised the appearance of bias but refused to quash the decision because the Gaming Board was not empowered to delegate the revocation decision to an independent panel. Hence the allegation of bias could not be cured by remitting the decision to the Gaming Board to be made again. On this basis, the European Court of Human Rights concluded that there had been a violation of art 6(1) because the High Court and the Court of Appeal did not have full jurisdiction within the meaning of the case law on art 6 when they reviewed the Board's decision. Widening the scope of review to encompass the merits of the decision would not have been the solution here, as the end result would still have been a quashing of the revocation, the issue being remitted again to the Gaming Board for consideration by means of the same flawed process.

Compare this with the judicial attitude towards the involvement of the Secretary of State in the determination of contentious planning applications and appeals. Under the relevant planning legislation, the Secretary of State is empowered to determine the outcome of such procedures even though applications may concern contentious policies, considerations for which the Secretary of State is responsible. In *R (On the Application of Holding and Barnes plc)* v *Secretary of State for the*

Environment, Transport and the Regions; R (On the Application of Alconbury Developments Ltd) v *Secretary of State for the Environment, Transport and the Regions; Secretary of State for the Environment, Transport and the Regions* v *Legal and General Assurance Society Ltd* [2001] 2 WLR 1389, it was contended that this process was in breach of art 6 because of the Secretary of State's obvious predisposition towards determining applications in a manner that fitted with his overall planning policy.

Rejecting the challenge, the House of Lords held that the minister was not intended to be an impartial figure in the planning process. A key feature of that process was that he was responsible for the development and execution of a national planning policy, for which he was answerable to Parliament. The Strasbourg jurisprudence recognised that the determination of some civil rights could be in the hands of elected representatives, provided adequate judicial safeguards were provided to challenge such decisions. Those judicial safeguards did not have to be procedures that provided for a complete rehearing of the case or a comprehensive challenge to the merits of a decision, as this would undermine the whole basis of giving the decision-making power to an elected representative. The application for judicial review procedure and the statutory rights of appeal provided in the relevant planning legislation did provide for adequate safeguards, as they allowed for challenges if the decision-maker erred in law, exceeded his powers or adopted an unfair procedure.

The key issue, therefore, is the extent to which appeal or review processes can 'cure' any failure to comply with the requirements of art 6. In *Adan* v *Newham London Borough Council* [2001] 1 All ER 930, the Court of Appeal considered statutory provisions that empowered a local housing authority to determine applications for assistance under the Housing Act 1996. Applications were determined by a housing officer, with a right of appeal to a appeal officer. A right to appeal on a point of law could be pursued further in the county court. Although it was accepted that the appeal officer did not possess the degree of impartiality required by art 6, the Court held that, viewing the process as a whole, the existence of a right of appeal to the county court ensured that the procedure was Convention compliant. By contrast, the Court held that where there was a dispute as to fact in respect of an appeal officer's findings, the existence of a right of appeal on a point of law would not suffice to satisfy art 6 as there would be no independent tribunal to determine such an issue. In *R (On the Application of Beeson)* v *Dorset County Council* (2001) The Times 21 December the Divisional Court held that a local authority review panel, making decisions as to whether or not an applicant was required to contribute to the cost of residential care, was not sufficiently independent of the council as a majority of its members were council members. This unfairness could not be remedied by judicial review, as the review panel was required to determine findings of fact – such as the assessing of the credibility of claimants. It was impossible for a court on judicial review to determine whether or not the review panel's findings would have been affected by its connection with one of the parties. A reviewing court could not become an appeal body in relation to the panel's decisions. See further *R (On the Application of McLellan)* v *Bracknell Forest Borough Council* [2002] 1 All ER 899.

Is the application of the rule against bias gradual or absolute?

It has been noted previously that the rules of natural justice and the duty to act fairly apply in varying degrees to different situations. Sometimes, what is at stake requires the full panoply of justice to be provided before a decision can be made; in other cases, a body is required to do little more than act in good faith.

Unlike the right to a fair hearing, the rule against bias, by its very nature, must be more absolute in its operation. A decision is either vitiated by bias or it is not: the rule against bias either applies or it does not. The authorities suggest that the rule may not apply to decisions that can be classified as purely administrative, in the sense that no substantive rights are yet affected by the decision. In *R* v *Secretary of State for Trade, ex parte Perestrello* [1981] QB 19 the applicant challenged the appointment of certain inspectors to investigate the affairs of a company that he owned on the ground that the same inspectors had been involved in investigating the affairs of other companies that he had owned, leading to their being wound up. Dismissing his application on the basis that bias had not been made out, the court added that, even if apparent bias had been established, it was not a situation where that would provide a valid ground of challenge. The investigating officers were in the position of potential prosecutors, in so far as their function was to ascertain whether the suspicions that had prompted the investigation were justified by what they found. They had to act fairly, but their actions could not be attacked on the basis of bias. See further *R* v *Chief Constable of South Wales, ex parte Thornhill* (1987) The Times 1 June.

The move towards a 'real danger' test for bias

The nature of the test applied by the courts in determining whether or not allegations of apparent bias are made out has gradually evolved, along with the development of judicial review, as a method of controlling executive action.

For some time the common law adopted a distinction between the test applied where the function impugned was judicial or quasi-judicial, and that applied where the function was more obviously administrative in nature. Of the two tests, the lower, in the sense that it was the more easily satisfied of the two, was the reasonable suspicion test, expounded in *R* v *Sussex Justices, ex parte McCarthy* (above) where Lord Hewart CJ stated:

> 'Nothing is to be done which creates even a suspicion that there has been an improper interference with the course of justice.'

This formulation tended to be applied to judicial or quasi-judicial proceedings, and was held, in *R* v *Liverpool City Justices, ex parte Topping* [1983] 1 WLR 119, to involve an examination of whether a reasonable and fair-minded person sitting in court and knowing all the facts would have a reasonable suspicion that a fair trial for the applicant was not possible.

The alternative test, and one which has generally placed a heavier evidential burden on the applicant, was that of 'real likelihood' of bias, a test that tended to be applied to administrative decision-making processes. In *Metropolitan Properties Co* v *Lannon* (above) Lord Denning MR expressed his preference for this test where he observed that it brought home the point that:

> '... in considering whether there was a real likelihood of bias, the court does not look at the mind of the justice himself or at the mind of the chairman of the tribunal ... It does not look to see if there was a real likelihood that he would, or did, in fact favour one side at the expense of the other ... the court looks at the impression which would be given to other people ... If right-minded persons would think that, in the circumstances there was a real likelihood of bias on (the part of the adjudicator) then he should not sit.'

There has since been a unification of the tests, as confirmed in *R* v *Gough* [1993] 2 WLR 883, and applied in decisions such as *R* v *Secretary of State for the Environment and Another, ex parte Kirkstall Valley Campaign* [1996] 3 All ER 304. Lord Goff, in *R* v *Gough*, criticised the emergence of the 'reasonable suspicion' test in judicial cases as being a misinterpretation of the decision in *ex parte McCarthy*, preferring instead the approach adopted in *R* v *Camborne Justices, ex parte Pearce* [1954] 2 All ER 850, which rejected 'reasonable suspicion' on the grounds that it presented too low a threshold for challenge, opening up the possibility of appeal on the flimsiest of pretexts.

Three types case were identified by the House of Lords in *R* v *Gough*. First, those cases where actual bias was alleged. In such cases the proceedings would be invalidated upon proof of bias. Second, where the allegation of bias rested upon a pecuniary or proprietary interest, the proceedings would be invalidated upon proof of the pecuniary or proprietary interest. Third, in cases of apparent bias, where there was no pecuniary or proprietary interest, the correct test was that of whether or not there was a real danger of bias. The term 'real danger' was preferred to real likelihood because of the desire to emphasis that the possibility of bias should be enough to impugn the validity of proceedings, as opposed to proof of probability.

Lord Goff went on to explain that the question of whether or not there was a real danger of bias in any particular case was to be assessed by the court in the light of the evidence before it. He rejected the notion of an objective 'reasonable man' test on the basis that:

> '... it is difficult to see what difference there is between the impression derived by a reasonable man to whom such knowledge has been imputed and the impression derived by the court, here personifying the reasonable man.'

Lord Goff also indicated that it was desirable that the real danger test should be applicable to all cases of apparent bias 'whether concerned with justices or members of other inferior tribunals, or with jurors or with arbitrators'; see further *AT & T*

Corporation v *Saudi Cable Co* (2000) The Times 23 May. These sentiments were echoed by Sedley J in *ex parte Kirkstall Valley Campaign* (above), confirming that, in applying the *Gough* test, no distinction is to be drawn on the one hand between decision-making that is judicial or quasi-judicial, and, on the other hand, the more general run of administrative decision-making. He was persuaded to this conclusion by the fact that, increasingly, administrative decisions could radically affect the interests of individual citizens just as much as those that might be categorised as judicial or quasi-judicial.

Criticism of R v Gough *in the context of the Human Rights Act 1998*

The approach adopted in *R* v *Gough* has not been without its critics. In *R* v *Bow Street Metropolitan Stipendiary Magistrate, ex parte Pinochet Ugarte (No 2)* [1999] 1 All ER 577 Lord Browne-Wilkinson did advert to the debate regarding the proper test to be applied where bias was alleged:

> '... it is unnecessary to determine whether the test of apparent bias laid down in *R* v *Gough* ... ("is there in the view of the court a real danger that the judge was biased?") needs to be reviewed in the light of subsequent decisions. Decisions in Canada, Australia and New Zealand have either refused to apply the test in *R* v *Gough*, or modified it so as to make the relevant test the question whether the events in question give rise to a reasonable apprehension or suspicion on the part of a fair-minded and informed member of the public that the judge was not impartial: see, for example, the High Court of Australia in *Webb* v *R* (1994) 181 CLR 41. It has also been suggested that the test in *R* v *Gough* in some way impinges on the requirement of Lord Hewart CJ's dictum that justice should appear to be done: see *R* v *Inner West London Coroner, ex parte Dallaglio* ...'

See further *Locabail (UK) Ltd* v *Bayfield Properties Ltd, etc* (above).

The matter received further scrutiny in *Director General of Fair Trading* v *Proprietary Association of Great Britain* (2001) The Times 2 February, where the issue before the court was whether the test in *R* v *Gough* was sufficient to satisfy the fair trial requirements under art 6 of the European Convention on Human Rights. It was noted that the approach of the European Court of Human Rights was to decide whether, on an objective appraisal, the material facts gave rise to a legitimate fear that the judge might not have been impartial. For these purposes, the material facts were not limited to those which were apparent to the applicant, but included those ascertained upon investigation by the court. This approach was approved by the House of Lords in *Magill* v *Porter; Weeks* v *Magill; Hartley* v *Magill; England* v *Magill; Phillips* v *Magill* (2001) The Times 14 December where the correct test to be applied by a court to determine whether or not there was a reasonable apprehension of bias (having first ascertained all the relevant circumstances) was confirmed as deciding whether those circumstances would lead a fair-minded and informed observer to conclude that there was a real possibility that the tribunal was biased.

Strictly speaking, this decision only alters the test for bias in those cases where

Convention rights are at stake, but it is hard to imagine a case where an applicant would be alleging bias that would not involve a determination of his civil rights. In any event, to have two different tests, one for domestic purposes and one for Convention cases, would be hard to defend.

Even with a single, tolerably clear test for apparent bias, the question of whether or not such bias had been established will depend on the facts of each case, regard being had to the proximity of the interest to the issue being decided. Where an apparent conflict of interest arises because a member of a decision-making body has an interest in the subject matter of the decision, or has a relevant pecuniary interest, the wise course of action for that member would be not only to abstain from partaking in the discussion and any voting, but also to withdraw whilst the remaining members of the decision-making body concluded their deliberations.

7

Reasonableness and Proportionality

7.1 Introduction

7.2 The development of unreasonableness and irrationality as grounds for review

7.3 The move towards proportionality

7.4 Proportionality and EC law

7.1 Introduction

The conventional ultra vires doctrine is based on the understanding that to abuse a delegated power is to exercise it in a manner that is unlawful. At common law the judges have, over many years, developed a core concept of unreasonableness to illustrate and explain what is meant by abuse of power, and have exercised the power of review to quash or prevent unreasonable administrative and executive action. The constitutional foundation for this is the contention that Parliament will rarely, if ever, specify that delegated discretion must be exercised reasonably. It is such an obvious restriction upon any delegated power that it does not need to be spelt out. Hence it is an implied limit on the power of public bodies. It is customary, for ease of exposition if for no other reason, to present 'categories' of ultra vires, such as breach of natural justice, unreasonableness or taking into account irrelevant considerations, but the reality is that they all merge into one another. A procedure might be so unfair that it is unreasonable for a decision-making body to adopt it. A decision can be unfair in the sense that it bears no relation to the evidence before the decision-making body, and in that sense it would be acceptable to also describe it as unreasonable. To arrive at a conclusion without taking into account relevant considerations is not only a specific manifestation of unreasonableness, it could also be characterised as a defective procedure, hence a breach of natural justice. The divisions are thus, to some extent, artificial and far from watertight, as many major decisions can as easily be placed under one heading as another.

Source of power

When considering the legality of the actions of a public body the starting point will normally be an examination of the source of its power. The source of the power will provide the parameters for the reviewing exercise. In most cases the source of the delegated discretion will be an enabling Act, but in some cases it might be an Order in Council issued under the Prerogative, and in others the decision-making body may have been constituted under private law, but may de facto exercise public law functions: see, for example, the consideration of the Panel on Take-overs and Mergers in *R* v *Panel on Take-overs and Mergers, ex parte Guiness plc* [1989] 2 WLR 863.

Types of power

Depending upon the degree of flexibility intended by the legislature, the powers of a public body may be drawn in narrow or broad terms. The body may be given powers to decide a matter, but only after taking certain matters into account. For example, under the Town and Country Planning Act 1990, local planning authorities must have regard to matters such as the development plans for their areas before exercising their discretion to grant planning permission. Failure to have regard to these matters could invalidate a decision. Powers may be worded in such a way as to appear to leave all discretion in the decision-making body, in the form of so-called subjectively worded powers. Typically these appear in the formulations indicating that the decision-making body may 'make such award as it thinks fit' or may 'impose such conditions upon the grant of a licence as it sees fit'. Prima facie it appears very difficult to see how a court could intervene to control the exercise of such a power, as the only criterion set by the legislature is that the minister should be satisfied that an award should be made. In *Liversidge* v *Anderson* [1942] AC 206 a majority of the House of Lords held that, as the Defence Regulation under consideration empowered the Home Secretary to detain a person if he had reasonable cause to believe him to be of hostile origin or associations, the minister's order detaining Liversidge could only be challenged on the ground of bad faith. The majority were unwilling to inquire into whether the Home Secretary had reasonable grounds for his belief. Even allowing for the fact that the decision was made during wartime, and involved issues that might have had a bearing upon national security, it was unsatisfactory in terms of its constitutional implications, raising as it did the prospect of the minister only having to satisfy himself that he had reasonable cause to believe that detention was necessary before authorising it.

This 'hands-off' approach to the exercise of subjectively worded powers by ministers and other administrative bodies no longer pertains. In *IRC* v *Rossminster Ltd* [1980] AC 952, the House of Lords considered the effect of a provision under which an officer was entitled to seize any material which he had reasonable cause to believe might be required as evidence. The Inland Revenue accepted that the courts could inquire into whether there were reasonable grounds for that belief. Lord Scarman stated that: 'The ghost of *Liversidge* v *Anderson* ... casts no shadow ... (and) I would think it need no longer haunt the law ... It is now beyond recall'.

Lord Wilberforce expressed the point somewhat more prosaically: 'Parliament by using such phrases as "is satisfied", "has reasonable cause to believe" must be taken to accept the restraint which the courts in many cases have held to be inherent in them'.

Much depends on context but, as will be seen below, the impact of the Human Rights Act 1998 indicates that judges arguably now have more power to intervene and closely scrutinise executive acts, at least where Convention rights are at stake, than they have ever possessed before.

7.2 The development of unreasonableness and irrationality as grounds for review

Unreasonableness as a basis for judicial review ha always been difficult to pin down because it is such a subjective concept. Opinions can obviously vary widely on whether a particular decision is reasonable or not. Judicial review has traditionally been concerned with the legality of the decision under review not its merits. Thus a public body can make a 'bad' decision with which people may disagree, but that does not necessarily mean it is an ultra vires decision. Determining the reasonableness of a decision may, however, involve questioning its merits, thus involving judges in the making of value judgments about the quality of the decision made by a public body. At this point merits and legality become intertwined. The incorporation of the European Convention on Human Rights by the enactment of the Human Rights Act 1998 has increased the incidence of such problems.

The 'Wednesbury' test and irrationality

For many years the basic test for reasonableness in English administrative law was that derived from the Court of Appeal's decision in *Associated Provincial Picture Houses Ltd* v *Wednesbury Corporation* [1948] 1 KB 223. The local authority had the power to grant permission for the opening of cinemas, subject to such conditions as they saw fit to impose. The plaintiff sought a declaration that a condition imposed on a grant of permission to open one of their cinemas, namely that no child under 15 was to be allowed in without an adult, was ultra vires. Lord Greene MR outlined the principles upon which the authority's decision might be open to attack. These were: not directing itself properly in law; not taking into account relevant considerations, or conversely taking into account irrelevant considerations; acting unreasonably; acting in bad faith; or acting in disregard of public policy. As regards the condition imposed by the defendant authority, Lord Greene thought it was important to bear in mind that Parliament had entrusted the local authority with the discretion to impose conditions because of its knowledge of the area's needs, and (impliedly) because having been elected it reflected the views of the area's inhabitants. He felt that courts should therefore be slow to intervene to quash a condition imposed by such a body, but should do so where a condition was seen to be unreasonable. This meant that the condition would have to be one that was so unreasonable, no reasonable authority would have imposed it, and to prove a case of that kind would require compelling evidence. He explained the concept in these terms:

> '... discretion must be exercised reasonably. Now what does that mean? ... It appears to me quite clear that the matter dealt with by this condition was a matter which a reasonable authority would be justified in considering when they were making up their mind what condition should be attached to the grant of this licence. Nobody, at this time of day, could say that the well-being and the physical and moral health of children is not a matter which a local authority, in exercising their powers, can properly have in mind when those questions are germane to what they have to consider ... It is clear that the local authority are entrusted by Parliament with the decision on a matter which the knowledge and experience of that authority can best be trusted to deal with. The subject matter with which the condition deals is one relevant for its consideration. They have considered it and come to a decision upon it. It is true to say that, if a decision on a competent matter is so unreasonable that no reasonable authority could ever have come to it ... It is not what the court considers unreasonable, a different thing altogether. If it is what the court considers unreasonable, the court may very well have different views to that of a local authority on matters of high public policy of this kind. Some courts might think that no children ought to be admitted on Sundays at all, some courts might think the reverse, and all over the country I have no doubt on a thing of that sort honest and sincere people hold different views. The effect of the legislation is not to set up the court as an arbiter of the correctness of one view over another. It is the local authority that are set in that position and, provided they act, as they have acted, within the four corners of their jurisdiction, this court, in my opinion, cannot interfere ...'

In his speech in *Council of Civil Service Unions* v *Minister for the Civil Service* [1984] 3 All ER 935 (the 'GCHQ' case), Lord Diplock took this concept further and identified what he saw as the three key heads of judicial review: 'illegality' 'irrationality' and 'procedural impropriety'. He went on to observe:

> 'By "irrationality" I mean what can by now be succinctly referred to as "*Wednesbury* unreasonableness" ... It applies to a decision which is so outrageous in its defiance of logic or of accepted moral standards that no sensible person who had applied his mind to the question to be decided could have arrived at it. Whether a decision falls within this category is a question that judges by their training and experience should be well equipped to answer, or else there would be something badly wrong with our judicial system ... "Irrationality" by now can stand on its own feet as an accepted ground on which a decision may be attacked by judicial review.'

Despite the difference in the language used, there is little to choose between the concepts of unreasonableness and irrationality, as post-GCHQ cases illustrate. Thus in a written reply to a Parliamentary question in 1985, the Home Secretary revealed that, although he would consult the relevant members of the judiciary with a view to establishing a 'tariff' of terms of imprisonment for prisoners convicted of certain serious offences, this consultation process would not begin until a prisoner had served at least three or four years of the sentence that had been imposed, and furthermore, that he would be prepared to proceed on the basis of his own views in preference to those of a trial judge where he thought fit. It was held, in *R* v *Secretary of State for the Home Department, ex parte Handscomb* (1988) 86 Cr App Rep 59 that it would be irrational for a minister never to refer cases to the trial judges for their comments until prisoners sentenced by them had served three years of their sentences, Watkins LJ observing that no satisfactory explanation was given by the minister for this delay. The court regarded the minister's decision to act upon his own views in preference to those of a trial judge as 'clearly irrational'. If the minister was not to accept the trial judge's view of the case, whose was he to follow?

Similarly in *R* v *Secretary of State for the Home Department, ex parte Norney and Others* [1995] Admin LR 861, the court ruled that the Home Secretary's policy of not referring the cases of prisoners serving life sentences for terrorist offences (for whom 20 years had been fixed as the tariff period element of such sentences, to reflect the degree of retribution and deterrence involved) for consideration by the Parole Board until after the expiry of the tariff period was unreasonable in the *Wednesbury* sense because it effectively increased the tariff period by the average length of time taken by the Parole Board to consider a case following referral (23 weeks). Further, as regards, prisoners who no longer posed a threat to society, the court felt that the policy was in breach of the common law and the European Convention on Human Rights.

Identifying and proving unreasonableness and irrationality: manifest unreasonableness and irrationality

There will always be those rare cases where the unreasonableness is so manifest that the courts will not hesitate to intervene. An example was provided by Warrington LJ in *Short* v *Poole Corporation* [1926] Ch 66, where he adverted to a school dismissing a teacher because she had red hair. Such cases border on being invalid because of bad faith, not mere unreasonableness. In *Williams* v *Giddy* [1911] AC 381, the Public Service Board of New South Wales awarded a retiring civil servant a gratuity of one penny per year of service. Not only was the award unreasonable but, the Privy Council noted, it was tantamount to a refusal to exercise discretion. In *Backhouse* v *Lambeth London Borough Council* (1972) 116 SJ 802, where a local authority increased the rent payable on a council property to £18,000 per week (this was part of a campaign against the Conservative government's 'Fair Rents' legislation), the court declared the action to be manifestly unreasonable – clearly it was a rent increase no reasonable authority would have sanctioned. Finally, in *R* v *Secretary of State for the Home Department, ex parte Cox* (1993) 5 Admin LR 17, the applicant, who had been convicted of murder in 1971 and released on licence in 1983, was charged during 1989 with making threats to kill a neighbour, and his licence was revoked although the charges were eventually dismissed. It was decided to release the applicant on licence again on 21 September 1990, but on 15

September he was arrested driving a car with an invalid tax disc and found to be in possession of a small quantity of cannabis. The Secretary of State cancelled the decision to release the applicant on the ground that he presented a risk of danger to the public. The Divisional Court quashed the Secretary of State's decision on the ground that it was unreasonable in the *Wednesbury* sense, bordering on the perverse.

Identifying and proving unreasonableness and irrationality: the evidential problem

Under domestic law establishing unreasonableness or irrationality has always placed a heavy evidential burden on the applicant for judicial review. It is a stringent test that leaves the ultimate discretion with the judiciary. The threshold for judicial intervention is set at a high level. To be 'unreasonable' an act must be of such a nature that no reasonable person could possibly entertain such a thing. As Lord Hailsham observed in *Re W (An Infant)* [1971] AC 682 at 700, in the course of illustrating the difficulty of sustaining an allegation that action is unreasonable, two reasonable persons can come to opposite conclusions on the same set of facts without forfeiting their title to be regarded as reasonable.

The task of determining whether the Secretary of State or the local education authority was proposing to act unreasonably fell to the House of Lords in *Secretary of State for Education and Science* v *Tameside Metropolitan Borough Council* [1977] AC 1014. In 1974 the Labour Party controlled the local education authority and decided to convert the state schools to the 'comprehensive' system of education. After the local elections in May 1976 the Conservative Party won control of the education authority and decided to retain the grammar/secondary school system. Section 68 of the Education Act 1944 gave the Secretary of State power to issue directions to a local education authority:

'... if ... satisfied ... that any local education authority ... have acted or are proposing to act unreasonably with respect to the exercise of any power conferred or the performance of any duty imposed by or under this Act.'

The Secretary of State directed the newly elected Conservative authority to retain the 'comprehensive' system. The authority refused and the Secretary of State sought an order of mandamus to compel compliance, on the basis that, in her view, it would not be possible for the authority to revert back to a selective system of schooling before the commencement of the new academic year without ensuing chaos. When the case was before the Court of Appeal Lord Denning observed (echoing the comment of Lord Hailsham, above) that:

'... two reasonable persons can reasonably come to opposite conclusions ... No one can properly be labelled as being unreasonableness unless he is not only wrong but unreasonably wrong, so wrong that no reasonable person could sensibly take that view ...'

His Lordship held that the Secretary of State must have misdirected herself on the interpretation of 'unreasonableness', as there was no evidence on which the Secretary of State could declare herself satisfied that the council was proposing to act unreasonably, ie he was satisfied that the authority could manage the change in the time available. The House of Lords upheld the Court of Appeal's decision.

Although the case appears to involve a choice between competing concepts of reasonableness, it is submitted that it could be seen as a case where the Secretary had no jurisdiction to make an order under s68 as the evidence that had to exist as a precondition for the exercise of that power was not before the court.

Generally, the current trend would appear to be for the courts not to intervene in relation to decisions of local authorities on matters of social policy that are within their control. As Lord Brightman commented in *R* v *Hillingdon London Borough Council, ex parte Puhlhofer* [1986] AC 484:

> 'Where the existence or non-existence of a fact is left to the judgment and discretion of a public body and that fact involves a broad spectrum ranging from the obvious to the debatable to the just conceivable, it is the duty of the court to leave the decision of that fact to the public body to whom Parliament has entrusted the decision-making power save in a case where it is obvious that the public body, consciously or unconsciously, are acting perversely.'

This passage was cited with approval by Ralph Gibson LJ in *West Glamorgan County Council* v *Rafferty* [1987] 1 WLR 457.

Identifying and proving unreasonableness and irrationality: the significance of context

As indicated above, judicial discretion as to whether or not to intervene is a key factor determining the success or failure of an application for judicial review on the grounds of unreasonableness or irrationality. The courts will be mindful not only of the merits of the decision, but also the desirability and appropriateness of judicial intervention. If a public body is deemed to be in a better position than the courts to determine an issue then, save for cases of manifest absurdity, the courts are unlikely to overturn its decisions.

A number of cases illustrate this point. In *R* v *Great Yarmouth Borough Council, ex parte Sawyer* (1987) The Times 18 June, the applicant, chairman of the local Taxi Proprietors' Association, sought judicial review of the respondent's decision to increase the number of hackney carriage licences granted. The Court of Appeal held, dismissing the application, that there was a very heavy burden indeed resting upon any applicant wishing to show that a public body, in the exercise of its discretion, had acted unreasonably. Woolf LJ explained that it could not be said in this case that the decision of the local authority, to allow market forces to determine the granting of licences, was perverse in the sense that no reasonable authority would have come to it. It was not for the courts to usurp the function of the authority simply because it disapproved of the decision. It could only intervene if it could be shown that the authority had arrived at its decision unlawfully. It is significant to note the importance attached by the courts to the purpose behind the relevant legislation. For a similar approach, albeit in a somewhat different context (decision not to re-let council properties to families on the council's waiting list), see *R* v *Hammersmith and Fulham London Borough Council, ex parte Beddowes* [1987] 2 WLR 263.

Second, in *Re Walker's Application* (1987) The Times 26 November, the applicant for review was a mother whose child urgently needed a heart operation. The health authorities in Birmingham had already postponed the operation five times due to a shortage of trained nursing staff. The basis of the application was the alleged failure of the authority to provide an adequate service. The Court of Appeal held, in rejecting the application, that whilst the health authorities were clearly public bodies amenable to review, the rationing of resources was a matter for them and not the courts. Only if it could be shown that the allocation of funds by the authority was unreasonable in the *Wednesbury* sense, or if there were breaches of public law duties, would the courts be prepared to intervene. The decision perhaps begs the question as to how bad the provision of a public service has to become before the courts would be willing to label an allocation of resources as perverse: see further *R* v *Camden London Borough Council, ex parte Gillan* (1988) 21 HLR 114, and *R* v *Cambridge District Health Authority, ex parte B* [1995] 1 WLR 898.

Cases such as *R* v *Secretary of State for the Environment, ex parte Hammersmith and Fulham London Borough Council* [1991] 1 AC 521 and *R* v *Secretary of State for the Environment, ex parte Nottinghamshire County Council* [1986] AC 240 suggest that the courts are less likely to accept a challenge based on the standard *Wednesbury* test to an exercise of ministerial discretion that has been expressly approved by the House of Commons. In these cases it was suggested that such action would only be declared ultra vires if it was manifestly absurd, motivated by bad faith or based on other improper motives. It is submitted, however, that there is little or no constitutional basis for such judicial reticence. A vote in the House of Commons as such has no legal significance in terms of validating administrative action, or making it proof against judicial review. In *R (On the Application of Javed)* v *Secretary of State for the Home Department* (2001) The Times 24 May, Lord Phillips MR observed that it would not be unconstitutional for a court to review the legality of subordinate legislation even though it had been approved by affirmative resolution of each House of Parliament. As to the approach to be taken to the scope for judicial review of subordinate legislation, he expressed the view that much depended on the nature and purpose of the Parent Act. In the '*Nottingham*' and '*Hammersmith*' cases the discretion had been exercised in the context of political and economic considerations to be evaluated by the minister – in such circumstances to contend that there was no scope for an attack on the exercise of the Secretary of State's exercise of discretion on the ground of irrationality in the absence of bad faith or manifest absurdity was no more than a statement of practical reality. It did not necessarily mean that those were the only grounds for review of an Order enacted following the affirmative resolution procedure.

The emergence of the 'super-Wednesbury' test

In the build up to the incorporation of the European Convention on Human Rights in the Human Rights Act 1998 the domestic courts began to develop a more rigorous application of the test for unreasonableness in those cases touching upon the fundamental rights of the citizen. As Lord Bridge observed in *R v Secretary of State for the Home Department, ex parte Bugdaycay* [1987] AC 514 at 531:

> '... the court must ... be entitled to subject an administrative decision to ... more rigorous examination ... according to the gravity of the issue which the decision determines. The most fundamental of all human rights is the individual's right to life and when an administrative decision under challenge is said to be one which may put the applicant's life at risk, the basis of the decision must surely call for anxious scrutiny.'

Similar sentiment where expressed by Sir Thomas Bingham MR in *R v Ministry of Defence, ex parte Smith* [1996] 2 WLR 305 at 337–8, where he noted:

> '... that the greater the policy content of a decision, and the more remote the subject matter of that decision from the ordinary judicial experience, the more hesitant the court must necessarily be in holding a decision to be irrational ... [and that] ... where decisions of a policy-laden, esoteric or security-based nature are in issue even greater caution than normal need be shown in applying [the test for reasonableness] ... the test itself is sufficiently flexible to cover all situations. The present cases [concerning the ban on homosexuals serving in the armed forces] ... do concern innate qualities of a very personal kind and the decisions of which the applicants complain have had a profound effect on their careers and prospects ... the court ... has the constitutional role and duty of ensuring that the rights of citizens are not abused by the unlawful exercise of executive power. While the court must properly defer to the expertise of responsible decision makers, it must not shrink from its fundamental duty to "... do right to all manner of people ...".'

These comments led to the court holding in *R v Lord Saville and Others, ex parte A and Others* [1999] 4 All ER 860 that it would be unreasonable for the inquiry in to the events of so-called 'Bloody Sunday' not to grant anonymity to soldiers giving evidence. Lord Woolf MR confirmed that where the decision in question involved something as basic as the right to life there would be very anxious scrutiny of the decision and the countervailing arguments.

7.3 The move towards proportionality

The enactment of the Human Rights Act 1998, and the consequent incorporation of most significant rights under the Convention, has meant that the doctrine of proportionality, as developed in the jurisprudence of the European Court of Human Rights, has to be taken into account by domestic courts considering applications for judicial review where Convention rights are in play. Section 2(1) of the 1998 Act provides that:

'A court or tribunal determining a question which has arisen in connection with a Convention right must take into account any –
(a) judgment, decision, declaration or advisory opinion of the European Court of Human Rights,
(b) opinion of the Commission given in a report adopted under art 31 of the Convention,
(c) decision of the Commission in connection with arts 26 or 27(2) of the Convention, or
(d) decision of the Committee of Ministers taken under art 46 of the Convention,
whenever made or given, so far as, in the opinion of the court or tribunal, it is relevant to the proceedings in which that question has arisen.'

Under s3(1) the court reviewing the exercise of statutory discretion will have to read and give effect to the enabling Act, so far as it is possible to do so, in a way which is compatible with the Convention rights. The extent to which this change would alter the judicial function was predicted by Lord Irvine LC, who observed:

'[Once the ECHR is incorporated in domestic law] The courts' decisions will be based on a more overtly principled, indeed moral, basis. The court will look at the positive right. It will only accept an interference with that right where a justification, allowed under the Convention, is made out. The scrutiny will not be limited to seeing if the words of an exception can be satisfied. The court will need to be satisfied that the spirit of this exception is made out. It will need to be satisfied that the interference with the protected right is justified in the public interests in a free democratic society. Moreover, the courts will in this area have to apply the Convention principle of proportionality. This means the court will be looking substantively at that question. It will not be limited to a secondary review of the decision-making process but at the primary question of the merits of the decision itself.

In reaching its judgment, therefore, the court will need to expand and explain its own view of whether the conduct is legitimate. It will produce in short a decision on the morality of the conduct and not simply its compliance with the bare letter of the law.'
(*Tom Sargant Memorial Lecture*, December 1997.)

The doctrine of proportionality provides that action will be unlawful if it is disproportionate in its effect, or relative to what is required. For example, to impose a very severe punishment in respect of a minor transgression would be seen as a breach of the proportionality doctrine. There is evidence to suggest that it has been recognised for some time in English administrative law, albeit as an offshoot of unreasonableness: see *R* v *Barnsley Metropolitan Borough Council, ex parte Hook* [1976] 1 WLR 1052 (market trader's licence revoked in response to allegations that he had urinated in the street). The doctrine received its most significant recognition, however, in Lord Diplock's speech in *Council of Civil Service Unions* v *Minister for the Civil Service* where he stated (at p410):

'... one can conveniently classify under three heads the grounds upon which administrative action is subject to control by judicial review. The first ground I would call "illegality", the second "irrationality" and the third "procedural impropriety". That is not to say that further development on a case by case basis may not in course of time add further grounds. I have in mind particularly the possible adoption in the future of the principle of "proportionality" which is recognised in the administrative law of several of our fellow members of the European Economic Community ...'

For a pre-incorporation example of its application see *R v Brent London Borough Council, ex parte Assegai* (1987) 151 LG Rev 891, where the decision to dismiss a school governor and ban him from attending meetings and entering local authority premises was quashed by Woolf LJ on the basis that such punishment was out of all proportion to the nature of the complaints made.

The need to move beyond *Wednesbury* or even super-*Wednesbury* as a basis for review where Convention rights were in play was confirmed by the European Court of Human Rights in *Smith and Grady v United Kingdom* (1999) 29 EHRR 493 and *Lustig-Prean and Beckett v United Kingdom* (1999) 29 EHRR 548. The Court, in the course of finding that the ban on homosexuals serving in the UK armed forces amounted to a violation of art 8, agreed with the submission that there had been a violation of art 13 in that judicial review had not provided an effective domestic remedy in respect of Convention rights, because the threshold set by domestic courts for proof of irrationality had been placed so high it had effectively denied the applicants any prospect of a remedy.

The House of Lords has now addressed the issue directly in *R (On the Application of Daly) v Secretary of State for the Home Department* [2001] 3 All ER 433. In a case concerning the legality of a policy of not allowing any prisoner to be present during a search of his cell, thus permitting prison staff to examine legal correspondence thoroughly in the absence of a prisoner, Lord Steyn addressed the difference between, on the one hand, the traditional *Wednesbury* approach to review and the heightened scrutiny in cases involving fundamental rights as formulated in *R v Ministry of Defence, ex parte Smith* (above), and, on the other, the approach of a reviewing court applying principles of proportionality in cases where Convention rights are at stake:

> 'What is the difference for the disposal of concrete cases? ... The starting point is that there is an overlap between the traditional grounds of review and the approach of proportionality. Most cases would be decided in the same way whichever approach is adopted. But the intensity of review is somewhat greater under the proportionality approach. Making due allowance for important structural differences between various Convention rights ... a few generalisations are perhaps permissible. I would mention three concrete differences without suggesting that my statement is exhaustive. First, the doctrine of proportionality may require the reviewing court to assess the balance which the decision-maker has struck, not merely whether it is within the range of rational or reasonable decisions. Secondly, the proportionality test may go further than the traditional grounds of review inasmuch as it may require attention to be directed to the relative weight accorded to interests and considerations. Thirdly, even the heightened scrutiny test developed in *R v Ministry of Defence, ex parte Smith* ... is not necessarily appropriate to the protection of human rights. It will be recalled that in *Smith* the Court of Appeal reluctantly felt compelled to reject a limitation on homosexuals in the army. The challenge based on art 8 of the Convention ... foundered on the threshold required even by the anxious scrutiny test. The European Court of Human Rights came to the opposite conclusion ... [that] court concluded:
>
> "... the threshold at which the High Court and the Court of Appeal could find the

Ministry of Defence policy irrational was placed so high that it effectively excluded any consideration by the domestic courts of the question of whether the interference with the applicants' rights answered a pressing social need or was proportionate to the national security and public order aims pursued, principles which lie at the heart of the court's analysis of complaints under art 8 of the Convention."

In other words, the intensity of the review, in similar cases, is guaranteed by the twin requirements that the limitation of the right was necessary in a democratic society, in the sense of meeting a pressing social need, and the question whether the interference was really proportionate to the legitimate aim being pursued.

The differences in approach between the traditional grounds of review and the proportionality approach may therefore sometimes yield different results. It is therefore important that cases involving Convention rights must be analysed in the correct way. This does not mean that there has been a shift to merits review. On the contrary, as Professor Jowell [[2000] PL 671, 681] has pointed out the respective roles of judges and administrators are fundamentally distinct and will remain so. To this extent the general tenor of the observations in *R (Mahmood) v Secretary of State for the Home Department* [2001] 1 WLR 840 are correct. And Laws LJ rightly emphasised in *Mahmood*, at p847, para 18, "that the intensity of review in a public law case will depend on the subject matter in hand". That is so even in cases involving Convention rights. In law context is everything.'

Does proportionality herald a shift to a merits basis for the review of administrative action?

In *R v Secretary of State for the Home Department, ex parte Brind* [1991] 2 WLR 588 Lord Ackner expressed the view that to import the concept of proportionality into English law would inevitably result in a blurring of the distinction between the courts proper supervisory role, and an improper appellate role. Although much of the significance of *ex parte Brind* has been swept away by the Human Rights Act 1998, the following observations are nonetheless useful in that they mark out what was thought to be the proper role of the reviewing court, and thus provide a basis for comparison with the situation pertaining in the wake of decisions such as *Daly* (above).

Emphasising the importance of the distinction between review on the grounds of legality and review on the grounds of merits, Lord Ackner in *ex parte Brind* observed:

'The [*Wednesbury*] standard of unreasonableness ... has been criticised as being too high. But it has to be expressed in terms that confine the jurisdiction exercised by the judiciary to a supervisory, as opposed to an appellate, jurisdiction. Where Parliament has given to a minister or other person or body a discretion, the court's jurisdiction is limited, in the absence of a statutory right of appeal, to the supervision of the exercise of that discretionary power, so as to ensure that it has been exercised lawfully. It would be a wrongful usurpation of power by the judiciary to substitute its, the judicial view, on the merits and on that basis to quash the decision. If no reasonable minister properly directing himself would have reached the impugned decision, the minister had exceeded his powers and thus acted unlawfully and the court in the exercise of its supervisory role will quash that decision. Such a decision is correctly, though unattractively, described as a "perverse" decision. To seek the court's intervention on the basis that the correct or objectively reasonable decision is other than the decision which the minister has made is to invite the court to adjudicate as if Parliament had provided a right of appeal against the decision that is, to invite an abuse of power by the judiciary.'

Lord Lowry was yet more forthright in his refusal to import what he saw as a 'European' concept into judicial review. He observed (at p609):

'In my opinion proportionality and the other phrases are simply intended to move the focus of discussion away from the hitherto accepted criteria for deciding whether the decision-maker has abused his power and into an area in which the court will feel more at liberty to interfere. The first observation I would make is that there is no authority for saying that proportionality in the sense in which the appellants have used it is part of the English common law and a great deal of authority the other way. This, so far as I am concerned, is not a cause for regret for several reasons: (1) The decision-makers, very often elected, are those to whom Parliament has entrusted the discretion and to interfere with that discretion beyond the limits as hitherto defined would itself be an abuse of the judges supervisory jurisdiction. (2) The judges are not, generally speaking, equipped by training or experience, or furnished with the requisite knowledge and advice, to decide the answer to an administrative problem where the scales are evenly balanced, but they have a much better chance of reaching the right answer where the question is put in a *Wednesbury* form. The same applies if the judge's decision is appealed. (3) Stability and relative certainty would be jeopardised if the new doctrine held sway, because there is nearly always something to be said against any administrative decision and parties who felt aggrieved would be even more likely than at present to try their luck with a judicial review application both at first instance and on appeal. (4) The increase in applications for judicial review of administrative action (inevitable if the threshold of unreasonableness is lowered) will lead to the expenditure of time and money by litigants, not to speak of the prolongation of uncertainty for all concerned with the decisions in question, and the taking up of court time which could otherwise be devoted to other matters. The losers in this respect will be members of the public, for whom the courts provide a service.'

Although the observations of Lord Steyn in *Daly*, noted above, may not quite be the death knell for the *Wednesbury* test it seems clear that, where the context warrants it, the courts will be willing to expand upon the traditional scope of review, examining more closely the merits of an impugned decision.

If Convention rights are interfered with the court will first ask whether the interference was necessary – ie could the public body have achieved its legitimate aims by adopting means that caused less interference with the applicant's rights? The fact that a policy, of necessity, interferes with Convention rights does not automatically mean that action taken in pursuance of that policy is therefore lawful: see the comments of Schiemann LJ in *R* v *Secretary of State for the Home Department, ex parte Isiko* (2001) The Times 20 February. If the interference is shown to be necessary the court will go on to consider the question of proportionality – did the interference go further than was necessary to achieve the legitimate aims of the public body? In considering this second question, the court will be considering whether the public body has struck a fair balance between the legitimate aims on the one hand and the affected person's Convention rights on the other. Allowing the public body an appropriate margin of appreciation, the court would intervene if the weight accorded to the legitimate aims was unfair and unreasonable: see further *R (On the Application of Samaroo)* v *Secretary of State for the Home Department* (2001) The Times 18 September. As Dyson LJ observed in that case, the level of scrutiny exercised by a court when following that process of review in the context of the Human Rights Act 1998 was 'undoubtedly' more intense that the traditional *Wednesbury* approach. The extent of the margin of appreciation is likely to vary with the circumstances of the case. Where a Secretary of State claims to be acting in a preventive and precautionary manner to protect state security, for example by deciding to deport an individual on the ground that such action would be conducive to the public good, the courts will recognise that a large element of policy is involved and show due deference to the decision-maker; see further *Secretary of State for the Home Department* v *Rehman* (2001) The Times 15 October.

As indicated above, such an approach inevitably leads the court into a closer examination of the factual basis for the actions of a public body, and hence the merits of the decision, although in a sense they will be doing what they have always done – looking to see whether the decision-maker has given sufficient weight to relevant factors, or too much weight to irrelevant factors. The role of the court in judicial review proceedings has not become one of substituting its view for that of the primary decision-maker, but it does have an enhanced role in assessing the legality of the decisions of public bodies where Convention rights are in issue.

For a further, recent illustration of this 'enhanced' approach, see *R (On the Application of W)* v *Broadmoor Hospital and Others* (2001) The Times 2 November. The Court of Appeal held that in reviewing a decision to administer medical treatment to a mental patient without his consent under s58(3)(b) of the Mental Health Act 1983, a court was entitled to reach its own view as to the merits of the medical decision and whether there would be any consequent infringement of the patient's human rights. Simon Brown LJ reiterated the two-stage necessity and proportionality approach, observing that the task could not be carried out properly unless the court was able to reach its own view on whether the applicant was capable of consenting to treatment, and whether such treatment would endanger his life in breach of art 2, be degrading in breach of art 3 or an unjustifiable and disproportionate invasion of his privacy under art 8.

It should not be assumed, however, that the courts will have any desire to usurp the functions of decision-makers. As Lord Clyde observed in *R (On the Application of Holding and Barnes plc)* v *Secretary of State for the Environment, Transport and the Regions; R (On the Application of Alconbury Developments Ltd)* v *Secretary of State for the Environment, Transport and the Regions; Secretary of State for the Environment, Transport and the Regions* v *Legal and General Assurance Society Ltd* [2001] 2 WLR

1389 the courts will be careful not to jeopardise 'the constitutional balance between the role of the courts and the role of the executive'. The change has been in respect of the evidence required to justify administrative action that impinges upon fundamental rights.

Is there a future for the Wednesbury *approach in domestic law?*

In a narrow sense the decision in *Associated Provincial Picture Houses* v *Wednesbury Corporation* is still good law as regards cases that do not involve an issue relating to Convention rights – but should the domestic courts continue to recognise this dichotomy, and is the *Wednesbury* test worth saving? It has, in recent years, been subjected to some trenchant criticism. In *R* v *Chief Constable of Sussex, ex parte International Trader's Ferry Ltd* [1999] 1 All ER 129, Lord Cooke observed:

> 'It seems to me unfortunate that *Wednesbury* and some *Wednesbury* phrases have become established incantations in the courts of the United Kingdom and beyond. *Associated Provincial Picture Houses Ltd* v *Wednesbury Corporation* ... an apparently briefly considered case, might well not be decided the same way today; and the judgment of Lord Greene MR twice uses (at 230 and 234) the tautologous formula "so unreasonable that no reasonable authority could ever have come to it." Yet judges are entirely accustomed to respecting the proper scope of administrative discretions. In my respectful opinion they do not need to be warned off the course by admonitory circumlocutions. When, in *Secretary of State for Education and Science* v *Tameside Metropolitan Borough Council* ... the precise meaning of "unreasonably" in an administrative context was crucial to the decision, the five speeches in the House of Lords, the three judgments in the Court of Appeal and the two judgments in the Divisional Court all succeeded in avoiding needless complexity. The simple test used throughout was whether the decision in question was one which a reasonable authority could reach. The converse was described by Lord Diplock (at 1064) as "conduct which no sensible authority acting with due appreciation of its responsibilities would have decided to adopt." These unexaggerated criteria give the administrator ample and rightful rein, consistently with the constitutional separation of powers.'

Lord Cooke in *Daly* echoed these sentiments, adding in respect of the 'degrees' of judicial review:

> 'Lord Steyn illuminates the distinctions between "traditional" (that is to say in terms of English case law, *Wednesbury*) standards of judicial review and higher standards under the European Convention or the common law of human rights. As he indicates, often the results are the same. But the view that the standards are substantially the same appears to have received its quietus in *Smith and Grady* v *United Kingdom* ... and *Lustig-Prean and Beckett* v *United Kingdom* ... And I think that the day will come when it will be more widely recognised that *Associated Provincial Picture Houses Ltd* v *Wednesbury Corporation* ... was an unfortunately retrogressive decision in English administrative law, insofar as it suggested that there are degrees of unreasonableness and that only a very extreme degree can bring an administrative decision within the legitimate scope of judicial invalidation. The depth of judicial review and the deference due to administrative discretion vary with the subject matter. It may well be, however, that the law can never be satisfied in any administrative field merely by a finding that the decision under review is not capricious or absurd.'

In *Holding and Barnes plc, etc* (above), Lord Slynn goes even further. In assessing the extent to which judicial review, as it had developed in recent years, has provided a sufficient judicial safeguard, he observes (in respect of the relationship between *Wednesbury* reasonableness as a ground for review and proportionality):

> 'There is a difference between [proportionality] and the approach of the English courts in *Associated Provincial Picture Houses Ltd* v *Wednesbury Corp* ... But the difference in practice is not as great as is sometimes supposed ... I consider that even without reference to the 1998 Act the time has come to recognise that this principle is part of English administrative law, not only when judges are dealing with community acts but also when they are dealing with acts subject to domestic law. Trying to keep the *Wednesbury* principle and proportionality in separate compartments seems to me to be unnecessary and confusing. Reference to the 1998 Act, however, makes it necessary that the court should ask whether what is done is compatible with Convention rights. That will often require that the question should be asked whether the principle of proportionality has been satisfied: see *R* v *Secretary of State for the Home Department, ex parte Turgut* [2001] 1 All ER 719; *R (On the Application of Mahmood)* v *Secretary of State for the Home Department* ...'

7.4 Proportionality and EC law

Proportionality as a ground of challenge is well established in the jurisprudence of the EC; see *Buitoni SA* v *Fonds d'Orientation et de Regularisation des Marches Agricoles* [1979] 2 CMLR 655. Where an application for judicial review alleges that a public body has acted unlawfully because it has infringed rights arising under EC law that are of direct effect (ie can be relied upon by a citizen in litigation with an emanation of the state) there is no doubt that the doctrine of proportionality, as developed by the European Court of Justice, will have to be applied. The matter was extensively considered in *R* v *Chief Constable of Sussex, ex parte International Trader's Ferry Ltd* (above), where one of the issues argued before the House of Lords was the extent to which the chief constable had acted unlawfully in refusing to provide resources to ensure the free movement of livestock exports from ports besieged by animal rights protestors. The applicant company contended, inter alia, that the refusal to provide protection amounted to a violation of art 34 of the EC Treaty, in as much as it had an effect equivalent to a quantitative restriction on exports. Upholding the lawfulness of the chief constable's decision, Lord Slynn relied upon the fact that any infringement that there might have been of art 34 was justified under art 36 because the chief constable had acted in the public interest to preserve law and order. He noted, however, that even if the chief constable's decisions survived scrutiny on the basis of the domestic law concept of *Wednesbury* reasonableness, it was not necessarily the case that they would also be lawful within the context of Community law, where a key question was whether they were proportionate to the problem they sought to deal with. On this basis the applicant pressed the point that, had more resources been devoted to the policing of the protests, the trade in livestock could have continued. Lord Slynn referred to the decision of the European Court of Justice in *Commission of the European Communities v French Republic* Case C–265/95 (1997) The Times 11 December where the Court found France to be in breach of its obligations under art 34 by not preventing public disorder on the part of those in France opposed to the importation of farm produce from other member states. The European Court of Justice had made it clear in that case that, whilst member states were required to take all necessary steps to ensure the free movement of goods, they also enjoyed a considerable margin of discretion in determining what measures were appropriate. Hence Lord Slynn accepted that a member state could not be expected to put money into preserving law and order to ensure the free movement of goods simply because the money was available in budgets set aside for other state activities such as education, health or defence. As he observed:

> '[That] would in any event require an investigation as to whether other competing claims for money allocated allowed moneys to be taken away from other areas of government. That is an impossible inquiry for the court to undertake and I think is an unreasonable exercise for the member state itself to be required to undertake. What is required in a case like the present where the chief constable has statutory and common law duties to perform is to ask whether he did all that proportionately and reasonably he could be expected to do with the resources available to him ... It seems to me that at the end of the day it is all a question of considering whether "appropriate measures" have been taken. That in turn involves an inquiry as to whether the steps taken were proportionate.'

Regarding the question of proportionality, and its relationship with *Wednesbury* reasonableness, he continued:

> 'In *ex parte Brind* ... the House treated *Wednesbury* reasonableness and proportionality as being different. So in some ways they are though the distinction between the two tests in practice is in any event much less than is sometimes suggested. The cautious way in which the European Court usually applies this test, recognising the importance of respecting the national authority's margin of appreciation, may mean that whichever test is adopted, and even allowing for a difference in onus, the result is the same. I am satisfied, as was the Court of Appeal, that the chief constable has shown here that what he did in providing police assistance was proportionate to what was required. To protect the lorries, in the way he did, was a suitable and necessary way of dealing with potentially violent demonstrators. To limit the occasions when sufficient police could be made available was, in the light of the resources available to him to deal with immediate and foreseeable events at the port, and at the same time to carry out all his other police duties, necessary and in no way disproportionate to the restrictions which were involved. Unlike the authorities in the case of France he was controlling and arresting violent offenders. He was, moreover, not dealing with a situation where no other way of exporting the animals was available. Dover was available and there were, and might be, other occasions when the lorries could get through. Far from failing to protect the appellants' trade he was seeking to do it in the most effective way available to him with his finite resources. It was only on rare and necessary, even dangerous, occasions that lorries were turned back. In the light of art 36 it is not open to ITF to say, as they at times seem to be saying, that they had an absolute right to export animals on seven days a week and there is no suggestion that with such a

short Channel crossing their claim was necessarily limited to one sailing a day. This case is quite different from *EC Commission* v *France* where "manifest and persistent failure" to control those interfering with imports was shown and where there was no evidence to show that those responsible could have acted.'

Lord Cooke proceeded on the basis that the actions of the chief constable did prima facie amount to an infringement of art 34, subject to any justification that might be made out under art 36. In this regard he stressed that the rights of the applicants under art 34 were directly enforceable by virtue of s2(1) of the European Communities Act 1972, and that arts 34 and 36 provided the basis for the application for judicial review to the extent that they imposed 'more rigorous scrutiny' of the chief constable's actions than would otherwise be the case under domestic law. Commenting on the relationship between the domestic law concept of reasonableness and proportionality he observed that the concepts of proportionality and margin of appreciation were likely to produce the same result as the *Wednesbury* principles. On this basis his Lordship was persuaded that the chief constable had achieved a fair and reasonable compromise between competing interests, notwithstanding that it did involve at least a partial triumph for those demonstrators willing to break the law in order to prevent movement of livestock: see further *R* v *Secretary of State for Health, ex parte Eastside Cheese Company* (1998) The Times 1 December (subordinate legislation declared invalid because the measure was disproportionate to the problem it sought to address).

8

Relevant and Irrelevant Factors

8.1 Getting the balance right

8.2 The aims and objects of the legislation

8.3 The exercise of discretion by local authorities

8.4 Acting on no evidence

8.1 Getting the balance right

The actions of a public body can be declared ultra vires where it is shown that the decision-maker has acted on the basis of irrelevant considerations, or where it can be shown that relevant considerations have been ignored. Arguably, as Lord Greene MR noted in the *Wednesbury* case, to do either of these things might also constitute acting unreasonably. A failure to advert to relevant considerations could mean that a decision-maker acts without the necessary evidence to justify his decision; similarly, where a decision-maker seeks to achieve some ulterior goal by using a power not intended for the purpose, he can be described as acting upon an irrelevant considerations. The basic principles under consideration were stated by Lord Esher MR in *R v St Pancras Vestry* (1890) 24 QBD 371 at 375, where he observed:

> '... [the decision-making body] must fairly consider [the case before it] and not take into account any reason for their decision which is not a legal one. If people who have to exercise a public duty by exercising their discretion take into account matters which the courts consider not to be proper for the exercise of their discretion, then in the eye of the law they have not exercised their discretion.'

The courts recognise that public bodies are frequently involved in the difficult task of balancing one set of considerations against another. The proper role of the courts is not to substitute its view of what are the most appropriate considerations to take into account for those of the decision-maker. An application for judicial review should not be granted unless there is evidence that the decision-making body has carried out the 'balancing act' unreasonably. As Lord Donaldson MR observed in *R v Secretary of State for Social Services, ex parte Wellcome Foundation* [1987] 2 All ER 1025:

'Good policy making, administration and decision-making involve studying problems from all angles. It is a practical process and must never be allowed, and still less induced, to become a theoretical and legalistic exercise. For my part I can find nothing whatsoever to criticise in the approach of a decision-maker which involves him in saying to himself, I do, not know whether, as a matter of law, factor A is or is not a relevant consideration. This is, or may be a difficult question, but I do not need to consider it further, because I am quite satisfied that other factors, which are admittedly relevant, are of such comparative weight, that my decision will be the same whether or not I take account of factor A.'

The nature of the problem is illustrated by the issues that were before the court in *R v Coventry Airport Ltd, ex parte Phoenix Aviation and Other Applications* [1995] 3 All ER 37, where a successful application for judicial review was made in respect of the decision of a number of port authorities to cease the use of their ports for the transportation of live animals. The authorities had acted in the light of the disruptive demonstrations that the trade had attracted at the ports, making the conduct of normal business virtually impossible. Notwithstanding that, under the terms of the legislation applicable to the ports in question, there did not appear to be any residual discretion vested in those operating the ports to impose a perpetual ban on any particular type of trade that was, in all other respects, lawful, Simon Brown LJ observed that, even if such a discretion existed, he was not satisfied on the facts that there would have been any grounds for imposing a ban. In his view, to permit the port authorities to rely upon the threat of unlawful public disorder by animal rights protesters as the basis for banning the export of animals for slaughter, would be to undermine the rule of law because it would serve to encourage widespread unlawful action by demonstrators, and would been seen as producing the desired result, ie would lead to increased activity at the remaining ports where the trade was still permitted. His Lordship also indicated that he had been influenced by wider considerations in coming to his conclusion, not least the devastating financial effect that a ban would have on the financial livelihood of thousands of farmers who depended on the trade. Hence, although the purely practical short-term trading considerations that motivated the ban were perfectly reasonable, they were outweighed, as far as the court was concerned, by the longer term constitutional considerations that the respondents had failed to take into account.

8.2 The aims and objects of the legislation

In assessing the lawfulness of administrative action based upon the exercise of statutory powers, the courts will be mindful of both the general principles of statutory interpretation and the more specific aims and objects that Parliament was seeking to achieve in enacting the particular legislation in question. In terms of general principles, it is assumed (in the absence of express terms to the contrary) that Parliament will not have intended to contravene international law; will not have intended to deprive individuals of their property without compensation; and will not have intended to impose criminal liability without proof of fault. Hence, any public body purporting to exercise a statutory power in a manner that contradicts any of the general assumptions regarding Parliament's legislative intent is likely to have its actions declared ultra vires.

In *R* v *Pierson* [1997] 3 All ER 577, the appellant, a prisoner sentenced to life imprisonment for murder, had been informed at the time of commencing his sentence that the tariff period (effectively the minimum period before being released on licence) would be 15 years. In 1993 the Home Secretary announced a change of policy, whereby the tariff set at the commencement of a life sentence was now to be regarded as an initial view that could be revised in order to ensure that the requirements of deterrence and retribution had been met, and that the penal element of the tariff might in fact be increased if necessary. The appellant was duly informed that in his case the tariff was being increased to 20 years. The House of Lords held (Lords Browne-Wilkinson and Lloyd dissenting) that the Home Secretary was acting unlawfully in purporting to increase tariffs established prior to the announcement of the new policy. In exercising his power to determine the tariff the Home Secretary was exercising a function analogous to a judge passing sentence on a convicted person. As such, the common law required that his powers be exercised fairly and with due regard to the rule of law. At common law, a sentenced once passed could not subsequently be increased by a judge who, on reflection, had decided that it was not severe enough. Similarly, the Home Secretary had no express or implied power, under s35 of the Criminal Justice Act 1991, to revise upwards the penal element of the tariff set for a life sentence that had been imposed at a time when a different policy (ie of not altering the tariff once fixed at the outset of a life sentence) applied. As Lord Steyn observed:

> 'Parliament has not expressly authorised the Home Secretary to increase tariffs retrospectively. If Parliament had done so that would have been the end of the matter. Instead Parliament has by s35(2) of the Criminal Justice Act 1991 entrusted the power to take decisions about the release of mandatory life sentence prisoners to the Home Secretary. The statutory power is wide enough to authorise the fixing of a tariff. But it does not follow that it is wide enough to permit a power retrospectively to increase the level of punishment. ... It contemplates a power unheard of in our criminal justice system until the 1993 policy statement of the Home Secretary. ... It would be wrong to assume that Parliament would have been prepared to give to the Home Secretary such an unprecedented power, alien to the principles of our law.'

He continued:

> 'Parliament does not legislate in a vacuum. Parliament legislates for a European liberal democracy founded on the principles and traditions of the common law. And the courts may approach legislation on this initial assumption.'

He then cited with approval the views expressed by Sir Rupert Cross in *Cross, Statutory Interpretation* (3rd ed, pp165–166):

> ' "Statutes often go into considerable detail, but even so allowance must be made for the

fact that they are not enacted in a vacuum. A great deal inevitably remains unsaid. Legislators and drafters assume that the courts will continue to act in accordance with well-recognised rules. ... Long-standing principles of constitutional and administrative law are likewise taken for granted, or assumed by the courts to have been taken for granted, by Parliament. Examples are the principles that discretionary powers conferred in apparently absolute terms must be exercised reasonably, and that administrative tribunals and other such bodies must act in accordance with the principles of natural justice. One function of the word 'presumption' in the context of statutory interpretation is to state the result of this legislative reliance (real or assumed) on firmly established legal principles. There is a 'presumption' that mens rea is required in the case of statutory crimes, and a 'presumption' that statutory powers must be exercised reasonably. These presumptions apply although there is no question of linguistic ambiguity in the statutory wording under construction, and they may be described as 'presumptions of general application'. ... These presumptions of general application not only supplement the text, they also operate at a higher level as expressions of fundamental principles governing both civil liberties and the relations between Parliament, the executive and the courts. They operate here as constitutional principles which are not easily displaced by a statutory text ..." '

Similarly, in *R* v *Secretary of State for the Home Department, ex parte Venables and Thompson* [1997] 3 All ER 97, the House of Lords held (Lord Lloyd dissenting), that the Home Secretary had acted unlawfully in taking public opinion (expressed in petitions and tabloid newspaper campaigns) into account in determining the minimum period of imprisonment to be served by the children convicted of murdering James Bulger. Whilst the majority thought that it would be legitimate for the Home Secretary to take into account public opinion regarding certain types of crime when developing sentencing policy, eg attitudes to sexual offences, race crimes or drugs offences, it was not appropriate when considering the punishment to be imposed in respect of a specific incident. It could be argued that difficulties arise here because, in discharging a sentencing function, the Home Secretary, although a member of the Executive and thus answerable to Parliament and the electorate, is exercising a judicial role. His political instincts will lead him to take into account matters that would not be pressing upon a trial judge, particularly the desire to appear tough on 'law and order' issues. As Lord Browne-Wilkinson observed (at p126d–h):

'Parliament has entrusted decisions relating to the future of these applicants to the Executive, not to the judiciary ... the court should be careful not to impose judicial procedures and attitudes on what Parliament has decided should be an Executive function. I understand it to be common ground that the Secretary of State, in setting the tariff, is entitled to have regard to "broader considerations of a public character" ... including ... public attitudes to criminal sentencing. How is the Secretary of State to discover what those attitudes are except from the media and from petitions? To seek to differentiate between the Secretary of State discovering public feeling generally (which is proper) and taking into account distasteful public reactions in a particular case (which is said to be unlawful) seems to me too narrow a distinction to be workable in practice. Public attitudes are ill-defined and are usually only expressed in relation to particular cases.'

In a sense the two cases above are examples of a minister seeking to exercise powers in a positive sense, but it is obvious that illegality can equally result from the refusal to exercise discretion, where the reasons for not doing so are illegitimate. A leading illustration is provided by *Padfield* v *Minister of Agriculture* [1968] AC 997, where the minister was empowered to order an investigation into complaints relating to the administration of the Milk Marketing Scheme as he thought fit. The litigation arose out of the minister's refusal to refer the plaintiff's complaint to a committee of inquiry, and the evidence indicated that the minister had been motivated by a fear that an inquiry might prove politically embarrassing. The House of Lords, by a majority, held that the minister was abusing his discretion so as to frustrate the aims and objects of the Parent Act, the Agricultural Marketing Act 1958. The minister had been granted subjectively worded powers, but the House of Lords made clear that these were not to be used to thwart the policy behind the legislation. Whilst the decision, in its time, was of great constitutional significance, confirming as it did the power of the judiciary to control the exercise of Executive discretion at the highest level, it also arguably exposed the futility of challenging administrative action in the courts. The complaint was eventually referred to a committee of inquiry, which upheld the complainant's case, but the minister refused to take any further action on the matter. It serves as a reminder that administrative law is primarily concerned with the proper procedures being followed, and not the execution of policy where those procedures are valid.

Taking Community law into account when exercising power

Section 2(1) of the European Communities Act 1972 has the undoubted effect of making certain aspects of EC law part of domestic law, either because they become directly applicable, as with Treaty provisions and regulations, or because they are subsequently given effect in domestic law by primary or subordinate legislation. Domestic courts are obliged to give effect to EC law regardless of whether conflicting domestic law was enacted before or after the 1972 Act came into effect: see generally Molan, *Constitutional Law: The Machinery of Government* (4th edn, 2003). A public body must, therefore have regard to the demands of EC law when exercising its discretion. Failure to do so can lead to its decisions being quashed. In *R* v *Chief Constable of Sussex, ex parte International Trader's Ferry Ltd* [1999] 1 All ER 129 the House of Lords examined the decision of the chief constable to allocate only enough manpower to keep the port of Shoreham open for the export of livestock two days a week in the light of protests by animal rights campaigners. Lord Hoffmann highlighted the difficulties in applying the doctrine of proportionality (a concept developed to test the legality of action or inaction on the part of EC member states) to a public body such as a chief constable.

> 'The difficulty lies in the fact that art 36 [which permits the imposition of restrictions on the free movement of goods such as livestock if it is in the public interest to do so]

involves a balancing of, on the one hand, the legitimate interests of the member state falling within the categories specified in art 36 and, on the other hand, the Community interest in free movement of goods. Measures taken by a member state which prima facie contravene art 30 or art 34 must be proportionate in the sense that they must not restrict the free movement of goods more than is necessary to protect such a legitimate interest. But the considerations taken into account in this balancing process are quite different from those involved in the domestic decision as to whether the chief constable acted reasonably in balancing the interests of ITF with the policing demands of the rest of Sussex. In European law, justification is seen in terms of the legitimate interests of the member state as a whole and for this purpose, all the institutions of the state are aggregated and treated as a single entity ... This reasoning is entirely appropriate when the question is the existence of justification for some measure taken by the member state or one of its institutions which prima facie infringes the prohibition in ... art 34, or the compliance by the member state with its positive obligation under art 5 in proceedings under s169 to which the member state itself is a party. In the former case, the issue is simply whether the validity of the measure has been struck down by art 30 or art 34 as supreme law. There is no question of the court ordering anything positive to be done. In the latter case, the court will declare that the member state, taken as a whole, has failed to comply with its obligations under art 5. But the reasoning makes little sense in proceedings brought against the chief constable, asserting a duty on his part to take positive steps which involve the use of resources. [Counsel for the applicants] saw the difficulty in making the cases on art 36 fit his contentions on the liability of the chief constable and suggested that ... the chief constable should be deemed to have access to all the resources of the United Kingdom. But I think it would be absurd for a court to make an order against an individual chief constable requiring him to take certain steps on the assumption that he has at his disposal all the resources of the United Kingdom. He plainly could not comply with such an order.'

Taking the European Convention on Human Rights into account when exercising power

The incorporation of the European Convention on Human Rights, as effected by the Human Rights Act 1998, has the effect that it becomes unlawful for any public authority to act in a way which is incompatible with a Convention right: s6(1). This duty is subject to the proviso that no unlawfulness will be held to have occurred if the public body was unable to avoid the incompatibility because of one or more provisions of primary or subordinate legislation. Hence, a public body, exercising its discretion, will now have to have regard to whether or not its decision is compatible with the Convention rights protected by the Act. Similarly, a court exercising its reviewing function will have to have such factors in mind, as it too is a public authority for these purposes and will act unlawfully if it fails to uphold the Convention rights. The extent to which this impacts on public bodies and the scope of judicial review remains to be seen. An early illustration of what we might expect was provided by the Divisional Court's ruling in *R v Secretary of State for the Home Department, ex parte Quaquah* (2000) The Times 21 January. Q arrived in the United Kingdom as an asylum seeker. His application to remain was refused and his appeal against refusal dismissed by a special adjudicator. Q was held at a detention centre where he was alleged to become involved in disturbances. Charges of riot and violent disorder were subsequently dropped when it became apparent that evidence given by prosecution witnesses was unreliable. Q was eventually released on bail and subsequently commenced an action for malicious prosecution. In the meantime the Home Office commenced proceedings to have Q removed from the United Kingdom. Q successfully sought judicial review of this decision on the basis that: (1) it contravened Home Office policy by impairing Q's ability to pursue his legal action; and (2) it was contrary to the principle of equality or arms, implicit in art 6(3) of the European Convention on Human Rights. Notwithstanding that the court could find no compelling argument to justify the interference with the applicant's right to a fair trial of the malicious prosecution action, the direction to remove the applicant was defective on the ground that there was no evidence that his need to remain in the jurisdiction to properly conduct the litigation had been taken into account.

Ulterior motives

Whereas there may be legitimate dispute as to whether a public body has correctly balanced competing considerations prior to the exercise of discretion, it is far easier to identify illegality when there is evidence that a public body has actually used a discretion given for one purpose to pursue a quite different one, outwith the scope of the Act. A decision-maker purporting to exercise a discretion, whilst in reality pursuing some ulterior goal, will be abusing his power, in the sense that he is flouting the aims and objects of the enabling Act, and acting on irrelevant considerations. A power given for one purpose cannot be used for another, even where the decision-maker may be acting from the best of intentions. An example of this type of illegality is provided by *Sydney Municipal Council* v *Campbell* [1925] AC 388 where the Privy Council held that compulsory purchase powers, vested in a local authority, were not to be used for speculating in property, even if the profit made was used to offset the rates. Similarly, in *R* v *Hillingdon London Borough Council, ex parte Royco Homes Ltd* [1974] QB 720, the respondent authority granted outline permission for houses, subject to conditions requiring that they should be designed so as to provide space and heating to the standards required by the government for council housing; that they should be constructed at a cost per dwelling not exceeding the limits normally allowed for council housing, to receive government subsidies; that they should be first occupied by persons on the authority's housing waiting list; and that they should for ten years from the first occupation be occupied by a person under the protection of the Rent Act 1968. Lord Widgery summarised Royco's arguments in this way:

> '... these four conditions were imposed to suit an ulterior purpose, a purpose ulterior to the duty of the council as planning authority ... their purpose was to ensure that, if a

private developer was allowed to develop this land, he should have to use it in such a way as to relieve the council of a significant part of its burden as housing authority to provide houses for the homeless ... they are ultra vires and bring the whole planning permission down.'

The Divisional Court held that the local planning authority could not use powers granted for 'planning purposes' to relieve the housing shortage in the area over which it had jurisdiction. In any event, the court regarded the conditions as so unreasonable that no reasonable planning authority would have imposed them. See further on this point *Newbury District Council* v *Secretary of State for the Environment* [1981] AC 578.

Where, in exercising a power, some incidental benefit accrues to the authority concerned, the courts will not declare action ultra vires simply because of the benefit. It may be a matter of looking for the dominant purpose in the exercise of the power. For example, in *Westminster Corporation* v *London and North Western Railway Co* [1905] AC 426 the local authority, which was empowered to build public conveniences, but not subways, constructed an underground convenience that effectively formed a subway under a particular street. The railway company argued that a power to build lavatories was being used to build subways. The House of Lords held that this was merely an incidental benefit arising from a legitimate use of the authority's powers.

It is an important constitutional issue that an authority cannot levy a tax or otherwise raise revenue without there being an express statutory power for the purpose. The courts will thus invalidate the exercise of discretion, even where the raising of revenue is merely a side effect of the decision. *Congreve* v *Home Office* [1976] QB 629, concerned the Secretary of State's announcement that the cost of a colour television licence was to be increased from £12 to £18, the increase taking effect on 1 April 1975. Congreve, along with another 20,000 licence holders, applied for a new licence shortly before the date set for the increase, even though his own licence had not expired, because he would still make an overall saving. Contemplating a substantial loss of revenue if this practice was allowed, the Secretary of State adopted a policy of revoking any new 'overlapping' licences after eight months if the extra £6 was not paid by the holder. The minister purported to act under s1(2) of the Wireless Telegraphy Act 1949 which states that a licence may be revoked by a notice in writing served on the holder. In an action seeking a declaration that the minister's action was unlawful the Court of Appeal held that the Secretary of State had acted ultra vires in using his statutory power of revocation for a purpose for which it was never intended, namely, the raising of revenue. Citing *Padfield* as authority, Lord Denning MR spoke of the courts having a duty to correct a misuse of power where a minister exercised discretion for reasons that were bad in law. The Master of the Rolls also adverted to the issue of taxation:

'There is yet another reason for holding that the demands for £6 to be unlawful. They were made contrary to the Bill of Rights. They were an attempt to levy money for the use of the Crown without the authority of Parliament: and that is quite enough to damn them: see *Attorney-General* v *Wilts United Dairies Ltd* (1921) 37 TLR 884.'

See further *R* v *Bowman* [1898] 1 QB 663.

8.3 The exercise of discretion by local authorities

In *R* v *Board of Education* [1910] KB 165 Farwell LJ took the view that allowing political considerations to influence decision-making would necessarily invalidate the process. They were, to his mind, 'pre-eminently extraneous'. Today such a view seems to be untenable. Local government is always dominated by party politics, and to that extent resolutions passed by majority groupings are bound to be motivated by adherence to one political viewpoint or another: see *Secretary of State for Education and Science* v *Tameside Metropolitan Borough Council* [1977] AC 1014 and *Cardiff Corporation* v *Secretary of State for Wales* (1971) 22 P & CR 718.

Decisions such as *Pickwell* v *Camden London Borough Council* [1983] 1 All ER 602, *R* v *Amber Valley District Council, ex parte Jackson* [1984] 3 All ER 501 and *R* v *Waltham Forest London Borough Council, ex parte Waltham Forest Ratepayers' Action Group* (1987) The Times 2 October, all indicate a more realistic and pragmatic approach being adopted by the courts to the decisions of local authorities. They reflect a willingness to accept the inevitability of local government being highly politicised, and an acknowledgement that the correct procedure for resolving disputes on policy is the democratic process of local elections. Inevitably, however, there are limits to what the courts are willing to permit in terms of local authorities pursuing overtly political objectives, and these were exceeded in *R* v *Ealing London Borough Council and Others, ex parte Times Newspapers Ltd* (1986) 85 LGR 316. A number of local authorities had resolved that the libraries under their control should not stock publications produced by Times Newspapers and others whilst the publishers were in dispute with sacked employees of the newspapers. The purpose of the ban was to show solidarity with the dismissed workers. The publishers, and a number of residents of each authority, applied for judicial review of the ban. It was held that the authorities had acted unlawfully. Watkins LJ recognised that the authorities had a discretion as to how they carried out their duties under the Public Libraries and Museums Act 1964, and that as a result it was not for the courts to readily usurp that function. His Lordship also observed that local government was a political arena and that it was not proper for the courts to adjudicate between one political philosophy and another. Neither of these factors, however, gave authorities an untrammelled discretion to come to decisions purely on the basis of political considerations. The ban imposed by the authorities was clearly related to an ulterior purpose, ie involvement in an industrial dispute. No rational authority could have thought that this was a proper way of discharging its duties under the 1964 Act. There was an alternative remedy available by way of s10 of the Act, under which the minister had certain default powers, but the courts would not be prevented from granting a remedy themselves where, as in the present case, there was a glaring example of abuse. See also *R v Liverpool City Council, ex parte Secretary of State for Employment* (1988) The Times 12 November and *R v Derbyshire County Council, ex parte Times Supplements Ltd* [1991] COD 129.

In both *Bromley London Borough Council v Greater London Council* [1983] 1 AC 768 (considered below) and *Tameside* the issues raised involved discussion of the significance to be given to the fact that a local authority may have been voted into power having promised to implement a particular policy. In *Tameside* the Conservative majority had given an undertaking to voters that, if elected, it would preserve grammar schools in the area. In holding that the local authority was not purporting to act unreasonably when it took steps to promulgate that policy, Lord Wilberforce laid much emphasis on the fact that it was an elected body, and that those who voted for the reverse of educational policy advocated by the Conservatives must be taken to have accepted some degree of disruption as a result of the implementation. His Lordship went on to suggest that having stood on a platform of ending comprehensivisation Conservative councillors were in a sense bound to implement the policy once in power. This is to be contrasted with his Lordship's approach to the same argument when relied upon by the Greater London Council (GLC) in *Bromley London Borough Council v Greater London Council* as justifying the implementation of a 25 per cent cut in London Transport fares, with a consequent rise in rates. The election mandate argument was rejected by Lord Wilberforce in this latter case because, he argued, in *Tameside* a power existed to restore grammar schools, and an election mandate to do so was a relevant factor in determining whether the exercise of that power was reasonable. In *Bromley London Borough Council v Greater London Council*, the GLC had no power to order London Transport to deliberately operate at a deliberate loss – thus the wishes of the electorate were irrelevant. An election mandate could not give the GLC a power it did not otherwise possess.

Local government finance: excessive expenditure

Despite the fact that the lion's share of local government income is supplied directly by central government grant, the courts will nevertheless expect local authorities to exercise discretion properly as regards spending. In particular, local authorities will have to show that they have paid sufficient regard to the interests of those who contribute to locally raised revenue. Formerly these would have been ratepayers. Since April 1993, following the abolition of the community charge, which in turn had replaced the old rating system, the basis for local taxation has been the council tax. It is submitted that the case law relating to the use of ratepayers' money is, nevertheless, equally applicable to the exercise of discretion in spending monies raise via the council tax.

A classic illustration of the competing interests at work when such spending decisions are made is provided by the House of Lords' ruling in *Roberts* v *Hopwood* [1925] AC 578. Poplar Borough Council, acting under statutory powers to pay its workers such wages as it thought fit, resolved to pay its male and female workers a wage of £4 per week. The payments made in pursuance of this resolution were challenged by the district auditor as being contrary to law, and this contention was eventually approved by the House of Lords. The local authority was held to have taken into account irrelevant considerations in wishing to set an example as a 'model employer'; further it had been motivated, wrongly, by considerations of 'socialist philanthropy, and feminist ambition'. The authority was also found to have failed to take into account the fact that during this period the cost of living was actually falling and therefore wages should have been reduced, not increased. The authority was also found to have failed to give sufficient regard to the interests of its ratepayers, who would in part have to finance the increases. In this regard the House of Lords took the view that the authority was under a fiduciary duty to spend ratepayers' money wisely.

The courts sought to apply the principles enunciated in *Roberts* v *Hopwood* in a number of cases involving disputes as to the legality of local authority spending, where the allegations were essentially a failure to take into account relevant considerations, usually the fiduciary duty owed to ratepayers. In *Prescott* v *Birmingham Corporation* [1955] Ch 210 a scheme to provide pensioners with free bus travel at the expense of local authority ratepayers was struck down by the courts. The authority was obliged to provide transport on business principles, and under the scheme was effectively making a gift to one section of the travelling public at the expense of ratepayers. Although viewed strictly the case involved a finding that the authority had breached the terms of a 'trust' upon which it held ratepayers' money, the decision can be viewed on wider terms as one where action was invalidated for failure to give due weight to the ratepayers' interest in securing value for money. Similarly, in *Bromley London Borough Council* v *Greater London Council*, the House of Lords invalidated a proposed scheme of public transport fare cuts that the GLC had intended to introduce. The scheme, if put into effect, would have resulted in a substantial increase in the level of rates due from ratepayers. The GLC argued, inter alia, that its controlling Labour group had been elected with a mandate to reduce fares by 25 per cent and were simply proposing to carry out the policy on which they had won the election. Among the grounds upon which the action of the GLC was held to be unlawful was the point that it had failed to have sufficient regard to the effect of the scheme on their ratepayers, and had placed too much emphasis on their election promises to cut fares.

Clearly these cases are not about spending decisions in the abstract. The sub-text is one of a clash of ideologies. Labour councils have, traditionally, sought to use local government expenditure to increase welfare provision and thereby redistribute wealth. Conservatives have tended to favour minimal local expenditure in favour of lower local taxation. Indications that the courts were becoming more realistic in their approach to these political battles was provided by decisions such as *Pickwell* v

Camden London Borough Council [1983] 1 All ER 602. Following a protracted national strike of local authority manual workers, Camden London Borough Council, concerned about the effect of refuse not being collected etc, entered into an agreement with its manual workers to increase their wages, as a result of which the strike ended in Camden. Some weeks later a national settlement was reached where lower wage increases were agreed to by the rest of the country's local authority manual workers. A year later, Camden London Borough Council, in line with other authorities, increased the wages of its manual workers again. The district auditor sought a declaration that this second increase in wages amounted to unlawful expenditure by the local authority who, it was argued, should not have raised wages again, but left them as they were so that wages in the rest of the country could rise to the same level. The court declined to declare the expenditure illegal, holding that the local authority had, quite legitimately, been concerned with the effect of the strike on its area. The authority had not, in fixing wage levels above the national average, been taking into account irrelevant considerations such as those of Poplar Borough Council in *Roberts* v *Hopwood*, of desiring to set an example as a model employer. The court placed great emphasis on the fact that the local authority was in the best position to judge the necessity of getting its refuse workers back to work. If its policies were unpopular the local electorate could show their displeasure at the next local elections.

Local government finance: taking account of financial constraints

Whilst many of the landmark cases in administrative law have been concerned with excessive or improper expenditure by local authorities, it should not be overlooked that local authorities and other public bodies might also fall foul of the law for refusing to incur expenditure, either because of a claimed lack of resources, or because the expenditure cannot be justified given the competing demands. The question arises as to the extent to which a public body can take into account its own resources when determining not to incur expenditure.

As a general principle it is submitted that, provided a public body is acting in good faith (as to which see the comments of Scarman LJ in *R* v *Bristol Corporation, ex parte Hendy* [1974] 1 WLR 498, considered in Chapter 11), and is genuinely trying to exercise discretion properly, the courts will not intervene: see *R* v *Cambridge District Health Authority, ex parte B* [1995] 1 WLR 898 – the courts being unlikely to want to take over the rationing of finite resources. By contrast if a rationing decision defies logic, or suggests wilful indifference to relevant considerations, the courts will intervene: see *R* v *North Derbyshire Health Authority, ex parte Fisher* (1997) The Times 2 September, where the Divisional Court quashed the authority's decision not to prescribe a drug on grounds of cost and granted an order compelling compliance with an NHS circular on provision within 14 days.

Much depends, however, on the statutory context. Where the statute is drawn in wider, more generalised, terms the courts may be able to grant an authority some flexibility. In *R* v *Gloucestershire County Council, ex parte Barry* [1997] 2 All ER 1 the House of Lords ruled (Lords Lloyd and Steyn dissenting) that, in determining whether or not a person had 'needs' that had to be met under s2(1) of the Chronically Sick and Disabled Persons Act 1970, a local authority was entitled to take into account its financial resources. It was the view of the majority that the evaluation of such needs involved the development, by the local authority, of a set of criteria to determine whether a particular disability generated a need for assistance. Those criteria would reflect what were generally accepted standards of living and also the balancing by the local authority of the costs of various forms of assistance measured against the relative benefits to the recipients. In determining what weight was to be given to the cost of any particular assistance a local authority was entitled to take into account its own resources. The determination of an applicant's needs could not, therefore, be determined in a vacuum from which all considerations of cost impact had been expelled. This reasoning was subsequently applied in *R* v *Sefton Metropolitan Borough Council, ex parte Help the Aged* [1997] 4 All ER 532, where the Court of Appeal held that a local authority was entitled to have regard to its own resourcing position in determining whether or not a person was in need for the purposes of s21 of the National Assistance Act of 1948 (residential accommodation for the elderly). Once a need is identified, however, lack of resources cannot be relied upon as a reason for not providing the necessary assistance. As Lord Woolf MR observed in *ex parte Help the Aged* (at pp542j–543c):

'While I fully accept in accordance with the decision in *ex parte Barry*, that it is possible to perform a cost benefit analysis in relation to a person's needs for services listed in s2(1) [of the Chronically Sick and Disabled Persons Act 1970] and then decide if they are necessary, taking into account the resources of the authority. I find it very much more difficult to perform the same exercise when deciding whether a person is in need of care and attention. However, having regard to the reasoning of Lord Nicholls and Clyde [in *ex parte Barry*], I am compelled to conclude that there is a limited subjective element in making the assessment of whether the ailments of the person concerned do or do not collectively establish a need for care and attention. ... However, in this case it is clear from the evidence that Sefton accepted that [Mrs Blanchard, one of the applicants] met their own threshold as a person in need of care and attention. What they were seeking to do was to say that because of their lack of resources, notwithstanding this, they were not prepared to meet the duty which was placed on them by the section. This they were not entitled to do. There is nothing in the speeches in the House of Lords in *ex parte Barry* to indicate to the contrary.'

Compare this with the approach taken in *R* v *East Sussex County Council, ex parte Tandy* [1998] 2 All ER 769, where the respondent authority had resolved that, as a consequence of central government spending policy that would result in it suffering a shortfall in its education budget of £3 million, cuts would have to be made in the provision of help to children with special needs. In an effort to contain its expenditure within its reduced budget, the authority reduced the extent of the home tuition (provided for the applicant under s298 of the Education Act 1993 –

now s19 of the Education Act 1996) from five hours per week to three. Under s298 an education authority was required to make arrangements for the provision of 'suitable education' for those children, such as the applicant who had special needs. At first instance the applicant applied successfully for an order of certiorari to quash this decision, but this was reversed on appeal by a majority of the Court of Appeal. The House of Lords, allowing the applicant's appeal, held that the availability of resources was an irrelevant consideration in determining what was a 'suitable education' for an individual pupil. The House of Lords reached this conclusion by reference to the fact that other sections of the 1993 Act did refer to the efficient use of resources, but s298 was silent as to this issue, hence the inference that resources were not relevant. The respondent authority sought to rely on *R v Gloucestershire County Council, ex parte Barry* (above) as authority for the proposition that resources could be taken into account in assessing need. Lord Browne-Wilkinson, however, distinguished that on the following grounds (at p776b–h):

'The question in *ex parte Barry* related to the questions what were the "needs" of the disabled person and whether it was necessary in order to meet those needs to make arrangements for the indicated benefits. It was held by Lord Nicholls that, in assessing the needs of the disabled person, the local authority had to have regard to the cost of what was to be provided and once regard was had to cost they must also have regard to the resources available to meet such cost. Depending on the authority's financial position the authority could be more or less stringent in the criteria it set as constituting need. Lord Clyde adopted a rather different approach. He apparently accepted that the local authority's resources were not relevant to deciding what were the needs of the applicant but held that they were relevant to the decision whether it was "necessary" to make arrangements to meet those needs: he accepted that there might be in one sense "unmet needs" if the local authority decided, in the light of its financial circumstances, that there was no necessity to meet those needs (see [1997] 2 All ER 1 at 16, 17, ...). Whichever approach was adopted, the statutory provision there under consideration was a strange one. The statutory duty was to arrange certain benefits to meet the "needs" of the disabled persons but the lack of certain of the benefits enumerated in the section could not possibly give rise to "need" in any stringent sense of the word. Thus it is difficult to talk about the lack of a radio or a holiday or a recreational activity as giving rise to a need: they may be desirable but they are not in any ordinary sense necessities. Yet, according to the section the disabled person's needs were to be capable of being met by the provision of such benefits. The statute provided no guidance as to what were the criteria by which a need of that unusual kind was to be assessed. There was no definition of need beyond the instances of the possible benefits. In those circumstances, it is perhaps not surprising that the majority of your Lordships looked for some other more stringent criteria enabling the local authority to determine what was to be treated as a need by reference to the resources available to it. The position in the present case is quite different. Under s298 the LEA is not required to make any prior determination of [the applicant's] need for education nor of the necessity for making provision for such education. The statute imposes an immediate obligation to make arrangements to provide suitable education. Moreover it then expressly defines what is meant by "suitable education" by reference to wholly objective educational criteria. For these reasons, in my judgment the decision in *ex parte Barry* does not affect the present case.'

The House of Lords accepted, however, that where there were various ways of providing a suitable education, regard could be had to the resources available in making choices, provided any decision was within the bounds of reasonableness. Lord Browne-Wilkinson noted that once the reasonableness became narrowed to how a local authority had decided to allocate scare financial resources, the local authority's decision became extremely difficult to review. In his words: 'The court cannot second-guess the local authority in the way in which it spends its limited resources'. On the facts the House of Lords felt that the respondent local education authority did have the resources. It had simply decided to spend them on other things. The House of Lords was not willing to allow this as a basis for denying the existence of a statutory duty. To do so would downgrade a duty to a discretion. Although the House of Lords found in favour of the applicant, Lord Browne-Wilkinson was mindful of the economic realities for local authorities. He observed (at p772b–c):

> 'Like all other local authorities, the respondent county council is in an unenviable position. It is now prevented from obtaining either from central government or from local taxation the financial resources necessary to discharge its functions as it would like to do. In a period when the aim of central government, of whatever political colour, has been to achieve a reduction in public spending, local authorities have not been relieved of statutory duties imposed upon them by Parliament in times past when different attitudes prevailed. Thus, in preparing its budget the respondent county council had to find ways of saving expenditure.'

Similarly, in *R* v *Birmingham City Council, ex parte Mohammed* [1998] 3 All ER 788, the Divisional Court held that the respondent authority could not refuse to make a disabled facilities grant under s23 of the Housing Grants, Construction and Regeneration Act 1996 because of limited financial resources. Again the court considered *ex parte Barry* but concluded that it did not assist the respondent authority. As Dyson J observed (at p797a–c):

> 'I do not consider that *ex parte Barry* provides the answer to the question that I have to decide. The important differences between the two statutes include the following. First, the needs mentioned in s23(1) of the 1996 Act are real needs for disabled occupants as defined. The observation by Lord Browne-Wilkinson [in *ex parte Barry*] that the lack of certain of the enumerated facilities could not possibly give rise to "need" in any stringent sense of the word is not applicable to the facilities enumerated in s23 of the 1996 Act. Secondly, none of the clues as to the intention of Parliament ... was present in the 1970 Act. I refer in particular to the legislative background, the contrast between the discretionary and mandatory grants, the references showing that the draftsman was alive to the issue of financial resources, and the existence of s24(3)(b) and (4) of the 1996 Act.'

Where any contentious budgeting decisions impinge upon rights protected by the Human Rights Act 1998 (see above) an applicant could now claim that the decision is unlawful because it is incompatible with his right to life (eg refusal of medical treatment) or his right to privacy and family life (eg provision of special assistance, or help needed to remain in his own home).

Race relations

Given that local authorities are under a statutory duty to promote good race relations within their areas (s71 of the Race Relations Act 1976), to what extent should they be permitted to take this into account in exercising statutory discretion? The question is particularly important given the 'dynamic' approach of some local authorities on this issue, evidenced by the adoption of high profile anti-racist policies, ranging from the eviction of council tenants found guilty of racial harassment to campaigns against apartheid. In *Wheeler* v *Leicester City Council* [1985] 2 All ER 1106 the House of Lords considered the validity of a local authority resolution banning a rugby football club from using a council recreation field because of the club's connections with South Africa. The local authority specifically objected to the fact that a number of club members had played in South Africa, something that the club had no power to prevent. Their Lordships held the ban to be unreasonable, not least because the club had not been guilty of any wrongdoing. It is noteworthy, however, that their Lordships did consider the promotion of good race relations a relevant factor in the exercise of the local authority's power, particularly in the light of the large number of individuals of Afro-Caribbean and Asian origin living in its area. Similarly, in *R* v *London Borough of Lewisham, ex parte Shell UK Ltd* [1988] 1 All ER 938, Lewisham London Borough Council had approved a resolution whereby it would boycott the products of Shell UK Ltd, provided alternative products were available at reasonable prices. The company applied for judicial review of the resolution, seeking a declaration that the resolution, and the campaign waged by the authority to dissuade other local authorities from using the company's products, were ultra vires; orders of certiorari to quash the resolution; and an injunction to stop the authority from implementing the resolution. Despite its reliance on s71 of the Race Relations Act 1976, the court held that the council could not use its contracting power to punish a company in relation to an activity that was not prohibited by English law. Neill LJ, commenting on the council's actions, observed:

> 'For my part, I do not accept ... that it was obligatory for the council to adduce evidence from ratepayers or others to prove that there was a body of public opinion in favour of the action taken by the council having regard to the fact that this is a multiracial borough, the council was entitled to decide on the basis of its own experience and perception that it was in the interests of good race relations that trading with a particular company should cease because of its links with apartheid. I shall therefore assume, though on the present evidence the matter must be very near the line, that the council's decision not to continue to trade with Shell UK, unless in effect it was obliged to do so, could not be successfully attacked as being unreasonable in a *Wednesbury* sense ... It seems to me to be quite clear, however ... that the purpose of the decision was not merely to satisfy public opinion in the borough or to promote good race relations in the borough, but was in order to put pressure on Shell UK and Shell Transport to procure a withdrawal of the Shell group from South Africa ... It is to be remembered that neither Shell UK nor any of the other UK Shell companies was acting in any way unlawfully. Nor is there any suggestion

whatever that Shell UK or any of the other UK companies was in any way in breach of the contract compliance scheme devised by the Commission for Racial Equality. The attitude which Shell UK and Shell Transport adopted was a responsible one. The council, and indeed a great many other people, may strongly disagree with the policy adopted by the Shell group and as to the efficacy of this policy in bringing about any change in the South African regime, but I find it impossible in the light of the authorities to escape from the conclusion that by seeking to bring pressure on Shell UK to change the Shell policy towards South Africa, the council was acting unfairly and in a manner which requires the court to intervene.'

As a result the court concluded that the wish to change the Shell policy towards South Africa was inextricably tied up with the desire to improve race relations in the borough, and had the effect of vitiating the decision as a whole. The court also noted that as a result of its decision on this point, the council's participation in a campaign to persuade other local authorities effectively to boycott trade with Shell UK and its associated companies was also ultra vires.

'Green' politics

Given the political changes in South Africa since the above cases were before the courts, councillors seeking a moral reference point from which to launch a programme of activism have increasingly turned to so-called 'green' politics, ie issues such as opposition to blood sports and the promotion of animal rights. Although the focus for campaigning shifts, the legal issues remain constant. If a local authority exercises its discretion having taken into account the opposition to blood sports, or the transport of live animals for export, has it acted unlawfully? Much turns on the wording of the power pursuant to which the action is taken. In *R* v *Somerset County Council, ex parte Fewings* [1995] 3 All ER 20 the Court of Appeal held (by a majority) that a resolution passed by the respondent authority prohibiting stag hunting on certain land within its ownership was unlawful. Sir Thomas Bingham MR, whilst rejecting the view of Laws J, in the court below, to the effect that the ethical arguments based on assertions that hunting was inherently cruel were necessarily extraneous to the local authority's exercise of its discretion, explained that the authority's councillors may have given undue weight to the moral question concerning the desirability of hunting, at the expense of the statutory requirement to manage the land for the benefit of the authority's area. In adopting a ban, the local authority would, in his view, have to demonstrate how its decision was conducive to this statutory objective. Evidence of the documentation circulated prior to the meeting at which the authority had arrived at its decision indicated that councillors might have underestimated the statutory constraints imposed upon a public landowner. Swinton Thomas LJ went further in expressing the view that the morality or otherwise of hunting was not a matter for public landowners, but a matter for Parliament to resolve by way of legislation if necessary. Note that Simon Brown LJ (dissenting) felt that, all other factors being properly considered, the councillors had been right to regard the ethical issue as decisive and he would have been prepared to uphold the legality of the authority's resolution on that basis. In the light of this case it might be tempting to advise local authorities that want to ban hunting on their land not to advert to any moral issues in justifying their actions, but merely to advance their cases on issues related to husbandry and land management. Arguably, only if an objector could show that a ban was irrational, or based on no evidence, could the courts intervene.

8.4 Acting on no evidence

To say that a decision-maker must have evidence upon which to base the exercise of his discretion is, of course, simply to highlight a particular facet of the requirement that a decision-maker should act reasonably – no reasonable decision-maker would come to a decision unsupported by evidence. Equally, the absence of evidence could be categorised as a relevant consideration to be taken into account when arriving at a determination (eg see *R* v *East Hertfordshire District Council, ex parte Beckman* [1997] NLJ 1185), or could be regarded as a jurisdictional precondition, in that there must be evidence before a decision-maker before he is entitled to exercise his powers. As a ground for review, acting on no evidence has the attraction that it depends less on the idiosyncrasies of individual judges, and their conceptions of reasonableness, or relevant considerations, and more on the establishment of objective criteria that have to be satisfied before powers can be exercised. Nevertheless, it is still for the reviewing court to adjudicate upon the sufficiency or otherwise of the evidence relied upon.

Broadly, two types of cases can be identified where a 'no evidence' challenge might be raised. The first is where there is insufficient evidence for what is essentially a policy decision. For example, in *R* v *Secretary of State for Foreign and Commonwealth Affairs, ex parte World Development Movement Ltd* [1995] 1 All ER 111, the court ruled that the provision of justifying evidence was a precondition to the Foreign Secretary exercising his discretion under s1(1) of the Overseas and Development Act 1980 to make a grant to the Malaysian government for the building of the Pergau Dam. The court was satisfied that both the original decision to grant aid, and the later decision not to withhold outstanding payments, were unlawful because the evidence of the Foreign Secretary had revealed that Pergau Dam project was so economically unsound that no economic argument in its favour could be constructed. The fact that Parliament had not limited the power under the 1980 Act by expressly specifying that it had to be exercised for a sound development purpose did not mean that it could, therefore, be used to promote unsound development. The court recognised that the respondent would have to take into account wider political and diplomatic considerations when deciding whether or not to honour a pledge to grant overseas aid, but those factors only became relevant once a proper purpose for granting aid arose under the 1980 Act. It could not be left to the respondent himself to determine whether or not a grant of aid under the 1980 Act would be lawful. Similarly, in *R v Derbyshire County Council, ex parte Times Supplements Ltd* (above), the respondent authority's decision to withdraw all future advertisements for teaching posts from the educational supplements published by the applicants was found to be unlawful because there was no evidence that, prior to the publication by the applicants of articles concerning the activities of the respondent council's leader, the respondent had been in any way dissatisfied by the service provided by the applicants in advertising council posts, and the court concluded that there was no valid grounds for the authority's decision. Watkins LJ expressed his view that the 'educational grounds' put forward by the councillors who gave evidence (ie that advertising in *The Times Educational Supplements* was no longer as effective as advertising in *The Guardian*) were implausible. He felt that the majority Labour grouping had taken the decision in bad faith, and had then sought to produce some 'evidence' to justify it in the hope that the court would be persuaded that this was a lawful consideration. Costs were awarded against the respondents on an indemnity basis, as it was felt that there had been an attempt to mislead the court. See further *Secretary of State for Education and Science v Tameside Metropolitan Borough Council* (above).

A second grouping of cases are those where a decision-maker acts in some appellate role, having to uphold or reverse a decision made by a tribunal of fact. For example, in *Burgesses of Sheffield v Minister of Health* (1935) 52 TLR 171, the owners of land subject to a compulsory purchase order issued by the local authority sought to challenge its confirmation by the minister on the ground that, contrary to the requirements of s3 of the Housing Act 1930, there was insufficient evidence that the acquisition was 'reasonably necessary for the purpose of securing a cleared area of convenient shape and dimensions, and ... for the satisfactory development or user of the cleared area'. Swift J, whilst satisfied that the necessary evidence existed in this particular case, went on to explain the role of the court thus:

> 'If [the local authority] go to the Minister asking for powers to buy land compulsorily which is not reasonably necessary for the satisfactory development of the land in the cleared area, they will not get those powers; the Minister would simply say to them: "This is not reasonably necessary." Even if the Minister gave them the powers asked for, the Court, should the matter come before it, could quash the order if satisfied that there was no material on which it could be said that the land was reasonably required or was reasonably necessary for the satisfactory development of the cleared area. It is for the corporation in the first place to say whether it is reasonably necessary or not; it is for the Minister in the second place to say whether it is reasonably necessary or not; and it is for the Court, if the matter is brought before it, to say whether there is any material on which the Minister could have come to the conclusion that it was reasonably necessary. If the Court comes to the conclusion that there is no such material, then it will not hesitate to quash the Minister's order ...'

See also *Coleen Properties v MHLG* [1971] 1 WLR 433, in which the Court of Appeal quashed a ministerial order confirming a slum clearance scheme – no evidence supporting the order had been offered at a public inquiry, and the inspector had recommended against it, thus there was no new evidence justifying the minister's departure from the inspector's conclusions; *R v Home Secretary, ex parte Zamir* [1980] AC 930, where the House of Lords held that an immigration officer, who had the power to refuse leave to enter the country if satisfied of certain facts was, on 'normal principles', not at liberty to refuse it if there was no evidence to support his decision; and *R v Secretary of State for the Home Department, ex parte Danaei* (1998) The Times 3 January, where the court quashed the minister's conclusion that the facts as found by the special adjudicator were implausible on the basis that he had no new evidence on which to come to such a conclusion, and in light of the fact that, unlike the minister, the special adjudicator had seen the applicant give evidence in person. As to what would have satisfied the evidential requirement in this latter case, the court gave, as an example, that it might be material indicating that the tribunal of fact had been misled by unreliable testimony. A distinction should be drawn, however, between those case where a minister comes to a different conclusion as to the credibility of a witness, and those where he differs with the tribunal of fact in relation to a more general issue, such as the political situation in a country from which an asylum seeker had fled, bearing in mind that the minister would have access to a wider range of evidence: see *R v Secretary of State for the Home Department, ex parte Alekesan* (1996) (unreported).

9

Fettering Discretion

9.1 Introduction

9.2 The rule against delegation

9.3 Fettering discretion by adoption of a policy

9.4 Fettering discretion by contract

9.5 Estoppel

9.1 Introduction

Ultra vires action is understandably seen as involving some positive act on the part of a public body. What this chapter examines are those situations where a public body can act unlawfully by deciding not to exercise its discretion at all. Four situations can be identified where this problem might arise. First, where a public body adopts a rigid policy regarding the exercise of its discretion; second where a public body divests itself of its discretion by delegating its decision-making functions to some other body, contrary to the intention of Parliament; third, where a public body enters into a contractual commitment that has the effect of restricting its power to act in the wider public interest; and, finally, where a public body, as a result of undertakings given, allegedly becomes estopped from exercising its discretion in a manner that is incompatible with the undertaking.

9.2 The rule against delegation

The basic principle is that where Parliament delegates a function to an inferior body, and bestows upon it the powers necessary for it to perform that function, the inferior body should not delegate that function to any other body.

There are a number of reasons for this rule, which is sometimes expressed as the latin maxim *delegatus non potest delegare*. The individual has the right to have decisions affecting his position made by the body empowered to do so. In selecting an inferior body to perform a particular function, Parliament will have had regard to its suitability and expertise. It would be thwarting the intention of Parliament to permit the function to be carried out by some other body. If a function is being discharged by a tribunal other than that authorised by the enabling Act, the tribunal purporting to act must be assuming a jurisdiction it does not in fact have, and therefore must be acting ultra vires.

A classic example of unlawful delegation is provided by the case of *Ellis* v *Dubowski* [1921] 3 KB 621, where a local authority with statutory powers to licence cinemas issued licences subject to the condition that only films approved by the British Board of Film Censors could be shown. The local authority was held to have unlawfully delegated its function of licensing films for public display as it had completely abdicated the function. Compare with the later decision in *Mills* v *London County Council* [1925] 1 KB 213, where a similar delegation of powers was upheld, the difference being that, regardless of the view of the Board, the LCC had taken care in its resolution to reserve to itself the ultimate choice as to whether a film should be shown or not. In effect it had retained a power to review the decisions of the British Board of Film Censors. The rule against delegation has also been applied to central government. In *H Lavender & Sons Ltd* v *MHLG* [1970] 3 All ER 871 the company applied for planning permission in order to extract certain minerals from an agricultural holding. Most of the holding was within a reservation area (ie was high quality agricultural land). The planning authority refused permission and the company appealed to the Minister under s23 of the Town and Country Planning Act 1962. In dismissing the appeal the Minister of Housing and Local Government stated his reasons, inter alia, as follows:

> 'It is the Minister's present policy that land in the reservations should not be released for mineral working unless the Minister of Agriculture, Fisheries and Food is not opposed to working. In the present case the agricultural objection has not been waived, and the Minister has therefore decided not to grant planning permission for the working of the appeal site.'

The company applied to the High Court under s179 of the Town and Country Planning Act 1962 for the Minister's decision to be quashed. The court held the abdication of power by the Ministry to be ultra vires. It could not defer to the views of another government department when exercising its discretionary powers. Note that the case could also be regarded as one involving the fettering of discretion by the adoption of an over-rigid policy, in this case, the policy of referring all such applications to the Ministry of Agriculture.

Government departments

Given the huge work load of many government departments, it is inconceivable that any minister should personally exercise all the powers and functions bestowed upon him, or her, by Parliament. This reality has to be reconciled with the theory, already expounded above, that power once delegated should not be delegated further.

The courts have accepted that, except where a statute expressly requires a

Secretary of State to act personally, his powers are frequently going to be exercised on his behalf by senior civil servants. The safeguard, and presumably the reason why the courts are willing to countenance such a practice, is that constitutionally the actions of civil servants are the actions of the minister, for which the minister is responsible to Parliament. Further, the fact that discretionary powers are exercised by a civil servant and not the minister does not prevent judicial review from operating in the event of illegality.

In *Carltona Ltd* v *Commissioners of Works* [1943] 2 All ER 560 the appellant's food factory was requisitioned by the Commissioners acting under reg 51(1) of the Defence (General) Regulations 1939 which provided that:

'A competent authority, if it appears to that authority to be necessary or expedient so to do in the interests of the public safety, the defence of the realm or the efficient prosecution of the war, or for maintaining supplies and services essential to the life of the community, may take possession of any land, and may give such directions as appear to the competent authority to be necessary or expedient in connection with the taking of possession of that land.'

On 4 November 1942 a Mr Morse signed the requisition notice on behalf of the Commissioners (in effect the Minister of Works and Planning). The appellants sought a declaration that the notice was invalid because of unlawful delegation of the Minister's functions to Mr Morse. The Court of Appeal rejected the claim of the appellants and made clear the principle that functions given to a Minister or Secretary of State were exercisable on his behalf by his department. As Lord Greene MR stated:

'It cannot be supposed that this regulation meant that, in each case, the minister in person should direct his mind to the matter. The duties imposed upon ministers and the powers given to ministers are normally exercised under the authority of the ministers by responsible officials of the department. Public business could not be carried on if that were not the case. Constitutionally, the decision of such an official is, of course, the decision of the minister. The minister is responsible. It is he who must answer before Parliament for anything that his officials have done under his authority, and, if for an important matter he selected an official of such junior standing that he could not be expected competently to perform the work, the minister would have to answer for that in Parliament. The whole system of departmental organisation and administration is based on the view that ministers, being responsible to Parliament, will see that important duties are committed to experienced officials. If they do not do that, Parliament is the place where complaint must be made against them.'

In *Point of Ayr Collieries Ltd* v *Lloyd-George* [1943] 2 All ER 546 a challenge to an order requisitioning a coal mine was challenged on grounds similar to those raised in *Carltona*. In upholding the order, Lord Greene commented that it might have been more appropriate for the Minister himself to sign the order, but this was not required as a matter of law. Further support for this position has been supplied in *Re Golden Chemical Products* [1976] 2 All ER 543, where officers acting for the Secretary of State for Trade presented a petition under s35 of the Companies Act

1967 for the winding-up of Golden Chemical Products Ltd. The company opposed the petition on the grounds that the power under s35 could only be exercised by the Secretary of State personally. The court rejected this argument, holding that it was established departmental practice that such functions be discharged by officials of the department. Brightman J stated that the fact that a s35 petition could have devastating effects for the company did not compel the conclusion that only the Minister could authorise such action.

The application of the rule against delegation within government departments may depend to a certain extent on the nature of the function being delegated. It has been suggested that where personal liberty is affected, the minister himself should act. The contention was considered in *R* v *Skinner* [1968] 2 QB 700, where the court considered the validity of using a breath-testing machine designed to measure blood alcohol levels of motorists suspected of driving with excess alcohol. Reliance on the readings produced by the machine was challenged when it became known that its use had been authorised by a senior civil servant on behalf of the Home Secretary, and not by the Home Secretary personally. The Court of Appeal had no doubt that the minister's function could be discharged by a senior official. The court pointed out that in certain circumstances it might be impolitic for the minister not to be seen to intervene personally, but whether or not he should do so was a matter for the minister: see *R* v *Governor of Brixton Prison, ex parte Enahoro (No 2)* [1963] 2 QB 455 and *Liversidge* v *Anderson* [1942] AC 206.

The question of what factors the court should consider when assessing the legality of the delegation of ministerial functions, in the absence of any express statutory restriction, was reviewed by the House of Lords in *R* v *Secretary of State for the Home Department, ex parte Oladehinde* [1990] 3 WLR 797. The applicants had been served with notices of intention to deport by immigration officers. The officers had been acting under the instructions of immigration inspectors to whom the function of making decisions to deport had been delegated by the Secretary of State. After appealing unsuccessfully to the adjudicator and the Immigration Appeal Tribunal, the applicants sought judicial review of the deportation decisions on the ground (inter alia) that the Secretary of State acted unlawfully in delegating his power of deportation under s3(5)(a) of the Immigration Act 1971 to immigration inspectors. The Divisional Court granted the application for review, quashing the deportation orders, on the grounds that it had been the intention of Parliament that the immigration officers should have had a distinct function, that of controlling entry to the country, whilst the Secretary of State was to be concerned with decisions relating to the right to remain and deportation. The Court of Appeal allowed the Secretary of State's appeal. The House of Lords, dismissing the appeals, held that there was nothing in the wording of s3(5)(a) which appeared expressly or impliedly to limit the Secretary of State's power to delegate his function of ordering deportations. In the absence of any such statutory restrictions, the factors to which the court would have regard were the seniority of the officers to whom the power had been delegated, the possibility of any conflict with their other statutory duties, and whether they had fully considered the applicant's cases. In all these respects it was established that the Secretary of State had acted lawfully. Note that the Secretary of State had been careful to avoid any allegation of intermingling of functions on the part of civil servants in the immigration service, by ensuring that the officials entrusted with the task of making the deportation orders had not been involved in the same cases as immigration officers.

Subject to a challenge on the grounds of irrationality, it is difficult to see how the delegation of functions by a Secretary of State, even in relation to matters such as sentencing, could now be shown to be ultra vires. With regard to the task of reviewing the release date for prisoners serving life sentences, the House of Lords in *R* v *Secretary of State for the Home Department, ex parte Doody and Others* [1993] 3 All ER 92 expressly approved the comments of Staughton LJ. Noting that the Home Secretary had to deal, on average, with 130 mandatory life sentence cases each year, Staughton LJ rejected the contention that it would be improper for him delegate such a function. He observed:

> 'Parliament must be well aware of the great burden that is placed on senior ministers who not only take charge of their departments but also speak for them in Parliament, attend meetings of the Cabinet and its committees, and see to their constituency affairs. ... I can see nothing irrational in the Secretary of State devolving [the consideration of minimum periods to be served by convicted murderers] upon junior ministers. They too are appointed by the Crown to hold office in the department, they have the same advice and assistance from departmental officials as the Secretary of State would have, and they too are answerable to Parliament.'

Local authorities

Local authorities have a very wide range of duties and, in enacting s101 of the Local Government Act 1972, Parliament has expressly recognised that the day-to-day business of local government cannot continue without a large scale delegation of those functions to committees, officers and even other local authorities, provided that a local authority always reserves to itself the right to exercise its powers if it so chooses: see further Chapter 3, section 3.8 and in particular *Credit Suisse* v *Waltham Forest London Borough Council.*

Even where the statutory power to delegate has not been invoked, the courts may adopt an indulgent attitude to the delegation of functions by a local authority, provided there is no evidence that it is seeking to flout statutory safeguards. Hence in *Provident Mutual Life Assurance Association* v *Derby City Council* [1981] 1 WLR 173 the appellants challenged the validity of a rating notice issued by the respondent authority on the ground that it had been made by the authority's principal rating assistant, and not its Treasurer. In rejecting the appellant's contentions, Lord Roskill stated:

> 'My Lords, the statutory conditions precedent to the imposition of a fiscal liability must obviously be properly complied with ... but Parliament has conferred very wide powers on

local authorities, and Parliament plainly contemplated that the actual machinery of enforcement and collection would not be operated personally by some senior local government official but would be so operated by the relevant senior official's staff.'

Compare with *R v St Edmundsbury Borough Council, ex parte Walton* (1999) The Times 5 May, where the court held that, in the absence of any formal delegation of the power to determine the issue, it had been unlawful for a planning officer to advise an applicant for planning permission that the proposed development would not require the formulation of an environmental statement. The decision was regarded by the court as being too important to be regarded merely as a procedural requirement.

Administrative functions

To the extent that such classifications continue to be important, it can generally be said that the courts adopt a liberal approach to the delegation of administrative functions, typically preparatory work, because at that stage of the administrative process no rights are directly affected.

In *Jeffs v New Zealand Dairy Production and Marketing Board* [1967] 1 AC 551 the Privy Council held that the Board, which was concerned with determining applications for permission to grow produce in zoned areas, could delegate to a committee the function of collecting evidence relating to how it should act, at least where the credibility of witnesses was not in question; this was essentially an administrative matter.

Similarly, in *Selvarajan v Race Relations Board* [1976] 1 All ER 12, it was held that the investigative functions of the Board could be delegated to a committee, especially in the light of the fact that it was a body with a large number of members, and it would be unrealistic to expect it to discharge such functions at a full meeting.

In *Attorney-General, ex rel McWhirter v IBA* [1973] QB 621 the court accepted that, even though the Authority was under a statutory duty to satisfy itself that programmes were suitable for broadcast within the terms of its enabling Act, it was entirely proper for the task of viewing programmes to be carried out by its staff.

Judicial functions

It is with regard to judicial functions, more than any other type of activity, that the rule against delegation is strictly applied. Note that in *Jeffs v New Zealand Dairy Production and Marketing Board* (above) the Privy Council held that the actual determination of applications for zoning was a judicial function that could not be delegated.

Barnard v National Dock Labour Board [1953] 2 QB 18 provides a classic illustration of the principle being applied. Under the Dock Workers (Regulations) Order 1947 a National Dock Labour Board was established with the duty, inter alia, of delegating the administration of as many aspects of the scheme as possible to local boards. Amongst the functions delegated was the operation of a disciplinary code.

Dock workers in London, who had been dismissed following a dispute about the unloading of raw sugar, sought a declaration that the dismissals were unlawful. Following discovery of documents it emerged that the local board had delegated its power of dismissal to its port manager. The Court of Appeal, granting the declaration sought, held that disciplinary functions, being judicial in nature because they affected persons rights, could not be delegated. Lord Denning MR stated the matter thus:

> 'While an administrative function can often be delegated, a judicial function rarely can be. No judicial tribunal can delegate its functions unless it is enabled to do so expressly or by necessary implication.'

This decision was subsequently approved by the House of Lords in *Vine* v *National Dock Labour Board* [1957] AC 488, where similar disciplinary powers had been delegated by the local board to a disciplinary committee. Their Lordships emphasised that in determining the legality of delegation of functions, the court should consider the nature of the duty in question and the characteristics of the body on whom it is put.

A more recent reiteration of this principle was provided by *R* v *Gateshead Justices, ex parte Tesco Stores Ltd* [1981] 2 WLR 419. Under r3 of the Justices' Clerks Rules 1970, the issuing of court summonses could be delegated from a single justice to the justice's clerk. Tesco Stores applied for an order of certiorari to quash a summons issued against it on the ground that the justice's clerk in question had unlawfully delegated this function to court officers. The Divisional Court granted the applications for certiorari, holding that there was no power to delegate a judicial function and therefore, since under the Rules of 1970 only a clerk to the justices could exercise the judicial function of a justice of the peace to consider an information, the informations had not been laid before a person who was authorised to consider them, and the convictions would be quashed. As Donaldson LJ stated:

> '... the requirement that a justice of the peace or the clerk to the justices as a justice of the peace shall take personal responsibility for the proprietory of taking so serious a step as to require the attendance of a citizen before a criminal court, is a constitutional safeguard of fundamental importance. We have no doubt that this function is judicial.'

See further *R* v *DPP, ex parte Association of First Division Civil Servants* (1988) The Times 26 May.

Human Rights Act 1998

Note that with the enactment of the 1998 Act, which has the effect of making it unlawful for any public authority to act in a way that is incompatible with the Convention rights protected thereunder, art 6 of the Convention becomes part of domestic law. This could have particular relevance to the delegation of judicial functions as it provides, inter alia, that:

'In the determination of his civil rights and obligations or of any criminal charge against him, everyone is entitled to a fair and public hearing within a reasonable time by an independent and impartial tribunal established by law.'

Where judicial powers are delegated, those adversely affected may contend that the decision-maker is not a tribunal established by law.

9.3 Fettering discretion by adoption of a policy

Administrative agencies vested with statutory powers are, in theory, supposed to consider each use of discretion in its own right, bearing in mind all relevant considerations. The benefits of individualised justice carry with them a potential cost in the form of inconsistency. The exercise of discretion is not normally governed by a system of precedent, hence a claimant denied a discretionary award cannot argue the refusal of his claim is unlawful simply because, in a previous similar application, an award was made. In order to promote fairness, consistency and efficiency many administrative bodies will develop policies as to how discretion is to be exercised, thus helping to ensure that like cases are treated alike.

Before proceeding to consider the legality of policies in more depth it should be noted that there may be situations where the adoption of a policy regarding the exercise of discretion is regarded as inappropriate per se. This will generally be the case were the context requires cases to be looked at on an individual basis.

For example, in *Attorney-General v Wandsworth London Borough Council, ex rel Tilley* [1981] 1 All ER 1162, the social services committee of a local authority passed a resolution that in cases where the housing department of the authority had determined that parents of a family with young children were intentionally homeless, and the family subsequently approached the social services department, assistance with accommodation would not be provided under the provisions of the Children and Young Persons Act 1963, although considerations would be given to receiving the children into care if the circumstances warranted it. Under the 1963 Act local authorities were placed under a duty to promote children's welfare by providing advice, guidance and assistance in order to diminish the need to receive children into care under the Children Act 1948. The Attorney-General, in a relator action brought on behalf of a ratepayer and a member of the local authority's council, sought a declaration that the local authority resolution was invalid as it amounted to a fetter on the discretion exercisable by the authority under s1(1) of the 1963 Act. The Court of Appeal, upholding the decision at first instance to grant the declaration, thought a strict policy was inappropriate where the welfare of children was at stake. As Templeman LJ observed:

'... a local authority, dealing with individual children, should not make a policy or an order that points towards fettering its discretion in such a way that the facilities offered to the child do not depend on the particular circumstances of that child or of its family but follow some policy which is expressed to apply in general cases.'

Similarly, in *R* v *Secretary of State for the Home Department, ex parte Venables and Thompson* [1997] 3 All ER 97 the House of Lords held (Lord Lloyd dissenting) that the Home Secretary, in adopting a policy (normally applicable to adult prisoners) that young offenders should serve a minimum period of imprisonment before being eligible for parole, had acted unlawfully. The intention of Parliament, as expressed in s44 of the Children and Young Persons Act 1933, required him to have regard to the welfare of the individual child detained at Her Majesty's pleasure.

The substantive issue: is the policy lawful in itself?

Assuming the adoption of a policy is appropriate to the decision-making function in question, the next issue to consider will be the lawfulness of the policy itself. In general terms the policy will be unlawful if it is ultra vires, ie irrational, based on irrelevant considerations, or devised in ignorance of relevant considerations. Hence in *Findlay* v *Secretary of State for the Home Department* [1984] 3 All ER 801 the House of Lords upheld the Home Secretary's policy of not considering certain categories of prisoners for parole unless they had served at least 20 years of their sentences. The House of Lords held that he was entitled to have a policy regarding the exercise of his discretion to grant parole, since it would be difficult for him to manage the complexities of his statutory duties in regard to parole without a policy. Furthermore, consideration of an individual case was not excluded by a policy which provided that exceptional circumstances or compelling reasons had to be shown for parole because of the weight attached to the nature of the offence, the length of the sentence and the factors of deterrence, retribution and public confidence, all of which it was the duty of the Secretary of State to consider. In *R* v *Southwark London Borough Council, ex parte Udu* (1995) The Times 30 October the Court of Appeal upheld the legality of a local education authority's policy of refusing to make any discretionary awards to law students with places on the Legal Practice Course at the College of Law. The court felt that the authority was entitled to have a policy regarding the provision of discretionary awards, provided the policy was rational and sufficiently flexible so as to take account of exceptional cases. The adoption of a policy not to fund study at private institutions was seen as essentially a political matter which the courts were not competent to comment upon, but in any event, in terms of the rationing of resources, a local authority could logically adopt the view that postgraduate students should not be given further access to local authority funds.

See further *R* v *Broadmoor Special Hospital Authority and Another, ex parte S* (1998) The Times 17 February (policy of searching mental patients was lawful given the risk of harm to others); *R* v *Secretary of State for the Home Department, ex parte Fielding* (1999) The Times 21 July (policy of not providing condoms to prison inmates as a matter of course held to be lawful – prison service did not wish to encourage homosexuality); *R* v *Chief Constable of the North Wales Police, ex parte AB* [1997] 4 All ER 691 (at first instance – policy of warning local people that convicted sex offenders had moved into their area declared lawful – appeal on other grounds: see [1998] 3 All ER 310); *R* v *Secretary of State for the Home Department, ex parte Mellor* (2001) The Times 1 May (policy of refusing artificial insemination facilities to prisoners serving life sentences lawful); *R* v *Secretary of State for the Home Department, ex parte Willis* (2000) The Times 22 March (policy of not considering prisoners on the sex offenders' register for early release under the 'electronic tagging' scheme) and *R (On the Application of T)* v *Secretary of State for the Home Department* (2001) The Times 1 August (policy of separating children born to mothers in prison after 18 months declared lawful).

By contrast a policy will fail the test of substantive validity if there is evidence that it unreasonable, serves no legitimate public policy, has been adopted to achieve an ulterior motive, fails to reflect relevant considerations, or is counter-productive in operation. In *R* v *Secretary of State for the Home Department, ex parte Jammeh and Others* (1997) The Times 11 September the Divisional Court held that the Home Secretary's policy of not permitting asylum seekers, awaiting the outcome of their appeals against the refusal of asylum, permission to seek work was unlawful. Owen J agreed with submissions made on behalf of the applicants to the effect that the policy was irrational on at least two grounds. First, given that it took nearly a year for an appeal against a refusal of asylum to be heard, it could result in an asylum seeker becoming destitute in the interim and, for the want of a very modest amount of money, being unable to exercise his right of appeal. Second, the policy meant that whilst it was lawful to give money to an asylum seeker who went begging for it, it was unlawful to give money to one who was willing to work for it. Similarly, in *R* v *Tower Hamlets London Borough Council, ex parte Khalique* (1994) The Times 16 March, the respondent authority's policy of regarding applications for housing from those more than £500 in arrears with payments of rent to the council as 'non-active' was declared unlawful on the basis, inter alia, that it prevented the applicant from putting his case, and because the existence of rent arrears was extraneous to the discharge of the statutory duty to provide secure accommodation.

In *R* v *Newham London Borough Council, ex parte Sacupima* (2000) The Times 12 January the respondent authority, by virtue of s188 of the Housing Act 1996, was under an interim duty to house homeless persons pending an inquiry into whether a duty to provide longer-term accommodation existed. Each of the applicants has been resident in Newham prior to becoming homeless. The respondent authority informed the applicants that it would not be providing temporary accommodation in its area, or in London, but would be relocating them to seaside resorts such as Brighton, Southend and Great Yarmouth. This decision was the result of the authority's policy of only regarding the provision of temporary accommodation out of the borough as unsuitable if there were 'serious reasons' for doing so – this being interpreted by the authority as only arising where it could be shown that there was a serious risk to the life or health of the homeless person or member of his family. In each case the applicants, who were on income support, found that the relocation made it impossible for them to continue with existing arrangements for work, education or medical care in Newham because of the cost of travelling from the resorts to the borough and the time involved in so doing. Not surprisingly the court held that the authority had acted unlawfully in pursuing its policy. Although the authority could have regard to the financial constraints in which it had to operate and the housing available to it, the issue of suitability of accommodation had to be considered relative to the needs of each applicant. Where, in light of those circumstances, the accommodation provided was such that no reasonable authority could regard it as suitable, the courts would intervene. In effect the respondent authority had adopted a policy regarding the provision of temporary accommodation that prevented it from being able to respond flexibly to individual cases. To disregard the effect of relocation on an applicant with children about to take important examinations in the borough's schools would be regarded as amounting to *Wednesbury* unreasonableness.

Finally, in *R v North Derbyshire Health Authority, ex parte Fisher* (1997) The Times 2 September, the Divisional Court declared unlawful the policy of a health authority not to prescribe a particular drug because of the impact on the authority's budget. Health authorities had been requested, by the Department of Health, to purchase and provide the drug, and whilst the terms of the circular were not legally binding on the authority, it was under a duty to take it into account when formulating its policy. It was evident from the terms of the policy adopted that it had made no serious attempt to do so.

The courts are sufficiently pragmatic in their approach to the realities of modern administration to accept the fact that the adoption of a policy will be well nigh essential where an administrative body has to deal with large number of applications, particularly where some benefit or privilege is being bestowed. Thus, in *British Oxygen Co Ltd v Minister of Technology* [1971] AC 610 Lord Reid accepted that 'a Ministry or large authority may have had to deal already with a multitude of similar applications … will almost certainly have evolved a policy'. Similarly, in *R v Camden London Borough Council, ex parte Mohammed* (1997) The Times 20 June, the Divisional Court upheld the legality of the policy adopted by respondent housing authority whereby it refused to grant applicants refused housing assistance any interim assistance with housing pending the outcome of any review of an applicant's case. The court noted that the adoption of a policy was appropriate given the large number of unsuccessful applicants who asked the respondent authority to review its decisions to refuse assistance, and the fact that the vast majority of such requests for review were unmeritorious.

The procedural issue: has the policy been lawfully implemented?

Even if the policy survives scrutiny on the grounds of substantive illegality, it must still be shown that it has been applied in a manner that is lawful. The basic rule here is that a decision-maker will act unlawfully if a policy is applied without sufficient flexibility being shown. Hence, in *ex parte Khalique*, the respondent authority's policy was also found to be unlawful because it was applied in an over-rigid fashion. Similarly, in *ex parte Fisher*, and *ex parte Jammeh*, there was little or no evidence of any exceptions being made, thus confirming suggestions that the policy was being used as a substitute for any real exercise of discretion. See also *R v North West Lancashire Health Authority, ex parte A* (1999) The Times 24 August.

Still a leading decision on how policies ought to be applied in practice is *R v Port of London Authority, ex parte Kynoch Ltd* [1919] 1 KB 176, where Kynoch Ltd applied to the Port of London Authority (PLA) for a licence (under s7 of the Port of London Act 1908 and s10 of the Thames Conservancy Act 1894) to construct a deep-water wharf and other works on land they owned, on the bank of the Thames. The PLA rejected the application on the ground that the accommodation applied for was of a character that Parliament had charged the Authority with providing in the port. Under s2 of the 1908 Act the PLA was under a duty to take into consideration the state of the river and the accommodation and facilities afforded in the Port of London and, subject to the provisions of the Act, to take such steps as it considered necessary for improvement. Under s2(2) the PLA had power (inter alia) to 'construct, equip, maintain, or manage any docks, quays, wharves and other works in connection therewith'. Kynoch Ltd appealed to the Board of Trade against the PLA's decision, but subsequently withdrew the appeal and applied instead for mandamus to compel the Authority to exercise its discretion according to law. The evidence included an affidavit showing that the merits of the application had been fully considered by two committees and the Authority itself. The court held that the PLA acted lawfully in rejecting the application, because it had fully considered the arguments raised by Kynoch Ltd and rejected them on their merits. The vital point, in the view of Banks LJ, was that the decision-making body must not shut its ears to an applicant who has something new to say. As he observed:

> 'There are on the one hand cases where a tribunal in the honest exercise of its discretion has adopted a policy, and without refusing to hear an applicant, intimates to him what its policy is, and that after hearing him it will in accordance with its policy decide against him, unless there is something exceptional in his case ... if the policy has been adopted for reasons which the tribunal may legitimately entertain, no objection could be taken to such a course. On the other hand there are cases where a tribunal has passed a rule, or come to a determination, not to hear any application of a particular character by whomsoever made. There is a wide distinction to be drawn between these two classes.'

This view was echoed in *British Oxygen Co Ltd v Minister of Technology* [1971] AC 610, where the House of Lords introduced more flexibility into Banks LJ's dictum by pointing out that the legality of adopting a rule to govern the exercise of discretion would vary with the context within which decisions were made. A rule could be adopted provided the decision-making body was still willing to listen to someone with something new to say. As Lord Reid explained:

> 'I do not think there is any great difference between a policy and a rule. ... What the authority must not do is refuse to listen at all ... a Ministry or large authority may have

had to deal already with a multitude of similar applications and then they will almost certainly have evolved a policy so precise that it could well be called a rule. There can be no objection to that, provided the authority is always willing to listen to anyone with something new to say.'

There may yet be a contradiction inherent in this advice: on the one hand inferior bodies are allowed to have policies to help speed up their administrative processes, whilst on the other they will still have to consider every case to see whether any applicant has anything new to say. The ideal is that by permitting exceptions, administrators should be able to develop more responsive and appropriate policies through application and experience. Examples of administrators retaining the correct degree of flexibility are provided by decisions such as *ex parte Mohammed* and *ex parte Udu* both noted above.

The link with natural justice

It should be noted that there is a clear link between challenging a decision on the basis that there has been a fettering of discretion by the adoption of an overrigid policy and challenging a decision on the basis that there has been a denial of a proper and fair hearing. The equation is a simple one; by refusing to consider representations from an individual who may have something new to say, the decision-making body has denied him the right to be heard. An example is provided by *R* v *Secretary of State for the Environment, ex parte Brent London Borough Council* [1982] 2 WLR 693, where the Divisional Court held that the Secretary of State had acted ultra vires in refusing to hear representations from local authorities who were about to suffer a significant loss of rate-support grant as a result of his policy on 'overspending' authorities. In refusing to hear what they might have to say, he was denying the authorities a fair hearing on a matter of considerable importance to them. Consider, on the same approach, *John* v *Rees* [1970] Ch 345 and *R* v *Police Complaints Board, ex parte Madden* [1983] 2 All ER 353.

There are other links with natural justice. A failure to comply with a stated policy does not necessarily render a decision unlawful (see *R* v *Avon County Council, ex parte Rexworthy* (1988) The Times 30 December), but a person affected thereby may claim to have a have a legitimate expectation that a policy will be followed: see further Chapter 5. Similarly, it is good practice to advertise a policy in advance so that applicants will know what criteria are important, and tailor their cases accordingly.

The incorporation of the European Convention on Human Rights has added a further dimension to the scrutiny of administrative policies – that of proportionality. Where a policy operates so as to interfere with rights protected by the Convention, the courts will inquire into whether or not the policy seeks to achieve an aim regarded as legitimate within the terms of the Convention. Even assuming it does, it will still be unlawful if the interference is a disproportionate response to the problem the policy seeks to address. Hence in *Lindsay* v *Customs and Excise Commissioners*

(2002) The Times 27 February the Court of Appeal held that the policy of automatic forfeiture of the vehicles used by those bringing in illegal quantities of tobacco back into the country via the channel ports was unlawful, as it interfered with the applicant's right to the peaceful enjoyment of his possessions as enshrined in art 1 of Protocol 1 to the European Convention on Human Rights. The prevention of smuggling was a legitimate aim that could be pursued by interfering with that right, but any such interference had to be proportionate. In particular, a policy of automatic forfeiture of vehicles ignored the relationship that the value of the car bore to the duty that should have been paid. See further *R (On the Application of Hirst)* v *Secretary of State for the Home Department* (2002) The Times 10 April – a policy of denying prisoners the right to contact the media by telephone to comment on matters of legitimate public interest relating to prisons and prisoners was held to be a violation of the right to freedom of expression as provided for by art 10 of the European Convention on Human Rights.

9.4 Fettering discretion by contract

All statutory bodies, in particular local authorities, have to be empowered to enter into contracts in order to be able to discharge their functions. The rule in public law is that a public body must not enter into a contract that results in the exercise of its discretion becoming unduly fettered, or which prevents it from carrying out its duties. Logically, the question to ask is whether or not the public body does have the discretion to enter into particular types of contract.

By virtue of s111 of the Local Government Act 1972, local authorities are empowered to do anything calculated to facilitate, or conducive to, the discharge of any of its functions, a power that will generally be relied upon to authorise the incurring of contractual obligations, but it must be viewed in the context of any other statutory limitations that might exist. Thus, in *Credit Suisse* v *Allerdale Borough Council* [1996] 4 All ER 129 and *Credit Suisse* v *Waltham Forest London Borough Council* [1996] 4 All ER 176, the Court of Appeal refused to allow the plaintiff bank to enforce guarantees that had been provided by the local authorities in each case, on the grounds that the relevant statutory provisions did not empower them to grant such guarantees, and no power to do so could be implied from s111. In both cases the guarantees were thus held to be void: see further Chapter 3, section 3.8 and *Morgan Grenfell & Co Ltd* v *Sutton London Borough Council* (1996) The Times 7 November (the local authority's contractual undertaking, to indemnify the plaintiff bank in the event of a housing association's failure to repay a loan, held to be ultra vires). Note also that s9 of the European Communities Act 1972 (persons dealing in good faith with companies) applies only to bodies incorporated under the Companies Acts legislation.

Assuming that a power to contract does exist, it has to be accepted that every contract entered into will, to some small degree, fetter the freedom of the body concerned, because it then commits it to a particular course of action, and invariably involves the allocation of limited resources to finance the contract. The issues, therefore, will be as to the compatibility of the contract, bearing in mind the other functions of the statutory body, and the extent to which the contract purports to limit discretion.

The problem of incompatibility

When trying to discern whether or not a contractual undertaking is incompatible with the status of a statutory body, regard must be had to the aims and objects of the enabling Act.

In *Ayr Harbour Trustees* v *Oswald* (1883) 8 App Cas 623 the Trustees were appointed under the Ayr Harbour Act 1879 for the management and improvement of the harbour and were empowered to take certain lands (including Oswald's) for this purpose. In order to reduce the amount of compensation payable to Oswald on taking this land the trustees agreed that the conveyance of the land should restrict their use of it so as not to interfere with access from Oswald's remaining land to the harbour. Oswald did not agree with this course of action and brought an action for a declaration that the trustees had to purchase the land absolutely. The House of Lords, affirming the decision of the Court of Session, held that the trustees had the power under the Act of 1879 then or at any time in the future to modify the land taken so as to destroy any access from Oswald's land to the harbour and that the trustees were not competent to dispense with the future exercise of their powers by themselves or their successors. The trustees had been given the powers of compulsory purchase so that they might be able to develop the harbour and surrounding land in the public interest, without having to defer to the private interests of individuals. An agreement to grant access to the land being acquired would be totally incompatible with the purpose for which the trustees had been vested with these powers. By contrast, in *Stourcliffe Estates* v *Bournemouth Corporation* [1910] 2 Ch 12, the defendant local authority unsuccessfully tried to argue that it was not bound by a covenant entered into when it purchased park land from the plaintiffs, to the effect that it would not carry out any building work on the land. The plaintiffs applied for an injunction to prevent the local authority from building public conveniences on the land, and the Court of Appeal held the covenants to be valid. Unlike the case of the *Ayr Harbour Trustees*, it could not to be said that a promise not to build on land was contrary to the purpose for which the local authority had been created; its functions were many and varied. For a more contemporary version of the *Ayr Harbour* problem, see *Trigg* v *Staines UDC* [1969] 1 Ch 10, wherein the court held that an agreement by a local authority not to use its powers of compulsory purchase in respect of a particular piece of land for a specified period was clearly incompatible with authority's duty to retain its full planning powers to be used in public interest.

Where a public body enters into what is essentially a normal commercial contract, the courts will not permit the public body to plead the fettering of discretion principle in order for it to be released from its obligations. The decision of the House of Lords in *Birkdale District Electric Supply Co Ltd* v *Southport Corporation* [1926] AC 355 is instructive. In 1901 the company, a statutory body, took over the local electricity supply from Birkdale Urban District Council and agreed, under seal, that the prices charged by it to private customers should not exceed those charged in an adjoining area by Southport Corporation. In 1911 Birkdale Urban District Council became a part of Southport Corporation. The company continued to supply electricity to the area. In 1923 the Corporation applied for an injunction to restrain the company from charging prices in excess of the Southport prices. The company argued that since it had a statutory power to charge what it wished, within certain limits, the 1901 agreement was invalid as an unlawful fetter on the exercise of this discretion. The House of Lords held that, far from being an unlawful fetter on the statutory body's discretion, the agreement was of a type that was commonly entered into by commercial bodies. The case could only begin to be equated with *Ayr Harbour Trustees* v *Oswald* (above) if the statutory body had, for example, entered into a contract not to generate electricity. In *Dowty Boulton Paul Ltd* v *Wolverhampton Corporation* [1971] 1 WLR 204 the local authority, having leased land to the plaintiff company in 1935 for 99 years, decided, in 1970, that it wanted to repossess the land in order to build housing. The plaintiff company argued that the lease was a valid contractual undertaking by which the local authority was bound. The court agreed, describing the suggestion of the local authority that the lease was subject to an implied condition enabling it to determine the lease at will as startling.

A local authority may not be bound by a commercial undertaking which, whilst not being incompatible with its other functions, goes too far in committing it to a particular course of action. In *York Corporation* v *Henry Leetham & Sons Ltd* [1924] 1 Ch 557 the plaintiff corporation was entrusted by statute with the control of navigation in parts of the Rivers Ouse and Foss, with power to charge such tolls, within limits, as the corporation deemed necessary to carry on the two navigations in which the public had an interest. The Corporation made two contracts with the defendants under which they agreed to accept, in consideration of the right to navigate the Ouse, a regular annual payment of £600 per annum in place of the authorised tolls. The agreements, which were perpetually renewable at the request of the defendants, were held by Russell J to be ultra vires, and thus void, because they purported to disable the Corporation, whatever emergency might arise, from exercising its statutory powers to increase tolls as from time to time might be necessary.

Further, a local authority cannot, by means of a commercial contractual undertaking, be prevented from exercising its legislative powers in the public interest. In *William Cory & Sons Ltd* v *London Corporation* [1951] 2 KB 476 the authority had entered into an agreement with the plaintiff company under which refuse would be transported in barges down the Thames. When the contract still had 20 years to run, the Corporation passed new bye-laws introducing more rigorous hygiene controls over refuse carried in open barges. The effect was to make the contract less profitable because modifications had to be made to the barges used by the plaintiffs in performance of the contract. The court held that it could not imply a term into the agreement to the effect that the Corporation would refrain from enacting legislation making the contract more onerous to perform. Such a term would have clearly been ultra vires.

Ultimately the courts are engaged in a balancing exercise, weighing the aims and objects of the relevant legislation on the one hand, with the need to ensure that public bodies have sufficient freedom to act as they think fit on the other. *R v Hammersmith and Fulham London Borough Council, ex parte Beddowes* [1987] 2 WLR 263 provides an excellent example of how controversial the court's assessment of where the balance lies can be. The Court of Appeal upheld, by a majority, negative covenants entered into by the council which prevented it from re-letting council flats to council tenants when they fell empty. The purpose of the covenants was to encourage owner-occupation of blocks of flats on derelict council estates. Fox LJ stated that the council's housing duty had to be considered in the light of the 'right to buy' legislation that had recently been introduced. His Lordship felt that this legislation indicated that a local authority might discharge its housing function by encouraging owner-occupation as well as by acting as a landlord, and that the courts had to be sympathetic to the efforts of a local authority attempting to take radical action to deal with a 'problem estate'. Hence the court held that the covenants did not amount to an unlawful fetter on the council's discretion, in that they were not incompatible with its housing powers and duties.

9.5 Estoppel

Reliance on estoppel to prevent a statutory body from exercising its public law powers gives rise to a particular difficulty in administrative law. An inferior body makes a promise to act in a particular way. The promisee relies on this statement and in most cases acts to his detriment on the strength of it. It is then discovered that what has been promised is beyond the power of the inferior body. The choice for the courts is a stark one between adherence to the ultra vires principle and unfairness to the promisee on the one hand, and holding that the inferior body is estopped from going back on its promise and in fact ordering it to act beyond its powers on the other.

Two situations may arise, both variants on the same theme. The first where the administrative body purports to exercise a power it simply does not possess. The second where the body does possess the power, but promises to use it in a manner that would be ultra vires.

Where no power exists

The basic principle here is that estoppel cannot operate so as to enable an authority to do that which it lacks the power to do, otherwise inferior bodies could acquire limitless jurisdiction by making promises to carry out acts beyond their powers.

In *Balbir Singh* v *Secretary of State for the Home Department* [1978] Imm AR 204, it was held that an immigrant did not acquire the right to appeal against a tribunal's decision simply because the Secretary of State's statement said that such a right existed. The right of appeal could only be provided by statute, and it was clearly beyond the powers of the Minister to confer such a right. Similarly, in *Islington Vestry* v *Hornsey Urban District Council* [1900] 1 Ch 695, a local authority which had permitted a neighbouring authority to use its sewers, despite the absence of any power to allow this, was not estopped from terminating this use, despite the reliance of the plaintiffs.

Where power does exist

The alternative problem arises where an inferior body does possess a power (eg to grant planning permission) but promises to use that power in a manner that would be ultra vires. *Southend-on-Sea Corporation* v *Hodgson (Wickford) Ltd* [1962] 1 QB 416 provides an example. The company wished to buy land for use as a builders' yard and, after making inquiries, was assured by the local authority surveyor that planning permission was not needed for such a use because of existing use rights. The company purchased the land, and started to use it as a builders' yard, only to be served with an enforcement notice ordering it to stop such use, the local planning authority claiming that planning permission had not been granted. The Divisional Court held that the local authority could not be estopped from issuing an enforcement notice by the surveyor's assurances, as this would be to prevent them using their powers for the benefit of their inhabitants generally. The decision represents the traditional approach of strict adherence to the ultra vires principle. The unauthorised representation of an official cannot bind an inferior body to act beyond its powers, to refrain from performing a statutory duty, or from exercising its discretion in the public interest. Notwithstanding the clear statement of principle that this case represented, a number of decision during the late 1960s and early 1970s suggested a more indulgent approach.

For example, in *Wells* v *MHLG* [1967] 2 All ER 1041 the plaintiff applied for planning permission, and received a letter from the local authority's surveyor stating that permission was not required for the development proposed. The building work was carried out by Wells, and evoked complaints from neighbours about its effect on the area. The local authority thereupon served an enforcement notice upon Wells claiming that he did not have planning permission for the works. The Court of Appeal held that although the precise statutory procedure had not been followed, the letter from the surveyor amounted to a determination by the authority that planning permission was not necessary under s53 Town and Country Planning Act 1971. The decision is clear authority for the view that a statutory body cannot waive minor procedural requirements, and then claim that it is not obliged to abide by its undertakings because precise statutory procedural requirements have not been followed.

In *Lever Finance Ltd* v *Westminster (City) London Borough Council* [1971] 1 QB 222 the company was granted planning permission to build a group of houses which, according to the plans, showed the development as being at least 40 feet away from the nearest existing building. During the course of construction, minor modifications were made to the plans, and on each occasion the local authority planning officer gave his approval on the nod (ie informally). When the development was nearing completion it became obvious that the sum total of the minor modifications was considerable. The new houses were now only 23 feet away from the nearest existing buildings. Neighbours complained and the company was advised to apply for formal planning permission for the changes. This was refused by the local authority. The company sought a declaration that it was entitled to continue with the work, the local authority being estopped by the actions of its planning officer. The Court of Appeal held that in the light of the fact that it was common practice for the planning officers to agree minor modifications to planning permission already granted, and the fact that the company had acted to its detriment on the strength of his statement, the local authority would be bound by its officer's decision. The Court of Appeal clearly considered it unfair that a member of the public might not otherwise be able to rely on statements made by council officers within the scope of their ostensible authority. But consider also the damage done to the interests of neighbouring land owners. By upholding an estoppel, the Court of Appeal prevented the local authority from exercising its planning powers in the best interest of its area and inhabitants.

This approach was developed further in *Western Fish Products Ltd* v *Penwith District Council* [1981] 2 All ER 204. In April 1976 the plaintiffs purchased a site that had previously been used for food processing, intending to develop the site for similar purposes. The chairman of the plaintiff company, in reply to his enquiries, received a letter from a planning officer of the defendant authority stating that the site had existing use rights for the various food processes the plaintiffs intended to carry out. As a result the plaintiff company carried out extensive work on the site, renovating and modifying the factory buildings thereon. Some months later the plaintiffs were asked to apply for planning permission for this work. At a full council meeting, this application was rejected, and enforcement notices issued. The plaintiffs then sought declarations that the defendant authority was not entitled to issue the enforcement notices in the light of its planning officer's statement. The Court of Appeal upheld the decision of the court below to dismiss the action. In the course of his decision Megaw LJ confirmed that the council's officers could not bind the authority by purporting to take decisions that only the council itself could take. To hold otherwise would be to run counter to the accepted principle that an estoppel could not be raised to prevent the exercise of a statutory discretion or to prevent or excuse the performance of a statutory duty. A local authority could, by s101 Local Government Act 1972, arrange for the discharge of its functions by, inter alia, its officers, but this had to be formally agreed within the authority. In the *Western Fish* case, the function of determining applications for planning permission had not been delegated to planning officers, and his Lordship saw no reason why the plaintiffs should ever have thought that the council's planning officer could bind the authority by anything said or written in this regard. Where a planning officer acts within the scope of the power properly delegated to him his actions will bind the authority for whom he acts but, beyond that, it could not be said that an authority would be bound by the actions of its officers, simply because they acted within the scope of their ostensible authority (ie the officers appeared to be entitled to take such decisions). In his Lordship's view, for estoppel to arise in this situation:

'... there must be some evidence justifying the person dealing with the planning officer for thinking that what the officer said would bind the planning authority. Holding an office, however senior, cannot, in our judgment, be enough by itself.'

The evidence required could be of a previous course of conduct whereby officers had in the past carried out functions on behalf of the local authority, with the authority's knowledge and approval, despite the formal delegation of functions not having been carried out. In the case of Penwith District Council, there was no evidence to suggest that the planning officer could determine applications for planning permission.

The natural justice argument

With the courts willing to recognise the operation of estoppel in only a very limited range of situations in public law, applicants have sought to challenge decisions on the grounds of breach of natural justice. In *R* v *Liverpool Corporation, ex parte LTFOA* [1972] 2 QB 299 Lord Denning MR was of the view that a local authority should be bound by a public undertaking given to taxi drivers within its area to the effect that only a limited number of new taxi licences would be granted, regarding the obligation to abide by the undertaking as virtually contractual. Similar thoughts were expressed by Hidden J in *R* v *North and East Devon Health Authority, ex parte Coughlan* [2001] QB 213, where a health authority had given oral assurances to the applicant to the effect that a home for the severely disabled, to which she was being moved, would be a 'home for life'. Describing the assurance as a 'clear promise' he was of the view that breaking the promise, if unfair to the applicant, was equivalent to a breach of contract. The court expressed the view that the health authority could only be permitted to resile from its undertaking if there was an overriding public interest demand that it should do so. No such public interest had been established by the authority, hence its decision was quashed. Although the courts in these cases refer to the issue of contractual liability, it is perhaps better to view them as cases concerning the observance of natural justice. Assurances can give rise to a legitimate expectation as to the way in which a public body will exercise its discretion. Failure to act as promised may result in unfairness: see further *Attorney-General of Hong Kong* v *Ng Yuen Shiu* [1983] 2 AC 629; *R* v *IRC, ex parte Preston* [1985] AC 835; and comments of Taylor LJ in *R* v *Secretary of State for Health, ex parte United States Tobacco International Inc* [1991] 3 WLR 529.

The issue of fairness may also be relevant were an individual faces the prospect of a criminal conviction having complied with advice given by public officials. In *Postermobile plc* v *Brent London Borough Council* (1997) The Times 8 December the appellant company met with planning officers employed by the respondent authority and were told that planning permission would not be required in respect of a number of temporary hoardings. Once the advertisement hoardings were erected the authority commenced proceedings against the appellants for displaying advertisements without obtaining the necessary planning consents. Following conviction, the appellants stated a case for consideration by the Divisional Court to the effect that, given the advice of the respondent's officers, it was an abuse of process to proceed with the prosecutions. Allowing the appeal, the Divisional Court held that the appellants had been correct to rely on the advice given. Expressing the view that, as a general principle, citizens should be able to rely on the statements of public officials, Schiemann LJ observed that it was not as if the appellants had sought advice on the matter from one of the council's gardeners. He went on to distinguish the case from *Western Fish Products* v *Penwith District Council* on the basis that that case had been concerned with permanent planning permission, whereas the case before him was concerned with temporary permission (ie one month or less). As regards the loss resulting from having to curtail the advertising campaign, would the appellants have an action in tort against the local authority based on negligent advice? See *Lambert* v *West Devon Borough Council* (1997) The Times 27 March.

The present position

The most recent decision of the House of Lords in this area suggests a severing of links between the private law concept of estoppel and the application of that doctrine to public law bodies taking public law decisions. In *R* v *East Sussex County Council, ex parte Reprotech Ltd* [2002] 4 All ER 58, where the House of Lords refused to accept that a local planning authority was estopped from requiring the claimants to apply for planning permission of the change of use of a waste treatment plant, Lord Hoffmann observed:

> '... I think that it is unhelpful to introduce private law concepts of estoppel into planning law. As Lord Scarman pointed out in *Newbury District Council* v *Secretary of State for the Environment; Newbury District Council* v *International Synthetic Rubber Co Ltd* [1981] AC 578 at 616, estoppels bind individuals on the ground that it would be unconscionable for them to deny what they have represented or agreed. But these concepts of private law

should not be extended into "the public law of planning control, which binds everyone" ... There is of course an analogy between a private law estoppel and the public law concept of a legitimate expectation created by a public authority, the denial of which may amount to an abuse of power (see *R* v *North and East Devon Health Authority, ex parte Coughlan (Secretary of State for Health Intervening)* [2001] QB 213). But it is no more than an analogy because remedies against public authorities also have to take into account the interests of the general public which the authority exists to promote. Public law can also take into account the hierarchy of individual rights which exist under the Human Rights Act 1998, so that, for example, the individual's right to a home is accorded a high degree of protection ... while ordinary property rights are in general far more limited by considerations of public interest ... It is true that in early cases such as *Well's* case and *Lever (Finance) Ltd* v *Westminster Corporation* [1971] 1 QB 222, Lord Denning MR used the language of estoppel in relation to planning law. At that time the public law concepts of abuse of power and legitimate expectation were very undeveloped and no doubt the analogy of estoppel seemed useful. In the *Western Fish* case the Court of Appeal tried its best to reconcile these invocations of estoppel with the general principle that a public authority cannot be estopped from exercising a statutory discretion or performing a public duty. But the results did not give universal satisfaction ... It seems to me that in this area, public law has already absorbed whatever is useful from the moral values which underlie the private law concept of estoppel and the time has come for it to stand upon its own two feet.'

It remains to be seen to what extent the courts adopt this reasoning as a basis for excluding the operation of estoppel.

Directory procedural requirements

One other situation in which an estoppel may be upheld arises where, for example, a planning authority waives a (directory) procedural requirement. As in *Wells* v *MHLG* (above), the authority will not be allowed to later claim that a grant of permission, or other determination, is invalid on these grounds. See further the House of Lords' decision in *Gowa* v *Attorney-General* [1985] 1 WLR 1003, where the Crown was estopped from denying an applicant's status as a British citizen even though it was granted in error by a colonial governor empowered to deal with such matters; and see *Minister of Agriculture and Fisheries* v *Hulkin* (unreported), cited in *Minister of Agriculture and Fisheries* v *Matthews* [1950] KB 148, at pp153–154.

10

The Application for Judicial Review

10.1 Control of power

The constitutional basis for administrative law, as will have been seen from Chapter 1, is the control of executive power. To this extent it can be seen as a manifestation of both the separation of powers (the judiciary reviewing the executive) and the rule of law (the concept that the executive is not above the law, but subject to it).

The mechanism by which that judicial control of executive power is put in train is normally the application for judicial review. The essence of judicial review is that an 'inferior' body (other expressions employed include subordinate body; administrative body, or administrative agency) has acted outside the scope of its power. The expressions used are:

- 'intra vires' – within its powers;
- 'ultra vires' – beyond its powers.

Because the powers (or jurisdiction) of these bodies are limited by reference to the terms of the statutes, royal charters, or prerogative orders, under which they are created, they can be referred to as 'bodies of limited jurisdiction'. Following the Court of Appeal's decision in *R* v *Panel on Take-overs and Mergers, ex parte Datafin plc* [1987] 2 WLR 699, it is arguable that the scope of judicial review has been extended to any 'entity' having de facto power to take decisions that affect the public. This matter is considered below at section 10.4.

252

10.2 When should judicial review be used?

Section 31(1) of the Supreme Court Act 1981 provides:

> '(1) An application to the High Court for one or more of the following forms of relief, namely –
> (a) an order of mandamus, prohibition or certiorari;
> (b) a declaration or injunction under subs(2) ...
> shall be made in accordance with rules of court by a procedure to be known as an application for judicial review.
> (2) A declaration may be made or an injunction granted under this subsection in any case where an application for judicial review, seeking that relief, has been made and the High Court considers that, having regard to –
> (a) the nature of the matters in respect of which relief may be granted by orders of mandamus, prohibition or certiorari;
> (b) the nature of the persons and bodies against whom relief may be granted by such orders; and
> (c) all the circumstances of the case,
> it would be just and convenient for the declaration to be made or the injunction to be granted, as the case may be.'

These provisions make it clear that where one of the prerogative orders is sought, judicial review must be used. Where one of the private law remedies of injunction or declaration is sought, judicial review may be used. The relevant procedural rules were to be found in the Rules of the Supreme Court (RSC) O.53: they are now to be found in the Civil Procedure Rules (CPR) 1998, Pt 54.

To understand the significance of these provisions it is necessary to look back at what the law relating to procedure in judicial review cases was prior to 1977.

Pre-1977

Traditionally there were two ways in which the actions of administrative agencies could be challenged.

Private law
An action started by writ, or originating summons, in the plaintiff's own name. The advantages were: flexible time limits, availability of discovery, no requirement to obtain the leave of the court to proceed. Remedies available were damages, declaration, and injunction.

Public law
An application had to be made for a prerogative order. Problems were the short time limits for bringing an application, locus standi requirements, unavailability of discovery, interrogation or cross-examination of deponents, and inflexibility regarding remedies.

Processes compared

Note the essential difference between proceeding by way of action and the application for judicial review. In the former the plaintiff was bringing the action in his own name. Hence the citation of such cases: *Ridge v Baldwin; Anisminic Ltd v Foreign Compensation Commission*. In the latter case the applicant seeking one of the prerogative orders, either certiorari, mandamus or prohibition, did so with the leave of the Crown, hence the citation in such cases: *R v Home Secretary, ex parte Santillo*. Today the citation would be *R (On the Application of Santillo) v Home Secretary*.

The 1977 reforms and their effects

The former procedure for applying for the prerogative orders was entirely replaced in 1977 with a reformed procedure for applying for judicial review, introduced by way of statutory instrument RSC (Amendment No 3) 1977 (SI 1977/1955). These changes were largely the result of recommendations made by the Law Commission in its *Report on Remedies in Administrative Law* (Law Com No 73, Cmnd 6407 (1976)). The effect of the changes was to substantially reduce the procedural handicaps imposed upon applicants for judicial review, and these reforms were later given the status of changes in substantive law by being enshrined in s31 of the Supreme Court Act 1981.

Initially it was thought that RSC O.53 had simply made the procedure for obtaining judicial review less burdensome, and if a plaintiff nevertheless still preferred to proceed by way of writ and seek damages, a declaration or an injunction against a public body he was free to do so. In a number of decisions, however, the courts began to question whether or not a plaintiff's proceeding by way of action, when judicial review would have been available, was an abuse of the processes of the court: see, for example, *Barrs v Bethell* [1981] 3 WLR 874 and *Re Tillmire Common, Heslington* [1982] 2 All ER 615.

The major decision on this issue came when the House of Lords gave its ruling in *O'Reilly v Mackman* [1983] 2 AC 237. The appellants were prisoners serving long sentences of imprisonment, who issued writs and originating summonses against members of the Board of Visitors of Hull Prison, seeking declarations that the disciplinary awards of forfeiture of remission made by the Board were null and void on the ground of breach of natural justice. The House of Lords held that the appellants had no private law rights as regards the Board, only a public law right to be given a fair hearing. Further, the Board was a public law body, deriving its status and powers from statute. As a result, it would be an abuse of the court's processes to proceed by way of action to challenge the Board's determinations. Hence the appellants should have proceeded by way of RSC O.53 to challenge the decision of the Board, although the time limit for applying for review had expired by the time the House of Lords handed down its decision.

The reasoning in O'Reilly v Mackman

Lord Diplock considered the problems associated with judicial review prior to 1977 and the changes instituted as a result of the Law Commission's Report, and concluded that many of the procedural handicaps that would previously have led a complainant to avoid having to apply for a prerogative order if at all possible, had since been removed. Specific improvements were:

1. discovery was now available;
2. interrogatories could now be administered;
3. deponents could now be cross-examined on affidavits;
4. a claim for damages could be added to the application;
5. a declaration, or injunction could now be included in an application for review.

The result was that there were no longer any compelling reasons for permitting a plaintiff to proceed by way of action in a public law matter. Further, there were sound policy reasons for insisting that RSC O.53 be used where the respondent was a public body, because of the procedural provided safeguards. Applications for review had to be made without delay, usually within three months of the action complained of; compare this with the six-year time limit on proceeding by way of action. It was important that a public body should know quickly of any significant challenge to the legality of its actions in public law so that third party interests were not adversely affected.

The requirement that those seeking review should have to possess 'sufficient interest' in the matter to which their application relates, and should have to obtain leave to apply for review, provided an important 'filter' of cases against public bodies. By the very nature of their activities such bodies were likely to attract the attention of 'cranks and busybodies'. If such persons were allowed to proceed by way of writ the defendant body would be put to the expense of instructing lawyers to put in a defence, no matter how worthless the allegation. The requirement of leave ensured that no participation from the respondent body was required until a prima facie case for review had been made out by the applicant.

The exceptions

From the foregoing it appeared that every case involving a public law body and a public law issue now had to be brought by way of RSC O.53. In his speech, however, Lord Diplock did contemplate exceptional situations where an action by writ would be allowed:

> 'My Lords, I have described this as a general rule; for, though it may normally be appropriate to apply it by the summary process of striking out the action, there may be exceptions, particularly where the invalidity of the decision arises as a collateral issue in a claim for infringement of a right of the plaintiff arising under private law, or where none of the parties objects to the adoption of the procedure by writ or originating summons.

Whether there should be other exceptions should, in my view, at this stage in the development of procedural public law, be left to be decided on a case to case basis.'

10.3 Public law and private law – making the distinction

As a result of the decision in *O'Reilly* v *Mackman* the choice of procedure became crucial for many litigants. The problem was that the correct choice of procedure rested in turn on being able to determine whether or not a decision-making body was public or private, or whether the issue of law arising was one of public law or private law. This proved troublesome because, as Lord Wilberforce memorably stated in *Davy* v *Spelthorne Borough Council* [1984] AC 262:

> 'The expressions "private law" and "public law" have recently been imported into the law of England from countries which, unlike our own, have separate systems concerning public law and private law. No doubt they are convenient expressions for descriptive purposes. In this country they must be used with caution, for typically, English law fastens not on principles but on remedies. The principle remains intact that public authorities and public servants are, unless clearly exempted, answerable in the ordinary courts for wrongs done to individuals. But by an extension of remedies and a flexible procedure, it can be said that something resembling a system of public law is being developed. Before the expression "public law" can be used to deny a subject a right of action in the court of his choice it must be related to a positive prescription of law, by statute or by statutory rules. We have not yet reached the point at which mere characterisation of a claim as a claim in public law is sufficient to exclude it from consideration by the ordinary courts; to permit this would be to create a dual system of law with the rigidity and procedural hardship for plaintiffs which it was the purpose of the recent reforms to remove.'

Similarly, in *Mercury Communications Ltd* v *Director General of Telecommunications* [1996] 1 WLR 48, Lord Slynn observed that:

> 'The precise limits of what is called "public law" and what is called "private law" are by no means worked out ... the working out of this distinction is not always an easy matter ... some flexibility as to the use of different procedures is necessary.'

10.4 Public law body – source of powers or functions test?

Lord Diplock's speech in *O'Reilly* v *Mackman* might be taken to suggest that a public body is one that derives its powers from statute, or at least the prerogative. In practice the courts have not adopted such a narrow view. The tendency has been to look at the functions discharged by the decision-making body with a view to assessing whether or not those functions have qualities that mark them out as those associated with a public body.

Partly as a result of moves towards deregulation, privatisation and the promotion of self-regulation, important powers are wielded by bodies that are not statutory in origin. Some derive their power from private contracts, some merely exercise de facto power only. The challenge for the courts has been to determine whether or not the concept of the public law body could be developed to encompass such decision-makers.

In this respect, the Court of Appeal's decision in *R v Panel on Take-overs and Mergers, ex parte Datafin plc* [1987] 2 WLR 699 is of crucial significance. It was held that the Panel was a body subject to review, even though it exercised no statutory or prerogative powers, and was not even based on a private contract or constitution. As the Master of the Rolls observed, it possessed no visible means of legal support. The court held that the Panel's functions were amenable to review, however, on the basis of the enormous de facto power it possessed to take decisions affecting the public and, significantly, the fact that there was no other means by which those affected by the decisions of the Panel could have challenged them in the courts.

The overriding issue here is one of control, ie the scope of the court's supervisory jurisdiction by way of judicial review. Once the court determines that the decision-making body should be brought within the scope of judicial review because, for example, of the inadequacy of other means of control, or the effect of its decisions, it follows that the decision-making body has to be classified as a public law body, as these are the only decision-makers that are amenable to judicial review.

This 'functionalist' approach (ie determining that a body is amenable to judicial review because of what it does, not the source of its powers) can be illustrated by a number of subsequent decisions.

1. *R v Ethical Committee of St Mary's Hospital, ex parte Harriot* (1987) The Times 27 October: the court held, apparently without any detailed consideration of the point, that an ad hoc committee comprised of professionals working at the hospital in question could be made subject to judicial review, where it was determining whether a patient should be permitted to undergo in vitro fertilisation treatment. The decision arguably illustrates both the 'functionalist' basis for review and the 'residual' basis for review, ie the absence of any other means of challenge.

2. *Bank of Scotland, Petitioner* (1988) The Times 21 November: the court held that the Investment Management Regulatory Organisation (IMRO), despite being a self regulatory body, established in the wake of the Financial Services Act 1986 as a company limited by guarantee, was nevertheless a body amenable to judicial review. The court confirmed that the determining factor when assessing the reviewability of such a body should be the public nature of its functions, rather that its legal character or constitution; this was true even where the action complained of allegedly took the form of a breach of contractual obligations.

3. *Scott v National Trust* [1998] 2 All ER 705: Robert Walker J confirmed that the National Trust could be a public law body for the purposes of judicial review because:

> 'The way in [which charitable bodies] exercise their powers and discretions may affect directly or indirectly many different sections of the public; and even members of the general public who are not personally affected financially or otherwise in any way, may still have very strong and sincerely held views about the rights or wrongs of decisions, whether by a charity or a local authority on a subject such as hunting. The court has jurisdiction to prevent misuse of public powers ... by judicial review ... the National Trust is a charity of exceptional importance to the nation, regulated by its own special Acts of Parliament. Its purposes and functions are of high public importance, as is reflected by the special statutory provisions (in the fields of taxation and compulsory acquisition) to which I have already referred. It seems to me to have all the characteristics of a public body which is, prima facie, amenable to judicial review, and to have been exercising its statutory public functions in making the decision which is challenged.'

4. *R* v *Advertising Standards Authority Ltd, ex parte The Insurance Service plc* (1989) 2 Admin LR 77: the Advertising Standards Authority Ltd (the ASA) was held to be amenable to judicial review, Glidewell LJ indicating that it exhibited many similarities with the Panel on Take-overs and Mergers. Like the Panel, it had no statutory or common law powers, although unlike the Panel it did have legal identity derived from its status as a company under the Companies Acts. The determining factors were: (a) if the ASA had not discharged the function of regulating the advertising industry, the task would almost certainly have been discharged by the Director General of Fair Trading. (b) There was no provision in the memorandum or articles of association of the ASA for any appeal against its rulings; (c) a ruling by the ASA that an advertisement was in breach of the code of advertising practice resulted in it being almost impossible for a company to continue with its campaign; and (d) the regulation of advertising was now supported by legislation in the form of the Control of Misleading Advertisements Regulations (SI 1988/915), implementing European Council Directive 84/450/EEC. The court seems to have been motivated to intervene here, partly on the basis that there was no other means of challenge, and partly because of the power exerted by the ASA, but note the importance attached to the 'governmental' nature of the functions.

5. *R* v *Football Association, ex parte Football League* [1993] 2 All ER 833: the Football League sought to challenge by way of judicial review the decision of the Football Association to form a Premier League and introduce consequent changes to its regulations. The Football League, which had a contractual agreement with the Football Association whereby it was permitted each year to operate the leagues, contended that the Football Association was amenable to review because it exercised monopoly control over the game and controlled the rules governing it. Dismissing the application, the court held that the Football Association was not discharging functions of a governmental nature and there was no evidence that its functions would be exercised by a governmental body if it did not exist.

6. *R* v *Disciplinary Committee of the Jockey Club, ex parte The Aga Khan* [1993] 1 WLR 909: Hoffmann and Farquharson LJJ felt that the Jockey Club fell outside

the scope of judicial review because its members agreed to be bound by its rules and it was thus to be regarded as a domestic body acting by consent. Sir Thomas Bingham MR refused to accept that the Jockey Club met the requirements of a public body for the purposes of review, because:

> '... [it] has not been woven into any system of governmental control of horse-racing ... while the ... Club's powers may be described as, in many ways, public, they are in no sense governmental ...'

As regards the question of whether or not the Jockey Club would ever be regarded as a public body for the purposes of review, Sir Thomas Bingham MR observed:

> 'Cases where the applicant ... has no contract on which to rely may raise different considerations and the existence or non-existence of alternative remedies may then be material.'

7. *R* v *Insurance Ombudsman Bureau and the Insurance Ombudsman, ex parte Aegon Life* (1994) The Independent 11 January: Rose LJ, declined to exercise the court's reviewing jurisdiction in respect of the Insurance Ombudsman on the basis that, even though such a person might be exercising governmental functions, the source of his jurisdiction was nevertheless the consensus of others to be bound by his findings. He observed:

> ' ... when Sir Thomas Bingham MR [in *The Aga Khan* case] spoke of the Jockey Club not being "woven into any system of governmental control" I do not accept that he was thereby indicating that such interweaving was in itself determinative ... the [Insurance Ombudsman Bureau's] power over its members is [despite the Financial Services Act 1986], solely derived from contract and it simply cannot be said that it exercises government functions. In a nutshell, even if it can be said that it has now been woven into a governmental system, the source of its power is still contractual.'

What then is the key issue? The function discharged? The absence of any other means of obtaining a remedy? The 'governmental' nature of the activity? At present it is a question that defies a simplistic answer. As Ognall J observed in *R* v *Legal Aid Board, ex parte Donn & Co* [1996] 3 All ER 1, a case concerned with the reviewability of a Legal Aid Board local committee's rejection of a tender from a firm of solicitors:

> 'The answer must, it seems to me, fall to be decided as one of overall impression, and one of degree. There can be no universal test ... I believe that the function exercised by [the local legal aid committee] ... the purpose for which they were empowered to act and the consequences of their decision-making processes, all demand the conclusion that it would be wrong to characterise this matter as one of private law. Even if there were to be arguably some private law remedy, or whether there is none, I am satisfied that, quite independently, the public dimensions of this matter are of a quality which make it justiciable in public law.'

Note that Ognall J was not persuaded to his conclusion merely by the existence of the statutory underpinning in this case, but also by the fact that the Legal Aid Board, through the local committee, was dispensing large sums of public money, and acted as the final arbiter (in the sense that it had a monopoly of jurisdiction) of the issue before it. On this basis, it is submitted, the decision in *ex parte The Aga Khan* is perhaps open to further questioning given that the court in that case was willing to concede that the Jockey Club enjoyed a virtual monopoly over the regulation of a significant national activity, exercised powers that affected the public, and appeared to accept that if the Jockey Club did not exist to carry out its functions the government would probably have created a public body for the purpose.

If decisions such as *Law* v *National Greyhound Racing Club Ltd* [1983] 3 All ER 300, *R* v *Disciplinary Committee of the Jockey Club, ex parte Massingberd Mundy* [1993] 2 All ER 207 and *R* v *Jockey Club, ex parte RAM Racecourses Ltd* [1992] 2 All ER 225, as well as those in *ex parte Aegon Life* and *ex parte The Aga Khan* are to be taken as indicative of the correct approach they mark a return to the 'source of power' test in determining reviewability. Suppose that the applicant in *ex parte The Aga Khan* had not been in a contractual relationship with the club, would that have been enough to persuade the court to exercise its reviewing powers? Why should the existence or otherwise of a contract determine the nature of the decision-making body? According to the court the club's functions would still not have been 'woven into any system of governmental control'. Such an approach is regrettable in that it seriously undermines the significance of *ex parte Datafin*, where it was the nature of the power being exercised and the presence or otherwise of any statutory underpinning that was regarded as more important. It is submitted that it would be better for the courts to claim supervisory jurisdiction on the basis of the 'functionalist' approach, as expounded in *ex parte Datafin*, but to decline to exercise it when an alternative remedy, such as the right to sue for breach of contract, was available.

Human Rights Act 1998

Section 6 of the Human Rights Act 1998 provides that public bodies are under a duty to uphold Convention rights. The only clue given to the meaning of the term 'public body' as it is used in this provision (beyond confirmation that it includes courts and tribunals) is that a public authority will include 'any person certain of whose functions are functions of a public nature' (s6(3)).

In *Poplar Housing and Regeneration Community Association Ltd* v *Donoghue* [2001] 4 All ER 604 the Court of Appeal had to consider whether or not a housing association, empowered by a local authority to discharge some of its housing obligations, was a public body bound by the provisions of the 1998 Act. Lord Woolf CJ observed:

> 'The purpose of s6(3)(b) is to deal with hybrid bodies which have both public and private functions. It is not to make a body, which does not have responsibilities to the public, a public body merely because it performs acts on behalf of a public body which would

constitute public functions were such acts to be performed by the public body itself ... while s6 of the 1998 Act requires a generous interpretation of who is a public authority, it is clearly inspired by the approach developed by the courts in identifying the bodies and activities subject to judicial review ... What can make an act, which would otherwise be private, public, is a feature or a combination of features which impose a public character or stamp on the act ... The more closely the acts that could be of a private nature are enmeshed in the activities of a public body, the more likely they are to be public. However, the fact that the acts are supervised by a public regulatory body does not necessarily indicate that they are of a public nature. This is analogous to the position in judicial review, where a regulatory body may be deemed public but the activities of the body which is regulated may be categorised private.'

On the facts he regarded the closeness of the relationship which existed between the local authority and the housing association, and the fact that the association had been set up by the authority, as key factors leading to the conclusion that the association fell within the scope of s6(1). He went on to emphasise, however, that as with applications for judicial review, there was no clear demarcation line to be drawn between public and private bodies and functions – in borderline cases the decision is very much one of fact and degree.

He returned to the issue in *R (On the Application of Heather and Another)* v *Leonard Cheshire Foundation* [2002] 2 All ER 936. The Leonard Cheshire Foundation (LCF) provided residential care home accommodation on behalf of a local authority. The claimants sought judicial review of the decision of the LCF to close one of its homes. It was contended, inter alia, that the decision would violate the claimants' art 8 rights, thus raising the issue of whether the LCF was bound by the European Convention on Human Rights. Explaining that the concept of 'public body' for the purposes of a Human Rights Act 1998 claim was not necessarily co-terminus with the concept as developed for the purposes of judicial review in domestic law, he observed:

'As is appropriately set out in Grosz, Beatson and Duffy, *Human Rights: The 1998 Act and the European Convention* (2000) p61, as to the relationship between the scope of the 1998 Act and the scope of judicial review:

"The law on the scope of judicial review cannot, however, be determinative. First, it will be necessary for the English courts to take into account the Strasbourg jurisprudence which identifies the bodies whose actions engage the responsibility of the state for the purpose of the Convention, which, as we shall see, differs from the judicial review criteria in material respects. That jurisprudence also makes clear that the Convention's reach is determined by reference to 'autonomous' concepts of Convention law and not by the manner in which national law classifies bodies or their acts. Secondly, notwithstanding the Home Secretary's statement that 'the concepts are reasonably clear', the way English courts have drawn the distinction between 'public' and 'private' for the purpose of judicial review produced a complicated and not altogether consistent body of cases, using a variety of tests. Thirdly, as will be seen, not all the acts of 'obvious' public authorities are treated as 'public' for the purposes of judicial review. In contrast, the [Human Rights Act 1998] will apply to all their acts. Nevertheless, the case law on the judicial review jurisdiction is instructive".'

Referring to *Poplar Housing and Regeneration Community Association Ltd* v *Donoghue*, and in particular the factors that led the Court in that case to conclude that the housing association was performing a public function, he concluded:

'If this were a situation where a local authority could divest itself of its art 8 obligations by contracting out to a voluntary sector provider its obligations [to provide accommodation under the National Assistance Act 1948] then there would be a responsibility on the court to approach the interpretation of s6(3)(b) [of the Human Rights Act 1998] in a way which ensures, so far as this is possible, that the rights under art 8 of persons in the position of the appellants are protected. This is not, however, the situation. The local authority remains under an obligation under ... the 1948 Act and retains an obligation under art 8 to the appellants even though it has used its powers under [the 1948 Act] to use LCF as a provider. In addition the appellants have their contractual rights against LCF in any event. There is also the possible protection which can be provided by the Attorney-General's role but this is not a significant factor.

... In our judgment the role that LCF was performing manifestly did not involve the performance of public functions. The fact that LCF is a large and flourishing organisation does not change the nature of its activities from private to public. (i) It is not in issue that it is possible for LCF to perform some public functions and some private functions. In this case it is contended that this was what has been happening in regard to those residents who are privately funded and those residents who are publicly funded. But in this case ... there is no material distinction between the nature of the services LCF has provided for residents funded by a local authority and those provided to residents funded privately. While the degree of public funding of the activities of an otherwise private body is certainly relevant as to the nature of the functions performed, by itself it is not determinative of whether the functions are public or private ... (ii) There is no other evidence of there being a public flavour to the functions of LCF or LCF itself. LCF is not standing in the shoes of the local authorities. Section 26 of the 1948 Act provides statutory authority for the actions of the local authorities but it provides LCF with no powers. LCF is not exercising statutory powers in performing functions for the appellants. (iii) In truth, all that [counsel for the claimants] can rely upon is the fact that if LCF is not performing a public function the appellants would not be able to rely upon art 8 as against LCF. However, this is a circular argument. If LCF was performing a public function, that would mean that the appellants could rely in relation to that function on art 8, but, if the situation is otherwise, art 8 cannot change the appropriate classification of the function. On the approach adopted in [*Donoghue*] it can be said that LCF is clearly not performing any public function.'

10.5 Public law issues: private law issues

Assuming that the courts accept that a decision-making body is, in principle, one that is amenable to judicial review (ie it is classified as a public law body), the courts will still be required to determine whether or not the issue at stake is one that falls within the scope of public law.

It will be noted that in *O'Reilly* v *Mackman* Lord Diplock expressed the view that the case involved a public law issue because the prisoners were asserting rights that did not exist in private law, such as the implied right to a fair hearing in respect of the Board of Visitors' discharging of its functions. This approach could be rationalised on the basis that, whilst there existed a general implied statutory duty to act fairly, it did not arise out of any personal relationship between the prisoners and the Board.

Discretion versus executive action

In *Cocks* v *Thanet District Council* [1982] 3 All ER 1135, a case decided on the same day as *O'Reilly* v *Mackman*, and clearly meant to provide an illustration of how the public/private dichotomy was to work in practice, the House of Lords held that a person claiming that a housing authority was in breach of its statutory duty to house him, pursuant to the Housing (Homeless Persons) Act 1977, would only be allowed to challenge the authority's decision by way of judicial review. Lord Bridge characterised the duty of the housing authority to inquire into the claimant's status to determine whether or not there was a duty to house, as a decision-making function falling within the sphere of public law.

In an attempt to delineate the distinction between public law and private law interests, however, Lord Bridge went on to observe that once the authority accepted that there was a duty to house an applicant it would be exercising its executive powers in relation to the discharge of that duty, creating, as his Lordship saw it, rights and obligations in the field of private law. Strictly speaking Lord Bridge's observations were obiter, not being necessary to dispose of the issue in *Cocks*, and may be questioned on the basis that Parliament may not have intended to create any private law rights that the homeless could enforce against housing authorities, for fear of the financial and administrative consequences. A cautious approach can be discerned in *Ali* v *Tower Hamlets London Borough Council* [1992] 3 WLR 208, where the respondent refused to accept accommodation offered by the appellant authority on the grounds that it was unsuitable. He believed that because of his disabilities and those of his wife, only a ground floor dwelling would be suitable. The authority accepted that the respondent was not intentionally homeless, and that he was a priority need case, but took the view that the sixth floor flat he had been offered was suitable. The respondent commenced proceedings against the authority in the county court, claiming breach of statutory duty (ss65 and 69 Housing Act 1985), and a mandatory injunction compelling the authority to provide suitable accommodation. On the preliminary issue of jurisdiction the Court of Appeal held that the respondent should have proceeded by way of judicial review, the court adopting the view that until the authority completed the process of deciding on suitable accommodation for a homeless person, it was still discharging a public law function, the suitability of any given accommodation being a matter to be determined by the authority using its own discretion and subjective judgment. Mindful of the comments of Lord Bridge in *Cocks*, to the effect that once the full housing duty was shown to exist a homeless person had private law rights that could be asserted vis-à-vis a housing authority, Nolan LJ sought to distinguish this case as one where the authority was still discharging its decision-making, as opposed to executive, functions. In his Lordship's view, the authority had to arrive at a decision as to the suitability of accommodation before it could perform the executive act of securing the accommodation.

A more significant retreat from the position adopted by Lord Bridge in *Cocks* can be seen in the speech of Lord Hoffmann in *O'Rourke* v *Camden London Borough Council* [1997] 3 All ER 23. The plaintiff was released from prison and applied to the defendant authority for accommodation. After an initial refusal, the authority provided the plaintiff with temporary accommodation. However, 12 days later the plaintiff was evicted from this accommodation by the authority and was thereafter refused any other assistance. The plaintiff's action for damages for breach of the statutory duty created by s63(1) of the Housing Act 1985 (which requires a local authority to provide accommodation for those in priority need) was struck out by the county court on the basis that it could only be pursued by way of an application for judicial review, a ruling subsequently upheld by the House of Lords. In determining that s63 was not to be construed as if it created a private law right to damages by way of an action for breach of statutory duty, Lord Hoffmann identified three key factors:

1. the Act created a scheme of social welfare (ie having no equivalence in the sphere of private law);
2. the Act conferred benefits on applicants at the public expense for the benefit of the applicants and society at large;
3. the provision of housing and the assessment of applicants' needs necessarily involved the exercise of discretion by a public body such as a housing authority, hence the appropriate way in which to assess the legality of such decisions was by way of reference to the principles of public law.

In particular Lord Hoffmann criticised Lord Bridge's observations in *Cocks* as to when private law rights would arise vis-à-vis a housing authority on the basis that Lord Bridge had not sufficiently explored the statutory intent behind s63. As Lord Hoffmann observed:

'The concept of a duty in private law which arises only when it has been acknowledged to exist is anomalous. It means that a housing authority which accepts that it has a duty to house the applicant but does so inadequately will be liable in damages but an authority which perversely refuses to accept that it has any such duty will not. This seems to me wrong. Of course a private law relationship may arise from the implementation of the housing authority's duty. The applicant may become the authority's tenant or licensee and so brought into a contractual relationship. But there seems to me no need to interpose a statutory duty actionable in tort merely to bridge the gap between the acknowledgement of the duty and its implementation ... the plaintiff has no private law action for breach of duty at all. It follows that in my view *Thornton* v *Kirklees MBC* [1979] QB 626, which held that he did have such a cause of action, was wrongly decided.'

The basis of these decisions, therefore, seems to be that the assessment of the claimant comes within a general statutory function, and is thus a public law matter, private law rights only arising when promises are made to the claimant, which creates something akin to a contractual relationship between the authority and that particular claimant.

Alternatively, the decisions could be seen as reflecting a desire on the part of the courts to ensure that any challenges to decision such as those relating to homelessness have to be pursued by way of an application for judicial review, thus providing housing authorities with additional procedural safeguards.

Although his decision on the substantive issue was reversed on appeal, the nature of the 'decision-making' versus 'executive powers' dichotomy was usefully summarised by Laws J in *British Steel plc* v *Customs and Excise Commissioners* [1996] 1 All ER 1002 (reversed on appeal [1997] 2 All ER 366):

> 'Where a complaint sought to be raised in litigation touches only on a public law issue, there being no question of a private right involved, the complainant must generally seek his remedy by way of judicial review ... [t]hough this looks like a rule of procedure ... it is in fact a rule of substance ... namely it would be an abuse of process to litigate such claims by ordinary private means. The concept of abuse of process is not a function of mere procedural regulation; it is a necessary safeguard against manipulation of court process ... Where statute confers what is plainly a private right, if on the Act's true construction the right enures only after and in consequence of a purely public law decision in favour of the claimant, any complaint directed to the public decision-making stage must be brought by O.53 ... I may ... add that this is by no means surprising: the public policy which requires that purely administrative decisions be subject only to the supervisory jurisdiction of the High Court in O.53 proceedings is in no sense weakened by the circumstance that the out-turn of a favourable decision may be to confer a private right ... Where a claimant enjoys a private right whose existence is not contingent upon the making of a prior public law decision in his favour ... the claimant may sue at private law even though he must assault an administrative or discretionary decision on the way (see *Roy*). Here again, the concept at the root of this jurisprudence, abuse of process, is in play. If the plaintiff stands in a relationship with the defendant whereby he enjoys a settled and existing private right, it cannot be abusive that he should seek to make it good by ordinary action merely because its value or quantification depends upon the defendant's opinion as to certain aspects given to him to decide.'

Commercial/contractual disputes and voluntary submission to self-regulation normally within the sphere of private law

It has already been noted that the existence of a contractual relationship can guide the courts in determining that a decision-maker is a private law body. Similarly, the fact that litigation turns upon the interpretation of a contract can lead the courts to determine that the issue involved is one of private law (ie between the parties) rather than public law.

In *Mercury Energy Ltd* v *Electricity Corporation of New Zealand Ltd* [1994] 1 WLR 521 the defendant organisation was held to be a public body amenable to judicial review on the basis that it was a designated state enterprise under the New Zealand State Owned Enterprises Act 1986, its shares were held by ministers, it carried on business in the interests of the public, and could make decisions adversely affecting the rights and liabilities of private individuals without affording them any redress. On the facts, however, its decision to terminate an electricity supply contract with the plaintiff was held not to be reviewable, given that there was no evidence of illegality, and that the express statutory duty and principle objective of the defendant body was the operation of a successful and efficient business enterprise. The Privy Council took the view that it was for the defendant to determine if those objectives could be achieved by terminating the contract with the plaintiff. On the basis that the courts should only intervene if the decision could be shown to be wrong in law, it was doubtful whether such a decision would ever be the subject of a successful application for judicial review unless the claimant could show fraud, corruption or bad faith. As Lord Templeman observed:

> 'Industrial disputes over prices and other related matters can only be solved by industry or by government interference and not by judicial interference in the absence of a breach of law.'

In *Mercury Communications Ltd v Director General of Telecommunications* [1996] 1 WLR 48 Lord Slynn observed that, although the Director's office was statutory and he shared some functions with the Secretary of State:

> 'That does not mean that what the Director does cannot lead to disputes which fall outside the realms of administrative law any more than a government department cannot enter into a commercial contract or commit a tort actionable before the court under its ordinary procedures.'

In support of his conclusion that the dispute was one that could be pursued by way of action he noted that the dispute between the parties was essentially about the terms of a contract, albeit one that took the form of a licence granted under statute.

An alleged breach of a contract of employment by an employer is generally regarded as falling within the sphere of private law, albeit a specialised area based on a body of legislative measures with adjudicatory functions being allocated to tribunals. Determining whether or not an employee of a public body can apply for review of the employer's decision to terminate his employment is not a straightforward task. It is perhaps safest to proceed on the basis of a rebuttable assumption that review would be inappropriate, unless the claimant can show that there is some particular statutory basis for his employment that justifies categorising the decision to dismiss as one of public law, that the dismissal raises wider constitutional issues going beyond the claimant's rights, or possibly that in the absence of judicial review he would have no other means of challenging the decision.

R v East Berkshire Health Authority, ex parte Walsh [1984] 3 WLR 818 illustrates the conventional approach to this issue, where the Court of Appeal held that it would be inappropriate for a senior nursing officer, employed under the National

Health Service, to challenge his dismissal by way of judicial review. As the Master of the Rolls explained, employment by a public authority per se did not inject an element of public law, neither did the interest of the public, although where a senior officer was involved more weight might be given to those factors. The applicant would have been able to seek a public law remedy if his conditions of service had differed from those laid down by the Whitely Council's regulations for the Health Service, as approved by the Secretary of State. As these had been incorporated into his contract of employment, any breach would be a matter of private law, falling outside the scope of judicial review. In the view of the Court, only if the authority refused to incorporate the Whitely Council regulations would a public law issue arise.

Two subsequent decisions bear out this analysis. In *R v Derbyshire County Council, ex parte Noble* [1990] ICR 808 a police surgeon sought unsuccessfully to challenge his dismissal on the basis that it was unfair and unreasonable, the court holding that the matter was not reviewable as it arose out of a private contract for services, with no statutory underpinning. Similarly, in *McClaren v Home Office* [1990] ICR 824, it was held that a prison officer, seeking a declaration regarding the legality of a revised shift system that he had been asked to work, was not obliged to do so by way of an application for judicial review: see also *Doyle v Northumbria Probation Committee*, considered below at 10.6.

The significance of voluntary submission to a self-regulatory scheme is illustrated by the decision in *R (On the Application of the Oxford Study Centre) v The British Council* [2001] EWHC Admin 207, where it was held that the respondent body was not a public law body, notwithstanding that it discharged a regulatory function. The key test was whether the respondent discharged a function that had been integrated into a system of governmental control. The accreditation scheme for language schools that it administered was a purely voluntary arrangement and as such did not satisfy that key test. Note that the court might have been willing to regard the respondent as a public body if there had been no basis for providing a contractual remedy.

For examples of other cases where the existence of a contractual relationship has persuaded the courts to permit a plaintiff to proceed by way of action, or to dismiss an application for review, see: *Law v National Greyhound Racing Club Ltd* (above) (stewards' authority arose from a contract, hence there was no public law element in their jurisdiction); *R v Disciplinary Committee of the Jockey Club, ex parte Massingberd Mundy* (above); and *R v Jockey Club, ex parte RAM Racecourses Ltd* (above).

Absence of a contract – residual function of public law

Logically, if the existence of a contractual relationship will persuade the court to classify an issue as one falling within the scope of private law, the absence of a contractual relationship will suggest that an issue is more likely to be regarded as falling within the sphere of public law. Whilst this could be described as a situation where the litigant has no private law rights, the decisions of the courts suggest that issues may be classified as coming within public law to ensure that the individual concerned has some means of challenge. For example, in *R* v *Birmingham City Council, ex parte Dredger* (1993) The Times 28 January, the Divisional Court rejected the local authority's contention that its decision to increase the rent to be paid by market traders was a private law matter based on commercial considerations, noting that the local authority had monopoly control over the letting of stalls, and that in the absence of judicial review there was no basis for any challenge by the applicant: see also *R* v *Lord Chancellor, ex parte Hibbit and Saunders* [1993] COD 326.

In this respect it is constructive to compare the decision of the court in *ex parte Walsh* (above) with that in *R* v *Secretary of State for the Home Department, ex parte Benwell* [1985] QB 554, where the applicant was a prison officer who sought to challenge the validity of his dismissal from the Prison Service. It was held that this would not be an inappropriate procedure, the distinguishing factors being that the applicant was subject to a statutory code of discipline which denied him any private law right to challenge the validity of his dismissal. In short, judicial review was the only means by which the Secretary of State's decision to uphold his dismissal could be challenged: see further *R* v *Lord Chancellor's Department, ex parte Nangle* [1991] ILR 343 (considered at Chapter 14, section 14.3), and *R* v *Crown Prosecution Service, ex parte Hogg* (1994) The Times 14 April.

In *R (On the Application of A)* v *Partnerships in Care Ltd* (2002) The Times 23 April it was held that a private hospital, making changes as to the provision of psychiatric care, was amenable to judicial review partly because the hospital was subject to specific statutory duties under the Registered Homes Act 1984, but also because the hospital's patients were admitted under compulsion by virtue of s3 of the Mental Health Act 1983. The patients had no private law relationship with the hospital grounded in contract. The treatment of patients was regarded as a matter of public concern, and decisions as to their care were therefore public law decisions: see also *The Great House at Sonning Ltd and Others* v *Berkshire County Council* (1996) The Times 25 March.

10.6 Exceptions to *O'Reilly* v *Mackman*

As noted above at section 10.2 Lord Diplock envisaged that there would be exceptions to the rule that public law issues would have to be pursued by way of judicial review. For example, he suggested that a matter could be pursued by way of action if the parties so wished, although this seemed to be at odds with the essential aspect of the decision in *O'Reilly* v *Mackman*, namely that it was for the courts to determine what procedure would be appropriate in any given case. If it would be an abuse of process to proceed by way of writ or originating summons, how could the consent of the parties rectify this? The comments of Dillon LJ in *Kent* v *University*

College London (1992) The Times 18 February clearly indicate that if a case involved substantive public law issues it would be inappropriate to proceed by way of action even if this was with the agreement of the parties, since the role of the court in private law proceedings would clearly be different from its role in public law proceedings, where its jurisdiction was limited to supervising the legality of action taken. Similarly, where parties to litigation agree between themselves that public law issues are involved and the matter should proceed as an application for judicial review, the court seized of the matter can still choose to transfer the case to proceed as if commenced by way of action: see *R* v *Durham City Council, ex parte Robinson* (1992) The Times 31 January.

Cases where the public law issue is merely collateral to the private law matter

This exception was considered by the House of Lords in *Davy* v *Spelthorne Borough Council* [1984] AC 262. In September 1977 the plaintiff, owner of premises used to produce concrete, applied to the council for permission to continue using his site for this purpose for another ten years. The application was rejected, but as a result of further negotiations with council officers an agreement was reached in November 1979 under which the council would issue an enforcement notice directing him to cease the use of the land, but the operation of this notice would be suspended for three years. In exchange the plaintiff promised not to exercise his statutory right of appeal against the notice, which had to be exercised within 35 days of its being issued. In October 1980 the notice was issued in accordance with the agreement. In August 1982 the plaintiff issued a writ against the council seeking an injunction to stop the notice taking effect; damages for negligent advice; and the setting aside of the notice. The Court of Appeal struck out the claim for an injunction and the application to have the notice set aside on the basis that such public law activities of the local authority were only challengeable by way of O.53, but allowed the claim for damages to survive. The council's appeal to the House of Lords was unsuccessful. Lord Wilberforce concluded that the action for damages was not a public law question because the plaintiff was no longer contesting the validity of the enforcement notice, but the nature of the advice that led to his failing to challenge it. If the case still had a public law element it was no more than collateral to the main action and this came within the exceptions envisaged by Lord Diplock in *O'Reilly* v *Mackman*. Furthermore, the court had no power (at the time – see now the Civil Procedure Rules, Pt 54) to transfer the action to proceed as if it had been commenced under O.53, with the result that if the writ had been struck out, the plaintiff would have had to start afresh with an application under O.53. This might have prejudiced the plaintiff as he would have been out of time; at the very least such a course of action would have been uncertain.

Lord Wilberforce's assertion that the plaintiff in *Davy* was no longer contesting the validity of the enforcement notice seems, in the light of subsequent decisions, to be a key factor. The difficulty, however, lay in drawing the line between cases where the plaintiff is primarily was asserting a private right, and those where he was effectively seeking to evade the strictures imposed by proceeding under O.53. In *The Great House at Sonning Ltd and Others* v *Berkshire County Council* (above) the Court of Appeal held that the plaintiffs were not entitled to proceed by way of writ with an action in negligence against highway authority that proposed to close a road pursuant to an order issued under s14 of the Road Traffic Regulations Act 1984. It was held that the order issued under the 1984 Act prevented any obstruction caused by the road closure from being a nuisance until such time as the order was shown to be invalid. No private law right of action arose until the order was quashed, and the order itself could only be challenged by way of an application for judicial review. Although the decision gave the impression of turning simply on the view that no private law rights were being asserted, it is submitted that, in the light of *Davy*, the dissenting judgment of Saville LJ is persuasive where he contends that the plaintiffs were simply asserting a private law right that arose because they could prove loss and damage over and above that sustained by the public at large as a consequence of the closure. In his view the plaintiffs should have been permitted to proceed on the basis of the 'broad' approach to the procedural dichotomy propounded by Lord Lowry in *Roy* v *Kensington and Chelsea etc* (see below).

Subsequent decisions revealed a discernible trend away from the rigid procedural dichotomy advocated in *O'Reilly* v *Mackman* where the plaintiff could show that he had a substantive private law right that he was seeking to vindicate. The courts appeared increasingly willing to accept that to force the litigant to use the judicial review procedure could actually result in a denial of justice. The following cases illustrate this trend.

1. *Doyle* v *Northumbria Probation Committee* [1991] 1 WLR 1340: the plaintiff probation officers proceeded by way of action claiming damages for breach of contract and a declaration as to their contractual rights. Since 1975 they had been paid a mileage allowance that compensated them for the cost of travel between work and home. In 1983, however, these payments were abolished, the defendant committee claiming that it had never had the power to make such payments under the Probation (Consolidation of Service) Rules 1975. The committee's application to have the proceedings struck out as an abuse of process, on the ground that the plaintiffs were essentially seeking to contest an issue of public law, ie the legality of the payments made under statutory authority, was dismissed. In rejecting the assertion that the plaintiffs should have sought review of the decision to phase out payments in 1983, Henry J observed:

   '... it is not incumbent on employees of a public authority faced with a prima facie breach of contract to investigate or prove that the public body which employed them had power to contract with them on the terms agreed ... the rule as set out [in *O'Reilly* v *Mackman*] does not cover this case and that is common ground. The reason for that is that the plaintiffs here do not seek to establish that they had any public law entitlement to the disputed allowance: their claim to it is purely contractual. Therefore they do not claim any remedy for infringement of their public law rights. Public law only comes into the action as a result of the committee's assertion by way of defence or anticipated assertion by way of defence that they had no power to pay the disputed allowance.'

2. *Roy* v *Kensington and Chelsea and Westminster Family Practitioner Committee* [1992] 1 All ER 705: the plaintiff, a general practitioner, sought payment from the defendant committee of part of his basic practice allowance that the committee had decided to withhold, having concluded that the plaintiff had failed to devote a substantial amount of his time to general practice. The committee, which derived its jurisdiction in this matter from the National Health Service (General Medical and Pharmaceutical) Regulations 1974, and the Statement of Fees and Allowances published thereunder, applied unsuccessfully to have the plaintiff's claim struck out as an abuse of process on the basis that he was seeking to challenge a public law decision. Lord Lowry, emphasising the extent to which an over-rigid adherence to the public law/private law dichotomy could prejudice the plaintiff's case, observed:

> 'An important point is that the court clearly has jurisdiction to entertain the doctor's action. Furthermore, even if one accepts the full rigour of *O'Reilly* v *Mackman*, there is ample room to hold that this case comes within the exceptions allowed for by Lord Diplock. It is concerned with a private law right, it involves a question which could in some circumstances give rise to a dispute of fact and one object of the plaintiff is to obtain an order for the payment (not by way of damages) of an ascertained or ascertainable sum of money. If it is wrong to allow such a claim to be litigated by action, what is to be said of other disputed claims for remuneration? I think it is right to consider the whole spectrum of claims which a doctor might make against the committee. The existence of any dispute as to entitlement means that he will be alleging a breach of his private law rights through a failure by the committee to perform their public duty. If the committee's argument prevails, the doctor must in all these cases go by judicial review, even when the facts are not clear. I scarcely think that this can be the right answer ...'

Lord Lowry went on to express the view that *O'Reilly* v *Mackman* should be seen as a decision that required a litigant to proceed by way of judicial review only when his private law rights where not at stake, rather than laying down a general requirement subject to limited exceptions.

3. *Trustees of the Dennis Rye Pension Fund and Another* v *Sheffield City Council* [1997] 4 All ER 747: the court refused to strike out as an abuse of process an action to recover unpaid improvement grants, on the basis that the case involved a dispute as to fact (whether or not improvement work had been completed as required) which could be more effectively resolved in an ordinary action than in proceedings for judicial review. Further, the action was, in effect, for the recovery of a debt (see as a further example *Steed* v *Secretary of State for the Home Department* [2000] 3 All ER 226, where the claimant allowed to proceed by way of summons to reclaim Home Office compensation for surrendered hand guns). There was nothing in *O'Reilly* v *Mackman* to suggest that judicial review

was intended to be used as a form of action for debt collecting – in that sense the case was analogous to *Roy* v *Kensington etc* in that the plaintiff sought to enforce a conditional right to payment. Lord Woolf MR stressed the need for flexibility in respect of choice of procedures and the need to ensure that a plaintiff who chose to proceed by way of action should not be deprived of his remedy on purely technical grounds. In his view, where a plaintiff did proceed by way of writ and there was an application to strike out on the basis that he should have made an application for judicial review, the trial judge should consider whether leave would have been granted had an application for review been made. If it would, that was an indication that proceeding by way of writ would not harm the interests that judicial review was designed to protect. See further on the 'practicalities' argument *R* v *Chief Constable for Warwickshire and Others, ex parte F* (1997) The Times 26 November (judicial review not appropriate where an individual complained of excessive seizure of material by police officers executing a search warrant).

Where the public law issue arises by way of a defence: civil proceedings

The possibility of a defendant in a civil action challenging, in the course of his defence, the vires of an administrative decision was not expressly referred to by Lord Diplock in *O'Reilly* v *Mackman*, but has subsequently emerged as a significant exception to the rule that such issues must be resolved by way of judicial review.

The key decision in this respect is that of the House of Lords in *Wandsworth London Borough Council* v *Winder* [1984] 3 All ER 976, wherein the local authority, acting under the Housing Act 1957, resolved to increase rents for its tenants. The appellant refused to pay the increased rent, arguing that the increase was ultra vires and void. A notice seeking possession of the property was served on the appellant for non-payment of rent, and in the subsequent possession proceedings he sought to rely on the defence that the increase was ultra vires. The authority applied to strike out the defence on the ground that it was an abuse of the court process to challenge a public law decision in a private law action. The defence was struck out at first instance in the county court, but the Court of Appeal allowed it to stand. The authority appealed unsuccessfully to the House of Lords, where it was held that the tenant was entitled to raise a defence based on allegations of ultra vires action in an action started by writ. There was no evidence that the defendant was attempting to abuse the process of the court, indeed he had not instigated the proceedings at all. Further, there was nothing in *O'Reilly* v *Mackman* to suggest that the House of Lords had intended to remove the right of a defendant to raise a public law issue by way of defence to a private law action. See further *Thrasyvoulou* v *Secretary of State for the Environment* [1988] 3 WLR 1, wherein it was held that, as regards the defending of enforcement notice proceedings, the House of Lords' decision in *O'Reilly* v *Mackman* did not exclude the right of a defendant to raise the invalidity of an enforcement notice, on the grounds of issue estoppel.

Whilst the ruling in *Winder* is significant, a distinction may be made by the courts where the defendant, seeking to raise a public law issue by way of a defence to civil proceedings for possession of property, is in law a trespasser on that property. In *Avon County Council* v *Buscott* [1988] 2 WLR 788 the appellants had been living as gypsies in a property owned by the respondent council. The council sought an eviction order against the appellants that was granted at first instance. In the course of the hearing the appellants had unsuccessfully requested an adjournment in order to prepare a defence based on the assertion that, because the council was in breach of its statutory duty in providing sites for gypsies, its decision to evict the appellants must be unreasonable. Upholding this ruling, the Master of the Rolls expressed his view that to have allowed the defence to be raised would have involved an abuse of the process of the court. The situation was to be distinguished from that in *Winder*, where the defendant had a 'true defence' in the sense that he was in lawful occupation of the land. Here the appellants readily conceded that they had no right to occupy the land in question. See further *Pawlowski* v *Dunnington* (1999) The Times 13 May (public law defence raised in county court proceedings for the collection of unpaid tax).

Where the public law issue arises by way of a defence: criminal proceedings

The validity of an order, notice or bye-law can arise as an issue in the course of criminal proceedings, typically where a defendant alleges that the order under which he is being prosecuted is in some way invalid, either on its face, or by reference to the procedure by which it was made. A strict adherence to the public/private dichotomy would suggest that a defendant should not be permitted to raise such a defence, but the courts have not adopted such an approach.

There are essentially two schools of thought in this issue. On the one hand there is the 'broad' view, which is that a defendant in criminal proceedings should be able to raise any defence, given the penal nature of the proceedings. For example, in *R* v *Crown Court at Reading, ex parte Hutchinson* [1988] QB 384, the applicants, arrested for allegedly breaching bye-laws relating to trespass on the air base at Greenham Common, were convicted before the magistrates' court and appealed to the Crown Court, where they contended that the bye-laws under which the prosecution had been brought were invalid on the grounds of substantive ultra vires. The Crown Court adjourned the proceedings pending a ruling on validity by the Divisional Court on an application for judicial review. The applicants objected to this course of action and applied successfully for an order of mandamus to compel the Crown Court to consider the validity of the bye-law and conclude the hearing of the appeal. Lloyd LJ held that the Crown Court had jurisdiction to inquire into the validity of bye-laws upon which the validity of a conviction rested since, in his view, neither the revisions to RSC O.53 nor the enactment of s31 Supreme Court Act 1981 had removed a defendant's right to raise such matters by way of defence to a criminal prosecution. The applicants could not be described as 'abusing the process of the court' as that phrase was used by Lord Diplock in *O'Reilly* v *Mackman*, as they were in the position of defendants, not plaintiffs or prosecutors. Note that the fine imposed in this case was £25. As Lloyd LJ observed (at 392):

> 'Coming to London to the High Court is inconvenient and expensive. Bye-laws are generally local laws which have been made for local people to do with local concerns. Magistrates' courts are local courts and there is one in every town of any size in England. The cost of proceedings in a magistrates' court are far less than in the High Court. I believe this egalitarian aspect of seeking recourse to the law in a magistrates' court to be an important sign of the availability of justice for all.'

Clearly the court was motivated by the fact that the legal fees would have easily outstripped the cost of the fine, resulting in an obvious disincentive to challenging the bye-law. Such a state of affairs would have been convenient for the Crown Prosecution Service, but did not justify the Crown Court's decision.

The 'narrow' view is that only allegations of substantive ultra vires should be entertained by the criminal courts where an order is impugned. The corollary being that allegations of procedural ultra vires should be pursued by way of an application for judicial review. Such was the view of the court in *Bugg* v *DPP; DPP* v *Percy* [1993] 2 WLR 628 (both cases involving challenge to the vires of bye-laws in criminal proceedings).

The matter has now received detailed consideration from the House of Lords in *Boddington* v *British Transport Police* [1998] 2 All ER 203. The defendant was convicted of the offence of smoking a cigarette in a railway carriage where smoking was prohibited, contrary to bye-law 20 of the British Railways Board's Bye-laws 1965, made under s67 of the Transport Act 1962, as amended. The bye-law prohibited smoking if notices were put up to that effect in train carriages. The defendant did not contest the facts and was fined £10 upon conviction. The defendant appealed by way of case stated contending that, although the bye-law itself might not be ultra vires, the complete ban effected by putting up notices in all train carriages on given lines was excessive, thus the bye-law had not been properly brought into effect. Although the conviction was upheld, the speeches of their Lordships very much reflect the 'broad' approach to permitting a vires challenge in criminal proceedings. On the basis that Parliament had not provided any particular procedure for challenging the order in question (as to which see *R* v *Wicks* below), Lord Irvine observed (at p209e–f):

> 'It would be a fundamental departure from the rule of law if an individual were liable to conviction for contravention of some rule which is itself liable to be set aside by a court as unlawful.'

Having considered *Wandsworth London Borough Council* v *Winder* [1984] 3 All ER 976 and having rejected the distinction drawn between challenges to statutory instruments based on 'latent' as opposed to 'patent' defects in *Bugg* v *DPP* [1993] 2 All ER 815, Lord Irvine continued [at p213e–h]:

'Subject to any statutory qualifications upon his right to do so, the citizen [faced with a threat of criminal proceedings for breach of a measure he considered to be invalid] could, in my judgment, choose to accept the risk of uncertainty, take no action at all, wait to be sued or prosecuted by the public body and then put forward his arguments on validity and have them determined by the court hearing the case against him. That is a matter of right in a case of ultra vires action by the public authority, and would not be subject to the discretion of the court: see *Wandsworth London BC* v *Winder*. In my judgment ... the reasoning of the Divisional Court in *Bugg*'s case, suggesting two classes of legal invalidity of subordinate legislation, is contrary both to the *Anisminic* case and the subsequent decisions of this House ... *Anisminic* ... established ... that there might be error of law within jurisdiction, that there was a single category of errors of law, all of which rendered a decision ultra vires. No distinction is to be drawn between a patent (or substantive) error of law or a latent (or procedural) error of law. An ultra vires act or subordinate legislation is unlawful simpliciter and, if the presumption in favour of its legality is overcome by a litigant before a court of competent jurisdiction, is of no legal effect whatsoever.'

Lord Irvine noted that in *Winder* the alleged error (taking into account irrelevant considerations when setting increased rent levels) would not have been 'patent' or clear from looking at the resolution itself, yet the House of Lords held that *Winder* could raise a vires argument by way of defence to civil proceedings. On this basis he felt that a defendant in criminal proceedings should not be prevented from similarly challenging the validity of a bye-law simply because the alleged defect was not apparent. He added (at p214f–g):

'Many different types of challenge, which shade into each other, may be made to the legality of bye-laws or administrative acts. The decision in the *Anisminic* case freed the law from a dependency on technical distinctions between different types of illegality. The law should not now be developed to create a new, and unstable, technical distinction between "substantive" and "procedural" invalidity.'

Whilst accepting that *R* v *Wicks*, and *Plymouth City Council* v *Quietlynn Ltd* [1988] QB 114 could be distinguished on the basis that, in both cases, there was a particular statutory scheme that justified limitations being placed upon the rights of the defendant to challenge the validity of the administrative acts in question, Lord Irvine observed that in both cases the courts were concerned with administrative orders directed specifically at the defendants. By contrast the present case concerned subordinate legislation of a general character directed at the world at large. A defendant might not become aware that a prohibition existed until charged with contravening it. The first opportunity to challenge it might arise in criminal proceedings. As he observed (at p216h–217a):

'A smoker might have made his first journey on the line on the same train as Mr Boddington; have found that there was no carriage free of no smoking signs and have chosen to exercise what he believed to be his right to smoke on the train. Such an individual would have had no sensible opportunity to challenge the validity of the posting of the no smoking signs throughout the train until he was charged, as Mr Boddington was, under bye-law 20. In my judgment in such a case the strong presumption must be that Parliament did not intend to deprive the smoker of an opportunity to defend himself in the criminal proceedings by asserting the alleged unlawfulness of the decision to post no smoking notices throughout the train. I can see nothing in s67 of the Transport Act 1962 or the bye-laws which could displace that presumption.'

Lord Steyn, expressing his agreement with Lord Irvine, addressed his attention to the failings of an application for judicial review as an alternative to raising a vires argument by way of defence to criminal proceedings (at p227a–c):

'The defendant may, however, be out of time [for applying for judicial review] before he becomes aware of the existence of the bye-law. He may lack the resources to defend his interests in two courts. He may not be able to obtain legal aid for an application for leave to apply for judicial review. Leave to apply for judicial review may be refused. At a substantive hearing his scope for demanding examination of witnesses in the Divisional Court may be restricted. He may be denied a remedy on a discretionary basis. The possibility of judicial review will, therefore, in no way compensate him for the loss of the right to defend himself by a defensive challenge to the bye-law in cases where the invalidity of the bye-law might afford him with a defence to the charge.'

Notwithstanding the views expressed in *Boddington*, it has to be recognised that there are a host of practical considerations to justify the 'narrow' view. The Divisional Court has the expertise to determine complex arguments regarding vires; the procedure for applying for judicial review involves significant safeguards for public bodies, such as time limits and the need to obtain leave; on an application for judicial review the public body would be a party to the proceedings, and thus able to give evidence; and there is the fact that an acquittal in the criminal court, on the basis that an order was invalid, would not be binding on the public body as regards third parties.

As indicated above, the task of the court will be easier in those cases where a vires challenge is raised in criminal proceedings and the legislation in question provides a means for the determination of such issues. In *R* v *Wicks* [1997] 2 All ER 801 W (defending criminal proceedings for non-compliance with an enforcement notice) contended that the issuing of the notice had been motivated by bad faith and irrelevant considerations. The trial judge ruled that W could only raise such arguments by way of judicial review of the notice and W changed his plea to guilty, and appealed. Dismissing the appeal the House of Lords was influenced by the fact that there was a statutory framework of appeal to the Secretary of State for challenging enforcement notices, and the provision of an alternative process militated against the conclusion that it could be challenged in criminal proceedings. Compare this case with *Dilieto* v *Ealing London Borough Council* [1998] 2 All ER 885, where the appellant was defending criminal proceedings brought for failing to comply with a breach of condition notice. At his trial before justices the appellant contended that he was not guilty because: the notice had been issued out of time; and the planning condition was a nullity because it was too vague to enforce. The appellant was convicted and appealed successfully by way of case stated. The Divisional Court held that the appellant could only be charged with failing to comply with a breach of condition notice if that notice was served within the prescribed time limits. There was no right of appeal to the Secretary of State against breach of condition notices, and it would be unfair to expect the recipient of a notice to challenge it by way of judicial review. Hence it was permissible to raise the validity of such a notice by way of defence to criminal proceedings for failure to comply (on the facts the condition was held not to be void for uncertainty). Sullivan J, having considered the speech of Lord Hoffmann in *R* v *Wicks*, cited what he saw as the relevant factors in determining that the appellant should be allowed to raise the vires argument before the justices (at pp897e–898c):

'I realise that one should not treat the various considerations mentioned in Lord Hoffmann's speech as though they were a set of criteria which are set out in an enactment, but it may nevertheless be helpful to apply them to the facts of this case ... First, in the case of breach of condition notices, there has been no progressive transfer of the right to appeal away from the magistrates to the Secretary of State. Second, the Act provides no comprehensive avenue of appeal against a breach of condition notice leaving only residual grounds for challenge by way of judicial review. Third, whilst an allegation of bad faith and improper purpose, or taking into consideration irrelevant considerations, is more appropriate for challenge by way of judicial review because of the complexity and sophistication of the relevant law, that is not true of an allegation that a breach of condition notice is out of time, for the reasons that I have set out above ... Fourth, so far as timing is concerned, since there is no right of appeal to the Secretary of State, there is no reason why a prosecution for a breach of condition notice should be delayed. Interposing a challenge by way of judicial review before any prosecution takes place may well lead to delay ... Fifth, whilst the purposes of the provisions for enforcement of enforcement notices and breach of condition notices by criminal proceedings are the same, hardship will be caused by requiring all challenges to breach of condition notices to be made by way of judicial review. One is not concerned here with "residual grounds" which would be needed only for the "rare case", but with basic defences to a breach of condition notice which a defendant should, in my view, be able to advance as of right and not subject to the discretion of the High Court in deciding whether or not to grant leave for judicial review. If the appellant had here wished to challenge the decision to serve the breach of condition notice on the basis that it was taken in bad faith or for improper motives, or was based on irrelevant considerations, then I would agree that such allegations are inappropriate in a criminal court, and should be raised by way of judicial review. But it does not follow that Parliament intended that any challenge to a breach of condition notice should be made by way of judicial review. In my judgment a breach of condition notice in s187A means a breach of condition notice which has been served within the time limits prescribed by s171B ... Some might consider it unsatisfactory that some challenges to a breach of condition notice may be made before magistrates whilst other challenges must proceed by way of judicial review, but that position is no different in principle from that which obtains in the case of enforcement notices. Most grounds of challenge go to the Secretary of State, other residual grounds must be advanced by way of judicial review. *R* v *Wicks* demonstrates that it may not be possible to define "the boundary"...'

Regarding the issue of issues that it might be appropriate for magistrates to consider, and those that ought more appropriately to be resolved by way of an application for judicial review, Sullivan J observed (at p898g–j):

> 'What about his claim that condition was so vague and imprecise as to be a nullity and hence to invalidate the notice? Such a contention could be advanced without any difficulty in judicial review proceedings, but if a defendant is charged with failing to comply with a notice alleging a breach of condition, it would require very clear words of exclusion to persuade me that he could not say to the magistrates: "but look at the condition, it is unlawful." No such words of exclusion are to be found in the Act. Such an argument can be advanced by simply looking at the face of the planning permission and construing the condition. It is wholly different from an allegation that service of a notice, which is valid on its face, was motivated by bad faith or improper purpose. It is also different from an allegation that a condition is undesirable on the planning merits, which is plainly not a matter for magistrates. Mr Baughan [counsel for the respondents] accepts that a defendant, in the position of this appellant, was entitled to challenge the lawfulness of the condition ... For the reasons that I have just given, I consider that the concession was correctly made. It follows that the appellant was entitled to raise his second argument before the magistrates. Whether it is a good argument, as a matter of law, is another matter, and one which this court is entitled to consider.'

10.7 The impact of the Civil Procedure Rules 1998

It is notable that Saville LJ, in the Court of Appeal in *British Steel plc* v *Customs and Excise Commissioners* [1996] 1 All ER 1002, likened the problems of determining whether to proceed by way of judicial review or by way of action to those associated with forms of action that bedevilled litigants in the nineteenth century. Expressing the view that much of the litigation on the public/private law dichotomy was in danger of bringing the legal system into disrepute, he observed (at p379):

> 'It reinforces the view held by the ordinary person that the law and our legal system are slow, expensive and unsatisfactory. In this day and age it is surely possible to devise procedures which avoid this form of satellite litigation, whilst safeguarding both the private rights of individuals and companies and the position and responsibilities of public authorities ...[this] case is yet another illustration of the fact that in this sphere we have allowed the law and our procedures to develop in such a way that the courts have to address difficult and complex questions which in my view, under a proper system, it should not be necessary even to ask, let alone answer.'

In *Clark* v *University of Lincolnshire and Humberside* [2000] 3 All ER 752, Lord Woolf MR referred (at p761) to the 'barren procedural disputes which generate satellite litigation' caused by the courts having to wrestle with the restrictions imposed by the public/private law dichotomy.

What the Civil Procedure Rules 1998 provide

Claims for judicial review are dealt with in the Administrative Court of the High Court.

The Civil Procedure Rules (CPR) 1998, in Pt 54.1, defines a 'claim for judicial review' as a claim to review 'the lawfulness of an enactment or a decision, action or failure to act in relation to the exercise of a public function'. The procedure must be used in a claim for judicial review where the claimant is seeking: a mandatory order; a prohibiting order; or a quashing order. The procedure may be used where the claimant is seeking a declaration or an injunction.

Under the CPR 1998 Pt 54.20, the court may order a claim to continue as if it had not been started by way of an application for judicial review, and where it does so, it may give directions about the future management of the claim; see CPR 1998 Pt 30 regarding transfers to and from the Administrative Court. Clearly this means that the court has a discretion to treat an application for judicial review as a private law claim if this is more appropriate. Alternatively, private law actions can be transferred to the Administrative Court if the judicial review procedure is more appropriate.

How the courts have applied the Civil Procedure Rules 1998

The introduction of the CPR 1998 Pt 54, in place of RSC O.53, has already had a significant impact on the procedural problems that have bedevilled judicial review since *O'Reilly* v *Mackman*. This is illustrated by decisions such as *Clark* v *University of Lincolnshire and Humberside* (above). The claimant (C), a humanities student at the respondent university, was awarded 0 per cent in a final year paper. Initially it was alleged that she had been guilty of plagiarism, but this allegation was subsequently dropped. C sued for breach of contract and the claim was struck out on the grounds that breaches of contract by universities were not justiciable in the courts. C appealed, having amended her statement of claim to include allegations that the respondent had breached its own student regulations. The respondent contended that C's action was an abuse of process, and that she should have proceeded by way of an application for judicial review – the time limit for which had long since passed. Allowing her appeal Sedley LJ observed that under the CPR 1998 the courts did not have to counter perceived abuses of process by resort to strict (procedural) exclusionary rules that might in themselves cause unfairness. Comparing the application with that in *O'Reilly* v *Mackman*, he stated (at p757):

'The critical decision for present purposes was in fact not *O'Reilly* v *Mackman*, where the issues were purely public law ones and the problem therefore entirely procedural, but the companion case of *Cocks* v *Thanet DC* [1982] 3 All ER 1135 ... which decided that where private law rights depended on prior public law decisions they too must ordinarily be litigated by judicial review. That this could not, however, be a universal rule was established not long afterwards ... [in] ... *Wandsworth London BC* v *Winder* [1984] 3 All ER 976 ... And in *Roy* v *Kensington and Chelsea and Westminster Family Practitioner Committee* [1992] 1 All ER 705 ... their Lordships made it clear that it was not necessarily an abuse of process to elect to sue in contract for statutory payments where the public law element was not dominant. The present class of case is if anything stronger from this point of view than *Roy*'s case, for where in *Roy*'s case a statutory relationship happened to include a contractual element, here it is a contractual relationship which happens to possess a public law dimension. Both are a long way from the situation in *Cocks v Thanet DC.*'

Turning to the impact of the CPR 1998, Sedley LJ stressed that the mode of commencement of proceedings should no longer be a determinant factor in assessing whether there had been an abuse of process:

'... what should matter is whether the choice of procedure ... is critical to the outcome. This focuses attention on what in my view is the single important difference between judicial review and civil suit, the differing time limits. To permit what is in substance a public law challenge to be brought as of right up to six years later if the relationship happens also to be contractual will in many cases circumvent the valuable provision of RSC O.53 ... Until the introduction of the CPR this was a dilemma which could be solved only by forbidding the use of the contractual route ... the CPR now enable the court to prevent the unfair exploitation of the longer limitation period for civil suits without resorting to a rigid exclusionary rule capable of doing equal and opposite injustice. Just as on a judicial review application the court may enlarge time if justice so requires, in a civil suit it may now intervene, notwithstanding the currency of the limitation period, if the entirety of circumstances – including of course the availability of judicial review, demonstrates that the court's processes are being misused, or if it is clear that because of the lapse of time or other circumstances no worthwhile relief can be expected.'

Lord Woolf MR went on to explain that under the CPR 1998:

'... if proceedings involving public law issues are commenced by an ordinary action under Pt 7 or Pt 8 [of the CPR] they are now subject to Pt 24. Part 24 is important because it enables the court, either on its own motion or on the application of a party, if it considers that a claimant has no real prospect of succeeding on a claim or an issue, to give summary judgment on the claim or issue. This is a markedly different position from that which existed when *O'Reilly* v *Mackman* was decided. If a defendant public body or an interested person considers that a claim has no real prospect of success an application can now be made under Pt 24. This restricts the inconvenience to third parties and the administration of public bodies caused by a hopeless claim to which Lord Diplock referred ... The distinction between proceedings under O.53 and an ordinary claim are now limited. Under O.53 the claimant has to obtain permission to bring the proceedings so that the onus is upon him to establish he has a real prospect of success. In the case of ordinary proceedings the defendant has to establish that the proceedings do not have a real prospect of success.'

Lord Woolf MR returned to this theme in *R (On the Application of Heather and Another)* v *Leonard Cheshire Foundation* (above), a case which raised, inter alia, the issue of whether an application for judicial review was the appropriate procedure for challenging the decision of a charity to close a residential home. Addressing the change of emphasis as regards the public/private law procedural dichotomy post the introduction of the CPR 1998, Lord Woolf CJ observed that in identifying cases appropriate for an application for judicial review, RSC O.53, had focussed on the nature of the application. The question for the court had been whether or not it was an application for an order of mandamus, prohibition or certiorari, or an application for a declaration or an injunction that could be granted on an application for judicial review. Would it, having regard to the nature and matters in respect of which relief could be granted by way of one of the prerogative remedies, be just and convenient for the declaration or injunction to be granted on an application for judicial review? In his view:

> '... CPR Pt 54.1 has changed the focus of the test so that it is also partly functions based ... These changes have not been reflected in any complementary change to s31 of the Supreme Court Act 1981, which still is in virtually the same language as RSC O.53. None the less, there was ... reflected in the decision of the court below ... with its reference to "A gap in judicial review", an idea that if the Leonard Cheshire Foundation [LCF] was not forming a public function, proceedings by way of judicial review were wrong. This is an echo of the old demarcation disputes as to when judicial review was or was not appropriate under RSC O.53. CPR Pt 54 is intended to avoid any such disputes which are wholly unproductive. In a case such as the present where a bona fide contention is being advanced (although incorrect) that LCF was performing a public function, that is an appropriate issue to be brought to the court by way of judicial review. Because LCF is a charity further procedural requirements may be involved ... We wish to make clear that the CPR provide a framework which is sufficiently flexible to enable all the issues between the parties to be determined.'

10.8 Procedure in applications for judicial review

The procedural requirements governing applications for judicial review are to be found in s31 Supreme Court Act 1981 and Pt 54 CPR 1998. As indicated above, an application for judicial review must be made if a claimant is seeking a mandatory order, a prohibiting order, or a quashing order. It may be used if a declaration or injunction is sought. Whether or not judicial review is the appropriate procedure has been considered above. Assuming it is the appropriate procedure, there are a number of procedural considerations that have to be borne in mind by the claimant.

Obtaining permission to apply for judicial review

Section 31(3) of the Supreme Court Act 1981 provides that: 'No application for judicial review shall be made unless the leave of the High Court has been obtained'.

Part 54.4 CPR 1998 similarly provides that the 'court's permission to proceed is required in a claim for judicial review whether started under this Part or transferred to the Administrative Court'.

Prior to October 2000 this 'permission' stage was known as applying for leave to apply for judicial review. The permission stage offers protection to public bodies in that the court will have an opportunity to 'weed out' unmeritorious cases at an early stage. The application is made ex parte to a judge who will generally determine the application without a hearing. The parties need not attend the permission hearing unless requested to do so by the court. Under Pt 54.12 CPR 1998, if the court refuses permission to proceed, or gives permission to proceed subject to conditions, without a hearing, it will serve its reasons for making the decision when it serves the order giving or refusing permission in accordance with the Rules. The claimant may not appeal against the permission decision but may request the decision to be reconsidered at a hearing. Part 54.13 further provides that if an order giving permission to proceed is granted neither the defendant nor any other person served with the claim form may apply to have it set aside.

In *R* v *Secretary of State for the Home Department, ex parte Angur Begum* (1989) The Times 3 April Lord Donaldson MR indicated that leave to apply for judicial review should be granted if it was felt that the matter disclosed a point suitable for further debate on an inter partes basis. Where it was clear that no arguable case was disclosed, the application should be dismissed. In intermediate cases, where a judge was unsure, the correct course of action might be to invite the putative respondent to attend the application hearing in order to make representations on the matter. The purpose of such a hearing should not be to trespass upon the full hearing, but to give the judge a 'bird's eye view' of the matter.

Parties to the application

In the claim form used to commence the application the claimant is required to state the name and address of any person he considers to be an interested party. The claim form must be served on the defendant and (subject to directions by the court) any person the claimant considers to be an interested party. Any party served with the claim form who wishes to take part in the judicial review must file an acknowledgment of service within 21 days of the claim form being served.

Although the court has a discretion to allow any person to make representations at a hearing of the judicial review, there may be a tactical significance in a party being made a respondent to an application. In *R* v *Liverpool City Council, ex parte Muldoon; Same, ex parte Kelly* (1996) The Times 11 July the applicants applied unsuccessfully for Housing Benefit, the refusal being based on the ground that access to the relevant premises by a rent officer had been denied. Judicial review was sought in relation to whether or not benefit could be refused where the denial of access had not been deliberate. The Secretary of State for Social Security sought unsuccessfully to issue a notice of motion for an order that he be joined as a respondent to the applications for judicial review. His motivation in so acting lay in the fact that, whilst Housing Benefit payments are made by local authorities, 95 per cent of the money paid out is recovered from central government. The Secretary of State was clearly concerned about the financial implications of a ruling in favour of the applicants. If the applicants were successful in their application for judicial review, the local authority might not be minded to contest the decision, given its limited financial interest. Whilst the Secretary of State could be heard in opposition to an application, he would have had to have been joined as a party to the proceedings if he was to have had the right to appeal against any ruling in favour of the applicants.

Exhausting alternative remedies

The application for judicial review has always been a remedy of last resort. This means that the court has a discretion to dismiss an application for review if it takes the view that there are, or were, alternative procedures open to the claimant. The most obvious example is where statute provides for a right of appeal against the decision of a public body. Judicial review in such cases is unlikely to be granted. The courts will take a broad view of what constitutes an alternative remedy. For example, in *Cowl* v *Plymouth City Council* (2002) The Times 8 January, Lord Woolf CJ observed that the claimants had wrongly concluded that the respondent authority's complaints procedure did not constitute an alternative remedy. He added that the Civil Procedure Rules 1998 could be invoked to require the parties to attend a hearing to determine whether or not it was necessary to resort to litigation.

Locus standi

The right to challenge the decisions of public bodies by way of judicial review is restricted to those who have some connection with the decision being impugned. Under s31(3) of the Supreme Court Act 1981 a court will not grant leave to make an application unless it considers that the applicant has a sufficient interest in the matter to which the application relates.

The 'sufficient interest' criterion, replacing the somewhat narrower 'person aggrieved' formulation used prior to the reforms of 1977, has presented the courts with an inevitable problem of interpretation. How is the balance to be struck between ensuring that vexatious litigants are denied access whilst bona fide pressure groups are permitted to assert the interests of those they represent?

The starting point for consideration of locus standi is now the decision of the House of Lords in *Inland Revenue Commissioners* v *National Federation of Self-Employed and Small Businesses* [1982] AC 617. In an effort to prevent large-scale tax evasion by casual workers in Fleet Street, the Revenue came to an understanding with the relevant trade unions, whereby it would agree to an amnesty as regards the investigation of unpaid tax in previous years, in return for the casual workers now providing accurate information when they registered for work so that tax could be collected. The Federation, which felt that its members were often unfairly harassed by the Revenue with regard to the collection of tax, sought a declaration that the amnesty was ultra vires the Revenue, and an order of mandamus to compel it to recover the tax due. In concluding that the Federation did not have locus standi to challenge the tax amnesty, Lord Wilberforce sought to outline how the matter should be addressed. He explained that the issue of sufficient interest was to be regarded as a mixed decision of fact and law for the courts to decide on legal principles, ie it was not simply a matter of judicial discretion. Further, that it should not be assumed that because one generic phrase was used as the test for standing it would necessarily be applied in the same way regardless of the remedy sought. As regards mandamus, for example, he agreed with the views expressed by the Lord Advocate to the effect that the courts should be guided by the definition of the duty, and should inquire whether expressly, or by implication, the definition indicates that the complaining applicant is within the scope or ambit of the duty.

His Lordship was at pains to emphasise that standing should not be viewed as a preliminary or threshold issue. As he observed:

> 'There may be simple cases in which it can be seen at the earliest stage that the person applying for judicial review has not interest at all, or no sufficient interest to support the application: then it would be quite correct at the threshold to refuse him leave to apply. The right to do so is an important safeguard against the courts being flooded and public bodies harassed by irresponsible applications. But in other cases this will not be so. In these it will be necessary to consider the powers or the duties in law of those against whom the relief is asked, the position of the applicant in relation to those powers or duties, and to the breach of those said to have been committed. In other words, the question of sufficient interest cannot, in such case, be considered in the abstract, or as an isolated point: it must be taken together with the legal and factual context.'

What was seen as fatal to the success of the Federation's application was not only its failure to establish any illegality on the part of the Revenue, but also the confidential nature of the relationship between the Revenue and any individual taxpayer. As Lord Wilberforce observed:

> 'As a matter of general principle I would hold that one taxpayer has no sufficient interest in asking the court to investigate the tax affairs of another taxpayer or to complain that the latter has been under-assessed or over-assessed: indeed, there is a strong public interest that he should not. And this principle applies equally to groups of taxpayers: an aggregate of individuals each of whom has no interest cannot of itself have an interest ...'

Lord Diplock sought to explain the rationale for the two-stage approach to the application for judicial review, and the way in which the assessment of standing might alter from one stage to another. He regarded the application for leave stage as involving the court in determining whether or not the case disclosed 'what might on further consideration turn out to be an arguable case in favour of granting to the applicant the relief claimed'. This was to be contrasted with the consideration of standing when the application for review was considered, with all the evidence in, and full argument delivered. Hence it would be perfectly possible for an claimant to be regarded as having standing for the purposes of the application for leave, but not for the full application for review.

The *Federation* case was hailed by many as indicative of a liberalisation of the rules on standing, a view borne out by a number of subsequent decisions. For example, in *R v IBA, ex parte Whitehouse* (1984) The Times 14 April, it was held that the applicant had locus standi to challenge the decision of the IBA to broadcast the film *Scum*, simply on the basis of her being a television licence holder (as opposed to her being chair of the National Viewers and Listeners Association). Similarly, in *R v HM Treasury, ex parte Smedley* [1985] 1 All ER 589, the Court of Appeal held that the applicant had locus standi to challenge the legality of a draft Order in Council authorising payments to the EEC, on the basis that he was a British taxpayer. The Divisional Court in *R v Felixstowe Justices, ex parte Leigh* [1987] 2 WLR 380 held that the applicant, a journalist, had locus standi to apply for a declaration that a justices' policy of maintaining anonymity was contrary to law, on the basis that the case raised issues of constitutional significance.

It is tempting to identify common factors that might explain the willingness of the courts to grant standing in some cases rather than others. The *Leigh* and *Smedley* cases suggest that identification of a constitutional issue of general importance will be persuasive. Can the same be said of a financial interest in the decision? *R v Legal Aid Board, ex parte Bateman* [1992] 1 WLR 711 suggests that whilst the existence of a financial interest in the outcome of an application is not a precondition of sufficient interest, its absence may persuade the court to find that locus standi is not established. In that case the applicant had received legal aid in respect of proceedings initiated to establish that she possessed a beneficial interest in certain property, the litigation being settled before coming to trial. Her solicitors, despite having agreed to limit their costs to such sums as were recovered under the consent order drawn up following the settlement, expressed their dissatisfaction with the taxation of their costs, and sought authority from the Legal Aid Board to apply to a judge for a further review of the costs order. This application was refused, whereupon the applicant applied for judicial review of the Board's refusal. Dismissing the application, the court noted that the applicant could not claim any financial interest in the decision, since if the Board ultimately ruled in favour of her solicitors on the issue of costs, the benefit would enure to them, not her. As Nolan LJ stated (at p718a–c):

> 'I accept that sufficient interest need not be a financial interest ... I fully accept the desirability of the courts recognising in appropriate cases the right of responsible citizens to enter the lists for the benefit of the public, or a section of the public, of which they themselves are members ... I cannot accept that the feelings of gratitude and sympathy which [the applicant] entertains for Makins (the applicant's solicitors) afford any sufficient justification for her, either in her own interest or in the public interest, to enter the lists on their behalf. It would be inaccurate as well as discourteous to describe her as a busybody, but her attempt to intervene is at best quixotic ...'

Jowitt J, arriving at the same conclusion, commented (at p721c–d):

> '... though the problem of definition is elusive, common sense should enable one to identify a sufficient interest when it presents itself, like the horse which is difficult to define but not difficult to recognise when one sees it. Nor do I regard the absence of any financial or legal interest as irrelevant to the issue of sufficient interest even though their absence cannot standing alone be fatal ... [N]othing of this amounts in my judgment to a sufficient interest. I have no doubt [that the applicant] will be disappointed if Mr Makin

> obtains no increase in his taxed costs, but her concern for him does not affect any personal interest of hers or her way of life or her environment. It does not relate to something which affects the public in general or any section of the public but only to Mr Makin who was perfectly well able to make his own application for leave and, if he is entitled to it, obtain the redress she wishes for him.'

Curiously no clear or convincing answer was given to the question of why the applicant was bringing these proceedings and not Makins. It may have been connected with the fact that she was granted legal aid to bring the application for judicial review, whereas, it is assumed, Makins would not have been so assisted.

The fact that an applicant has been involved in a decision-making process as an interested party, and possibly consulted during that process, does not necessarily give that party sufficient interest for the purposes of review, especially where there are other parties better placed to contribute to the decision-making process. Hence, in *R* v *Secretary of State for the Home Department, ex parte Bulger* [2001] 3 All ER 449, the Divisional Court rejected the contention that the father of James Bulger, the two-year-old child murdered by Thompson and Venables, had sufficient interest to intervene to challenge the decision of the Lord Chief Justice regarding the defendants' eligibility for parole. The court held that, in criminal cases, the two parties with an interest were the Crown and the defendant. The rule of law could be maintained through those two parties. There was, therefore, no need for a third party to intervene. As Rose LJ observed:

> 'It is true ... that the threshold for standing in judicial review has generally been set by the courts at a low level. This, as it seems to me, is because of the importance in public law that someone should be able to call decision-makers to account, lest the rule of law break down and private rights be denied by public bodies ... But in the present matter the traditional and invariable parties to criminal proceedings, namely the Crown and the defendant, are both able to, and do, challenge those judicial decisions which are susceptible to judicial review as ... It follows that in criminal cases there is no need for a third party to seek to intervene to uphold the rule of law. Nor, in my judgment, would such intervention generally be desirable. If the family of a victim could challenge the sentencing process, why not the family of the defendant? Should the Official Solicitor be permitted to represent the interests of children adversely affected by the imprisonment of their mother? Should organisations representing victims or offenders be permitted to intervene? In my judgment, the answer in all these cases is that the Crown and the defendant are the only proper parties to criminal proceedings. A proper discharge of judicial functions in relation to sentencing requires that the judge take into account ... the impact of the offence and the sentence on the public generally, and on individuals, including the victim and the victim's family and the defendant and the defendant's family. The nature of that impact is properly channelled through prosecution or defence.'

As the *Federation* case itself shows, the interpretation of the phrase 'sufficient interest' is of especial significance to campaigning pressure groups who, by their very nature, may not be directly affected by the decision being challenged, but will represent those who have a concern about the issues involved. It is perhaps not unfair to describe the development of the law on this issue as a case of 'two steps forwards, one step back'. Decisions such as that in *R v Secretary of State for Social Services, ex parte Child Poverty Action Group; Same, ex parte GLC* [1990] 2 QB 540 displayed a broadly rational approach, and suggest that if there is a sufficient nexus between the pressure group and those affected by the decision the courts will normally find the locus standi requirement satisfied. Against this, there was what can only be described as the somewhat aberrant decision of Schiemann J in *R v Secretary of State for the Environment, ex parte Rose Theatre Trust Company* [1990] 1 All ER 754, where he refused to accept that a pressure group, which had formed itself into a company solely for the purpose of challenging the minister's failure to grant the site of the Rose Theatre protected status, had locus standi to challenge the minister's decision. It was his view that merely because an applicant asserted that he or she had an interest did not of itself create such an interest; that a company would not necessarily have sufficient interest simply because it was formed by persons sharing a common view, even if the company's memorandum empowered it to campaign on a particular issue; that the company could have no greater claim to standing than that possessed by individual members of the campaign prior to its incorporation; that the minister's decision was not one in respect of which the ordinary citizen had sufficient interest so as to entitle him to apply for judicial review. In his Lordship's view, the law was not there for every individual who wished to challenge the legality of an administrative decision, and on the facts 'no individual [had] the standing to apply for judicial review'.

Regardless of the view one might take as to the narrow question of whether or not the applicants had sufficient interest, the assertion that there are some executive decisions that no one has sufficient interest to challenge cannot be correct. It subverts the notion of the rule of law to contend that a manifestly ultra vires decision should go unchecked for the want of an applicant with sufficient standing.

Lord Diplock in the *Federation* case was willing to accept that if the Federation had been able to make out its claim of ultra vires action by the Revenue he would have held that this was a matter in which the Federation had a sufficient interest in obtaining an appropriate order. As he stated:

> 'It would, in my view, be a grave lacuna in our system of public law if a pressure group, like the Federation, or even a single public-spirited taxpayer, were prevented by outdated technical rules of locus standi from bringing the matter to the attention of the court to vindicate the rule of law and get the unlawful conduct stopped.'

Significantly, the Divisional Court refused to follow the decision of Schiemann J in *R v Inspectorate of Pollution and Another, ex parte Greenpeace Ltd (No 2)* [1994] 4 All ER 329. British Nuclear Fuels (BNFL), which was authorised to discharge radioactive waste resulting from its undertakings by virtue of permission granted by the Inspectorate of Pollution and the Ministry of Agriculture, acting pursuant to the Radioactive Substances Act 1960 sought, in 1992, further authorisation to discharge waste resulting from the operation of its thermal oxide reprocessing plant. Prior to the granting of these new authorisations BNFL sought variations to its existing authorisations in order to test its new plant before it came into operation. The applicants applied for judicial review, seeking an order of certiorari to quash the respondents' decision to grant the variation, and an injunction to prevent the new authorisations from taking effect. Leave to apply for review was granted but the court refused to grant a stay on the implementation of the authorisations. On the hearing of the application for review the respondents unsuccessfully contended that the applicants lacked locus standi to challenge the variations. Otton J explained his ruling on standing in favour of the applicants on the grounds that the court would take into account the nature of the applicant body, the extent of its interest, the remedies sought, the extent to which the applicant was a responsible body, its consultative status if any, the extent of its membership and support and whether the applicant body would have any other viable means of challenging the matter in question. He explained further that he was also mindful of the fact that if the objections to the authorisations had not been consolidated and organised by a pressure group such as Greenpeace the proceedings could have been far lengthier and more expensive. Although this was a decision of the High Court Otton J felt at liberty not to follow the decision of the Court of Appeal in *ex parte Rose Theatre Trust Co* on the ground that in that case:

> '... the circumstances were different, the interest group had been formed for the exclusive purpose of saving the Rose Theatre site and no individual member could show any personal interest in the outcome.'

Note that this ruling on standing was arrived at despite the fact that the substantive application failed on its merits. The public interest trend has been maintained by the Divisional Court in decisions such as *R v Secretary of State for Foreign Affairs, ex parte World Development Movement Ltd* [1995] 1 WLR 386, wherein it was held that the applicants had sufficient interest to challenge the provision of grants to the Malaysian government for the building of the Pergau Dam. Rose LJ recognised that, whilst the dominant factor was the merit of the application itself, other significant matters included the need to uphold the rule of law, the fact that no other organisation was likely to launch such a challenge, and the key role played by the applicants in giving advice, guidance and assistance regarding aid. In particular it was felt that if the applicant in *R v Secretary of State for Foreign and Commonwealth Affairs, ex parte Rees-Mogg* [1994] 2 WLR 115 was properly regarded as having had locus standi on the basis of his 'sincere concerns for constitutional issues', then a fotiori the applicants in the present case should have standing, given their track record in promoting aid for under-developed nations.

The House of Lords has itself added to the weight of authority recognising the legitimacy of bona fide interested organisations, albeit without citing either the *Rose Theatre* or *Greenpeace* cases, by way of its ruling in *R v Secretary of State for Employment, ex parte Equal Opportunities Commission and Another* [1994] 2 WLR 409. The Equal Opportunities Commission (EOC) made representations to the Secretary of State to the effect that existing domestic law relating to redundancy and unfair dismissal was contrary to EC law as it indirectly discriminated against female employees by offering reduced protection to part-time workers. The Secretary of State rejected these assertions, whereupon the EOC applied for judicial review (seeking a declaration and an order of mandamus) of the Secretary of State's decision not to act in this matter, with a view to challenging the differential in the qualifying dates for redundancy compensation, and his failure to amend the law to take into account an earlier period of full-time employment in calculating the amount of redundancy payment due. The House of Lords held (inter alia) (Lord Jauncy dissenting) that the EOC did have locus standi, as the litigation concerned the extent to which the legislation ensured equality of treatment of employees. As Lord Keith observed:

> '... it would be a very retrograde step now to hold that the EOC has no locus standi to agitate in judicial review proceedings questions related to sex discrimination which are of public importance and affect a large section of the population. The determination of this issue turns essentially upon a consideration of the statutory duties and public law role of the EOC as regards which no helpful guidance is to be gathered from decided cases ...'

The significance of the decision may the extent to which it encourages statutory bodies to adopt a dynamic role in applying for declarations concerning the compatibility of domestic and EC law, rather than waiting for a suitable case to arise as a vehicle for such a challenge. The extent to which the Court of Appeal is willing to endorse the Divisional Court's approach in the *ex parte Greenpeace* case, and take its cue from the majority of their Lordships in the *Equal Opportunities* case, remains to be seen.

Where the respondent is a local authority it is generally assumed that a person who is an elector of, and council taxpayer to, the council would have locus standi. Note, however, that in cases where malpractices have come to light in respect of the activities of council members, the courts have been prepared to allow council leaders to apply for judicial review of their own authorities: see *R* v *Bassetlaw District Council, ex parte Oxby* (1997) The Times 18 December. As Nolan J observed in *R* v *Port Talbot Borough Council, ex parte Jones* [1988] 2 All ER 207 (at p215), where unlawful conduct by a local authority is alleged, the council itself can hardly be both applicant and respondent. Note that the nature of the role of the applicant will be one of the factors taken into account at the substantive hearing in deciding whether to grant the remedy sought. As indicated above, a court hearing an application for judicial review also has the discretion to hear any person who wishes to file evidence or make representations at the hearing.

Applications for review based on the Human Rights Act 1998

An application for judicial review can be made where the applicant alleges that a public authority has acted unlawfully: s6. Under s7(3) an applicant for judicial review 'is to be taken to have a sufficient interest in relation to the unlawful act only if he is, or would be, a victim of that act'. Section 7(7) further provides that an applicant can only be a victim for these purposes if he would be so regarded for the purposes of art 34 of the European Convention on Human Rights.

Delay in applying for relief

Broadly stated, the time limit for applying for judicial review is three months. The rationale for such a short time limit for challenging executive decisions in public law was partly explained by Lord Diplock in *O'Reilly* v *Mackman* (above) where he stated:

> 'The public interest in good administration requires that public authorities and third parties should not be kept in suspense as to the legal validity of a decision the authority has reached in purported exercise of decision-making powers for any longer period than is absolutely necessary in fairness to the person affected by the decision ... the public policy that underlies the grant of those protections [is] ... the need, in the interests of good administration and of third parties who may be indirectly affected by the decision, for speedy certainty as to whether [a] ... decision ... is valid in public law. An action for a declaration or injunction need not be commenced until the very end of the limitation period ... unless such an action can be struck out summarily at the outset as an abuse of the process of the court the whole purpose of the public policy to which the change in O.53 was directed would be defeated.'

The application of the time limit for applications for review is not an entirely straightforward matter, as it is governed by two provisions. Section 31(6) of the Supreme Court Act 1981 provides:

> 'Where the High Court considers that there has been undue delay in making an application for judicial review, the court may refuse to grant (a) leave for the making of the application; or (b) any relief sought on the application, if it considers that the granting of the relief sought would be likely to cause substantial hardship to, or substantially prejudice the rights of, any person or would be detrimental to good administration.'

Part 54.5 CPR 1998 provides that the claim form must be filed 'promptly; and in any event not later than three months after the grounds to make the claim first arose'. It further specifies that the time limit may not be extended by agreement between the parties, and that it does not apply when any other enactment specifies a shorter time limit for making the claim for judicial review. The Practice Direction that accompanies Pt 54 provides that: 'Where the claim is for a quashing order in respect of a judgment, order or conviction, the date when the grounds to make the claim first arose, for the purposes of Pt 54.5, is the date of that judgment, order or conviction'. The issue of when the grounds for the application first arose may be the subject of some dispute, particularly where there are a number of stages in an administrative process.

The key seems to lie in identifying the stage in the decision-making process where the legal rights and obligations of the claimant are first affected. For example, in *R (On the Application of Burkett)* v *Hammersmith and Fulham London Borough Council* [2002] 3 All ER 97, the local planning authority passed a resolution in favour of granting planning permission to a property developer in November 1999. In May 2000 the claimants submitted an application for judicial review of that resolution. On 12 May 2000 the developer met the conditions precedent and outline planning permission was granted. On 18 May 2000 the claimant's application for judicial review was refused both on its merits and due to the delay in bringing the challenge to the November 1999 resolution. On appeal the House of Lords held that the time limit for applying for judicial review ran from the date of the grant of planning permission, not the date of the resolution. The application for review could be amended so as to be directed at the grant of planning permission. As regards the issue of whether time should run from the date of the resolution, Lord Steyn observed:

'In law the resolution is not a juristic act giving rise to rights and obligations. It is not inevitable that it will ripen into an actual grant of planning permission. In these circumstances it would be curious if, when the actual grant of planning permission is challenged, a court could insist by retrospective judgment that the applicant ought to have moved earlier for judicial review against a preliminary decision "which is the real basis of his complaint" ... Moreover, an application to declare a resolution unlawful might arguably be premature and be objected to on this ground. And in strict law it could be dismissed ... For my part the substantive position is straightforward. The court has jurisdiction to entertain an application by a citizen for judicial review in respect of a resolution before or after its adoption. But it is a jump in legal logic to say that he must apply for such relief in respect of the resolution on pain of losing his right to judicial review of the actual grant of planning permission which does affect his rights. Such a view would also be in tension with the established principle that judicial review is a remedy of last resort.

At this stage it is necessary to return to the point that the rule of court applies across the board to judicial review applications. If a decision-maker indicates that, subject to hearing further representations, he is provisionally minded to make a decision adverse to a citizen, is it to be said that time runs against the citizen from the moment of the provisional expression of view? That would plainly not be sensible and would involve waste of time and money. Let me give a more concrete example. A licensing authority expresses a provisional view that a licence should be cancelled but indicates a willingness to hear further argument. The citizen contends that the proposed decision would be unlawful. Surely, a court might as a matter of discretion take the view that it would be premature to apply for judicial review as soon as the provisional decision is announced. And it would certainly be contrary to principle to require the citizen to take such premature legal action. In my view the time limit under the rules of court would not run from the date of such preliminary decisions in respect of a challenge of the actual decision. If that is so, one is entitled to ask: what is the qualitative difference in town planning? ... Undoubtedly, there is a need for public bodies to have certainty as to the legal validity of their actions. That is the rationale of O.53, r4(1) [the forerunner of CPR Pt 54.5.]. On the other hand, it is far from clear that the selection of the actual grant of planning permission as the critical date would disadvantage developers and local authorities.

For my part the arguments in favour of time running from the date of resolution in the present case have been given undue weight by the Court of Appeal. In any event, there are a number of countervailing policy considerations to be considered ... legal policy favours simplicity and certainty rather than complexity and uncertainty. In the interpretation of legislation this factor is a commonplace consideration. In choosing between competing constructions a court may presume, in the absence of contrary indications, that the legislature intended to legislate for a certain and predictable regime. Much will depend on the context. In procedural legislation, primary or subordinate, it must be a primary factor in the interpretative process, notably where the application of the procedural regime may result in the loss of fundamental rights to challenge an unlawful exercise of power. The citizen must know where he stands. And so must the local authority and the developer. For my part this approach is so firmly anchored in domestic law that it is unnecessary, in this case, to seek to reinforce it by reference to the European principle of legal certainty ... I am satisfied that the words "from the date when the grounds for the application first arose" refer to the date when the planning permission was granted.'

Whether there has been what s31 of the 1981 Act refers to as 'undue delay' will clearly depend upon the facts of each case. For example, in *R v Stratford-upon-Avon District Council, ex parte Jackson* [1985] 1 WLR 1319, the Court of Appeal allowed the appellant to apply for judicial review outside the usual time limits where the delay in applying arose from difficulties in being granted legal aid. In *R v Secretary of State for Foreign and Commonwealth Affairs, ex parte World Development Movement Ltd* (above), the application for review was allowed to proceed despite the fact that it related in part to a decision taken in July 1991, and was hence technically out of time, because the court accepted the assertion that the applicants could not have been aware of the material matters providing the basis for their challenge until early 1994. Given the importance of the matters raised the court was persuaded that there had been good reasons for the delay in applying.

It should not be assumed, however, that establishing evidence of good reasons for delay will be decisive of the matter. The court will still have regard to the further issues referred to in s31(6) Supreme Court Act 1981, in particular the possibility of causing substantial hardship to a third party, causing substantial prejudice to the rights of any person, or that permitting an application would be detrimental to good administration: see, as an example of the latter, *R v Director of Passenger Rail Franchising, ex parte Save Our Railways* (1995) The Times 18 December.

Permitting an application to be brought outside the three-month limit can adversely affect third party rights where, for example, the decision challenged concerns the allocation of a finite resource. In *R v Dairy Produce Quota Tribunal, ex parte Caswell* [1990] 2 WLR 1320 the applicants were granted a quota by the Dairy Produce Quota Tribunal (the DPQT) under which they were permitted to produce milk from a herd of 70 cows. They had intended to increase the size of the milking herd to 150 in due course and believed they would obtain the necessary increase in their quota when this occurred. In 1987 the applicants, who had by this time increased the size of their herd to 150, were charged a super levy for overproduction of milk. The applicants discovered that the quota they had been granted in 1985 could not be increased to take account of the increase in the size of their herd. Before both the Divisional Court and the Court of Appeal, the applicants were refused judicial review on the grounds of delay in making the application. These refusals were upheld on appeal to the House of Lords, where it was held that, where the words 'an application for judicial review' appeared in s31(6) and (7) of the 1981 Act and RSC O.53 r4 (the forerunner to Pt 54 CPR), they were to be interpreted as referring to the application for leave to apply for judicial review, the combined effect of RSC O.53 r4 and s31 being that if an application was not made within the three-month time limit, or was not made promptly, any delay was to be regarded as undue delay within the meaning given to that phrase in s31(6). Leave might still be refused, or where leave had been granted relief might be refused, even if the court accepted that there were good reasons for the undue delay, if nevertheless, the court was of the opinion that the granting of either leave or of relief was likely to have a detrimental effect on good administration, or would cause hardship or prejudice within the terms of s31(6). The House of Lords appears to have concluded that to allow the Caswells to contest the DPQT's determinations would have encouraged others to act similarly, with consequent problems for the administration of the quota system, concerned as it was with the allocation of a limited resource. Is this a good reason for denying the citizen relief in respect of a dubious exercise of power by a public body? Taken to its logical conclusion the reasoning suggests that if only a small number of persons are affected by an impugned decision, a late application for review might be permitted if there are good reasons for the delay. Where, however, the decision affects a large number of persons the daunting prospect of resolving the ensuing chaos justifies a denial of relief. A similarly restrictive approach can be discerned in *R* v *Secretary of State for Health, ex parte Furneaux* [1994] 2 All ER 652.

   Where permission has been granted, it is not open to a judge hearing a substantive application for judicial review to dismiss the application solely on the ground that there had been undue delay in applying for leave: *R* v *Criminal Injuries Compensation Board, ex parte A* [1999] 2 AC 330. Assuming an applicant establishes a claim regarding the illegality of the administrative action, delay in applying for review can only come back into play as a factor if there is evidence that granting the relief sought would be likely to cause hardship, prejudice or detriment to others. If such is the case the court will then be engaged in a balancing act – determining whether the applicant should have to suffer the consequences of the impugned decision, or whether the respondent and others should have to deal with the consequences of the decision being quashed. The relevant factors would be the length of the delay, whether the delay had been caused by the applicant, the extent of the hardship caused to others by allowing the application to succeed, and whether the applicant has mislead the court at the permission stage. As Simon Brown LJ explained when the matter was before the Court of Appeal (see *R* v *Criminal Injuries Compensation Board, ex parte A* [1997] 3 WLR 776):

'In short, quite different questions arise with regard to delay depending on whether the point is raised at the leave stage or at the substantive hearing. At the leave stage (putting s31(6)(a) aside), the question is whether there is "good reason" for extending time and allowing the substantive application to be made. This involves both consideration of the reasons for the delay and the apparent merits of the challenge: the better the prospects of success, the readier will the court be to extend time even where the delay is unjustifiable, ie the merits themselves can contribute to or even supply the "good reason". At the substantive hearing, however, the question is whether, in a case where there was initially "undue delay" (which may have been wholly justifiable), the merits of the challenge (by now actually established) should be overridden by the hardship, prejudice or detriment that would result from the grant of relief.'

See further *R* v *Bassetlaw District Council, ex parte Oxby* (above).

Even if an application is brought within the three-month time limit, it can still be refused, or the relief sought denied, if the court is nevertheless of the opinion that there has been undue delay: see *R* v *Customs and Excise, ex parte Eurotunnel plc* (1995) The Independent 23 February and *R* v *Swale Borough Council, ex parte The Royal Society for the Protection of Birds* (1990) 2 Admin LR 790. In *R* v *Secretary of State for Trade and Industry, ex parte Greenpeace Ltd* [1998] COD 59 Laws J held that delay should be measured from the date when the grounds for the application arose, not the date when the impugned decision was made. He also indicated that delay would be less readily tolerated in public interest litigation: see further *R* v *Secretary of State for Trade and Industry, ex parte Greenpeace Ltd* (2000) The Times 19 January.

Note that although the time limit for bringing proceedings alleging that a public authority has acted unlawfully (by acting in a manner incompatible with Convention rights) is stated by s7(5)(a) of the Human Rights Act 1998 to be 12 months, this time limit applies 'subject to any rule imposing a stricter time limit in relation to the procedure in question'. Hence the rules and policies relating to delay in applying for judicial review discussed above will still apply, notwithstanding that an application for review is based on an alleged breach of Convention rights.

Costs

As a general rule the unsuccessful party in judicial review proceedings will have to bear the cost of the proceedings. The prospect of such a financial burden may act as a disincentive to certain worthwhile applications being brought. In *R* v *Lord Chancellor, ex parte Child Poverty Action Group; R* v *DPP, ex parte Bull* [1998] 2 All ER 755 various pressure groups who were planning to make applications for judicial review in respect of what they regarded as 'public interest' cases, made interlocutory applications for pre-emptive costs orders, ie orders to the effect that, whatever the outcome of the substantive judicial review proceedings, no order for costs would be made against the applicants. The gist of their submissions was that it would be wrong for a pressure group to have to bear the risk of costs being awarded when making 'public interest' applications for judicial review. Dismissing the application, the Divisional Court held that courts should only exercise the discretion to make a pre-emptive costs order where the issues raised were truly of general public importance, and the court had a sufficient appreciation of the merits of the claim to be able to conclude that it was in the public interest to make such an order. A further factor was the ability of the respondent to bear the costs when compared to the applicant. Given the approach taken to standing, ie that it is not simply a threshold issue, but one that has to be considered in the light of all the evidence put forward at the substantive hearing, it is not surprising that the court was unwilling to accept the argument that the issue of costs might be determined without hearing both sides' arguments.

11

Remedies

11.1 Introduction

11.2 Injunction

11.3 Declaration

11.4 Damages

11.5 Quashing order (certiorari) and prohibiting order (prohibition)

11.6 Mandatory order (mandamus)

11.1 Introduction

Prior to the introduction of O.53 and the application for judicial review, litigants seeking to challenge the decisions of public bodies would have had to proceed by way of action in order to obtain a declaration, injunction or damages, or would have had to apply for one of the public law remedies, the prerogative orders of mandamus, prohibition or certiorari. One of the major changes introduced by the reforms of 1977 was that, for the first time, all six remedies became available to an applicant seeking judicial review of administrative action. In theory, even after 1977, a litigant could have chosen between proceeding by way of action for a declaration that a public body had acted unlawfully, and applying for judicial review under O.53. As has been explained in Chapter 10, however, the effect of *O'Reilly* v *Mackman* was to force litigants to use the application for judicial review where the respondent was a public body and the issue in the case was primarily one of public law. Some relaxation of this strict procedural dichotomy has followed the introduction of the Civil Procedure Rules 1998, but it is still the case that the 'prerogative orders' will only be available by way of an application for judicial review. The purpose of this Chapter is, therefore, to examine the availability of the six remedies on an application for review, and to examine what the remedies can achieve.

The court's discretion

When considering the issue of remedies by way of judicial review, it is important to

296

bear in mind that the court has an enormous discretion as regards the granting of relief. Even if a prima facie case of ultra vires action has been made out, there are a number of grounds upon which the court may decide to refuse relief. Some of these have already been considered elsewhere in this text, eg lack of standing (Chapter 10); non-justiciability (Chapter 1, section 1.6); and futility of granting a hearing (Chapter 6, section 6.3).

The court may view the applicant as 'undeserving': see *Ward* v *Bradford Corporation* (1972) 70 LGR 27 (trainee teacher living with a man whilst unmarried) and *Cinnamond* v *British Airports Authority* [1980] 1 WLR 582 (unlicensed taxi drivers touting at airports). Generally, if appears to the court that the applicant has been largely responsible for bringing about the decision that he now seeks to have quashed, the court will not grant a remedy: see further *R* v *Secretary of State for Education and Science, ex parte Birmingham District Council* (1984) The Times 18 July and *R* v *South Holland Drainage Committee Men* (1838) 8 Ad & El 429.

The court may decline to grant a remedy because of the undesirable consequences that would flow from so doing. This may be the case where there has been delay: see Chapter 10, and observations made in *Glynn* v *Keele University* [1971] 1 WLR 487. The courts will, on occasion, be mindful of the administrative consequences of intervention, as in *R* v *Brent Health Authority, ex parte Francis* [1984] 3 WLR 1317, where relief was refused on the ground that to quash the financial resolutions of the authority would plunge it into even deeper chaos, and that could not be justified on the basis of the applicant's allegation of procedural impropriety: see further Chapter 3, section 3.5 and *R* v *Secretary of State for Social Services, ex parte Association of Metropolitan Authorities* [1986] 1 WLR 1 (reluctance to throw housing benefit claim system into chaos). Alternatively, the court may be reluctant to set a precedent that opens up certain decision-making bodies to review in the courts: see *R* v *Preston Supplementary Benefit Appeal Tribunal, ex parte Moore* [1975] 1 WLR 624 (Lord Denning MR reluctant to allow tribunals to be come a 'happy hunting ground for lawyers').

Possibly the most important ground for the court declining to grant relief is that another more suitable remedy has been provided by statute, typically a default power, right of appeal or other form of referral to an administrative agency. Hence, in *R* v *Chief Adjudication Officer, ex parte Bland* (1985) The Times 6 February, Taylor J held that judicial review would not be available as an alternative to a specialised statutory system of appeals unless special reasons for not using the statutory procedure were advanced. Similarly, in *ex parte P* (1998) The Times 31 March, minister's default powers were held to be more appropriate than judicial review regarding a local authority's duties to asylum seekers: see further *R* v *Paddington Valuation Officer, ex parte Peachey Property Corporation* [1966] 1 QB 380 at 400 and *R* v *Epping and Harlow General Commissioners, ex parte Goldstraw* [1983] 3 All ER 257. The issue is considered further in relation to each of the prerogative orders at sections 11.5 and 11.6 below.

11.2 Injunction

An injunction is an order of the court directed at a defendant or respondent, ordering that party not to proceed with particular action, or in the case of a mandatory injunction, an order to act in a particular way. Until the procedural reforms of 1977 (see again Chapter 10) an injunction was only available by way of a private action and, as an equitable remedy, was only granted where damages would not provide sufficient relief. Since 1977 the position has been that a litigant may apply for an injunction, by way of an application for judicial review, in circumstances where a prerogative order would be available.

An injunction may be applied for as a final remedy (ie a perpetual injunction) or as an interim form of relief, by way of an interlocutory application. In particular, an interim injunction can be granted to prevent a public body from taking action, pending the determination of the issue by the court. In deciding whether or not to grant such interim relief by way of judicial review proceedings the courts will have regard to the principles established by the House of Lords in *American Cyanamid Co v Ethicon Ltd* [1975] AC 396 (ie the applicant must have an arguable case, there has to be a serious question to decide), but regard will also be had to the fact that the application is being made in the public law context. In *R* v *Ministry of Agriculture, Fisheries and Food, ex parte Monsanto plc* (1998) The Times 12 October the Divisional Court held that in deciding where the balance of convenience lay it would be persuaded by the following factors: the presumption against granting an application if it would have the effect of restricting free competition; the public interest that a decision of a public body should have effect until set aside by the courts; whether damages would be a sufficient remedy for the party against whom the injunction was sought in the event that the interim injunction was discharged; and the availability of other safeguards or relief available to the applicant.

As regards final conclusive orders, a prohibiting order would have the same effect as a standard injunction, and a mandatory order the same effect as a mandatory injunction.

The jurisdiction of the courts in relation to the granting of such relief was the key question in a number of landmark decisions: *R* v *Secretary of State for Transport, ex parte Factortame* [1989] 2 WLR 997 (and, when considering a reference back by the European Court of Justice, in *R* v *Secretary of State for Transport, ex parte Factortame (No 2)* [1990] 3 WLR 818) and *M* v *Home Office* [1993] 3 All ER 537.

The *Factortame* litigation arose out of attempts by the United Kingdom government to limit the impact of the common fisheries policy on its domestic fishing industry by the enactment of the Merchant Shipping Act 1988 (Pt II), which purported to restrict the number of vessels whose catch could be counted against the British quota. The Secretary of State issued regulations under the Act that required any vessel wishing to fish as part of the British fleet to be registered under the 1988 Act, registration being contingent upon a vessel's owner being a British citizen or domiciled in Britain. Where the vessels were owned by companies, the shareholders would have to meet these requirements. The applicants were British registered companies operating fishing vessels in British waters who now found it impossible to obtain registration because their shareholders and directors were Spanish. The applicants contended that the regulations effectively prevented them from exercising their rights under Community law to fish as part of the British fleet. The Secretary of State contended that Community law did not prevent the United Kingdom from introducing domestic legislation determining which companies were 'British nationals' and which were not.

The applicants sought judicial review of the minister's decision that their registration should cease; his determination that their vessels were no longer 'British' ships; and of the relevant parts of the Act and Regulations which would have the effect of preventing them from fishing. As to remedies, the applicants sought, inter alia, an interim injunction suspending the operation of the legislation pending the ruling of the European Court of Justice as to its compatibility with EC law. Regarding the interpretation of Community law, the Divisional Court requested a preliminary ruling under art 177 of the Treaty of Rome (now art 234 EC Treaty) so that the questions relating to the applicants' rights could be resolved. Pending that ruling, the court granted the applicants interim relief in the form of an injunction to suspend the operation of the legislation by restraining the minister from enforcing it, thus enabling the applicants to continue fishing. The Secretary of State challenged the order for interim relief, which was set aside by the Court of Appeal. The applicants appealed unsuccessfully to the House of Lords, their Lordships holding that an English court had no power to grant interim relief to prevent the operation of a statute passed by Parliament.

Lord Bridge put forward two grounds for denying the remedy. First, if the ultimate decision of the European Court of Justice went against the applicants they would have enjoyed approximately two years (the length of time it would take for that court to resolve the matter) unjust enrichment by being allowed to continue fishing. On that basis no interim relief would be given, unless it was shown that there was some overriding principle of Community law which provided that member states should provide some form of relief to litigants who claimed that their rights were being interfered with, pending a decision of the European Court of Justice. Second, Lord Bridge sought to deny the availability of the relief sought, by reference to ss21(2) and 23(2)(b) of the Crown Proceedings Act 1947, holding that these provisions preserved what had been the common law position, ie that such relief was not available in judicial review proceedings on the Crown side. Lord Bridge expressed the view that it was not surprising that the Crown Proceedings Act 1947 Act did not expressly state that injunctions were not available in proceedings on the Crown side of the Queen's Bench Division; they had not been before 1947, so why should the statute have bothered to re-state the existing law? His Lordship drew support for his analysis from the fact that the Law Commission, in its *Report on Remedies in Administrative Law* (Law Com No 73, Cmnd 6407) had looked at the problem of obtaining an interim injunction by way of an application for judicial review, and had assumed that, given s21 of the 1947 Act, such an order would not be possible. The Law Commission had drafted an amended s21 which it appended to its report, but as O.53 was concerned with procedure and practice, it would have been outside the jurisdiction of the Rules Committee to institute such a far-reaching change by way of delegated legislation, and the change was therefore not adopted.

In arriving at these conclusions, Lord Bridge expressly rejected the reasoning in two earlier decisions, *R* v *Secretary of State for the Home Department, ex parte Herbage* [1987] 1 QB 872 and *R* v *Licensing Authority, ex parte Smith Kline & French Laboratories Ltd (No 2)* [1990] 1 QB 574. The question of whether or not EC law required the provision of such an interim form of relief was referred by the House of Lords to the European Court of Justice under art 177.

By way of response, the European Court of Justice held that Community law did require the courts of member states to give effect to the directly enforceable provisions of Community law, such Community laws rendering any conflicting national law inapplicable. A court which would grant interim relief, but for a rule of domestic law, should set aside that rule of domestic law in favour of observing Community obligations. When the matter returned to the House of Lords, therefore, the question for consideration was no longer that of whether or not relief was available in principle, but whether or not it should be granted in that particular case. The House took the view that the determining factor should not be the availability of damages as a remedy, but the balance of convenience, taking into account the importance of upholding duly enacted laws. It noted that damages were not available against a public body exercising its powers in good faith, and expressed the view that a domestic court should not restrain a public authority from enforcing an apparently valid law unless it was satisfied, having regard to all the circumstances, that the challenge to the validity of the law was, prima facie, so firmly based as to justify so exceptional a course being taken. As regards the Spanish trawlermen, it was felt that the applicants did have a strong case for relief being granted, particularly with regard to the provisions requiring residence and domicile of owners. The balance of convenience was found to favour the granting of such relief.

Issues of interim injunctive relief may also arise where an applicant seeks to prevent the promulgation of domestic legislation giving effect to an EC directive prior to the directive's implementation date. The House of Lords was asked to advise as to the correct approach in such cases in *R* v *Secretary of State for Health and Others, ex parte Imperial Tobacco Ltd and Others* (2000) The Times 20 December. The directive in question was concerned with the ban on the advertising of tobacco products. It came into force in July 1998, obliging member states to comply with its terms by the end of July 2001. Despite the fact that Germany commenced direct action to have the directive annulled in the European Court of Justice, in December 1998 the United Kingdom government announced its intention to implement the directive by means of secondary legislation and the applicant companies, manufacturers of tobacco products, were granted leave to apply for judicial review of that decision. In February 1999 an order was granted for a reference to the European Court of Justice in respect of the directive. The applicants sought an injunction to prevent the respondent from making the regulations that would give effect to the directive on the ground that the directive was itself unlawful under the terms of the EC Treaty. A specific criticism of the directive was that it was essentially a public health matter being promulgated under a Treaty provision related to the approximation of laws and regulations for the effective working of the internal market. The injunction was granted at first instance, a ruling against which the Secretary of State appealed successfully (Laws LJ dissenting). The majority in the Court of Appeal had held that the grant of interim relief had to be decided applying Community law principles as enunciated in *Zuckerfabrik Süderdithmarschen AG* v *Hauptzollamt Itzehoe* [1991] ECR I–415. Under Community law the test was whether the applicants could show that they would suffer serious and irreparable damage if the relief was not granted, financial damage not being considered irreparable for these purposes. The Court of Appeal had also expressed concerns about the Court usurping the political judgment of the government's decision to promote public health by granting the relief sought. On 30 July 2000 the Advocate-General delivered an opinion to the effect that the directive was ultra vires and the government accepted that the regulations could not be promulgated until the ruling of the European Court of Justice was known. The European Court of Justice subsequently ruled the directive to be ultra vires. The House of Lords was nevertheless asked to give its opinion on the availability of interlocutory relief where a challenge was made to regulations introduced pursuant to an EC directive. Lord Slynn, for the majority, explained that where a domestic court was asked to grant an injunction to restrain the government from introducing regulations purporting to give effect to an EC directive, a reference to the European Court of Justice would be required to determine whether domestic or Community law was applicable. He expressed the view that there should be a Community-wide approach to the application, even via national regulations, of Community law. He felt that the adoption of such an approach could be undermined by the granting of interim injunctive relief by domestic courts. Regardless of what member states might or might not do in adopting or refusing to adopt Community directives as a matter of policy, the majority of their Lordships felt that the courts ought to adopt a consistent approach. Accepting that the test laid down in *Zuckerfabrik Süderdithmarschen AG* v *Hauptzollamt Itzehoe* represented an appropriate starting point, Lord Slynn went on to consider the extent to which it might be said to differ from the approach in domestic law as laid down in *American Cyanamid Co* v *Ethicon Ltd* [1975] AC 396. He observed that, whilst there were common factors, such as the need to show urgency, and the need to avoid serious and irreparable harm, there were points of divergence, such as the relevance of financial damage. Lord Slynn, therefore, concluded that if, in the present case, it had been necessary to consider whether Community law applied and the scope of its application, it would have been necessary and obligatory for the House to have referred a question to the ECJ under art 234 (formerly 177) of the EC Treaty.

Lord Hoffmann, dissenting, expressed the view that no issue as to uniformity of application arose where interim relief was sought during the implementation period as, by definition, Community law did not require the uniform application of directives prior to the implementation date. Lord Millett (also dissenting) expressed his profound disagreement with observations made in the court below, to the effect that the granting of relief might amount to an impermissible attempt to interfere with the government's legislative programme. His Lordship observed that it was the proper role of the judiciary to test the validity of any law that was invoked by the state to support its actions.

Although the case bears similarities with the *Factortame* litigation, a key difference is that in *Factortame* the applicants were challenging the validity of domestic law. Here the tobacco companies were effectively challenging the validity of (putative) Community law. See further *R v Secretary of State for the Environment, ex parte Royal Society for the Protection of Birds* (1995) 7 Admin LR 434, where an interim injunction was refused after the court had conducted a balance of convenience assessment, on the basis that it might result in enormous economic loss and the applicants were not in a position to give any cross-undertaking in damages.

The outcome of the *Factortame* litigation appeared to be, therefore, that the courts could grant interim relief to prevent the application of the provisions of an Act of Parliament, where adherence to it was likely to result in a violation of rights protected by Community law, but the position of the litigant seeking to protect rights arising solely under domestic law remained unclear until clarified by the House of Lords in *M v Home Office* [1993] 3 WLR 433. The applicant (M) had arrived in the United Kingdom from Zaire seeking political asylum, but was not granted permission to remain following the Home Secretary's finding that M had not established the required 'well grounded fear of persecution' in Zaire. M was due to be returned to Zaire on 1 May 1991, the flight leaving London at 6.30pm. Judicial review proceedings to challenge the Secretary of State's decision on asylum were heard on 1 May, and at 5.55pm Garland J indicated that, as in his view there was an arguable case to be considered, M should not be removed from the country until there had been a full hearing of the case. Counsel for the Home Office indicated that it would seek to prevent M's removal from the country, although he had not been instructed to give an undertaking that M's removal would be prevented. M did depart on the flight to Zaire, and later that evening the judge granted a mandatory order compelling the Home Office to ensure the return of M to the United Kingdom. The Home Secretary declined to obey the order, and instead challenged its validity in the courts. During these proceedings Garland J accepted that he did not have the power to issue what amounted to mandatory injunctions against ministers, but suggested that he had been seeking to ensure compliance with the earlier undertaking given by counsel for the Secretary of State to the effect that the judicial review proceedings would not be rendered otiose by M's removal from the jurisdiction. M brought proceedings for contempt against the Secretary of State based on his failure to comply with the court's order whilst it had been in force. The applicant's motion was dismissed at first instance but he was partly successful before the Court of Appeal. The House of Lords held, inter alia, that s31 of the Supreme Court Act 1981 empowered the courts to grant coercive orders against a minister of the Crown acting in his official capacity.

Lord Woolf, in a closely argued speech, found himself unable to agree with the reasoning that had led Lord Bridge to conclude that interim injunctive relief was, subject to the demands of Community law, not available in respect of ministers of the Crown acting in an official capacity because of s21 of the 1947 Act. He expressed the view that the purpose of s21 had been to prevent any extension of the availability of injunctive relief against the Crown to circumstances where it had not been available prior to 1947. The 1947 Act did not affect the right of an individual to seek injunctive relief against an individual Crown servant acting in his official capacity. In particular, he was persuaded by the argument that, by virtue of s38(2) of the 1947 Act, s21 had not been intended by Parliament to apply to proceedings on the Crown side of the Queen's Bench Division, and proceedings for the prerogative orders were brought on the Crown side. The prerogative orders had never been available against the Crown, therefore when s31(2) of the Supreme Court Act 1981 extended the prerogative jurisdiction to include the granting of injunctions, including interim injunctions, by way of judicial review proceedings, it was not creating a conflict with s21 of the 1947 Act (ie it did not create the possibility of injunctions being granted against the Crown where previously they had not been). Even prior to 1947, however, it had been recognised that the prerogative orders were available in respect of a minister of the Crown acting in an official capacity. Hence the effect of s31(2) was to make injunctive relief available in situations where there was jurisdiction to grant a prerogative order, although in Lord Woolf's view the power to do so should be exercised sparingly. Further, there was no serious doubt as to the availability of declaratory relief against a minister acting in his official capacity. If a declaration was now available in such cases it would be curious if an (interim) injunction was not.

As will be seen in Chapter 14, some doubt may still surround the availability of injunctive relief where what is challenged is an exercise of (delegated) prerogative power. Traditionally the relief granted in such cases has been declaratory, on the basis that it would be incongruous to grant a prerogative order against the Crown. Lord Woolf specifically relies on the argument that, since injunctions and the prerogative orders are now available via the same procedure, the courts should have the jurisdiction to grant an injunction wherever they have the jurisdiction to grant a prerogative order. If, therefore, the courts have declined in the past to grant prerogative orders in respect of the exercise of prerogative power, congruity would suggest that the courts would also decline to grant injunctive relief. Lord Woolf comments in *M* v *Home Office* that, in the light of the GCHQ case, 'a distinction probably no longer has to be drawn between duties which have a statutory and those which have a prerogative source.' Note that in the GCHQ case, however, the applicants originally sought an order of certiorari to quash the Prime Minister's instruction on union membership, but at the first hearing this was amended to become a request for declaratory relief. The remedy sought in both *R* v *Criminal Injuries Compensation Board, ex parte Lain* [1967] 2 QB 864 and *R* v *Secretary of State for Foreign and Commonwealth Affairs, ex parte Everett* [1989] 2 WLR 224 was an order of certiorari, but it could be contended that both cases involved the exercise of delegated prerogative power, where the decision-maker has to act within the terms of the delegation. If a minister exercising prerogative power is to be regarded as being amenable to the prerogative orders, it raises the question of when, if ever, action is taken by the Crown as such. The Crown, other than when the monarch acts in person, can only act via its ministers. The issue is not entirely academic as difficulties could arise as regards a challenge to the creation of regulations by way of Order in Council. Would the courts be willing to grant interim relief to prevent this exercise of prerogative power?

Aside from the issue of injunctive relief, the courts may, in any event, be able to achieve much the same result by granting a stay of proceedings. In *R* v *Secretary of State for Education and Science, ex parte Avon County Council* [1991] 2 WLR 702 the Court of Appeal expressed the view that, under O.53 r3(10)(a) (see now Pt 54.1(2) CPR 1998), the term 'proceedings' should be construed widely so as to encompass the procedures by which administrative bodies arrived at their decisions: see further *R* v *Secretary of State for the Home Department, ex parte Muboyayi* [1992] QB 244 and *R* v *Inspectorate of Pollution and Another, ex parte Greenpeace Ltd (No 2)* [1994] 4 All ER 329.

11.3 Declaration

A declaration is an order of the court stating the legal position between two parties, and can be sought to provide some clarification on a disputed point of law: see *Attorney-General* v *Able* [1984] 1 All ER 277. Although it has no coercive force, and refusal to act in accordance with a declaration will not be a contempt, a public body is most unlikely to ignore the implications of any declaratory relief granted by the courts: see *Webster* v *Southwark London Borough Council* [1983] QB 698. The declaration is a particularly flexible remedy as regards the challenging of executive action. In theory it permits the citizen to question proposed executive action, rather than wait for it to happen and attempt to have it quashed. In *Dyson* v *Attorney-General* [1911] QB 410 and [1912] 1 Ch 158 the court held that it was permissible for the plaintiff to question the validity of tax assessment notices (on the ground that they were ultra vires the enabling Act) prior to the notices being issued, rather than having to dispute the claim for tax when made: see further *Gillick* v *West Norfolk and Wisbech Area Health Authority* [1986] AC 112. Reliance on a declaration in a case involving a challenge to the exercise of prerogative powers might also avoid the problems adverted to above, as regards whether or not the prerogative orders are available in respect of such action.

Any doubt as to whether declaratory relief can be obtained in situations where prerogative orders cannot has been resolved by the House of Lords' decision in *R* v *Secretary of State for Employment, ex parte Equal Opportunities Commission and Another* [1994] 2 WLR 409. The Commission made representations to the Secretary of State to the effect that existing domestic law relating to redundancy and unfair dismissal was contrary to EC law as it indirectly discriminated against female employees by offering reduced protection to part-time workers. The Secretary of State rejected these assertions, whereupon the Commission applied for judicial review (seeking a declaration and an order of mandamus) of the Secretary of State's decision not to act in this matter, with a view to challenging the differential in the qualifying dates for redundancy compensation and a declaration and order of mandamus in respect of Secretary of State's failure to amend the law to take into account an earlier period of full-time employment in calculating the amount of redundancy payment due. A majority of their Lordships held that even though the case was not one where the court would have been empowered to grant a prerogative order, as there was no 'decision' of the Secretary of State to quash, reference to the *Factortame* series of cases confirmed that the Commission was entitled to apply for a declaration as to the extent to which the provisions of the 1978 Act relating to redundancy and compensation for unfair dismissal were compatible with Community law. Such an application would not involve a declaration that the United Kingdom or the Secretary of State was in breach of Community obligations, as the Commission's purpose could be served simply by a declaration confirming the incompatibility of domestic law and Community law. Lord Browne-Wilkinson in particular charted the history of declaratory relief, and observed that if the availability of declaratory relief was co-terminus with the availability of the prerogative remedies litigants would have been seriously disadvantaged by decisions such as *O'Reilly* v *Mackman*. As he stated:

'... under O.53 any declaration as to public rights which could formerly be obtained in civil proceedings in the High Court can now also be obtained in judicial review proceedings. If this were not so, the effect of the purely procedural decision in *O'Reilly* v *Mackman*, requiring all public law cases to be brought by way of judicial review, would have had the effect of thenceforward preventing a plaintiff who previously had locus standi to bring civil proceedings for a declaration as to public rights (even though there was no decision which could be the subject of a prerogative order) from bringing any proceedings for such a declaration. No statutory provision has ever removed the right to seek such a declaration ... O.53 r1(2) does not say that a declaration is only to be made in lieu of a prerogative order. All it requires is that the court should have regard to "the nature of the matters in respect of which" prerogative orders can be made.'

See further *R* v *Secretary of State for Employment, ex parte Seymour Smith* (1997) The Times 14 March.

Availability

In theory the applicant for a declaration need not have any subsisting cause of action, but as Lord Diplock observed in *Gouriet* v *Union of Post Office Workers* [1978] AC 435:

'... the jurisdiction of the court is not to declare the law generally or give advisory opinions; it is confined to declaring contested legal rights, subsisting or future, of the parties represented in the litigation before it.'

Thus in *Malone* v *Metropolitan Police Commissioner* [1979] Ch 344, where the plaintiff sought a declaration that the tapping of his telephone by the police constituted an invasion of his right to privacy, as enshrined in the European Convention on Human Rights, the Vice-Chancellor refused to grant the declaration sought because, in his view, the case did not raise any issues concerning rights protected by English law. He expressed the view that it would have been an unwarranted usurpation of the functions of the legislature for him to have laid down any legal principles applicable to this matter. In *Gillick* v *West Norfolk Area Health Authority* (above) Lord Bridge observed that the court should exercise the 'utmost restraint' in granting a remedy by way of a declaration. It should certainly not exercise its jurisdiction to grant the remedy if there was some other equally convenient remedy available to the applicant. This reasoning was cited with approval by Woolf J in *R* v *Secretary of State for the Environment, ex parte Greater London Council* (1985) The Times 30 December, where his Lordship expressed the view that the power to grant declarations should not be used merely as a means of improving the reasoning for decisions of administrative bodies where the decision itself was unobjectionable.

A declaration will not be granted where there is no longer alive issue in the case. In *Williams* v *Home Office (No 2)* [1982] 1 All ER 1151 a prisoner who had been transferred to a special control unit sought a declaration that his transfer had been in breach of natural justice, as he had not committed any offences against prison discipline, and had not been told of the reasons for the transfer. By the time the matter reached the court, however, the prisoner had been returned to his usual cell. The court refused to grant the declaration sought on the basis that the matter was now only of 'academic' interest. In the same spirit, the courts will refuse a declaration if the issues involved do not raise the possibility of any legal consequence. Hence, in *Maxwell* v *Department of Trade and Industry* [1974] QB 523, a declaration that departmental inspectors had acted in breach of natural justice in compiling a report was refused because the report alone could not produce any legal consequences, it was merely preparatory to further action: see further *R* v *Inland Revenue Commissioners, ex parte Bishop etc* [1999] NLJ 682.

A declaration will not be granted where the effect would be to provide a 'second opinion' in respect of a matter that an administrative body has already lawfully dealt with. Hence, in *Healey* v *Minister of Health* [1955] 1 QB 221, where the plaintiff sought a declaration that he was a 'mental health officer' and thus entitled to a certain level of superannuation, the Court of Appeal refused to grant declaratory relief. The minister, who was designated under the relevant Act to determine such matters, had already announced his decision to the contrary. The plaintiff was not alleging any ultra vires act on the part of the minister, or error of law, so that, even if the court granted the declaration sought, it would not effect the minister's decision. The court saw no purpose in simply producing two conflicting decisions. Similarly, in *Punton* v *Ministry of Pensions and National Insurance* [1963] 1 All ER 275, a declaration that the plaintiff was 'not a person directly interested in a trade dispute' was refused, because it would simply have resulted in a decision conflicting with that already made by the National Insurance Commissioner. A declaration cannot quash a decision that the applicant seeks to overturn. In such cases an order of certiorari must be requested.

A declaration may, however, achieve the same effect in certain circumstances. Hence, in *R* v *Bassetlaw District Council, ex parte Oxby* (1997) The Times 18 December, declarations were granted to the effect that certain planning consents were void on the ground of bias, thus relieving the local authority of the need to formally revoke the consents under the Town and Country Planning Act 1990 and pay compensation to the landowners concerned.

Declarations under the Human Rights Act 1998

Following the enactment of the Human Rights Act 1998 a reviewing court is now able to grant a declaration that the action or inaction of a public authority is incompatible with the Convention rights protected by the 1998 Act. The 1998 Act introduces a new power, however, where the incompatibility with Convention rights arises from the operation of a provision in primary legislation, or in a provision in subordinate legislation that cannot be avoided because of the wording of primary legislation. In such cases the House of Lords, the Judicial Committee of the Privy Council, the Courts-Martial Appeal Court, the High Court or the Court of Appeal will be empowered to grant a declaration of incompatibility: s4. Where such a declaration is made it does not 'affect the validity, continuing operation or enforcement of the provision in respect of which it is given; and ... is not binding on the parties to the proceedings in which it is made': s4(6). Note that only the 'victim' of an alleged infringement of Convention rights can apply for judicial review: see Chapter 10. Where a declaration of incompatibility has been made and rights of appeal have been exhausted, abandoned or become time-barred, or it appears to a minister that (in the light of a finding of the European Court of Human Rights) a provision of legislation is incompatible with obligations under the Convention, a minister may, if he considers that there are compelling reasons for so doing, make orders to amend the relevant legislation to the extent that considers necessary to remove the incompatibility: see s10(1) and (2).

11.4 Damages

Subject to the exceptions considered in Chapter 14, damages may be awarded against public bodies in actions commenced by way of writ in respect of the normal range of private law liabilities. Part 54.3(2) CPR 1998 provides that a 'claim for judicial review may include a claim for damages but may not seek damages alone'. Section 31(4) of the Supreme Court Act 1981 sets out the circumstances in which the court may award damages on a claim for judicial review – ie where the applicant can show that had he proceeded by way of action he would have been able to establish a private law right to damages. Note that it was never the intention to create a new right to damages as a remedy in administrative law – the procedural rules simply save the litigant the trouble of pursuing two actions (the application for review and the action for damages).

Whilst a private law action for damages might lie against a public body in respect of its giving negligent advice, it seems very doubtful whether an action will succeed on the basis that the public body has negligently acted ultra vires. In *Dunlop* v *Woollahra Municipal Council* [1982] AC 158 Lord Diplock went so far as to doubt whether any private law duty of care is owed by a public authority when exercising its statutory discretion. Similar doubts are raised by the Privy Council in *Rowling* v *Takaro Properties* [1988] 1 All ER 163. It would appear that the only remedy in such cases is to apply for judicial review to have the ultra vires decision quashed: see further *R* v *Knowsley Borough Council, ex parte Maguire* [1992] NLJ 1375. The litigant is caught in a vicious circle as he will not be able to add a claim for damages to his application for review, as he would not have been able to claim damages for the ultra vires action in proceedings commenced by way of writ. On the basis of *Bourgoin SA* v *Ministry of Agriculture, Fisheries and Food* [1985] 3 All ER 585 and *Three Rivers District Council* v *Bank of England (No 3)* [2000] 3 All ER 1 it would appear that damages are available by way of action where a public officer deliberately acts ultra vires (malicious abuse of power), hence if the litigant wanted to proceed by way of an application for review a claim for damages could be made: see further Chapter 14. Other matters are still uncertain. How, for example, should a litigant pursue an action for breach of statutory duty, where there appears to be a right to a remedy by way of damages? Presumably if the litigant has the option of proceeding by way of writ he will not go out of his way, given the need to obtain leave within three months etc to seek judicial review instead. In *R* v *Northavon District Council, ex parte Palmer* (1993) The Times 17 August the applicant, who had been incorrectly refused housing by the respondent authority, applied for judicial review of the decision, seeking, inter alia, damages for breach of its housing duty. Whilst the matter was adjourned the authority reconsidered her case and determined it properly in her favour. The applicant thereupon amended her claim and requesting a declaration that she had been wrongly denied housing, and damages. The Divisional Court held that even though the application for prerogative relief had become redundant, the claim for a declaration would be allowed to proceed since it provided a basis on which the court could consider the claim for damages. If the application were struck out, the applicant would be forced to pursue her claim for damages by way of action, thus running the risk that her writ might be struck out as an abuse of process, since her claim was founded on a public law issue.

The Human Rights Act 1998 does not create a new right to damages as such (beyond the possibility of damages being awarded in respect of breach of the statutory duty not to act in a way that is incompatible with the Convention rights protected by the Act). Subsection 8(2) provides that 'damages may be awarded only by a court which has power to award damages, or to order the payment of compensation, in civil proceedings'. Under s8(3) no award of damages will be made unless (having taking account of all the circumstances of the case, including any other relief or remedy granted) the court considers that such an award is necessary to afford just satisfaction to the person in whose favour it is made.

A court contemplating an award of damages in respect of action incompatible with Convention rights must also have regard to 'the principles applied by the European Court of Human Rights in relation to the award of compensation under art 41 of the Convention': see s8(4).

11.5 Quashing order (certiorari) and prohibiting order (prohibition)

The prerogative orders formerly known by the terms certiorari, prohibition and mandamus are only available by way of an application for judicial review; see Pt 54 CPR 1998. Note that in October 2000 the names of these orders were changed, as apart of the process of modernising the court procedures, and with effect from that date were renamed quashing order, prohibiting order and mandatory order respectively.

Whilst Pt 54 states that an application for a mandatory order, a prohibiting order or a quashing order *shall* be made by way of an application for judicial review, r1(2) provides that an application for a declaration or an injunction *may* be made by way of an application for judicial review.

Where such an application is made the court may grant the declaration or injunction claimed if it considers that, having regard to the nature of the matters in respect of which relief may be granted by way of order of mandatory order, prohibiting order or quashing order; the nature of the persons and bodies against whom relief may be granted by way of such an order; and all the circumstances of the case, it would be just and convenient for the declaration or injunction to be granted on an application for judicial review.

Quashing order

The effect of a quashing order is to quash the decision of an inferior body on the basis that the decision is either ultra vires, or vitiated by an intra vires error of law.

The effect of quashing a decision in this way is to render it null and void. Given that judicial review is concerned with the legality of the decision making process, and not the substantive merits of a decision properly arrived at, the court in granting a quashing order will not be substituting its own decision for that of the inferior body. Part 54.19 provides, however, that where the relief sought is a quashing order, and the court is satisfied that there are grounds for quashing the decision to which the application relates, the court may, in addition to quashing it, remit the matter to the court, tribunal, or authority concerned with a direction to reconsider it and reach a decision in accordance with the findings of the court.

Availability of quashing order

The starting point for any examination of the availability of quashing order is the dictum of Atkin LJ in *R* v *Electricity Commissioners, ex parte London Electricity Joint Committee Co (1922) Ltd* [1924] 1 KB 171 (hereinafter the *Electricity Commissioners* case). As he observed:

'The operation of the writs [of prohibiting order and quashing order] has extended to control the proceedings of bodies which do not claim to be and would not be recognised as courts of justice. Whenever any body of persons having legal authority to determine questions affecting the rights of subjects, and having the duty to act judicially, act in excess of their legal authority, they are subject to the controlling jurisdiction of the King's Bench Division exercised in these writs.'

As will be seen from the above passage, there are essentially three criteria that must be satisfied for a quashing order to issue. First, the decision-making body must act with legal authority. Historically this has meant that a quashing order has been available in respect of bodies exercising statutory power, typically local authorities, tribunals and ministers, as opposed to decisions of domestic tribunals or private companies registered under the Companies Act 1948: see *R* v *BBC, ex parte Lavelle* [1983] 1 All ER 241 and *Law* v *National Greyhound Racing Club Ltd* [1983] 3 All ER 300. It is now clear that the exercise of prerogative power falls within the scope of judicial review but, as outlined above, there may still be uncertainty as to the suitability of the prerogative orders as the appropriate form of relief. In *R* v *Criminal Injuries Compensation Board, ex parte Lain* [1967] 2 QB 864 Diplock LJ observed that the Criminal Injuries Compensation Board's jurisdiction to discharge the quasi-judicial function of awarding compensation was not derived from any agreement between the Crown and applicants for compensation:

'... but from instructions by the executive government, that is, by prerogative act of the Crown. The appointment of the board and the conferring upon it of jurisdiction ... and ... authority to make payments ... are acts of government, done without statutory authority but nonetheless lawful for that.'

Regardless of the position in relation to prerogative power, however, the scope of a quashing order as a remedy has been significantly widened by the Court of

Appeal's decision in *R* v *Panel on Take-overs and Mergers, ex parte Datafin* [1987] 2 WLR 699. The Court held that the remedy would be available against a body lacking statutory or prerogative powers (in fact lacking any de jure power) on the basis that its decisions were nevertheless of great significance and affected the public – those dealing in companies quoted on the Stock Exchange. A key factor, it is submitted, was the fact that there was no other means of legal challenge to the Panel's decisions. It confirms that courts will be less concerned with the source of a body's power, and more with the effect of its decisions.

Second, the decision-making body must be empowered to deal with questions affecting the rights of subjects. The issue here is in determining the nature of the rights that fall to be protected by the courts on an application for review. In *R* v *Hull Prison Board of Visitors, ex parte St Germain* [1979] QB 425, the Court of Appeal held that certiorari was available to quash a decision of the Board because it adjudicated upon rights of prisoners that fell to be protected by public law. The Board's contention that no question of rights arose because its decisions only effected remission, was rejected, the court taking the view that the Board's decisions were effectively punishments, and that a prisoner, therefore, had the right to be dealt with in accordance with the rules of natural justice; see further *R* v *Board of Visitors of Blundeston Prison, ex parte Fox Taylor* [1982] 1 All ER 646.

In *R* v *Criminal Injuries Compensation Board, ex parte Lain* (above) it had been argued by the Board that certiorari was not available to quash its decisions because its determination gave rise to no enforceable rights, all awards being discretionary. The Divisional Court held that this was too narrow an interpretation of the Atkin dictum, which was not simply limited to enforceable rights but would apply to decisions taken as a step towards the creation of legally enforceable rights.

The applicant should only fail in his bid to establish that his public law rights are affected by the decision being challenged if the court concludes that the case raises primarily private law issues. Lord Parker CJ in *ex parte Lain* observed:

> '... the exact limits of ... [a quashing order] ... have never been and ought not to be specifically defined. They have varied from time to time being extended to meet changing conditions. At one time the writ only went to an inferior court. Later its ambit was extended to statutory tribunals determining a lis inter partes. Later again it extended to cases where there was no lis in the strict sense of the word but where immediate or subsequent rights of citizens were affected. The only constant limits throughout were that it was performing a public duty. Private ... tribunals have always been outside the scope of [a quashing order] ... We have as it seems to me reached the position when the ambit of [a quashing order] can be said to cover every case in which a body of persons of a public as opposed to a purely private or domestic character has to determine matters affecting subjects provided always that it has a duty to act judicially.'

As will have been seen in Chapter 10, making the distinction between public law rights and private law rights is far from straight forward. In *R* v *Barnsley Metropolitan Borough Council, ex parte Hook* [1976] 1 WLR 1052 (revocation of a market traders' licence) it was held that certiorari would be granted because, although the relationship between the parties was essentially contractual, the matter also involved a public law element, the regulation of a public market. In *R v Basildon District Council, ex parte Brown* (1981) 79 LGR 655, however, a completely contrary conclusion was arrived at, certiorari being refused on the ground that the relationship between the market trader and the local authority as a licensing agency was contractual and did not therefore raise any public law issues.

Consider further the decisions in *R v East Berkshire Health Authority, ex parte Walsh* [1984] 3 WLR 818 and *R v Secretary of State for the Home Department, ex parte Benwell* [1985] QB 554.

The third criterion for the granting of a quashing order, namely that the decision-making body must being under a duty to act judicially, was one of the chief causes of the restricted development of natural justice prior to *Ridge v Baldwin* [1964] AC 40. It was thought that only courts, or administrative bodies deciding a dispute between two parties concerning rights traditionally protected by law, were under a duty to act judicially and therefore amenable to a quashing order. In *Ridge v Baldwin* Lord Reid changed the course of the law's development by holding that in order to determine whether there existed a duty to act judicially the court should have regard to the nature of the power being exercised and the rights thereby affected. The change in emphasis to what is at stake for the applicant has significantly widened the scope of the remedy. Hence, in *R v Barnsley Metropolitan Borough Council, ex parte Hook* (above), some members of the Court of Appeal inferred the duty to act judicially from the fact that the local authority was a statutory body having the power to determine the rights of others.

Alternative remedy available

A quashing order, like the other prerogative orders, is a discretionary remedy and in particular it will not be granted if a more suitable alternative remedy exists. In *R v Peterkin, ex parte Soni* [1972] Imm AR 253, certiorari was refused when an application was made to quash the determination of an immigration adjudicator, because an appeal lay from his decision to an immigration appeal tribunal. Lord Widgery LJ pointed out that the courts should normally allow statutory appellate machinery to work, where it had been provided, in preference to certiorari. The prerogative orders were not to be used as an alternative form of appeal. The courts, before deciding to grant or refuse a quashing order, will consider the suitability of the alternatively remedy. In *R v Chief Immigration Officer, Gatwick Airport, ex parte Kharrazi* [1980] 3 All ER 373 the applicant sought an order of certiorari to quash the decision refusing him entry as he would have had to return to Iran in order to invoke the appeal procedure provided by statute. As Lord Denning MR observed:

'If there is a convenient remedy by way of appeal to an adjudicator, then [a quashing order] may be refused: and the applicant left to his remedy by way of appeal. But it has been held on countless occasions that the availability of appeal does not debar the court from quashing an order by prerogative writs ... It depends on the circumstances of each case. In the present case the remedy by way of appeal is useless. This boy's education – indeed, his whole future – will be ruined if he is sent off by plane to Tehran. Rather than his future be ruined, it is better to quash the refusal – and let the Home Secretary reconsider the case.'

See also *R* v *Paddington Valuation Officer, ex parte Peachey Property Corporation* [1966] 1 QB 380.

As indicated above a quashing order will not be available if, for example, a minister has been provided with a default power that provides a more appropriate remedy than judicial review (see *ex parte P*), or if the respondent has agreed to comply with the applicant's demands: see *R* v *Secretary of State for the Home Department, ex parte Harry* [1998] 3 All ER 360.

Prohibiting order

A prohibiting order is a prerogative order directed at an inferior body, compelling it to refrain from a course of action, in effect the public law equivalent of an injunction. Non-observance of a prohibiting order by an inferior body amounts to contempt of court. The criteria for the granting of prohibiting orders are essentially the same as those for the granting of quashing orders, as laid down in the *Electricity Commissioners* case (above), in which it was one of the remedies sought. By its very nature, it is only of use where an individual is able to produce evidence that an inferior body proposes to act beyond its jurisdiction. In *R* v *Liverpool Corporation, ex parte Liverpool Taxi Fleet Operators' Association* [1972] 2 QB 299 the applicants sought an order of prohibition to prevent the local authority from reneging on a public undertaking that the number of licensed cab drivers in the city would not be increased. In granting the relief sought, Lord Denning MR stated:

'We have considered what the actual relief should be. On the whole we think it is sufficient in this case to let prohibition issue. The order should prohibit the corporation or their committee or sub-committee from acting on the resolutions of 16 November 1971, 8 December 1971 and 22 December 1971; in particular, from granting any further number of licences pursuant to s37 of the Town Police Clauses Act 1847 over and above the 300 currently existing, without first hearing any representations which may be made by or on behalf of any persons interested therein, including the applicants in this case and any other matters relevant thereto, including the undertaking recorded in the two clerk's letters of 11 August 1971. If prohibiting order goes in those terms, it means that the relevant committees, sub-committees and the corporation themselves, can look at the matter afresh. They will hear all those interested and come to a right conclusion as to what is to be done about the number of taxicabs on the streets of Liverpool. I would say that the trouble has arisen because the corporation was advised that this undertaking was not binding on them, whereas it certainly was binding unless overridden by some imperative public interest. I am sure that all concerned have been acting as best they can, but nevertheless prohibiting order in my view should issue so as to prevent the corporation committee acting on those resolutions.'

11.6 Mandatory order (mandamus)

A mandatory order is a prerogative order, directed at an inferior body, compelling it to act in accordance with duties to which it is subject. It will only lie against a public body, in relation to public law duties. A court will not grant a mandatory order compelling the exercise of discretion in a particular way, since judicial review is concerned with the legality of actions, not their merits. If, for example, a tribunal is given the power to award licences to whoever it thinks fit, the court will not compel it by mandatory order to award a licence to a particular person. What the court will order such a body to do, however, is to exercise its discretion according to law, for example by taking into account relevant considerations or providing reasons for its decisions. A mandatory order will lie, therefore, in respect of statutory duties and implied common law duties, such as the duty to exercise power according to law. The most significant example of the latter is provided by *Padfield* v *Minister of Agriculture* [1968] AC 997, where mandamus was granted against the minister, compelling him to consider a complaint about the milk-marketing scheme, according to law, despite the fact that the enabling Act appeared to leave the holding of an inquiry to his discretion.

Simply because a duty has been expressly stated in an enabling Act does not mean that a mandatory order will necessarily issue to compel its performance. Certain statutory duties are drafted in such wide, vague terms, that they are not amenable to orders of mandatory order. The courts will not grant the remedy unless compliance with the order can be supervised. Without supervision it would be impossible to know whether or not the order was being complied with, and hence, whether any contempt was being committed. In short, the courts will not act in vain; a mandatory order will not be granted unless something can be achieved by making the order.

Lack of funds on the part of a public body will generally not be accepted as justification for failing to comply with a public law duty. In *R* v *Poplar Borough Council, ex parte London County Council (No 2)* [1922] 1 KB 95 mandamus was issued to compel a London borough to pay the precept due to the London County Council, despite its arguments that due to the poverty of the borough it was unable to pay. As Younger LJ observed:

> '[The Councillors of Poplar are] by law left with no discretion as to their action in this matter ... If the rate directed be excessive in its amount, or burdensome in its incidence on Poplar, that is a justification for an alteration in the law, but it is no justification for disobedience to the law before it is altered. If the appellants will not carry out the duties they have undertaken by accepting election to this body, it is their duty to make way for others who will. Deliberate disobedience to this order cannot, in my judgment, be overlooked or excused'

Where the failure to perform a statutory duty appears to be motivated by the desire to make a political point, the courts are unlikely to restrain themselves from ordering that the duties be discharged. This view is supported by the decision of the Divisional Court in *R* v *Camden London Borough Council, ex parte Gillan and Others* (1988) 21 HLR 114. The Housing Act 1985 imposed a duty upon Camden London Borough Council (the authority) to hear and adjudicate upon applications from homeless persons for accommodation. The evidence submitted by the applicants indicated that the authority was providing only very limited opportunities for such applications to be made. The authority's homeless persons unit was not attended at night or over weekends, and homeless persons could not talk to housing officers face to face, but only via the telephone. Further evidence suggested that telephones in the unit were either constantly engaged or left unanswered. The applicants sought judicial review of the authority's discharging of its duties under the 1985 Act, and in particular sought orders of mandamus to compel the authority to comply with the requirements of the Act. The authority contended that rate-capping imposed by central government had left it without the funds to provide a better service to the homeless. Allowing the applications, and granting the remedies sought, the court held that the impecuniosity of the authority, whether arising from a reduction in income from rates or any other source, could not excuse the cavalier fashion in which it had failed to discharge its duties to the homeless under the 1985 Act. The court was of the opinion that in an area with as high a population density as Camden the local authority should be providing a 24-hour service. Whilst the decision has its encouraging aspects it begs the question of how effectively the court was able to supervise the authority's compliance with the mandatory order. Compare with the approach of the court in *R* v *Secretary of State for Social Services, ex parte Hincks* (1980) (unreported) where, although the Secretary of State was under a duty to provide certain welfare services, the court rejected out of hand any argument that he was, as a consequence, under a duty to secure from Parliament sufficient funds to provide adequate welfare services. What the authorities do confirm is that if the court perceives the public body to be doing its best, in good faith, to discharge a duty that is not absolute in nature, it may give it the benefit of the doubt and not intervene. In *R* v *Bristol Corporation, ex parte Hendy* [1974] 1 WLR 498 the local authority, acting under s39(1) of the Land Compensation Act 1973, offered the applicant temporary accommodation following the closing order that had been made in respect of his flat. The applicant sought an order of mandamus to compel the authority to comply with its duty under s39 to provide him with 'suitable alternative residential accommodation on reasonable terms'. Refusing the order sought, Scarman LJ stated:

> 'If there is evidence that a local authority is doing all that it honestly and honourably can to meet the statutory obligation, and that its failure, if there be failure, to meet that obligation arises really out of circumstances over which it has no control, then I would think it would be improper for the court to [grant a mandatory order] compelling it to do that which either it cannot do or which it can only do at the expense of other persons not before the court who may have equal rights with the applicant.'

Alternative remedy available

As with a quashing order, a mandatory order will not be granted where it appears that Parliament has supplied a more suitable alternative remedy, in particular, default powers vested in a minister. In *Pasmore* v *Oswaldtwistle Urban District Council* [1898] AC 387 the court held that it was not open to an individual to seek an order of mandamus compelling the local authority to comply with its duty to provide sewers, because statutory default powers had been vested in the minister and he was the correct person to apply for such an order. In *Watt* v *Kesteven County Council* [1955] 1 QB 408 it was held that the existence of ministerial default powers, which could be used in the event of a local education authority failing to provide sufficient schools for its area, militated against mandamus being available at the suit of a private individual to compel performance of the duty. Similarly, in *R* v *ILEA, ex parte Ali* [1990] COD 317, where the applicant sought an order of mandamus to compel the local education authority to provide an adequate number of primary school places in Tower Hamlets. Despite the fact that the minister had refused to exercise his statutory powers to intervene the court refused to grant the relief sought. The statutory duty in question was not regarded as being absolute, but merely one that required ILEA to do its best. The court appreciated that the authority might be at the mercy of unforeseen circumstances, such as teacher shortages. Furthermore, although the minister's default power under s99 of the Education Act 1944 did not oust the jurisdiction of the court to order a mandatory order, until such ministerial directives were issued and ignored it became difficult to see how a mandatory order could issue, given the wide nature of the duties in question. In the final analysis it was felt that an order of mandamus added nothing to ILEA's duties, nor did it clarify them, as that body fully accepted what they were. Given the imminent demise of ILEA, an order of mandamus would have been, in any event, somewhat redundant.

Mandatory order inappropriate

There have been situations where, despite mandamus clearly being available, the courts, in the exercise of their discretion, have refused to grant the remedy, on the ground that it would be inappropriate for the court to intervene. In *R* v *Metropolitan Police Commissioner, ex parte Blackburn* [1968] 2 QB 118 the Court of Appeal refused to grant a mandatory order to compel the Metropolitan Police Commissioner to prosecute persons involved in illegal gaming, although it was stated, obiter, that a policy decision not to enforce a particular law would be challengeable in the courts. Lord Denning MR commented that:

> '... it is for the Commissioner of Police of the Metropolis, or the chief constable, as the case may be, to decide in any particular case whether inquiries should be pursued, or whether an arrest should be made, or a prosecution brought. It must be for him to decide on the disposition of his force and the concentration of his resources on any particular crime or area.'

Similarly, in *R* v *Chief Constable of Devon and Cornwall, ex parte Central Electricity Generating Board* [1981] 3 WLR 967, in refusing to grant mandamus to compel the Chief Constable to clear protesters from the proposed site of a nuclear power station, Lord Denning MR observed:

'... I would not give any orders to the chief constable or his men. It is of the first importance that the police should decide on their own responsibility what action should be taken in any particular situation ... The decision of the chief constable not to intervene in this case was a policy decision with which I think the courts should not interfere ... I hope he will decide to use his men to clear the obstructors off the site or at any rate help the board to do so.'

See further the reluctant refusal of a mandatory order in *Chief Constable of the North Wales Police* v *Evans* [1982] 3 All ER 141.

12

Exclusion of Review

12.1 Introduction

12.2 Errors of law and ouster clauses

12.3 Partial ouster clauses

12.4 The Human Rights Act 1998

12.1 Introduction

Much has been made of the constitutional importance of judicial review as part of the essential system of checks and balances whereby the judiciary can ensure that the Executive acts within the scope of its powers. It may come as a surprise, therefore, to discover that, from time to time, Parliament has enacted measures (sometimes referred to as ouster clauses) expressly designed to prevent the courts from carrying out this reviewing function. Perhaps two general points need to be made. The first is that, even without such statutory provisions, there are many ways in which a litigant might be prevented from seeking judicial review of a public law body. The applicant may not have locus standi, may be out of time, may not be granted leave, or may be denied a remedy at the discretion of the court. Second, there will nearly always be a clear rationale, either apparent in the legislation or made plain by government policy statements, as to why judicial challenge is being prevented. The rationale may be that a particular tribunal has a finite fund of money to distribute and Parliament seeks prevent any challenge to the tribunal's decisions once the fund has been allocated. It may be that planning decisions need to be settled and beyond any legal challenge before development can safely take place. The constitutional implications of such clauses are, however, stark. Without recourse to the courts how is the rule of law to be maintained? To seek to prevent judicial review runs counter to the development of public law in latter half of the twentieth century.

Despite the fact that where access to the courts is excluded some other form of administrative control is sometimes provided, the courts have not been altogether willing to take such legislative provisions at face value. As will be seen, despite Parliament's efforts, ouster clauses have only been permitted a very limited range of operation.

Finality clauses

One device that has been used in the past is the finality clause, whereby a statute simply declares a tribunal's decision to be 'final'. The effectiveness of such provisions was considered by the Divisional Court in *R* v *Medical Appeal Tribunal, ex parte Gilmore* [1957] 1 QB 574. The applicant sought to quash the decision of a medical appeal tribunal. Such decisions were protected by s36(3) of the National Insurance (Industrial Injuries) Act 1946, which provided that 'any decision of a claim or question ... shall be final'. Allowing the applicant's appeal against the Divisional Court's refusal to grant certiorari to quash the decision of the tribunal on the basis of error of law, Denning LJ, on behalf of the Court of Appeal, explained that the granting of certiorari could only be excluded by the use of very clear words. In his view the words 'shall be final' were not enough, and the decision could still be quashed where there was an error of law, even though the decision might be 'final' as regard findings of fact.

'No certiorari' clauses

Parliament has attempted to exclude review by expressly providing in legislation that a decision is not to be subject to an order of certiorari. Rather like finality clauses, they have been rendered largely ineffective by the courts. As Denning LJ explained in *R* v *Medical Appeal Tribunal, ex parte Gilmore* (above):

> 'In contrast to the word "final" I would like to say a word about the old statutes which used in express words to make away the remedy by certiorari by saying that the decision of the tribunal "shall not be removed by certiorari". Those statutes were passed chiefly between 1680 and 1848, in the days when the courts used certiorari too freely and quashed decisions for technical defects of form. In stopping this abuse the statutes proved very beneficial, but the court never allowed those statutes to be used as a cover for wrongdoings by tribunals. If tribunals were to be at liberty to exceed their jurisdiction without any check by the courts, the rule of law would be at an end. Despite express words taking away certiorari, therefore, it was held that certiorari would still lie if some of the members of the tribunals were disqualified from acting ... So, also, if the tribunal exceeded its jurisdiction: see *ex parte Bradlaugh* (1878) 3 QBD 508; or if its decision was obtained by fraud: see *R* v *Gillyard* (1848) 12 QB 527, the courts would still grant certiorari. I do not pause to consider those cases further, for I am glad to notice that modern statutes never take away, in express words, the right to certiorari without substituting an analogous remedy. This is probably because the courts no longer use it to quash for technical defects but only in case of a substantial miscarriage of justice. Parliament nowadays more often uses the words "final" or "final and conclusive" or some such words which leave intact the control of the Queen's courts by certiorari.'

In this regard, note s12 of the Tribunals and Inquiries Act 1992 considered at Chapter 4.

Conclusive evidence clauses

In *R* v *Registrar of Companies, ex parte Esal (Commodities) Ltd (in liquidation)* [1985] 2 All ER 79 the court had to consider the effect of s98(2) of the Companies Act 1948, which provided:

> 'The registrar shall give a certificate under his hand of the registration of any charge registered in pursuance of this Part of this Act, stating the amount thereby secured, and the certificate shall be conclusive evidence that the requirements of this part of this Act have been complied with.'

A bank wished to register a charge in respect of the company's assets. Paperwork was submitted to the registrar on 29 February 1984, but it was incorrectly filled in, and certain details were lacking. On 29 March 1984 the paperwork was resubmitted in its proper form and the charge was registered without the company's knowledge. On 7 November 1984 the company was made the subject of a winding-up order, and its creditors sought judicial review of the registrar's decision to register the bank's charge, on the basis that he had lacked jurisdiction to do so. Inter alia, it was alleged that the registrar had erred in law in regarding the original paperwork as 'prescribed paperwork' within the Act. The registrar relied on s98(2), arguing that his certificate had to be regarded as conclusive in the interests of commercial certainty. The court held that, despite s98(2), the registrar's certificate was reviewable in the courts. He was a person amenable to judicial review, in the sense that he exercised statutory powers affecting the rights of others, and the decisions of public officials had to be amenable to scrutiny by way of judicial review for either error of law or breach of natural justice. The need to promote commercial certainty was, to some extent, seen as being protected by the time limits in applying for judicial review.

12.2 Errors of law and ouster clauses

There may be occasions when a public body embarks on the task of determining an issue that lies within its jurisdiction, but in the course of so doing makes an error of law. What is the status of such a decision? In one sense the decision is not ultra vires because the public body has been addressing an issue within its jurisdiction, albeit it has applied the law incorrectly to a given set of facts. On the other hand it is not right that a decision based on erroneous application of the law should be allowed to stand. Where a statutory right of appeal exists there is no problem. The appellate body can rectify the error. Where there is no appeals framework the choice is between letting the error stand, or permitting judicial review. The courts have always been concerned that 'inferior' bodies, especially those having no particular legal expertise, should apply the law correctly. Judicial review for error of law on the face of the record was the ancient remedy invoked to deal with such errors, although, as will be seen it has had something of a chequered history, and may indeed be of only academic significance in modern administrative law.

Despite its history of being used to call up and quash the decisions of inferior bodies, such as Justices of the Peace during the eighteenth and nineteenth centuries, certiorari appeared to have been forgotten as a means of controlling errors of law in the first half of the twentieth century. In *Racecourse Betting Control Board* v *Secretary for Air* [1944] Ch 114 the Court of Appeal went so far as to deny that it would be available to quash a mistake of law made in an award of a statutory tribunal.

The remedy was revived, however, by the Court of Appeal in *R* v *Northumberland Compensation Appeal Tribunal, ex parte Shaw* [1952] 1 KB 338. The tribunal in question appealed unsuccessfully against the grant of certiorari by the Divisional Court to quash its decision for error of law. In explaining the availability of certiorari as a remedy for dealing with errors of law made by statutory bodies, Lord Denning (then Denning LJ) stated:

> '... the court of King's Bench has an inherent jurisdiction to control all inferior tribunals, not in an appellate capacity, but in a supervisory capacity. This control extends not only to seeing that the inferior tribunals keep within their jurisdiction but also to seeing that they observe the law. The control is exercised by means of a power to quash any determination by the tribunal which on the face of it offends against the law. The King's Bench does not substitute its own views for those of the tribunal, as a court of appeal would do. It leaves it to the tribunal to hear the case again, and in a proper case may command it to do so. When the King's Bench exercises its control over tribunals in this way, it is not usurping a jurisdiction which does not belong to it. It is only exercising a jurisdiction it has always had.'

There must be an error of law

The problem of deciding whether an error is one of law or fact is exceedingly complex. It can be safely assumed that the interpretation to be given to a word in a statute is a question of law, but cases coming before the courts are rarely that simple. Instead one has to develop a sense of what the courts are likely to regard as an error of law by looking at decided cases. To arrive at a conclusion unsupported by the facts could constitute an error of law: see *R* v *Medical Appeal Tribunal, ex parte Gilmore* (above). In a sense this is a variant on the 'no evidence' ground of review. Failing to apply the correct legal test to the facts will constitute an error of law. For example, see *R* v *Minister of Housing and Local Government, ex parte Chichester Rural District Council* [1960] 2 All ER 407, where a minister's decision was quashed for error of law after he applied the wrong test to determine whether or not land was 'capable of reasonably beneficial use'. Procedural irregularities, such as wrongly refusing to grant an adjournment so that an applicant can prepare his case properly, have been held to amount to an error of law, for example in *R* v *Medical Appeal Tribunal, ex parte Carrarini* [1966] 1 WLR 883. Generally, the courts seemed to give a wide meaning to the expression error of law, so as to maintain the usefulness of the remedy. Consider further the meaning given to the expression 'appeal on a point of law' in the context of an appeal under s11 of the Tribunals and Inquiries Act 1992.

What constitutes the 'record'?

As with the interpretation of error of law, the meaning of the phrase 'face of the record' has been liberally interpreted by the courts. As Griffiths LJ observed in *R* v *Knightsbridge Crown Court, ex parte International Sporting Club Ltd* [1982] QB 304:

> 'Although the old authorities do show a stricter approach to what constituted the "record", the modern authorities show that the judges have relaxed the strictness of that rule and taken a broader view of the "record" in order that certiorari may give relief to those against whom a decision has been given which is based upon a manifest error of law.'

In *ex parte Shaw* (above) Denning LJ stated that the record would comprise at least the documents initiating the proceedings, the pleadings if any, and the adjudication. In *R* v *Greater Birmingham Supplementary Benefit Appeal Tribunal, ex parte Khan* [1979] 3 All ER 759 the concept of 'record' was extended to include a letter sent by the tribunal to the applicant containing the reasons for the tribunal's decision. In *ex parte International Sporting Club Ltd* (above) the record was held to include the judgment, the reasons for the judgment, and the affidavit evidence upon which it was based.

The Anisminic *case*

Anisminic was a company that owned property in Egypt valued at approximately £4 million. During the Suez crisis in 1956 the Egyptian authorities seized the property, and Anisminic entered into a contract to sell the property to an Egyptian company for a fraction of its true value. After the cessation of hostilities, the United Kingdom government received £27.5 million by way of compensation. The task of distributing the fund was given to the Foreign Compensation Commission (the FCC). The FCC rejected Anisminic's claim to a share of this fund on the erroneous basis that the successor in title to the expropriated property should have been of British nationality at a specific date. Anisminic sought a declaration that the determination of the FCC was a nullity because it had misconstrued the terms of the relevant statutory Order. Section 4(4) of the Foreign Compensation Act 1950 Act provided that no determination of the FCC was to be called into question in any court of law.

The House of Lords held, by a majority, that what the FCC had done was to make an error of law in the course of its deliberations. In basing its decision on a matter it had no right to take into account, or making an inquiry that the Order did not empower it to make, the FCC had exceeded its powers. The nature of the error of law was such that its 'determination' was, therefore, ultra vires: see *Anisminic* v *Foreign Compensation Commission* [1969] 2 AC 147. The reasoning leading to this conclusion can be deconstructed in the following way.

1. The FCC was a statutory body with jurisdiction to consider claims for compensation.
2. In rejecting Anisminic's claim the FCC had misconstrued the terms of an Order in Council, something that would normally be regarded as an error of law and, although intra vires, reviewable by way of error of law on the face of the record.
3. The clause excluding the jurisdiction of the courts referred to 'determinations' of the FCC. The House of Lords interpreted this as meaning 'valid determinations'. A valid determination was one that was intra vires. An ultra vires decision would only be a 'purported' determination, and therefore not protected by the exclusion clause.
4. Returning to the FCC's decision, if it was only an error of law that vitiated its decision, it was an intra vires decision and therefore 'valid', and therefore protected by the exclusion clause.
5. The House of Lords (by a majority) avoided this conclusion by holding that what the FCC had committed was not an 'ordinary' intra vires error of law, but an error of law going to jurisdiction. In short an ultra vires error of law.
6. The result was then predictable. As the error of law took the FCC beyond its jurisdiction, its decision was ultra vires, and therefore only a 'purported' determination, and therefore not one protected by the exclusion clause.

The decision can be seen as a startling assertion of judicial power in the face of a statutory provision intended to exclude judicial intervention. In that sense it provides evidence of the judges showing greater allegiance to the doctrine of the rule of law (ie the doctrine that no body should be above the law) than to the doctrine of parliamentary sovereignty. Interestingly Parliament responded by enacting the Foreign Compensation Act 1969 which provided for appeal on a point of law to the Court of Appeal.

The consequences of Anisminic v Foreign Compensation Commission

The response of many commentators, in the wake of *Anisminic*, was to sound the death knell of review for error of law on the face of the record. If one could now argue that an error of law was one resulting in a decision being ultra vires, why bother with the more limited remedy of review for an intra vires error? For example, in *Pearlman* v *Keepers and Governors of Harrow School* [1979] QB 56, the plaintiff sought a county court declaration that the installation of central heating in his property was a 'structural alteration' resulting in rateable value of his property being reduced. The county court refused the declaration, finding that the works carried out did not constitute a 'structural alteration'. By statute the decision of the county court judge was declared to be 'final and conclusive'. In the Court of Appeal Lord Denning held that the error of law made by the trial judge was one going to his jurisdiction and therefore not protected by the exclusion clause, ie an ultra vires error of law. In any event, Lord Denning felt that the distinction between intra vires errors of law and those going to jurisdiction was so fine that it ought to be discarded. In his view the correct approach was to say that no inferior tribunal had the jurisdiction to make a mistake of law upon which its decision depended.

Note that Geoffrey Lane LJ, dissenting, struck a much more cautious note, his view being that there was still scope for errors of law that could be intra vires. This cautious approach was subsequently vindicated to some extent by the Privy Council in *South East Asia Firebricks Sdn Bhd* v *Non-Metallic (etc) Union* [1981] AC 363, where it was held that the decision of the Industrial Court of Malaysia was protected by the relevant ouster clause. In the course of his speech, Lord Fraser referred to Lord Denning's approach to the problem in *Pearlman*:

> '... if the inferior tribunal has merely an error of law which does not affect its jurisdiction, and if its decision is not a nullity for some reason such as breach of the rules of natural justice then the ouster clause will be effective. In *Pearlman* Lord Denning MR suggested that the distinction between an error of law which affected jurisdiction and one which did not, should now be discarded. Their Lordships do not accept that suggestion. They consider that the law was correctly applied to the circumstances of that case in the dissenting opinion of Geoffrey Lane LJ when he said:
>
> > " ... the only circumstances in which this court can correct what is to my mind the error of the County Court judge is if he was acting in excess of his jurisdiction as opposed to merely making an error of law in his judgment by misinterpreting the meaning of structural alteration ... or addition ..." '

The position was clarified to some extent by the House of Lords' decision in *Re Racal Communications Ltd* [1981] AC 374. An application was made to a High Court judge for an order authorising inspection of a company's books on the grounds that reasonable cause existed to believe that a person, whilst an officer of the company, had committed certain offences. The High Court judge declined to grant the order, on the basis that he did not think the individual alleged to be involved in illegal activities was an 'officer' of the company, and he did not think the wrongdoings alleged were of the sort that justified the making of the order sought. By the statute in question the judge's decision was stated as being 'non-appealable'. The Court of Appeal nevertheless reversed this decision, holding that the judge at first instance had wrongly declined to exercise his jurisdiction, that this constituted an error of law going to jurisdiction, and the decision was therefore ultra vires and not protected by the ouster clause. The Court of Appeal granted the Order requested. Note that the leading judgment in the Court of Appeal was that of Lord Denning, relying heavily on his own previous decision in *Pearlman*.

The House of Lords unanimously reversed the decision of the Court of Appeal on a number of grounds. First, on the ground that it was only sensible to talk of errors 'going to jurisdiction' when dealing with an inferior body, the jurisdiction of which was limited by an enabling Act. High Court judges had unlimited common law jurisdiction, making it illogical to describe them as making errors going to jurisdiction. Second, on the ground that the Court of Appeal was purporting to exercise a reviewing function in stating the judge's decision to be ultra vires. This was an error as the Court of Appeal had no inherent power of review; it was a statutory body with jurisdiction to hear certain types of appeals only.

Lord Diplock sought to explain the circumstances in which the courts would regard an error of law as one going to jurisdiction, and therefore reviewable. He drew a distinction between decisions of 'administrative' bodies, such as the FCC, and judicial bodies, such as county court judges. The former had no expertise in law, therefore the courts would be more likely to intervene to deal with an error of law committed by such a body, notwithstanding the existence of an ouster clause. Judicial bodies were more likely to have expertise on matters of law and the courts would be slow to interfere with their decisions. That is why the decision in *Anisminic* was still good law, and the decision of the majority in *Pearlman* was not. Hence the *Anisminic* principle of regarding errors of law as jurisdictional was one that would apply to the decisions of inferior courts and tribunals. Hence, for example, in *R* v *Greater Manchester Coroner, ex parte Tal* [1984] 3 All ER 240 it was held that *Anisminic* principle applied to inferior courts, such as coroners' courts. Not surprisingly the courts have ruled that ministers come within the category of 'administrative' decision-makers, with the result that their actions are not normally protected by such ouster clauses. In *R* v *Secretary of State for the Home Department, ex parte Mohammed Al Fayed* [1997] 1 All ER 228 the Court of Appeal (Kennedy LJ dissenting) held that s44(2) of the British Nationality Act 1981, which provides that the refusal of citizenship by the Secretary of State 'shall not be subject to appeal to, or review in, any court', could not prevent judicial review on the ground that the minister had unfairly withheld details of the case against the applicants prior to making his decision: see further *Attorney-General* v *Ryan* [1980] AC 718.

In *O'Reilly* v *Mackman* [1983] 2 AC 237, Lord Diplock referred to the significance of *Anisminic* in the following terms:

> 'The breakthrough that *Anisminic* made was the recognition by the majority of this House that if a tribunal whose jurisdiction was limited by statute or subordinate legislation mistook the law applicable to the facts as it had found them, it must have asked itself the wrong question, ie one into which it was not empowered to enquire and so had no jurisdiction to determine. Its purported "determination" not being a "determination" within the meaning of the empowering legislation, was accordingly a nullity.

More recently, in *Boddington* v *British Transport Police* [1998] 2 All ER 203, Lord Irvine expressed the view that the effect of *Anisminic* had been to render obsolete the historic distinction between errors of law on the face of the record and other errors of law by extending the doctrine of ultra vires to any misdirection in law. Lord Browne-Wilkinson expressed similar views in *R* v *Lord President of the Privy Council, ex parte Page* [1992] 3 WLR 1112, to the effect that any error of law made by an administrative tribunal or inferior court could be quashed for error of law. The point is of more than academic significance. Decisions vitiated by an error of law on the face of the record were regarded as voidable – ie valid until quashed by the court. Hence anyone acting in defiance of such a decision (prior to its being quashed) would have contravened the law. According to Lord Irvine, however, such distinctions can now be discarded and a decision vitiated by an error of law is to regarded as void ab initio. Hence, it can be ignored even without it being formally quashed by the courts. It is submitted that, whilst review for error of law on the face of the record may indeed have become nothing more than an academic possibility in practice, two points should be borne in mind. First, Lord Irvine's comments regarding such decisions being void ab initio were obiter, and not expressly supported by Lord Browne-Wilkinson or Lord Slynn. Second, the *Anisminic* approach to errors of law is only really necessary where there is an ouster clause that purports to prevent judicial review of the impugned decision. To describe the error of law as one that goes to jurisdiction, thus rendering a decision ultra vires, is nothing more than a juristic device to enable the ouster clause to be circumvented. Where there is no ouster clause why not retain the concept of intra vires error of law, and accept that review of such errors is the one exception to the ultra vires doctrine as the basis for review?

Limits of the Anisminic principle

In *R* v *Lord President of the Privy Council, ex parte Page* (above) the House of Lords held that the Lord President of the Privy Council, acting on behalf of a university visitor, upholding the decision of a university to terminate a lecturer's employment on the ground of redundancy, was not amenable to judicial review in respect of any ruling in fact or law that he might make in the course of exercising that jurisdiction. Lord Browne-Wilkinson relied upon two lines of reasoning to justify non-intervention on the grounds of error of law. The first related to the peculiar type of law applied by the visitor:

> 'Although the general rule is that decisions affected by errors of law made by industrial tribunals or inferior courts can be quashed, in my judgment there are two reasons why that rule does not apply in the case of visitors. First, as I have sought to explain, the constitutional basis of the courts' power to quash is that the decision of the inferior tribunal is unlawful on the grounds that it is ultra vires. In the ordinary case, the law applicable to a decision made by such a body is the general law of the land. Therefore, a tribunal or inferior court acts ultra vires if it reaches its conclusion on a basis erroneous under the general law. But the position of decisions made by a visitor is different. As the authorities which I have cited demonstrate, the visitor is applying not the general law of the land but a peculiar, domestic law of which he is the sole arbiter and of which the courts have no cognisance. If the visitor has power under the regulating documents to enter into the adjudication of the dispute (ie is acting within his jurisdiction in the narrow sense) he cannot err in law in reaching this decision since the general law is not the applicable law. Therefore he cannot be acting ultra vires and unlawfully by applying his view of the domestic law in reaching his decision. The court has no jurisdiction either to say that he erred in his application of the general law (since the general law is not applicable to the decision) or to reach a contrary view as to the effect of the domestic law (since the visitor is the sole judge of such domestic law).'

The second line of reasoning related to Lord Diplock's speech in *Re Racal Communications* [1981] AC 374, at p384B–D and pp390F–391D, where the distinction between administrative and judicial bodies was drawn with reference to the greater readiness of the courts to intervene and quash decisions on the grounds of error of law where the decision-making body was classified as administrative as opposed to judicial. Lord Browne-Wilkinson viewed the Visitor to a university as coming within the 'judicial' class of decision-maker. Thus, if a statutory ouster clause had been enacted to protect the decisions of the Visitor, the courts would have been slow to disregard it. The reality under the common law was that the courts had for 300 years treated decisions of university Visitors as being final and conclusive and thus unchallengeable in the courts. His Lordship saw no reason for departing from that line of authority on this occasion.

Ex parte Page was followed by the Court of Appeal in *R v Visitors to the Inns of Court, ex parte Calder; Same, ex parte Persuad* [1993] 3 WLR 287, where the applicants, practising barristers who had been found guilty of professional misconduct by the disciplinary tribunal of the Council of the Inns of Court and subsequently disbarred, sought to challenge the decisions of High Court judges, sitting as Visitors, to uphold the tribunal's decisions. The Divisional Court held that judges performing the visitorial function were still acting judicially to maintain the proper administration of justice in the courts, and as such their functions were not amenable to review. The Court of Appeal allowed the appeals on the basis that, prior to the enactment of the Supreme Court of Judicature Act 1873, judges exercising a visitorial function in respect of the Inns of Court had done so as members of a domestic tribunal, in the sense that they had not sat as 'judges', and the effect of s12 of the 1873 Act had been to transfer this visitorial function to all judges of the High Court; thus the decisions of judges sitting as visitors to the Inns were reviewable if they exceeded their jurisdiction, acted in breach of natural justice, or abused their powers. In relation to the 'narrow' issue of intervention on grounds of error of law, however, Sir Donald Nicholls V-C observed that:

> '... the principle enunciated [in *Page*] regarding the finality of the visitorial jurisdiction is applicable to visitors to the Inns of Court ...'

His Lordship was led to this conclusion by the fact that the visitors to the Inns would not be applying the ordinary law of the land, but the Bar's Code of Conduct.

Protecting errors as to jurisdiction

The rationale for the courts disregarding purported 'ouster' clauses has, in many cases, been the belief on the part of the judges that Parliament did not mean what it appeared to say when enacting the relevant statutory provisions. It remains to be seen whether the courts will respect a statutory provision that does indicate that even jurisdictional errors should be immune from challenge in the courts. One such example is provided by s67(8) of the Regulation of Investigatory Powers Act 2000 which provides, as regards the tribunal established to hear complaints regarding unauthorised surveillance:

> 'Except to such extent as the Secretary of State may by order otherwise provide, determinations, awards, orders and other decisions of the tribunal (*including decisions as to whether they have jurisdiction*) shall not be subject to appeal or be liable to be questioned in any court.' (emphasis added)

12.3 Partial ouster clauses

The only type of clause purporting to exclude review to have been granted any real effectiveness by the courts is that which allows a period during which a decision can be challenged before the ouster clause takes effect. In *Smith* v *East Elloe Rural District Council* [1956] AC 736 the plaintiff sought to challenge the validity of a compulsory purchase order which had been made in respect of her property some five years earlier. Under the Acquisition of Land (Authorisation Procedure) Act 1946 a court could quash an order where it appeared to be beyond the powers of the enabling Act, or the procedural requirements of the enabling Act had not been complied with, causing the applicant substantial prejudice. Applications to the High Court to challenge compulsory purchase orders under the Act had to be submitted within six weeks of the order being made. The House of Lords held, by a majority, that the ouster clause prevented challenge on any ground beyond the six-week time limit. Lord Reid, dissenting, said that the order must remain challengeable at any time for bad faith; he could not accept that it was the intention of Parliament to protect such decisions.

An almost identical provision fell to be considered by the Court of Appeal in *R* v *Secretary of State for the Environment, ex parte Ostler* [1977] QB 122. The applicant sought leave to apply for an order of certiorari to quash a stopping-up order under the Highways Act 1959 and a compulsory purchase order under the Acquisition of Land (Authorising Procedure) Act 1946 (whose wording was identical to that considered in the *East Elloe* case). A preliminary objection was taken by the Secretary of State that, whatever the facts (and in this case the applicant alleged bad faith which amounted to fraud), any attack on the validity of the orders was barred in any legal proceedings whatsoever because the statutory prescribed six-week period had expired. The Divisional Court considered that the speeches in *Anisminic* undermined the reasoning in *East Elloe*, and the Secretary of State appealed to the Court of Appeal on this question as a preliminary point of law. Holding that the clause was still effective to exclude challenge outside the six-week time limit, Lord Denning sought to explain why the decision of the House of Lords in *Anisminic* could not be taken to have reduced the authority of *East Elloe*.

First, in *Anisminic* the ouster clause was complete, in the present case the clause was a partial ouster. Second, in *Anisminic* the House of Lords was considering the determination of a judicial body (a view subsequently contradicted by Lord Diplock in *Re Racal Communications*); in *East Elloe* the courts were considering an administrative decision which affected the rights of third parties, ie the general public. Third, *Anisminic* concerned an actual determination, whereas *East Elloe* concerned the validity of the process by which a decision was reached.

Ex parte Ostler and *East Elloe* have since been reaffirmed by the Court of Appeal in *R* v *Secretary of State for the Environment, ex parte Kent* [1990] JPL 124 and *R* v *Cornwall County Council, ex parte Huntington and Another* [1994] 1 All ER 694. In *ex parte Kent* the court refused to allow a challenge outside the statutory six-week time limit where a local authority had failed to notify persons likely to be affected by development of a planning application, with the result that objectors had not been able to make representations to the local authority or the Secretary of State. Regarding the case as indistinguishable from *ex parte Ostler*, Parker LJ indicated the reluctance with which he had arrived at his conclusion, but trusted that there would be very few cases such as this where an objector was denied the right of legal challenge through no fault of his own.

In *ex parte Huntington* the applicants sought to challenge the decisions of local authorities with respect to the amendment of definitive maps and statements regarding the making of right of way orders under the Wildlife and Countryside Act 1981. The Act provided for notice to be given of the making of the order by the local authority, the holding of a public inquiry into objections, and publication of the Secretary of State's decision following the inquiry. Paragraph 12 of Sch 15 to the 1981 Act provided for any challenge to such an order to be made within 42 days on the grounds specified in that paragraph, with the proviso that 'Except as provided by this paragraph, the validity of an order shall not be questioned in any legal proceedings whatsoever.' The applicants, who were awaiting the outcome of the public inquiry, applied unsuccessfully for leave to apply for judicial review to quash the right of way order on the grounds that in making it the local authority had acted ultra vires. Although the matter was technically obiter (no legal challenge was possible until the orders had been confirmed, therefore the court did not have jurisdiction to entertain any challenge prior to confirmation), Simon Brown LJ cited with approval the comments of Mann LJ at first instance, to the effect that;

> 'The intention of Parliament when it uses an *Anisminic* clause is that questions as to validity are not excluded. ... [W]hen paragraphs such as those considered in *Ex p Ostler* are used, then the legislative intention is that questions as to invalidity may be raised on the specified grounds in the prescribed time and in the prescribed manner, but otherwise the jurisdiction of the court is excluded in the interests of certainty.'

12.4 The Human Rights Act 1998

Regard should be had to the effect that the Human Rights Act 1998 might have on the operation of ouster clauses. Article 6, which becomes part of domestic law with the enactment of the 1998 Act, provides that: '... In the determination of his civil rights and obligations ... everyone is entitled to a fair and public hearing ...'. Where an ouster clause totally excludes access to the courts a litigant may thus contend that the provision is incompatible with art 6. The duty of any court or tribunal faced with an ouster clause will be to give effect to the provision in a way that is compatible with Convention rights. It remains to be seen how creative the courts are prepared to be. In those cases where the incompatibility cannot be avoided the court can make a 'declaration of incompatibility' (see Chapter 11, section 11.3), thus prompting the introduction of remedial legislation. Where an ouster clause protects 'judicial acts' (ie a judicial act of a court) the right to bring proceedings under s7(1) of the 1998 Act is declared (by s9(2)) not to affect any rule of law which prevents a court from being the subject of judicial review.

13

The Parliamentary Commissioner for Administration

13.1 Introduction

13.2 Jurisdiction of the Parliamentary Commissioner for Administration

13.3 Parliamentary supervision of the Parliamentary Commissioner for Administration

13.4 Judicial review of the Parliamentary Commissioner for Administration

13.5 The work of the Parliamentary Commissioner for Administration

13.6 Improving the effectiveness of the Parliamentary Commissioner for Administration

13.7 Complaining to the Ombudsman – advantages over judicial review

13.8 The other ombudsmen

13.1 Introduction

The concept of an independent officer to investigate complaints against the administration is not new. Scandinavian countries had appointed such persons, known popularly as 'ombudsmen', as early as 1809. The appointment of such an officer in the United Kingdom is, however, a comparatively recent development, dating from 1967.

Previously, the traditional methods by which complaints against government departments would be pursued were either to complain to a Member of Parliament, or to seek what is now referred to as judicial review of the decision complained of. Both courses of actions had their limitations. Members of Parliament could not mount a very effective investigation into the workings of government departments, and had to limit themselves largely to asking questions of ministers in the House of Commons. Judicial review could only be invoked by those with locus standi, and was limited to dealing with ultra vires action. The need for some form of central investigative agency to inquire into instances of unsatisfactory executive action gradually became more obvious, given the rapid growth of state involvement in everyday life, and the very considerable powers being vested in ministers.

A classic illustration of these problems was provided by what became known as the 'Crichel Down Affair'. Land had been compulsorily acquired by the Ministry of Defence shortly before the Second World War, and an undertaking had been given to the owner at the time of acquisition that, if the land was found to be surplus to requirements, he would be given the opportunity to repurchase. After the war, the Ministry of Defence ceased to have any use for the land and it was transferred to the Ministry of Agriculture. The land was then offered for sale in an auction and a bid from the son-in-law of the pre-war owner, who now farmed land adjoining that which had been compulsorily purchased, was rejected. Following complaints, an inquiry was set up to discover what had happened. It discovered evidence of serious improprieties on the part of civil servants involved, who had determined for personal reasons that the land should not be resold to the original owner's family at any price. The matter was eventually debated in the House of Commons, resulting in the resignation of the incumbent minister, Sir Thomas Dugdale.

The whole affair is typical of the sort of matter that would now be the subject of an investigation by the Parliamentary Commissioner for Administration (PCA). The second factor giving considerable impetus to the creation of the PCA was the Justice report in 1961, known popularly as the Whyatt Report, which strongly advocated the creation of an ombudsman along Scandinavian lines to investigate complaints of maladministration in central government departments. There was at the time considerable opposition to the concept, principally for two reasons. The first was the fear that it would undermine the doctrine of ministerial responsibility. The second was that it would be a threat to the traditional role of Members of Parliament in receiving complaints from their constituents and questioning ministers on the matters raised during question time in the House of Commons – a fear that is a factor in the continued existence of the MP filter created by the 1967 legislation.

13.2 Jurisdiction of the Parliamentary Commissioner for Administration

The main legislative provisions dealing with the functions and jurisdiction of the PCA are the Parliamentary Commissioner Act 1967, the Parliamentary and Health Service Commissioners Act 1987 and the Parliamentary Commissioner Act 1994.

Constitution, appointment, and tenure

Under s1 of the 1967 Act the PCA is appointed by the Queen, on the advice of the Prime Minister, and holds office 'during good behaviour', ie effectively on the same basis as a High Court judge. The PCA may be relieved of office by the Queen at his own request, or can be removed from office by the Queen in consequence of

Addresses from both Houses of Parliament. The statutory retirement age is 65. The 1987 Act amends s1 of the 1967 Act by providing for the removal of the PCA on grounds of incapacity.

Staffing arrangements are governed by s3 of the 1967 Act which provides that the PCA may appoint 'such officers as he may determine with the approval of the Treasury as to numbers and conditions of service'. The 1987 Act provides for the appointment of acting Commissioners where necessary.

Jurisdiction

The PCA cannot investigate instances of maladministration of his own volition, he can only respond to complaints from members of the public. The government departments subject to investigation by the PCA are listed in Sch 2 to the 1967 Act as amended by the 1987 Act. Not surprisingly the schedule includes all the major government departments, and one of the major changes introduced by the 1987 Act was the extension of the PCA's jurisdiction to 'quangos'. Not all such bodies are included, however. Bodies subject to control by the Council on Tribunals are still excluded, as are bodies performing only advisory functions, charitable bodies under the control of the Charity Commissioners, the nationalised industries and professional bodies. The result is that bodies such as the Criminal Injuries Compensation Board and the Civil Aviation Authority are excluded on the basis that they are, in reality, tribunals. Similarly, the Boundary Commission and the Monopolies and Mergers Commission are excluded on the basis that they perform a purely advisory role. Any action taken on the basis of advice given by these bodies is itself the subject of ministerial responsibility. The schedule remains alterable by way of statutory instrument. Note that reference to a government department includes reference to ministers, members and officers of the department.

Section 110(1) of the Courts and Legal Services Act 1990 added a new subs(6) to s5 so as to extend the jurisdiction of the Parliamentary Commissioner to 'administrative functions exercisable by any person appointed by the Lord Chancellor as a member of the *administrative* [emphasis added] staff of any court or tribunal'. The Parliamentary Commissioner Act 1994 goes further by adding a new subs(7) which extends jurisdiction to the administrative functions of the administrative staff of any 'relevant tribunal' where those members of staff are appointed by, or with the consent of, a government department or other designated authority. The relevant tribunals are those listed in Sch 4 to the 1967 Act (added by the 1994 Act) and include tribunals set up under the Vaccine Damage Payment Act 1979, the Child Support Act 1991 and ss41, 43 and 50 of the Social Security Administration Act 1992. The 1994 Act extended the PCA's jurisdiction to include complaints arising from the Code of Practice on Access to Government Information.

Section 5(3) of the Act prohibits the PCA from investigating any of the matters referred to in Sch 3 to the Act. These include action taken in matters certified by a secretary of state or other minister of the Crown to affect relations or dealings between the government of the United Kingdom and any other government or any international organisation of states or governments. The following matters are also excluded from his jurisdiction.

1. Action taken in connection with the administration of the government of any country or territory outside the United Kingdom which forms part of Her Majesty's dominions or in which Her Majesty has jurisdiction.
2. Action taken by the Secretary of State under the Extradition Act 1870 or the Fugitive Offenders Act 1881.
3. Action taken by the Secretary of State for the purposes of investigating crime or of protecting the security of the state, including action so taken with respect to passports.
4. The commencement or conduct of civil or criminal proceedings before any court of law in the United Kingdom, of proceedings at any place under the Naval Discipline Act 1957, the Army Act 1955 or the Air Force Act 1955, or of proceedings before any international court or tribunal.
5. Any exercise of the prerogative of mercy or of the power of a Secretary of State to make a reference in respect of any person to the Court of Appeal, the High Court of Justiciary or the Courts-Martial Appeal Court.
6. Action taken on behalf of the Minister of Health or the Secretary of State by a (regional health authority, an area health authority, a district health authority, a special health authority except the Rampton Hospital Review Board, a family practitioner committee, a health board or the Common Services Agency for the Scottish Health Service) or by the Public Health Laboratory Service Board.
7. Action taken by any person appointed by the Lord Chancellor as a member of the administrative staff of any court or tribunal, so far as that action is taken at the discretion, or on the authority of any person acting in a judicial capacity or in his capacity as a member of the tribunal. Similarly, any action taken by any member of the administrative staff of a relevant tribunal.
8. Action taken in matters relating to contractual or other commercial transactions, whether within the United Kingdom or elsewhere, being transactions of a government department or authority to which the Act applies, not being transactions for or relating to the acquisition of land compulsorily or in circumstances in which it could be acquired compulsorily or the disposal as surplus of land acquired compulsorily.
9. Action taken in respect of appointments or removals, pay, discipline, superannuation or other personnel matters, in relation to service in any of the armed forces of the Crown, including reserve and auxiliary and cadet forces; service in any office or employment under the Crown or under any authority listed in Sch 2 of the 1967 Act; or service in any office or employment, or under any contract for service, in respect of which power to take action, or to determine or approve the action to be taken, in such matters is vested in Her Majesty, or any minister of the Crown.

10. The grant of honours, awards or privileges within the gift of the Crown, including the grant of Royal Charters.

Under s110 of the Courts and Legal Services Act 1990, s5 and Sch 3 of the 1967 Act are amended to exclude from the PCA's jurisdiction action taken by any person appointed by the Lord Chancellor as a member of the administrative staff of any court or tribunal, so far as that action is taken at the direction of any person acting in a judicial capacity or in his capacity as a member of the tribunal.

As regards those departments subject to his investigation, the PCA is limited by s5(1) to investigating 'any action taken by or on behalf of a government department or other authority to which this Act applies, being action taken in the exercise of administrative functions of that department or authority.' The effect of this is that he cannot carry out any investigation of complaints relating to the exercise of legislative functions, such as the preparation or creation of delegated legislation, although he could investigate complaints into the way in which a scheme set up by way of delegated legislation was actually being administered.

Section 12(3) of the Act provides:

> 'It is hereby declared that nothing in this Act authorises or requires the Commissioner to question the merits of a decision taken without maladministration by a government department or other authority in the exercise of a discretion vested in that department or authority ...'

Despite earlier views to the contrary, (see Sir Edmund Compton's approach) this section is now seen as meaning that the PCA cannot actually question the merits of a decision taken without maladministration (ie he cannot question government policy as such), but he can investigate maladministration in administrative processes and the decisions resulting therefrom (ie the execution of that policy).

Who may complain?

This is governed principally by s6 of the 1967 Act, which provides that a complaint can be made by any person, or body corporate (excluding local authorities, other bodies constituted for purposes of public service or local government, or any body whose members are appointed by Her Majesty or any Minister of the Crown or government department, or whose revenues consist wholly or mainly of moneys provided by Parliament). Normally a complaint must be made by the 'person aggrieved' unless he is unable to act for himself.

The 'hurdles' – MP filter

A person wishing to have a complaint considered by the PCA must first clear a number of procedural and jurisdictional hurdles. Each complaint must be in writing. Complaints must be submitted in the first instance to a Member of Parliament. This is the so-called 'MP filter' which is supposed to serve two functions. First, it provides the MP with an opportunity to deal with the complaint if he sees fit; second, it is a means by which clearly inappropriate or unmeritorious complaints can be rejected before reaching the PCA, thus reducing his workload. In reality MPs are reluctant to reject complaints in this manner for fear of appearing unhelpful to their constituents.

The 'hurdles' – maladministration

Complaints must be of injustice sustained in consequence of maladministration, a term not defined in the 1967 Act, but one memorably illustrated by the late Richard Crossman in his so-called 'catalogue' as involving rudeness, ineptitude, delay, wrong advice and loss of documents. In 1994 William Reid, a serving PCA, attempted his own definition which encompassed: neglecting to inform a complainant on request of his or her rights or entitlement; ignoring valid advice or overruling considerations which would produce an uncomfortable result for the overruler; offering no redress for manifestly disproportionate redress; failure by management to monitor compliance with adequate procedures; cavalier disregard of guidance which was intended to be followed in the interests of equitable treatment of those who use a service; and failure to mitigate the effects of rigid adherence to the letter of the law where that produces manifestly inequitable treatment.

The PCA's website refers visitors to examples such as: avoidable delay, faulty procedures or failing to follow correct procedures, not telling applicants about rights of appeal, prejudice, giving advice which is misleading or inadequate, refusing to answer reasonable questions, discourtesy and failure to apologise properly for errors and mistakes in handling claims, and not offering an adequate remedy where one is due.

The 'hurdles' – alternative remedy

A complainant will not have his complaint investigated if it appears that it is 'any action in respect of which the person aggrieved has or had right of appeal, reference or review to or before a tribunal constituted by or under any enactment or by virtue of Her Majesty's prerogative; or any action in respect of which the person aggrieved has or had a remedy by way of proceedings in any court of law': see s5(2).

The proviso to s5(2) does permit the PCA to conduct an investigation notwithstanding that the complainant has or had such a right or remedy if the PCA is nevertheless satisfied that, in the particular circumstances, it is not reasonable to expect the complainant to resort or have resorted to it. In *Congreve* v *Home Office* [1976] QB 629 the plaintiff successfully applied for a declaration that the Home Office had acted illegally in revoking the television licences of those who had renewed their licences early to avoid paying the new higher fee. In fact, the action of the Home Office had already been condemned in a special report by the PCA, illustrating the overlap between the powers of the courts and the role of the PCA in policing maladministration.

The 'hurdles' – time limits and location

The lodging of complaints is subject to time limits. Under s6(3) a complaint will not be entertained unless it is made to an MP within 12 months from the day on which the complainant first had notice of the matters alleged in the complaint. The PCA nevertheless has the discretion to conduct an investigation pursuant to a complaint not made within that period if he considers that there are special circumstances that make it proper to do so.

Complainants must be resident in the United Kingdom, or the action complained of must have taken place in relation to the complainant whilst he was present in the United Kingdom. Complaints may be accepted in relation to the actions of consular staff abroad, provided the aggrieved person is a United Kingdom citizen: see s6(5).

Investigative procedure

Under s5(5) it is for the PCA to use his discretion to determine the manner in which a complaint should be investigated. This discretion is not, of course, unlimited but the courts have shown themselves unwilling to question his decisions as to whether to investigate a complaint or not: see *Re Fletcher's Application* [1970] 2 All ER 527. It should be noted that the PCA adopts an investigatory approach to complaints, if possible promoting a friendly settlement between the private individual and government department. Under s7 the PCA must ensure that the principal officer of the department or authority concerned, and any other person alleged in the complaint to have taken or authorised the action complained of, has an opportunity to comment on any allegations contained in the complaint. Investigations will be conducted in private, but the PCA is at liberty to obtain information from such persons and in such manner, and make such inquiries, as he thinks fit: s7(2). Those being questioned may be represented, by counsel or solicitor or otherwise, in the investigation if appropriate.

The PCA has powers similar to those of the High Court as regards securing the presence of witnesses and the production of documents. Under s8(1) the PCA may require 'any Minister, officer or member of the department or authority concerned or any other person who in his opinion is able to furnish information or produce documents relevant to the investigation to furnish any such information or produce any such document.' Evidence can be taken on oath. Significantly, under s8(3), no obligation to maintain secrecy or other restriction upon the disclosure of information obtained by or furnished to persons in Her Majesty's service, whether imposed by any enactment or by any rule of law, shall apply to the disclosure of information for the purposes of an investigation under the 1967 Act. Further the Crown is not be entitled, in relation to any such investigation, to any such privilege in respect of the production of documents or the giving of evidence as is allowed by law in legal proceedings (although note that s8(4) excludes the production of Cabinet or Cabinet committee papers).

The PCA is protected in the conduct of his investigations by the laws relating to contempt of court (see s9(1)), and is empowered to reimburse complainants and witnesses for their expenses, and compensation for the time they have given up to help his investigation: see s7(3). On completing his investigations, the PCA must report on his findings to the Member of Parliament who referred the complaint to him, and to the principal officer of the government department against whom the complaint was made: see s10(3).

Note that under s76 of the Freedom of Information Act 2000, following consideration of a complaint relating to a public body's handling of a request for disclosure of information, the Information Commissioner may disclose to the Parliamentary Ombudsman, the Health Service Ombudsman or local government ombudsman any information if it appears to the Information Commissioner that the information relates to a matter which could be the subject of an investigation by an ombudsman.

Enforcement

The PCA cannot have any of his recommendations put into effect by force of law. If he conducts an investigation and concludes that maladministration has occurred, and that the complainant has suffered injustice as a result, he can lay a special report on the matter before both Houses of Parliament. Everything is then left to the doctrine of ministerial responsibility, the assumption being that the minister will be asked questions about the matter and will have to take some appropriate action. In reality such reports are not often necessary because a mutually agreed settlement can be reached. Government departments and other executive agencies falling within the remit of the PCA generally co-operate with his investigations and accept his findings, in part justifying the absence of any coercive powers as regards remedies. There have been instances where PCA findings have been ignored, most notably in the case of the collapse of the Court Line holiday company, where the PCA criticised the minister concerned for leading the public into believing that the company was sound and that they should continue to book holidays with them. Many members of the public suffered financial loss when the company went into liquidation, but the government department denied any fault on its part.

13.3 Parliamentary supervision of the Parliamentary Commissioner for Administration

A Select Committee oversees the work of the PCA, the Health Service Commissioner and the Northern Ireland Commissioner, examining the reports that each is required to lay each year before each House of Parliament. The reports contain a general summary on the performance of the Commissioners' functions under their various enabling Acts and do not identify complainants, ministers or civil servants. The PCA may also produce special reports that are laid before each House of Parliament and these too can be considered by the committee. Since 1967 the Select Committee has made a number of suggestions as to the way in which the PCA should carry out his functions, such as the correct approach under s12(3) of the 1967 Act, and the widening of his powers to deal with the actions of United Kingdom consular officials.

13.4 Judicial review of the Parliamentary Commissioner for Administration

The PCA is a creature of statute and is, therefore, amenable to judicial review along with other bodies of limited jurisdiction. In practice the courts have been reluctant to interfere with the way in which the PCA has exercised his discretion in the handling of complaints. For example, in *R v Local Commissioner for Administration for the North and East Area of England, ex parte Bradford Metropolitan County Council* [1979] QB 287, the court refused to grant an order of prohibition to prevent the Local Government Commissioner from conducting an investigation. In *R v Parliamentary Commissioner, ex parte Dyer* [1994] 1 WLR 621 the applicant had complained to the PCA in relation to the mishandling of her claim for invalidity benefit and other related welfare benefits. Subsequent to his investigation the Department of Social Security agreed to offer the applicant an apology and an ex gratia payment of £500 plus her expenses. The PCA reported to the applicant's MP, and the department, that he considered this a satisfactory outcome. The applicant sought judicial review of the PCA's alleged failure to investigate all of her complaints, his failure to seek her comments on the settlement and his view that he was precluded from re-opening the complaint. The PCA contended that either his decisions were unreviewable as he was answerable to Parliament for the discharge of his functions, or alternatively that his decisions could only be reviewed in the exceptional case where he had abused his discretion. The court noted that although the PCA's decisions were reviewable, in practice, given the wide discretion vested in him by the 1967 Act, any court would be reluctant to intervene. Consequently the PCA's decision only to select certain of the applicant's complaints for investigation would not be overturned. His practice of submitting a draft report to the department being investigated, but not to the complainant, was not contrary to natural justice, given that it was the department being investigated that would have to defend its action if it was found to have been guilty of maladministration. Having submitted his report to the relevant government department and to the relevant MP the PCA had no remaining power to re-open the complaint as he was functus officio. The only decisions where the PCA has been found to have abused his powers both arose out of the same complaint: see *R* v *Parliamentary Commissioner, ex parte Balchin* [1997] COD 146 and *R* v *Parliamentary Commissioner, ex parte Balchin* (1999) 24 June (unreported).

In 1996 the Balchins had their first success in seeking judicial review of the PCA, when the Divisional Court accepted their argument that the PCA (then Sir William Reid) had acted unlawfully in rejecting their complaints into a proposed dual carriageway that had blighted their property with consequent loss in value for which they were not compensated. A second investigation took place (under Michael Buckley) which again came down in favour of the Department of Transport. Again the Balchins successfully sought judicial review of the PCA's ruling, the court accepting the contention that the reasons given for the PCA's decision were inadequate.

13.5 The work of the Parliamentary Commissioner for Administration

Apart from the more notable investigations, primarily those with significant political repercussions that are reported in the press, the main source of information concerning the nature of the PCA's workload, the extent to which he succeeds in improving the quality of the administrative process and the extent to which he is able to obtain tangible compensation for complainants, are annual and special reports prepared by the PCA for Parliament.

Amongst the high profile cases are the 'Sachsenhausen case', and the investigation into the 'Barlow Clowes' affair. In the former, an Anglo-German Agreement of 1964 provided for £1 million to be paid in compensation to UK citizens who suffered from Nazi persecution during the Second World War. Distribution of this money was left to the discretion of the UK government and in 1964 the Foreign Secretary (then Mr Butler) approved rules for the distribution. Later the Foreign Office withheld compensation from 12 persons who claimed to be within these rules because of their detention within the Sachsenhausen concentration camp. Pressure from many MPs failed to get this decision reversed and a complaint of maladministration was referred to the PCA. By this time the whole of the £1 million had been distributed to other claimants. After extensive investigations the PCA reported that there were defects in the administrative procedures by which the Foreign Office reached its decisions and subsequently defended them, and that this maladministration had damaged the reputation of the claimants. When this report was debated in the Commons, the Foreign Secretary (Mr George Brown) assumed personal responsibility for the decisions of the Foreign Office, which he maintained were correct. He nonetheless made available an additional £25,000 in order that the claimants might receive the same rate of compensation as successful claimants on the fund. Similarly, the Barlow Clowes investigation into the granting of credit licences by the Department of Trade and Industry led, eventually, to the payment of compensation (over £150 million) to those who had lost their investments because of the company's fraudulent activities.

Other examples of maladministration uncovered by PCA investigations include the following.

1. The failure of the Home Office to review the convictions of over 1,500 prisoners who had been sentenced to imprisonment on the strength of the discredited evidence of Home Office forensic scientist Dr Alan Clift. The report included severe criticism of that department for not acting more quickly in the light of what he described as an 'unprecedented pollution of justice'.
2. The handling of the 1994 crisis in the poultry industry by the Ministry of Agriculture resulting in the payment of compensation to poultry farmers.
3. Planning blight caused by the handling of the Channel tunnel rail link project.
4. The operation of certain aspects of the work of the Child Support Agency (1994 and 1995 reports), the PCA highlighting maladministration in the form of the wrongful release of confidential information to potentially violent estranged husbands, the wrongful labelling of fathers as potentially violent, the failure to spot palpably false paternity claims and misdirecting correspondence.
5. The conduct of a British ambassador in response to complaints about the service offered by a British consulate (December 1998).
6. Failure of the Ministry of Defence to release non-sensitive information (May 2000).
7. Delays in payments made to farmers under the EC Arable Areas Payments Scheme (July 2000).

Even though many of the complaints investigated have resulted in only modest levels of compensation being paid, they are nevertheless important in providing the individual concerned with an assurance that his concerns are taken seriously and can result in improvements in the way that the executive conducts its business. For example, customs officials had advised that a car could be temporarily imported into the United Kingdom without payment of purchase tax but, on arrival, the owner was made to pay the £167 purchase tax which was, in reality, due. The PCA persuaded the department, which had refused any concession, to refund the full amount. In another case a complainant, who had been encouraged by the Board of Trade to suppose that his company would be eligible for an investment grant if it installed a grain-processing plant, found that the plant was ruled ineligible after it had been installed and the expenditure incurred. The PCA persuaded the Board to pay compensation of £950. The 1995 Report revealed that the Child Support Agency had been persuaded to make an ex gratia payment of £250 to a man who had been sent a child maintenance form in error.

The 1995 Report was notable in its more general comments on the effects of staff reductions on the quality of work carried out by civil servants. Observing that civil service numbers had dropped below 500,000 for the first time in 50 years, William Reid commented that:

'Reductions in staff numbers, organisational changes and new working practices will continue for some time to place individual civil servants under stress ... there is a real risk that fewer staff will lead to a slower service and to more mistakes because civil servants will have less time for thought to enable them to pursue considered and prudent action.'

The PCA's 1999/2000 Annual Report reveals that he received 1,601 complaints, of which 313 resulted in full investigation reports to Members of Parliament. Of these complaints 93 per cent were wholly or partially upheld. An informal resolution was achieved in respect of 121 cases. The Department of Social Security continued to attract the highest number of complaints (660), followed by the Inland Revenue (134) and the DETR (121). Financial redress was obtained in 251 cases.

13.6 Improving the effectiveness of the Parliamentary Commissioner for Administration

In 1993 the Select Committee on the Parliamentary Commissioner undertook an investigation into the operation of the Parliamentary and Health Service Ombudsman systems, in an effort to identify workable reforms that would improve the effectiveness of those offices. The report was published at the end of 1993 – see *The Powers, Work and Jurisdiction of the Ombudsman* (HC 33–1 (1993)) – and the government's response and further comments from the Select Committee were published in July 1994. The main issues to emerge from this exercise are summarised below.

Procedure

The continued existence of the 'MP filter' has been subject to criticism on the basis that some MPs may adopt a policy of automatically referring complaints to the PCA, and because it may serve to distance the PCA from the public. The Select Committee recommended that the current system be retained, partly because it attached some constitutional significance to the role of the MP in dealing with constituents' complaints, but also because it meant that MPs would be aware of the types of complaints being made about the executive by the public. A further concern was the likely impact on the resources of the PCA's office if the filter was removed. Where complaints are received direct from members of the public there is, in any event, nothing to prevent the PCA from submitting them to Members of Parliament so that they can be re-submitted to him.

Jurisdiction

The Select Committee suggested that the PCA should be given an inclusive jurisdiction, ie the 1967 Act should be amended to provide that the PCA can investigate all complaints other than those relating to matters specifically excluded.

In particular it was felt that commercial contracts and personnel matters should be included in his remit. The government rejected this proposal, indicating that more could be done via publicity to ensure that the public had a higher level of awareness as to the role of the PCA. The level of complaints rejected because they fall outside the jurisdiction of the PCA indicates that more needs to be done to educate the public in respect of the PCA's role.

Publicity

The need for increased awareness of the PCA's work, not least amongst MPs, was highlighted by the Select Committee, which proposed the circulation of an informal newsletter containing details of the PCA's caseload, the amendment of legislation so that references to the Parliamentary Commissioner for Administration and the Health Service Commissioner would become references to the 'Parliamentary Ombudsman' and 'Health Service Ombudsman' respectively, and the provision of parliamentary time for a debate on the work of the PCA in each parliamentary session. The government accepted the proposals for statutory amendment regarding nomenclature and the publication of a newsletter, but rejected the proposal for debating time, arguing that there was insufficient evidence that MPs wanted such a debate. The government also noted its intention to amend literature concerning the Citizen's Charter so as to ensure that it carried on it appropriate references to the role played by the PCA.

Operation

As regards the independence and funding of the ombudsmen, the Committee recommended that appointment should be by the Crown on an address of the House of Commons, no motion being made for such an address except by the Prime Minister with the agreement of the chair of the Select Committee and the Leader of the Opposition, and that the ombudsmen should be paid out of moneys voted for directly by Parliament. The government accepted these recommendations. The Select Committee was critical of the average length of time taken to complete a case investigation by the PCA, noting that although the target was nine months, the average until 1989 had been 15 months and by 1992 had only dropped to 12 months. The government noted these criticisms and hinted that in might be necessary, in due course, to consider allocating the role of PCA and Health Service Ombudsman to two different persons. Other proposals finding favour with the Select Committee, but not the government, were that the PCA should be empowered to conduct an administrative audit of a department or agency where he received complaints indicating a pattern of under-performance, and that the PCA should be able to carry out an investigation following an informal suggestion by the Select Committee.

13.7 Complaining to the Ombudsman – advantages over judicial review

Jurisdictional

Judicial review is, with the exception of error of law, limited to ensuring that public bodies act intra vires, yet there are many forms of maladministration which can cause problems for the public without amounting to ultra vires action. These may be beyond the control of the courts, but matters such as delay, incompetence, stupidity, rudeness, and loss of documents fall squarely within the ambit of the PCA. In short the PCA can reach problems of administration beyond the reaches of judicial review.

Many of the matters dealt with would not warrant litigation even if they were within the scope of judicial review, but are nevertheless a problem to those affected. For example, a complaint may result in a form being made more comprehensible, or a process being speeded up.

Practical

A complaint to the PCA costs the price of a postage stamp. All other costs are borne by the taxpayer, which compares favourably with judicial review. As will have been noted, the PCA can even award complainants out-of-pocket expenses. As the investigation is conducted by the PCA no effort is required on the part of the complainant to prepare a prima facie case, unlike the application for judicial review. The time limit for bringing a complaint (12 months) is more liberal than the three months allowed under Pt 54.5 CPR 1998.

As the PCA procedure is conciliatory as opposed to adversarial, the dispute is unlikely to be exacerbated by his investigation, and those called to give evidence are less likely to be defensive, given that their anonymity is assured.

Remedies

The PCA works towards an amicable settlement between the complainant and the government department. The result of this settlement may be something that could not have been obtained on an application for judicial review. This ranges from an ex-gratia payment (remember damages are not available for ultra vires action), the reversal of a decision (judicial review can only quash a decision, not substitute a new one), or the alteration of an administrative process (some court decisions about improper administrative processes are simply not implemented). Decisions by courts on applications for judicial review only directly affect the case of individual litigants involved; a wider significance can only be obtained if the decision is widely reported and followed by administrators. Where, by contrast, the PCA investigates and reports that a particular administrative process is improper, the department concerned may well agree to amend its procedures in future cases – the so-called 'ripple' effect. The finding in relation to one complaint may affect the treatment of hundreds or thousands of similar cases where no complaint has actually been made.

13.8 The other ombudsmen

Following the partial devolution of power to Scotland and Wales effected by the Scotland Act 1998 and the Government of Wales Act 1998, complaints about maladministration by various public bodies involved in Scottish and Welsh matters are now investigated by the Scottish Parliamentary Commissioner for Administration or the Welsh Administration Ombudsman as appropriate. It is significant that the number of complaints received by the Welsh Administration Ombudsman in respect of matters devolved to the Welsh Assembly has increased dramatically since the removal of the 'MP filter'.

The Local Government Act 1974

The 1974 Act established two Commissions for Local Administration, one for England and one for Wales (the Commission for Local Administration in Wales). A similar Commission was created for Scotland. The Commissioner for Local Government (CLG) investigates complaints of maladministration in connection with the execution of administrative functions performed by a local authority. Note that any matter that affects all or most of the authority's inhabitants is outside the jurisdiction of the CLG.

Normally complaints must be in writing and submitted in the first instance to a member of the authority against whom the complaint is made, although since 1989 the CLG has been able to accept complaints directly if he sees fit. Under s26(6) Local Government Act 1974 the local government ombudsman is not permitted to entertain a complaint in relation to any issue in respect of which the complainant has a viable remedy before the courts: see *R* v *Commissioner for Local Administration, ex parte Croydon London Borough Council* [1989] 1 All ER 1033.

The CLG uses the same concept of maladministration as is used by the PCA. In the event that a local authority is found guilty of maladministration that has resulted in injustice, the CLG will issue a report, copies of which must be kept available by the local authority concerned for public inspection. The authority concerned will be required to indicate the action it intends to take in light of the finding. If an authority fails to respond to criticisms made in a CLG report, he can make a further report. His findings are unenforceable, as is the case with the PCA, the vital difference being the absence of any equivalent of ministerial responsibility at local government level to cajole councils into action. Under s92 of the Local Government Act 2000, if a local authority considers that action taken by or on behalf of the authority amounts to, or may amount to, maladministration, and that a person has been, or may have been, adversely affected by that action, the authority may, if it thinks fit, pay compensation.

The refusal of some local authorities to comply with the findings of the CLG has, in the past, been the subject of concern. In *Administrative Justice: Some Necessary Reforms*, published by Justice in 1988, the authors observed that:

'The local commissioners are treated contemptuously by some local authorities and the public are repeatedly being made aware of their inability to achieve results.'

The report went on to point out that of the 160 reports issued by the local government commissioners up to 31 March 1986, 120 had failed to produce a satisfactory conclusion.

Simply because an application for judicial review may be available to challenge the legality of action taken by a local authority, it does not mean that the CLG is therefore prevented from carrying out an investigation. In *R v Local Commissioner for Administration for the North and East Area of England, ex parte Liverpool City Council* [2001] 1 All ER 462 the Court of Appeal held that the CLG was right to entertain complaints that councillors in Liverpool had acted improperly in approving a planning application brought by Liverpool FC when councillors approving the decision were season ticket holders at the club. The court approved of the CLG's intervention not least because, even though judicial review was available, those adversely affected might not have the means to mount an effective legal challenge, and also because the judicial review procedure might not have revealed the evidence uncovered by the Commissioner for Local Government's investigation. As Henry LJ observed:

'Serious allegations of maladministration … could best be investigated by the resources and powers of the commissioner, with her powers to compel both disclosure of documents, and the giving of assistance to the investigation. The commissioner was in a position to get to the bottom of a prima facie case of maladministration, and the ratepayers would be unlikely to have reached that goal, having regard to the weaknesses of the coercive fact-finding potential of judicial review. As she found, it would be very difficult, if not impossible, for the complainants to obtain the necessary evidence in judicial review proceedings. Additionally, the complainants were a group in modest housing, unlikely to have the means to pursue the remedy. The commissioner was clearly right to use the proviso to continue with her investigation. This case is a good example of a case where the commissioner's investigation and report can provide the just remedy when judicial review might fail to; and can reach facts which might not emerge under the judicial review process.'

The courts have, nevertheless, shown themselves to be willing to intervene as regards decisions of the local government ombudsman, for example in *R v Local Commissioner for Administration for the South (etc), ex parte Eastleigh Borough Council* [1988] 3 WLR 113, where the Court of Appeal held (the Master of the Rolls dissenting) that the local government ombudsman had exceeded his powers in making certain reports, because it had not been established that the complainant had suffered injustice in consequence of maladministration: see also *R* v *Commissioner for Local Administration, ex parte Croydon London Borough Council* [1989] 1 All ER 1033.

Under the Local Government Act 2000 (s67) Local Commissioners are given a role to play in the investigation of complaints against council members relating to unethical behaviour. Under ss68 and 69 the Commission for Local Administration in Wales has further powers to issue guidance and investigate breaches of the code of conduct for local authority members: see further Chapter 3.

Northern Ireland

In 1969 the ombudsman principle was extended to the Province, and it should be noted that the Commissioner for Complaints Act (Northern Ireland) 1969 provides for decisions of the Northern Ireland Parliamentary Commissioner for Administration to be enforceable by way of a complainant applying to the county court for damages, injunction or other appropriate order. He also has jurisdiction to investigate complaints about public sector employment matters.

The Health Service Commissioners

The National Health Service Reorganisation Act 1973 and National Health Service (Scotland) Act 1972 created three Health Service ombudsmen (one each for England, Wales and Scotland respectively). The relevant statutory provisions were subsequently re-enacted in the National Health Service Act 1977 and the National Health Service Act (Scotland) 1978, and have now been consolidated in the Health Service Commissioners Act 1993.

The Health Service Commissioners are appointed by the Queen on the advice of the Prime Minister, and hold office during good behaviour, retiring at the age of 65. It has been past practice for the same person to occupy all four posts (Parliamentary Commissioner and Health Service Commissioners).

The Health Service Commissioner for England can investigate complaints made against regional health authorities, district health authorities, specified special health authorities, NHS trusts, family health service authorities, the Dental Practice Board and the Public Health Laboratory Service Board. The provisions for Wales and Scotland are broadly similar. A complaint must allege that a person has sustained injustice or hardship in consequence of: a failure in a service provided by a health service body; the failure of such a body to provide a service that it was a function of that body to provide; maladministration connected with any other action taken by or on behalf of such a body. As with the Parliamentary Commissioner, the Health Service Commissioners are not authorised to question the merits of a decision taken without maladministration by a health service body in the exercise of a discretion vested in that body: s3.

A complaint can be made by an individual or organisation, whether incorporated or not, provided that the complainant is not a 'public authority' as defined in s8(2).

Complaints must be made in writing, normally within a year of the matter complained of being made aware to the complainant, and the body that is the subject of the complaint must normally have been given an opportunity to respond to it before the Commissioner acts. In contrast to the procedure to be followed in respect of the Parliamentary Commissioner, the Health Service Commissioners have the power to accept complaints directly from members of the public and organisations.

Investigations are conducted in private, with the health body concerned being given an opportunity to comment on the allegations. The exact procedure to be adopted is largely within the discretion of the relevant commissioner. Health service bodies under investigation, and any other person who may be able to assist the investigation can be compelled to produce evidence, and those who obstruct the inquiry can be subject to punishment for contempt of court.

The Health Service Commissioners cannot normally entertain complaints where the complainant has the right to obtain redress in respect of the matter complained of before a court or tribunal. Under s5 of the 1993 Act the Commissioners were specifically excluded from investigating complaints that related to the diagnosis of illness or the care or treatment of a patient, where, in the opinion of the Commissioner, the action complained of was taken solely in consequence of the exercise of clinical judgment. This jurisdictional barrier has now been repealed by s6 of the Health Service Commissioners (Amendment) Act 1996, which repeals s5 of the 1993 Act.

On completion of his investigation the Commissioner will send a copy of his report to (inter alia) the complainant, any MP involved in the making of the complaint and the health service body concerned.

14

Liability of the Crown and Public Bodies in Contract and Tort

14.1 Introduction to Crown liability

14.2 The Crown Proceedings Act 1947

14.3 Actions against the Crown in contract

14.4 Crown liability in tort

14.5 Public interest immunity

14.6 Remedies

14.7 The liability of local authorities and other public bodies in contract and tort

14.8 Nuisance

14.9 Breach of statutory duty

14.10 Liability in negligence

14.11 Misfeasance in public office

14.12 Liability of individual council officers

14.1 Introduction to Crown liability

Prior to the enactment of the Crown Proceedings Act 1947, the position of the Crown as regards its legal liabilities was governed by the common law doctrine that 'the Crown can do no wrong'. The effect of this was that the monarch, in his or her personal capacity, could not be subjected to the judicial process, and that the Crown could not be liable in tort for the actions of its servants. Such legal proceedings as could be brought against the Crown, such as actions for damages in respect of debts and other property matters, could only be brought by means of a petition of right, subject to the grant of the royal fiat. In order to circumvent the restriction on proceedings against the Crown in tort a legal fiction was resorted to, whereby the plaintiff would sue a nominal Crown servant in his personal capacity, and the relevant government department would subsequently reimburse its servant in the event of any damages being awarded. Note that the immunity belonged to the Crown, not the minister or official concerned: see *Entick* v *Carrington* (1765) 19 St Tr 1030. A Crown servant could be sued in a personal capacity, for example where a minister authorised the unlawful action of a Crown servant: see *Raleigh* v *Goschen* [1898] 1 Ch 73 and *Tamaki* v *Baker* [1901] AC 561. The courts eventually rejected this resort to legal fiction, see *Royster* v *Cavey* [1947] KB 204, and it became obvious that a wholesale revision of the law was necessary. Given the increased number of important activities undertaken by state agencies, Parliament felt that the time was right to set the law on a more rational basis.

14.2 The Crown Proceedings Act 1947

The principal aim of the legislation was to place the Crown in the same situation as any other legal entity as regards proceedings in tort. Whilst the Act largely achieves this by introducing significant changes to the scope of the Crown's tortious liability, no changes are made in respect of contractual liability. The only difference for an individual proceeding against the Crown for breach of contract after 1947, as compared to before 1947, would be in respect of the procedure to be utilised. Section 1 of the Crown Proceedings Act 1947 states:

> 'Where any person has a claim against the Crown after the commencement of this Act, and if this Act had not been passed, the claim might have been enforced, subject to the grant of His Majesty's fiat, by petition of right, or might have been enforced by a proceeding provided by any statutory provision repealed by this Act, then, subject to the provisions of this Act, the claim may be enforced as of right, and without the fiat of His Majesty, by proceedings taken against the Crown for that purpose in accordance with the provisions of this Act.'

To assess Crown liability in contract, therefore, it is necessary to consider the position at common law.

14.3 Actions against the Crown in contract

It could be argued that normal contractual relationships with the Crown are impossible, given the inequality of bargaining power and the residual power of the Crown to render obligations void by means of retrospective legislation, thus undermining the principle that both sides should be equally bound by the transaction. Notwithstanding these theoretical issues, the fact remains that the Crown enters into numerous 'contracts' in the carrying out of government business, and the vast majority are discharged without any problems. From the case law it is possible, however, to identify a number of areas where a litigant may be denied a remedy should the Crown decide to terminate the agreement in question.

Where money must be provided

Government spending must be authorised by Parliament, and this is normally achieved by way of an Appropriation Act. Once the money has been allotted to departments they are free, within political and legal constraints, to spend it. In the majority of cases, therefore, no problem arises, in the sense that a government department cannot cease performance of a contract on the ground of lack of funds, when in fact these have already been provided.

An exceptional problem arose in *Churchward v R* (1865) LR 1 QB 173, where the plaintiff had entered into a contract with the Admiralty to provide a mail service between Dover and the continent for 11 years. An annual sum was to be provided by Parliament as consideration. After the contract had run for four years, the Admiralty terminated the agreement, and in that year the relevant Appropriation Act provided that no sum was to be made available by Parliament to provide any further payment. The plaintiff thereupon sought damages from the Crown for breach of contract in respect of the income he would have received had the agreement run its full course. The court held that the provision of funds by Parliament was a condition precedent to the enforceability of the contractual undertaking, and the court had no power to compel Parliament to vote in favour of making such funds available. As Luon J observed:

'... I think it is in the highest degree improbable that any department of the public service would pledge the Crown to a given course of action for a series of years, in the management of any branch of the public service, especially one for which they have to go to Parliament year by year for supplies, without at all events reserving the right of putting an end to it, if the public service required it, or if Parliament disapproved of it.'

Cockburn C J stated that the existence of sufficient funds voted by Parliament was a condition precedent to the enforceability of the contract. Where the funds have been allocated by Parliament, however, there should be no reason why, in the ordinary run of commercial contracts, the Crown should not be held to its undertakings.

In *New South Wales v Bardolph* (1934) 52 CLR 455 the New South Wales government, following a change of policy, determined not to continue with a series of tourism advertisements booked in the plaintiff's publication. The plaintiff nevertheless continued to run the advertisements and at the end of the contract period claimed the sum due. Although the contract had not been expressly authorised by the State Legislature, the relevant Appropriation Acts had made sums available for 'government advertising', and the amount available far exceeded that sought by the plaintiff. The High Court held that the plaintiff was therefore entitled to succeed in his action for damages.

Evatt J summarised the position thus:

'In the absence of some controlling statutory provision, contracts are enforceable against the Crown if;
(a) the contract is entered into in the ordinary or necessary course of Government administration,

(b) it is authorized by the responsible Ministers of the Crown, and
(c) the payments which the contractor is seeking to recover are covered by or referable to
a parliamentary grant for the class of service to which the contract relates.'

Note the distinction between the court declaring the existence of contractual rights and enforcement of those rights. It is probably true to say that a contract can be sued on before sums have been appropriated to it, provided there is no express provision prohibiting payment, but there may be problems in gaining anything other than declaratory relief as the courts will not be able to grant any coercive order against the Crown to enforce judgment.

Executive necessity

The effect of this doctrine is that the Crown will not be bound by a contract where there is an overriding need for it to be free to act in the national interest. In *Rederiaktiebolaget Amphitrite* v *R* [1921] 3 KB 500 the owners of the vessel *Amphitrite* were given assurances by the British government, acting through diplomatic channels, that if the ship docked at a British port it would not be detained in the way that similar vessels were under wartime measures. Nevertheless, whilst docked at Hull, the ship was detained by the Crown and eventually had to be sold by the owners. After the war, the owners sued the Crown for damages for breach of contract. The court held that even if there was a contract in this case (which was dubious) the petition would fail, on the ground that the government had to remain free to take what action was necessary in the national interest, and could not be hampered by the restraints of contract in this respect. Rowlatt J expressed the view that normally commercial undertakings would be binding on the Crown, but went on to observe that:

'... this was not a commercial contract; it was an arrangement whereby the Government purported to give an assurance as to what its executive action would be in the future in relation to a particular ship in the event of her coming to this country with a particular kind of cargo. And that is, to my mind, not a contract for the breach of which damages can be sued for in a Court of law ... it is not competent for the Government to fetter its future executive action, which must necessarily be determined by the needs of the community when the question arises. It cannot by contract hamper its freedom of action in matters which concern the welfare of the State.'

The precise extent of 'executive necessity' as a basis for releasing the Crown from its contractual liabilities has never been settled. Clearly, as the above case demonstrates, it extends to acting in the national interest during wartime. Similarly, in *Crown Lands Commissioners* v *Page* [1960] 2 QB 274, the doctrine was invoked to uphold the validity of the Crown's actions in leasing land to Page, requisitioning it under wartime powers, then suing him for the rent that he had not paid during the period of requisition. The court refused to imply into the lease any right to quiet enjoyment of the property. The Crown had to be free to recover the land whenever necessary. Devlin J indicated that he would have come to the same conclusion even if a covenant to that effect had been express. He stated:

> 'When the Crown in dealing with one of its subjects, is dealing as if it too were a private person and is granting leases or buying and selling as ordinary persons do, it is absurd to suppose that it is making any promise about the way in which it will conduct the affairs of the nation. No one can imagine, for example, that when the Crown makes a contract which could not be fulfilled in time of war, it is pledging itself not to declare war for so long as the contract lasts.'

Authorities such as *The Steaua Romana* [1944] P 43, and obiter statements of Lord Denning in *Robertson* v *Ministry of Pensions* [1949] 1 KB 227, display a reluctance to extend the doctrine of executive necessity to commercial contracts. The Crown could not, of course, be prevented from enacting legislation that would frustrate the performance of a commercial contract, nor does it mean that the Crown should ensure the enactment of legislation to facilitate the performance of such a contract: see *Board of Trade* v *Temperley Steam Shipping Co Ltd* (1926) 26 Ll LR 76.

Suppliers of goods to the Crown, entering into long-term contracts involving much expenditure and capital outlay on their part, may subsequently find that, following a change of government, the new administration, as a matter of policy, determines not to provide any more public funds for various contracts. As has been outlined above, there is very little that the private party to the contract can do in such situations. A government seeking to ensure that its policies are carried out, even after it leaves office, might consider the inclusion of a liquidated damages clause enuring to the benefit of the contractor in the event a later administration seeking to terminate the agreement. In this regard it should be noted that the placing of government contracts is not subject to any statutory procedure, and is a matter expressly excluded from the jurisdiction of the Parliamentary Commissioner for the Administration.

Crown employment

Crown servants are, traditionally, 'dismissable at will'. The theory is that the Crown should not be forced to continue the employment of some individual who is no longer suitable, as this would be contrary to the public interest. In some senses, at least, the proposition can be regarded as an extension of executive necessity, although there is some doubt as to whether or not Crown servants are employed pursuant to a contract of employment. The fact that Crown servants are dismissable at will militates against there being a contractual relationship, but on the other hand, as Lord Atkin stated in *Reilly* v *R* [1934] AC 176 at 179: 'A power to determine a contract at will is not inconsistent with the existence of a contract until it is so determined.' To some extent this view is reflected in *Dunn* v *R* [1896] 1 QB 116, where the plaintiff had been appointed as a consular official in what was then Niger, for three years. Before the expiry of this period he was dismissed and consequently sought damages for breach of contract. The court held that no damages were payable since, as a Crown servant, he was dismissable at pleasure, but Lord Herschell's observations seem to assume the existence of a contract:

> 'I take it that persons employed as the petitioner was in the service of the Crown, except in cases where there is some statutory provision for a higher tenure of office, are ordinarily engaged on the understanding that they hold their employment at the pleasure of the Crown. So I think that there must be imported into the contract for the employment of the petitioner the term which is applicable to civil servants in general, namely, that the Crown may put an end to the employment at its pleasure. ... The cases cited show that, such employment being for the good of the public, it is essential for the public good that it should be capable of being determined at the pleasure of the Crown, except in certain exceptional cases where it has been deemed to be more for the public good that some restriction should be imposed on the power of the Crown to dismiss its servants ...'

There is evidence to support both sides of this argument. In *Council of Civil Service Unions* v *Minister for the Civil Service* [1984] 3 All ER 935, by the time the case had reached the House of Lords, both sides appeared to have agreed that the relationship was not contractual. Further support for this view is provided by *R* v *Civil Service Appeal Board, ex parte Bruce* [1988] 3 All ER 686. A civil servant employed by the Inland Revenue was given notice terminating his employment and sought judicial review of the Appeal Board's decision to uphold his dismissal. Although counsel for the Crown had contended that there could be a contract between the Crown and its servants, albeit one which was not intended to be legally binding, the court held that there was no contract. The decision was influenced by the fact that the applicant had not been appointed pursuant to any statutory power, evidence that there had never been any intention to enter into contractual obligations on the part of the Crown, and that the whole matter was under review by the government, through a Cabinet Office reappraisal of the status of Crown servants.

Against this one should consider older cases, such as *Rodwell* v *Thomas* [1944] KB 596. The court proceeded on the basis that a civil servant did have a contract of employment but that the courts would never imply or incorporate into the contract any provisions/agreements which purported to limit the power of the Crown to dismiss. Similarly, in *Riordan* v *War Office* [1959] 3 All ER 552, where the plaintiff was dismissed from his post as a civil servant without being given the 14 days' notice required under Order in Council regulations, the court refused to incorporate the regulations into his contract of employment if they acted as a fetter on the Crown's discretion. Finally, in *Kodeeswaran* v *Attorney-General of Ceylon* [1970] AC 1111, the Privy Council, being asked to consider whether a civil servant had any right of action against the Crown in respect of salary due for services rendered, held that a civil servant could bring an action, under the common law of Ceylon, against the Crown to recover arrears of wages. As to the existence of a contract Lord Diplock observed that:

'Their Lordships thus see nothing inconsistent with British constitutional theory in the Governor of Ceylon being empowered by the Proclamation of 1799 to enter into a contract on behalf of the Crown with a person appointed to an office in the civil administration of the colony as to the salary payable to him, provided that such contract was terminable at will. ... A right to terminate a contract of service at will coupled with a right to enter into a fresh contract of service may in effect enable the Crown to change the terms of employment in future if the true inference to be drawn from the communication of the intended change to the servant and his continuing to serve thereafter is that his existing contract has been terminated by the Crown and a fresh contract entered into on the revised terms. But this cannot affect any right to salary already earned under the terms of his existing contract before its termination.'

For the moment, the tide of judicial opinion seems to be running in favour of the view that a contract can exist but may not always do so. In *McClaren* v *Home Office* [1990] ICR 824 the plaintiff was a prison officer who had been involved in a dispute with the Home Office over working conditions that had culminated in his suspension without pay. He sought a declaration, by way of an action in the Chancery Division, that his conditions of employment could not be altered by his employers in breach of collective agreements, and claimed compensation for loss of salary. At first instance it was held that his statement of claim would be struck out as it disclosed no claim in private law, because the plaintiff had no individual contract of employment with the Home Office that could give rise to rights in the private law of contract. *Ex parte Bruce* was cited with approval in support of this conclusion. The Court of Appeal allowed the plaintiff's appeal against this decision on the basis that his action did raise questions of private law. Dillon LJ, in the Court of Appeal, was influenced by the fact that McClaren's appointment had been made under a statutory power, namely s3 of the Prison Act 1952. His Lordship expressed the view that in appointing prison officers the Home Office was in a position analogous to that of a nationalised industry or health authority, and as such had the power to enter into contractual relationships with staff. In his view the exercise of the statutory power of appointment was free from the restrictions inherent in an exercise of prerogative power. The question of whether or not there was a contract between McClaren and the Home Office was actually left open by the court, but it did regard the question as one which could be properly resolved by way of a private action.

A more definite opinion as to the existence of a contract was expressed by Stuart-Smith LJ in *R* v *Lord Chancellor's Department, ex parte Nangle* [1991] IRLR 343. The applicant had faced internal disciplinary hearings following allegations that he had sexually harassed a female colleague. The question for the Divisional Court was whether or not the applicant was employed under a contract of employment, as the existence of such a contract would militate against the existence of any public law rights to be protected by way of judicial review.

Stuart-Smith LJ held that a contract did exist in this case since all the required elements were present: offer, acceptance, consideration and, crucially, an intention to be legally bound. Interestingly, his Lordship chose to ignore para 14 of the Civil Service Pay and Conditions Code which provided that no contract existed between civil servants and the Crown, regarding this as a mistaken assumption.

The existence of a contract may also be of significance where the Crown seeks to enforce its rights as against a Crown servant. In *Attorney-General* v *Blake* [2000] 4 All ER 385 the House of Lords held that the Crown had the right to sue a former member of the intelligence services for breach of contract where he had submitted the manuscript of his autobiography for publication without obtaining clearance.

Allied to the question of whether or not a contract exists is that of the procedure the aggrieved Crown servant should use. A simplistic analysis suggests that if a contract does exist, he or she should proceed by way of action and, in the absence of a contract, by way of an application for judicial review. Such an analysis may be flawed, since even if there is no contract there may not be a sufficient public law issue to warrant the intervention of the courts by way of judicial review: see comments of Stuart-Smith LJ *in ex parte Nangle*, and see further *R* v *Derbyshire County Council, ex parte Noble* [1990] ICR 808.

The Employment Protection (Consolidation) Act 1978

Crown servants are permitted to take disputes relating to their employment to industrial tribunals. The matter is governed by s138 of the Employment Protection (Consolidation) Act 1978 Act, in which Crown employment is defined (in subs(2)) as:

> '... employment under or for the purposes of a government department or any officer or body exercising on behalf of the Crown functions conferred by an enactment.'

Subsection 138(3) expressly excludes members of the armed forces from the benefits provided by the section. Note also that the Act is silent as to the existence of a contract of employment. Under s138(4) a minister may certify that the employment of a particular Crown servant is of such a nature that he should not be permitted to take his case to an industrial tribunal as this would be prejudicial to national security.

Agency

The normal principles of agency, which apply where a Crown servant acts on behalf of the Crown, would appear to be as follows. First, the Crown is clearly bound by a servant acting with real authority. Second, the Crown will be bound where a servant has apparent, or ostensible authority, provided it can be shown that the Crown represented the agent as having more authority than he in reality possessed. If no such representation by the Crown (as principal) has been made, it will not be bound. In *Attorney-General for Ceylon* v *Silva* [1953] AC 461 the Principal Collector of Customs of Ceylon obtained the permission of the Chief Secretary of Ceylon to sell, by auction, certain steel plates, which were on customs premises. The Principal

Collector was unaware that the plates had already been sold by the Crown some two months earlier. Permission to auction the steel plates had been granted to the Principal Collector under the provisions of the Ceylon Customs Ordinance. The plaintiff, Silva, purchased the steel plates at the auction and claimed damages when delivery was refused because of the prior sale. The Privy Council held that the Ordinance under which the goods were sold did not bind the Crown, therefore the Principal Collector had had no actual authority to sell the steel plates at the auction because they were Crown property. The argument that he had been acting within the scope of his apparent authority, and that the Crown was therefore still bound by his actions, was also rejected on the basis that no public officer, unless he possessed some special power, could hold out on behalf of the Crown that he had the right to enter into a contract in respect of the property of the Crown when in fact no such right existed.

Finally, a Crown servant cannot be sued for breach of warranty of authority, that is be sued personally for entering into contracts he in fact had no power to make: see *Dunn* v *MacDonald* [1897] 1 QB 555.

14.4 Crown liability in tort

As stated above, the primary aim of the 1947 Act was to amend the law and place the Crown in the same position as any other individual as regard liability in tort. It has largely achieved this goal, as s2(1)(a) provides:

> 'Subject to the provisions of this Act, the Crown shall be subject to all those liabilities in tort to which, if it were a private person of full age and capacity, it would be subject ...'

Liability is extended by s2(1)(b) as regards any breach of those duties which a person owes to his servants or agents at common law by reason of being their employer; s2(1)(c) extends the Crown's liability to any breach of the duties attaching at common law to the ownership, occupation, possession or control of property; and s2(2) provides that:

> 'Where the Crown is bound by a statutory duty which is binding also upon persons other than the Crown and its officers, then, subject to the provisions of this Act, the Crown shall, in respect of a failure to comply with that duty, be subject to all those liabilities in tort (if any) to which it would be so subject if it were a private person of full age and capacity.'

Third party, or joint, liability is provided for by s4, which states that, in so far as liability is imposed by the 1947 Act, the law relating to indemnity and contribution shall be enforceable by or against the Crown in respect of the liability to which it is so subject as if the Crown were a private person of full age and capacity.

The Crown's liability in tort will of necessity be vicarious in nature, as it can only act through its servants and agents. For this purpose s2(6) of the 1947 Act defines a Crown servant as a person who:

'... has been directly or indirectly appointed by the Crown and was at the material time paid in respect of his duties as an officer of the Crown wholly out of the Consolidated Fund of the United Kingdom, moneys provided by Parliament, the Road Fund, or any other Fund certified by the Treasury for the purposes of this subsection or was at the material time holding an office in respect of which the Treasury certify that the holder thereof would normally be so paid.'

The nature of this vicarious liability is adverted to by s2(3) which provides that:

'Where any functions are conferred or imposed upon an officer of the Crown as such either by any rule of the common law or by statute, and that officer commits a tort while performing or purporting to perform those functions, the liabilities of the Crown in respect of the tort shall be such as they would have been if those functions had been conferred or imposed solely by virtue of instructions lawfully given by the Crown.'

Clearly the vicarious liability of the Crown depends upon the liability of the individual Crown servant, thus s2(4) provides that:

'Any enactment which negatives or limits the amount of the liability of any Government department or officer of the Crown in respect of any tort committed by that department or officer shall, in the case of proceedings against the Crown under this section in respect of a tort committed by that department or officer, apply in relation to the Crown as it would have applied in relation to that department or officer if the proceedings against the Crown had been proceedings against that department or officer.'

And the proviso to s2 makes it clear that no proceedings shall lie against the Crown in respect of any act or omission of a servant or agent unless the act or omission would in any event have given rise to a cause of action in tort against the servant or agent. The effect of this latter provision is that unless the individual Crown servant or agent can be sued, the Crown will not be vicariously liable. In some cases it may be very difficult to identify the civil servant responsible for one's loss. It also means that if, for some reason, as in *Corney* v *Minister of Labour* (1959) PL 170, no action can be taken against the individual tortfeasor, then no action is maintainable against the Crown.

The problem was also adverted to in *Racz* v *Home Office* [1994] 2 WLR 23, where a prisoner sought damages for assault, battery, negligence and misfeasance in respect of his treatment whilst detained. The Home Office applied unsuccessfully to have the claim of misfeasance struck out on the ground that it could not be held vicariously liable for such actions. Lord Jauncey observed that in order to determine whether or not a department of state could be vicariously liable for the misfeasance of an officer of the Crown, the court would distinguish between a situation on the one hand, where the officer was performing authorised acts by means of a misguided or unauthorised means, and on the other where he was committing acts which had no connection with his duties. In the latter case there would not normally be any question of vicarious liability.

Liability in negligence

Whilst as a matter of fact it may be possible to establish that a plaintiff has been adversely affected by the actions of Crown servant, and thus construct an argument that the servant's negligence has caused the plaintiff's loss, and that the loss was the foreseeable result of that negligence, it does not necessarily follow that the courts will recognise the existence of any private law duty of care.

Where the defendant is a public body, such as a department of state, which is vicariously liable for the torts of its Crown servants, the courts will additionally have to consider whether there is a relationship of proximity between the parties, and whether or not there are any public policy reasons for holding that, in all the circumstances, it would be fair, just and reasonable to impose a private law duty of care. Key consideration as regards these public policy issues are: whether or not the imposition of a private law duty of care would actually have a salutary effect on the manner in which public powers are exercised or duties discharged; whether there are other more appropriate routes by which remedies can be obtained; and whether a side-effect of imposing a private law duty of care would be to unleash a tide of time-consuming and expensive litigation. For examples: see *W* v *Home Office* (1997) The Times 14 March, where the court refused to impose a private law duty of care on an immigration officer deciding whether or not to release an asylum seeker from custody; and *OLL Ltd* v *Secretary of State for Transport* [1997] 3 All ER 897, where the Divisional Court, applying *Capital and Counties plc* v *Hampshire County Council etc* [1997] 2 All ER 865, held that HM Coastguard, as an emergency service, was under no enforceable private law duty to respond to emergency calls. There is also the question of how best the exercise of loss distribution should be carried out, ie whether the taxpayer should fund an award of damages, or whether a loss should lay where it falls.

A useful starting point for the examination of these issues is the House of Lords' decision in *Home Office* v *Dorset Yacht Co Ltd* [1970] AC 1004. Several borstal trainees, being detained under 'open conditions', escaped from supervision and damaged property belonging to the respondents. The relaxed detention regime had been adopted following a change of policy at the Home Office, the rationale being that if the boys were trusted and given more freedom they would become more responsible and mature. The respondents argued that the borstal officers owed neighbouring property owners a duty of care to ensure that none of the detainees would escape, the existence of this duty of care being tried as a preliminary matter. The House of Lords held (Viscount Dilhorne dissenting) that a duty of care was owed by the borstal officers to neighbouring property owners (ie those who were sufficiently 'proximate'), to the extent that they should use reasonable care to prevent an escape of detainees where there was a manifest risk of this. Lord Diplock made it clear, however, that in his view no duty of care was owed by the minister or his officials in exercising policy-making powers. The majority view reflects the opinion that the law should not necessarily apply the standard common law rules of negligence in an unqualified form to government departments because their functions were unlikely to have any parallel in private law – for example the decision as to whether or not to release a felon. The majority concluded that if harm resulted because of acts or omissions of a borstal officer (ie from something that could be identified as falling within the operational rather than policy sphere) the first inquiry should be as to whether or not he had exceeded his powers (ie acted ultra vires). If this was the case then the common law principles of negligence could be applied – but even then only a very limited duty of care (in terms of its geographic scope) could arise.

The obvious difficulty here lies in determining whether a given activity falls within the policy or operational sphere. In *Rowling* v *Takaro Properties Ltd* [1988] 1 All ER 163 the Privy Council issued a clear warning against adopting an overly simplistic approach to the policy/operational dichotomy as the determinant of whether a private law action for negligence is maintainable against the Crown. Underpinning the decision is the assumption that if the exercise of discretion by a public body appears to have been invalid, the matter can be quickly rectified by way of an application for judicial review. Any losses resulting from this delay should, in theory, be minimal, given the speed with which a ruling can be obtained. As a result, there should be no need for a plaintiff to launch, in addition, an action for negligence. Lord Keith, delivering the advice of the Board, commented that, on the broader issue of when a private law duty of care would arise in relation to the exercise of public law powers, the distinction between policy and operational decisions was not the only relevant factor. His Lordship felt that the question of whether there was a duty of care should be approached pragmatically, with reference to the availability of judicial review in respect of the action, the likelihood of negligence actually being established and the danger of inducing undue caution amongst administrators.

The comments of Lord Keith in *Rowling* v *Takaro Properties Ltd* did not subsequently inhibit the Vice-Chancellor, Sir Nicholas Browne-Wilkinson, in *Lonrho plc* v *Tebbit and the Department of Trade and Industry* [1991] 4 All ER 973, from concluding that a minister could face an action for negligence in the respect of the exercise of ministerial powers. The plaintiff company's cause of action arose from the Secretary of State's delay in releasing it from an undertaking not to acquire shares in a particular company. By the time the release was granted a rival company had already won the take-over battle. The Vice-Chancellor took the view that the decision to release Lonrho from its undertaking could be characterised as operational, rather than one falling within the sphere of policy, and as such it would be regarded as a governmental activity in respect of which a private law duty of care could be said to exist. In this respect his Lordship paid considerable attention to the issue of proximity and, given that the issue arose out of an agreement between the plaintiff and the defendants, felt that there were grounds for arguing that the economic loss suffered by the plaintiff might be reasonably foreseeable. It was clearly a case where a trial of the facts was required so that the question of proximity could be resolved, and hence the defendant's application to have the action struck out was dismissed. On appeal ([1992] 4 All ER 280) Dillon LJ, whilst confirming the decision at first instance, was careful to point out that the court was ruling only on the procedural issues. He noted that on the substantive issue of negligence, the plaintiffs might yet face serious difficulties in persuading a court to depart from the constraints on liability indicated by Lord Keith in *Rowling*. Leave to appeal to the House of Lords was refused. As to the principles applicable to determining the nature of liability for economic loss see the comments of Lord Bridge in *Caparo Industries plc* v *Dickman* [1990] 1 All ER 568 at 573–4. For further consideration of the policy/operational dichotomy in the context of the liability of local authorities in negligence: see section 14.10, below.

It should be noted that if there is evidence that a minister has deliberately acted ultra vires in the knowledge that he could adversely affect the interests of another, an action for the tort of misfeasance may be possible.

Judicial immunity

Section 2(5) of the 1947 Act excludes Crown liability in respect of acts of a 'judicial nature'. It provides:

> 'No proceedings shall lie against the Crown by virtue of this section in respect of anything done or omitted to be done by any person while discharging or purporting to discharge any responsibilities of a judicial nature vested in him, or any responsibilities which he has in connection with the execution of judicial process.'

The problem here is identifying responsibilities of a judicial nature. Where individuals such as judges enjoy immunity in their own right, then it is clear that the Crown cannot be vicariously liable. The difficulty arises with persons such as tribunal chairmen, inquiry inspectors and others discharging functions of a quasi-judicial nature. Statements made by tribunal members will sometimes be privileged, thus preventing any action in defamation, but there is no clear authority stating the ambit of s2(5). Cases that may be of assistance in deciding whether proceedings are judicial are: *Sirros* v *Moore* [1975] QB 118; *Royal Aquarium Society* v *Parkinson* [1892] 1 QB 431; and *Trapp* v *Mackie* [1979] 1 All ER 489. In *Jones* v *Department of Employment* [1988] 2 WLR 493 the Court of Appeal held that an employment benefit adjudication officer could not be described as falling within the scope of the judicial immunity referred to in s2(5) of the 1947 Act as regards his giving advice to benefit claimants. The court went further, however, in rejecting the contention that a common law duty of care should be imposed on such an officer, holding that the only private law action that might be sustainable in such circumstances was an action for misfeasance. It was felt that to allow an action for negligence to proceed would run counter to the aims and objects of the relevant legislation which had established a framework of appeals from decisions of adjudication officers, appeal lying ultimately to the Social Security Commissioner whose decision was to be regarded as final on all matters other than questions of law.

At common law there will be immunity from civil action in respect of actions that are closely associated with the judicial process itself. For example a decision not to grant bail (see *Gizzonio* v *Chief Constable of Derbyshire Constabulary* (1998) The Times 29 April) and the preparation of evidence (see *Docker* v *Chief Constable of West Midlands Police* (1998) The Times 29 April). On the other hand, it has been held that s2(5) would not provide protection from an action in negligence in respect of a solicitor employed by the Crown Prosecution Service carrying out administrative tasks prior to the presentation of a case before a magistrates' court: see further *Welsh* v *Chief Constable of the Merseyside Police* [1993] 1 All ER 692 and *Elguzouli-Daf* v *Commissioner of Police of the Metropolis* [1995] NLJ 151.

Provisions relating to the armed forces

Section 10 of the 1947 Act provides that the Crown will not be liable in negligence in respect of death or personal injury occurring to a member of the armed forces caused by the act of another member of the armed forces. The immunity is subject to a number of conditions. First, the death or injury must be occur whilst the victim is either on duty as a member of the armed forces of the Crown or is, though not on duty as such, on any land, premises, ship, aircraft or vehicle for the time being used for the purposes of the armed forces of the Crown. Second, the Secretary of State for Social Security must certify that the death or injury is attributable to service for the purposes of entitlement to an award under the Royal Warrant Order in Council or Order of His Majesty relating to the disablement or death of members of the force of which he is a member.

If a member of the armed forces causes death or injury to another member of the armed forces as a result of an act or omission not connected with the execution of his duties as a member of those forces, there is no immunity from an action in negligence, although it should be noted that in such cases the Crown is unlikely to be vicariously liable.

The rationale for s10 of the 1947 Act was that it was not thought appropriate for members of the armed forces to be encouraged to think in terms of bringing actions in the courts in respect of the conduct of the their colleagues. Training and warfare being inherently dangerous activities, the imposition of a private law duty of care was seen as incongruous. When s10 was enacted the medical and financial benefits available to disabled servicemen compared favourably with the award of damages that would have been obtained through litigation. Increasingly, however, the restriction on litigation imposed by s10 became subject to considerable criticism, not least because the compensation paid to injured military personnel failed to keep pace with the awards of damages being made in the courts, particularly to serving police officers and firemen injured by the negligence of their colleagues.

Bowing to the pressure for reform, Parliament enacted the Crown Proceedings

(Armed Forces) Act 1987 which has the effect of suspending the operation of s10, but also empowers the Secretary of State to reactivate the section at any time in the future should it be considered necessary. The 1987 Act is not retrospective in operation and thus does not, for example, affect the claims made by servicemen suing in respect of injuries sustained whilst present at nuclear tests in the Pacific region during the 1950s, some of which were considered by the House of Lords in *Pearce* v *Secretary of State for Defence* [1988] 2 All ER 348. In the event, it was held that the Crown was not entitled to rely on the immunity that had been created by s10 of the 1947 Act, as the tests had actually been conducted by the United Kingdom Atomic Energy Authority, the liabilities of which had been transferred to the Crown by subsequent legislation. At the time of the tests the Authority had not been covered by the immunity created by s10, thus the Crown could not now rely on it; but see *Derry* v *Ministry of Defence* (1999) The Times 30 March (no liability for misdiagnosis of cancer by army doctor made prior to the suspension of s10).

Even though s10 is not currently in effect, it should not be assumed that the common law rules on liability in negligence apply in full to the Crown as regards the actions of service personnel. On the basis of *Mulcahy* v *Ministry of Defence* [1996] 2 WLR 474, it seems clear that a serving soldier, acting in battle conditions, owes no common law duty of care to a fellow serving soldier, and hence the Crown is not vicariously liable for any harm so caused. In *Mulcahy* the plaintiff contended that the injuries he had incurred, whilst serving as one of a team of soldiers manning a Howitzer gun during the Gulf War, had been caused by the negligence of the gun commander. Applying *Shaw Savill and Albion Co Ltd* v *The Commonwealth* (1940) 66 CLR 344 and *Burmah Oil Co Ltd* v *Lord Advocate* [1965] AC 75, the Court of Appeal ruled, on the basis that no duty of care was owed, that the case disclosed no cause of action and should thus be struck out. Neill J expressed the view that, even in the absence of the previous decisions in *Shaw Savill and Albion Co Ltd* v *The Commonwealth* and *Burmah Oil Co Ltd* v *Lord Advocate*, he would, as a matter of policy, have declined to impose any duty of care at common law on the basis that, in the words of Gibbs CJ in *Groves* v *Commonwealth of Australia* (1982) 150 CLR 113 at p117, such a conclusion accorded with 'common sense and sound policy'.

In *Matthews* v *Ministry of Defence* [2002] 3 All ER 513 the Court of Appeal confirmed that s10 of the Crown Proceedings Act 1947 was not incompatible with art 6 of the European Convention on Human Rights. The claimant had contended that s10 operated so as to deny him his right of access to the courts. The Court held that s10 was substantive, as opposed to procedural, in its effect. If the terms of s10 were met a claimant had no cause of action in negligence. The issuing of a certificate under s10 that prevented any cause of action arising gave rise to a defence that existed as a matter of substantive law. There had, therefore, been no violation of art 6. As Lord Phillips MR explained:

'Article 6(1) is essentially concerned with judicial process. Its effects include an entitlement to a fair, public and reasonably prompt hearing in respect of any assertion of an infringement of a civil right. A claim that a civil right has been infringed may involve a seminal question of law of whether the civil right, which the claimant asserts has been infringed, exists at all ... Whether a civil right exists is a matter of the substantive law of the contracting states ... The Bill, which became the 1947 Act, was introduced into the House of Lords by the Lord Chancellor. The debate there shows that the Bill was always subject to the s10 exception, which was not initially qualified by the requirement for a certificate. Provision was made for the "conclusive" certificates under s10(3) and there was considerable discussion about these. The requirement for the s10(1) and (2) certificate was introduced in the committee stage by the Attorney-General. In moving these amendments the Lord Chancellor explained (151 HL Official Report (5th series), col 849, 31 July 1947):

> "The substance of these Amendments is this, and I think that it is valuable. It is quite plain that a soldier does not lose his right of action against a fellow soldier through whom he has been injured, unless the Minister of Pensions certifies that the injury he has sustained is attributable to war service, or that he can get a pension. In other words, we must see that before we deprive a man of his right of action we give him a co-relative right, by way of pension."

... It is thus apparent that it was never intended that the question of whether or not a serviceman should enjoy a right of action against a fellow serviceman or the Crown for personal injuries sustained in service should be at the option of the Secretary of State. The requirement for a certificate was introduced as a prerequisite to the loss of the cause of action in order to establish conclusively that the circumstances which had deprived the serviceman of a cause of action had entitled him, provided other relevant criteria were satisfied, to a pension. While reference to Hansard makes this quite clear, it is the conclusion to which we would have come without that assistance ...'

Act of State

The courts may decline jurisdiction if the Crown claims that the actions complained of by the plaintiff fall within the scope of the 'Act of State' doctrine. An Act of State is generally accepted as being an act of the Executive carried out as part of the conduct of foreign affairs policy in dealings with other states. In practice it means that a servant of the Crown will have a defence in respect of an act otherwise tortious or criminal committed abroad provided that the act was authorised or subsequently ratified by the Crown: see *Buron* v *Denman* (1848) 2 Ex 167. Act of State may not be pleaded against British subjects within the territories of the Crown; see *Walker* v *Baird* [1892] AC 491. The temporary allegiance owed to the Crown by a friendly alien who is resident can deprive the Crown of the defence of Act of State in an action brought by a friendly alien: see *Johnston* v *Pedlar* [1921] 2 AC 262. The defence of Act of State may be available in respect of Executive acts taken against enemy aliens within the territories of the Crown: see *R* v *Bottrill, ex parte Kuechenmeister* [1947] KB 41 and *R* v *Vine Street Police Station, ex parte Liebmann* [1916] 1 KB 268. The position regarding the availability of the plea of Act of State against British subjects outside the territories of the Crown is unclear. In *Nissan* v *Attorney-General* [1970] AC 179 the plaintiff was a citizen of the United Kingdom seeking compensation for damage caused by the occupation of his hotel on Cyprus (an independent republic within the Commonwealth) by British troops acting as part of an international peace-keeping force. The House of Lords held that the plaintiff was not prevented from bringing an action for compensation by the defence of Act of State, because the occupation of the hotel was not an act in the nature of an Act of State. On the one hand Lord Reid expressed the view that Act of State could not be pleaded as a defence where the plaintiff was a British subject, whilst on the other Lord Wilberforce found it impossible to accept such a broad proposition. The position, therefore, remains unclear.

14.5 Public interest immunity

As stated above, the 1947 Act replaced the petition of right by permitting a litigant to proceed by way of writ. Such writs are issued in the normal way, and documents served on solicitors for the relevant government department. By s17(3):

> 'Civil proceedings against the Crown shall be instituted against the appropriate authorised Government department, or, if none of the authorised Government departments is appropriate or the person instituting the proceedings has any reasonable doubt whether any and if so which of those departments is appropriate, against the Attorney-General.'

Who makes the claim?

A plaintiff bringing an action against a government department or other public body will not be able to discharge the burden of proof resting upon him unless he can adduce the evidence necessary to support his claims. In the course of civil litigation the purpose of the procedure known as discovery is for each party to the litigation to receive relevant documents from the other. This helps to avoid trial by ambush, in which one side produces a devastating piece of evidence at the trial, which destroys the case of the other; it is also intended to promote an early settlement of the dispute by both sides being better informed as to the strength of the other side's case. For information on the detailed procedure to be followed see Pt 31 CPR 1998; what follows is a brief account.

In a High Court action, the parties to litigation will exchange a list of documents that relate to the dispute, in theory, within 14 days of the close of pleadings, provided they are, or have been, in the possession or custody of the parties. In this listing each party indicates the documents he is willing to disclose and those for which he claims privilege. All relevant documents must be disclosed, ie their existence admitted, but those for which privilege is claimed may be protected from inspection. The criteria for disclosure are generally set out in *Compagnie Financière et Commerciale du Pacifique* v *Peruvian Guano Co* (1882) 11 QBD 55. To be relevant for the purposes of discovery the documents must contain information which may enable one's opponent to advance his own case or damage one's own case or which may fairly lead him to a train of inquiry which may have either of these two consequences: see further *Air Canada* v *Secretary of State for Trade (No 2)* [1983] 1 All ER 910.

It is at this stage in the litigation that a public body defending a civil action may seek to resist the disclosure of documents on the ground of public interest immunity. In the case of a government department this is done by a minister providing a certificate that explains why certain documents should not be revealed. In some cases a claim arises from an affidavit sworn by a senior official of a local authority or police force. As to the issue of who might raise an objection to the discovery of documents Lord Reid, in *Rodgers* v *Home Secretary* [1973] AC 388, observed:

> 'The ground put forward has been said to be Crown privilege. I think that that expression is wrong and may be misleading. There is no question of any privilege in the ordinary sense of the word. The real question is whether the public interest requires that the letter shall not be produced and whether that public interest is so strong as to override the ordinary right and interest of a litigant that he shall be able to lay before a court of justice all relevant evidence. A Minister of the Crown is always an appropriate and often the most appropriate person to assert this public interest, and the evidence or advice which he gives to the court is always valuable and may sometimes be indispensable. But, in my view, it must always be open to any person interested to raise the question and there may be cases where the trial judge should himself raise the question if no one else has done so. In the present case the question of public interest was raised by both the Attorney-General and the Gaming Board. In my judgment both were entitled to raise the matter. Indeed I think that in the circumstances it was the duty of the board to do as they have done.'

Where a minister takes the view that a document should not be disclosed he will, having taken legal advice from the Attorney-General, sign a public interest immunity certificate (PIIC) to that effect. If accepted by the court, the documents in question will not be admissible in evidence, notwithstanding that they may contain evidence vital to the plaintiff's case.

Public interest immunity: the impact of the Scott Report

Historically ministers, and other public bodies, have resisted the disclosure of documents either because they belonged to a class, eg Cabinet papers, communications with other sovereign states etc, that ought not to be disclosed as a matter of principle, or because of the contents of the documents, eg blueprints of military equipment. In December 1996, following the publication of the Scott Report (*Inquiry into the Export of Defence Equipment and Dual-Use Goods to Iraq and Related Prosecutions* (1995–96) HC 115), and the criticisms contained therein of the reliance by ministers on PIICs to suppress evidence during the 'Matrix-Churchill' trial that could have been useful to the defendants, the Government announced a revised policy on the signing of PIICs.

As Lord Mackay LC stated in the House of Lords:

'The Government are committed to the principle that there should be the maximum disclosure consistent with protecting essential public interests. ... Public interest immunity is needed because of the potential conflict between two important public interests: the clear public interest in the administration of justice, in a criminal case the fair trial of an accused, and what is sometimes also the clear public interest in the confidentiality of certain documents or information. But your Lordships will bear in mind that the so-called immunity is subject to the ruling of the court, and that in a criminal case where government documents are in issue, the judge himself examines any such document and makes the actual decision on disclosure in the light of the facts of the case. In their proposals for the future, the Government have had particular regard both to the recommendations of Sir Richard Scott and to the many responses received during the consultation process. The Government's conclusions represent a new approach. ... Ministers will focus directly on the damage that disclosure would cause. The former division into class and contents claims will no longer be applied. Ministers will only claim public interest immunity when it is believed that disclosure of a document would cause real damage or harm to the public interest. This new approach constitutes a change in the practice to be adopted by Ministers but fully respects existing legal principles, as developed by the courts, and is subject to the supervision of the courts. It also accords with the view expressed by the present Lord Chief Justice that:

"... public interest immunity should only be claimed for the bare minimum of documents for which the claim of serious harm can be seen to be clearly justified."

This new, restrictive approach will require, so far as possible, the way in which disclosure could cause real damage to the public interest to be clearly identified. Public interest immunity certificates will in future set out in greater detail than before both what the document is and what damage its disclosure would be likely to do, unless to do so would itself cause the damage which the certificate aims to prevent. This will allow even closer scrutiny of claims by the court, which is always the final arbiter. ... Many public interest immunity claims are not the responsibility of government. Although the Government believe that their approach can be applied more widely, [this new policy] ... only restricts Government claims.'

Grounds for resisting disclosure: proof of harm

Under the new regime for claiming public interest immunity outlined by Lord Mackay LC it is envisaged that a PIIC would only be signed in relation to a document, the disclosure of which could undermine the safety of an individual, such as an informant, interfere significantly with a regulatory process or result in damage to international relations by the disclosure of confidential diplomatic communications. To justify a PIIC the harm would normally have to be direct and immediate, eg harm to the nation's economic interests or relations with a foreign state. In each case the nature of the harm will have to be clearly explained. As Lord Mackay LC explained:

'The new emphasis on the test of serious harm means that Ministers will not, for example, claim public interest immunity to protect either internal advice or national security material merely by pointing to the general nature of the document. The only basis for claiming public interest immunity will be a belief that disclosure will cause real harm ... a document will not attract public interest immunity simply because it falls into a pre-defined category.'

Grounds for resisting disclosure: regulatory procedures

In relation to regulatory procedures, such as those dealing with complaints against police officers, the courts had already begun to loosen the constraints previously imposed by reliance on public interest immunity. *R* v *Chief Constable of West Midlands, ex parte Wiley; R* v *Chief Constable of Nottinghamshire Police, ex parte Sunderland* [1994] 3 WLR 433 arose out of two separate trials in which the applicants were acquitted following the decision of the prosecution to offer no evidence. Both applicants instituted complaints to the Police Complaints Authority and civil actions for damages. Given the state of the law at the time, neither applicant was allowed access to the complaints file in order to prepare for the civil action, hence solicitors for the applicants had sought undertakings from the respondents to the effect that they would not rely on, or make use of, any information provided by the applicants in the course of their complaints to the authority. The undertakings were refused, and the applicants sought judicial review of these refusals; the second applicant also sought an injunction to prevent the Chief Constable from using the material in question. At first instance Popplewell J granted the relief sought and the Chief Constables' appeals to the Court of Appeal were dismissed. On appeal to the House of Lords it was argued by both sides that public interest immunity did not attach to the documents collated in the course of an investigation into complaints against the police under Part IX of the Police and Criminal Evidence Act 1984. Allowing the appeals, and in the process overruling *Neilson* v *Laugharne* [1981] QB 736, *Hehir* v *Commissioner of Police of the Metropolis* [1982] 1 WLR 715, *Makanjuola* v *Commissioner of Police of the Metropolis* [1992] 3 All ER 617 and *Halford* v *Sharples* [1992] 1 WLR 736, the House of Lords held that there was no compelling case for the creation of a new category of class-based public interest immunity in respect of statements made during police complaints investigations, as had been suggested in the earlier cases. The House of Lords did not, however, rule out the possibility of statements made during complaints investigations attracting immunity on a contents basis, as may be the position with, for example, statements made by police informers. In agreement, Lord Woolf added that despite Lord Hailsham's comments in *D* v *National Society for the Prevention of Cruelty to Children* [1978] AC 171, to the effect that the categories of public interest were not closed and must alter from time to time as social changes required, no sufficient case had been made out to justify the class of public interest immunity erroneously created by the Court of Appeal in *Neilson*. See further *R* v *Secretary of State for the Home Department, ex parte Hickey* [1995] 1 WLR 734 and *Kaufmann and Others* v *Credit Lyonnais Bank* (1995) The Times 1 February. Note that there is a Human Rights Act 1998 dimension to this issue – a litigant denied access to evidence may claim that his Convention rights are being infringed. In *R (On the Application of Green) v Police Complaints Authority* (2002) The Times 16 January the Court of Appeal confirmed that denying a complainant access to eyewitness statements relating to complaints against the police could result in a failure to comply with the provisions of the 1998 Act.

Notwithstanding the reluctance of the House of Lords in *ex parte Wiley* to recognise class based claims for immunity, a distinction has been drawn by the courts between witness statements made in the course of investigations, and reports made by officers involved in such investigations. In *Taylor v Anderton (Police Complaints Authority)* [1995] 1 WLR 447 the plaintiff brought an action against the defendant for malicious prosecution, misfeasance in public office and conspiracy. At the discovery stage the defendant listed among the relevant documents in his possession reports made by investigating officers pursuant to complaints made in relation to police conduct under the provisions of the Police and Criminal Evidence Act 1984. The defendant resisted disclosure of these reports on the basis that, as a class, they were protected by public interest immunity. The plaintiff sought an order compelling production of the documents by the defendant, and the trial judge allowed the Police Complaints Authority (PCA) to intervene so as to assist the defendant's case. Following argument, the trial judge granted the order for production, a ruling in respect of which the defendant and the PCA appealed successfully. Although the court doubted whether disclosure of the reports was necessary on the facts, the reports did belong to a class of documents to which public interest immunity attached, as the public interest lay in the proper functioning of the PCA's procedures. The matter had not been determined by the House of Lords' decision in *ex parte Wiley*, as that case had dealt with statements of fact made by witnesses. Here the need was to ensure that the opinions of the investigating officers (who were required to comment on the veracity of evidence given, inter alia, by colleagues) were not disclosed for fear that they would be inhibited and thus make the investigation less effective. Similarly, in *O'Sullivan v Commissioner of Police of the Metropolis* (1995) The Times 3 July, the plaintiff, who was suing for damages for wrongful arrest and malicious prosecution, sought discovery of a document known as form 151, which contained a summary of the case against the plaintiff prepared by the investigating officer for consideration by the Crown Prosecution Service. The officer was required to give his opinion on various matters related to the case, including the veracity of witnesses etc. The Commissioner of the Police of the Metropolis was successful in resisting disclosure on the basis that the form belonged to a class of documents subject to public interest immunity. The court noting that *ex parte Wiley* was not binding as that case had been concerned with disclosure of witness statements provided in the course of an investigation into complaints against the police, and not the summarising report of an investigating officer, relied upon *Evans v Chief Constable of Surrey* [1988] 1 QB 588, in which it had been held that public interest immunity attached to reports prepared by the police for consideration by the DPP, and regarded it as unaffected by *ex parte Wiley*. See further *Kelly* v *Commissioner of Police of the Metropolis* (1997) The Times 20 August.

Grounds for resisting disclosure: government papers

The new policy clearly indicates that PIICs should, in future, be signed because of the contents of a document, rather than the class to which it belongs, raising the theoretical possibility of Cabinet papers being adduced as evidence. In reality, however, it is likely that any Cabinet paper could be suppressed because of the broader constitutional implications of granting disclosure. For example, collective responsibility is generally regarded as being an essential constitutional convention, thus in *Attorney-General* v *Jonathan Cape Ltd* [1976] QB 752, Lord Widgery CJ stated that 'no court will compel production of Cabinet papers in the course of discovery in an action.' And Lord Reid in *Conway* v *Rimmer* [1968] AC 910 observed:

> 'Virtually everyone agrees that Cabinet minutes and the like ought not to be disclosed until such time as they are only of historical interest. But I do not think that many people would give as the reason that premature disclosure would prevent candour in the Cabinet. To my mind the most important reason is that such disclosure would create or fan ill-informed or captious public or political criticism. The business of government is difficult enough as it is, and no government could contemplate with equanimity the inner workings of the government machine being exposed to the gaze of those ready to criticise without adequate knowledge of the background and perhaps with some axe to grind. And that must, in my view, also apply to all documents concerned with policy-making within departments including, it may be, minutes and the like by quite junior officials and correspondence with outside bodies. Further it may be that deliberations about a particular case require protection as much as deliberations about policy.'

Further, in *Burmah Oil* v *Bank of England* [1980] AC 1090, the House of Lords considered claims of privilege relating to documents concerned with the formation of government policy and documents containing information given in confidence by businessmen to the Bank of England. Lord Wilberforce felt that given the obvious importance of the documents as regards policy-formulation, there was no question of them being produced. The majority expressed a variety of views, all of which were in favour of inspection, but in the event the documents were found not to have anything recorded in them that needed to be disclosed for fairly disposing of the case. Lords Scarman and Keith both doubted the excessive weight given in past cases to the need to secure secrecy for those giving information in confidence, or for civil servants who needed to feel free to state their opinions. Lord Scarman felt that the 'candour' argument (ie that documents ought to be protected if candid views were to be expressed) was only really appropriate where a civil servant was advising a minister on a matter of national security.

Grounds for resisting disclosure: national security

It remains to be seen whether or not, in the wake of Lord Mackay's announcement referred to above, the courts adopt a bolder approach in respect of PIICs signed in the interest of national security. To date the courts have allowed ministers a wide margin of appreciation. For example, in *Balfour* v *Foreign and Commonwealth Office* [1994] 1 WLR 681, the applicant, who had been dismissed by his employers, the Foreign and Commonwealth Office, took his case to an industrial tribunal, and in support of his claim sought various documents, production of which was resisted by both the Foreign Secretary and the Home Secretary on the ground that the documents related to national security. The tribunal chairman's refusal to order disclosure was upheld on appeal by the Court of Appeal, where it was held that once a minister had demonstrated the potential harm to national security that might be caused by disclosure, a court should not exercise its right to inspect. Having referred to dicta in *Conway* v *Rimmer* [1968] AC 910 and *Council of Civil Service Unions* v *Minister for the Civil Service* [1985] AC 374, highlighting the importance of the courts showing due deference to ministerial claims to be acting to protect national security, Russell LJ observed:

> '[Counsel for the appellant] boldly invites this court to depart from these powerful dicta, contending that they were obiter and that in the society in which we now live the time is right for what he described as a more open approach when issues of national security are raised by the appropriate ministers. Even if not constrained by authority we firmly decline to accept that invitation, for it seems to us to be contrary to principle and to good sense. In this case the court has not abdicated its responsibility, but it has recognised the constraints placed upon it by the terms of the certificates issued by the executive. There must always be vigilance by the courts to ensure that public interest immunity of whatever kind is raised only in appropriate circumstances and with appropriate particularity, but once there is an actual or potential risk to national security demonstrated by an appropriate certificate the court should not exercise its right to inspect.'

Grounds for resisting disclosure: information given in confidence

The courts have always been willing to accept that it may not be in the public interest to admit certain documents in evidence if to do so would reveal the identity of anyone who has given information in confidence, and who might thus be at risk of harm if identified, or where the supply of information to law enforcement agencies would be adversely affected. In *Rodgers* v *Home Secretary* [1973] AC 388 documents containing information given by police informers to the Gaming Board were held to be privileged, on the grounds that anonymity had been promised to the informers and that the Board would be unable to function properly if its supply of information were to dry up. Similarly, in *Alfred Crompton Amusement Machines Ltd* v *Customs and Excise Commissioners (No 2)* [1974] AC 405, information given in confidence to the Inland Revenue was held to be privileged. Again, the fear that such information might become difficult to obtain if sources were disclosed was a paramount consideration: see also *D* v *NSPCC* [1978] AC 171, where the identity of an informant supplying evidence of alleged child abuse was held to be privileged, again to protect the continued supply of information. The principle has more recently been reaffirmed in *Bookbinder* v *Tebbit* [1992] 1 WLR 217, where the court refused to order disclosure of statements and other documents from Audit Commission employees who had been investigating a local authority's finances. The plaintiff, the leader of the local authority concerned, sought to use the documents in support of a libel action. Drake J expressed the view that public interest immunity should extend to evidence obtained by the Audit Commission during its investigations, particularly that which might disclose the identity of informants, since the Commission performed a public duty of inquiring into the legality of public expenditure, and the performance of that duty may be hampered if informants felt less at ease about coming forward.

The courts as the final arbiters of disclosure

Even if a minister does sign a PIIC in respect of a document, a court will not be bound to accept it. For the first half of the twentieth century the courts adopted what might be called an administration-minded approach to ministerial claims of public interest immunity, tending to accept the minister's word that documents needed to be suppressed in the public interest: see *Duncan* v *Cammell Laird & Co Ltd* [1942] AC 624 and *Ellis* v *Home Office* [1953] 2 QB 135. A significant turning point, however, was the decision of the House of Lords in *Conway* v *Rimmer*, where it was held that the documents in question should be produced, notwithstanding the fact that the Home Secretary had certified that their production could be injurious to the public interest. The House of Lords made it clear that the courts should not always allow a ministerial certificate to be conclusive. As Lord Reid stated:

> 'I would ... propose that the House ought now to decide that courts have, and are entitled
> to exercise, a power and a duty to hold a balance between public interest, as expressed by
> a Minister, to withhold certain documents and other evidence, and the public interest in
> ensuring the proper administration of justice.'

Lord Reid accepted that there were certain matters of which a minister would be a better judge than the courts, such as whether documents should be suppressed on grounds of national security, and that in any event great weight would always be given to any ministerial view. Documents such as Cabinet papers, he felt, would not be disclosed until they were of historical interest only. On other matters, such as the effect of disclosure of documents on the smooth running of a public service, the courts were in just as good a position as the minister to decide what should and should not be produced.

14.6 Remedies

The remedies available

The 1947 Act provides for certain key restrictions upon the availability of remedies, perhaps most significantly in s21 which provides:

> 'In any civil proceedings by or against the Crown the court shall, subject to the provisions of this Act, have power to make all such orders as it has power to make in proceedings between subjects, and otherwise to give such appropriate relief as the case may require.
>
> Provided that: where in any proceedings against the Crown any such relief is sought as might in proceedings between subjects be granted by way of injunction of specific performance, the court shall not grant an injunction or make an order for specific performance, but may in lieu thereof make an order declaratory of the rights of the parties; and in any proceedings against the Crown for the recovery of land or other property the court shall not make an order for the recovery of the land or the delivery of the property, but may in lieu thereof make an order declaring that the plaintiff is entitled as against the Crown to the land or property or to the possession thereof.'

Subsection (2) adds:

> 'The court shall not in any civil proceedings grant any injunction or make any order against an officer of the Crown if the effect of granting the injunction or making the order would be to give any relief against the Crown which could not have been obtained in proceedings against the Crown.'

This provision has been the cause of considerable confusion, much of it exacerbated by uncertainty as to the meaning to be given to the term 'the Crown'.

This difficult question was considered at some length by the House of Lords in *Town Investments Ltd* v *Department of the Environment* [1978] AC 359. The majority view expressed by Lord Diplock was that:

> 'Where ... we are concerned with the legal nature of the exercise of executive powers of government, I believe that some of the more Athanasian like features of the debate in your Lordships' House could have been eliminated if instead of speaking of "the Crown" we were to speak of "the government" – a term appropriate to embrace both collectively and individually all of the ministers of the Crown and parliamentary secretaries under whose direction the administrative work of government is carried on by the civil servants employed in the various government departments. It is through them that the executive powers of Her Majesty's government in the United Kingdom are exercised, sometimes in the more important administrative matters in Her Majesty's name, but most often under their own official designation. Executive acts of government that are done by any of them are acts done by "the Crown" in the fictional sense in which that expression is now used in English public law.'

Lord Morris dissented from this view:

> 'The expression "the Crown" may sometimes be used to designate Her Majesty in a purely personal capacity. It may sometimes be used to designate Her Majesty in her capacity as Head of the Commonwealth. It may sometimes be used to designate Her

Majesty in her capacity as the constitutional monarch of the United Kingdom. Thus laws are enacted by Her Majesty in Parliament. The expression may sometimes be used in a somewhat broad sense in reference to the functions of government and the public administration. It may sometimes be used in reference to the rule of law. The case for the prosecution is the case for "the Crown". The government of the day is Her Majesty's Government. A Minister of the Crown is and is constantly referred to as a servant of the Crown. But it cannot be suggested that the Minister is or becomes "the Crown". Even if the grandiloquent description of being an "emanation" of the Crown is applied to him he remains separate from the Crown and is not and does not become the Crown. When acting on behalf of or for the purpose of "the Crown" some of the well recognised immunities of "the Crown" may cover what he does ...'

It would appear that, prior to the enactment of the 1947 Act, injunctions, both interim and final, were available against Crown servants acting in a personal capacity: see *Ellis* v *Earl Grey* (1833) 6 Sim 214, *Rankin* v *Hukisson* (1830) 4 Sim 13, *Tamaki* v *Baker* (above), and *Attorney-General for New South Wales* v *Trethowan* [1932] AC 526.

Injunctions were not available against the Crown as such, as this would have created difficulties in relation to enforcement, hence the use of the declaration in such cases. In any event there were, and still are, good policy reasons for the Crown being free to exercise prerogative power in the national interest without fear of restraint by the courts. The confusion arises as a result of s21 being read as an extension of the Crown's immunity, as regards injunctions, to Crown servants acting in an official capacity: see *Merricks* v *Heathcoat Amory* [1955] Ch 567. The argument that the 1947 Act, despite its overriding purpose of removing Crown immunities in litigation, should have succeeded in extending the immunity of ministers as regards injunctive relief was criticised in *R* v *Secretary of State for the Home Department, ex parte Herbage* [1987] QB 872 and *R* v *Licensing Authority, ex parte Smith Kline & French Laboratories Ltd (No 2)* [1988] 3 WLR 896. The contention that found support in these cases was that if prerogative orders could lie against a minister, why not injunctive relief? As regards the views expressed on the availability of injunctive relief, both of these decisions were overruled by the House of Lords decision in *R* v *Secretary of State for Transport, ex parte Factortame* [1989] 2 All ER 692, but their Lordships interpretation of s21 has been the subject of trenchant academic criticism. In any event, as a result of the ruling of the European Court of Justice, considered by the House of Lords in *R* v *Secretary of State for Transport, ex parte Factortame (No 2)* [1991] 1 All ER 70, the House of Lords had to concede that Community law required the granting of an interim injunction against a minister where the applicant sought to protect a purported right arising as an incident of Community membership. It is respectfully submitted that the luminous analysis provided by Professor Wade ('The Crown – Old Platitudes and New Heresies' [1992] NLJ 1275 and 1315) should be adopted. He reveals that the true purposes of s21, as the Notes on Clauses provided by the parliamentary draughtsman reveal, was to prevent the immunity of the Crown being circumvented by the grant of injunctive relief against a minister. Thus a minister enforcing an Order in Council could not be the subject of an injunction, because he would be acting as an agent of the Crown. If, however, he was purporting to exercise his statutory power by promulgating regulations thought to be invalid, or in breach of Community law, the court would not be restrained by s21 from granting interim relief. Wade's view has, to some extent, been adopted by the House of Lords in *M v Home Office* [1993] 3 WLR 433, where it was held that an injunction could be granted to prevent a minister flouting a court order preventing the deportation of an alleged political refugee.

Lord Woolf recognised that s21 of the Crown Proceedings Act 1947 had not been intended to affect the right of an individual to seek injunctive relief against an individual Crown servant, acting in his official capacity, to prevent the commission of a tort. He explained further that, as the prerogative orders have never been available against the Crown, when s31(2) of the Supreme Court Act 1981 extended the prerogative jurisdiction to include the granting of injunctions, including interim injunctions, by way of judicial review proceedings, it was not creating a conflict with s21 of the 1947 Act (ie it did not create the possibility of injunctions being granted against the Crown as such). The provision merely created a procedure by which an injunction could be obtained against a minister exercising statutory power in his official capacity. It was obvious that prior to 1947 prerogative orders had been available in respect of a minister of the Crown acting in an official capacity. Hence the effect of s31(2) was to make injunctive relief available in such cases although, in Lord Woolf's view, the power to do so should be exercised sparingly.

Although no finding of contempt could be made against the Crown, if a minister flouted a coercive order, contempt proceedings could be maintained against the minister in his official capacity, and his department. It followed that although the sanctions for such contempt could not be personal or punitive, the court's finding of contempt would be an indication that the minister had acted improperly, an appropriate order as to costs could be made, and there would in all likelihood be repercussions for the minister in terms of parliamentary scrutiny.

Similarly, s25(4) of the 1947 Act, which provides that no execution or attachment shall issue from any court for enforcing payment by the Crown of any damages or costs awarded, should be read as preventing proceedings for enforcement being brought against ministers and civil servants in order to recover such sums in circumstances where enforcement would not be possible against the Crown. It should not be interpreted as extending the Crown's immunities from enforcement to ministers exercising statutory powers.

Remedies under the Human Rights Act 1998

Section 7(1)(b) of the Human Rights Act provides that a person who claims that a public authority has acted unlawfully by taking action incompatible with the Convention rights protected by the 1998 Act may rely on Convention rights in any legal proceedings provided he is (or would be) the victim of the unlawful act. It is possible that a claim against the Crown in contract or tort could raise such issues. Action could also be taken against a court that failed to uphold Convention rights, given the wide definition given to the term 'public authority' under s6(3)(a), but not against a minister failing to introduce or lay legislation before Parliament. Breach of the Convention rights by the Crown will not of itself give rise to a right to damages. Section 8(2) provides that 'damages may be awarded only by a court which has power to award damages, or to order the payment of compensation, in civil proceedings.' Section 8(3) adds the following:

> 'No award of damages is to be made unless, taking account of all the circumstances of the case, including –
> a) any other relief or remedy granted, or order made, in relation to the act in question (by that or any other court), and
> b) the consequences of any decision (of that or any other court) in respect of that act,
> the court is satisfied that the award is necessary to afford just satisfaction to the person in whose favour it is made.'

Hence the plaintiff will have to have a subsisting claim in contract or tort in order to receive damages for a violation of his Convention rights. In determining the availability of damages and the level of damages the court must have regard to the principles applied by the European Court of Human Rights in relation to the award of compensation under art 41 of the Convention: see s8(4). As an illustration of how these issues can arise consider *Osman* v *United Kingdom* [1998] BHRC 293 (considered below at section 14.10), where the European Court of Human Rights upheld the applicant's claim that the application of the rule in *Hill* v *Chief Constable of West Yorkshire* [1989] AC 53 amounted to a violation of art 6(1) of the European Convention on Human Rights.

14.7 The liability of local authorities and other public bodies in contract and tort

Local authorities are, with the exception of the Corporation of the City of London, statutory bodies. As such they are, in principle, liable to be sued for breach of contract, or in respect of a range of tortious behaviour in much the same way as any other real or artificial legal entity. The same applies to other public bodies with overtly 'public' functions such as police forces (as legally embodied in the person of the chief constable), fire brigades (ie fire authorities) and health authorities. All such bodies would satisfy the definition of 'public authority' as that expression is used in s6 of the Human Rights Act 1998, hence there is the prospect of issues relating to the protection of Convention rights arising in the course of proceedings to which a local authority is a party. The purpose of this chapter is to examine how private law concepts are applied to asses the liability of public bodies, with emphasis on situations where principles of public law apply so as to limit the scope of liability.

There is no equivalent of the Crown Proceedings Act 1947 governing the liability of local authorities and similar bodies in contract and tort, largely because they have never historically enjoyed the immunities from suit that attached to the Crown a common law.

Liability in contract

Generally, local authorities are in the same position as any other corporate body as regards entering into contractual obligations. Section 111 of the Local Government Act 1972 empowers an authority to do anything which is reasonably incidental to the discharge of its functions, and this extends to incurring contractual obligations. Being statutory bodies, local authorities must act within the limits of their power and will not be bound by any ultra vires agreements. Section 9 of the European Communities Act 1972 does not apply to local authorities. A contract is likely to be regarded as ultra vires on the common law principles that it is incompatible with the public law duties placed upon a local authority, for example where a planning authority agrees not to grant planning permission, or where it goes too far in fettering the discretion of the authority, such as the granting of a perpetually renewable lease. This issue is dealt with in more detail in Chapter 9, section 9.4.

When entering into contracts, especially for goods and services, local authorities will have to observe standing orders relating to tenders, price paid and selection of contractor: for example see s135 Local Government Act 1972. The fiduciary duty owed to council tax payers must be borne in mind, and refusing to accept tenders from firms having non-unionised work forces, for example, may be of dubious legality.

Tortious liability

As indicated above, local authorities are potentially liable for the full range of torts from negligence, nuisance and defamation, through to trespass: see for example *Cooper* v *Wandsworth Board of Works* (1863) 14 CBNS 180, where the plaintiff's property was demolished without adequate notice being given. The tortious liability of local authorities is of interest to administrative lawyers because the status and functions of such bodies bring into play a number of policy considerations not necessarily encountered when considering the liability of private parties. Not least is the fact that local authorities have duties placed upon them, and powers vested in them, that have no counterpart in private law, and this begs the question as to the extent, if at all, that the normal common law principles on tortious liability need to be adapted and modified when dealing with local authorities. The question of compensation and cost distribution is never very far from the minds of judges dealing with actions in negligence, especially where a case raises a novel issue, and in the context of local authority liability the problem is often one of whether or not the public, in the form of the taxpayer, should be called upon to provide the compensation sought. Judges will also have in mind the question of whether or not the imposition of tortious liability is the most effective mechanism for persuading a local authority to alter its behaviour so as to prevent loss and harm being caused in future.

14.8 Nuisance

The common law of nuisance applies to local authorities as it does to all other legal persons, but it will often be the case that a local authority, by virtue of the duties placed upon it, or discretion vested in it, will engage in activities that are particularly likely to cause a nuisance to others, eg dealing with refuse, ensuring road safety, providing social services. If an action in nuisance is brought in respect of an activity expressly provided for by Parliament, the local authority may be able to rely upon the defence of statutory authority. The rationale being that, provided the nuisance is an inevitable consequence of the powers being exercised, no right to compensation at common law arises because Parliament must have contemplated that nuisance would result from the activity. Clearly it would be open to Parliament to provide for a scheme of statutory compensation for those suffering from the exercise of powers in these circumstances if it saw fit.

In *Dormer* v *Newcastle upon Tyne Corporation* [1940] 2 KB 204 the defendants, purporting to exercise their powers under s22 of the Newcastle-upon-Tyne Improvement Act 1865, placed guard rails, in front of Grainger House, in the highway between the pavement and the road for a distance of about 138 feet, in order to protect pedestrians. The defendants relied on a plea of 'inevitable nuisance', citing the provisions of s22 as empowering it to place barriers for the prevention of accidents and so as to make the crossing less dangerous to pedestrians. The court held that the action failed because the nuisance complained of was a result of steps expressly authorised by statute, the guard rails would have been less effective if placed elsewhere: see further *Goldberg & Sons Ltd* v *Liverpool Corporation* (1900) 82 LT 362 and *Allen* v *Gulf Oil Refining Ltd* [1981] 2 WLR 141.

Where a local authority has a number of options as to how and where it will exercise its powers, and it is clear that the amount of nuisance caused will vary with the choice made, it is required to select the option likely to create the least nuisance, so far as that is reasonably possible, if it wishes to be able to rely on the defence of statutory authority. *Metropolitan Asylum District* v *Hill* (1881) 6 App Cas 193 raised the question of whether the appellants could rely on the defence of statutory authority in respect of nuisance found to have been caused by the building of a hospital for sufferers from contagious diseases. The appellants had built the hospital pursuant to their powers under the Metropolitan Poor Act 1867. Dismissing the appeal, the court accepted that the provision of the hospital would necessarily cause some nuisance, but the powers in the relevant Act were permissive not imperative.

The appellants had failed to show that they had no choice but to build on the site chosen. As Lord Watson observed:

'... the Respondents did not dispute that if the Appellants or the Local Government Board had been, by the Metropolitan Poor Act, 1867, expressly empowered to build the identical hospital which they have erected at Hampstead, upon the very site which it now occupies, and that with a view to its being used for the treatment of patients suffering from small-pox, the Respondents would not be entitled to the judgment which they have obtained. ... I am disposed to hold that if the Legislature, without specifying either plan or site, were to prescribe by statute that a public body shall, within certain defined limits, provide hospital accommodation for a class or classes of persons labouring under infectious disease, no injunction could issue against the use of an hospital established in pursuance of the Act, provided that it were either apparent or proved to the satisfaction of the Court that the directions of the Act could not be complied with at all, without creating a nuisance. In that case, the necessary result of that which they have directed to be done must presumably have been in the view of the Legislature at the time when the Act was passed. ... On the other hand, I do not think that the Legislature can be held to have sanctioned that which is a nuisance at common law, except in the case where it has authorized a certain use of a specific building in a specified position, which cannot be used without occasioning nuisance, or in the case where the particular plan or locality not being prescribed, it has imperatively directed that a building shall be provided within a certain area and so used, it being an obvious or established fact that nuisance must be the result. In the latter case the onus of proving that the creation of a nuisance will be the inevitable result of carrying out the directions of the Legislature, lies upon the persons seeking to justify the nuisance. Their justification depends upon their making good these two propositions – in the first place, that such are the imperative orders of the Legislature; and in the second place, that they cannot possibly obey those orders without infringing private rights. If the order of the Legislature can be implemented without nuisance, they cannot, in my opinion, plead the protection of the statute; and, on the other hand, it is insufficient for their protection that what is contemplated by the statute cannot be done without nuisance, unless they are also able to show that the Legislature has directed it to be done. Where the terms of the statute are not imperative, but permissive, when it is left to the discretion of the persons empowered to determine whether the general powers committed to them shall be put into execution or not, I think the fair inference is that the Legislature intended that discretion to be exercised in strict conformity with private rights, and did not intend to confer licence to commit nuisance in any place which might be selected for the purpose.'

See also *Manchester Corporation* v *Farnworth* [1930] AC 171 (local authority could not rely on statutory authority as a defence to an action in nuisance caused by pollution from an electricity generating station, having failed to exercise all due diligence to prevent the pollution) and *Tate & Lyle Ltd* v *GLC* [1983] 1 All ER 1159 (defendant authority not permitted to rely on statutory authority as a defence to an action in nuisance arising out of siltation of the River Thames, which rendered stretches of it unnavigable, because they had not shown that they had taken all reasonable care to prevent the siltation and had not shown sufficient regard for the interests of members of the public likely to be affected).

Where statute provides a self-contained code for dealing with the abatement of statutory nuisances by a local authority, the courts will generally be unwilling to recognise any common law right to bring proceedings for damages in respect of the loss and suffering caused by that nuisance: see *Issa* v *Hackney London Borough Council* [1997] 1 WLR 956.

14.9 Breach of statutory duty

There are innumerable pieces of legislation placing local authorities under a duty of one sort or another. If a local authority fails to comply with such a duty, is the failure actionable? Depending on the nature of the duty, and the identity of the complainant, it may be possible to challenge the failure by means of an action for judicial review, in particular by requesting a mandatory order to the effect that the duty be performed: see further Chapter 10 and Chapter 11. An application for judicial review may not, however, be as attractive to the complainant as an action for breach of statutory duty. Judicial review is discretionary, as are the remedies, and the court may decide that it is not an appropriate case for the granting of a mandatory order, either because some other more suitable remedy exists, or because the duty is worded in such broad, vague terms, supervision of its (non) performance would be impossible. The applicant for a mandatory order will have to establish that he has locus standi to apply and, if he wishes to add a request for damages to his application, an order will only be granted if he can show that such a remedy would have been available in an action started by writ. Further, an application for review must normally be made within three months of the breach of duty complained.

Whilst the tort of breach of statutory duty has been recognised for many years by the courts, it is not necessarily the case that every such breach will give rise to a right to damages. There are a number of hurdles that the plaintiff will have to clear. First, the right to proceed by way of action may be expressly removed by statute as, for example, is the case with s18 of the Civic Amenities Act 1967 which provides that no action for damages shall lie against a local authority arising from its failure to provide refuse tips.

Second, even where the statute is silent as to the right to bring an action, the court will have to engage in the task of determining whether or not Parliament intended such duties to be enforceable at the behest of the individual: see further *R* v *Deputy Governor of Parkhurst Prison, ex parte Hague* [1991] 3 All ER 733, *Cutler* v *Wandsworth Stadium Ltd* [1949] AC 398 and *West Wiltshire District Council* v *Garland and Others* [1995] 2 All ER 17.

The House of Lords considered this issue in *X (Minors)* v *Bedfordshire County Council* [1995] 3 WLR 152, an appeal concerning the statutory and common law duties owed by local authorities to children in the context of social welfare and special educational needs. Lord Browne-Wilkinson observed that an action for breach of statutory duty might be permissible where there was no other means of enforcing the performance of the duty, and where Parliament intended to protect an ascertainable class – otherwise the statute could not provide the protection it intended to confer. On the facts of the cases giving rise to these particular appeals, he was persuaded that no such action should lie where statutory provision established a regulatory framework or scheme of social welfare for the benefit of the public at large. As he stated:

'Although regulatory or welfare legislation affecting a particular area of activity does in fact provide protection to those individuals particularly affected by that activity, the legislation is not to be treated as being passed for the benefit of those individuals but for the benefit of society in general. ... The cases where a private right of action for breach of statutory duty have been held to arise are all cases in which the statutory duty has been very limited and specific as opposed to general administrative functions imposed on public bodies and involving the exercise of administrative discretions.'

An important, although not necessarily deciding, factor will be whether or not there is provision in the Act of some other means of enforcing the performance of the duty. It is generally assumed that Parliament cannot have intended a breach of duty to be actionable at the suit of an individual where, for example, it has expressly provided for the imposition of criminal sanctions in the event of non-performance: see *Keating* v *Elvan Reinforced Concrete Co Ltd* [1968] 2 All ER 139 and *Cutler* v *Wandsworth Stadium Ltd* (above). The same applies where the statute provides a right of appeal. In *R* v *Knowsley Borough Council, ex parte Maguire and Others* [1992] NLJ 1375 the court rejected the assertion that an action for breach of statutory duty might lie in respect of a local authority's decision not to grant taxi cab licences, on the basis that if a licence was refused there was a right of appeal to the Crown Court and, if a condition attached to the grant of a licence was challenged, proceedings could be taken in the magistrates' court.

Another common device is for Parliament to provide some other administrative body with default powers that can be exercised in cases on failure to perform a statutory duty. Again this will militate against the existence of any private law right to damages. As Lord Denning observed in *Southwark London Borough Council* v *Williams* [1971] Ch 734, confirming that the only way of enforcing a local authority's duty towards its homeless population was through default powers provided in the relevant Act:

'Seeing that [the default power] is the remedy given by the statute, I do not think there is any other remedy available. The case falls within the principle that: "... where an Act creates an obligation, and enforces the obligation in a specified manner, we take it to be a general rule that performance cannot be enforced in any other manner": see *Doe d Rochester (Bp)* v *Bridges* (1831) 1 B & Ad 847, 859. A good instance of that principle is *Pasmore* v *Oswaldtwistle Urban District Council* [1898] AC 387, where a local authority was put by statute under an obligation to make sewers for draining their district. It was held by the House of Lords that the only remedy was the specific remedy given by the statute, namely, a complaint to the Local Government Board. Policy and convenience dictated that decision in the case of sewers. Likewise here in the case of temporary accommodation for those in need. It cannot have been intended by Parliament that every person who was in need of temporary accommodation should be able to sue the local authority for it: or to take the law into his own hands for the purpose.'

Similarly, in *R* v *ILEA, ex parte Ali* [1990] COD 317, the applicant unsuccessfully sought damages in respect of ILEA's failure to provide an adequate number of primary school places in Tower Hamlets, despite the fact that the minister had refused to invoke his default powers provided under the Education Act 1944. The court took the view that ILEA's statutory duty was not absolute. It had to do its best to discharges its duty, but might not be able to do so because of unforeseen circumstances. The court concluded that Parliament had not intended to provide a member of the public with a private law right to compensation: see further *Wyatt* v *Hillingdon London Borough Council* (1978) 76 LGR 727.

Despite the above, the courts will not regard themselves as powerless to act simply because a default power exists, especially where there is evidence of an ultra vires refusal to exercise such default powers. In *Meade* v *Haringey London Borough Council* [1979] 1 WLR 637 the local authority had closed its schools due to a caretakers' strike, and a number of parents brought an action claiming that the authority was in breach of its duty under s8 of the Education Act 1944 to provide sufficient schools in its area. Section 99 of the 1944 Act provided the Secretary of State with powers to compel performance of this duty which he declined to exercise after concluding that the authority was not in breach of its duty. Although the Court of Appeal dismissed the parents' action, Lord Denning expressed the view that:

> '... although that section does give a remedy – by complaint to a Minister – it does not exclude any other remedy. To my mind it leaves open all the established remedies which the law provides in cases where a public authority fails to perform its statutory duty either by an act of commission or omission. ... I am clearly of opinion that if the borough council of Haringey, of their own free will, deliberately closed one school in their borough for one week – without just cause or excuse – it would be ultra vires: and each of the parents whose child suffered thereby would have an action for damages. All the more so if they closed it for five weeks or more. Or for all schools. No one can suppose that Parliament authorised the borough council to renounce their duties to such an extent as deliberately to close the schools without just cause or excuse. To use Lord Reid's words, it was their duty "not to act so as to frustrate the policy and objects of the Act".'

As indicated above, public authorities are subject to the requirements of the Human Rights Act 1998, s6(1) providing that: 'It is unlawful for a public authority to act in a way which is incompatible with a Convention right.' This opens the way for the courts to allow plaintiffs to bring actions for breach of statutory duty against an authority alleged to have failed to meet the requirements of s6(1). The 1998 Act does not provide a free-standing right to damages as such, but does provide that a court may grant such remedies as lie within its powers that it considers to be appropriate, and that damages may be awarded in proceedings brought under the 1998 Act by a court empowered to order the payment of compensation in civil proceedings: see s8(1) and (2). This is subject to the proviso that an award should be 'necessary to afford just satisfaction to the person in whose favour it is made': s8(3).

14.10 Liability in negligence

As a general proposition it is true to say that a local authority can be either directly liable in negligence, or vicariously liable for the actions, and in some cases the omissions of it officers and employees according to the general common law principles established in a line of authorities stretching back to, and beyond, *Donoghue* v *Stevenson* [1932] AC 562. A plaintiff seeking damages will have to establish that: a duty of care was owed; that the duty had been breached; and that the breach had caused the harm. On the basis of *Caparo Industries plc* v *Dickman* [1990] 2 AC 605 the question of whether a common law duty of care arises will depend upon whether the damage was reasonably foreseeable; the degree of proximity between the plaintiff and defendant; and the extent to which the imposition of a duty of care can be seen as just and reasonable.

The fact that a local authority discharges its functions through officers and employees does not of itself offer any particular immunity: see *Mersey Docks and Harbour Board* v *Gibbs* (1866) LR 1 HL 93. Suppose that the driver of a local authority refuse lorry, acting in the course of his employment, negligently fails to keep a proper look out and reverses over P causing him to be injured. The local authority will be liable in negligence. The driver owes P a duty of care, which he has breached, causing the harm. As will be seen below, however, simply because a local authority employee is discharging his duties to his employer does not automatically mean that he owes a private law duty of care to those affected by his actions. Policy considerations will come into play to determine whether the recognition of any such duty of care is desirable: see for example *Phelps* v *Hillingdon London Borough Council* [2000] 4 All ER 504 (considered below).

Given the above, why is the issue of the tortious liability of local authorities of interest and relevance to administrative lawyers? The answer lies in the fact that, over the last 40 years, the courts have recognised that in certain circumstances there may be sound policy reasons for not applying the common principles to local authorities and similar bodies, without some modification. This is not to suggest that these public bodies are in any way above the law as far as potential tortious liability is concerned, merely that there may be situations where to permit an action for damages to succeed would be counter to the wider public interest. In particular, special consideration may have to be given to the fact that local authorities (as is the case with government departments) often have to discharge functions that have no parallel in private law, in the sense that no private body would be placed under a duty to perform them or empowered to engage in them. Examples might include the formulation of policies on education or welfare matters, the approval of plans for buildings, the inspection of building foundations, the designing and laying of public sewers, the painting of white lines on roads, road improvement schemes or the provision of care to children with special needs. These tend to be social or regulatory activities that are performed on behalf of public for the general good of the public. If harm results from the exercise of these powers should the taxpayer have to reimburse the injured party?

Limiting the scope of the duty of care: was the harm foreseeable and was the relationship one of sufficient proximity?

An action in negligence will fail if the court rules that there is insufficient proximity between the plaintiff and defendant for a duty of care to arise. Traditionalists would perhaps adopt the language of the 'neighbour' principle, but it is submitted that by using the term proximity it is perhaps easier for the courts to mask what are essentially policy decisions about the potential liability of public bodies. For example, in *Hill* v *Chief Constable of West Yorkshire* [1989] AC 53 a negligence action was brought against the defendant in respect of his force's failure to apprehend Peter Sutcliffe (alias 'the Yorkshire Ripper') before he murdered the plaintiff's daughter. The House of Lords rejected the claim on a number of grounds. First, it was held that no general duty of care was owed by the police in respect of the policies adopted regarding the investigation of crime, as this was largely a matter within the discretion of police officers that the courts were not well versed to comment upon. Second, because there was insufficient proximity between the plaintiff and the defendant's action, in hunting for Sutcliffe the police were seeking to protect the public at large, not the plaintiff's daughter in particular. For consideration of the compatibility of this ruling with the European Convention on Human Rights: see *Osman* v *United Kingdom*, considered below.

Failure to satisfy the test for proximity was also a key factor in the Court of Appeal's ruling in *John Munroe (Acrylics) Ltd* v *London Fire and Civil Defence Authority and Others* [1997] 3 WLR 331, where it was held that, in the absence of any special relationship, a fire authority did not owe the owner of any property a common law duty of care that required an authority to respond to a call for assistance. The court at first instance (see [1996] 4 All ER 318), rejecting the contention that an authority's decision to respond to such a call could, of itself, create a common law duty of care, confirmed that such a duty would not arise unless an individual could show that, by its actions, a fire authority had assumed a personal responsibility towards that person. Where an emergency call is made to an ambulance service the courts may be more prepared to accept that there is a relationship of proximity, given the nature of the service provided: see *Kent* v *Griffiths and Others* [2000] 2 All ER 474.

Limiting the scope of the duty of care: is the imposition of a duty of care just, reasonable and in the public interest?

As the House of Lords made clear in *X (Minors)* v *Bedfordshire County Council* [1995] 2 AC 633, an important variable in the process of determining whether or not a private law duty of care exists is the question of whether or not it would be fair, just and reasonable to impose such a duty. This in turn requires an examination of the intention of Parliament in devolving powers to a public body, the context in which those powers are to be exercised, and whether the imposition of a private law duty of care would be an appropriate way of ensuring that those powers are exercised as intended by Parliament. Essentially this question will involve the courts in carrying out a balancing exercise, weighing the need to secure justice for the litigant who has suffered loss on the one hand against the wider public interest on the other. It is submitted that there are no settled rules here as to how this balancing task is to be carried out; on the contrary the courts would wish to retain as much flexibility as possible so as to approach each case largely on its own facts. A number of illustrations, however, help to give an indication of the factors that the courts will give weight to.

Imposition of a duty of care held not to be just, reasonable or in the public interest

Two factors in particular can be determined in the decisions of the courts where they have declined to impose a private law duty of care on a public body on the basis that it would be unreasonable or against the public interest to do so. The first is that the imposition of a duty of care would be inappropriate given the relevant statutory framework of supervisory mechanisms. The second is that it would be counter-productive in terms of improving the quality of service or administration: see generally *X (Minors)* v *Bedfordshire County Council* [1995] 2 AC 633.

Hence in *Hill* v *Chief Constable of West Yorkshire* (above) the House of Lords held that it was not in the public interest to subject the police to a duty of care as regards the methods chosen to search for a dangerous suspect. There was no evidence that the imposition of such a duty would be an effective mechanism for improving detection rates or preventing crime. In *Cowan* v *Chief Constable of Avon and Somerset* (2001) The Independent 21 November it was held that police officers, called by the claimant to prevent his being evicted from his rented accommodation contrary to the Protection from Eviction Act 1977, owed him no duty of care to prevent such an unlawful eviction. Following *Costello* v *Chief Constable of Northumbria Police* [1999] ICR 752, a duty of care would only be imposed upon the police in respect of a specific individual where a sufficiently close relationship had been established. There was no evidence that by attending at the scene of the eviction the police officers had assumed any such responsibility for the claimant – compare with *Capital and Counties plc* v *Hampshire County Council* [1997] QB 1004 – and there was no evidence that the police officers assumed any responsibility to prevent the claimant from being evicted. Their purpose in attending at the scene was merely to prevent a breach of the peace. There were no compelling countervailing policy arguments in favour of imposing a duty of care. Similar sentiments, albeit in a different context, were expressed as regards the likely effect of imposing a private law duty of care upon ministers regarding the exercise of discretion in *Rowling* v *Takaro Properties Ltd* [1988] AC 473 and *Lonrho plc* v *Tebbit and the Department of Trade and Industry* [1991] 4 All ER 973.

In *John Munroe (Acrylics) Ltd* v *London Fire and Civil Defence Authority and Others* (above) the Court of Appeal, in rejecting the imposition of a duty of care, adverted to the following factors as being persuasive in arriving at that conclusion: there was no evidence that the imposition of such a duty would encourage a higher level of performance on the part of the fire authority's officers; that it might encourage an over-cautious attitude on the part of officers that could result in an uneconomic deployment of resources; that the efficacy of a public service, provided for collective welfare, ought to be assessed through administrative means and not by way of private law claims for damages; and that the imposition of a duty of care could open the 'floodgates' to a host of similar claims. In *Clunis* v *Camden and Islington Health Authority* [1998] 3 All ER 180 the plaintiff sought damages on the basis that if he had been assessed by the defendant authority's psychiatrist he would have been detained and thus would not have been at liberty to carry out an unlawful killing for which he was subsequently detained. Notwithstanding the public policy consideration that the courts would not normally assist a litigant who sought to base his action on his own immoral or illegal conduct, the Court of Appeal held that the imposition of a private law duty of care was inappropriate given that, under the Mental Health Act 1983, the performance of s117 obligations (after-care for mental patients released into the community) could be enforced by way of complaint to the Secretary of State. See further *Jarvis* v *Hampshire County Council* (1999) The Times 23 November, where a similar claim was struck out on the basis that no duty of care existed.

Imposition of a duty of care held to be just, reasonable and in the public interest

The range of cases where the courts have held that it is just and reasonable to impose a duty of care on a public body tend to have one common factor – reliance by the claimant on the assurances, advice or service offered by the public body to that particular claimant. For example, in *W and Others* v *Essex County Council* [1998] 3 All ER 111, the plaintiff parents agreed with the defendant authority that they would act as foster parents for an adolescent boy. Prior to taking on this responsibility they sought, and were given, undertakings to the effect that the boy was not a known sex abuser of other children. During the one-month period when the boy was living with the plaintiffs he sexually abused each of their children. The plaintiffs (the parents and their abused children) commenced proceedings against the local authority for (inter alia) negligence by breach of statutory duty, negligent misstatement, breach of the fostering agreement, damages for psychiatric harm and misfeasance by the social worker for whom the authority was vicariously liable. The defendant authority brought proceedings to strike out the action. At first instance the parents' action was struck out but not that brought by their children as far as their claims alleged negligence by breach of statutory duty, vicarious liability for the social worker and damages for psychiatric harm consequent upon the abuse. The parents appealed against the striking out of their claims and the authority cross-appealed against the decision to allow the children's actions to proceed. Both appeals were dismissed by the Court of Appeal (Stuart-Smith LJ dissenting), holding that, whilst, as a general principle, it would not be just and reasonable to impose a common law duty of care where a statutory framework existed for the protection of children at risk, the policy reasons for not imposing a common law duty of care did not apply as regards children who were not actually in the care of a local authority (such as the plaintiff children) and who thus fell outside the statutory framework. Given that the defendant authority had given express assurances regarding the history of the child to be placed with the plaintiffs it was just and reasonable in the circumstances to allow the children's action to proceed. The House of Lords subsequently held that parents' claim should also be allowed to proceed: see *W and Others* v *Essex County Council* (2000) The Times 17 March.

In *Kent* v *Griffiths and Others* (above) the Court of Appeal was willing to accept that it might be just, reasonable and in the public interest to impose a duty of care on an ambulance service responding to emergency calls because: physical harm was likely to result from the failure of an ambulance to arrive, not just economic loss; the physical harm could result in loss that might not be recoverable under a policy of insurance; once an ambulance had been called there was, arguably, a relationship of proximity between the plaintiff and the ambulance authority; and there was the policy consideration that, once an ambulance had been called, those acting to assist the person in need would normally abandon their search to secure other means of transporting the injured person to hospital. Note that the court was simply allowing an appeal against a striking out, not determining these issues. See further the issue of reliance on fire fighters once at the scene of a crime considered in *Capital and Counties plc* v *Hampshire County Council* (below).

Similarly, in *Welton* v *North Cornwall District Council* [1997] 1 WLR 570, the defendant authority was found liable in negligence in respect of unnecessary building work carried out by the plaintiffs on the basis of the authority's environmental health officer's instructions. Again the issue of reliance on advice was seen as significant. Following the reasoning of Lord Browne-Wilkinson in *X* v *Bedfordshire County Council*, Rose LJ observed that the imposition of a duty of care was in no way inconsistent with the statutory duties placed upon the defendant authority and would not impede the authority in discharging its day-to-day functions. He also regarded it as significant that, in purporting to impose conditions on the plaintiffs, the defendant's officer had been acting outwith the scope of the power delegated to him.

Finally, in *Phelps* v *Hillingdon London Borough Council* [2000] 4 All ER 504, the House of Lords held that a local education authority could be vicariously liable for the negligent discharge of statutory duties on its behalf by an educational psychologist employed by the authority who failed to diagnose the plaintiff's dyslexia. The House of Lords accepted that there could be situations where the imposition of such a duty of care could be counter-productive and result in an interference in the proper discharge of an authority's function, but the plaintiff's case was one where a person was exercising a particular skill and professional judgment in circumstances where it was foreseeable that harm would be caused if due skill and care were not exercised. There was no justification for a blanket immunity in the case of teachers or education officers dealing with pupils with special needs. The House of Lords regarded it as especially significant that the educational psychologist called in this case had been asked to give specific advice and guidance in relation to the plaintiff. It was clear that the plaintiff's parents would act on that advice, hence, prima facie, a duty of care arose. The House of Lords rejected the contention that the imposition of a duty of care would hamper the provision of the specialist advice service. It was noted in passing that if the educational psychologist had been acting for a private client there would have been no doubt as to the existence of a duty of care. Neither was the imposition of a duty of care seen as imposing unreasonably high standards: see further *S* v *Gloucestershire County Council* [2000] 3 All ER 346.

Limiting the scope of the duty of care: policy decisions and the careless exercise of discretion

Traditionally the courts have recognised a distinction between the actions of public bodies falling within the sphere of policy-making, and action that might be described as operational, ie the steps taken to execute that policy. The significance of the distinction lies in the proposition that an exercise of discretion that involves the adoption of a policy will not normally give rise to liability in negligence, no mater how wrong-headed the policy. The legality or otherwise of policies should be challenged by way of judicial review, on public law grounds. By contrast, if a claimant can show that his loss is consequent upon the negligent exercise of discretion in the execution of a policy, he will stand a better chance of establishing a private law duty of care.

As Lord Wilberforce observed in *Anns* v *Merton London Borough Council* [1978] AC 728:

> 'Most, indeed probably all, statutes relating to public authorities or public bodies, contain in them a large area of policy. The courts call this "discretion" meaning that the decision is one for the authority or body to make, and not for the courts. Many statutes also prescribe or at least presuppose the practical execution of policy decisions: a convenient description of this is to say that in addition to the area of policy or discretion, there is an operational area. Although this distinction between the policy area and the operational area is convenient, and illuminating, it is probably a distinction of degree; many "operational" powers or duties have in them some element of "discretion". It can safely be said that the more "operational" a power or duty may be, the easier it is to superimpose upon it a common law duty of care ...'

Hence the House of Lords in *X (Minors)* v *Bedfordshire County Council* (above), held that if negligence could be said to have occurred at an operational level concerning the welfare of school pupils (the provision of counselling services, supervision of educational progress by a headmaster and identification of special needs cases) a duty of care could exist at common law, although the courts will still have regard to whether or not the imposition of a duty of care is actually in the public interest: see *Phelps* v *Hillingdon London Borough Council* (above).

The nature of the policy/operational dichotomy was reconsidered in *Barrett* v *Enfield London Borough Council* [1999] 3 All ER 193, where the plaintiff challenged the decision to strike out his claim in negligence in respect of the treatment he had received having been taken into care by the defendant local authority. Lord Slynn reviewed the various test for imposing liability and, having referred to *Dorset Yacht Co Ltd* v *Home Office* and *Anns* v *Merton London Borough Council*, continued (p210g–211h):

> 'On this basis, if an authority acts wholly within its discretion – ie it is doing what Parliament has said it can do, even if it has to choose between several alternatives open to it, then there can be no liability in negligence. It is only if a plaintiff can show that what has been done is outside the discretion and the power, then he can go on to show the authority was negligent. But if that stage is reached, the authority is not exercising a statutory power, but purporting to do so and the statute is no defence.
>
> This, however, does not in my view mean that if an element of discretion is involved in an act being done subject to the exercise of the overriding statutory power, common law negligence is necessarily ruled out. Acts may be done pursuant and subsequent to the exercise of a discretion where a duty of care may exist – as has often been said even knocking a nail into a piece of wood involves the exercise of some choice or discretion and yet there may be a duty of care in the way it is done. Whether there is an element of discretion to do the act is thus not a complete test leading to the result that, if there is, a claim against an authority for what it actually does or fails to do must necessarily be ruled out.
>
> Another distinction which is sometimes drawn between decisions as to "policy" and as to "operational acts" sounds more promising. A pure policy decision where Parliament has entrusted the decision to a public authority is not something which a court would normally be expected to review in a claim in negligence. But again this is not an absolute test. Policy and operational acts are closely linked and the decision to do an operational act may easily involve and flow from a policy decision ... Where a statutory power is given to a local authority and damage is caused by what it does pursuant to that power, the ultimate question is whether the particular issue is justiciable or whether the court should accept that it has no role to play. The two tests (discretion and policy/operational) to which I have referred are guides in deciding that question. The greater the element of policy involved, the wider the area of discretion accorded, the more likely it is that the matter is not justiciable so that no action in negligence can be brought. It is true that Lord Reid and Lord Diplock in the *Dorset Yacht* case accepted that before a claim can be brought in negligence, the plaintiffs must show that the authority is behaving so unreasonably that it is not in truth exercising the real discretion given to it. But the passage I have cited was, as I read it, obiter, since Lord Reid made it clear that the case did not concern such a claim, but rather was a claim that Borstal officers had been negligent when they had disobeyed orders given to them.
>
> Moreover, I share Lord Browne-Wilkinson's reluctance to introduce the concepts of

administrative law into the law of negligence, as Lord Diplock appears to have done. But in any case I do not read what either Lord Reid or Lord Wilberforce in the *Anns* case (and in particular Lord Reid) said as to the need to show that there has been an abuse of power before a claim can be brought in negligence in the exercise of a statutory discretion as meaning that an action can never be brought in negligence where an act has been done pursuant to the exercise of the discretion. A claim of negligence in the taking of a decision to exercise a statutory discretion is likely to be barred, unless it is wholly unreasonable so as not to be a real exercise of the discretion, or if it involves the making of a policy decision involving the balancing of different public interests; acts done pursuant to the lawful exercise of the discretion can, however, in my view be subject to a duty of care, even if some element of discretion is involved. Thus accepting that a decision to take a child into care pursuant to a statutory power is not justiciable, it does not in my view follow that, having taken a child into care, an authority cannot be liable for what it or its employees do in relation to the child without it being shown that they have acted in excess of power. It may amount to an excess of power, but that is not in my opinion the test to be adopted: the test is whether the conditions in the *Caparo* case [ie foreseeability, proximity and just and reasonable to impose a duty of care] have been satisfied ... Both in deciding whether particular issues are justiciable and whether if a duty of care is owed, it has been broken, the court must have regard to the statutory context and to the nature of the tasks involved. The mere fact that something has gone wrong or that a mistake has been made, or that someone has been inefficient does not mean that there was a duty to be careful or that such duty has been broken. Much of what has to be done in this area involves the balancing of delicate and difficult factors and courts should not be too ready to find in these situations that there has been negligence by staff who largely are skilled and dedicated.'

For further support for the view that an exercise of discretion has to be irrational in order to establish a private law duty of care, see *Larner* v *Solihull MBC* (2001) The Times 6 February.

It may be the case that the policy/operational dichotomy survives but in another guise. It might be more appropriate to argue now that policy decisions do not give rise to a private law duty of care because of the lack of proximity. Positively negligent acts by the employees of public authorities will be viewed as giving rise to liability if there are no compelling public policy reasons to the contrary and there is sufficient proximity. In a sense negligence, such the fire officer's decision to switch off the sprinkler system at the scene of a fire in *Capital and Counties plc* v *Hampshire County Council* (above), can be characterised as operational and thus more likely to give rise to liability. As Judge Havery QC (at first instance) observed in *Capital and Counties plc* v *Hampshire County Council* [1996] 4 All ER 336:

'... decisions made on site fighting a fire may be said to include tactical or strategic decisions, but they are entirely operational; they do not include the decision of questions of priority in the allocation of resources between one fire and another ... Whilst I do not accept that the fire brigade in any way warrant the success of their fire-fighting operations, I accept that the provision as to their exclusive control of those operations while they are carrying them out, which may prevent anyone else from fighting the fire at the same time, is a consideration against immunity on the ground of public policy. It is also a consideration supporting the fairness, justice and reasonableness of the existence of a duty of care.'

The ruling at first instance was upheld by the Court of Appeal: see [1997] 3 WLR 331.

The impact of the European Convention on Human Rights: the need for flexibility

Notwithstanding the policy considerations that underpin the decisions of the courts to restrict the liability of public authorities, care should be taken to maintain a degree of flexibility, not least because of the rights and duties arising under the European Convention on Human Rights, as incorporated in part by the Human Rights Act 1998.

A legal rule that prevents a claimant from pursuing an action for compensation against a public body may amount to a denial of rights under art 6 of the Convention.

The matter was considered by the European Court of Human Rights in *Osman* v *United Kingdom* [1998] BHRC 293, where it upheld the applicant's claim that the immunity principles in *Hill* v *Chief Constable of West Yorkshire* (above) amounted to a violation of art 6(1) rights. The applicants alleged that the Metropolitan Police had negligently failed to apprehend a suspect before he killed her husband and seriously injured her son. The evidence indicated that the suspect had formed an obsessional attachment to her son and was behaving in a very uncontrolled manner. The domestic court had held that, following *Hill*, the case disclosed no reasonable cause of action and should be struck out. The European Court of Human Rights, whilst acknowledging that the exclusionary rule in *Hill* might be justifiable in terms of public policy (ie maintaining the effectiveness of a police force) held that it had to be applied proportionately, with regard to its scope and especially its application in the case at issue. The applicant had a right to have the issue (of whether or not an action in negligence should proceed) determined by the courts by reference to the issues of proximity, foreseeability and whether it was fair, just and reasonable to apply the exclusionary rule, hence the applicant was asserting a right that fell to be protected by art 6(1). In asserting that the case fell squarely within the exclusionary rule in *Hill*, and treating that rule as 'watertight', the Court of Appeal had denied the applicant access to a hearing of the substantive issues. The European Court of Human Rights concluded that, as applied by the Court of Appeal, the rule in *Hill* conferred a blanket immunity on the police for their acts and omissions during the investigation and suppression of crime and amounted to an unjustifiable restriction on an applicant's rights under art 6(1). The factors that persuaded the Court that the applicant's case could be distinguished from that in *Hill* were: the issue of proximity; the fact that a child was involved; the catalogue of acts and omissions which amounted to grave negligence as opposed to minor acts of incompetence; and the applicant's allegation that the police had assumed responsibility for the safety of her family. Note that there was no suggestion in the Court's judgment that, had the case gone to trial, the applicant would necessarily have succeeded.

The ruling of the European Court of Human Rights in *Osman* was subsequently subjected to the trenchant and illuminating criticisms of Lord Browne-Wilkinson in *Barrett* v *Enfield London Borough Council* [1999] 3 All ER 193. He observed that it was flawed insofar as it presupposed that the applicant in *Osman* had enjoyed a pre-existing legal right to bring an action in the courts that the ruling in *Hill* prevented him from exercising. He commented (at p198j–199d):

> '[The ruling of the European Court of Human Rights] … seems to treat the Osmans as having a right under English law to go to court for a declaration that, apart from the public policy preventing suits against the police, they would have had a claim in negligence against the police and further, that it was not fair, just and reasonable in the circumstances of that case to apply the "exclusionary rule", ie the rule excluding negligence actions against the police.
>
> Having so defined the ambit of art 6, the Strasbourg court held that there was in the *Osman* case a breach of such right of access to the English court, such breach lying in the application of a blanket exclusionary rule which excludes all claims against the police for negligent failure to investigate or protect from crime. In the view of the Strasbourg court, apparently, the applicability of such exclusionary rule has to be decided afresh in each individual case. If this is not done then it is impossible to determine whether the public interest in an efficient police force is or is not proportionate to the seriousness of the harm suffered by the plaintiff in the individual case … The problems in applying this reasoning to the English law of negligence are many and various. For example, the correct answer to the following points is not immediately apparent: 1. Although the word "immunity" is sometimes incorrectly used, a holding that it is not fair, just and reasonable to hold liable a particular class of defendants whether generally or in relation to a particular type of activity is not to give immunity from a liability to which the rest of the world is subject. It is a prerequisite to there being any liability in negligence at all that as a matter of policy it is fair, just and reasonable in those circumstances to impose liability in negligence. 2. In a wide range of cases public policy has led to the decision that the imposition of liability would not be fair and reasonable in the circumstances, eg some activities of financial regulators, building inspectors, ship surveyors, social workers dealing with sex abuse cases. In all these cases and many others the view has been taken that the proper performance of the defendant's primary functions for the benefit of society as a whole will be inhibited if they are required to look over their shoulder to avoid liability in negligence. In English law the decision as to whether it is fair, just and reasonable to impose a liability in negligence on a particular class of would-be defendants depends on weighing in the balance the total detriment to the public interest in all cases from holding such class liable in negligence as against the total loss to all would-be plaintiffs if they are not to have a cause of action in respect of the loss they have individually suffered. 3. In English law, questions of public policy and the question whether it is fair and reasonable to impose liability in negligence are decided as questions of law. Once the decision is taken that, say, company auditors though liable to shareholders for negligent auditing are not liable to those proposing to invest in the company … that decision will apply to all future cases of the same kind. The decision does not depend on weighing the balance

between the extent of the damage to the plaintiff and the damage to the public in each particular case.'

He went on, however, to conclude that, given the 'unsatisfactory state of affairs' created by the decision in the *Osman* case the plaintiff would probably succeed in Strasbourg if the House of Lords were to uphold the striking-out decision – hence his reluctant conclusion that the claim should be allowed to proceed.

A distinction can be drawn between an exclusionary rule that prevents a court from assessing the merits of a case, and a substantive rule that operates so as to prevent a duty of care from arising. When the claimants in *X (Minors)* v *Bedfordshire County Council* took their case to Strasbourg, the European Court of Humans Rights, whilst upholding the application on other grounds, held that the situation whereby the applicants could not sue a local authority in negligence in respect of the harm suffered through neglect did not arise from any procedural bar or from the operation of any immunity which restricted access to court. Instead it resulted from the application by the domestic courts of substantive law principles. The European Court of Human Rights was not competent to rule on the appropriate content of domestic law: see *Z and Others* v *United Kingdom (Application No 29392/95)* [2001] FCR 246.

Limiting the scope of the duty of care: who should bear the cost of alleged negligence?

The imposition of liability in tort is also an exercise in loss distribution. The courts will be mindful of this, and it may determine whether a loss should be borne by the inured party (in reality an insurer), or defrayed though the public purse. The clearest recognition of this arose in the ruling of the House of Lords in *Stovin* v *Wise; Norfolk County Council (Third Party)* [1996] 3 WLR 388. The plaintiff motorcyclist was injured in a collision with a car. The plaintiff's visibility at the junction where the collision occurred had been obscured by a raised bank of earth to his left. The local highway authority was aware of the dangerous nature of the junction and the fact that a number of accidents had occurred there in the recent past. Efforts had been made to secure the agreement of the landowner to the levelling of the ground to improve visibility at the junction, but by the time of the accident no response had been received. The plaintiff's action against the motorist was settled, but he joined the highway authority as a third party alleging that it was to blame for not having taken more steps to improve safety at the junction. At first instance the court ruled that the highway authority had breached its common law duty of care and that it was 30 per cent to blame for the collision. The Court of Appeal dismissed the authority's appeal, which was renewed before the House of Lords. By a majority (Lords Slynn and Nicholls dissenting) the appeal was allowed. In the course of a speech with which Lords Goff and Jauncey concurred, Lord Hoffmann provided a detailed analysis of the legal, political and economic basis for the decision of the majority. He stressed that, whilst a public body would almost always have a duty in public law to consider whether or not to exercise its powers, it did not necessarily mean that it owed a duty of care which might require that the power be exercised. As he put it:

'Upon what principles can one say of a public authority that not only did it have a duty in public law to consider the exercise of the power but that it would thereupon have been under a duty in public law to act, giving rise to a claim in compensation against public funds for its failure to do so?'

Observing that public bodies were often subject to statutory or common law duties to provide services, but not necessarily liable in damages in the event of a breach of any such duty, he added:

'It is one thing to provide a service at the public expense. It is another to require the public to pay compensation when a failure to provide the service has resulted in loss ... the same is true of an omission to perform a statutory duty. In the case of a mere statutory power there is the further point that the legislature has chosen to confer a discretion rather than create a duty ... I ... do not say that a statutory "may" can never give rise to a common law duty of care ... [B]ut the fact that Parliament has conferred a discretion must be some indication that the policy of the Act conferring the power was not to create a right to compensation.'

Lord Hoffmann was willing to recognise that exceptions might be made, and a duty of care identified, in cases of general or specific reliance. By general reliance he had in mind:

'... [the] ... general expectations in the community ... [A] widespread assumption that a statutory power will be exercised [that] may affect the general pattern of economic and social behaviour. For example, insurance premiums may take into account the expectation that statutory powers of inspection or accident prevention will ordinarily prevent certain kinds of risks from materialising ... [I]t appears to be essential to the doctrine of general reliance that the benefit or service provided under statutory powers should be of a uniform and routine nature, so that one can describe exactly what the public authority was supposed to do. Powers of inspection for defects fall clearly into this category ... if a particular service is provided as a matter of routine, it would be irrational for a public authority to provide it in one case and arbitrarily withhold it in another. This was obviously the main ground upon which this House in *Anns* considered that the power of the local authority to inspect foundations should give rise to a duty of care.'

Even in cases of reliance, however, the court would still have to be satisfied that, as a matter of policy, it was appropriate to provide financial compensation for the failure to exercise power.

Lord Hoffmann went on to summarise the minimum pre-conditions for basing a duty of care upon the existence of a statutory power as being:

'... first, that it would in the circumstances have been irrational not to have exercised the power, so that there was in effect a public law duty to act, and secondly, that there are exceptional grounds for holding that the policy of the statute requires compensation to be paid to persons who suffer loss because the power was not exercised.'

Turning to the facts giving rise to the appeal, Lord Hoffmann observed that, as a matter of law, the highway authority was not under a duty to render the junction less dangerous, and thus there was no basis for the imposition of a private law duty of care. There was no evidence that the case came within any 'general reliance' exception because the case did not involve the provision of a uniform identifiable service. As Lord Hoffmann observed:

> 'Every hazardous junction, intersection or stretch of road is different and requires a separate decision as to whether anything should be done to improve it ...'

His Lordship also had in mind the broader consequences of imposing a duty of care, notably that local authorities might increase expenditure on highways to avoid large claims for damages at the expense of education and social service budgets, and felt that the courts ought not develop policies on the imposition of liability that would cause such budgetary distortions.

The clear implication here is that the financial impact of any loss should be provided for through private arrangements with insurance companies. As Stuart-Smith LJ observed in *Capital and Counties plc* v *Hampshire County Council*, adverting to Lord Hoffmann's use of the 'general reliance' doctrine as a determinant of liability:

> '... Lord Hoffmann ... is suggesting that there is not a general expectation that fires will necessarily be extinguished by the fire brigade; there is no doubt a hope that they will; but they may arrive too late to be of practical use, or they may not arrive at all; instead, for the most part people rely upon insurance for indemnification in case of loss ... If, therefore [the fire brigade] fail to turn up, or fail to turn up in time, because they have carelessly misunderstood the message, got lost on the way or run into a tree, they are not liable ...'

Exactly the same philosophy underpins the decision in *Philcox* v *Civil Aviation Authority* (1995) The Times 8 June, where the court dismissed a claim in negligence against the defendant authority brought after the plaintiff's plane had crashed. The plaintiff based his action on the fact that his plane had only just been inspected by the Civil Aviation Authority and given a certificate of airworthiness. The court held that the Civil Aviation Authority was under a duty to supervise civil aviation for the benefit of the public at large. It had not been created to protect the owners of aircraft from the consequences of their own failure to maintain their machines, and owed them no private law duty of care in respect of such inspections, ie it was not intended to act as an insurance scheme funded by the taxpayer. By contrast, a third party suffering injury or loss as a result of such a plane crash might, it is submitted, have a right of action against the Civil Aviation Authority.

Economic loss

The scope of a local authority's liability for economic loss has been significantly curtailed in a number of decisions relating to the allegedly negligent approval of building plans. In *Investors in Industry Commercial Properties* v *South Bedfordshire District Council and Others* [1986] 1 All ER 787 the plaintiffs were owners of a number of warehouses built on the site of a former rubbish tip that had rapidly disintegrated due to the inadequacy of the foundations. The plans for the warehouses had been approved by the defendant local authority and the foundations inspected and approved. The plaintiffs argued, inter alia, that the local authority had been negligent but the court, relying on *Anns* and *Governors of Peabody Donation Fund* v *Sir Lindsay Parkinson & Co Ltd* [1985] AC 210 (in which the court had held that the plaintiffs could not recover in negligence because the statutory power of inspection had been conferred on the local authority to safeguard the occupiers of houses and not to protect developers from economic losses), held that the local authority owed no duty of care to the plaintiffs. In the course of his judgment Slade LJ stated three propositions that now applied to this situation. First, the supervisory powers given to local authorities in relation to building plans and inspection of foundations were for the benefit of members of the public, and the occupants of such buildings, not to safeguard the developer, or anyone else, from purely economic loss. Second, it was possible that a local authority could be regarded as owing a duty of care to a subsequent occupier other than the original building owner to take reasonable care to ensure that a building was erected in accordance with the building regulations so as not to endanger life or health. Third, in the majority of situations, the original owner of a property (ie the developer) would not normally be able to recover damages from a local authority if plans and foundations were negligently approved, as it was incumbent on the original owner to ensure that the building complied with the building regulations, a fortiori where the owner had had the benefit of the advice of architects, engineers and contractors: see further *Curran* v *Northern Ireland Co-Ownership Housing Association Ltd* [1987] 2 All ER 13. These decisions were followed by that of the House of Lords in *Murphy* v *Brentwood District Council* [1990] 3 WLR 414, where it was held that the principle in *Donoghue* v *Stevenson* should not be extended to impose liability for pure economic loss on local authorities supervising plans to ensure compliance with building regulations. See further *Welton* v *North Cornwall District Council* (above).

Causation

The plaintiff must show that the local authority's exercise of power has actually caused damage that would not otherwise have occurred. In *Sheppard* v *Glossop Corporation* [1921] 3 KB 132 (where the plaintiff had fallen and been injured in an unlit street, the council having adopted a policy of extinguishing the lights at 9 o'clock in the evening in the interests of economy) Banks LJ observed that, the authority had not, by its policy, rendered the street any more dangerous than it would have been. As he stated:

'If in lighting the district they act negligently, if for instance they should erect a lamp post and leave it unprotected in the middle of a highway or so close by the highway as to be a danger to persons passing along unless it was properly protected, or allow their gas to escape into some one's house, those would be negligent acts in the course of doing that which the Legislature has authorised ... This is not a case of a statutory power, like a power to make a reservoir and maintain a sufficient supply of water therein, negligently exercised; the appellants have merely exercised the discretion vested in them by the Legislature. They were under no obligation to place a lamp post at this particular spot; and if they kept it there they were not bound to supply it with gas, and are not to be made liable for merely extinguishing the light at any particular hour.'

For further authority on this point, see *East Suffolk Rivers Catchment Board* v *Kent* [1941] AC 74.

Defences

Local authorities are entitled to raise any defence to an action in negligence that would be available to any private party, but it should be noted that the defence of statutory authority, considered above in relation to nuisance is unlikely to be available in respect of an allegation of negligence, as the law does not recognise negligence as 'inevitable'. For example, in *Geddis* v *Proprietors of Bann Reservoir* (1878) 3 App Cas 430, where the plaintiff successfully sued for damages consequent to the flooding of his land following the failure of the defendants to cleanse a channel leading from a reservoir that they had constructed pursuant to statutory authority, Lord Blackburn observed:

'... an action does lie for doing that which the legislature has authorised, if it be done negligently. And I think that if by a reasonable exercise of the powers, either given by statute ... or ... at common law ... the damage could have been prevented, it is, within this rule, "negligence" not to make such reasonable exercise of their powers.'

Similarly, in *Capital and Counties plc* v *Hampshire County Council* (above), the court noted that, whilst s30(1) of the Fire Services Act 1947 did provide fire authorities with a degree of immunity against actions in tort in respect of harm caused by applying water to burning buildings, trespassing on land to obtain water from a hydrant, or switching sprinkler systems on and off, but that immunity did not extend to actions which were in themselves negligent.

14.11 Misfeasance in public office

Ultra vires action is normally challenged by way of an application for judicial review. Where, however, there is evidence that a public officer has exceeded his powers and caused loss to another party, an action for tort of misfeasance in public office may be sustainable if the preconditions for liability are made out. The elements of the tort where considered by the House of Lords in *Three Rivers District Council and Others* v *Governor and Company of the Bank of England (No 3)* [2000] 3 All ER 1.

The plaintiffs, along with 6,018 other depositors, brought an action against the defendant as a result of having lost money deposited with the Bank of Credit and Commerce International (BCCI) at the time of its collapse. Regarding that aspect of the claim that alleged misfeasance in licensing BCCI as a deposit taker, or in failing to revoke its licence when irregularities came to light, the House of Lords held that the tort could be made out in one of two situations. The first was where the public officer concerned acted with 'targeted malice' (ie he had acted with the intention to injure the interests of a specific person or organisation). In such cases there would be bad faith on the part of the public officer who would be acting on the basis of some ulterior motive. A classic example of targeted malice is provided by the Canadian case of *Roncarelli* v *Duplessis* (1959) 16 DLR (2d) 689, where the Canadian premier purported to revoke a liquor licence because the holder had regularly provided sureties for Jehovah's Witnesses who had been arrested by the police. The premier was clearly exercising a power he did not possess and was motivated by a desire to adversely affect the interests of the citizen.

The second basis for misfeasance was where the public officer acted with no honest belief that he was entitled to exercise his powers as he had done. Taking his lead from decisions such as *Northern Territory* v *Mengel* (1995) 69 AJLR 527, *Garrett* v *Attorney-General* [1997] 2 NZLR 332 and *Rawlinson* v *Rice* [1997] 2 NZLR 651, Lord Steyn concluded that recklessness on the part of the public officer would suffice in such cases. In practice this meant that the public officer would have to be shown to have been aware of the risk that his act would be unlawful. Where damages for consequential financial losses were sought, the test to be applied was whether or not the public officer knew that his actions would probably injure the plaintiff's interests. In effect recklessness as to the consequences of the action. Lord Steyn expressed the view that this test would ensure that the correct balance was struck between the need to provide some remedy for abuse of power and the need to protect public officers from unmeritorious claims.

Establishing the tort places a heavy evidential burden on the plaintiff and successful cases are rare, but a good example is provided by *Bourgoin SA* v *Minister of Agriculture, Fisheries and Food* [1985] 3 All ER 585, where the United Kingdom government imposed a ban on the importation of turkeys from countries where particular methods of dealing with disease amongst turkeys were in use. One consequence of this was that French turkey producers were unable to export to the United Kingdom. The plaintiffs claimed that the import ban was in breach of the Treaty of Rome, and could not be justified on public health grounds, and in 1982 the European Court of Justice ruled that the importation ban was in breach of art 30 of the Treaty of Rome, and the ban was removed by the United Kingdom government. The plaintiffs successfully sought damages in the English courts to compensate them for the economic loss that they had suffered: see further *Asoka Kumar David* v *MAMM Abdul Cader* [1963] 3 All ER 579, *Jones* v *Swansea City Council* [1990] 3 All ER 737; *Davies* v *Bromley Corporation* [1908] 1 KB 170; and *Bennett* v *Commissioner of Police of the Metropolis* (1997) The Times 24 October.

Procedural considerations

As indicated above where a public officer acts in bad faith it is certain that he will have acted ultra vires because he has been motivated by irrelevant considerations (a desire to harm the plaintiff) or has acted ultra vires because he has failed to take into account the adverse consequences of has actions on a third party: see further Chapter 8. In theory the party suffering loss could seek redress by way of an action for judicial review, given that the respondent is a public law body, and the case will inevitably involve a substantial point of public law. Two points should, however, be noted. First, following *O'Reilly* v *Mackman* [1983] 2 AC 237, such an action could be regarded as coming within the scope of one of Lord Diplock's exceptions, in that the public law issue involved arises as a collateral matter: see further *Davy* v *Spelthorne BC* [1984] AC 262. Second, there are a number of tactical reasons, not least the time limit for applying for review, that explain why the plaintiff will almost always seek to proceed by way of action: see further Chapter 10.

Where an individual officer of a public body can be identified as having been responsible for misfeasance the plaintiff can proceed against him in his personal capacity. Hence, in *Smith* v *East Elloe Rural District Council* [1956] AC 736, the House of Lords, whilst refusing to allow the plaintiff to challenge a compulsory purchase order that had been made in respect of her property because she was out of time, did suggest that if she felt that the order had been made in bad faith she could proceed with an action for malicious abuse of power against the officer concerned. Acting upon this advice, Mrs Smith subsequently brought such an action against the clerk to the council in *Smith* v *Pywell* (1959) 173 EG 1009. The action failed on its merits, however. In the vast majority of cases the public body will be vicariously liable for the misfeasance of its officer and will be the more attractive defendant in financial terms.

14.12 Liability of individual council officers

In some situations, largely as a result of the wording of the relevant legislation, it may be the individual council officer who is to be held liable in tort and not the employing authority. In *Stanbury* v *Exeter Corporation* [1905] 2 KB 838 an inspector appointed by the defendant authority, but acting under a duty imposed by central government, ordered the destruction of the plaintiff's sheep. The plaintiff claimed that the local authority was vicariously liable for the inspector's negligence in ordering the destruction of the animals. The court held that the defendants were not vicariously liable as the inspector was not acting in pursuance of duties imposed by them. In *Ministry of Housing and Local Government* v *Sharp* [1970] 2 QB 223 a landowner applied unsuccessfully for planning permission and was paid compensation by the Ministry. A compensation notice was placed on the register of local land charges so that if planning permission was later granted the Ministry could be reimbursed. Planning permission was later granted to the owner who sold the land. The purchaser had requested a search of the local land register, and this was conducted negligently by a local authority clerk, with the result that the purchaser bought the land with no notice of the charge. The purchaser was thus entitled to refuse to reimburse the Ministry. The Ministry then sought damages from the registrar, Mr Sharp, for breach of statutory duty, and against the local authority on the basis that they were vicariously liable for their clerk's negligence. At first instance Fisher J held that the registrar was in breach of his statutory duty, that the clerk who made the search knew or ought to have known that if he did not use proper care any incumbrancer against whom the certificate was conclusive would be damaged; that accordingly the clerk owed a duty of care to the minister and was in breach of it; and that the local authority was vicariously liable for the negligence of the clerk. The Court of Appeal (Lord Denning MR dissenting) held that the Registrar was not under an absolute statutory duty to issue accurate certificates, and as he himself has not been negligent no action would lie against him. The clerk, on the other hand, had been negligent and the local authority was vicariously liable for his actions. Salmon LJ observed:

> 'The real question is whether Parliament intended that in the event of a search being inaccurate and the certificate failing to set out the relevant entries in the register, the registrar should be personally liable to the incumbrancer for the financial loss which this failure may have caused him ... There have been numerous attempts in the books to lay down guidelines as to when a civil action may be brought claiming damages for breach of an absolute statutory obligation against the person upon whom such an obligation is imposed ... If the Legislature had intended to make the registrar absolutely liable for any damage caused (through no fault of his or anyone else) by an inaccurate certificate, I am convinced that it would have imposed that liability in very much clearer language than that used in s17 ... I can see no reason why the Legislature should impose such a liability upon a registrar, however tender it may be to purchasers and incumbrancers. It does not seem to me to be any answer to say that the Crown would probably stand behind the registrar. No doubt it would, but only as a matter of grace ... I hope that nothing I have said can be taken to mean that I consider that anyone in this country is allowed to shelter behind any kind of droit administratif. Indeed I consider that one of the most important functions of our courts is vigilantly to protect the rights of the individual against unlawful encroachment by public officers and by the administration. The courts' powers to this end might well, in my view, be enlarged. Certainly such powers as we possess should be vigorously exercised. I do not suggest that the registrar escapes liability because he is a public officer. The question is not: Can the registrar escape from some absolute obligation which the statute imposes upon him?; but: What obligation (if any) does the statute impose upon him?...'

Note that s101 of the Local Government Act 2000 empowers the Secretary of State to makes orders providing for the indemnification of local authority members and officers in respect of any damages, costs or expenses reasonably incurred in connection with membership or employment by a local authority.

Glossary of Terms

Administrative Agency

See Administrative Body.

Administrative Body

A body, usually created by statute, but sometimes by prerogative powers, to carry out a particular task, such as the resolution of disputes or promotion of central government policy.

Appeal

Appeal only exists where statute so provides. On appeal an appellate body can substitute its own decision for the original. An appeal can be launched against the merits of a decision – compare with judicial review.

Audi Alteram Partem

One of the two limbs of natural justice, the rule that no man shall be denied a fair hearing – otherwise described as the right to be heard.

Declaration

Originally only available as a private law remedy, now available on an application for judicial review. Simply states the court's view of the law on the issues raised. Has no coercive force.

Delegated Legislation

A generic term for orders made by bodies given the powers to do so by Parliament. Includes statutory instruments and bye-laws. Not all matters actually described as delegated legislation are actually legislative in effect.

Directory Requirements

Statutory procedural requirements that should normally be followed, however failure to do so will not necessarily be fatal to consequent action.

Enabling Act

The primary Act that gives an inferior body the powers to act, and consequently lays down the limits of its power, eg the Civil Aviation Act 1971 is the enabling Act of the Civil Aviation Authority.

Estoppel

An estoppel arises where A makes a promise or representation to B, upon which B acts to his detriment. A may then be estopped from going back on his promise. In public law an estoppel will not normally be upheld against a public body where it would result in that body acting ultra vires, or where it would conflict with that body's public duty.

Express Limits on Power

The wording of the enabling Act detailing the limits of an inferior body's power.

Fettering Discretion

Where a body refuses to use its powers as Parliament contemplated. The fettering may arise from a contract, policy, delegation of power, or estoppel.

Implied Limits

Limits placed on the powers of inferior bodies by the courts, as opposed to the enabling Act, eg that a body must act reasonably.

Inferior Body

A body of limited jurisdiction, and therefore capable of acting ultra vires and being reviewed by the courts; see Administrative Body.

Intra Vires

Within the powers delegated to an inferior body. Intra vires actions are not normally reviewable, save for error of law on the face of the record.

Judicial Activism

Where the judiciary have decided to create new grounds for reviewing administrative action previously thought unreviewable, eg *Padfield* v *Minister of Agriculture*; *Ridge* v *Baldwin*.

Judicial Review

Supervision of inferior bodies by the courts. Concerned only with the legality of their actions not the merits. Reviewing court cannot substitute a new decision for the one reviewed. Procedure under Pt 54 CPR 1998 must be used.

Jurisdiction

Power to act. Jurisdiction will be laid down in a body's enabling Act. Acting beyond jurisdiction is ultra vires.

Jurisdictional Error

Where a body makes a mistake on a matter of fact or law upon which its jurisdiction depends.

Justices

Magistrates – who frequently perform licensing functions.

Justiciable Matter

An issue upon which the courts are competent to pronounce, as opposed to non-judiciable matters such as defence policy, or the conduct of foreign affairs.

Locus Standi

An applicant for judicial review must have locus standi – meaning he has sufficient interest in the matter to which his application relates. The standing requirements are to prevent applications from persons with no connection to the issue.

Mandatory Order

One of the three prerogative orders (previously known as mandamus), compels a public body to perform its duties.

Mandatory Requirements

Procedural requirements laid down in an inferior body's enabling Act which must be complied with. Failure to comply renders subsequent action ultra vires.

Ministerial Orders

Includes codes, guidance, and directives. See delegated legislation.

Nemo Judex in Causa Sua

One of the two rules of natural justice, that no man should be a judge in his own cause. Also referred to as the rule against bias.

Ombudsman

Formally referred to as the Parliamentary Commissioner for Administration (PCA).

Ouster Clause

A statutory provision purporting to exclude recourse to the courts by an individual wishing to challenge the decision of an inferior body.

Parent Act

See Enabling Act.

Part 54 CPR 1998

The Civil Procedure Rules governing the process by which applications for judicial review must be made.

Petition of Right

The pre Crown Proceedings Act procedure by which action against the Crown in contract were proceeded with.

Prerogative Order

The public law remedy available by way of judicial review to deal with ultra vires action. They are available at the discretion of the court. Being prerogative orders they are clearly not available against the Crown. See quashing order, mandatory order or prohibiting order.

Prerogative Power

The power still remaining in the Crown, ie not now transferred to statute eg the power to declare war, or sign treaties.

Primary Act

See Enabling Act.

Prohibiting Order

One of the prerogative orders (previously known as prohibition), intended to stop an inferior body from acting ultra vires.

Public Body

A body created by statute having public law functions.

Public Corporation

A body created by statute to perform a particular function, either commercial or regulatory.

Quashing Order

Originally known as certiorari (one of the prerogative orders), only available by way of judicial review against a public body having the power to determine questions affecting rights. Has the effect of quashing an ultra vires decision, or intra vires decision vitiated by error of law on the face of the record.

Statutory Corporation

See Public Body, or Public Corporation.

Subordinate Body

See Inferior Body.

Subordinate Legislation

See Delegated Legislation.

Ultra Vires

Acting beyond jurisdiction; outside the express and implied limits on power.

Void

Of no effect – as a result of being declared ultra vires by the court.

Void ab Initio

Void retrospectively, ie never of any effect.

Voidable

A decision that is effective, but could be invalidated because of some vitiating factors such as an error of law.

Index

Law Update 2004 edition – due March 2004

An annual review of the most recent developments in specific legal subject areas, useful for law students at degree and professional levels, others with law elements in their courses and also practitioners seeking a quick update.

Published around March every year, the Law Update summarises the major legal developments during the course of the previous year. In conjunction with Old Bailey Press textbooks it gives the student a significant advantage when revising for examinations.

Contents

Administrative Law • Civil and Criminal Procedure • Commercial Law • Company Law • Conflict of Laws • Constitutional Law • Contract Law • Conveyancing • Criminal Law • Criminology • Employment Law • English and European Legal Systems • Equity and Trusts • European Union Law • Evidence • Family Law • Jurisprudence • Land Law • Law of International Trade • Public International Law • Revenue Law • Succession • Tort

For further information on contents or to place an order, please contact:

Mail Order
Old Bailey Press
at Holborn College
Woolwich Road
Charlton
London
SE7 8LN

Telephone No: 020 8317 6039
Fax No: 020 8317 6004
Website: www.oldbaileypress.co.uk

ISBN 1 85836 518 X
Soft cover 246 x 175 mm
400 pages approx
£10.95
Due March 2004

Unannotated Cracknell's Statutes for use in Examinations

New Editions of Cracknell's Statutes

£11.95 due 2003

Cracknell's Statutes provide a comprehensive series of essential statutory provisions for each subject. Amendments are consolidated, avoiding the need to cross-refer to amending legislation. Unannotated, they are suitable for use in examinations, and provide the precise wording of vital Acts of Parliament for the diligent student.

Constitutional and Administrative Law
ISBN: 1 85836 511 2

Equity and Trusts
ISBN: 1 85836 508 2

Contract, Tort and Remedies
ISBN: 1 85836 507 4

Land: The Law of Real Property
ISBN: 1 85836 509 0

English Legal System
ISBN: 1 85836 510 4

Law of International Trade
ISBN: 1 85836 512 0

For further information on contents or to place an order, please contact:

Mail Order
Old Bailey Press
at Holborn College
Woolwich Road
Charlton
London
SE7 8LN

Telephone No: 020 8317 6039
Fax No: 020 8317 6004
Website: www.oldbaileypress.co.uk

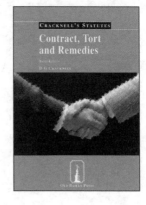

Suggested Solutions to Past Examination Questions 2001–2002

The Suggested Solutions series provides examples of full answers to the questions regularly set by examiners. Each suggested solution has been broken down into three stages: general comment, skeleton solution and suggested solution. The examination questions included within the text are taken from past examination papers set by the London University. The full opinion answers will undoubtedly assist you with your research and further your understanding and appreciation of the subject in question.

Only £6.95 due November 2003

Company Law
ISBN: 1 85836 519 8

Evidence
ISBN: 1 85836 521 X

Employment Law
ISBN: 1 85836 520 1

Family Law
ISBN: 1 85836 525 2

European Union Law
ISBN: 1 85836 524 4

For further information on contents or to place an order, please contact:

Mail Order
Old Bailey Press
at Holborn College
Woolwich Road
Charlton
London
SE7 8LN

Telephone No: 020 8317 6039
Fax No: 020 8317 6004
Website: www.oldbaileypress.co.uk

Company Law

2001–2002 LLB Examination Questions
and Suggested Solutions

University of London
External Examinations

Solutions by Susan Barber

Old Bailey Press

The Old Bailey Press integrated student law library is tailor-made to help you at every stage of your studies from the preliminaries of each subject through to the final examination. The series of Textbooks, Revision WorkBooks, 150 Leading Cases and Cracknell's Statutes are interrelated to provide you with a comprehensive set of study materials.

You can buy Old Bailey Press books from your University Bookshop, your local Bookshop, direct using this form, or you can order a free catalogue of our titles from the address shown overleaf.

The following subjects each have a Textbook, 150 Leading Cases/Casebook, Revision WorkBook and Cracknell's Statutes unless otherwise stated.

Administrative Law
Commercial Law
Company Law
Conflict of Laws
Constitutional Law
Conveyancing (Textbook and 150 Leading Cases)
Criminal Law
Criminology (Textbook and Sourcebook)
Employment Law (Textbook and Cracknell's Statutes)
English and European Legal Systems
Equity and Trusts
Evidence
Family Law
Jurisprudence: The Philosophy of Law (Textbook, Sourcebook and
    Revision WorkBook)
Land: The Law of Real Property
Law of International Trade
Law of the European Union
Legal Skills and System
    (Textbook)
Obligations: Contract Law
Obligations: The Law of Tort
Public International Law
Revenue Law (Textbook,
    Revision WorkBook and
    Cracknell's Statutes)
Succession

Mail order prices:	
Textbook	£15.95
150 Leading Cases	£11.95
Revision WorkBook	£9.95
Cracknell's Statutes	£11.95
Suggested Solutions 1999–2000	£6.95
Suggested Solutions 2000–2001	£6.95
Suggested Solutions 2001–2002	£6.95
Law Update 2003	£10.95
Law Update 2004	£10.95

Please note details and prices are subject to alteration.

To complete your order, please fill in the form below:

Module	Books required	Quantity	Price	Cost
		Postage		
		TOTAL		

For Europe, add 15% postage and packing (£20 maximum).
For the rest of the world, add 40% for airmail.

ORDERING

By telephone to Mail Order at 020 8317 6039, with your credit card to hand.

By fax to 020 8317 6004 (giving your credit card details).

Website: www.oldbaileypress.co.uk

By post to: Mail Order, Old Bailey Press at Holborn College, Woolwich Road, Charlton, London, SE7 8LN.

When ordering by post, please enclose full payment by cheque or banker's draft, or complete the credit card details below. You may also order a free catalogue of our complete range of titles from this address.

We aim to despatch your books within 3 working days of receiving your order.

Name

Address

Postcode   Telephone

Total value of order, including postage: £

I enclose a cheque/banker's draft for the above sum, or

charge my   ☐ Access/Mastercard   ☐ Visa   ☐ American Express
Card number

☐☐☐☐ ☐☐☐☐ ☐☐☐☐ ☐☐☐☐

Expiry date   ☐☐☐☐

Signature: ....Date: ....